Microsoft

W9-BZB-160

Inside Microsoft® SQL Server® 2008: T-SQL Programming

Itzik Ben-Gan
Dejan Sarka, Greg Low
Ed Katibah, Isaac Kunen
and Roger Wolter

PUBLISHED BY
Microsoft Press
A Division of Microsoft Corporation
One Microsoft Way
Redmond, Washington 98052-6399

Library of Congress Control Number: 2009932820

Printed and bound in the United States of America.

1 2 3 4 5 6 7 8 9 QWT 4 3 2 1 0 9

Distributed in Canada by H.B. Fenn and Company Ltd.

A CIP catalogue record for this book is available from the British Library.

Microsoft Press books are available through booksellers and distributors worldwide. For further information about international editions, contact your local Microsoft Corporation office or contact Microsoft Press International directly at fax (425) 936-7329. Visit our Web site at www.microsoft.com/mspress. Send comments to tkinput@microsoft.com.

Acquisitions Editor: Ken Jones
Developmental Editor: Denise Bankaitis
Project Editor: Denise Bankaitis
Editorial Production: Ashley Schneider, S4Carlisle Publishing Services
Technical Reviewer: Steve Kass; Technical Review services provided by Content Master, a member of CM Group, Ltd.
Cover: Tom Draper Design

Body Part No. X15-74121

To my siblings, Ina & Mickey

—Itzik

Table of Contents

What do you think of this book? We want to hear from you!

Microsoft is interested in hearing your feedback so we can continually improve our books and learning resources for you. To participate in a brief online survey, please visit:

www.microsoft.com/learning/booksurvey/

What do you think of this book? We want to hear from you!

Microsoft is interested in hearing your feedback so we can continually improve our books and learning resources for you. To participate in a brief online survey, please visit:

www.microsoft.com/learning/booksurvey/

Foreword

Let me start with a few words about the lead author of this book, Itzik Ben-Gan. He is a mentor, consultant, presenter, teacher, and writer. All his roles have a common theme—Microsoft SQL Server programming. But wait—there's even more: he is an MVP (officially "Microsoft Valued Professional," but often interpreted as Most Valuable Programmer) and a close partner with many SQL Server developers in Redmond, Washington. The combination of these traits puts Itzik into a unique position when writing a book about SQL Server programming. He knows what works and what does not. He knows what performs and what does not. He knows what questions people ask when he is teaching. And he knows what people grasp easily and what they don't when it comes to introducing more complex concepts of SQL Server programming.

Itzik invited several coauthors to write parts of this book. He does not hesitate to tap the resources of the SQL Server development team when it comes to introducing the newest SQL Server technologies. This was the case with spatial data chapter written by Ed Katibah (a.k.a. "Spatial Ed") and Isaac Kunen and with the Service Broker chapter written by Roger Wolter. Dejan Sarka helped with CLR and XML, and contributed the fascinating chapter on temporal support in the relational model, where he pokes at SQL Server developers about usefulness of PACK and UNPACK relational operators still missing in SQL Server. Greg Low untangled the many ways one can go about tracking access and changes to data and metadata. Both Dejan and Greg are SQL Server veterans and Itzik's colleagues in Solid Quality Mentors.

I personally believe in hands-on learning when it comes to programming. This book has many examples and they are all presented in a way that allows you to run them on your own SQL Server installation. If you don't have your own SQL Server installation, you can go to *http://www.microsoft.com/sql* and download the evaluation version of SQL Server 2008 (you must have a Windows Live ID; the evaluation version is Enterprise and it is good for 180 days). Preferably you should be using the Enterprise or Developer edition of SQL Server to run the examples. And no, you don't need to retype all code segments in the book! You can download the source code from *http://www.InsideTSQL.com*.

If you are new to the SQL language you should start with the earlier published book, *Microsoft SQL Server 2008: T-SQL Fundamentals*. If you are new to SQL Server but you have used other SQL supporting products you may want to start with the companion book *Inside Microsoft SQL Server 2008: T-SQL Querying*. But you can jump right into this book as well; it will give you great insight into SQL Server–specific programming. You can use the examples in the book to find out whether you need to study specific statements where SQL Server has a different implementation from your previous experiences and you can use these books for reference.

Even if you are a seasoned SQL Server developer I'm sure this book will show you new and more efficient ways to perform your tasks. For example, I agree with Dejan that there are few CLR UDTs in production systems. And this is not only true for UDTs—few UDFs, triggers, and stored procedures are written in CLR languages. The book provides numerous examples of C# and Microsoft Visual Basic solutions. Most of the examples are presented in both C# and Visual Basic, which are the most popular CLR languages. The authors are careful about CLR recommendations because of performance implications. Itzik not only provides general performance guidelines, but he also tells you how long the alternatives took to execute on his computer. Of course, you will try it on your computer!

Performance considerations are not restricted to CLR. You will find performance improvement tips in every single chapter of this book. For example, in Chapter 7, "Temporary Tables and Table Variables," you will learn when it is better to use temporary tables and when it is better to use table variables. Itzik uses simple examples, interpreting query plans and showing how to use IO counters when comparing different solutions for the same task.

I mentioned that Chapter 12— Dejan's "Temporal Support in the Relational Model" chapter—is fascinating. Why? Let me share a little secret. Some time ago we considered implementing special support for temporal data inside SQL Server. The work was intense and the SQL Server development team got help from leading academic sources as well. One development lead even personalized the license plate on his car to "TIME DB." What happened with the project? The implementation was complex and costly. Some of the alternatives were repeatedly re-evaluated without providing a clear winner. And there was always a counter-argument—"you can use a workaround." Whenever this argument was challenged someone wrote a piece of code showing how a particular temporal task could be achieved using *existing* features in SQL Server. But I don't know anybody who did as complete a job as Dejan in Chapter 12 of this book!

I worked with Roger Wolter on the same team when he was responsible for developing the brand new Service Broker in SQL Server 2005. His chapter (Chapter 16) is great reflection of his personality—deep with very accurate details in perfect structure. If you are new to Service Broker you may want to start reading this chapter from the end, where you will learn which scenarios you can use Service Broker with, along with a brief comparison of Service Broker with messaging solutions delivered by Microsoft Message Queue (MSMQ), BizTalk, and Windows Communication Foundation (WCF). Bank Itau in Brazil and MySpace are two examples of SQL Server customers who use Service Broker for very different purposes. Bank Itau uses Service Broker for batch processing. In MySpace, Service Broker creates a communication fabric among hundreds of SQL Servers behind the MySpace.com social networking site.

I'm confident you will find this book useful and worth reading whether you are a new or seasoned SQL Server user. It is an invaluable reference for developers, data architects, and administrators.

Lubor Kollar
Group Program Manager
SQL Server Customer Advisory Team
Microsoft, Redmond, Washington U.S.A.

Acknowledgments

Several people contributed to the T-SQL Querying and T-SQL Programming books and I'd like to acknowledge their contributions. Some were involved directly in writing or editing the books, whereas others were involved indirectly by providing advice, support, and inspiration.

To the coauthors of *Inside Microsoft SQL Server 2008: T-SQL Querying*—Lubor Kollar, Dejan Sarka, and Steve Kass; and to the coauthors of *Inside Microsoft SQL Server 2008: T-SQL Programming*—Dejan Sarka, Roger Wolter, Greg Low, Ed Katibah, and Isaac Kunen, it is a great honor to work with you. It is simply amazing to see the level of mastery that you have over your areas of expertise, and it is pure joy to read your texts. Thanks for agreeing to be part of this project.

To Lubor, besides directly contributing to the books by writing a chapter for T-SQL Querying and the foreword to *T-SQL Programming,* you provide support, advice, friendship, and are a great source of inspiration. I always look forward to spending time with you—hiking, drinking, and talking about SQL and other things.

To Dejko, your knowledge of the relational model is admirable. Whenever we spend time together I learn new things and discover new depths. I like the fact that you don't take things for granted and don't blindly follow the words of those who are considered experts in the field. You have a healthy mind of your own, and see things that very few are capable of seeing. I'd like to thank you for agreeing to contribute texts to the books. I'd also like to thank you for your friendship; I always enjoy spending time with you. We need to do the beer list thing again some time. It's been almost 10 years!

To the technical editor of the books, Steve Kass, your unique mix of strengths in mathematics, SQL, and English are truly extraordinary. I know that editing both books and also writing your own chapters took their toll. Therefore I'd like you to know how much I appreciate your work. I know you won't like my saying this, but it is quite interesting to see a genius at work. It kept reminding me of Domingo Montoya's work on the sword he prepared for the six-fingered man from William Goldman's *The Princess Bride.*

To Umachandar Jayachandran (UC), many thanks for helping out by editing some of the chapters. Your mastery of T-SQL is remarkable, and I'm so glad you could join the project in any capacity. I'd also like to thank Bob Beauchemin for reviewing the chapter on spatial data. I enjoy reading your texts; your insights on SQL Server programmability are always interesting and timely.

To Cesar Galindo-Legaria, I feel honored that you agreed to write the foreword for the *T-SQL Querying* book. The way you and your team designed SQL Server's optimizer is simply a marvel. I'm constantly trying to figure out and interpret what the optimizer does, and whenever I manage to understand a piece of the puzzle, I find it astonishing what a piece of software is capable of. Your depth of knowledge, your pleasant ways, and your humility are an inspiration.

To the team at Microsoft Press: Ken Jones, the product planner: I appreciate the personal manner in which you handle things, and always look forward to Guinness sessions with you. I think that you have an impossible job trying to make everyone happy and keep projects moving, but somehow you still manage to do it.

To Sally Stickney, the development editor, thanks for kicking the project off the ground. I know that the T-SQL Querying book was your last project at Microsoft Press before you started your new chosen path in life, and am hopeful that it left a good impression on you. I wish you luck and happiness in your new calling.

To Denise Bankaitis, the project editor, you of all people at Microsoft Press probably spent the most time working on the books. Thanks for your elegant project management, and for making sure things kept flowing. It was a pleasure to work with you.

I'd also like to thank DeAnn Montoya and Ashley Schneider, the project managers for the vendor editorial team, S4Carlisle, and Becka McKay, the copy editor. I know you spent countless hours going over our texts, and I appreciate it a lot.

To Solid Quality Mentors, being part of this amazing company and group of people is by far the best thing that happened to me in my career. It's as if all I did in my professional life led me to this place where I can fulfill my calling, which is teaching people about SQL. To Fernando Guerrero, Brian Moran, Douglas McDowell: the company grew and matured because of your efforts, and you have a lot to be proud of. Being part of this company, I feel a part of something meaningful, and that I'm among family and friends—among people that I both respect and trust.

I'd like to thank my friends and colleagues from the company: Ron Talmage, Andrew J. Kelly, Eladio Rincón, Dejan Sarka, Herbert Albert, Fritz Lechnitz, Gianluca Hotz, Erik Veerman, Jay Hackney, Daniel A. Seara, Davide Mauri, Andrea Benedetti, Miguel Egea, Adolfo Wiernik, Javier Loria, Rushabh Mehta, Greg Low, Peter Myers, Randy Dyess, and many others. I'd like to thank Jeanne Reeves and Glen McCoin for making many of my classes possible, and all the back-office team for their support. I'd also like to thank Kathy Blomstrom for managing our writing projects and for your excellent edits.

I'd like to thank the members of the SQL Server development team that are working on T-SQL and its optimization: Michael Wang, Michael Rys, Eric Hanson, Umachandar Jayachandran (UC), Tobias Thernström, Jim Hogg, Isaac Kunen, Krzysztof Kozielczyk, Cesar Galindo-Legaria, Craig Freedman, Conor Cunningham, Yavor Angelov, Susan Price, and many others. For better or worse, what you develop is what we have to work with, and so far the results are outstanding! Still, until we get a full implementation of the OVER clause, you know I won't stop bothering you.

I'd like to thank Dubi Lebel and Assaf Fraenkel from Microsoft Israel, and also Ami Levin who helps me run the Israeli SQL Server users group.

To the team at *SQL Server Magazine*: Megan Bearly, Sheila Molnar, Mary Waterloo, Michele Crockett, Mike Otey, Lavon Peters, Anne Grubb; being part of this magazine is a great privilege. Congratulations on the tenth anniversary of the magazine! I can't believe that 10 years passed so quickly, but that's what happens when you have fun.

To my fellow SQL Server MVPs: Erland Sommarskog, Alejandro Mesa, Aaron Bertrand, Tibor Karaszi, Steve Kass, Dejan Sarka, Roy Harvey, Tony Rogerson, Marcello Poletti (Marc), Paul Randall, Bob Beauchemin, Adam Machanic, Simon Sabin, Tom Moreau, Hugo Kornelis, David Portas, David Guzman, Paul Nielsen, and many others: Your contribution to the SQL Server community is remarkable. Much of what I know today is thanks to our discussions and exchange of ideas.

To my fellow SQL Server MCTs: Tibor Karaszi, Chris Randall, Ted Malone, and others: We go a long way back, and I'm glad to see that you're all still around in the SQL teaching community. We all share the same passion for teaching. Of anyone, you best understand the kind of fulfillment that teaching can bestow.

To my students: Without you my work would be meaningless. Teaching is what I like to do best, and the purpose of pretty much everything else that I do with SQL—including writing these books—is to support my teaching. Your questions make me do a lot of research, and therefore I owe much of my knowledge to you.

To my parents, Emilia and Gabriel Ben-Gan, and to my siblings, Ina Aviram and Michael Ben-Gan, thanks for your continuous support. The fact that most of us ended up being teachers is probably not by chance, but for me to fulfill my calling I end up traveling a lot. I miss you all when I'm away and I always look forward to our family reunions when I'm back.

To Lilach, you're the one who needs to put up with me all the time, and listen to my SQL ideas that you probably couldn't care less about. It's brainwashing, you see—at some point you will start asking for more, and before you know it you will even start reading my books. Not because I will force you, rather because you will want to, of course. That's the plan, at least… Thanks for giving meaning to what I do, and for supporting me through some rough times of writing.

Introduction

This book and its prequel—*Inside Microsoft SQL Server 2008: T-SQL Querying*—cover advanced T-SQL querying, query tuning, and programming in Microsoft SQL Server 2008. They are designed for experienced programmers and DBAs who need to write and optimize code in SQL Server 2008. For brevity, I'll refer to the books as *T-SQL Querying* and *T-SQL Programming*, or just as *these books*.

Those who read the SQL Server 2005 edition of the books will find plenty of new material covering new subjects, new features, and enhancements in SQL Server 2008, plus revisions and new insights about the existing subjects.

These books focus on practical common problems, discussing several approaches to tackle each. You will be introduced to many polished techniques that will enhance your toolbox and coding vocabulary, allowing you to provide efficient solutions in a natural manner.

These books unveil the power of set-based querying, and they explain why it's usually superior to procedural programming with cursors and the like. At the same time, they teach you how to identify the few scenarios where cursor-based solutions are superior to set-based ones.

The prequel to this book—*T-SQL Querying*—focuses on set-based querying and query tuning, and I recommend that you read it first. This book—*T-SQL Programming*—focuses on procedural programming and assumes that you read the first book or have sufficient querying background.

T-SQL Querying starts with five chapters that lay the foundation of logical and physical query processing required to gain the most from the rest of the chapters in both books.

The first chapter covers logical query processing. It describes in detail the logical phases involved in processing queries, the unique aspects of SQL querying, and the special mind-set you need to adopt to program in a relational, set-oriented environment.

The second chapter covers set theory and predicate logic—the strong mathematical foundations upon which the relational model is built. Understanding these foundations will give you better insights into the model and the language. This chapter was written by Steve Kass, who was also the main technical editor of these books. Steve has a unique combination of strengths in mathematics, computer science, SQL, and English that make him the ideal author for this subject.

The third chapter covers the relational model. Understanding the relational model is essential for good database design and helps in writing good code. The chapter defines relations and tuples and operators of relational algebra. Then it shows the relational model from a different perspective called *relational calculus*. This is more of a business-oriented perspective, as the logical model is described in terms of predicates and propositions. Data integrity is crucial for transactional systems; therefore, the chapter spends time discussing all kinds of constraints. Finally, the chapter introduces normalization—the formal process of improving database design. This chapter was written by Dejan Sarka. Dejan is one of the people with the deepest understanding of the relational model that I know.

The fourth chapter covers query tuning. It introduces a query tuning methodology we developed in our company (Solid Quality Mentors) and have been applying in production systems. The chapter also covers working with indexes and analyzing execution plans. This chapter provides the important background knowledge required for the rest of the chapters in both books, which as a practice discuss working with indexes and analyzing execution plans. These are important aspects of querying and query tuning.

The fifth chapter covers complexity and algorithms and was also written by Steve Kass. This chapter particularly focuses on some of the algorithms used often by the SQL Server engine. It gives attention to considering worst-case behavior as well as average case complexity. By understanding the complexity of algorithms used by the engine you can anticipate, for example, how the performance of certain queries will degrade when more data is added to the tables involved. Gaining a better understanding of how the engine processes your queries equips you with better tools to tune them.

The chapters that follow delve into advanced querying and query tuning, addressing both logical and physical aspects of your code. These chapters cover the following subjects: subqueries, table expressions, and ranking functions; joins and set operations; aggregating and pivoting data; TOP and APPLY; data modification; querying partitioned tables; and graphs, trees, hierarchies, and recursive queries.

The chapter covering querying partitioned tables was written by Lubor Kollar. Lubor led the development of partitioned tables and indexes when first introduced in the product, and many of the features that we have today are thanks to his efforts. These days Lubor works with customers that have, among other things, large implementations of partitioned tables and indexes as part of his role in the SQL Server Customer Advisory Team (SQL CAT).

Appendix A covers logic puzzles. Here you have a chance to practice logical puzzles to improve your logic skills. SQL querying essentially deals with logic. I find it important to practice pure logic to improve your query problem-solving capabilities. I also find these puzzles fun and challenging, and you can practice them with the entire family. These puzzles are a compilation of the logic puzzles that I covered in my T-SQL column in *SQL Server Magazine*. I'd like to thank *SQL Server Magazine* for allowing me to share these puzzles with the book's readers.

This book—*T-SQL Programming*—focuses on programmatic T-SQL constructs and expands its coverage to treatment of XML and XQuery, and the CLR integration. The book's chapters cover the following subjects: views, user-defined functions, stored procedures, triggers, transactions and concurrency, exception handling, temporary tables and table variables, cursors, dynamic SQL, working with date and time, CLR user-defined types, temporal support in the relational model, XML and XQuery (including coverage of open schema), spatial data, tracking access and changes to data, and Service Broker.

The chapters covering CLR user-defined types, temporal support in the relational model, and XML and XQuery were written by Dejan Sarka. As I mentioned, Dejan is extremely knowledgeable in the relational model, and has very interesting insights into the model itself and the way the constructs that he covers in his chapters fit in the model when used sensibly.

The chapter about spatial data was written by Ed Katibah and Isaac Kunen. Ed and Isaac are with the SQL Server development team, and led the efforts to implement spatial data support in SQL Server 2008. It is a great privilege to have this chapter written by the designers of the feature. Spatial data support is new to SQL Server 2008 and brings new data types, methods, and indices. This chapter is not intended as an exhaustive treatise on spatial data nor an encyclopedia of every spatial method which SQL Server now supports. Instead, this chapter will introduce core spatial concepts and provide the reader with key programming constructs necessary to successfully navigate this new feature to SQL Server.

The chapter about tracking access and changes to data was written by Greg Low. Greg is a SQL Server MVP and the managing director of SolidQ Australia. Greg has many years of experience working with SQL Server—teaching, speaking, and writing about it—and is highly regarded in the SQL Server community. This chapter covers extended events, auditing, change tracking, and change data capture. The technologies that are the focus of this chapter track access and changes to data and are new in SQL Server 2008. At first glance, these technologies can appear to be either overlapping or contradictory and the best use cases for each might be far from obvious. This chapter explores each technology, discusses the capabilities and limitations of each, and explains how each is intended to be used.

The last chapter, which covers Service Broker (SSB) was written by Roger Wolter. Roger is the program manager with the SQL Server development team and led the initial efforts to introduce SSB in SQL Server. Again, there's nothing like having the designer of a component explain it in his own words. The "sleeper" feature of SQL Server 2005 is now in production in a wide variety of applications. This chapter covers the architecture of SSB and how to use SSB to build a variety of reliable asynchronous database applications. The SQL 2008 edition adds coverage of the new features added to SSB for the SQL Server 2008 release and includes lessons learned and best practices from SSB applications deployed since the SQL Server 2005 release. The major new features are Queue Priorities, External Activation, and a new SSB troubleshooting application that incorporates lessons the SSB team learned from customers who have already deployed applications.

Hardware and Software Requirements

To practice all the material in these books and run all code samples it is recommended that you use Microsoft SQL Server 2008 Developer or Enterprise edition, and Microsoft Visual Studio 2008 Professional or Database edition. If you have a subscription to MSDN, you can download SQL Server 2008 and Visual Studio 2008 from *http://msdn.microsoft.com*. Otherwise, you can download a 180-day evaluation copy of SQL Server 2008 Enterprise edition free from: *http://www.microsoft.com/sqlserver/2008/en/us/trial-software.aspx*, and a 90-day free trial of Visual Studio 2008 Professional edition from: *http://www.microsoft.com/visualstudio/en-us/try/default.mspx*.

You can find the system requirements for SQL Server 2008 at the following link: *http://msdn.microsoft.com/en-us/library/ms143506.aspx*, and for Visual Studio 2008 at the following link: *http://www.microsoft.com/visualstudio/en-us/products/default.mspx*.

Companion Content and Sample Database

These books feature a companion Web site that makes available to you all the code used in the books, the errata, additional resources, and more. The companion Web site is *http://www.insidetsql.com*.

For each of these books the companion Web site provides a compressed file with the book's source code, a script file to create the books' sample database, and additional files that are required to run some of the code samples.

After downloading the source code, run the script file InsideTSQL2008.sql to create the sample database InsideTSQL2008, which is used in many of the books' code samples. The data model of the InsideTSQL2008 database is provided in Figure I-1 for your convenience.

Find Additional Content Online

As new or updated material becomes available that complements your books, it will be posted online on the Microsoft Press Online Developer Tools Web site. The type of material you might find includes updates to books content, articles, links to companion content, errata, sample chapters, and more. This Web site is available at *http://microsoftpresssrv.libredigital.com/serverclient/* and is updated periodically.

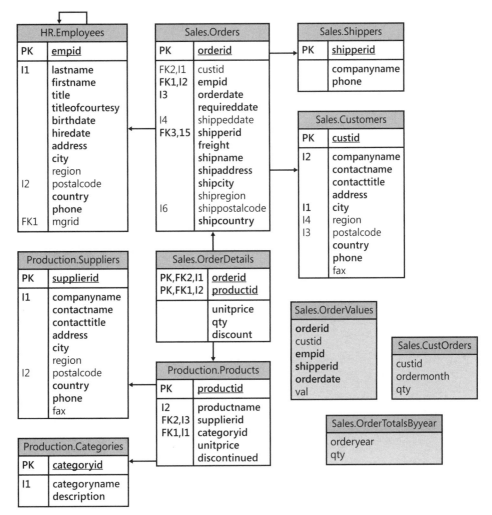

FIGURE I-1 Data model of the InsideTSQL2008 database

Support for These Books

Every effort has been made to ensure the accuracy of these books and the contents of the companion Web site. As corrections or changes are collected, they will be added to a Microsoft Knowledge Base article.

Microsoft Press provides support for books at the following Web site:

http://www.microsoft.com/learning/support/books/.

Questions and Comments

If you have comments, questions, or ideas regarding the books, or questions that are not answered by visiting the sites listed previously, please send them to me via e-mail to

itzik@SolidQ.com

or via postal mail to

Microsoft Press
Attn: *Inside Microsoft SQL Server 2008: T-SQL Querying and Inside Microsoft SQL Server 2008: T-SQL Programming* Editor
One Microsoft Way
Redmond, WA 98052-6399

Please note that Microsoft software product support is not offered through the above addresses.

Chapter 1
Views

Itzik Ben-Gan

This book is the sequel to *Inside Microsoft SQL Server 2008: T-SQL Querying* (Microsoft Press, 2009) and I assume that you've read its prequel or have equivalent querying knowledge. Throughout the book I will refer to the books in short as *T-SQL Querying* and *T-SQL Programming*. The T-SQL programming book focuses on programmatic T-SQL constructs, and I think it makes sense to start with a chapter that covers views—a construct that is considered by some a programmatic construct and by others a querying construct.

This chapter starts with a brief description of views and their uses. As the chapter progresses, I'll discuss details of working with views. Among other things, I'll cover the use of views to simplify your queries and indexed views to improve the performance of your database.

What Are Views?

A view is a named virtual table that is defined by a query and used as a table. Unlike permanent tables, a view has no physical representation of its data unless you create an index on it. Whenever you issue a query against a nonindexed view, SQL Server in practice has to access the underlying tables. Unless specified otherwise, the discussions in this chapter involve nonindexed views.

When you create a view, you specify a name for the view and a query. Microsoft SQL Server stores only metadata information about the view, describing the object, its columns, security, dependencies, and so on. When you query a view—by retrieving or modifying data—the query processor replaces a view reference with its definition; in other words, the query processor "expands" the view definition and generates an execution plan accessing the underlying objects.

Views play important roles in the database. One of the more valuable uses of views is as an abstraction mechanism. For example, you can use views to make it easier to provide a more or less normalized picture of the underlying data, where appropriate, without changing the normalization of the actual data. You can use views to simplify your solutions by applying a modular approach—solving complex problems one step at a time. You can use views as a security layer (to some degree) by granting access to filtered or manipulated data only through views, and not directly against the base tables (provided that the owner of the view and the owner of the underlying objects are the same).

Views can also play a performance role if you create an index on them. Creating a clustered index on the view materializes its data on disk, giving the view a physical dimension, as opposed to its normal virtual role. I'll describe indexed views later in the chapter in a dedicated section. For now, the important point is that without an index, a view typically has no special performance impact—negative or positive.

As with any other table expression—such as a derived table, a common table expression (CTE), or inline table-valued user-defined function (UDF)—the query defining the view must meet three requirements:

- ORDER BY cannot be used in the view's query unless there is also a TOP or FOR XML specification in the definition.

- All result columns must have names.

- All result column names must be unique.

An ORDER BY clause without TOP or FOR XML specification is not allowed in the query defining the view because a view is supposed to represent a table. A table is a logical entity that has no order to its rows—as opposed to a cursor, which is a physical object that does have order to its records. Naturally, all columns must have names in a valid table, and the names must be unique. You can assign column names to the target columns of a view either in parentheses following the view name or as inline column aliases following the individual expressions.

As an example, run the following code to create the CustsWithOrders view in the InsideTSQL2008 sample database (see the book's Introduction for details on the sample database):

```
SET NOCOUNT ON;
USE InsideTSQL2008;

IF OBJECT_ID('Sales.CustsWithOrders', 'V') IS NOT NULL
  DROP VIEW Sales.CustsWithOrders;
GO
CREATE VIEW Sales.CustsWithOrders
AS

SELECT custid, companyname, contactname, contacttitle,
  address, city, region, postalcode, country, phone, fax
FROM Sales.Customers AS C
WHERE EXISTS
  (SELECT * FROM Sales.Orders AS O
  WHERE O.custid = C.custid);
GO
```

This view contains customers that placed orders. The view's query uses the EXISTS predicate to return customers that have at least one order in the Orders table.

> **Tip** Even though the use of the asterisk (*) is generally a bad practice, you can use it safely
> with the EXISTS predicate. The optimizer knows that the EXISTS predicate does not refer to a
> particular attribute from the row. Rather, it cares only about existence; therefore, it ignores the
> SELECT list. You can deduce this by examining execution plans for such queries and noticing that
> if there's an index on the filtered column (*O.custid* in the preceding example), it will be used and
> there won't be additional lookup operations. Another way to demonstrate that the SELECT list is
> ignored by the optimizer is by specifying expressions that would normally cause an error, such as:
>
> ```
> IF EXISTS(SELECT 1/0) PRINT 'no error';
> ```
>
> This code runs with no error, demonstrating that SQL Server didn't evaluate the expression.
> If SQL Server had evaluated the expression, you would have received an error. Some resolution
> overhead may be involved in expanding the * to check column permissions, but this cost is likely
> so negligible that you will hardly ever notice it. I find the use of * more natural and clear than
> specifying a constant, and clarity of code is an important aspect of programming.

The following sections will explore various aspects of views in more detail, starting with the
reasoning behind disallowing an ORDER BY clause without a TOP or FOR XML specification in
the view's query.

ORDER BY in a View

As I mentioned earlier, there is a reason behind disallowing an ORDER BY clause in the view's
query. A view is similar to a table in the sense that it represents a logical entity with no
predetermined order to its rows—unlike a cursor that has order to its records.

Try running the following code, which attempts to introduce an ORDER BY clause in the
CustsWithOrders view:

```
ALTER VIEW Sales.CustsWithOrders
AS

SELECT country, custid, companyname, contactname, contacttitle,
  address, city, region, postalcode, phone, fax
FROM Sales.Customers AS C
WHERE EXISTS
  (SELECT * FROM Sales.Orders AS O
  WHERE O.custid = C.custid)
ORDER BY country;
GO
```

The attempt fails, generating the following error:

```
Msg 1033, Level 15, State 1, Procedure CustsWithOrders, Line 10
The ORDER BY clause is invalid in views, inline functions, derived tables, subqueries,
and common table expressions, unless TOP or FOR XML is also specified.
```

Notice that the error doesn't say that ORDER BY is disallowed altogether; rather, it indicates a couple of exceptions where it is allowed—when TOP or FOR XML is also specified. Remember that both TOP and FOR XML are T-SQL extensions, not standard SQL elements. TOP and ORDER BY or ORDER BY and FOR XML are part of the result set specification, whereas ORDER BY alone is not, and only specifies a detail of presentation. Hence, TOP and ORDER BY or ORDER BY and FOR XML are allowed in a view definition, whereas ORDER BY alone is not.

If you need to return sorted data to the client, or declare a cursor object that allows processing the rows one at a time in certain order, you can always specify an ORDER BY clause in the outer query against the view:

```
SELECT country, custid, companyname
FROM Sales.CustsWithOrders
ORDER BY country;
```

Note that when using the TOP option in an outer query, the ORDER BY clause serves two purposes: the first is to determine for the TOP option which rows to pick, and the second is to determine the order of the records in the result cursor. However, when the ORDER BY clause is used with the TOP option in a table expression (for example, in a view's query), it is guaranteed to serve only one purpose—determining for the TOP option which rows to pick. In such a case, the view still represents a valid table (a set). When querying the view, there's no guarantee that the rows will be returned in any particular order unless the outer query against the view has an ORDER BY clause as well. When TOP is also specified, the ORDER BY clause is allowed within a view (or other table expressions) because it is guaranteed to serve only a logical purpose for TOP and not a physical one. Understanding this detail can help you develop correct code and avoid using table expressions in ways they really weren't designed to work.

For example, an attempt to create a "sorted view" is wrong to begin with because a view is a table and a table has no order to its rows. Programmers who don't understand this—and don't realize that a view with a TOP query and an ORDER BY clause gives no guarantees in terms of presentation ordering—might try something like this:

```
ALTER VIEW Sales.CustsWithOrders
AS

SELECT TOP (100) PERCENT
   country, custid, companyname, contactname, contacttitle,
   address, city, region, postalcode, phone, fax
FROM Sales.Customers AS C
WHERE EXISTS
   (SELECT * FROM Sales.Orders AS O
   WHERE O.custid = C.custid)
ORDER BY country;
GO
```

So what is the meaning of the ORDER BY clause in the view's query? Things are fuzzy here because the TOP option is not standard. But if you try to think in terms of sets, the ORDER BY clause is meaningless because you're selecting all rows that meet the filter expression.

When querying the view, SQL Server does not have to guarantee any order of the output unless the outer query has an ORDER BY clause. SQL Server 2008 Books Online has a helpful statement describing this behavior: "The ORDER BY clause is used only to determine the rows that are returned by the TOP clause in the view definition. The ORDER BY clause does not guarantee ordered results when the view is queried, unless ORDER BY is also specified in the query itself."

Run the following query in SQL Server 2008 (after altering the view to include the TOP (100) PERCENT specification and ORDER BY clause):

```
SELECT country, custid, companyname
FROM Sales.CustsWithOrders;
```

When I ran this query on my system, I got the following unsorted output:

```
country             custid       companyname
---------------     -----------  ---------------
Germany             1            Customer NRZBB
Mexico              2            Customer MLTDN
Mexico              3            Customer KBUDE
UK                  4            Customer HFBZG
Sweden              5            Customer HGVLZ
Germany             6            Customer XHXJV
France              7            Customer QXVLA
Spain               8            Customer QUHWH
France              9            Customer RTXGC
Canada              10           Customer EEALV
...
```

In both SQL Server 2008 and SQL Server 2005 the optimizer will realize that it can ignore both the TOP specification and the ORDER BY clause in the view definition because TOP (100) PERCENT is specified. In SQL Server 2000, however, the optimizer fell into the trap, so to speak, and sorted the rows even though the outer query against the view did not have an ORDER BY clause.

Examining the execution plans in the different versions of SQL Server shows that in version 2000 (in a similar scenario with a view against the Customers and Orders tables in the Northwind sample database) the optimizer sorts the data (see Figure 1-1) and in versions 2008 and 2005 it doesn't (see Figure 1-2).

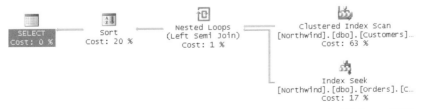

FIGURE 1-1 Execution plan for a query against a view with ORDER BY in SQL Server 2000

FIGURE 1-2 Execution plan for a query against a view with ORDER BY in SQL Server 2008 and SQL Server 2005

You can see that the plan in SQL Server 2000 uses a sort operator, sorting the data by *Country*. On the other hand, the SQL Server 2008 optimizer completely ignored the combination of TOP (100) PERCENT and the ORDER BY clause. The optimizer realized that TOP and ORDER BY are meaningless here; therefore, it didn't bother to sort the data by *country*. Unfortunately, programmers accustomed to the SQL Server 2000 behavior might consider this change in behavior a bug, even though the whole premise for creating such a view is wrong. Those who already upgraded from SQL Server 2000 to SQL Server 2005 have already faced this issue, but for organizations that waited with their upgrades for the release of SQL Server 2008 this issue is new and needs to be addressed. In SQL Server 2008, the code needs to be revised to incorporate an ORDER BY clause in the outer query to guarantee presentation ordering.

> **Note** The view designer in SQL Server Management Studio (SSMS) has a place to specify the order of a view, yielding a view definition with a TOP (100) PERCENT specification and an ORDER BY clause. This might have been how programmers discovered this loophole. Although the SQL Server 2008 query optimizer ignores this combination, this unfortunate usage will probably continue, because the SSMS view designer encourages it. It will simply create more confusion. I hope that you will realize that such use is absurd and refrain from it altogether.

When you're done, run the following code to drop the CustsWithOrders view:

```
IF OBJECT_ID('Sales.CustsWithOrders', 'V') IS NOT NULL
  DROP VIEW Sales.CustsWithOrders;
```

Refreshing Views

When you create a view, SQL Server stores metadata information describing the view, its columns, security, dependencies, and so on. Schema changes in underlying objects are not reflected in the view's metadata information. After applying such schema changes, it's a good practice to refresh the view's metadata information using the *sp_refreshview* stored procedure so that the changes are reflected in the view.

To demonstrate what can happen when you make schema changes and don't refresh the view's metadata information, first run the following code, which creates the table T1 and the view V1 in the tempdb database for demonstration purposes:

```
USE tempdb;
IF OBJECT_ID('dbo.V1', 'V') IS NOT NULL DROP VIEW dbo.V1;
IF OBJECT_ID('dbo.T1', 'U') IS NOT NULL DROP TABLE dbo.T1;
GO
CREATE TABLE dbo.T1(col1 INT, col2 INT);
INSERT INTO dbo.T1(col1, col2) VALUES(1, 2);
GO
CREATE VIEW dbo.V1
AS
SELECT * FROM dbo.T1;
GO
```

As a practice, avoid using * in your SELECT statements. I'm using it here just for demonstration purposes. When V1 was initially created, SQL Server stored metadata information about the columns that existed at that point in time—*col1* and *col2*. Run the following code to query the view:

```
SELECT * FROM dbo.V1;
```

You get the following output with both columns:

```
col1        col2
----------- -----------
1           2
```

Next, add a column to T1:

```
ALTER TABLE dbo.T1 ADD col3 INT;
```

The schema change in T1 was not reflected in the view's metadata information. As far as SQL Server is concerned, the view still has just two columns. If you execute the previous SELECT query again, you still get only two columns in the output:

```
col1        col2
----------- -----------
1           2
```

To refresh the view's metadata information, run the *sp_refreshview* stored procedure against V1:

```
EXEC sp_refreshview 'dbo.V1';
```

Execute the previous SELECT query again, and you get the following output, which includes the new column—*col3*:

```
col1        col2        col3
----------- ----------- -----------
1           2           NULL
```

This is just one example where a schema change in the underlying objects is not reflected in the view's metadata information. You might find it to be a good practice to refresh all views' metadata information after applying schema changes to objects in the database. To avoid the tedious process of writing the *sp_refreshview* statements you can use the following query:

```
SELECT
  N'EXEC sp_refreshview '
    + QUOTENAME(SCHEMA_NAME(schema_id) + N'.' + QUOTENAME(name), '''')
    + ';' AS cmd
FROM sys.views
WHERE OBJECTPROPERTY(object_id, 'IsSchemaBound') = 0;
```

The query generates as its output the lines of code with the *sp_refreshview* statements against all views in the database that are not schema-bound.

> **Warning** Make sure that you examine the output carefully before running it. Someone with permission to create views can maliciously plant specially crafted view names to subvert this maintenance code into doing damage.

When you're done, drop V1 and T1:

```
USE tempdb;
IF OBJECT_ID('dbo.V1', 'V') IS NOT NULL DROP VIEW dbo.V1;
IF OBJECT_ID('dbo.T1', 'U') IS NOT NULL DROP TABLE dbo.T1;
```

Modular Approach

You can use views to develop solutions in a modular way. You solve each step of the problem with a query, and define a view based on that query. This process simplifies the solution by allowing you to focus on a single step at a time.

I'll demonstrate a modular approach through an example. First, run the following code to create and populate the Sales table in the tempdb database:

```
SET NOCOUNT ON;
USE tempdb;
IF OBJECT_ID('dbo.Sales', 'U') IS NOT NULL DROP TABLE dbo.Sales;
GO
CREATE TABLE dbo.Sales
(
  mnth DATE NOT NULL PRIMARY KEY,
/* Note: The DATE type is new in SQL Server 2008.
   In earlier versions use DATETIME. */
  qty  INT  NOT NULL
);

INSERT INTO dbo.Sales(mnth, qty) VALUES
/* Note: Table Value Constructor (enhanced VALUES clause) is new
   in SQL Server 2008. In earlier versions use a separate
   INSERT VALUES statement for each row. */
```

```
('20071201', 100),
('20080101', 110),
('20080201', 120),
('20080301', 130),
('20080401', 140),
('20080501', 140),
('20080601', 130),
('20080701', 120),
('20080801', 110),
('20080901', 100),
('20081001', 110),
('20081101', 100),
('20081201', 120),
('20090101', 130),
('20090201', 140),
('20090301', 100),
('20090401', 100),
('20090501', 100),
('20090601', 110),
('20090701', 120),
('20090801', 110),
('20090901', 120),
('20091001', 130),
('20091101', 140),
('20091201', 100);
```

> **Note** This code uses features that were introduced in SQL Server 2008. Those are the DATE
> data type and the enhanced VALUES clause that allows inserting multiple rows using a single
> INSERT VALUES statement. If you're running this code on an earlier version of SQL Server, use the
> DATETIME data type and a separate INSERT statement for each row.

The table contains one row per month with the sales quantity (column *qty*) and month
(column *mnth*). Notice that I used the DATE data type to store a month to support
date-related calculations. Even though I care only about the year and month elements of
the value, I had to specify something in the day portion. So I specified the first day of each
month as the day. When you need to present the data, you can always extract the relevant
elements from the full date value.

The task at hand is to return groups of consecutive months that have the same sales trend;
that is, identify ranges of months with the same trend (up, same, down, or unknown), and
indicate the trend with a string column—*trend*. The trend for a given month is based on its
qty value minus the *qty* value of the previous month. If the difference is positive, the trend is
'up'; if it's negative, the trend is *'down'*; if it's zero, the trend is *'same'*; otherwise, the trend is
'unknown'. The following is the desired result:

```
start_range end_range trend
----------- --------- -------
200712      200712    unknown
200801      200804    up
```

```
200805      200805      same
200806      200809      down
200810      200810      up
200811      200811      down
200812      200902      up
200903      200903      down
200904      200905      same
200906      200907      up
200908      200908      down
200909      200911      up
200912      200912      down
```

Trying to develop a single query to solve the problem can be too complex. Instead, break the solution into steps. I'll show a couple of different solutions—one based on subqueries and another based on ranking calculations.

First, calculate the sign of the difference between the current month's *qty* and the previous month's. This can be achieved by creating the SalesTrendSgn view, as follows:

```
IF OBJECT_ID('dbo.SalesTrendSgn', 'V') IS NOT NULL DROP VIEW dbo.SalesTrendSgn;
GO
CREATE VIEW dbo.SalesTrendSgn
AS

SELECT mnth, qty,
  SIGN((S1.qty -
          (SELECT TOP (1) qty
           FROM dbo.Sales AS S2
           WHERE S2.mnth < S1.mnth
           ORDER BY S2.mnth DESC))) AS sgn
FROM dbo.Sales AS S1;
GO

SELECT * FROM dbo.SalesTrendSgn;
```

This code generates the following output:

```
mnth          qty          sgn
------------  -----------  -----------
2007-12-01    100          NULL
2008-01-01    110          1
2008-02-01    120          1
2008-03-01    130          1
2008-04-01    140          1
2008-05-01    140          0
2008-06-01    130          -1
2008-07-01    120          -1
2008-08-01    110          -1
2008-09-01    100          -1
2008-10-01    110          1
2008-11-01    100          -1
2008-12-01    120          1
2009-01-01    130          1
2009-02-01    140          1
```

```
2009-03-01   100         -1
2009-04-01   100         0
2009-05-01   100         0
2009-06-01   110         1
2009-07-01   120         1
2009-08-01   110         -1
2009-09-01   120         1
2009-10-01   130         1
2009-11-01   140         1
2009-12-01   100         -1
```

The SIGN function returns 1 for a positive input, 0 an input of zero, –1 for a negative input, and NULL for a NULL input. The *sgn* column actually represents the sales trend of the current month. At this point, you want to group all consecutive months that have the same sales trend. To do so, you first need to calculate a grouping factor—a value that identifies the group. One option for the grouping factor is the earliest future month in which the trend is different from the current month's trend. If you think about it, you can see that such a value will be the same for all consecutive months that have the same trend.

Run the following code to create the SalesGrp view, which calculates the grouping factor:

```
IF OBJECT_ID('dbo.SalesGrp', 'V') IS NOT NULL DROP VIEW dbo.SalesGrp;
GO
CREATE VIEW dbo.SalesGrp
AS

SELECT mnth, sgn,
  (SELECT MIN(mnth) FROM dbo.SalesTrendSgn AS V2
    WHERE V2.sgn <> V1.sgn
      AND V2.mnth > V1.mnth) AS grp
FROM dbo.SalesTrendSgn AS V1;
GO

SELECT * FROM dbo.SalesGrp;
```

This code generates the following output:

```
mnth          sgn          grp
------------  -----------  ----------
2007-12-01    NULL         NULL
2008-01-01    1            2008-05-01
2008-02-01    1            2008-05-01
2008-03-01    1            2008-05-01
2008-04-01    1            2008-05-01
2008-05-01    0            2008-06-01
2008-06-01    -1           2008-10-01
2008-07-01    -1           2008-10-01
2008-08-01    -1           2008-10-01
2008-09-01    -1           2008-10-01
2008-10-01    1            2008-11-01
2008-11-01    -1           2008-12-01
2008-12-01    1            2009-03-01
2009-01-01    1            2009-03-01
```

2009-02-01	1	2009-03-01
2009-03-01	-1	2009-04-01
2009-04-01	0	2009-06-01
2009-05-01	0	2009-06-01
2009-06-01	1	2009-08-01
2009-07-01	1	2009-08-01
2009-08-01	-1	2009-09-01
2009-09-01	1	2009-12-01
2009-10-01	1	2009-12-01
2009-11-01	1	2009-12-01
2009-12-01	-1	NULL

You can observe that the *grp* column values are unique for each consecutive group of months that have the same trend. The only exception is the two NULLs. You received a NULL for December 2007 because that month showed an unknown trend. You received a NULL for December 2009 because no data exists after that date. The two NULLs belong to two different consecutive trend groups, but you can easily solve the problem by using both *sgn* (representing the trend) and *grp* to define the group.

The last part is straightforward—group the data by *sgn* and *grp*, return *MIN(mnth)* as the start of the range, and return *MAX(mnth)* as the end of the range. Also, use a CASE expression to convert the *sgn* value to a more descriptive representation of the trend.

Run the following code to create the SalesTrends view implementing this step:

```
IF OBJECT_ID('dbo.SalesTrends', 'V') IS NOT NULL
  DROP VIEW dbo.SalesTrends;
GO
CREATE VIEW dbo.SalesTrends
AS

SELECT
  CONVERT(VARCHAR(6), MIN(mnth), 112) AS start_range,
  CONVERT(VARCHAR(6), MAX(mnth), 112) AS end_range,
  CASE sgn
    WHEN -1 THEN 'down'
    WHEN  0 THEN 'same'
    WHEN  1 THEN 'up'
    ELSE            'unknown'
  END AS trend
FROM dbo.SalesGrp
GROUP BY sgn, grp;
GO
```

If you query SalesTrends as shown in the following code, you get the desired results:

```
SELECT start_range, end_range, trend
FROM dbo.SalesTrends
ORDER BY start_range;
```

You can provide a more efficient solution for this problem by using ranking calculations. First create a view called SalesRN with row numbers assigned to the rows from Sales based on the order of *mnth*:

```
IF OBJECT_ID('dbo.SalesRN', 'V') IS NOT NULL
  DROP VIEW dbo.SalesRN;
GO
CREATE VIEW dbo.SalesRN
AS

SELECT mnth, qty, ROW_NUMBER() OVER(ORDER BY mnth) AS rn
FROM dbo.Sales;
GO

SELECT * FROM dbo.SalesRN;
```

This code generates the following output:

```
mnth          qty          rn
------------  -----------  --------------------
2007-12-01    100          1
2008-01-01    110          2
2008-02-01    120          3
2008-03-01    130          4
2008-04-01    140          5
2008-05-01    140          6
2008-06-01    130          7
2008-07-01    120          8
2008-08-01    110          9
2008-09-01    100          10
2008-10-01    110          11
2008-11-01    100          12
2008-12-01    120          13
2009-01-01    130          14
2009-02-01    140          15
2009-03-01    100          16
2009-04-01    100          17
2009-05-01    100          18
2009-06-01    110          19
2009-07-01    120          20
2009-08-01    110          21
2009-09-01    120          22
2009-10-01    130          23
2009-11-01    140          24
2009-12-01    100          25
```

In the SalesTrendSgn view, you join two instances of SalesRN to match each current row with the row for the previous month. You then have access to both the current month's and previous month's *qty* values, and you calculate the sign of their difference. Here's the code for the new version of the SalesTrendSgn view that relies on the row numbers from the SalesRN view:

```
IF OBJECT_ID('dbo.SalesTrendSgn', 'V') IS NOT NULL
  DROP VIEW dbo.SalesTrendSgn;
GO
CREATE VIEW dbo.SalesTrendSgn
AS
```

```
SELECT Cur.mnth, Cur.qty, SIGN(Cur.qty - Prv.qty) AS sgn
FROM dbo.SalesRN AS Cur
  LEFT OUTER JOIN dbo.SalesRN AS Prv
    ON Cur.rn = Prv.rn + 1;
GO
```

You can further optimize the solution by revising the SalesGrp view, which calculates the grouping factor, as follows:

```
IF OBJECT_ID('dbo.SalesGrp', 'V') IS NOT NULL
  DROP VIEW dbo.SalesGrp;
GO
CREATE VIEW dbo.SalesGrp
AS

SELECT mnth, sgn,
  DATEADD(month,
    -1 * ROW_NUMBER() OVER(PARTITION BY sgn ORDER BY mnth),
    mnth) AS grp
FROM dbo.SalesTrendSgn;
GO
```

The logic behind the calculation of the grouping factor here is a bit tricky. You calculate a row number (*rn*) based on the order of *mnth*, partitioned by *sgn* (trend). This means that, for each trend, you can have multiple consecutive groups, naturally with gaps between them. Now try to think of the way the *mnth* value increments within a particular trend versus how *rn* increments. Both continue to increment by one unit as long as you're still in the same consecutive group. Once you have a gap, *mnth* increments by more than one unit, whereas *rn* keeps incrementing by one. You can conclude that if you subtract *rn* months from *mnth*, the result for each consecutive group will be constant and unique. As I mentioned, the logic here is tricky and can be hard to grasp. To better understand it, I suggest that you pull SalesGrp's query aside and play with it. For example, return the row number itself (as opposed to using it in a calculation), and so on.

Finally, create the SalesTrends view to group the data by *sgn* and *grp*, returning the ranges of consecutive months with the same trend.

```
IF OBJECT_ID('dbo.SalesTrends', 'V') IS NOT NULL
  DROP VIEW dbo.SalesTrends;
GO
CREATE VIEW dbo.SalesTrends
AS

SELECT
  CONVERT(VARCHAR(6), MIN(mnth), 112) AS start_range,
  CONVERT(VARCHAR(6), MAX(mnth), 112) AS end_range,
  CASE sgn
    WHEN -1 THEN 'down'
    WHEN  0 THEN 'same'
    WHEN  1 THEN 'up'
    ELSE         'unknown'
  END AS trend
```

```
FROM dbo.SalesGrp
GROUP BY sgn, grp;
GO
```

Query the SalesTrends view and you get the desired result:

```
SELECT start_range, end_range, trend
FROM dbo.SalesTrends
ORDER BY start_range;
```

Remember that SQL Server 2008 supports CTEs, which also allow you to develop solutions applying a modular approach. In fact, you can think of CTEs as inline views that exist only in the scope of the outer query. If you think about it, other than allowing a modular development approach, you have no real reason to create the intermediate views in the solution. Instead, you should just create the final one—SalesTrends—which will be defined by a CTE developed using a modular approach. Run the following code to alter the SalesTrends view, implementing it with multiple CTEs defined in the same WITH statement instead of defining multiple views:

```
ALTER VIEW dbo.SalesTrends
AS

WITH SalesRN AS
(
  SELECT mnth, qty, ROW_NUMBER() OVER(ORDER BY mnth) AS rn
  FROM dbo.Sales
),
SalesTrendSgn AS
(
  SELECT Cur.mnth, Cur.qty, SIGN(Cur.qty - Prv.qty) AS sgn
  FROM SalesRN AS Cur
    LEFT OUTER JOIN SalesRN AS Prv
      ON Cur.rn = Prv.rn + 1
),
SalesGrp AS
(
  SELECT mnth, sgn,
    DATEADD(month,
      -1 * ROW_NUMBER() OVER(PARTITION BY sgn ORDER BY mnth),
      mnth) AS grp
  FROM SalesTrendSgn
)
SELECT
  CONVERT(VARCHAR(6), MIN(mnth), 112) AS start_range,
  CONVERT(VARCHAR(6), MAX(mnth), 112) AS end_range,
  CASE sgn
    WHEN -1 THEN 'down'
    WHEN  0 THEN 'same'
    WHEN  1 THEN 'up'
    ELSE         'unknown'
  END AS trend
FROM SalesGrp
GROUP BY sgn, grp;
GO
```

If you query SalesTrends using the following code, you get the desired output:

```
SELECT start_range, end_range, trend
FROM dbo.SalesTrends
ORDER BY start_range;
```

In short, developing solutions with the modular approach simplifies the process and reduces the chances of bugs and errors.

When you're done, run the following cleanup code:

```
IF OBJECT_ID('dbo.SalesTrends', 'V') IS NOT NULL DROP VIEW dbo.SalesTrends;
IF OBJECT_ID('dbo.SalesGrp', 'V') IS NOT NULL DROP VIEW dbo.SalesGrp;
IF OBJECT_ID('dbo.SalesTrendSgn', 'V') IS NOT NULL DROP VIEW dbo.SalesTrendSgn;
IF OBJECT_ID('dbo.SalesRN', 'V') IS NOT NULL DROP VIEW dbo.SalesRN;
IF OBJECT_ID('dbo.Sales', 'U') IS NOT NULL DROP TABLE dbo.Sales;
```

Updating Views

Remember that a view is a virtual table, and remember that when you submit a query against a view, SQL Server expands the view's select statement and issues the query against the underlying tables. A view is not limited to being a target of SELECT queries; it can be a target for modifications, too. When you submit a modification against a view, SQL Server modifies the underlying tables. The view in such a case acts as an agent or a vehicle. Of course, you can limit the data that you're exposing through the view by allowing modifications through the view but not directly against the underlying tables. This way, the view can play a security role to some degree in terms of privacy and disclosure.

For example, one way to achieve row-level security is by using views.

> **Caution** In this section, I'll show the simple use of views to provide row-level security. Note that the technique I will demonstrate is imperfect and might be useful for applications in which security is not a firm requirement. For details about row-level security and the disclosure risk of this security mechanism, please refer to the following white paper: *http://technet.microsoft.com/ en-us/library/cc966395.aspx*.

The following code creates a table called UserData with a column called *loginname* that accepts a default value from the SUSER_SNAME function (current login name). The code creates a view that exposes all attributes except *loginname* only to the current user by using the filter *loginname = SUSER_SNAME()*. The code denies data manipulation language (DML) permissions against the table to public, and it grants permissions against the view to public:

```
USE tempdb;
IF OBJECT_ID('dbo.CurrentUserData', 'V') IS NOT NULL
  DROP VIEW dbo.CurrentUserData;
IF OBJECT_ID('dbo.UserData', 'T') IS NOT NULL
  DROP TABLE dbo.UserData;
GO
```

```
CREATE TABLE dbo.UserData
(
  keycol    INT        NOT NULL IDENTITY PRIMARY KEY,
  loginname sysname    NOT NULL DEFAULT (SUSER_SNAME()),
  datacol   VARCHAR(20) NOT NULL,
  /* ... other columns ... */
);
GO
CREATE VIEW dbo.CurrentUserData
AS

SELECT keycol, datacol
FROM dbo.UserData
WHERE loginname = SUSER_SNAME();
GO

DENY SELECT, INSERT, UPDATE, DELETE ON dbo.UserData TO public;
GRANT SELECT, INSERT, UPDATE, DELETE ON dbo.CurrentUserData TO public;
```

With these restrictions in place, users can access and manipulate only their own data.

Modifications against views have the following limitations:

- You cannot insert data through a view if the view doesn't include even one column from the underlying table that doesn't get its value implicitly. A column can get a value implicitly if it allows NULLs, has a default value, has an IDENTITY property, or is typed as ROWVERSION.

- If the view is defined by a join query, an UPDATE or INSERT statement is allowed to affect only one side of the join; that is, an INSERT statement must specify a target column list that belongs only to one side of the join. Similarly, the columns that an UPDATE statement modifies must all belong to one side of the join. However, you are allowed to refer to any column you want to elsewhere in the query—on the right side of an assignment, in the query's filter, and so on. You cannot delete data from a view defined by a join query.

- You cannot modify a column that is a result of a calculation. This limitation includes both scalar expressions and aggregates. SQL Server doesn't make an attempt to reverse-engineer the calculation.

- If WITH CHECK OPTION was specified when the view was created or altered, INSERT or UPDATE statements that conflict with the view's query filter will be rejected. I will elaborate on this point later in this chapter in the "View Options" section.

Data modification statements in violation of these limitations can be issued if there is an INSTEAD OF trigger on the view. An INSTEAD OF trigger replaces the original modification with your own code. For example, you can write your own code to reverse-engineer modifications of columns that result from a calculation and issue the modification directly against the underlying tables. I will discuss triggers in Chapter 4, "Triggers."

Be especially careful when you allow modifications against a view defined by a join query. Users who are not aware that the target object for their modifications is a view and not a table might find the effect of their modifications surprising in some cases—for example, when they modify the "one" side of a one-to-many join.

As an example, run the following code to create the Customers and Orders tables and the CustOrders view that joins the two:

```
SET NOCOUNT ON;
USE tempdb;
IF OBJECT_ID('dbo.CustOrders', 'V') IS NOT NULL DROP VIEW dbo.CustOrders;
IF OBJECT_ID('dbo.Orders', 'U') IS NOT NULL DROP TABLE dbo.Orders;
IF OBJECT_ID('dbo.Customers', 'U') IS NOT NULL DROP TABLE dbo.Customers;
GO

CREATE TABLE dbo.Customers
(
  cid    INT         NOT NULL PRIMARY KEY,
  cname VARCHAR(25) NOT NULL,
  /* other columns */
)
INSERT INTO dbo.Customers(cid, cname) VALUES
  (1, 'Cust 1'),
  (2, 'Cust 2');

CREATE TABLE dbo.Orders
(
  oid INT NOT NULL PRIMARY KEY,
  cid INT NOT NULL REFERENCES dbo.Customers,
  /* other columns */
)
INSERT INTO dbo.Orders(oid, cid) VALUES
  (1001, 1),
  (1002, 1),
  (1003, 1),
  (2001, 2),
  (2002, 2),
  (2003, 2);
GO

CREATE VIEW dbo.CustOrders
AS

SELECT C.cid, C.cname, O.oid
FROM dbo.Customers AS C
  JOIN dbo.Orders AS O
    ON O.cid = C.cid;
GO
```

Query the view:

```
SELECT cid, cname, oid FROM dbo.CustOrders;
```

You get the following output:

```
cid          cname                     oid
-----------  ------------------------  -----------
1            Cust 1                    1001
1            Cust 1                    1002
1            Cust 1                    1003
2            Cust 2                    2001
2            Cust 2                    2002
2            Cust 2                    2003
```

Notice that customer attributes, such as the company name (*cname*), are duplicated for each matching order.

Suppose that a user who was granted UPDATE permissions against the view wants to modify the company name to *'Cust 42'*, where the order ID (*oid*) is equal to 1001. The user submits the following update:

```
UPDATE dbo.CustOrders
   SET cname = 'Cust 42'
WHERE oid = 1001;
```

Of course, if the target of the update was a table and not a view, you would have seen only one row with *'Cust 42'* in *cname* when querying the table. However, the target of the update is a view, and SQL Server modifies the Customers table underneath the covers. In practice, *cname* is modified for customer 1. Now query the CustOrders view using the following code:

```
SELECT cid, cname, oid FROM dbo.CustOrders;
```

You get the following output:

```
cid          cname                     oid
-----------  ------------------------  -----------
1            Cust 42                   1001
1            Cust 42                   1002
1            Cust 42                   1003
2            Cust 2                    2001
2            Cust 2                    2002
2            Cust 2                    2003
```

What happened was that the *cname* value was changed for order 1001. The view's *cname* value for order 1001 was the *cname* value from the Customers table associated with order 1001's customer (customer number 1, as stored in the Orders table). The view returned customer number 1's *cname* value for all three of customer number 1's orders.

When you're done, run the following cleanup code:

```
USE tempdb;
IF OBJECT_ID('dbo.CurrentUserData', 'V') IS NOT NULL
   DROP VIEW dbo.CurrentUserData;
IF OBJECT_ID('dbo.UserData', 'U') IS NOT NULL
   DROP TABLE dbo.UserData;
```

```
IF OBJECT_ID('dbo.CustOrders', 'V') IS NOT NULL
  DROP VIEW dbo.CustOrders;
IF OBJECT_ID('Sales.Orders', 'U') IS NOT NULL
  DROP TABLE Sales.Orders;
IF OBJECT_ID('Sales.Customers', 'U') IS NOT NULL
  DROP TABLE Sales.Customers;
```

View Options

When you create or alter a view, you can specify options that will control the view's behavior and functionality. The options ENCRYPTION, SCHEMABINDING, and VIEW_METADATA are specified in the view's header, and the CHECK OPTION is specified after the query.

ENCRYPTION

The ENCRYPTION option is available for views, UDFs, stored procedures, and triggers. If you don't specify the ENCRYPTION option, SQL Server stores the text defining the body of the object/routine as clear text in *sys.sql_modules*. If you specify the ENCRYPTION option, the object's text will be converted to an obfuscated format. But don't rely on this option as an encryption mechanism to protect your intellectual property. People have found ways to decrypt text stored for objects created with the ENCRYPTION option. Even in SQL Server 2008 the object's text will be accessible to privileged users through the dedicated administrator connection (DAC), direct access to the database files, or from memory using a debugger. For details on the ENCRYPTION option, please refer to SQL Server Books Online.

SCHEMABINDING

The SCHEMABINDING option binds the view or UDF to the schema of the underlying objects. If you create a view with the SCHEMABINDING option, SQL Server rejects attempts to drop underlying objects or make any schema modification to referenced columns. This option has two syntactical requirements in terms of the query defining the view: you must use two-part names for all objects (for example, Sales.Orders, not just Orders), and the use of * is not allowed in the SELECT list—instead, all column names must be specified explicitly.

As an example of using both ENCRYPTION and SCHEMABINDING, the following code re-creates the CustsWithOrders view, which I used earlier in my examples:

```
USE InsideTSQL2008;
IF OBJECT_ID('Sales.CustsWithOrders') IS NOT NULL
  DROP VIEW Sales.CustsWithOrders;
GO

CREATE VIEW Sales.CustsWithOrders WITH ENCRYPTION, SCHEMABINDING
AS
```

```
SELECT custid, companyname, contactname, contacttitle,
  address, city, region, postalcode, country, phone, fax
FROM Sales.Customers AS C
WHERE EXISTS
  (SELECT 1 FROM Sales.Orders AS O
   WHERE O.custid = C.custid);
GO
```

> **Note** If the view already exists, it's wiser to use ALTER VIEW than to drop and re-create the view, because ALTER VIEW preserves permissions.

Notice that I substituted the * I used originally in the EXISTS subquery with the constant 1 to meet the requirements of the SCHEMABINDING option.

Try to get the text of the view:

```
EXEC sp_helptext 'Sales.CustsWithOrders';
```

You get the following output:

```
The text for object 'Sales.CustsWithOrders' is encrypted.
```

Similarly, try to query the object definition using the OBJECT_DEFINITION function:

```
SELECT OBJECT_DEFINITION(OBJECT_ID('Sales.CustsWithOrders'));
```

You get NULL as the output.

Try to alter one of the referenced columns:

```
ALTER TABLE Sales.Customers DROP COLUMN address;
```

You get the following error:

```
Msg 5074, Level 16, State 1, Line 1
The object 'CustsWithOrders' is dependent on column 'address'.
Msg 4922, Level 16, State 9, Line 1
ALTER TABLE DROP COLUMN address failed because one or more objects access this column.
```

The error indicates which objects depend on the column that you're trying to drop. Using SQL Server 2008, you can query new dynamic management objects that provide reliable dependency information to identify object dependency before you attempt a schema change. For example, query the *sys.dm_sql_referencing_entities* function to find out which objects depend on the one you're about to alter or drop, like so:

```
SELECT referencing_schema_name, referencing_entity_name
FROM sys.dm_sql_referencing_entities('Sales.Customers', 'OBJECT');
```

Or query the *sys.sql_expression_dependencies* view to find out which objects depend on a column you're about to alter or drop, like so:

```
SELECT
  OBJECT_SCHEMA_NAME(referencing_id) AS referencing_schema_name,
  OBJECT_NAME(referencing_id) AS referencing_entity_name
FROM sys.sql_expression_dependencies
WHERE referenced_schema_name = N'Sales'
  AND referenced_entity_name = N'Customers'
  AND COL_NAME(referenced_id, referenced_minor_id) = N'address';
```

Both queries return *'Sales'* as the referencing schema name and *'CustsWithOrders'* as the referencing object name, telling you that the Sales.CustsWithOrders view depends on the Sales.Customers table, and more specifically on the *Sales.Customers.address* column.

CHECK OPTION

Specifying WITH CHECK OPTION when creating a view prevents INSERT and UPDATE statements that conflict with the view's query filter. Without this option, a view normally accepts modifications that do not meet the query's filter. For example, the CustsWithOrders view accepts the following INSERT, even though it inserts a new customer that has no orders yet:

```
INSERT INTO Sales.CustsWithOrders(
        companyname, contactname, contacttitle, address, city, region,
        postalcode, country, phone, fax)
  VALUES(N'Customer ABCDE', N'ABCDE', N'ABCDE', N'ABCDE', N'ABCDE',
        N'ABCDE', N'ABCDE', N'ABCDE', N'ABCDE', N'ABCDE');
```

The new customer was added to the Customers table, but obviously when you query the view, you don't see the new customer because the view contains only customers with orders:

```
SELECT custid, companyname
FROM Sales.CustsWithOrders
WHERE companyname = N'Customer ABCDE';
```

This query returns an empty set.

If you query the Customers table directly, you see the new customer:

```
SELECT custid, companyname
FROM Sales.Customers
WHERE companyname = N'Customer ABCDE';
```

This query returns information about customer ABCDE.

Next, run the following code to add WITH CHECK OPTION to the view's definition:

```
ALTER VIEW Sales.CustsWithOrders WITH ENCRYPTION, SCHEMABINDING
AS
```

```
SELECT custid, companyname, contactname, contacttitle,
  address, city, region, postalcode, country, phone, fax
FROM Sales.Customers AS C
WHERE EXISTS
  (SELECT 1 FROM Sales.Orders AS O
   WHERE O.custid = C.custid)
WITH CHECK OPTION;
GO
```

> **Note** When altering the view, you must specify again all options that you want to preserve—in our case, ENCRYPTION and SCHEMABINDING. If you don't mention them in the ALTER statement, they will no longer be in effect.

Now try to insert a row that conflicts with the filter:

```
INSERT INTO Sales.CustsWithOrders(
        companyname, contactname, contacttitle, address, city, region,
        postalcode, country, phone, fax)
  VALUES(N'Customer FGHIJ', N'FGHIJ', N'FGHIJ', N'FGHIJ', N'FGHIJ',
        N'FGHIJ', N'FGHIJ', N'FGHIJ', N'FGHIJ', N'FGHIJ');
```

You get the following error:

```
Msg 550, Level 16, State 1, Line 1
The attempted insert or update failed because the target view either specifies WITH CHECK
OPTION or spans a view that specifies WITH CHECK OPTION and one or more rows resulting from
the operation did not qualify under the CHECK OPTION constraint.
The statement has been terminated.
```

When you're done, issue the following cleanup code:

```
DELETE FROM Sales.Customers
WHERE custid > 91;

DBCC CHECKIDENT('Sales.Customers', RESEED, 91);
```

VIEW_METADATA

SQL Server can control client requests to query or modify data through a view only when the request ends up generating T-SQL code with the view as the target. However, clients that request browse-mode metadata through the DB-Library, ODBC, or OLEDB APIs might cause trouble. Browse-mode metadata is additional metadata about the base tables and columns in the result set that SQL Server returns to these client-side APIs. Of course, if the client chooses to construct statements with the base table as the target instead of the view, user requests might not work as expected.

Suppose that a user was granted permission against a view but not against the underlying tables. The user tries to perform some activity against the view. If the client tool constructs a statement against the base table because it requested browse-mode metadata, such a statement will fail on a security violation. On the other hand, if a user attempts to modify data through a view, and the modification conflicts with a CHECK OPTION defined with the view, such a modification might succeed if submitted directly against the underlying table.

If you want SQL Server to send metadata information about the view and not the underlying tables when browse mode metadata is requested by the client APIs, specify the VIEW_ METADATA option when you create or alter the view, as shown here:

```
ALTER VIEW Sales.CustsWithOrders
  WITH ENCRYPTION, SCHEMABINDING, VIEW_METADATA
AS

SELECT custid, companyname, contactname, contacttitle,
  address, city, region, postalcode, country, phone, fax
FROM Sales.Customers AS C
WHERE EXISTS
  (SELECT 1 FROM Sales.Orders AS O
  WHERE O.custid = C.custid)
WITH CHECK OPTION;
GO
```

When you're done, issue the following cleanup code:

```
IF OBJECT_ID('Sales.CustsWithOrders', 'V') IS NOT NULL
  DROP VIEW Sales.CustsWithOrders;
```

Indexed Views

Remember that without an index, a view does not have any physical representation of its data—rather, it just has metadata information pointing to the underlying objects. However, SQL Server will physically materialize a view's data if you create a unique clustered index on the view. SQL Server keeps the indexed view in sync with modifications against the underlying tables. You cannot request to synchronize the view's contents on demand or on scheduled basis. An indexed view is very much like a table index in terms of data integrity.

Indexed views can give you great performance benefits for queries that retrieve data. Indexed views can substantially reduce the amount of I/O required to return data and the processing time required for expensive calculations. Substantial performance gains can be achieved, for example, for data aggregation queries or expensive joins. However, keep in mind that modifications to an indexed view's underlying tables require changes to the indexed (and therefore materialized) view, degrading the performance of your modifications.

The long list of requirements and restrictions for creating an indexed view often prevents indexed views from being a viable option. The requirement list in SQL Server 2008 did not get any shorter than in previous versions.

The first index that you create on a view must be unique and clustered. After creating a clustered index on a view, you can create additional nonclustered indexes. The view must be created with the SCHEMABINDING option; therefore, you must use the two-part naming convention for object names and explicitly specify column names in the SELECT list. If the view's query aggregates data, its select list must include the COUNT_BIG(*) aggregate function. COUNT_BIG is the same as COUNT, except that its result type is BIGINT. This count allows SQL Server to keep track of the number of rows that were aggregated in each group, and it is also used to calculate other aggregates. Some SET options in the session must be in a certain state. The list of requirements and restrictions goes on. Please refer to SQL Server Books Online for the gory details.

For example, suppose that you want to optimize queries that request aggregated data from the Orders and OrderDetails tables for employees. One way to do this is to create a materialized view containing the aggregates you expect to request. The following code creates the EmpOrders indexed view based on a query that joins Orders and OrderDetails, groups the data by *empid*, and calculates the sum of *qty* and the count of rows for each employee:

```
USE InsideTSQL2008;
IF OBJECT_ID('dbo.EmpOrders', 'V') IS NOT NULL DROP VIEW dbo.EmpOrders;
IF OBJECT_ID('dbo.EmpOrders', 'U') IS NOT NULL DROP TABLE dbo.EmpOrders;
GO
CREATE VIEW dbo.EmpOrders WITH SCHEMABINDING
AS

SELECT O.empid, SUM(OD.qty) AS totalqty, COUNT_BIG(*) AS cnt
FROM Sales.Orders AS O
  JOIN Sales.OrderDetails AS OD
    ON OD.orderid = O.orderid
GROUP BY O.empid;
GO
CREATE UNIQUE CLUSTERED INDEX idx_uc_empid ON dbo.EmpOrders(empid);
```

Notice that the view was created with the SCHEMABINDING option, the tables are referenced with two-part names, the COUNT_BIG function is used because it's a query that calculates aggregates, and the index created on the view is both clustered and unique.

SQL Server doesn't regenerate the whole index whenever the underlying tables are modified; rather, it maintains the index in a smarter manner. When you insert data, SQL Server identifies the affected row of the view and increments the aggregate values *totalqty* and *cnt* for that row. When you delete data, SQL Server decrements these values. When you update data in the underlying tables, SQL Server updates the aggregate values accordingly.

To observe the performance benefit indexed views can give you, run the following query after turning on the STATISTICS IO option and the Include Actual Execution Plan in SSMS:

```
SET STATISTICS IO ON;
SELECT empid, totalqty, cnt FROM dbo.EmpOrders;
```

Here's the output of this query:

```
empid       totalqty    cnt
----------- ----------- --------------------
1           7812        345
2           6055        241
3           7852        321
4           9798        420
5           3036        117
6           3527        168
7           4654        176
8           5913        260
9           2670        107
```

Figure 1-3 shows the query's execution plan.

FIGURE 1-3 Execution plan for a query against the EmpOrders view

The plan shows that the view's clustered index was scanned. For this small view, which contains only nine rows, the total I/O was two logical reads. If you're using the Enterprise edition of SQL Server (or the Developer edition, which is equivalent in its feature set), the query optimizer will consider using the indexed view for queries against the view without specifying any hints, and for queries against the base tables. For example, the following query generates the execution plan shown in Figure 1-4:

```
SELECT O.empid, SUM(OD.qty) AS totalqty, AVG(OD.qty) AS avgqty, COUNT_BIG(*) AS cnt
FROM Sales.Orders AS O
  JOIN Sales.OrderDetails AS OD
    ON OD.orderid = O.orderid
GROUP BY O.empid;
```

FIGURE 1-4 Execution plan for a query against the Orders and OrderDetails tables

As you can see, the indexed view was used, and again the I/O cost was only two logical reads. Interestingly, the query requested the aggregate *AVG(OD.qty)*, which was not part of the view, yet the indexed view was used. Remember that the sum and the count were calculated. If you expand the properties of the Compute Scalar operator in the plan, you find the following expression, which calculates the average from the sum and the count:

```
[Expr1005] = Scalar Operator(CASE WHEN [InsideTSQL2008].[dbo].[EmpOrders]
  .[cnt]=(0) THEN NULL ELSE [InsideTSQL2008].[dbo].[EmpOrders].[totalqty]/
  CONVERT_IMPLICIT(int,[InsideTSQL2008].[dbo].[EmpOrders].[cnt],0) END),
  [Expr1006] = Scalar Operator([InsideTSQL2008].[dbo].[EmpOrders].[cnt])
```

Note If you're not working with the Enterprise or Developer edition of SQL Server, an indexed view will not be considered by default even when you query the view directly. To use the index, you must specify the NOEXPAND hint.

SQL Server 2005 introduced several optimization enhancements in regards to indexed views, whereas SQL Server 2008 introduces improved support for partitioned tables. The optimization enhancements in SQL Server 2005 include support for subintervals (for example, you can use an index when the view's query has the filter *col1 > 5* and the outer query has the filter *col1 > 10*) and logically equivalent expressions (for example, you can use an index when the view's query has the filter *col1 = 5* and the outer query has *5 = col1*), and others. SQL Server 2008 improves support for partitioned tables by allowing more types of operations on partitioned tables without requiring dropping and re-creating the index on the view, as was required in some cases in SQL Server 2005. SQL Server 2008 supports a feature called *partition-aligned indexed views*, which means that the query processor automatically maintains an indexed view created on a partitioned table when a new partition is switched in. When you switch a partition in or out of a partitioned table, you are no longer required to drop the index on the view and re-create it later.

More Info For detailed information about indexed views in SQL Server 2008 and improvements over previous versions, please refer to the white paper "Improving Performance with SQL Server 2008 Indexed Views" by Eric Hanson and Susan Price, which can be found at *http://msdn.microsoft.com/en-us/library/dd171921.aspx*.

You can use indexed views for purposes other than performance. For example, T-SQL's UNIQUE constraint treats two NULLs as equal. If you create a UNIQUE constraint on a nullable column, the constraint allows only one instance of a NULL in that column. Suppose that you want to enforce uniqueness for known (that is, NOT NULL) values only, but allow multiple NULLs—the way a UNIQUE constraint defined by ANSI SQL is supposed to behave. You can achieve this by using a trigger, but such a trigger has a cost. If the trigger rolls back, it's as if the modification that fired it was done twice—or, more accurately, done and then undone. Instead of using a trigger, you can enforce such an integrity rule by using an indexed view. Create an indexed view based on a query that filters only the non-NULL values from the source column. Remember that the clustered index created on a view must be unique. Such an index prevents duplicate known values from entering the base table, but it allows multiple NULLs because NULLs are not part of the unique index.

To demonstrate this, run the following code, which creates the table T1 with the column *keycol*, and an indexed view based on a query that filters only known *keycol* values from T1:

```
USE tempdb;
IF OBJECT_ID('dbo.V1', 'V') IS NOT NULL DROP VIEW dbo.V1;
IF OBJECT_ID('dbo.T1', 'U') IS NOT NULL DROP TABLE dbo.T1;
```

```
GO
CREATE TABLE dbo.T1
(
  keycol  INT         NULL,
  datacol VARCHAR(10) NOT NULL
);
GO
CREATE VIEW dbo.V1 WITH SCHEMABINDING
AS

SELECT keycol FROM dbo.T1 WHERE keycol IS NOT NULL;
GO
CREATE UNIQUE CLUSTERED INDEX idx_uc_keycol ON dbo.V1(keycol);
```

Next, issue the following INSERT statements:

```
INSERT INTO dbo.T1(keycol, datacol) VALUES(1,    'a');
INSERT INTO dbo.T1(keycol, datacol) VALUES(1,    'b'); -- fails
INSERT INTO dbo.T1(keycol, datacol) VALUES(NULL, 'c');
INSERT INTO dbo.T1(keycol, datacol) VALUES(NULL, 'd');
```

Notice that the second attempt to insert a row with the value 1 in *keycol* fails, but both NULLs are accepted. Query T1:

```
SELECT keycol, datacol FROM dbo.T1;
```

You get the following output:

```
keycol      datacol
----------- ----------
1           a
NULL        c
NULL        d
```

Observe that both NULLs reached the table.

SQL Server 2008 allows you to achieve this task in an even simpler manner by using a new feature called *filtered indexes*. Filtered indexes are table indexes defined on a subset of rows from the base table identified by a predicate that you specify in a WHERE clause as part of the index definition, much like in a query's WHERE clause.

To accomplish the task at hand, simply define a unique filtered index on *keycol* that filters only rows where *keycol* is not NULL. This way, uniqueness is enforced only for known values. To demonstrate using a filtered index to achieve the task, first drop the view you created earlier by running the following code:

```
IF OBJECT_ID('dbo.V1', 'V') IS NOT NULL DROP VIEW dbo.V1;
```

Next, create the aforementioned filtered index by running the following code:

```
CREATE UNIQUE INDEX idx_keycol_notnull ON dbo.T1(keycol)
  WHERE keycol IS NOT NULL;
```

Now run the following code to insert a couple of rows with a NULL in *keycol*, and attempt to insert another row with a non-NULL value that already exists in the table:

```
INSERT INTO dbo.T1(keycol, datacol) VALUES(NULL, 'e');
INSERT INTO dbo.T1(keycol, datacol) VALUES(NULL, 'f');
INSERT INTO dbo.T1(keycol, datacol) VALUES(1, 'g');
```

The rows with the NULL make it to the table, but the duplicate known value doesn't. Query the table by running the following code:

```
SELECT keycol, datacol FROM dbo.T1;
```

You get the following output:

```
keycol      datacol
----------- ----------

1           a
NULL        c
NULL        d
NULL        e
NULL        f
```

When done, run the following code for cleanup:

```
USE InsideTSQL2008;
IF OBJECT_ID('dbo.EmpOrders', 'V') IS NOT NULL DROP VIEW dbo.EmpOrders;

USE tempdb;
IF OBJECT_ID('dbo.V1', 'V') IS NOT NULL DROP VIEW dbo.V1;
IF OBJECT_ID('dbo.T1', 'U') IS NOT NULL DROP TABLE dbo.T1;
```

Conclusion

Views give you great power. They allow you to provide a desired logical representation of your relations, they give you some degree of security enforcement, they allow you to develop simpler solutions in a modular approach, and they can help you improve the performance of your queries when you index them. Keep in mind that a view represents a table and, as such, does not have any guaranteed order to its rows. Do not attempt to produce a "sorted" view because the entire premise for adopting such an approach is wrong. If you need to send data from a view to the client in a particular order, specify an ORDER BY clause in the outer query. Remember to refresh views' metadata information after applying schema changes to underlying objects in the database.

Chapter 2
User-Defined Functions

Itzik Ben-Gan and Dejan Sarka

User-defined functions (UDFs) are routines that perform calculations/computations and return a value—scalar (singular) or a table. Microsoft SQL Server 2008 allows you to develop UDFs using either T-SQL or a .NET language of your choice based on the common language runtime (CLR) integration in the product. You can incorporate UDFs in queries, computed columns, and constraints.

This chapter explores the types of UDFs that are supported by SQL Server: scalar-valued UDFs, which return a single value, and table-valued UDFs (inline and multiple-statement), which return a table. I'll provide sample code for CLR UDFs in both C# and Microsoft Visual Basic.

Most of the .NET routines in this book were originally developed by Dejan Sarka.

> **Note** This chapter is the first of four chapters (2, 3, 4, and 8) that cover CLR routines. Some of the steps involved in building and deploying CLR code into a database are common to any type of CLR routine that you create in SQL Server and are also very technical. To avoid repetition of such technical steps in the text and to allow you to focus on the code of the routines, I compiled all the relevant information about CLR routines into Appendix A.
>
> In Appendix A, you will find instructions for creating a test database called CLRUtilities, which you will use to test all CLR routines covered in these four chapters. You will also find step-by-step instructions required to develop, build, deploy, and test all the CLR routines.
>
> The appendix also gathers in one place all the code of CLR routines that is scattered throughout these four chapters. I recommend that before you read the remainder of this chapter, you follow the instructions in Appendix A, in which you will create in advance all the routines you will use in these four chapters. Then return to this chapter and continue reading, focusing on the code of the CLR routines instead of on the common technical steps.

Some Facts About UDFs

UDFs can be embedded in queries, constraints, and computed columns. The code that defines a UDF may not cause side effects that affect the database state outside the scope of the function—that is, the UDF's code is not allowed to modify data in tables or to invoke a function that has side effects (for example, RAND). In addition, the UDF's code can only create table variables and cannot create or access temporary tables. Also, the UDF's code is not allowed to use dynamic SQL.

When creating or altering a UDF, you can specify function options in the header. T-SQL UDFs support the ENCRYPTION and SCHEMABINDING options, which I described in the previous chapter when discussing views. Both T-SQL and CLR UDFs can be created with the EXECUTE AS clause, which lets you define the security context of the execution of the function. This option is not available to inline table-valued UDFs. An inline table-valued UDF is very similar to a view with the exception that it can accept arguments. It consists of a single query that defines the table returned by the function. With scalar UDFs (both T-SQL and CLR), you can also specify one of these two options: RETURNS NULL ON NULL INPUT or CALLED ON NULL INPUT (the default). The former option tells SQL Server not to invoke the function at all if a parameter value is NULL; in this case, the function result will be NULL. The latter option tells SQL Server that you want it to invoke the function even when one of the input parameters is NULL.

It is a good practice to create all your UDFs with both the SCHEMABINDING and RETURNS NULL ON NULL INPUT options when it is the desired behavior. SCHEMABINDING prevents dropping underlying objects and schema changes to referenced columns. RETURNS NULL ON NULL INPUT can improve the performance of your code by bypassing the function logic and returning NULL when one of the inputs is NULL.

Scalar UDFs

Scalar UDFs return a single (scalar) value. They can be specified where scalar expressions are allowed—for example, in a query, constraint, computed column, and so on. Scalar UDFs have several syntactical requirements:

- They must have a BEGIN/END block defining their body.

- They must be schema qualified when invoked (unless invoked as stored procedures with EXEC, as in *EXEC myFunction 3, 4*).

- They do not allow omitting optional parameters (ones that have default values) when invoked; rather, you must at least specify the DEFAULT keyword for those.

The following sections explore both T-SQL and CLR UDFs.

T-SQL Scalar UDFs

T-SQL UDFs are typically faster than CLR UDFs when the main cost of their activity pertains to set-based data manipulation, as opposed to procedural logic and computations. This is the case with any type of routine—not just UDFs. In the function's header you specify its name, define the input parameters, and define the data type of the returned value. As an example of a scalar UDF, the following code creates the *ConcatOrders* function, which accepts a customer ID as input and returns a string with the concatenated order IDs for the input customer:

```
SET NOCOUNT ON;
USE InsideTSQL2008;

IF OBJECT_ID('dbo.ConcatOrders', 'FN') IS NOT NULL
  DROP FUNCTION dbo.ConcatOrders;
GO

CREATE FUNCTION dbo.ConcatOrders
  (@custid AS INT) RETURNS VARCHAR(MAX)
```

```
AS
BEGIN
  DECLARE @orders AS VARCHAR(MAX);
  SET @orders = '';

  SELECT @orders = @orders + CAST(orderid AS VARCHAR(10)) + ';'
  FROM Sales.Orders
  WHERE custid = @custid;

  RETURN @orders;
END
GO
```

The function declares the *@orders* variable and initializes it with an empty string. The query in the function uses a special T-SQL assignment SELECT syntax. It scans the qualifying rows, and for each row it assigns a value to the *@orders* variable. The value is the current content of *@orders* concatenated with the current *orderid* value and a semicolon as the separator.

> **Important** Microsoft has no official documentation describing this aggregate concatenation technique that is based on the assignment SELECT syntax. The behavior described here is based on observation alone. The current implementation of the *ConcatOrders* function doesn't incorporate an ORDER BY clause and does not guarantee the order of concatenation. According to a blog entry by Microsoft's Conor Cunningham, it seems that SQL Server will respect an ORDER BY clause if specified (*http://blogs.msdn.com/sqltips/archive/2005/07/20/441053.aspx*). Conor is a very credible source, but I should stress that besides this blog entry I haven't found any official documentation describing how a multi-row assignment SELECT should behave—with or without an ORDER BY clause.

To test the *ConcatOrders* function, run the following query:

```
SELECT custid, dbo.ConcatOrders(custid) AS orders
FROM Sales.Customers;
```

This generates the following output, shown here in abbreviated form with line wrapping:

```
custid      orders
----------- ------------------------------------------------------------
1           10835;10952;11011;10692;10702;10643;
2           10625;10759;10926;10308;
3           10677;10365;10682;10856;10535;10507;10573;
4           10453;10558;10743;10768;10793;10707;10741;10864;10920;10355;
            10383;10953;11016;
5           10524;10626;10689;10733;10280;10384;10444;10445;10572;10778;
            10924;10875;10654;10866;10278;10857;10672;10837;
6           10582;10509;10956;10614;10501;10853;11058;
7           10265;10436;10449;10360;10584;10628;10297;10559;10826;10679;
            10566;
8           10326;10801;10970;
9           10340;10525;10827;10663;10362;10715;10732;10470;10511;10755;
            11076;10730;10876;10932;10940;10331;10871;
11          11023;10471;10484;10947;10578;10943;10539;10599;10289;10538;
...
```

The task of string concatenation can be achieved with another very efficient solution based on the FOR XML PATH option. This solution is much more elegant than the one based on assignment SELECT, it is fully supported, and it provides full control over ordering. The fast and nifty concatenation technique was originally devised by Michael Rys, a program manager with the Microsoft SQL Server development team, and Eugene Kogan, a technical lead on the Microsoft SQL Server Engine team. Credit also goes to SQL Server MVP Tony Rogerson who added logic for handling special characters. The PATH mode provides an easier way to mix elements and attributes than the EXPLICIT directive. Here's the complete solution:

```
SELECT custid,
  COALESCE(
    (SELECT CAST(orderid AS VARCHAR(10)) + ';' AS [text()]
     FROM Sales.Orders AS O
     WHERE O.custid = C.custid
     ORDER BY orderid
     FOR XML PATH(''), TYPE).value('.[1]', 'VARCHAR(MAX)'), '') AS orders
FROM Sales.Customers AS C;
```

The outer query returns the customer IDs of all customers from the Customers table. The correlated subquery returns all order IDs from the Orders table for the current customer in the outer row. The purpose of the FOR XML option is to return a single XML instance made of the values returned by the query. To achieve this, the FOR XML option needs to concatenate all values. The combination of providing an empty string as input to the PATH mode and aliasing the expression in the SELECT list as *[text()]* means that you get simple concatenation of the values returned by the query without tags. The COALESCE function is then used to convert a NULL to an empty string in case the customer has no orders.

Note that the use of AS [text()] will apply various XML requirements to special characters, like &, <, and >, converting them to their representative tags (*&*, *<*, and *>*, respectively). Our specific query concatenates order IDs that are originally integers, hence there's no chance to find special characters in the data. Still, I added logic to address special characters to the query so that you will be able to use it when relevant. This extra logic involves using the TYPE directive that tells SQL Server to returned an XML type instance, and the *.value* method that retrieves a value from the XML instance, converting the tags back to the original special characters.

CLR user-defined aggregates (UDAs) can also solve this problem. I provide detailed coverage of the aforementioned techniques to achieve string concatenation, as well as other custom aggregates in *Inside T-SQL Querying*.

When you're done, run the following code for cleanup:

```
IF OBJECT_ID('dbo.ConcatOrders', 'FN') IS NOT NULL
  DROP FUNCTION dbo.ConcatOrders;
```

Performance Issues

You should be aware that invoking scalar UDFs in queries has a high cost when you provide the function with attributes from the outer table as inputs. Even when the function only has a RETURN clause with a scalar expression, it is not considered inline. The overhead of the function call per row involves a high cost. You can run a simple performance test to realize the high cost involved with UDFs compared to inline expressions in a query.

Before you run the performance test, run the code in Listing 2-1 to create an auxiliary table of numbers called Nums and populate it with 1,000,000 numbers. Note that this book makes frequent use of this helper table, so you may want to keep it around after creating it.

LISTING 2-1 Creating and Populating Auxiliary Table of Numbers

```
SET NOCOUNT ON;
USE InsideTSQL2008;

IF OBJECT_ID('dbo.Nums', 'U') IS NOT NULL DROP TABLE dbo.Nums;

CREATE TABLE dbo.Nums(n INT NOT NULL PRIMARY KEY);
DECLARE @max AS INT, @rc AS INT;
SET @max = 1000000;
SET @rc = 1;

INSERT INTO Nums VALUES(1);
WHILE @rc * 2 <= @max
BEGIN
  INSERT INTO dbo.Nums SELECT n + @rc FROM dbo.Nums;
  SET @rc = @rc * 2;
END

INSERT INTO dbo.Nums
  SELECT n + @rc FROM dbo.Nums WHERE n + @rc <= @max;
```

Turn on the Discard results after execution in SQL Server Management Studio (SSMS), so that your measurements do not include the time it takes to generate the output.

> **Note** There are two ways to turn the option Discard results after execution on or off in SSMS. One option is from the current session's Query Options dialog box (choose the Query Options item from the Query menu or choose Query Options in the session's shortcut menu). This option affects the current editor window. Another option is from the Options dialog box. (Go to Tools, then Options, then on the left pane navigate to Query Results, SQL Server, and then to Results to Grid or Results to Text, depending on your current setting.) This option affects only new editor windows that you open and not the current one.

Start by running a query against a million rows from Nums, with an inline expression that adds 1 to *n*:

```
SELECT n, n + 1 AS n_plus_one FROM dbo.Nums WHERE n <= 1000000;
```

Figure 2-1 shows the execution plan for this query.

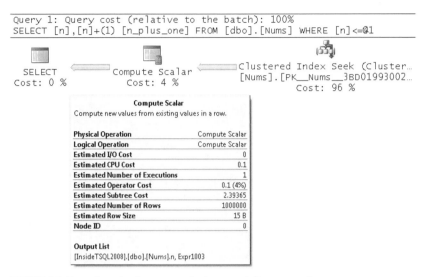

```
Query 1: Query cost (relative to the batch): 100%
SELECT [n],[n]+(1) [n_plus_one] FROM [dbo].[Nums] WHERE [n]<=@1
```

Compute Scalar	
Compute new values from existing values in a row.	
Physical Operation	Compute Scalar
Logical Operation	Compute Scalar
Estimated I/O Cost	0
Estimated CPU Cost	0.1
Estimated Number of Executions	1
Estimated Operator Cost	0.1 (4%)
Estimated Subtree Cost	2.39365
Estimated Number of Rows	1000000
Estimated Row Size	15 B
Node ID	0
Output List	
[InsideTSQL2008].[dbo].[Nums].n, Expr1003	

FIGURE 2-1 Execution plan for a query that uses an inline expression

Observe that in the plan the Compute Scalar operator calculates a scalar variable called *Expr1003*. In the Properties dialog box for this operator you will find that the expression used to assign a value to this variable is: *[Expr1003] = Scalar Operator([InsideTSQL2008].[dbo] .[Nums].[n]+(1))*. This is an inline expression that was evaluated as part of the query, and didn't involve any special cost.

Note that the first invocation of the code might have had to scan the data physically. Now that the data is loaded into cache, run the query a second time and measure the run time. When I ran this code on my system, it finished in less than a second.

Next, create the *AddOne* scalar UDF:

```
IF OBJECT_ID('dbo.AddOne', 'FN') IS NOT NULL
  DROP FUNCTION dbo.AddOne;
GO
CREATE FUNCTION dbo.AddOne(@i AS INT) RETURNS INT
AS
BEGIN
  RETURN @i + 1;
END
GO
```

Now run the query using *AddOne*:

```
SELECT n, dbo.AddOne(n) AS n_plus_one FROM dbo.Nums WHERE n <= 1000000;
```

Figure 2-2 shows the execution plan for this query.

```
Query 1: Query cost (relative to the batch): 100%
SELECT n, dbo.AddOne(n) AS n_plus_one FROM dbo.Nums WHERE n <= 1000000
```

```
                                          Clustered Index Seek (Cluster...
   SELECT         Compute Scalar           [Nums].[PK__Nums__3BD01993002...
  Cost: 0 %         Cost: 4 %                     Cost: 96 %
```

Compute Scalar	
Compute new values from existing values in a row.	
Physical Operation	Compute Scalar
Logical Operation	Compute Scalar
Actual Number of Rows	1000000
Estimated I/O Cost	0
Estimated CPU Cost	0.1
Number of Executions	1
Estimated Number of Executions	1
Estimated Operator Cost	0.1 (4%)
Estimated Subtree Cost	2.39365
Estimated Number of Rows	1000000
Estimated Row Size	15 B
Actual Rebinds	0
Actual Rewinds	0
Node ID	0
Output List	
[InsideTSQL2008].[dbo].[Nums].n, Expr1003	

FIGURE 2-2 Execution plan for a query that uses a scalar UDF

Observe that also in this plan the Compute Scalar operator calculates a scalar variable called *Expr1003*. However, if you examine the Properties dialog box for this operator, you will find that the expression that is assigned to the variable is different than in the previous plan: *[Expr1003] = Scalar Operator([InsideTSQL2008].[dbo].[AddOne]([InsideTSQL2008].[dbo] .[Nums].[n]))*. The difference is that this time you see the call to the *AddOne* UDF and not the expression *n + 1*. At first you might not think this makes any difference—after all, the query does have an expression that invokes the UDF. However, the fact that the UDF call appears in the plan is an indication that the function's expression wasn't inlined in the query. In other words, SQL Server makes a separate call to the UDF per each row, and each such invocation bears some extra cost compared to the corresponding inline expression. To give you a sense of what this extra cost translates to, this query ran for five seconds on my system—remember that the query that had the expression inline ran for under a second.

The high cost of the last query has to do with the overhead of each function call. You can easily observe the multiple invocations of the UDF by running a SQL Server Profiler trace with the *SP:Completed* (or *SP:Starting*) event while the query is running. To limit the size of the trace, you might want to test the query against fewer rows—for example, with the filter *n <= 10*. Figure 2-3 shows the events I got when I traced this query.

The encapsulation of your code in UDFs give you some important programmatic benefits, such as simplifying your code, reusability of logic, and so on. But you need to consider the negative impact on performance. Does this mean you must make a choice between programmatic benefits and performance? Fortunately, there is a solution that allows you

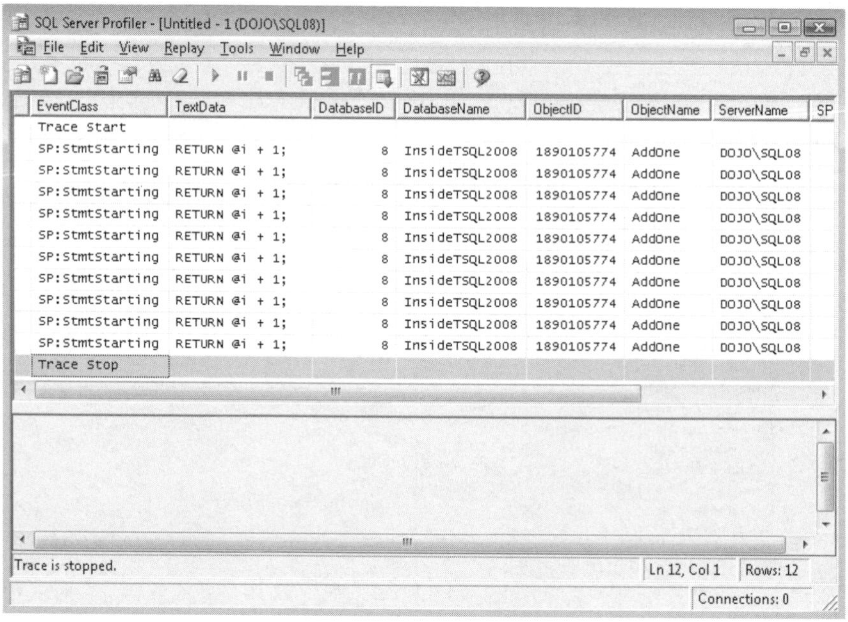

FIGURE 2-3 Profiler trace of multiple scalar UDF invocations

to avoid making such a choice—a solution that allows you to create a UDF without negatively effecting the performance of the query.

The solution is applicable only when the function is based on a single expression, as opposed to having a full body with flow. Instead of defining a scalar UDF, define an inline table-valued UDF that returns a query with no FROM clause, with a single column based on the expression of interest. I'll provide more details about inline table-valued UDFs later in the chapter, in the section "Table-Valued UDFs." For now, suffice to say that an inline table-valued UDF is very much like a view that can accept input parameters. Here's the inline table-valued UDF version of *AddOne*:

```
IF OBJECT_ID('dbo.AddOneInline', 'IF') IS NOT NULL
  DROP FUNCTION dbo.AddOneInline;
GO
CREATE FUNCTION dbo.AddOneInline(@n AS INT) RETURNS TABLE
AS
RETURN SELECT @n + 1 AS val;
GO
```

Because this UDF is table-valued, you can't just call it as part of an expression—you have to query it. Therefore, to write a scalar expression based on the function call, you have to use a scalar subquery, like so:

```
SELECT n, (SELECT val FROM dbo.AddOneInline(n) AS F) AS n_plus_one
FROM dbo.Nums WHERE n <= 1000000;
```

Even though you may find this form a bit awkward, in my opinion the benefits outweigh this awkwardness. Inline table-valued UDFs are by definition inline. This means that SQL Server expands the function's definition and incorporates its inner references inline in the query—as if the UDF weren't really there. If you look at the plan for this query, you will find that it is identical to the plan shown earlier in Figure 2-1 for the query that did not contain any function call, but instead contained the original inline expression *n + 1*. Of course, as a result, this query also ran for under a second, just like the query with the inline expression.

The ability to refer to a table UDF within a subquery and pass attributes from the outer table as input is like an implicit use of the APPLY operator functionality. If you prefer, as an alternative you could use the APPLY operator explicitly, like so:

```
SELECT Nums.n, A.val AS n_plus_one
FROM dbo.Nums
  CROSS APPLY dbo.AddOneInline(n) AS A
WHERE n <= 1000000;
```

You get the same execution plan as the one shown earlier in Figure 2-1. At this point, you can turn off the Discard results after execution option in SSMS.

Some tasks that are usually implemented as UDFs might seem—at least at first glance—impossible to rewrite as inline expressions in the query, because they appear to require iterative or procedural logic with multiple statements. With a little creativity, though, you might be able to find a solution that is based on a single expression that can be inlined. For example, try to think how you would implement a task to count the number of occurrences of one string within another. The following code demonstrates how this task can be implemented with an inline expression. The query counts the number of occurrences of *@find* in the *companyname* column for each row of the Customers table:

```
DECLARE @find AS NVARCHAR(40);
SET @find = N'n';

SELECT companyname,
  (LEN(companyname+'*') - LEN(REPLACE(companyname, @find, '')+'*'))
    / LEN(@find) AS cnt
FROM Sales.Customers;
```

This generates the following output, shown here in abbreviated form:

```
companyname      cnt
---------------  -----------
Customer AHPOP   0
Customer AHXHT   0
Customer AZJED   0
Customer BSVAR   0
Customer CCFIZ   0
Customer CCKOT   0
Customer CQRAA   0
Customer CYZTN   1
```

```
Customer DTDMN  1
Customer DVFMB  0
Customer EEALV  0
Customer EFFTC  0
Customer ENQZT  1
Customer EYHKM  0
Customer FAPSM  0
Customer FEVNN  2
Customer FRXZL  0
Customer FVXPQ  0
...
```

The expression uses the REPLACE function to calculate this count. The logic is that you can figure out how many times *@find* appears in a string by seeing how much shorter the string would get if each instance were removed (that is, replaced with "). Notice that '*' is appended to both strings before their lengths are measured to avoid getting an incorrect length when the string has trailing spaces.

UDFs Used in Constraints

You can use scalar UDFs in constraints. The following sections discuss and demonstrate how you can use UDFs in DEFAULT, CHECK, PRIMARY KEY, and UNIQUE constraints.

DEFAULT Constraints

You can use scalar UDFs in DEFAULT constraints. The only limitation that you should be aware of is that a UDF cannot accept columns from the table as inputs when used in a DEFAULT constraint. For example, the following code creates a table called T1 and a UDF called *T1_getkey*, which returns the minimum missing key in T1:

```
IF OBJECT_ID('dbo.T1', 'U') IS NOT NULL DROP TABLE dbo.T1;

CREATE TABLE dbo.T1
(
  keycol INT NOT NULL CONSTRAINT PK_T1 PRIMARY KEY CHECK (keycol > 0),
  datacol VARCHAR(10) NOT NULL
);

IF OBJECT_ID('dbo.T1_getkey', 'FN') IS NOT NULL
  DROP FUNCTION dbo.T1_getkey;
GO
CREATE FUNCTION dbo.T1_getkey() RETURNS INT
AS
BEGIN
  RETURN
    CASE
      WHEN NOT EXISTS(SELECT * FROM dbo.T1 WHERE keycol = 1) THEN 1
      ELSE (SELECT MIN(keycol + 1)
            FROM dbo.T1 AS A
            WHERE NOT EXISTS
```

```
              (SELECT *
               FROM dbo.T1 AS B
               WHERE B.keycol = A.keycol + 1))
      END;
END
GO
```

The following code adds a DEFAULT constraint to *keycol*, which invokes the *T1_getkey* function:

```
ALTER TABLE dbo.T1 ADD DEFAULT(dbo.T1_getkey()) FOR keycol;
```

> **Note** Note that this DEFAULT constraint will do its job only for single row inserts, not for multiple-row inserts. Also, reusing key values is almost never advisable in actual business scenarios. I'm using this example here for demonstration purposes only.

The following code inserts three rows, generating the keys 1, 2, and 3; deletes the row with the key 2; and inserts another row, generating the key 2:

```
INSERT INTO dbo.T1(datacol) VALUES('a');
INSERT INTO dbo.T1(datacol) VALUES('b');
INSERT INTO dbo.T1(datacol) VALUES('c');
DELETE FROM dbo.T1 WHERE keycol = 2;
INSERT INTO dbo.T1(datacol) VALUES('d');
```

Query the table by using the following code:

```
SELECT * FROM dbo.T1;
```

This generates the following output:

```
keycol      datacol
----------- ----------
1           a
2           d
3           c
```

Notice that key 2 was assigned to the row that was inserted last (*datacol* = *'d'*), because the row with the key 2 was previously deleted.

CHECK Constraints

Unlike UDFs used in DEFAULT constraints, UDFs used in CHECK constraints are allowed to refer to columns from the table as inputs. CHECK constraints with UDFs give you great power in enforcing integrity rules, allowing you in some cases to avoid using triggers, which are typically more expensive. Later in this chapter I will demonstrate using UDFs that match input strings based on regular expressions in CHECK constraints.

PRIMARY KEY and UNIQUE Constraints

You can create a UNIQUE or PRIMARY KEY constraint on a computed column that invokes a UDF. Keep in mind that both constraints create a unique index under the covers. This means that the target computed column and the UDF it invokes must meet indexing guidelines. For example, the UDF must be schema bound (created with the SCHEMABINDING option); the computed column must be deterministic and precise or deterministic and persisted, and so on. You can find the details about indexing guidelines for computed columns and UDFs in SQL Server Books Online.

The following code attempts to add to T1 a computed column called *col1*—which invokes the *AddOne* UDF—and create a UNIQUE constraint on that column:

```
ALTER TABLE dbo.T1
  ADD col1 AS dbo.AddOne(keycol) CONSTRAINT UQ_T1_col1 UNIQUE;
```

The attempt fails with the following error:

```
Msg 2729, Level 16, State 1, Line 1
Column 'col1' in table 'dbo.T1' cannot be used in an index or statistics or as a partition
key because it is non-deterministic.
Msg 1750, Level 16, State 0, Line 1
Could not create constraint. See previous errors.
```

The error occurs because the function doesn't meet one of the requirements for indexing, which says that the function must be schema bound. As you can see, the error message itself is not too helpful in indicating the cause of the error or in suggesting how to fix it. You need to realize that to fix the problem, you should alter the function by adding the SCHEMABINDING option:

```
ALTER FUNCTION dbo.AddOne(@i AS INT) RETURNS INT
  WITH SCHEMABINDING
AS
BEGIN
  RETURN @i + 1;
END
GO
```

Try adding the computed column with the UNIQUE constraint again. This time your code runs successfully:

```
ALTER TABLE dbo.T1
  ADD col1 AS dbo.AddOne(keycol) CONSTRAINT UQ_T1_col1 UNIQUE;
```

It's a bit trickier when you try to create a PRIMARY KEY constraint on such a computed column. To see how this works, first drop the existing PRIMARY KEY from T1:

```
ALTER TABLE dbo.T1 DROP CONSTRAINT PK_T1;
```

Next, attempt to add another computed column called *col2* with a PRIMARY KEY constraint:

```
ALTER TABLE dbo.T1
  ADD col2 AS dbo.AddOne(keycol)
    CONSTRAINT PK_T1 PRIMARY KEY;
```

The attempt fails, generating the following error:

```
Msg 1711, Level 16, State 1, Line 1
Cannot define PRIMARY KEY constraint on column 'col2' in table 'T1'. The computed column has
to be persisted and not nullable.
Msg 1750, Level 16, State 0, Line 1
Could not create constraint. See previous errors.
```

You must explicitly guarantee that *col2* never ends up with a NULL. You can achieve this by defining the column as PERSISTED and NOT NULL:

```
ALTER TABLE dbo.T1
  ADD col2 AS dbo.AddOne(keycol) PERSISTED NOT NULL
    CONSTRAINT PK_T1 PRIMARY KEY;
```

When you're done, run the following code for cleanup:

```
IF OBJECT_ID('dbo.T1', 'U') IS NOT NULL
  DROP TABLE dbo.T1;
IF OBJECT_ID('dbo.T1_getkey', 'FN') IS NOT NULL
  DROP FUNCTION dbo.T1_getkey;
IF OBJECT_ID('dbo.AddOne', 'FN') IS NOT NULL
  DROP FUNCTION dbo.AddOne;
IF OBJECT_ID('dbo.AddOneInline', 'IF') IS NOT NULL
  DROP FUNCTION dbo.AddOneInline;
```

CLR Scalar UDFs

This section covers CLR scalar UDFs and compares them with T-SQL UDFs where relevant. Remember that Appendix A provides the instructions you need to follow to develop, build, deploy, and test the CLR routines. In this chapter, as well as in other sections in the book where I cover CLR routines, I'll focus only on the routines' code. The appendix provides the namespace definitions and the *CLRUtilities* class that contains the routines. Here's the C# version of the namespace definitions and the header of the *CLRUtilities* class:

```
using System;
using System.Data;
using System.Data.SqlClient;
using System.Data.SqlTypes;
using Microsoft.SqlServer.Server;
using System.Text;
using System.Text.RegularExpressions;
using System.Collections;
using System.Collections.Generic;
using System.Diagnostics;
using System.Reflection;
```

```
public partial class CLRUtilities
{
    ... routine definitions go here ...
}
```

And here's the Visual Basic version:

```
Imports System
Imports System.Data
Imports System.Data.SqlClient
Imports System.Data.SqlTypes
Imports Microsoft.SqlServer.Server
Imports System.Text
Imports System.Text.RegularExpressions
Imports System.Collections
Imports System.Collections.Generic
Imports System.Diagnostics
Imports System.Reflection
Imports System.Runtime.InteropServices

Partial Public Class CLRUtilities
    ... routine definitions go here ...
End Class
```

I won't repeat the definition of the namespaces and the class. I also won't provide instructions that are as detailed as those in the appendix for the common technical steps involved.

CLR Routines

The ability to develop CLR routines in SQL Server gives you great power, but at the same time it introduces great risk. The procedural .NET languages give you a richer programming vocabulary and better performance than T-SQL in areas that T-SQL was never designed to cope with efficiently. These areas include complex calculations, iterative and procedural logic, string manipulation, external access to operating system resources, and so on. T-SQL is a declarative language. It's typically much more powerful and better performing than .NET when the task at hand is data manipulation with set-based queries. The danger with .NET integration is that it is also a vehicle for programmers who have not yet adopted a SQL mindset, enabling them to introduce poorly performing code with inappropriate tools. In this book, I'll give examples of where routines should be developed with .NET.

 More Info For information about set-based querying and efficient set-based solutions, please refer to *Inside T-SQL Querying*, which covers those topics in great detail.

String Manipulation

One area where procedural languages such as .NET are faster and richer than T-SQL is string manipulation. The following sections demonstrate how to handle string manipulation–related tasks such as string matching, string replacement, and formatting date and time values in SQL Server.

Matching Based on Regular Expressions   Regular expressions give you a powerful way to match patterns of text with concise and flexible notation. *Regular expression* is a standard and meaningful term that has been around a long time. ANSI SQL defines a SIMILAR TO predicate that provides support for regular expressions, but unfortunately SQL Server 2008 hasn't yet implemented this predicate in T-SQL. However, you can take advantage of regular expressions in .NET code. For example, the following C# code defines a function called *RegexIsMatch*:

```
// RegexIsMatch function
// Validates input string against regular expression
[SqlFunction(IsDeterministic = true, DataAccess = DataAccessKind.None)]
public static SqlBoolean RegexIsMatch(SqlString input,
  SqlString pattern)
{
    if (input.IsNull || pattern.IsNull)
        return SqlBoolean.Null;
    else
        return (SqlBoolean)Regex.IsMatch(input.Value, pattern.Value,
            RegexOptions.CultureInvariant);
}
```

The attributes in the header tell SQL Server that the function is deterministic and that no data access is involved. Note the usage of the *RegexOptions.CultureInvariant* option to get a culture-independent match. If the match was culture-dependent, the function would not be deterministic. (See *http://msdn.microsoft.com/en-us/library/z0sbec17.aspx* for details.)

The function accepts a string (*input*) and a regular expression (*pattern*) as input. The return type of this function is *SqlBoolean*, which has three possible values: 0, 1, and Null; the return value is Null if *input* or *pattern* is Null, 1 if the pattern *pattern* was found in *input*, and 0 otherwise. As you can see, the function's code is very simple. The code first tests for Null input parameters and returns Null if either parameter is Null. If neither input parameter is Null, the function returns the result of the *Regex.IsMatch* method. This method checks whether the string provided as the first parameter contains the pattern provided as the second parameter. The *Regex.IsMatch* method returns a .NET *System.Boolean* value, which must be explicitly converted to *SqlBoolean*.

Here's the function's code using Visual Basic, in case that's your language of preference:

```
' RegexIsMatch function
' Validates input string against regular expression
<SqlFunction(IsDeterministic:=True, DataAccess:=DataAccessKind.None)> _
Public Shared Function RegexIsMatch(ByVal input As SqlString, _
  ByVal pattern As SqlString) As SqlBoolean
    If (input.IsNull Or pattern.IsNull) Then
        Return SqlBoolean.Null
    Else
        Return CType(Regex.IsMatch(input.Value, pattern.Value, _
            RegexOptions.CultureInvariant), SqlBoolean)
    End If
End Function
```

If you followed all the instructions described in Appendix A, you're ready to test and use the function. Those instructions include enabling CLR in SQL Server (disabled by default), creating a test database called CLRUtilities, developing your code in Microsoft Visual Studio 2008, building an assembly in a .dll file on disk, loading the Intermediate Language (IL) code from the assembly into a SQL Server database, and registering routines from the assembly in the database. Here's the code you need to run to enable CLR in SQL Server and create the CLRUtilities test database, in case you haven't yet done so:

```
SET NOCOUNT ON;
USE master;
EXEC sp_configure 'clr enabled', 1;
RECONFIGURE;
GO
IF DB_ID('CLRUtilities') IS NOT NULL
  DROP DATABASE CLRUtilities;
GO
CREATE DATABASE CLRUtilities;
GO
USE CLRUtilities;
```

Note By turning on the *'clr enabled'* server configuration option (disabled by default) you specify that user assemblies can be run by SQL Server at the instance level. You cannot control this option at a more granular level, so by enabling this option, you enable it for the whole SQL Server instance. Enabling this option might impose a security risk. The level of risk depends on what you will allow each individual assembly to do. When creating assemblies with the CREATE ASSEMBLY command, you can control code access permissions by setting the PERMISSION_SET option to SAFE, EXTERNAL_ACCESS, *or* UNSAFE. The following security note from SQL Books Online describes all three:

SAFE is the recommended permission setting for assemblies that perform computation and data management tasks without accessing resources outside an instance of SQL Server.

We recommend using EXTERNAL_ACCESS for assemblies that access resources outside of an instance of SQL Server. EXTERNAL_ACCESS assemblies include the reliability and scalability protections of SAFE assemblies, but from a security perspective are similar to UNSAFE assemblies. This is because code in EXTERNAL_ACCESS assemblies runs by default under the SQL Server service account and accesses external resources under that account, unless the code explicitly impersonates the caller. Therefore, permission to create EXTERNAL_ACCESS assemblies should be granted only to logins that are trusted to run code under the SQL Server service account. For more information about impersonation, see CLR Integration Security.

Specifying UNSAFE enables the code in the assembly complete freedom to perform operations in the SQL Server process space that can potentially compromise the robustness of SQL Server. UNSAFE assemblies can also potentially subvert the security system of either SQL Server or the common language runtime. UNSAFE permissions should be granted only to highly trusted assemblies. Only members of the sysadmin fixed server role can create and alter UNSAFE assemblies.

None of the functions discussed in this chapter requires external access, so the assembly will be created with the SAFE permission. In the following chapters, I will demonstrate a stored procedure that requires EXTERNAL_ACCESS and a trigger that requires UNSAFE, but I'll do so only for demonstration purposes. When demonstrating those routines, I'll alter the assembly to support the required permission. Bear in mind the security risk involved in allowing external access to your assembly.

In all the following examples in the book, I'll assume that the CLRUtilities database exists and that you have already built the assembly from Visual Studio.

Now run the following code to load the assembly into the database if you haven't done so yet:

```
USE CLRUtilities;

CREATE ASSEMBLY CLRUtilities
FROM 'C:\CLRUtilities\CLRUtilities\bin\Debug\CLRUtilities.dll'
WITH PERMISSION_SET = SAFE;
-- If no Debug folder, use instead:
-- FROM 'C:\CLRUtilities\CLRUtilities\bin\CLRUtilities.dll'
```

Of course, if the CLRUtilities.dll file containing the assembly was created in a different folder, specify the relevant folder instead. The CREATE ASSEMBLY command loads the IL code from the .dll file into the database. After it's loaded, you no longer need the external file. Note that if you rebuild the assembly later after adding routines and do not use the automatic deployment option from Visual Studio Professional edition, you will need to issue an ALTER ASSEMBLY command or the DROP and CREATE ASSEMBLY commands manually to reload the IL code into the database. This step is not necessary if you followed the instructions in Appendix A and already created all routines that are discussed in the book. I will not refer further to this step.

Whenever I discuss a new routine, I will provide the T-SQL code required to register it in the database (CREATE FUNCTION | PROCEDURE | TRIGGER command), although you don't actually need to run such code if you followed the instructions in Appendix A fully.

Here's the code you need to run to register the C# version of the *RegexIsMatch* function in the CLRUtilities database:

```
USE CLRUtilities;
IF OBJECT_ID('dbo.RegexIsMatch', 'FS') IS NOT NULL
  DROP FUNCTION dbo.RegexIsMatch;
GO
CREATE FUNCTION dbo.RegexIsMatch
  (@inpstr AS NVARCHAR(MAX), @regexstr AS NVARCHAR(MAX))
RETURNS BIT
EXTERNAL NAME CLRUtilities.CLRUtilities.RegexIsMatch;
GO
```

And here's the code that registers the Visual Basic version:

```
CREATE FUNCTION dbo.RegexIsMatch
  (@inpstr AS NVARCHAR(MAX), @regexstr AS NVARCHAR(MAX))
RETURNS BIT
EXTERNAL NAME CLRUtilities.[CLRUtilities.CLRUtilities].RegexIsMatch;
GO
```

Note Notice the discrepancy between the external name specified when registering a function developed with C# and one developed with Visual Basic (*CLRUtilities.CLRUtilities.RegexIsMatch* versus *CLRUtilities.[CLRUtilities.CLRUtilities].RegexIsMatch*). This is quite confusing. The reason for this discrepancy is that Visual Basic creates a root namespace and C# does not. To make the T-SQL code consistent regardless of the .NET language you used, you must prevent the creation of the root namespace when programming with Visual Basic. In Visual Studio, right-click the project, select Properties, and then select the Application page. Clear the Root Namespace text box. In this book I will assume that you did not clear this option; hence, when registering objects you will see a discrepancy in the specified external names.

As I mentioned earlier, if you want the function to return a NULL if any of its inputs is NULL, you can specify the option RETURNS NULL ON NULL INPUT when registering the function. When any of the inputs is NULL, SQL Server won't bother to invoke the function—it simply will return NULL. Here's the code you would use to register the function, specifying the RETURNS NULL ON NULL INPUT option:

```
IF OBJECT_ID('dbo.RegexIsMatch', 'FS') IS NOT NULL
   DROP FUNCTION dbo.RegexIsMatch;
GO
CREATE FUNCTION dbo.RegexIsMatch
   (@inpstr AS NVARCHAR(MAX), @regexstr AS NVARCHAR(MAX))
RETURNS BIT
WITH RETURNS NULL ON NULL INPUT
EXTERNAL NAME CLRUtilities.CLRUtilities.RegexIsMatch;
GO
```

At this point, you can start using the *RegexIsMatch* function.

More Info You can find many useful regular expressions on the Internet—for example, at *http://www.regexlib.com*.

As an example of using your new function, suppose that you want to check whether a certain e-mail address is valid. To do so, use this regular expression:

N'^([\w-]+\.)?[\w-]+@[\w-]+\.([\w-]+\.)*?[\w]+$'*

The regular expression determines whether the address starts with a word, contains the at symbol (@), and has at least two words delimited with a dot (.) after the @. It can have additional dot-separated words before and after the @ symbol. Note that this regular expression is simplistic and is provided here for demonstration purposes. To learn how to write more robust and complete regular expressions, I suggest that you visit *http://www.regularexpressions.info/*.

The following code returns 1 because the e-mail address provided is valid:

```
SELECT dbo.RegexIsMatch(
  N'dejan@solidq.com',
  N'^([\w-]+\.)*?[\w-]+@[\w-]+\.([\w-]+\.)*?[\w]+$');
```

And the following code returns 0 because the address is invalid:

```
SELECT dbo.RegexIsMatch(
  N'dejan#solidq.com',
  N'^([\w-]+\.)*?[\w-]+@[\w-]+\.([\w-]+\.)*?[\w]+$');
```

> **Tip** You might want to create functions that serve a generic purpose such as making the *RegexIsMatch* function accessible in all databases without the need to database-qualify the function name (CLRUtilities.dbo.RegexIsMatch). To achieve this, create a synonym for the function in each database where you want to make it available. For example, to make the function available in a database called MyDB, run the following code:
>
> ```
> USE MyDB;
> ```
>
> ```
> CREATE SYNONYM dbo.RegexIsMatch FOR CLRUtilities.dbo.RegexIsMatch;
> ```
>
> If you create a synonym in the model database, the synonym will be created in every new database that you create in the future because a new database is created as a copy of model. This also applies to the tempdb database, which is created every time you restart SQL Server.

You can also use RegexIsMatch in a CHECK constraint. For example, the following code creates the table TestRegex with a CHECK constraint that limits the values of the *jpgfilename* column to filenames with the extension *jpg*:

```
IF OBJECT_ID('dbo.TestRegex', 'U') IS NOT NULL DROP TABLE dbo.TestRegex;

CREATE TABLE dbo.TestRegex
(
  jpgfilename NVARCHAR(4000) NOT NULL
  CHECK(dbo.RegexIsMatch(jpgfilename,
    N'^(([a-zA-Z]:)|(\\{2}\w+)\$?)(\\(\w[\w ]*.*))+\.(jpg|JPG)$')
      = CAST(1 As BIT))
);
```

The values in the *jpgfilename* column must meet the following pattern: the value must start with either a letter in the range A through Z followed by a colon (drive letter), or with two backslashes and a word (network share). Then the value must have at least one backslash denoting the root folder of the drive or the share. After that, the value can have additional backslash-word combinations denoting multiple subfolders. Finally, after the last word there must be a dot followed by the letters *jpg* (uppercase or lowercase).

The following INSERT statements containing valid JPEG file names are accepted:

```
INSERT INTO dbo.TestRegex(jpgfilename) VALUES(N'C:\Temp\myFile.jpg');
INSERT INTO dbo.TestRegex(jpgfilename) VALUES(N'\\MyShare\Temp\myFile.jpg');
INSERT INTO dbo.TestRegex(jpgfilename) VALUES(N'\\MyShare\myFile.jpg');
INSERT INTO dbo.TestRegex(jpgfilename) VALUES(N'C:\myFile.jpg');
```

The following INSERT statements that do not contain valid JPEG file names are rejected:

```
INSERT INTO dbo.TestRegex(jpgfilename) VALUES(N'C:\Temp\myFile.txt');
INSERT INTO dbo.TestRegex(jpgfilename) VALUES(N'\\MyShare\\Temp\myFile.jpg');
INSERT INTO dbo.TestRegex(jpgfilename) VALUES(N'\\myFile.jpg');
INSERT INTO dbo.TestRegex(jpgfilename) VALUES(N'C:myFile.jpg');
```

Replacement Based on Regular Expressions   In addition to matching strings based on patterns, you might also need to perform string replacement based on patterns. Unfortunately, T-SQL gives you very little help in this area. Take a simple task such as removing all characters of a given pattern from an input string. Here's an implementation of this task using a T-SQL UDF called *RemoveChars*:

```
IF OBJECT_ID('dbo.RemoveChars', 'FN') IS NOT NULL
  DROP FUNCTION dbo.RemoveChars;
GO

CREATE FUNCTION dbo.RemoveChars
  (@string AS NVARCHAR(MAX), @pattern AS NVARCHAR(MAX))
  RETURNS NVARCHAR(MAX)
AS
BEGIN
  DECLARE @pos AS INT;
  SET @pos = PATINDEX(@pattern, @string);

  WHILE @pos > 0
  BEGIN
    SET @string = STUFF(@string, @pos, 1, N'');
    SET @pos = PATINDEX(@pattern, @string);
  END

  RETURN @string;
END
GO
```

The function accepts two inputs: the string to operate on (*@string*) and the pattern of a character (*@pattern*). The code uses the PATINDEX function to find the position of the first occurrence of the pattern in the input string and stores that position in the variable *@pos*. As long as the pattern is found in the string, the code uses the STUFF function to remove the character in the position indicated by *@pos*, and looks again for the first position of the pattern in the input string. The code finally returns the string after the removal of all characters that match the pattern.

As an example of using the function, the following code queries the Sales.Customers table in the InsideTSQL2008 database, and returns the customer phone numbers after removing characters that are not digits or alphabetic:

```
SELECT custid, phone,
  dbo.RemoveChars(phone, N'%[^0-9a-zA-Z]%') AS cleanphone
FROM InsideTSQL2008.Sales.Customers;
```

This generates the following output, shown here in abbreviated form:

```
custid      phone             cleanphone
----------- ---------------   -----------
1           030-3456789        0303456789
2           (5) 789-0123       57890123
3           (5) 123-4567       51234567
4           (171) 456-7890     1714567890
5           0921-67 89 01      0921678901
6           0621-67890         062167890
7           67.89.01.23        67890123
8           (91) 345 67 89     913456789
9           23.45.67.89        23456789
10          (604) 901-2345     6049012345
...
```

Note that because T-SQL doesn't support regular expressions it has to resort to the far inferior patterns supported by T-SQL's PATINDEX function. The types of patterns supported by the PATINDEX function are similar to those supported by the LIKE predicate. Also, iterations in T-SQL are far slower than iterations performed in .NET.

You can implement a .NET function that uses regular expressions to do pattern-based replacement; that is, you can replace all occurrences of a pattern within a string with another pattern. Here's the C# definition of the *RegexReplace* function, which invokes the *Replace* method of a *Regex* object:

```csharp
// RegexReplace function
// String replacement based on regular expression
[SqlFunction(IsDeterministic = true, DataAccess = DataAccessKind.None)]
public static SqlString RegexReplace(
    SqlString input, SqlString pattern, SqlString replacement)
{
  if (input.IsNull || pattern.IsNull || replacement.IsNull)
      return SqlString.Null;
  else
    return (SqlString)Regex.Replace(
      input.Value, pattern.Value, replacement.Value);
}
```

And here's the Visual Basic definition of the function:

```vbnet
' RegexReplace function
' String replacement based on regular expression
<SqlFunction(IsDeterministic:=True, DataAccess:=DataAccessKind.None)> _
Public Shared Function RegexReplace( _
  ByVal input As SqlString, ByVal pattern As SqlString, _
  ByVal replacement As SqlString) As SqlString

  If (input.IsNull Or pattern.IsNull Or replacement.IsNull) Then
    Return SqlString.Null
  Else
    Return CType(Regex.Replace( _
      input.Value, pattern.Value, replacement.Value), SqlString)
  End If
End Function
```

The function accepts three input arguments: *input, pattern,* and *replacement.* After input validation, the function simply invokes the *Regex.Replace* method, which substitutes each occurrence of *pattern* within the string *input* with the *replacement* pattern. You don't need to express the iterations yourself to handle all occurrences of the pattern. Also, this function handles patterns representing strings of any length, while the T-SQL version handled only patterns representing a single character.

Use the following code to register the C# version of the *RegexReplace* function:

```
IF OBJECT_ID('dbo.RegexReplace', 'SF') IS NOT NULL
  DROP FUNCTION dbo.RegexReplace;
GO
CREATE FUNCTION dbo.RegexReplace(
  @input       AS NVARCHAR(MAX),
  @pattern     AS NVARCHAR(MAX),
  @replacement AS NVARCHAR(MAX))
RETURNS NVARCHAR(MAX)
WITH RETURNS NULL ON NULL INPUT
EXTERNAL NAME CLRUtilities.CLRUtilities.RegexReplace;
GO
```

And use the following code if you implemented the function with Visual Basic:

```
CREATE FUNCTION dbo.RegexReplace(
  @input       AS NVARCHAR(MAX),
  @pattern     AS NVARCHAR(MAX),
  @replacement AS NVARCHAR(MAX))
RETURNS NVARCHAR(MAX)
WITH RETURNS NULL ON NULL INPUT
EXTERNAL NAME CLRUtilities.[CLRUtilities.CLRUtilities].RegexReplace;
GO
```

Here's the revised query that produces "clean" phone numbers, this time using the *RegexReplace* function:

```
SELECT phone, dbo.RegexReplace(phone, N'[^0-9a-zA-Z]', N'') AS cleanphone
FROM InsideTSQL2008.Sales.Customers;
```

Even though you can see some resemblance to the pattern I used earlier with the T-SQL function, the CLR version uses a regular expression. With regular expressions you can do so much more than with the patterns supported by T-SQL's PATINDEX function. The CLR version of the function is also significantly faster than the T-SQL version.

Later in the chapter, in the section "SQL Signature," I'll present more sophisticated uses of the *RegexReplace* function.

Formatting Date and Time Values   Another example of a string manipulation–related task that is very cumbersome and slow to achieve in T-SQL is formatting date and time values based on an input format string. T-SQL provides the CONVERT function, which allows you to convert a date and time value to a character string, but you can only choose from a small set of predetermined style numbers. T-SQL doesn't support specifying a format string the way that many procedural languages do. To support such an option you have to implement your own function. If you've ever tried achieving this task with T-SQL, you know how difficult it is and how poorly it performs.

Implementing the task with a CLR function is ridiculously simple. You write a function that accepts a date and time value (of a *SqlDateTime* type) and a format string (of a *SqlString* type) as inputs. The function's definition is based on a single line of code that applies the *.Value.ToString* methods to the input date and time value, passing the format string as input to the method.

> **Note** An important difference between CONVERT and the CLR routine is that CONVERT will behave according to the SQL Server session's SET LANGUAGE setting, but the CLR routine will behave according to the current thread culture. If you use the CLR routine, SET LANGUAGE will have no effect (except on how strings are converted to passed parameters before the CLR routine is called).

Here's the C# definition of the function:

```
// FormatDatetime function
// Formats a DATETIME value based on a format string
[Microsoft.SqlServer.Server.SqlFunction]
public static SqlString FormatDatetime(SqlDateTime dt, SqlString formatstring)
{
  if (dt.IsNull || formatstring.IsNull)
    return SqlString.Null;
  else
    return (SqlString)dt.Value.ToString(formatstring.Value);
}
```

And here's the Visual Basic definition:

```
' FormatDatetime function
' Formats a DATETIME value based on a format string
<SqlFunction(IsDeterministic:=True, DataAccess:=DataAccessKind.None)> _
Public Shared Function FormatDatetime( _
  ByVal dt As SqlDateTime, ByVal formatstring As SqlString) As SqlString

  If (dt.IsNull Or formatstring.IsNull) Then
    Return SqlString.Null
  Else
    Return CType(dt.Value.ToString(formatstring.Value), SqlString)
  End If
End Function
```

Use the following code to register the C# version of the function:

```
IF OBJECT_ID('dbo.FormatDatetime', 'SF') IS NOT NULL
  DROP FUNCTION dbo.FormatDatetime;
GO
```

```
CREATE FUNCTION dbo.FormatDatetime
  (@dt AS DATETIME, @formatstring AS NVARCHAR(500))
RETURNS NVARCHAR(500)
WITH RETURNS NULL ON NULL INPUT
EXTERNAL NAME CLRUtilities.CLRUtilities.FormatDatetime;
GO
```

And the following code to register the Visual Basic version:

```
CREATE FUNCTION dbo.FormatDatetime
  (@dt AS DATETIME, @formatstring AS NVARCHAR(500))
RETURNS NVARCHAR(500)
WITH RETURNS NULL ON NULL INPUT
EXTERNAL NAME CLRUtilities.[CLRUtilities.CLRUtilities].FormatDatetime;
GO
```

You can now start using the *FormatDatetime* function, specifying your choice of a format string, such as:

```
SELECT dbo.FormatDatetime(GETDATE(), 'MM/dd/yyyy');
```

For details about date and time format strings, please visit *http://msdn.microsoft.com/en-us/library/97x6twsz.aspx*.

When you're done, run the following code for cleanup:

```
IF OBJECT_ID('dbo.TestRegex','U') IS NOT NULL
  DROP TABLE dbo.TestRegex;
IF OBJECT_ID('dbo.RegexIsMatch', 'FS') IS NOT NULL
  DROP FUNCTION dbo.RegexIsMatch;
IF OBJECT_ID('dbo.RemoveChars', 'FN') IS NOT NULL
  DROP FUNCTION dbo.RemoveChars;
IF OBJECT_ID('dbo.RegexReplace', 'FS') IS NOT NULL
  DROP FUNCTION dbo.RegexReplace;
IF OBJECT_ID('dbo.FormatDatetime', 'SF') IS NOT NULL
  DROP FUNCTION dbo.FormatDatetime;
```

Explicit vs. Implicit Conversions

When you develop CLR objects in SQL Server 2008, you might think that you can use either .NET native types or .NET SQL types for your input/output parameters and variables. .NET SQL types map more accurately to SQL Server types. Using .NET native types in the routines' interfaces causes implicit casting of the values when passed from or to SQL Server. Some programmers prefer to stick to .NET SQL types because they believe that there's overhead in the implicit conversions. Such a choice limits you in some cases because .NET SQL types are not as rich as .NET native types in their functionality. For example, the .NET native *System. String* type (*string* in C#, *String* in Visual Basic) has the *Substring* method, but the .NET SQL type *SqlString* doesn't.

Performance is not what makes a real difference. Using SQL types in .NET code for CLR objects inside a database is highly recommended because native .NET types do not support NULL values. With SQL types you can use the *IsNull* method to check whether the input is NULL and react appropriately, but .NET native types do not support this method. If you try to invoke a CLR routine from T-SQL and pass a NULL to an argument of a .NET native type, you will get an exception (unless you registered the function with the RETURNS NULL ON NULL INPUT option). If you need additional functionality provided by .NET native types, you have to do some explicit casting. Alternatively, you can get the value in .NET native type using the *Value* property of a SQL type variable, store this value in another variable of the native .NET type, and then use any properties or methods of the native type. In the *RegexIsMatch* function, the *Regex.IsMatch* method expects native .NET string types as input; therefore, the *Value* property of the .NET SQL types is used. The return type of the method is a .NET native Boolean value, so the code casts it explicitly to *SqlBoolean*.

This section will show you that the performance difference between implicit and explicit casting is not significant. The following C# code defines the functions *ImpCast*, which uses .NET native types and implicit conversion, and *ExpCast*, which uses .NET SQL types and explicit conversion:

```
// Compare implicit vs. explicit casting
[SqlFunction(IsDeterministic = true, DataAccess = DataAccessKind.None)]
public static string ImpCast(string inpStr)
{
    return inpStr.Substring(2, 3);
}

[SqlFunction(IsDeterministic = true, DataAccess = DataAccessKind.None)]
public static SqlString ExpCast(SqlString inpStr)
{
    return (SqlString)inpStr.ToString().Substring(2, 3);
}
```

And here's the Visual Basic code that defines the functions:

```
' Compare implicit vs. explicit casting
<SqlFunction(IsDeterministic:=True, DataAccess:=DataAccessKind.None)> _
Public Shared Function ImpCast(ByVal inpStr As String) As String
    Return inpStr.Substring(2, 3)
End Function

<SqlFunction(IsDeterministic:=True, DataAccess:=DataAccessKind.None)> _
Public Shared Function ExpCast(ByVal inpStr As SqlString) As SqlString
    Return CType(inpStr.ToString().Substring(2, 3), SqlString)
End Function
```

Here's code that registers the C# functions in the database:

```
IF OBJECT_ID('dbo.ImpCast', 'FS') IS NOT NULL
  DROP FUNCTION dbo.ImpCast;
IF OBJECT_ID('dbo.ExpCast', 'FS') IS NOT NULL
  DROP FUNCTION dbo.ExpCast;
GO
```

```
-- Create ImpCast function
CREATE FUNCTION dbo.ImpCast(@inpstr AS NVARCHAR(4000))
RETURNS NVARCHAR(4000)
EXTERNAL NAME CLRUtilities.CLRUtilities.ImpCast;
GO
-- Create ExpCast function
CREATE FUNCTION dbo.ExpCast(@inpstr AS NVARCHAR(4000))
RETURNS NVARCHAR(4000)
EXTERNAL NAME CLRUtilities.CLRUtilities.ExpCast;
GO
```

Here's code that registers the Visual Basic functions:

```
-- Create ImpCast function
CREATE FUNCTION dbo.ImpCast(@inpstr AS NVARCHAR(4000))
RETURNS NVARCHAR(4000)
EXTERNAL NAME CLRUtilities.[CLRUtilities.CLRUtilities].ImpCast;
GO
-- Create ExpCast function
CREATE FUNCTION dbo.ExpCast(@inpstr AS NVARCHAR(4000))
RETURNS NVARCHAR(4000)
EXTERNAL NAME CLRUtilities.[CLRUtilities.CLRUtilities].ExpCast;
GO
```

The following code invokes the *ImpCast* function a million times in a loop, running for 17 seconds on my system:

```
SET NOCOUNT ON;

DECLARE @a AS NVARCHAR(4000);
DECLARE @i AS INT;
SET @i = 1;
WHILE @i <= 1000000
BEGIN
 SET @a = dbo.ImpCast(N'123456');
 SET @i = @i + 1;
END
```

The following code invokes the *ExpCast* function, running for 18 seconds:

```
DECLARE @a AS NVARCHAR(4000);
DECLARE @i AS INT;
SET @i = 1;
WHILE @i <= 1000000
BEGIN
 SET @a = dbo.ExpCast(N'123456');
 SET @i = @i + 1;
END
```

As you can see, the difference is not significant, and in this test the implicit casting method even performs a bit better than the explicit casting method.

When you're done, run the following code for cleanup:

```
IF OBJECT_ID('dbo.ImpCast', 'FS') IS NOT NULL
  DROP FUNCTION dbo.ImpCast;
IF OBJECT_ID('dbo.ExpCast', 'FS') IS NOT NULL
  DROP FUNCTION dbo.ExpCast;
```

SQL Signature

The following section provides T-SQL and CLR implementations of a function that returns a signature of a query string. The idea is to receive a query string as an input and return a string that represents the query signature or template. In that signature, all literals that appeared in the input query string are replaced with a common symbol (in our case, #). For example, assume you are using the following query string:

```
N'SELECT * FROM dbo.T1 WHERE col1 = 3 AND col2 > 78;'
```

You want to get the following string back:

```
N'SELECT * FROM dbo.T1 WHERE col1 = # AND col2 > #'
```

Such a function can be very handy when you want to aggregate query performance data from traces after inserting the trace data to a table. If you group the data by the original query string, queries that are logically the same end up in different groups. Aggregating performance data by the query signature gives you more useful and valuable information.

T-SQL SQL Signature UDF

The following code has the T-SQL implementation of the SQL Signature function:

```
IF OBJECT_ID('dbo.SQLSigTSQL', 'FN') IS NOT NULL
  DROP FUNCTION dbo.SQLSigTSQL;
GO

CREATE FUNCTION dbo.SQLSigTSQL
  (@p1 NVARCHAR(MAX), @parselength INT = 4000)
RETURNS NVARCHAR(4000)

-- This function was developed at Microsoft
-- and included in this book with their permission.
--
-- This function is provided "AS IS" with no warranties,
-- and confers no rights.
-- Use of included script samples are subject to the terms specified at
-- http://www.microsoft.com/info/cpyright.htm
--
-- Strips query strings
AS
BEGIN
  DECLARE @pos AS INT;
  DECLARE @mode AS CHAR(10);
  DECLARE @maxlength AS INT;
```

```
DECLARE @p2 AS NCHAR(4000);
DECLARE @currchar AS CHAR(1), @nextchar AS CHAR(1);
DECLARE @p2len AS INT;

SET @maxlength = LEN(RTRIM(SUBSTRING(@p1,1,4000)));
SET @maxlength = CASE WHEN @maxlength > @parselength
                      THEN @parselength ELSE @maxlength END;
SET @pos = 1;
SET @p2 = '';
SET @p2len = 0;
SET @currchar = '';
set @nextchar = '';
SET @mode = 'command';

WHILE (@pos <= @maxlength)
BEGIN
  SET @currchar = SUBSTRING(@p1,@pos,1);
  SET @nextchar = SUBSTRING(@p1,@pos+1,1);
  IF @mode = 'command'
  BEGIN
    SET @p2 = LEFT(@p2,@p2len) + @currchar;
    SET @p2len = @p2len + 1 ;
    IF @currchar IN (',','(',' ','=','<','>','!')
      AND @nextchar BETWEEN '0' AND '9'
    BEGIN
      SET @mode = 'number';
      SET @p2 = LEFT(@p2,@p2len) + '#';
      SET @p2len = @p2len + 1;
    END
    IF @currchar = ''''
    BEGIN
      SET @mode = 'literal';
      SET @p2 = LEFT(@p2,@p2len) + '#''';
      SET @p2len = @p2len + 2;
    END
  END
  ELSE IF @mode = 'number' AND @nextchar IN (',',')',' ','=','<','>','!')
    SET @mode= 'command';
  ELSE IF @mode = 'literal' AND @currchar = ''''
    SET @mode= 'command';

  SET @pos = @pos + 1;
END
RETURN @p2;
END
GO
```

> **Note** I'd like to thank Stuart Ozer, who authored the function, for allowing me to cover it in this book. Stuart is with the Microsoft SQL Server Customer Advisory Team (SQL CAT).

The *SQLSigTSQL* function accepts two input parameters: *@p1* is the input query string, and *@parselength* is the maximum number of characters that you want to parse. If *@parselength* is smaller than the length of the query string stored in *@p1*, the function parses only the

@parselength leftmost characters. The function iterates through the characters of the string one at a time. It keeps a state value in a variable called *@mode*, which has three possible values: *'command'*, *'number'*, and *'literal'*.

Command is the default state, and it simply means that the current character will be concatenated to the output string as is. *Number* means that a number literal is identified, in which case the # symbol will be concatenated. A *number* literal is identified when a digit follows a comma, an opening parenthesis, a space, or an operator. The state changes from *number* to *command* when the next character is a comma, a closing parenthesis, a space, or an operator. *Literal* means that a character string literal is identified, in which case the string '#' will be concatenated. A character string literal is identified when an opening quote is detected. The state changes from *literal* to *command* when a closing quote is detected.

To test the *SQLSigTSQL* function, run the following code:

```
SELECT dbo.SQLSigTSQL
  (N'SELECT * FROM dbo.T1 WHERE col1 = 3 AND col2 > 78', 4000);
```

You will get the following output:

```
SELECT * FROM dbo.T1 WHERE col1 = # AND col2 > #
```

CLR SQL Signature UDF

The following code has the C# implementation of the SQL Signature function:

```
// SQLSigCLR Funcion
// Produces SQL Signature from an input query string
[SqlFunction(IsDeterministic = true, DataAccess = DataAccessKind.None)]
public static SqlString SQLSigCLR(SqlString inpRawString,
  SqlInt32 inpParseLength)
{
    if (inpRawString.IsNull)
        return SqlString.Null;
    int pos = 0;
    string mode = "command";
    string RawString = inpRawString.Value;
    int maxlength = RawString.Length;
    StringBuilder p2 = new StringBuilder();
    char currchar = ' ';
    char nextchar = ' ';
    int ParseLength = RawString.Length;
    if (!inpParseLength.IsNull)
        ParseLength = inpParseLength.Value;
    if (RawString.Length > ParseLength)
    {
        maxlength = ParseLength;
    }
    while (pos < maxlength)
    {
        currchar = RawString[pos];
```

```
        if (pos < maxlength - 1)
        {
            nextchar = RawString[pos + 1];
        }
        else
        {
            nextchar = RawString[pos];
        }
        if (mode == "command")
        {
            p2.Append(currchar);
            if ((",( =<>!".IndexOf(currchar) >= 0)
                &&
                (nextchar >= '0' && nextchar <= '9'))
            {
                mode = "number";
                p2.Append('#');
            }
            if (currchar == '\'')
            {
                mode = "literal";
                p2.Append("#'");
            }
        }
        else if ((mode == "number")
                &&
                (",( =<>!".IndexOf(nextchar) >= 0))
        {
            mode = "command";
        }
        else if ((mode == "literal") && (currchar == '\''))
        {
            mode = "command";
        }
        pos++;
    }
    return p2.ToString();
}
```

And the following code has the Visual Basic implementation of the function:

```
' SQLSigCLR Funcion
' Produces SQL Signature from an input query string
<SqlFunction(IsDeterministic:=True, DataAccess:=DataAccessKind.None)> _
Public Shared Function SQLSigCLR(ByVal inpRawString As SqlString, _
  ByVal inpParseLength As SqlInt32) As SqlString
    If inpRawString.IsNull Then
        Return SqlString.Null
    End If
    Dim pos As Integer = 0
    Dim mode As String = "command"
    Dim RawString As String = inpRawString.Value
    Dim maxlength As Integer = RawString.Length
    Dim p2 As StringBuilder = New StringBuilder()
    Dim currchar As Char = " "c
    Dim nextchar As Char = " "c
    Dim ParseLength As Integer = RawString.Length
```

```
        If (Not inpParseLength.IsNull) Then
            ParseLength = inpParseLength.Value
        End If
        If (RawString.Length > ParseLength) Then
            maxlength = ParseLength
        End If
        While (pos < maxlength)
            currchar = RawString(pos)
            If (pos < maxlength - 1) Then
                nextchar = RawString(pos + 1)
            Else
                nextchar = RawString(pos)
            End If
            If (mode = "command") Then
                p2.Append(currchar)
                If ((",( =<>!".IndexOf(currchar) >= 0) _
                    And _
                    (nextchar >= "0"c And nextchar <= "9"c)) Then
                    mode = "number"
                    p2.Append("#")
                End If
                If (currchar = "'"c) Then
                    mode = "literal"
                    p2.Append("#")
                End If
            ElseIf ((mode = "number") And _
                    (",( =<>!".IndexOf(nextchar) >= 0)) Then
                mode = "command"
            ElseIf ((mode = "literal") And _
                    (currchar = "'"c)) Then
                mode = "command"
            End If
            pos = pos + 1
        End While
        Return p2.ToString
    End Function
```

The .NET versions of the function are adaptations of Stuart's algorithm. These adaptations were developed by Andrew J. Kelly and Dejan Sarka, both of whom are mentors with Solid Quality Mentors and distinguished SQL Server MVPs. The .NET versions of the function described here are logically similar to the T-SQL version shown earlier and are provided for performance testing and comparison purposes only. They do not represent good CLR writing. Later in this chapter, I'll describe a much more powerful CLR-based solution using regular expressions to produce query signatures.

Use the following code to register the C# version of the *SQLSigCLR* function:

```
IF OBJECT_ID('dbo.SQLSigCLR', 'FS') IS NOT NULL
  DROP FUNCTION dbo.SQLSigCLR;
GO
CREATE FUNCTION dbo.SQLSigCLR
  (@rawstring AS NVARCHAR(MAX), @parselength AS INT)
RETURNS NVARCHAR(MAX)
EXTERNAL NAME CLRUtilities.CLRUtilities.SQLSigCLR;
GO
```

And use the following code if you implemented the function with Visual Basic:

```
CREATE FUNCTION dbo.SQLSigCLR
  (@rawstring AS NVARCHAR(MAX), @parselength AS INT)
RETURNS NVARCHAR(MAX)
EXTERNAL NAME CLRUtilities.[CLRUtilities.CLRUtilities].SQLSigCLR;
GO
```

Run the following code to test the *SQLSigCLR* function:

```
SELECT dbo.SQLSigCLR
  (N'SELECT * FROM dbo.T1 WHERE col1 = 3 AND col2 > 78', 4000);
```

You will get the following output:

```
SELECT * FROM dbo.T1 WHERE col1 = # AND col2 > #
```

Compare Performance of T-SQL and CLR SQL Signature UDFs

Remember that .NET code is much faster than T-SQL in string manipulation. The SQL Signature function is a perfect example for demonstrating the performance difference, especially because both versions implement the same algorithm. You will be able to observe the net performance difference in string manipulation.

First, run the following code to create the table Queries and populate it with 100,000 query strings:

```
IF OBJECT_ID('dbo.Queries', 'U') IS NOT NULL
  DROP TABLE dbo.Queries;
GO
SELECT CAST(N'SELECT * FROM dbo.T1 WHERE col1 = '
          + CAST(n AS NVARCHAR(10))
        AS NVARCHAR(MAX)) AS query
INTO dbo.Queries
FROM dbo.Nums
WHERE n <= 100000;
```

Use the Discard results after execution option in SSMS.

When I ran the following code with the T-SQL version of the function, it took 64 seconds to finish:

```
SELECT dbo.SQLSigTSQL(query, 4000) FROM dbo.Queries;
```

The CLR C# version finished in one second, and the Visual Basic version finished in two seconds:

```
SELECT dbo.SQLSigCLR(query, 4000) FROM dbo.Queries;
```

Turn off the Discard results after execution option in SSMS.

As you can see, the CLR version of the function is dozens of times faster than the T-SQL version.

As I mentioned earlier, the *SQLSigCLR* function implements the same algorithm implemented by the *SQLSigTSQL* function and is provided mainly for purposes of performance comparison. You can implement a much more powerful CLR-based solution using regular expressions. Earlier I explained how you can perform string replacement and parsing based on regular expressions. I provided an implementation of a function called *RegexReplace* that invokes the *Regex.Replace* method. Here's an example of how you can use the function to generate query signatures out of the query strings stored in the Queries table:

```
SELECT
  dbo.RegexReplace(query,
    N'([\s,(=<>!](?![^\]]+[\]]))(?:(?:(?:(?#       expression coming
     )(?:([N])?('')(?:[^'']|'''')*(''))(?#       character
     )|(?:0x[\da-fA-F]*)(?#                       binary
     )|(?:[-+]?(?:(?:[\d]*\.[\d]*|[\d]+)(?#       precise number
     )(?:[eE]?[\d]*)))(?#                         imprecise number
     )|(?:[~]?[-+]?(?:[\d]+))(?#                  integer
     ))(?:[\s]?[\+\-\*\/\%\&\|\^][\s]?)?)+(?#     operators
     ))',
    N'$1$2$3#$4')
FROM dbo.Queries;
```

The pattern is self-documenting with inline comments. It identifies (and substitutes with a # symbol) more types of literals than the *SQLSigCLR* function did. It identifies character literals, binary ones, precise numbers, imprecise numbers, and even folds expressions involving literals and substitutes them with a # symbol. This solution has another advantage over the *SQLSigCLR* function—you can maintain the regular expressions yourself and enhance them to support more cases without having to alter the definition of the function. However, the enhanced capabilities you get from regular expressions do come at a certain cost; the preceding query ran in about four seconds—4 times slower than the *SQLSigCLR* function, but still 16 times faster than the *SQLSigTSQL* function.

When you're done, run the following code for cleanup:

```
IF OBJECT_ID('dbo.SQLSigTSQL', 'FN') IS NOT NULL
  DROP FUNCTION dbo.SQLSigTSQL;
IF OBJECT_ID('dbo.SQLSigCLR', 'FS') IS NOT NULL
  DROP FUNCTION dbo.SQLSigCLR;
```

Table-Valued UDFs

Table-valued UDFs are UDFs that return a table and are typically specified in the FROM clause of an outer query. This section will describe inline table-valued UDFs, multistatement table-valued UDFs, and CLR table-valued UDFs.

Inline Table-Valued UDFs

Inline table-valued UDFs are similar to views in the sense that their returned table is defined by a query specification. However, a UDF's query can refer to input parameters, while a view cannot. So you can think of an inline UDF as a "parameterized view." SQL Server actually treats inline UDFs very similarly to views. The query processor replaces an inline UDF reference with its definition; in other words, the query processor "expands" the UDF definition and generates an execution plan accessing the underlying objects.

Unlike scalar and multistatement table-valued UDFs, you don't specify a BEGIN/END block in an inline UDF's body. All you specify is a RETURN clause and a query. In the function's header, you simply state that it returns a table. For example, the following code creates in InsideTSQL2008 the *CustOrders* function, which accepts a customer ID as an input and returns the input customer's orders:

```
SET NOCOUNT ON;
USE InsideTSQL2008;

IF OBJECT_ID('dbo.CustOrders', 'IF') IS NOT NULL
  DROP FUNCTION dbo.CustOrders;
GO
CREATE FUNCTION dbo.CustOrders
  (@custid AS INT) RETURNS TABLE
AS
RETURN
  SELECT orderid, custid, empid, orderdate, requireddate,
    shippeddate, shipperid, freight, shipname, shipaddress, shipcity,
    shipregion, shippostalcode, shipcountry
  FROM Sales.Orders
  WHERE custid = @custid;
GO
```

Run the following query to match the orders of customer 1 (returned by the function) with their order details:

```
SELECT O.orderid, O.custid, OD.productid, OD.qty
FROM dbo.CustOrders(1) AS O
  JOIN Sales.OrderDetails AS OD
    ON O.orderid = OD.orderid;
```

This generates the following output:

```
orderid      custid       productid    qty
-----------  -----------  -----------  ------
10835        1            59           15
10835        1            77           2
10952        1            6            16
10952        1            28           2
11011        1            58           40
11011        1            71           20
10692        1            63           20
10702        1            3            6
```

10702	1	76	15
10643	1	28	15
10643	1	39	21
10643	1	46	2

Like views, inline UDFs can be a target of a modification statement. You can assign any DML permission on the function to users. Of course, the underlying tables absorb the actual modification. For example, the following code sets the *shipperid* attribute in all of customer 1's orders to *2* and shows you the state of the orders before and after the update:

```
BEGIN TRAN
  SELECT orderid, shipperid FROM CustOrders(1) AS O;
  UPDATE dbo.CustOrders(1) SET shipperid = 2;
  SELECT orderid, shipperid FROM CustOrders(1) AS O;
ROLLBACK
```

The code is invoked in a transaction and then rolled back just for demonstration purposes, to avoid applying the change permanently in the InsideTSQL2008 sample database. The following output shows customer 1's orders before the update:

```
orderid     shipperid
----------- -----------
10643       1
10692       2
10702       1
10835       3
10952       1
11011       1
```

And the following output shows customer 1's orders after the update:

```
orderid     shipperid
----------- -----------
10643       2
10692       2
10702       2
10835       2
10952       2
11011       2
```

Similarly, you can delete data through the function, assuming that you have appropriate permissions. For example, the following code (don't run it) would delete customer 1's orders placed in 2007:

```
DELETE FROM dbo.CustOrders(1) WHERE YEAR(orderdate) = 2007;
```

Don't run this code because it will fail with a foreign key violation. I just wanted to provide you with a code sample.

When you're done, run the following code for cleanup:

```
IF OBJECT_ID('dbo.CustOrders', 'IF') IS NOT NULL
  DROP FUNCTION dbo.CustOrders;
```

Split Array

This section provides both T-SQL and CLR implementations of a function that accepts a string containing an array of elements as input and returns a table with the individual elements, each in a separate result row. This section also covers the new ORDER option for CLR table-valued UDFs that was introduced in SQL Server 2008.

T-SQL Split UDF

Run the following code to create the *SplitTSQL* inline table-valued function:

```
USE CLRUtilities;

IF OBJECT_ID('dbo.SplitTSQL', 'IF') IS NOT NULL
  DROP FUNCTION dbo.SplitTSQL;
GO
CREATE FUNCTION dbo.SplitTSQL
  (@string NVARCHAR(MAX), @separator NCHAR(1) = N',') RETURNS TABLE
AS
RETURN
  SELECT
    (n - 1) - DATALENGTH(REPLACE(LEFT(@string, n - 1), @separator, ''))/2
      + 1 AS pos,
    SUBSTRING(@string, n,
      CHARINDEX(@separator, @string + @separator, n) - n) AS element
  FROM dbo.Nums
  WHERE n <= DATALENGTH(@string)/2 + 1
    AND SUBSTRING(@separator + @string, n, 1) = @separator;
GO
```

The function accepts two input parameters: *@string* and *@separator*. The *@string* parameter holds the input array, and *@separator* holds the character used to separate the elements in the array. The function queries the Nums auxiliary table to generate as many copies of *string* (the input array) as the number of elements. The query's filter finds a match for each *@separator* value that appears in *@separator* + *@string*. In other words, *@string* is duplicated once for each element, and *n* from Nums represents the starting position of the element.

The SELECT list has an expression invoking the SUBSTRING function to extract the element starting at the *n*th character up until the next occurrence of *@separator* in *@string*. The SELECT list has another expression that uses the technique I described earlier in the chapter to count occurrences of a substring within a string. In our case, the technique is used to count the number of occurrences of *@separator* in the first *n* characters within *@string*. This count plus one is, in fact, the position of the current element within *@string*.

To test the *SplitTSQL* function, run the following code:

```
SELECT pos, element FROM dbo.SplitTSQL(N'a,b,c', N',') AS F;
```

This generates the following output:

```
pos  element
---- --------
1    a
2    b
3    c
```

You can use the function in interesting ways. For example, suppose that a client application needs to send SQL Server a comma-separated list of order IDs as input to a stored procedure, and expects to get back information about orders whose keys appear in the list. A common way to achieve this task is to pass the stored procedure the comma-separated list of values as an input string, concatenate the input as part of a query string, and use dynamic SQL to run the query and return the requested orders. However, this approach suffers from both security and performance problems. In terms of security, such an implementation exposes your environment to SQL injection. In terms of performance, such an implementation does not provide efficient reuse of previously cached execution plans. With your new function, you can answer such a need with a static query that can reuse a previously cached execution plan:

```
DECLARE @arr AS NVARCHAR(MAX) = N'10248,10249,10250';

SELECT O.orderid, O.custid, O.empid, O.orderdate
FROM dbo.SplitTSQL(@arr, N',') AS F
  JOIN InsideTSQL2008.Sales.Orders AS O
    ON CAST(F.element AS INT) = O.orderid;
```

This generates the following output:

```
orderid     custid      empid       orderdate
----------- ----------- ----------- -----------------------
10248       85          5           2006-07-04 00:00:00.000
10249       79          6           2006-07-05 00:00:00.000
10250       34          4           2006-07-08 00:00:00.000
```

For brevity, this example uses a local variable. Normally you would call this function from your stored procedure and pass the input list you got to the stored procedure as the input to the function.

Note that SQL Server 2008 introduces a new feature called *table-valued parameters* that allows another solution to the task at hand—a solution that is both secure and efficient. I'll describe this feature in detail in Chapter 3, "Stored Procedures."

CLR Split UDF

The CLR implementation of the split function is simpler, although it actually uses two methods. Here's the C# definition of the *SplitCLR* function:

```csharp
// Struct used in SplitCLR function
struct row_item
{
    public string item;
    public int pos;
}
```

```
// SplitCLR Function
// Splits separated list of values and returns a table
// FillRowMethodName = "ArrSplitFillRow"
[SqlFunction(FillRowMethodName = "ArrSplitFillRow",
 DataAccess = DataAccessKind.None,
 TableDefinition = "pos INT, element NVARCHAR(4000) ")]
public static IEnumerable SplitCLR(SqlString inpStr,
    SqlString charSeparator)
{
    string locStr;
    string[] splitStr;
    char[] locSeparator = new char[1];
    locSeparator[0] = (char)charSeparator.Value[0];
    if (inpStr.IsNull)
        locStr = "";
    else
        locStr = inpStr.Value;
    splitStr = locStr.Split(locSeparator,
        StringSplitOptions.RemoveEmptyEntries);
    //locStr.Split(charSeparator.ToString()[0]);
    List<row_item> SplitString = new List<row_item>();
    int i = 1;
    foreach (string s in splitStr)
    {
        row_item r = new row_item();
        r.item = s;
        r.pos = i;
        SplitString.Add(r);
        ++i;
    }
    return SplitString;
}

public static void ArrSplitFillRow(
  Object obj, out int pos, out string item)
{
    pos = ((row_item)obj).pos;
    item = ((row_item)obj).item;
}
```

The function's header sets the *FillRowMethodName* attribute to *ArrSplitFillRow,* which is a method (defined after the *SplitCLR* function's definition) that simply converts the input object to a string. The header also defines the schema of the output table in the *TableDefinition* attribute. This attribute is needed only if you deploy the function automatically using Visual Studio. If you deploy the function manually using T-SQL, you don't need to specify this attribute.

The function simply invokes the built-in *Split* method of the *string* type to split the input array (after converting the input array from a .NET SQL type *SqlString* to a .NET native type *string*). It uses the *StringSplitOptions.RemoveEmptyEntries Split* method option, so the return value does not include array elements that contain an empty string.

Here's the Visual Basic version of the *SplitCLR* function:

```vb
'Struct used in SplitCLR function
Structure row_item
    Dim item As String
    Dim pos As Integer
End Structure

' SplitCLR Function
' Splits separated list of values and returns a table
' FillRowMethodName = "ArrSplitFillRow"
<SqlFunction(FillRowMethodName:="ArrSplitFillRow", _
  DataAccess:=DataAccessKind.None, _
  TableDefinition:="pos INT, element NVARCHAR(4000) ")> _
Public Shared Function SplitCLR(ByVal inpStr As SqlString, _
  ByVal charSeparator As SqlString) As IEnumerable
    Dim locStr As String
    Dim splitStr() As String
    Dim locSeparator(0) As Char
    locSeparator(0) = CChar(charSeparator.Value(0))
    If (inpStr.IsNull) Then
        locStr = ""
    Else
        locStr = inpStr.Value
    End If
    splitStr = locStr.Split(locSeparator, _
      StringSplitOptions.RemoveEmptyEntries)
    Dim SplitString As New List(Of row_item)
    Dim i As Integer = 1
    For Each s As String In splitStr
        Dim r As New row_item
        r.item = s
        r.pos = i
        SplitString.Add(r)
        i = i + 1
    Next
    Return SplitString
End Function

Public Shared Sub ArrSplitFillRow( _
ByVal obj As Object, <Out()> ByRef pos As Integer, _
  <Out()> ByRef item As String)
    pos = CType(obj, row_item).pos
    item = CType(obj, row_item).item
End Sub
```

Use the following code to register the C# version of the function in the database:

```sql
IF OBJECT_ID('dbo.SplitCLR', 'FT') IS NOT NULL
  DROP FUNCTION dbo.SplitCLR;
GO
CREATE FUNCTION dbo.SplitCLR
  (@string AS NVARCHAR(4000), @separator AS NCHAR(1))
RETURNS TABLE(pos INT, element NVARCHAR(4000))
EXTERNAL NAME CLRUtilities.CLRUtilities.SplitCLR;
GO
```

Use the following code to register the Visual Basic version:

```
CREATE FUNCTION dbo.SplitCLR
  (@string AS NVARCHAR(4000), @separator AS NCHAR(1))
RETURNS TABLE(pos INT, element NVARCHAR(4000))
EXTERNAL NAME CLRUtilities.[CLRUtilities.CLRUtilities].SplitCLR;
GO
```

Run the following query to test the *SplitCLR* function:

```
SELECT pos, element FROM dbo.SplitCLR(N'a,b,c', N',');
```

To test the function against a table of arrays, first run the following code, which creates the Arrays table and populates it with some sample arrays:

```
IF OBJECT_ID('dbo.Arrays', 'U') IS NOT NULL DROP TABLE dbo.Arrays;

CREATE TABLE dbo.Arrays
(
  arrid INT            NOT NULL IDENTITY PRIMARY KEY,
  arr   NVARCHAR(4000) NOT NULL
);
GO

INSERT INTO dbo.Arrays(arr) VALUES
  (N'20,220,25,2115,14'),
  (N'30,330,28'),
  (N'12,10,8,8,122,13,2,14,10,9'),
  (N'-4,-6,1050,-2');
```

Use the following query to apply the function to each array from the Arrays table:

```
SELECT arrid, pos, element
FROM dbo.Arrays AS A
  CROSS APPLY dbo.SplitCLR(arr, N',') AS F;
```

This generates the following output:

```
arrid       pos         element
----------- ----------- --------
1           1           20
1           2           220
1           3           25
1           4           2115
1           5           14
2           1           30
2           2           330
2           3           28
3           1           12
3           2           10
3           3           8
3           4           8
3           5           122
```

3	6	13
3	7	2
3	8	14
3	9	10
3	10	9
4	1	-4
4	2	-6
4	3	1050
4	4	-2

Compare Performance of T-SQL and CLR Split

To compare the performance of the T-SQL and CLR splitting techniques, first duplicate the current contents of Arrays 100,000 times by running the following code:

```
INSERT INTO dbo.Arrays
  SELECT arr
  FROM dbo.Arrays, dbo.Nums
  WHERE n <= 100000;
```

The Arrays table is now populated with 400,004 rows.

Use the following query (with results discarded) to apply the T-SQL splitting technique:

```
SELECT arrid,
  (n - 1) - DATALENGTH(REPLACE(LEFT(arr, n - 1), ',', ''))/2 + 1 AS pos,
  CAST(SUBSTRING(arr, n, CHARINDEX(',', arr + ',', n) - n)
        AS INT) AS element
FROM dbo.Arrays
  JOIN dbo.Nums
    ON n <= DATALENGTH(arr)/2 + 1
    AND SUBSTRING(',' + arr, n, 1) = ',';
```

Notice that I didn't use the *SplitTSQL* UDF here because you can use the same technique directly against the Arrays table. This code ran for 19 seconds on my system. The CLR version ran for four seconds—almost five times faster than the T-SQL version. You can find another, even faster, CLR-based implementation of the split functionality by SQL Server MVP Adam Machanic here: *http://sqlblog.com/blogs/adam_machanic/archive/2009/04/26/faster-more-scalable-sqlclr-string-splitting.aspx*.

ORDER Option for CLR Table-Valued UDFs

SQL Server 2008 introduces a new option called ORDER in the CREATE FUNCTION command that is applicable to CLR table-valued UDFs. When registering a UDF, you can specify this option along with an order by list to indicate to SQL Server the order in which the rows are produced by the function. Registering a UDF with this option can give you performance benefits when an operator in the query's execution plan needs to consume the UDF rows in the specified order—for example, to process an ORDER BY clause, GROUP BY, DISTINCT, merge join, and so on. Knowing that the UDF produces rows in the desired order, the optimizer can avoid the need for a sort operation, for example.

> **Note** The ORDER option does not guarantee that a SELECT query from the function will produce an ordered result set to the user. As with all tables, views, and table-valued functions, the only way to guarantee the ordering of rows in the result set of a SELECT query is to include an ORDER BY clause in the outermost SELECT query.

For example, recall that earlier you created a CLR UDF called *SplitCLR* that splits an input separated list of values to its individual elements. The function returns a row for each element with the position of the element in the list (*pos*) and the element itself (*element*). The function *SplitCLR* was designed and written so that the rows are produced in the order of the *pos* attribute—but without any special indication, SQL Server is not aware of this fact. If you specify the new ORDER option the optimizer can produce efficient plans for your queries by taking advantage of this fact.

Run the following code to register a function called *SplitCLR_OrderByPos* based on the same C# routine you used to register the function *SplitCLR* earlier. This time, specify the option ORDER(pos) to indicate that your implementation of the function incorporates logic to produce the rows in the order of the *pos* attribute:

```
CREATE FUNCTION dbo.SplitCLR_OrderByPos
  (@string AS NVARCHAR(4000), @separator AS NCHAR(1))
RETURNS TABLE(pos INT, element NVARCHAR(4000))
ORDER(pos)
EXTERNAL NAME CLRUtilities.CLRUtilities.SplitCLR;
GO
```

Use the following code to register the function if you used Visual Basic to develop the routine:

```
CREATE FUNCTION dbo.SplitCLR_OrderByPos
  (@string AS NVARCHAR(4000), @separator AS NCHAR(1))
RETURNS TABLE(pos INT, element NVARCHAR(4000))
ORDER(pos)
EXTERNAL NAME CLRUtilities.[CLRUtilities.CLRUtilities].SplitCLR;
GO
```

To demonstrate the performance benefit in the new ORDER option I'll use a query whose plan needs to consume the UDF rows in *pos* order—for example, by specifying ORDER BY *pos*. Here's such a query run against both versions of the UDF:

```
SELECT *
FROM dbo.SplitCLR(N'a,b,c,d,e,f,g,h,i,j,k,l,m,n,o,p,q,r,s,t,u,v,w,x,y,z', N',')
ORDER BY pos;

SELECT *
FROM dbo.SplitCLR_OrderByPos(N'a,b,c,d,e,f,g,h,i,j,k,l,m,n,o,p,q,r,s,t,u,v,w,x,y,z', N',')
ORDER BY pos;
```

The execution plans for both queries and their respective cost ratios are shown in Figure 2-4.

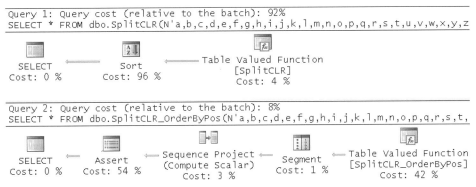

FIGURE 2-4 Execution plan for UDF—first without and then with the ORDER option

Observe that in the case of the *SplitCLR* function (Query 1) that was registered without the ORDER option, the optimizer wasn't aware of the order in which the rows are returned from the function—hence it had to apply a sort operation. In the case of the *SplitCLR_OrderByPos* function, the optimizer was aware that the rows were returned in *pos* order; therefore, it didn't bother to sort them. The respective cost ratios in the plans indicate that the first query is more than 10 times as expensive as the second.

Note that you cannot fool the optimizer by registering a UDF with an ORDER option that in practice is not guaranteed. As part of the execution plan, SQL Server monitors the order in which the rows are returned. If the specified order is violated, the Assert operator in the plan fails the query. Because some extra work is required to validate the ORDER option, it is recommended that you do not use this option when the plans for your queries don't need to consume the function's rows in order. Of course, if some of your queries will benefit from the ORDER option and some won't, you can always register two versions of the function in SQL Server for the same CLR routine—one with and one without the option, just like I did.

When you're done, run the following code for cleanup:

```
IF OBJECT_ID('dbo.Arrays', 'U') IS NOT NULL
  DROP TABLE dbo.Arrays;
IF OBJECT_ID('dbo.SplitTSQL', 'IF') IS NOT NULL
  DROP FUNCTION dbo.SplitTSQL;
IF OBJECT_ID('dbo.SplitCLR', 'FT') IS NOT NULL
  DROP FUNCTION dbo.SplitCLR;
IF OBJECT_ID('dbo.SplitCLR_OrderByPos', 'FT') IS NOT NULL
  DROP FUNCTION dbo.SplitCLR_OrderByPos;
```

Multistatement Table-Valued UDFs

A multistatement table-valued UDF is a function that returns a table variable. The function has a body with the sole purpose of populating the table variable. You develop a multistatement table-valued UDF when you need a routine that returns a table, and the implementation of the routine cannot be expressed as a single query—instead, it requires multiple statements; for example, flow elements such as loops.

A multistatement table-valued UDF is used in a similar manner to an inline table-valued UDF, but it cannot be a target of a modification statement; that is, you can use it only in the FROM clause of a SELECT query. Internally, SQL Server treats the two completely differently. An inline UDF is treated more like a view—as a table expression; a multistatement table-valued UDF is treated more like a stored procedure. As with other UDFs, a multistatement table-valued UDF is not allowed to have side effects.

As an example of a multistatement table-valued UDF, you will create a function that accepts an employee ID as input and returns details about the input employee and its subordinates in all levels. First, run the following code to create the Employees table and populate it with some sample data:

```
SET NOCOUNT ON;
USE tempdb;

IF OBJECT_ID('dbo.Employees', 'U') IS NOT NULL DROP TABLE dbo.Employees;

CREATE TABLE dbo.Employees
(
  empid    INT         NOT NULL PRIMARY KEY,
  mgrid    INT         NULL     REFERENCES dbo.Employees,
  empname  VARCHAR(25) NOT NULL,
  salary   MONEY       NOT NULL
);
GO

INSERT INTO dbo.Employees(empid, mgrid, empname, salary) VALUES
    (1,  NULL, 'David',   $10000.00),
    (2,  1,    'Eitan',   $7000.00),
    (3,  1,    'Ina',     $7500.00),
    (4,  2,    'Seraph',  $5000.00),
    (5,  2,    'Jiru',    $5500.00),
    (6,  2,    'Steve',   $4500.00),
    (7,  3,    'Aaron',   $5000.00),
    (8,  5,    'Lilach',  $3500.00),
    (9,  7,    'Rita',    $3000.00),
    (10, 5,    'Sean',    $3000.00),
    (11, 7,    'Gabriel', $3000.00),
    (12, 9,    'Emilia' , $2000.00),
    (13, 9,    'Michael', $2000.00),
    (14, 9,    'Didi',    $1500.00);

CREATE UNIQUE INDEX idx_unc_mgrid_empid ON dbo.Employees(mgrid, empid);
```

Run the following code to create the multistatement *Subordinates* UDF, which uses an implementation based on loops:

```
IF OBJECT_ID('dbo.Subordinates', 'TF') IS NOT NULL
   DROP FUNCTION dbo.Subordinates;
GO
CREATE FUNCTION dbo.Subordinates(@mgrid AS INT) RETURNS @Subs Table
(
  empid  INT NOT NULL PRIMARY KEY NONCLUSTERED,
  mgrid  INT NULL,
```

```
    empname VARCHAR(25) NOT NULL,
    salary  MONEY        NOT NULL,
    lvl     INT NOT NULL,
    UNIQUE CLUSTERED(lvl, empid)
)
AS
BEGIN
  DECLARE @lvl AS INT;
  SET @lvl = 0;                    -- Init level counter with 0

  -- Insert root node to @Subs
  INSERT INTO @Subs(empid, mgrid, empname, salary, lvl)
    SELECT empid, mgrid, empname, salary, @lvl
    FROM dbo.Employees WHERE empid = @mgrid;

  WHILE @@rowcount > 0             -- While prev level had rows
  BEGIN
    SET @lvl = @lvl + 1;          -- Increment level counter

    -- Insert next level of subordinates to @Subs
    INSERT INTO @Subs(empid, mgrid, empname, salary, lvl)
      SELECT C.empid, C.mgrid, C.empname, C.salary, @lvl
      FROM @Subs AS P               -- P = Parent
        JOIN dbo.Employees AS C -- C = Child
          ON P.lvl = @lvl - 1   -- Filter parents from prev level
          AND C.mgrid = P.empid;
  END

  RETURN;
END
GO
```

The function accepts the *@mgrid* input parameter, which is the ID of the input manager. The function returns the @Subs table variable, with details about the input manager and all its subordinates in all levels. In addition to the employee attributes, @Subs also has a column called *lvl* that keeps track of the level distance from the input manager (0 for the input manager and increasing by one unit for each level).

The function keeps track of the current level in the *@lvl* local variable, which is initialized with zero.

The function first inserts into @Subs the row from Employees with ID equal to *@mgrid*.

Then, in a loop, if the last insert affected more than zero rows, the code increments the *@lvl* variable's value by one and inserts the next level of employees—in other words, direct subordinates of the managers found in the previous level—into @Subs.

The *lvl* column is important because it allows you to isolate the employees who were inserted into @Subs in the last iteration. To return only subordinates of the employees found in the previous level, the join condition filters from @Subs only rows where the *lvl* column is equal to the previous level (*@lvl – 1*).

To test the function, run the following code, which returns information about employee 3 and her subordinates:

```
SELECT empid, mgrid, empname, salary, lvl
FROM dbo.Subordinates(3) AS S;
```

This generates the following output:

```
empid  mgrid  empname   salary   lvl
------ ------ --------- -------- ----
3      1      Ina       7500.00  0
7      3      Aaron     5000.00  1
9      7      Rita      3000.00  2
11     7      Gabriel   3000.00  2
12     9      Emilia    2000.00  3
13     9      Michael   2000.00  3
14     9      Didi      1500.00  3
```

Interestingly, the task of returning subordinates can also be achieved with an inline table-valued UDF that is based on a recursive query, like so:

```
IF OBJECT_ID('dbo.Subordinates') IS NOT NULL
  DROP FUNCTION dbo.Subordinates;
GO
CREATE FUNCTION dbo.Subordinates(@mgrid AS INT) RETURNS TABLE
AS
RETURN
  WITH Subs
  AS
  (
    -- Anchor member returns a row for the input manager
    SELECT empid, mgrid, empname, salary, 0 AS lvl
    FROM dbo.Employees
    WHERE empid = @mgrid

    UNION ALL

    -- Recursive member returns next level of children
    SELECT C.empid, C.mgrid, C.empname, C.salary, P.lvl + 1
    FROM Subs AS P
      JOIN dbo.Employees AS C
        ON C.mgrid = P.empid
  )
  SELECT * FROM Subs;
GO
```

The inline UDF applies logic similar to the multistatement UDF, except that it uses recursive common table expressions (CTEs). It's simpler in the sense that you don't need to define the returned table explicitly or filter the previous level's managers.

The first query in the CTE's body returns the row from Employees for the given root employee. It also returns zero as the level of the root employee. In a recursive CTE, a query that doesn't have any recursive references is known as an *anchor member*.

The second query in the CTE's body (following the UNION ALL set operation) has a recursive reference to itself. This makes it a *recursive member*, and it is treated in a special manner. The recursive reference to the CTE's name (*Subs*) represents the result set returned previously. The recursive member query joins the previous result set representing the managers in the previous level with the Employees table to return the next level of employees. The recursive query also calculates the level value as the employee's manager level plus one. The first time that the recursive member is invoked, *Subs* stands for the result set returned by the anchor member (root employee). There's no explicit termination check for the recursive member—it is invoked repeatedly until it returns an empty set. Thus, the first time it is invoked, it returns direct subordinates of the subtree's root employee. The second time it is invoked, *Subs* represents the result set of the first invocation of the recursive member (first level of subordinates), so it returns the second level of subordinates. The recursive member is invoked repeatedly until there are no more subordinates, in which case it returns an empty set and recursion stops.

The reference to the CTE name in the outer query represents the UNION ALL of all the result sets returned by the invocation of the anchor member and all the invocations of the recursive member.

To test the function, run the following query:

```
SELECT empid, mgrid, empname, salary, lvl
FROM dbo.Subordinates(3) AS S;
```

> **More Info** For more details about querying hierarchical data, such as an employee organizational chart, please refer to *Inside T-SQL Querying*.

When you're done, run the following code for cleanup:

```
IF OBJECT_ID('dbo.Employees', 'U') IS NOT NULL
  DROP TABLE dbo.Employees;
IF OBJECT_ID('dbo.Subordinates', 'IF') IS NOT NULL
  DROP FUNCTION dbo.Subordinates;
```

Per-Row UDFs

Nondeterministic functions are functions that are not guaranteed to return the same output when invoked multiple times with the same input. When you invoke nondeterministic built-in functions in a query (such as RAND and GETDATE), those functions are invoked once for the whole query and not once per row. The only exception to this rule is the NEWID function, which generates a globally unique identifier (GUID). NEWID is the only nondeterministic built-in function that will be invoked once per row.

To demonstrate this behavior of nondeterministic functions, run the following code, which queries the Orders table in the InsideTSQL2008 database and invokes the functions RAND, GETDATE, and NEWID:

```
USE InsideTSQL2008;

SELECT n, RAND() AS rnd, GETDATE() AS dt, NEWID() AS guid
FROM dbo.Nums
WHERE n <= 10;
```

This generates the following output:

```
n    rnd                dt                       guid
---  ---------------    ----------------------   ------------------------------------
1    0.67882771079132   2009-02-09 10:56:11.227  A9A2DCB2-5005-4308-BC30-DC67599E2B72
2    0.67882771079132   2009-02-09 10:56:11.227  32CD827C-38E2-4F12-A609-10F6AFA3E110
3    0.67882771079132   2009-02-09 10:56:11.227  E796A4A9-9B64-4D5A-A634-C52F2650168C
4    0.67882771079132   2009-02-09 10:56:11.227  82EEC0C1-8A29-4936-BB11-092C884952AA
5    0.67882771079132   2009-02-09 10:56:11.227  A1C243BD-9B0E-455B-A101-EC6C79C4EC85
6    0.67882771079132   2009-02-09 10:56:11.227  0CBAD293-AB5F-4054-A8C3-204CDC47DE4D
7    0.67882771079132   2009-02-09 10:56:11.227  E0648D48-E452-4F95-B35E-63FF980DB080
8    0.67882771079132   2009-02-09 10:56:11.227  FDDAF9E3-BB62-4EBE-9EB0-DDAC3EDA1659
9    0.67882771079132   2009-02-09 10:56:11.227  5E03C18D-BEDF-4D5E-AB8B-DEA8791E5587
10   0.67882771079132   2009-02-09 10:56:11.227  A97E907D-2292-4222-A11B-92340C8D99ED
```

You can observe that both RAND and GETDATE were invoked only once for the whole query, and their result values were copied to all rows. On the other hand, NEWID was invoked once per row, generating a different value in each row.

Suppose that you needed to invoke the RAND function for each row. You might have thought of invoking RAND from a UDF and then invoking the UDF in an outer query, knowing that a UDF is invoked once per row. Here's an attempt to create such a UDF called *PerRowRand*:

```
IF OBJECT_ID('dbo.PerRowRand', 'FN') IS NOT NULL
  DROP FUNCTION dbo.PerRowRand;
GO
CREATE FUNCTION dbo.PerRowRand() RETURNS FLOAT
AS
BEGIN
  RETURN RAND();
END
GO
```

However, this attempt fails and produces the following error:

```
Msg 443, Level 16, State 1, Procedure PerRowRand, Line 4
Invalid use of a side-effecting operator 'rand' within a function.
```

The error tells you that your function is not allowed to have side effects, and the RAND function does change an internal state (for use in a subsequent invocation of RAND).

A back door allows you to implicitly invoke RAND from a UDF. Create a view that invokes RAND and query the view from the UDF, like so:

```
IF OBJECT_ID('dbo.VRand', 'V') IS NOT NULL
  DROP VIEW dbo.VRand;
GO
```

```
CREATE VIEW dbo.VRand AS SELECT RAND() AS r;
GO

IF OBJECT_ID('dbo.PerRowRand', 'FN') IS NOT NULL
  DROP FUNCTION dbo.PerRowRand;
GO
CREATE FUNCTION dbo.PerRowRand() RETURNS FLOAT
AS
BEGIN
  RETURN (SELECT r FROM dbo.VRand);
END
GO
```

You can test the *PerRowRand* UDF by invoking it in a query against the Orders table, like so:

```
SELECT n, dbo.PerRowRand() AS rnd
FROM dbo.Nums
WHERE n <= 10;
```

This generates the following output:

```
n           rnd
----------- ---------------------
1           0.372112088734625
2           0.351204240953987
3           0.534180551426038
4           0.0494653055888316
5           0.387218774605993
6           0.585318509610502
7           0.640748344596822
8           0.741752879888198
9           0.120974678583898
10          0.768738750832328
```

Note that SQL Server 2008 cares about side effects but not about nondeterminism. For example, the GETDATE function is nondeterministic, but it doesn't have any side effects. Therefore, SQL Server allows you to use the GETDATE function in a UDF:

```
IF OBJECT_ID('dbo.PerRowGetdate') IS NOT NULL
  DROP FUNCTION dbo.PerRowGetdate;
GO
CREATE FUNCTION dbo.PerRowGetdate() RETURNS DATETIME
AS
BEGIN
  RETURN GETDATE();
END
GO
```

To demonstrate that the GETDATE function is evaluated only once when invoked directly in a query, run the following code querying 1,000,000 rows and applying DISTINCT to the GETDATE values:

```
SELECT DISTINCT GETDATE() AS dt
FROM dbo.Nums
WHERE n <= 1000000;
```

The output has only one row:

```
dt
-----------------------
2009-02-12 10:59:28.873
```

Try a similar query using the *PerRowGetdate* UDF that in its body calls the GETDATE function:

```
SELECT DISTINCT dbo.PerRowGetdate() AS dt
FROM dbo.Nums
WHERE n <= 1000000;
```

This time you get multiple distinct values in the result, proving that GETDATE was invoked multiple times:

```
dt
-----------------------
2009-02-12 11:00:32.370
2009-02-12 11:00:32.540
2009-02-12 11:00:35.193
2009-02-12 11:00:35.223
2009-02-12 11:00:33.057
2009-02-12 11:00:34.757
2009-02-12 11:00:32.493
2009-02-12 11:00:32.900
2009-02-12 11:00:34.630
2009-02-12 11:00:31.610
...
```

When you're done, run the following code for cleanup:

```
IF OBJECT_ID('dbo.VRand', 'V') IS NOT NULL
  DROP VIEW dbo.VRand;
IF OBJECT_ID('dbo.PerRowRand', 'FN') IS NOT NULL
  DROP FUNCTION dbo.PerRowRand;
IF OBJECT_ID('dbo.PerRowGetDate', 'FN') IS NOT NULL
  DROP FUNCTION dbo.PerRowGetDate;
```

Conclusion

User-defined functions can be embedded in queries, constraints, and computed columns. This capability allows you to enhance the functionality of your queries while still preserving a high level of readability and simplicity. SQL Server 2008 supports .NET integration and the ability to create functions with CLR code. You can create both scalar and table-valued CLR UDFs. Remember to use CLR UDFs wisely. They are especially good for tasks that T-SQL is not built to cope with efficiently, including procedural logic, complex calculations, string manipulation, and so on. On the other hand, .NET code should not be the choice when the task mainly involves set-based data manipulation. T-SQL will typically be simpler and perform much better for such tasks.

Chapter 3
Stored Procedures

Itzik Ben-Gan and Dejan Sarka

Stored procedures are executable server-side routines. They give you great power and performance benefits if used wisely. Unlike user-defined functions (UDFs), stored procedures are allowed to have side effects; that is, they are allowed to change data in tables, and even alter object definitions. Stored procedures can be used as a security layer. You can control access to objects by granting execution permissions on stored procedures and not to underlying objects. You can perform input validation in stored procedures, and you can use stored procedures to allow activities only if they make sense as a whole unit, as opposed to allowing users to perform activities directly against objects.

Stored procedures also give you the benefits of encapsulation; if you need to change the implementation of a stored procedure because you developed a more efficient way to achieve a task, you can issue an ALTER PROCEDURE statement. As long as the procedure's interface remains the same, the users and the applications are not affected. On the other hand, if you implement your business logic in the client application, the impact of a change can be very painful.

Stored procedures also provide many important performance benefits. By default, a stored procedure will reuse a previously cached execution plan, saving the CPU resources and the time it takes to parse, resolve, and optimize your code. Network traffic is minimized by shortening the code strings that the client submits to Microsoft SQL Server—the client submits only the stored procedure's name and its arguments, as opposed to the full code. Moreover, all the activity is performed at the server, avoiding multiple roundtrips between the client and the server. The stored procedure passes only the final result to the client through the network.

This chapter explores stored procedures. It starts with brief coverage of the different types of stored procedures supported by SQL Server 2008 and then delves into details. The chapter covers the stored procedure's interface, resolution process, compilation, recompilations and execution plan reuse, plan guides, the EXECUTE AS clause, and common language runtime (CLR) stored procedures.

Types of Stored Procedures

SQL Server 2008 supports different types of stored procedures: user-defined, system, and extended. You can develop user-defined stored procedures with T-SQL or with the CLR. This section briefly covers the different types.

User-Defined Stored Procedures

A user-defined stored procedure is created in a user database and typically interacts with the database objects. When you invoke a user-defined stored procedure, you specify the EXEC (or EXECUTE) command and the stored procedure's schema-qualified name and arguments:

```
EXEC dbo.Proc1 <arguments>;
```

As an example, run the following code to create the *GetSortedShippers* stored procedure in the InsideTSQL2008 database:

```
USE InsideTSQL2008;

IF OBJECT_ID('dbo.GetSortedShippers', 'P') IS NOT NULL
  DROP PROC dbo.GetSortedShippers;
GO
-- Stored procedure GetSortedShippers
-- Returns shippers sorted by requested sort column
CREATE PROC dbo.GetSortedShippers
  @colname AS sysname = NULL
AS

DECLARE @msg AS NVARCHAR(500);

-- Input validation
IF @colname IS NULL
BEGIN
  SET @msg = N'A value must be supplied for parameter @colname.';
  RAISERROR(@msg, 16, 1);
  RETURN;
END

IF @colname NOT IN(N'shipperid', N'companyname', N'phone')
BEGIN
  SET @msg =
    N'Valid values for @colname are: '
    + N'N''shipperid'', N''companyname'', N''phone''.';
  RAISERROR(@msg, 16, 1);
  RETURN;
END

-- Return shippers sorted by requested sort column
IF @colname = N'shipperid'
  SELECT shipperid, companyname, phone
  FROM Sales.Shippers
  ORDER BY shipperid;
ELSE IF @colname = N'companyname'
  SELECT shipperid, companyname, phone
  FROM Sales.Shippers
  ORDER BY companyname;
ELSE IF @colname = N'phone'
  SELECT shipperid, companyname, phone
  FROM Sales.Shippers
  ORDER BY phone;
GO
```

The stored procedure accepts a column name from the Sales.Shippers table in the InsideTSQL2008 database as input (@*colname*); after input validation, it returns the rows from the Shippers table sorted by the specified column name. Input validation here involves verifying that a column name was specified, and that the specified column name exists in the Shippers table. Later in the chapter, I will discuss the subject of parameterizing sort order in more detail; for now, I just wanted to provide a simple example of a user-defined stored procedure. Run the following code to invoke *GetSortedShippers* specifying *N'companyname'* as input:

```
EXEC dbo.GetSortedShippers @colname = N'companyname';
```

This generates the following output:

```
shipperid   companyname     phone
----------- --------------- ---------------
2           Shipper ETYNR   (425) 555-0136
1           Shipper GVSUA   (503) 555-0137
3           Shipper ZHISN   (415) 555-0138
```

You can leave out the keyword EXEC if the stored procedure is the first statement of a batch, but I recommend using it all the time. You can also omit the stored procedure's schema name (*dbo* in our case), but when you neglect to specify it, SQL Server must resolve the schema. The resolution in SQL Server 2008 occurs in the following order (adapted from SQL Server Books Online):

1. The sys schema of the current database.

2. The caller's default schema if executed in a batch or in dynamic SQL. Or, if the nonqualified procedure name appears inside the body of another procedure definition, the schema containing this other procedure is searched next.

3. The dbo schema in the current database.

   For example, suppose that you connect to the InsideTSQL2008 database and your user's default schema in InsideTSQL2008 is called Sales. You invoke the following code in a batch:

   ```
   EXEC GetSortedShippers @colname = N'companyname';
   ```

The resolution takes place in the following order:

1. Look for *GetSortedShippers* in the sys schema of InsideTSQL2008 (*sys. GetSortedShippers*). If found, execute it; if not, proceed to the next step (as in our case).

2. If invoked in a batch (as in our case) or dynamic SQL, look for *GetSortedShippers* in Sales (*Sales.GetSortedShippers*). Or, if invoked in another procedure (say, *Production. AnotherProc*), look for *GetSortedShippers* in *Production* next. If found, execute it; if not, proceed to the next step (as in our case).

3. Look for *GetSortedShippers* in the *dbo* schema (*dbo.GetSortedShippers*). If found (as in our case), execute it; if not, generate a resolution error.

As I mentioned earlier, you can use stored procedures as a security layer. You can control access to objects by granting execution permissions on stored procedures and not on underlying objects. For example, suppose that there's a database user called user1 in the InsideTSQL2008 database. You want to allow user1 to invoke the *GetSortedShippers* procedure, but you want to deny user1 direct access to the Shippers table. You can achieve this by granting the user EXECUTE permissions on the procedure, and denying SELECT (and possibly other) permissions on the table, as in:

```
DENY SELECT ON Sales.Shippers TO user1;
GRANT EXECUTE ON dbo.GetSortedShippers TO user1;
```

SQL Server allows user1 to execute the stored procedure. However, if user1 attempts to query the Shippers table directly:

```
SELECT shipperid, companyname, phone
FROM Sales.Shippers;
```

SQL Server generates the following error:

```
Msg 229, Level 14, State 5, Line 1
The SELECT permission was denied on the object 'Shippers', database 'InsideTSQL2008', schema
'Sales'.
```

This security model gives you a high level of control over the activities that users will be allowed to perform.

I'd like to point out other aspects of stored procedure programming through the *GetSortedShippers* sample procedure:

- Notice that I explicitly specified column names in the query and didn't use SELECT *. Using SELECT * is a bad practice. In the future, the table might undergo schema changes that cause your application to break. Also, if you really need only a subset of the table's columns and not all of them, the use of SELECT * prevents the optimizer from utilizing covering indexes defined on that subset of columns.

- The query is missing a filter. This is not a bad practice by itself—it's perfectly valid if you really need all rows from the table. But you might be surprised to learn that in performance-tuning projects at Solid Quality Mentors, we still find production applications that need filtered data but filter it only at the client. Such an approach introduces extreme pressure on both SQL Server and the network. Filters allow the optimizer to consider using indexes, which minimizes the I/O cost. Also, by filtering at the server, you reduce network traffic. If you need filtered data, make sure you filter it at the server; use a WHERE clause (or ON, HAVING where relevant)!

- Notice the use of a semicolon (;) to suffix statements. Although not a requirement of T-SQL for all statements, the semicolon suffix is an ANSI requirement. In SQL Server 2008, you are required to suffix some statements with a semicolon to avoid ambiguity of your code. For example, the WITH keyword is used for different purposes—to define a CTE, to specify a table hint, and so on. SQL Server requires you to suffix the statement preceding the CTE's WITH clause to avoid ambiguity. Similarly, the MERGE keyword is used for different purposes—to specify a join hint and to start a MERGE statement. SQL Server requires you to terminate a MERGE statement with a semicolon to avoid ambiguity. Getting used to suffixing all statements with a semicolon is a good practice.

Now let's get back to the focus of this section—user-defined stored procedures.

As I mentioned earlier, to invoke a user-defined stored procedure, you specify EXEC, the schema-qualified name of the procedure, and the parameter values for the invocation if there are any. References in the stored procedure to system and user object names that are not fully qualified (that is, without the database prefix) are always resolved in the database in which the procedure was created. If you want to invoke a user-defined procedure created in another database, you must database-qualify its name. For example, if you are connected to a database called db1 and want to invoke a stored procedure called *dbo.Proc1*, which resides in db2, you would use the following code:

```
USE db1;
EXEC db2.dbo.Proc1 <arguments>;
```

Invoking a procedure from another database wouldn't change the fact that object names that are not fully qualified would be resolved in the database in which the procedure was created (db2, in this case).

If you want to invoke a remote stored procedure residing in another instance of SQL Server, you would use the fully qualified stored procedure name, including the linked server name: *server.database.schema.proc*.

When done, run the following code for cleanup:

```
IF OBJECT_ID('dbo.GetSortedShippers', 'P') IS NOT NULL
  DROP PROC dbo.GetSortedShippers;
```

Special Stored Procedures

By *special* stored procedure I mean a stored procedure created with a name beginning with *sp_* in the master database. A stored procedure created in this way has a special behavior.

> ⚠ **Important** Note that Microsoft strongly recommends against creating your own stored procedures with the *sp_* prefix. This prefix is used by SQL Server to designate system stored procedures. In this section, I will create stored procedures with the *sp_* prefix to demonstrate their special behavior.

As an example, the following code creates the special procedure *sp_Proc1*, which prints the database context and queries the INFORMATION_SCHEMA.TABLES view—first with dynamic SQL, then with a static query:

```
USE master;
IF OBJECT_ID('dbo.sp_Proc1', 'P') IS NOT NULL DROP PROC dbo.sp_Proc1;
GO

CREATE PROC dbo.sp_Proc1
AS
PRINT 'master.dbo.sp_Proc1 executing in ' + DB_NAME();

-- Dynamic query
EXEC('SELECT TABLE_CATALOG, TABLE_SCHEMA, TABLE_NAME
FROM INFORMATION_SCHEMA.TABLES
WHERE TABLE_TYPE = N''BASE TABLE'';');

-- Static query
SELECT TABLE_CATALOG, TABLE_SCHEMA, TABLE_NAME
FROM INFORMATION_SCHEMA.TABLES
WHERE TABLE_TYPE = 'BASE TABLE';
GO
```

One of the unique aspects of a special procedure is that you don't need to database-qualify its name when connected to another database. For example, you can be connected to InsideTSQL2008 and still be able to run it without database-qualifying its name:

```
USE InsideTSQL2008;
EXEC dbo.sp_Proc1;
```

The PRINT command returns *master.dbo.sp_Proc1 executing in InsideTSQL2008*. The database name in the printed message was obtained by the DB_NAME function. It seems that DB_NAME "thinks" that the database context is InsideTSQL2008 (the current database) and not master. Similarly, dynamic SQL also assumes the context of the current database; therefore, the EXEC command (which invokes a query against INFORMATION_SCHEMA.TABLES) returns table names from the InsideTSQL2008 database. In contrast to the previous two statements, the static query against INFORMATION_SCHEMA.TABLES seems to "think" that it is running in master—it returns table names from the master database and not InsideTSQL2008. Similarly, if you refer with static code to user objects (for example, a table called T1), SQL Server looks for them in master. If that's not confusing enough, static code referring to compatibility views (for example, sys.objects) is normally resolved in master, but if the catalog view is a backward-compatibility one (for example, sys.sysobjects) the code is resolved in the current database.

Interestingly, the *sp_* prefix also works magic with other types of objects in addition to stored procedures.

Caution The behavior described in the following section is undocumented and you should not rely on it in production environments.

For example, the following code creates a table with the *sp_* prefix in master:

```
USE master;
IF OBJECT_ID('dbo.sp_Globals', 'U') IS NOT NULL
  DROP TABLE dbo.sp_Globals;

CREATE TABLE dbo.sp_Globals
(
  var_name sysname     NOT NULL PRIMARY KEY,
  val       SQL_VARIANT NULL
);
```

And the following code switches between database contexts and always manages to find the table even though the table name is not database-qualified.

```
USE InsideTSQL2008;
INSERT INTO dbo.sp_Globals(var_name, val)
  VALUES('var1', 10);

USE AdventureWorks2008;
INSERT INTO dbo.sp_Globals(var_name, val)
  VALUES('var2', CAST(1 AS BIT));

USE tempdb;
SELECT var_name, val FROM dbo.sp_Globals;
```

This generates the following output:

```
var_name  val
--------- ----
var1      10
var2      1
```

For cleanup, run the following code:

```
USE master;
IF OBJECT_ID('dbo.sp_Globals', 'U') IS NOT NULL
  DROP TABLE dbo.sp_Globals;
```

Do not drop *sp_Proc1* yet; we'll use it in the following section.

System Stored Procedures

System stored procedures are procedures that were shipped by Microsoft. Historically, system stored procedures resided in the master database, had the *sp_* prefix, and were marked as system objects with a special flag (MS Shipped). In SQL Server 2008, system stored procedures reside physically in an internal hidden Resource database, and they exist logically in every database.

A special procedure (*sp_* prefix, created in master) that is also marked as a system procedure gets additional unique behavior. You can mark a procedure as a system procedure by using the undocumented procedure *sp_MS_marksystemobject*.

> **Caution** You should not use the *sp_MS_marksystemobject* stored procedure in production because you won't get any support if you run into trouble with it. Also, the behavior you get by marking your procedures as *system* isn't guaranteed to remain the same in future versions of SQL Server, or even future service packs. I'm going to use it here for demonstration purposes to show additional behaviors that system procedures have.

Run the following code to mark the special procedure *sp_Proc1* also as a system procedure:

```
USE master;
EXEC sp_MS_marksystemobject 'dbo.sp_Proc1';
```

If you now run *sp_Proc1* in databases other than master, you will observe that all code statements within the stored procedure assume the context of the current database:

```
USE InsideTSQL2008;
EXEC dbo.sp_Proc1;

USE AdventureWorks2008;
EXEC dbo.sp_Proc1;

EXEC InsideTSQL2008.dbo.sp_Proc1;
```

As a practice, avoid using the *sp_* prefix for user-defined stored procedures. Remember that if a local database has a stored procedure with the same name and schema as a special procedure in master, the user-defined procedure will be invoked. To demonstrate this, create a procedure called *sp_Proc1* in InsideTSQL2008 as well:

```
USE InsideTSQL2008;
IF OBJECT_ID('dbo.sp_Proc1', 'P') IS NOT NULL DROP PROC dbo.sp_Proc1;
GO

CREATE PROC dbo.sp_Proc1
AS
PRINT 'InsideTSQL2008.dbo.sp_Proc1 executing in ' + DB_NAME();
GO
```

If you run the following code, you will observe that when connected to InsideTSQL2008, *sp_Proc1* from InsideTSQL2008 was invoked:

```
USE InsideTSQL2008;
EXEC dbo.sp_Proc1;

USE AdventureWorks2008;
EXEC dbo.sp_Proc1;
```

Drop the InsideTSQL2008 version so that it doesn't interfere with the following examples:

```
USE InsideTSQL2008;
IF OBJECT_ID('dbo.sp_Proc1', 'P') IS NOT NULL DROP PROC dbo.sp_Proc1;
```

Interestingly, system procedures have an additional unique behavior: They also resolve user objects in the current database, not just system objects. To demonstrate this, run the following code to re-create the *sp_Proc1* special procedure—which queries a user table called Sales.Orders—and to mark the procedure as system:

```
USE master;
IF OBJECT_ID('dbo.sp_Proc1', 'P') IS NOT NULL DROP PROC dbo.sp_Proc1;
GO

CREATE PROC dbo.sp_Proc1
AS
PRINT 'master.dbo.sp_Proc1 executing in ' + DB_NAME();
SELECT orderid FROM Sales.Orders;
GO

EXEC sp_MS_marksystemobject 'dbo.sp_Proc1';
```

Run *sp_Proc1* in InsideTSQL2008, and you will observe that the query ran successfully against the Sales.Orders table in InsideTSQL2008:

```
USE InsideTSQL2008;
EXEC dbo.sp_Proc1;
```

Make a similar attempt in AdventureWorks2008:

```
USE AdventureWorks2008;
EXEC dbo.sp_Proc1;
```

You get the following error:

```
master.dbo.sp_Proc1 executing in AdventureWorks2008
Msg 208, Level 16, State 1, Procedure sp_Proc1, Line 4
Invalid object name 'Sales.Orders'.
```

The error tells you that SQL Server looked for a Sales.Orders table in AdventureWorks2008 but couldn't find one.

When you're done, run the following code for cleanup:

```
USE master;
IF OBJECT_ID('dbo.sp_Proc1', 'P') IS NOT NULL DROP PROC dbo.sp_Proc1;

USE InsideTSQL2008
IF OBJECT_ID('dbo.sp_Proc1', 'P') IS NOT NULL DROP PROC dbo.sp_Proc1;
```

Other Types of Stored Procedures

SQL Server also supports other types of stored procedures:

- **Temporary stored procedures**   You can create temporary procedures by prefixing their names with a single number symbol or a double number symbol (# or ##).

A single number symbol makes the procedure a local temporary procedure; two number symbols make it a global one. Local and global temporary procedures behave in terms of visibility and scope like local and global temporary tables, respectively.

> **More Info** For details about local and global temporary tables, please refer to Chapter 7, "Temporary Tables and Table Variables."

- **Extended stored procedures**   These procedures allow you to create external routines with a programming language such as C using the Extended Stored Procedure API. These were used in older versions of SQL Server to extend the functionality of the product. External routines were written using the Extended Stored Procedure API, compiled to a .dll file, and registered as extended stored procedures in SQL Server. They were used like user-defined stored procedures with T-SQL. In SQL Server 2008, extended stored procedures are supported for backward compatibility and will be removed in a future version of SQL Server. Now you can rely on the .NET integration in the product and develop CLR stored procedures, as well as other types of routines. I'll cover CLR procedures later in the chapter.

The Stored Procedure Interface

This section covers the interface (that is, the input and output parameters) of stored procedures. Stored procedures accept three kinds of parameters: scalar input parameters, table-valued input parameters, and scalar output parameters.

Scalar Input Parameters

A scalar input parameter must be provided with a value when the stored procedure is invoked, unless you assign the parameter with a default value. For example, the following code creates the *GetCustOrders* procedure, which accepts a customer ID and datetime range boundaries as inputs, and returns the given customer's orders in the given datetime range:

```
USE InsideTSQL2008;
IF OBJECT_ID('dbo.GetCustOrders', 'P') IS NOT NULL
  DROP PROC dbo.GetCustOrders;
GO

CREATE PROC dbo.GetCustOrders
  @custid   AS INT,
  @fromdate AS DATETIME = '19000101',
  @todate   AS DATETIME = '99991231'
AS

SET NOCOUNT ON;
```

```
SELECT orderid, custid, empid, orderdate
FROM Sales.Orders
WHERE custid = @custid
  AND orderdate >= @fromdate
  AND orderdate < @todate;
GO
```

> **Tip** The SET NOCOUNT ON option tells SQL Server not to produce the message saying how many rows were affected for data manipulation language (DML) statements. Some client database interfaces, such as OLEDB, absorb this message as a row set. The result is that when you expect to get a result set of a query back to the client, you instead get this message of how many rows were affected as the first result set. By issuing SET NOCOUNT ON, you avoid this problem in those interfaces, so you might want to adopt the practice of specifying it.

When invoking a stored procedure, you must specify inputs for those scalar parameters that were not given default values in the definition (for *@custid* in our case). There are two formats for assigning values to parameters when invoking a stored procedure: *unnamed* and *named*. In the unnamed format, you just specify values without specifying the parameter names. Also, you must specify the inputs by declaration order of the parameters. You can omit inputs only for parameters that have default values and that were declared at the end of the parameter list. You cannot omit an input between two parameters for which you do specify values. If you want such parameters to use their default values, you need to specify the DEFAULT keyword for those.

As an example, the following code invokes the procedure without specifying the inputs for the two last parameters, which will use their default values:

```
EXEC dbo.GetCustOrders 1;
```

This generates the following output:

```
orderid     custid      empid       orderdate
----------- ----------- ----------- -----------------------
10692       1           4           2007-10-03 00:00:00.000
10702       1           4           2007-10-13 00:00:00.000
10643       1           6           2007-08-25 00:00:00.000
10835       1           1           2008-01-15 00:00:00.000
10952       1           1           2008-03-16 00:00:00.000
11011       1           3           2008-04-09 00:00:00.000
```

If you want to specify your own value for the third parameter but use the default for the second, specify the DEFAULT keyword for the second parameter:

```
EXEC dbo.GetCustOrders 1, DEFAULT, '20100212';
```

And, of course, if you want to specify your own values for all parameters, just specify them in order:

```
EXEC dbo.GetCustOrders 1, '20070101', '20080101';
```

This produces the following output:

```
orderid      custid       empid        orderdate
-----------  -----------  -----------  -----------------------
10643        1            6            2007-08-25 00:00:00.000
10692        1            4            2007-10-03 00:00:00.000
10702        1            4            2007-10-13 00:00:00.000
```

These are the basics of stored procedures. You're probably already familiar with them, but I decided to include this coverage to lead to a recommended practice. Many maintenance-related issues can arise when you use the unnamed assignment format. You must specify the arguments in order; you must not omit an optional parameter; and by looking at the code, it might not be clear what the inputs actually mean and to which parameter they relate. Therefore, it's a good practice to use the named assignment format, in which you specify the name of the argument and assign it with an input value, as in the following example:

```
EXEC dbo.GetCustOrders
  @custid   = 1,
  @fromdate = '20070101',
  @todate   = '20080101';
```

The code is much more readable, you can play with the order in which you specify the inputs, and you can omit any parameter that you like if it has a default value.

Table-Valued Parameters

SQL Server 2008 introduces table types and table-valued parameters. A table type allows you to store the definition of a table structure as a user-defined object in the database and later use it as the type for table variables and table-valued parameters. A table type definition can include most common elements of a table definition, including column names; types; NULLability; properties such as IDENTITY and COLLATE; and constraint definitions such as PRIMARY KEY, UNIQUE, and CHECK (but not FOREIGN KEY).

For example, the following code creates a table type called dbo.OrderIDs in the InsideTSQL2008 database:

```
USE InsideTSQL2008;

IF TYPE_ID('dbo.OrderIDs') IS NOT NULL DROP TYPE dbo.OrderIDs;

CREATE TYPE dbo.OrderIDs AS TABLE
(
  pos INT NOT NULL PRIMARY KEY,
  orderid INT NOT NULL UNIQUE
);
```

The type defines orders with attributes called *pos* and *orderid* representing a position for sorting purposes and an order ID, respectively. Once created, you can use OrderIDs as the type for table variables , like so:

```
DECLARE @T AS dbo.OrderIDs;

INSERT INTO @T(pos, orderid)
  VALUES(1, 10248),(2, 10250),(3, 10249);

SELECT * FROM @T;
```

This generates the following output:

```
pos         orderid
----------- -----------
1           10248
3           10249
2           10250
```

Such use of table types as the type for table variables prevents you from the need to repeat the table definition. Of course, it's not just about code brevity. The real news in supporting table types is that you can use those as types for input parameters in stored procedures and UDFs. Client APIs were also enhanced to support passing table-valued parameters to routines, so you are not restricted to using T-SQL to invoke such routines.

Note that when defining a table-valued parameter in a routine, you have to specify the attribute READONLY, indicating that you can only read from the parameter but not write to it. For now, this attribute is mandatory. I hope that in the future SQL Server will also support writable table-valued parameters.

As an example, the following code creates a stored procedure called *GetOrders* that accepts an input table-valued parameter called @T of the OrderIDs type, and returns the orders from the Sales.Orders table whose IDs appear in @T, sorted by *pos*:

```
IF OBJECT_ID('dbo.GetOrders', 'P') IS NOT NULL DROP PROC dbo.GetOrders;
GO

CREATE PROC dbo.GetOrders(@T AS dbo.OrderIDs READONLY)
AS

SELECT O.orderid, O.orderdate, O.custid, O.empid
FROM Sales.Orders AS O
  JOIN @T AS K
    ON O.orderid = K.orderid
ORDER BY K.pos;
GO
```

To invoke the procedure from T-SQL, first declare and populate a local table variable of the OrderIDs type in the calling batch, then call the procedure and pass the variable as the input parameter, like so:

```
DECLARE @Myorderids AS dbo.OrderIDs;

INSERT INTO @Myorderids(pos, orderid)
  VALUES(1, 10248),(2, 10250),(3, 10249);

EXEC dbo.GetOrders @T = @Myorderids;
```

This generates the following output:

```
orderid     orderdate               custid      empid
----------- ----------------------- ----------- -----------
10248       2006-07-04 00:00:00.000 85          5
10250       2006-07-08 00:00:00.000 34          4
10249       2006-07-05 00:00:00.000 79          6
```

The input parameter is passed by reference, meaning that SQL Server gets a pointer to the parameter, rather than internally generating a copy. This makes the use of table-valued parameters very efficient. SQL Server can also efficiently reuse a previously cached plan of our stored procedure for subsequent invocations of the procedure.

Internally, SQL Server treats table-valued parameters very much like table variables. This means that SQL Server does not maintain distribution statistics (histograms) on them. The downside of not having distribution statistics on table variables is that the optimizer can't come up with accurate selectivity estimates for filters. The upside is that you get fewer recompiles, because no refreshes of statistics would trigger plan optimality–related recompiles.

Note that unlike with scalar input parameters, SQL Server won't generate an error if you omit an input table-valued parameter when executing the procedure. In such a case, SQL Server simply uses an empty table by default. This means that if you omit such a parameter by mistake, you will have a logical bug in the code that might go unnoticed. For example, run the following code:

```
EXEC dbo.GetOrders;
```

You don't get an error—instead, the stored procedure uses an empty table by default, producing an empty set as the output:

```
orderid     orderdate               custid      empid
----------- ----------------------- ----------- -----------

(0 row(s) affected)
```

When you're done, run the following code for cleanup:

```
IF OBJECT_ID('dbo.GetOrders', 'P') IS NOT NULL DROP PROC dbo.GetOrders;
IF TYPE_ID('dbo.OrderIDs') IS NOT NULL DROP TYPE dbo.OrderIDs;
```

Output Parameters

Output parameters allow you to return output values from a stored procedure. A change made to the output parameter within the stored procedure is reflected in the variable from the calling batch that was assigned to the output parameter. The concept is similar to a pointer in C or a *ByRef* parameter in Visual Basic.

As an example, the following code alters the definition of the *GetCustOrders* procedure, adding to it the output parameter *@numrows*:

```
USE InsideTSQL2008;
GO

ALTER PROC dbo.GetCustOrders
  @custid   AS INT,
  @fromdate AS DATETIME = '19000101',
  @todate   AS DATETIME = '99991231',
  @numrows  AS INT OUTPUT
AS

SET NOCOUNT ON;

DECLARE @err AS INT;

SELECT orderid, custid, empid, orderdate
FROM Sales.Orders
WHERE custid = @custid
  AND orderdate >= @fromdate
  AND orderdate < @todate;

SELECT @numrows = @@rowcount, @err = @@error;

RETURN @err;
GO
```

@numrows returns the number of rows affected by the query. Notice that the stored procedure also uses a RETURN clause to return the value of the *@@error* function after the invocation of the query.

To get the output parameter back from the stored procedure when invoking it, you need to assign it with a variable defined in the calling batch and mention the keyword OUTPUT. To get back the return status, you also need to provide a variable from the calling batch right before the procedure name and an equal sign, as in the following example:

```
DECLARE @myerr AS INT, @mynumrows AS INT;

EXEC @myerr = dbo.GetCustOrders
  @custid   = 1,
  @fromdate = '20070101',
  @todate   = '20080101',
  @numrows  = @mynumrows OUTPUT;

SELECT @myerr AS err, @mynumrows AS rc;
```

This generates the following output:

```
orderid      custid       empid        orderdate
-----------  -----------  -----------  -----------------------
10643        1            6            2007-08-25 00:00:00.000
10692        1            4            2007-10-03 00:00:00.000
10702        1            4            2007-10-13 00:00:00.000


err          rc
-----------  -----------
0            3
```

The stored procedure returns the applicable orders, plus it assigns the return status *0* to
@myerr and the number of affected rows (in this case, *3*) to the *@mynumrows* variable.

If you want to manipulate the row set returned by the stored procedure with T-SQL, you
need to create a table first and use the INSERT/EXEC syntax, by running the following code:

```
IF OBJECT_ID('tempdb..#CustOrders', 'U') IS NOT NULL
  DROP TABLE #CustOrders;

CREATE TABLE #CustOrders
(
  orderid    INT     NOT NULL PRIMARY KEY,
  custid INT NOT NULL,
  empid INT       NOT NULL,
  orderdate  DATETIME NOT NULL
);
GO

DECLARE @myerr AS INT, @mynumrows AS INT;

INSERT INTO #CustOrders(orderid, custid, empid, orderdate)
  EXEC @myerr = dbo.GetCustOrders
    @custid   = 1,
    @fromdate = '20070101',
    @todate   = '20080101',
    @numrows  = @mynumrows OUTPUT;

SELECT orderid, custid, empid, orderdate
FROM #CustOrders;

SELECT @myerr AS err, @mynumrows AS rc;
```

When you're done, run the following code for cleanup:

```
IF OBJECT_ID('dbo.GetCustOrders', 'P') IS NOT NULL
  DROP PROC dbo.GetCustOrders;
IF OBJECT_ID('tempdb..#CustOrders', 'U') IS NOT NULL
  DROP TABLE #CustOrders;
```

Resolution

When you create a stored procedure, SQL Server first parses the code to check for syntax errors. If the code passes the parsing stage successfully, SQL Server attempts to resolve the names it contains. The resolution process verifies the existence of object and column names, among other things. If the referenced objects exist, the resolution process will take place fully—that is, it also checks for the existence of the referenced column names.

If an object name exists but a column within it doesn't, the resolution process produces an error and the stored procedure is not created. However, if the object doesn't exist at all, SQL Server creates the stored procedure and defers the resolution process to run time, when the stored procedure is invoked. Of course, if a referenced object or a column is still missing when you execute the stored procedure, the code will fail. This process of postponing name resolution until run time is called *deferred name resolution*.

I'll demonstrate the resolution aspects I just described. First run the following code to make sure that the *Proc1* procedure, the *Proc2* procedure, and the table T1 do not exist within tempdb:

```
USE tempdb;
IF OBJECT_ID('dbo.Proc1', 'P') IS NOT NULL DROP PROC dbo.Proc1;
IF OBJECT_ID('dbo.Proc2', 'P') IS NOT NULL DROP PROC dbo.Proc2;
IF OBJECT_ID('dbo.T1', 'U') IS NOT NULL DROP TABLE dbo.T1;
```

Run the following code to create the stored procedure *Proc1*, which refers to a table named T1, which doesn't exist:

```
CREATE PROC dbo.Proc1
AS

SELECT col1 FROM dbo.T1;
GO
```

Because table T1 doesn't exist, resolution was deferred to run time, and the stored procedure was created successfully. If T1 does not exist when you invoke the procedure, it fails at run time. Run the following code:

```
EXEC dbo.Proc1;
```

You get the following error:

```
Msg 208, Level 16, State 1, Procedure Proc1, Line 4
Invalid object name 'dbo.T1'.
```

Next, create table T1 with a column called *col1*:

```
CREATE TABLE dbo.T1(col1 INT);
INSERT INTO dbo.T1(col1) VALUES(1);
```

Invoke the stored procedure again:

```
EXEC dbo.Proc1;
```

This time it will run successfully.

Next, attempt to create a stored procedure called *Proc2*, referring to a nonexistent column (*col2*) in the existing T1 table:

```
CREATE PROC dbo.Proc2
AS

SELECT col2 FROM dbo.T1;
GO
```

Here, the resolution process was not deferred to run time because T1 exists. The stored procedure was not created, and you got the following error:

```
Msg 207, Level 16, State 1, Procedure Proc2, Line 4
Invalid column name 'col2'.
```

When you're done, run the following code for cleanup:

```
USE tempdb;
IF OBJECT_ID('dbo.Proc1', 'P') IS NOT NULL DROP PROC dbo.Proc1;
IF OBJECT_ID('dbo.Proc2', 'P') IS NOT NULL DROP PROC dbo.Proc2;
IF OBJECT_ID('dbo.T1', 'U') IS NOT NULL DROP TABLE dbo.T1;
```

Dependency Information

Prior to SQL Server 2008, dependency information between objects was not reliable. Dependency information was recorded only if the referenced object existed when the referencing object was created. But if the referenced object didn't exist when the referencing object was created, and SQL Server ended up using deferred name resolution, object dependency simply wasn't recorded. So when asking for dependency information prior to SQL Server 2008 (by querying the *sys.sql_dependencies* or *sys.sysdepends* compatibility views, or by executing the *sp_depends* system procedure) the information that you got was incomplete and thus not reliable.

SQL Server 2008 addresses this problem by providing reliable dependency information. When you create an object, SQL Server parses its text and records dependency information regardless of whether the referenced object exists . SQL Server exposes dependency information through three objects: the *sys.sql_expression_dependencies* catalog view and the *sys.dm_sql_referenced_entities* and *sys.dm_sql_referencing_entities* dynamic management functions (DMFs). I will explain the purpose of each object shortly. When querying these objects, if a referenced object doesn't exist, you get only object name information. If a referenced object exists, you get both object name and ID information. Dependency information keeps track of all relevant parts, including server, database, schema, object, and even column.

Note that SQL Server records only dependency information for references that appear in static T-SQL code. It doesn't record dependency information for references that appear in dynamic SQL and CLR code.

To demonstrate retrieving reliable dependency information in SQL Server 2008, first run the following code, which creates a few objects with dependencies:

```
USE tempdb;

IF OBJECT_ID('dbo.Proc1', 'P') IS NOT NULL DROP PROC dbo.Proc1;
IF OBJECT_ID('dbo.Proc2', 'P') IS NOT NULL DROP PROC dbo.Proc2;
IF OBJECT_ID('dbo.V1', 'V') IS NOT NULL DROP VIEW dbo.V1;
IF OBJECT_ID('dbo.V2', 'V') IS NOT NULL DROP VIEW dbo.V2;
IF OBJECT_ID('dbo.T1', 'U') IS NOT NULL DROP TABLE dbo.T1;
IF OBJECT_ID('dbo.T2', 'U') IS NOT NULL DROP TABLE dbo.T2;
GO

CREATE PROC dbo.Proc1
AS
SELECT * FROM dbo.T1;
EXEC('SELECT * FROM dbo.T2');
GO
CREATE PROC dbo.Proc2
AS
SELECT * FROM dbo.T3;
GO
CREATE TABLE dbo.T1(col1 INT);
CREATE TABLE dbo.T2(col2 INT);
GO
CREATE VIEW dbo.V1
AS
SELECT col1 FROM dbo.T1;
GO
CREATE VIEW dbo.V2
AS
SELECT col1 FROM dbo.T1;
GO
```

Observe that the procedure *Proc1* has a dependency on the table T1 in static code and on the table T2 in dynamic code. Also notice that the procedure is created before the referenced tables are created. The procedure *Proc2* has a reference to the table T3 in static code, but the table doesn't exist. The views V1 and V2 refer to the column *col1* in T1.

Next I'll describe the purpose of the three objects that give you dependency information, or more accurately, information about references by name. The *sys.sql_expression_dependencies* view gives you object dependency information by name. Run the following code in the tempdb database:

```
SELECT
  OBJECT_SCHEMA_NAME(referencing_id) AS srcobjschema,
  OBJECT_NAME(referencing_id) AS srcobjname,
  referencing_minor_id AS srcminorid,
```

```
    referenced_schema_name AS tgtschema,
    referenced_id AS tgtobjid,
    referenced_entity_name AS tgtobjname,
    referenced_minor_id AS tgtminorid
FROM sys.sql_expression_dependencies;
```

You get the following output:

```
srcobjschema  srcobjname  srcminorid  tgtschema  tgtobjid    tgtobjname  tgtminorid
------------  ----------  ----------  ---------  ----------  ----------  ----------
dbo           Proc1       0           dbo        2098106515  T1          0
dbo           Proc2       0           dbo        NULL        T3          0
dbo           V1          0           dbo        2098106515  T1          0
dbo           V2          0           dbo        2098106515  T1          0
```

Observe that you got only dependency information for references that appear in static code. The reference in *Proc1* to T2 in the dynamic SQL code wasn't recorded. Also observe that for referenced objects that exist (for example, T1) you get both name and ID information, but for objects that don't exist (for example, T3) you get only name information. For objects that exist, you get the object ID even if the dependency was established before the object existed—the ID is effectively "filled in" when known.

If you attempt to run code that refers to a nonexistent object, you get a Level 16 resolution error. If you want to know which objects a certain object depends on, query the *sys.dm_sql_referenced_entities* function and provide the referencing object name as the first input and OBJECT as the second input, like so:

```
SELECT
    referenced_schema_name AS objschema,
    referenced_entity_name AS objname,
    referenced_minor_name  AS minorname,
    referenced_class_desc  AS class
FROM sys.dm_sql_referenced_entities('dbo.Proc1', 'OBJECT');
```

You get the following output, indicating that *Proc1* depends on the table T1 and on the column *col1* within T1:

```
objschema  objname  minorname  class
---------  -------  ---------  -----------------
dbo        T1       NULL       OBJECT_OR_COLUMN
dbo        T1       col1       OBJECT_OR_COLUMN
```

If you want to know which objects depend on a certain object—for example before dropping an object—query the *sys.dm_sql_referencing_entities* function and provide the referenced object name as the first input and 'OBJECT' as the second input, like so:

```
SELECT
    referencing_schema_name AS objschema,
    referencing_entity_name AS objname,
    referencing_class_desc  AS class
FROM sys.dm_sql_referencing_entities('dbo.T1', 'OBJECT');
```

This generates the following output indicating that *Proc1*, V1, and V2 depend on T1:

```
objschema  objname  class
---------- -------- -----------------
dbo        Proc1    OBJECT_OR_COLUMN
dbo        V1       OBJECT_OR_COLUMN
dbo        V2       OBJECT_OR_COLUMN
```

> **Important** These objects contain a bit less than full dependency information—they give you information about references by name (with some exceptions, such as references to temporary tables). If there's an indirect dependency (e.g., *Proc3* calls *Proc1*, and *Proc1* references T1 by name), the simple calls to these objects won't reveal it (here, *Proc3* depends on T1). However, an indirect dependency like this may be just as important to know about as a direct named reference. If you want to know what will be affected when you drop an object, for example, you have to follow the dependencies yourself. The good news is that in SQL Server 2008, you can.

When you're done experimenting with object dependency information run the following code for cleanup:

```
IF OBJECT_ID('dbo.Proc1', 'P') IS NOT NULL DROP PROC dbo.Proc1;
IF OBJECT_ID('dbo.V1', 'V') IS NOT NULL DROP VIEW dbo.V1;
IF OBJECT_ID('dbo.V2', 'V') IS NOT NULL DROP VIEW dbo.V2;
IF OBJECT_ID('dbo.T1', 'U') IS NOT NULL DROP TABLE dbo.T1;
IF OBJECT_ID('dbo.T2', 'U') IS NOT NULL DROP TABLE dbo.T2;
```

Compilations, Recompilations, and Reuse of Execution Plans

Earlier I mentioned that when you create a stored procedure, SQL Server parses your code and then attempts to resolve it. If resolution was deferred, it will take place at first invocation. Upon first invocation of the stored procedure, if the resolution phase finished successfully, SQL Server analyzes and optimizes the queries within the stored procedure and generates an execution plan. An execution plan holds the instructions to process the query. These instructions include which order to access the tables in; which indexes, access methods, and join algorithms to use; whether to spool interim sets; and so on. SQL Server typically generates multiple permutations of execution plans and will choose the one with the lowest cost out of the ones that it generated.

Note that SQL Server won't necessarily create all possible permutations of execution plans; if it did, the optimization phase might take too long. SQL Server limits the optimizer by calculating a threshold for optimization based on the sizes of the tables involved as well as other factors.

Stored procedures can reuse a previously cached execution plan, thereby saving the resources involved in generating a new execution plan. This section will discuss the reuse of execution plans, cases when a plan cannot be reused, parameter and variable sniffing issues, and plan guides.

Reuse of Execution Plans

The process of optimization requires mainly CPU resources. SQL Server will, by default, reuse a previously cached plan from an earlier invocation of a stored procedure, without investigating whether it is actually a good idea to do so.

To demonstrate plan reuse, first run the following code, which creates the *GetOrders* stored procedure:

```
USE InsideTSQL2008;
IF OBJECT_ID('dbo.GetOrders', 'P') IS NOT NULL DROP PROC dbo.GetOrders;
GO

CREATE PROC dbo.GetOrders
  @odate AS DATETIME
AS

SELECT orderid, custid, empid, orderdate /* 33145F87-1109-4959-91D6-F1EC81F8428F */
FROM Sales.Orders
WHERE orderdate >= @odate;
GO
```

The stored procedure accepts an order date as input (*@odate*) and returns orders placed on or after the input order date. I embedded a comment with a GUID in the code to be able to easily track down cached plans that are associated with this query.

Turn on the STATISTICS IO option to get back I/O information for your session's activity:

```
SET STATISTICS IO ON;
```

Run the stored procedure for the first time, providing an input with *high selectivity* (that is, an input for which a small percentage of rows will be returned):

```
EXEC dbo.GetOrders '20080506';
```

This generates the following output:

```
orderid     custid      empid       orderdate
----------- ----------- ----------- -----------------------
11074       73          7           2008-05-06 00:00:00.000
11075       68          8           2008-05-06 00:00:00.000
11076       9           4           2008-05-06 00:00:00.000
11077       65          1           2008-05-06 00:00:00.000
```

Examine the execution plan produced for the query, shown in Figure 3-1.

Because this is the first time the stored procedure is invoked, SQL Server generated an execution plan for it based on the selective input value and cached that plan.

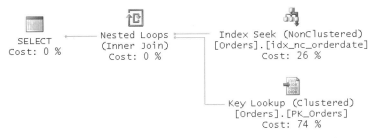

FIGURE 3-1 Execution plan showing that the index on *orderdate* is used

The optimizer uses cardinality and density information to estimate the cost of the access methods that it considers applying, and the selectivity of filters is an important factor. For example, a query with a highly selective filter can benefit from a nonclustered, noncovering index, whereas a *low selectivity* filter (that is, one that returns a high percentage of rows) would not justify using such an index.

For highly selective input such as that provided to our stored procedure, the optimizer chose a plan that uses a nonclustered, noncovering index on the *orderdate* column. The plan first performed a seek within that index (Index Seek operator), reaching the first index entry that matches the filter at the leaf level of the index. This seek operation caused two page reads, one at each of the two levels in the index. In a larger table, such an index might contain three or four levels.

Following the seek operation, the plan performed a partial ordered forward scan within the leaf level of the index (which is not seen in the plan but is part of the Index Seek operator). The partial scan fetched all index entries that match the query's filter (that is, all *orderdate* values greater than or equal to the input *@odate*). Because the input was very selective, only four matching *orderdate* values were found. In this particular case, the partial scan did not need to access additional pages at the leaf level beyond the leaf page that the seek operation reached, so it did not incur additional I/O.

The plan used a Nested Loops operator, which invoked a series of Clustered Index Seek operations to look up the data row for each of the four index entries that the partial scan found. Because the clustered index on this small table has two levels, the lookups cost eight page reads: *2 × 4 = 8*. In total, there were 10 page reads: *2 (seek) + 2 × 4 (lookups) = 10*. This is the value reported by STATISTICS IO as logical reads.

That's the optimal plan for this selective query with the existing indexes.

Remember that I mentioned earlier that stored procedures will, by default, reuse a previously cached plan. Now that you have a plan stored in cache, additional invocations of the stored procedure will reuse it. That's fine if you keep invoking the stored procedure with a highly selective input. You will enjoy the fact that the plan is reused, and SQL Server will not waste resources on generating new plans. That's especially important with systems that invoke stored procedures very frequently.

However, imagine that the stored procedure's inputs vary considerably in selectivity—some invocations have high selectivity whereas others have low selectivity. For example, the following code invokes the stored procedure with an input that has low selectivity:

```
EXEC dbo.GetOrders '20060101';
```

Because a plan is in cache, it will be reused, which is unfortunate in this case. I provided an input value earlier than the earliest *orderdate* in the table. This means that all rows in the table (830) qualify. The plan will require a clustered index lookup for each qualifying row. This invocation generated 1,664 logical reads, even though the whole Orders table resides on 21 data pages. Keep in mind that the Orders table is very small and that in production environments such a table would typically have millions of rows. The cost of reusing such a plan would then be much more dramatic given a similar scenario. For example, take a table with 1,000,000 orders residing on about 25,000 pages. Suppose that the clustered index contains three levels. Just the cost of the lookups would then be 3,000,000 reads: $1,000,000 \times 3 = 3,000,000$.

Obviously, in a case such as this, with a lot of data access and large variations in selectivity, it's a very bad idea to reuse a previously cached execution plan.

Similarly, if you invoke the stored procedure for the first time with a low selectivity input, you get a plan that is optimal for that input—one that issues a table scan (unordered clustered index scan)—and that plan would be cached. Then, in later invocations, the plan would be reused even when the input has high selectivity.

You can observe the fact that an execution plan was reused by querying the *sys.syscacheobjects* view, which contains information about execution plans:

```
SELECT cacheobjtype, objtype, usecounts, sql
FROM sys.syscacheobjects
WHERE sql NOT LIKE '%sys%'
  AND sql LIKE '%33145F87-1109-4959-91D6-F1EC81F8428F%';
```

As you can see, planting a GUID in a comment embedded in the query makes it very easy to filter only the plans of interest. This code generates the following output:

```
cacheobjtype    objtype  usecounts  sql
--------------  -------- ---------- ----------------------------
Compiled Plan   Proc     2          CREATE PROC dbo.GetOrders...
```

Notice that one plan was found for the *GetOrders* procedure in cache, and that it was used twice (*usecounts* = 2).

One way to solve the problem is to create two stored procedures—one for requests with high selectivity and a second for low selectivity. You create another stored procedure with flow logic, examining the input and determining which procedure to invoke based on the input's selectivity that your calculations estimate. The idea is nice in theory, but it's very difficult to implement in practice. It can be very complex to calculate the boundary point dynamically without consuming additional resources. Furthermore, this stored procedure accepts only one input, so imagine how complex things would become with multiple inputs.

Another way to solve the problem is to create (or alter) the stored procedure with the RECOMPILE option, as in:

```
ALTER PROC dbo.GetOrders
  @odate AS DATETIME
WITH RECOMPILE
AS

SELECT orderid, custid, empid, orderdate /* 33145F87-1109-4959-91D6-F1EC81F8428F */
FROM Sales.Orders
WHERE orderdate >= @odate;
GO
```

The RECOMPILE option tells SQL Server to create a new execution plan every time it is invoked. This option actually tells SQL Server not to bother to cache the plan, hence every invocation of the procedure ends up creating a new plan because it won't find an existing one. It is especially useful when the cost of the recompiles is lower than the extra cost associated with reusing suboptimal plans.

First, run the altered procedure specifying an input with high selectivity:

```
EXEC dbo.GetOrders '20080506';
```

You get the plan shown earlier in Figure 3-1, which is optimal in this case and generates an I/O cost of 10 logical reads.

Next, run it specifying an input with low selectivity:

```
EXEC dbo.GetOrders '20060101';
```

You get the plan in Figure 3-2, showing a table scan (unordered clustered index scan), which is optimal for this input. The I/O cost in this case is 21 logical reads.

FIGURE 3-2 Execution plan showing a table scan (unordered clustered index scan)

As mentioned, when creating a stored procedure with the RECOMPILE option, SQL Server doesn't even bother to keep the execution plan for it in cache. If you now query *sys.syscacheobjects*, you will get no plan back for the *GetOrders* procedure:

```
SELECT cacheobjtype, objtype, usecounts, sql
FROM sys.syscacheobjects
WHERE sql NOT LIKE '%sys%'
  AND sql LIKE '%33145F87-1109-4959-91D6-F1EC81F8428F%';
```

If you had multiple queries in your stored procedure, the RECOMPILE procedure option would cause all of them to get recompiled every time the procedure ran. Of course, that's a waste of resources if only some of the queries would benefit from recompiles whereas others would benefit from plan reuse.

SQL Server 2008 supports statement-level recompiles. Instead of having all queries in the stored procedure recompiled, SQL Server can recompile individual statements. You can request a statement-level recompile by specifying a query hint called RECOMPILE (not to be confused with the RECOMPILE procedure option). This way, other queries can benefit from reusing previously cached execution plans if you don't have a reason to recompile them every time the stored procedure is invoked.

Run the following code to alter the procedure, specifying the RECOMPILE query hint:

```
ALTER PROC dbo.GetOrders
  @odate AS DATETIME
AS

SELECT orderid, custid, empid, orderdate /* 33145F87-1109-4959-91D6-F1EC81F8428F */
FROM Sales.Orders
WHERE orderdate >= @odate
OPTION(RECOMPILE);
GO
```

In our case, there's only one query in the stored procedure, so it doesn't really matter whether you specify the RECOMPILE option at the procedure or the query level. But try to think of the advantages of this hint when you have multiple queries in one stored procedure.

Note There is a certain difference between the RECOMPILE procedure option and the RECOMPILE query hint that might be worth noting, and it is regarding estimated execution plans. When the procedure is created with the RECOMPILE procedure option, there is no cached plan. Consequently, a new plan is generated when the estimated plan is requested. If the RECOMPILE query option is used, however, a plan is cached, as mentioned, and the RECOMPILE query option forces a recompile at run time, but not at estimated-plan-generation time. In other words, estimated and actual query plans may not match when statement-level OPTION (RECOMPILE) is present. They will match if the procedure-level RECOMPILE option is used instead.

To see that you get good plans, first run the procedure specifying an input with high selectivity:

```
EXEC dbo.GetOrders '20080506';
```

You will get the plan in Figure 3-1 and an I/O cost of 10 logical reads.

Next, run it specifying an input with low selectivity:

```
EXEC dbo.GetOrders '20060101';
```

You will get the plan in Figure 3-2 and an I/O cost of 21 logical reads.

Don't be confused by the fact that *syscacheobjects* shows a plan with the value *2* as the *usecounts*:

```
SELECT cacheobjtype, objtype, usecounts, sql
FROM sys.syscacheobjects
WHERE sql NOT LIKE '%sys%'
  AND sql LIKE '%33145F87-1109-4959-91D6-F1EC81F8428F%';
```

This generates the following output:

```
cacheobjtype    objtype   usecounts   sql
--------------  --------  ----------  ---------------------------
Compiled Plan   Proc      2           CREATE PROC dbo.GetOrders...
```

Remember that if other queries were in the stored procedure, they could potentially reuse the execution plan.

At this point, you can turn off the STATISTICS IO option:

```
SET STATISTICS IO OFF;
```

Recompilations

As I mentioned earlier, as a rule a stored procedure will reuse a previously cached execution plan by default. There are some exceptions to this rule, and in certain situations there is a recompilation even when there is a plan in cache. Remember that in SQL Server 2008, a recompilation occurs at the statement level.

Such exceptions might be caused by issues related to plan stability (correctness) or plan optimality. Plan stability issues include schema changes in underlying objects (for example, adding or dropping a column, adding or dropping an index, and so on) or changes to SET options that can affect query results (for example, ANSI_NULLS, CONCAT_NULL_YIELDS_ NULL, and so on). Plan optimality issues that cause recompilation include making data changes in referenced objects to the extent that a new plan might be more optimal—for example, as a result of a statistics update.

Both types of causes for recompilations have many particular cases. At the end of this section, I will provide you with a resource that describes them in great detail.

Naturally, if a plan is removed from cache after a while for lack of reuse, SQL Server generates a new one when the procedure is invoked again.

To see an example of a cause of a recompilation, first run the following code, which creates the stored procedure *CustCities*:

```
IF OBJECT_ID('dbo.CustCities', 'P') IS NOT NULL
  DROP PROC dbo.CustCities;
GO
```

```
CREATE PROC dbo.CustCities
AS

SELECT custid, country, region, city, /* 97216686-F90E-4D5A-9A9E-CFD9E548AE81 */
  country + '.' + region + '.' + city AS CRC
FROM Sales.Customers
ORDER BY country, region, city;
GO
```

The stored procedure queries the Customers table, concatenating the three parts of the customer's geographical location: *country*, *region*, and *city*. By default, the SET option CONCAT_NULL_YIELDS_NULL is turned ON, meaning that when you concatenate a NULL with any string, you get a NULL as a result.

Run the stored procedure for the first time:

```
EXEC dbo.CustCities;
```

This generates the following output, shown here in abbreviated form:

```
custid  country     region  city             CRC
-------  ----------  ------  ---------------  -------------------------
12       Argentina   NULL    Buenos Aires     NULL
54       Argentina   NULL    Buenos Aires     NULL
64       Argentina   NULL    Buenos Aires     NULL
20       Austria     NULL    Graz             NULL
59       Austria     NULL    Salzburg         NULL
50       Belgium     NULL    Bruxelles        NULL
76       Belgium     NULL    Charleroi        NULL
61       Brazil      RJ      Rio de Janeiro   Brazil.RJ.Rio de Janeiro
67       Brazil      RJ      Rio de Janeiro   Brazil.RJ.Rio de Janeiro
34       Brazil      RJ      Rio de Janeiro   Brazil.RJ.Rio de Janeiro
31       Brazil      SP      Campinas         Brazil.SP.Campinas
88       Brazil      SP      Resende          Brazil.SP.Resende
81       Brazil      SP      Sao Paulo        Brazil.SP.Sao Paulo
21       Brazil      SP      Sao Paulo        Brazil.SP.Sao Paulo
15       Brazil      SP      Sao Paulo        Brazil.SP.Sao Paulo
...
```

As you can see, whenever *region* was NULL, the concatenated string became NULL. SQL Server cached the execution plan of the stored procedure for later reuse. Along with the plan, SQL Server also stored the state of all SET options that can affect query results. You can observe those in a bitmap called *setopts* in *sys.syscacheobjects*.

Set the CONCAT_NULL_YIELDS_NULL option to OFF, telling SQL Server to treat a NULL in concatenation as an empty string:

```
SET CONCAT_NULL_YIELDS_NULL OFF;
```

Rerun the stored procedure:

```
EXEC dbo.CustCities;
```

This generates the following output:

```
custid  country     region  city             CRC
------- ----------  ------- ---------------  -------------------------
12      Argentina   NULL    Buenos Aires     Argentina..Buenos Aires
54      Argentina   NULL    Buenos Aires     Argentina..Buenos Aires
64      Argentina   NULL    Buenos Aires     Argentina..Buenos Aires
20      Austria     NULL    Graz             Austria..Graz
59      Austria     NULL    Salzburg         Austria..Salzburg
50      Belgium     NULL    Bruxelles        Belgium..Bruxelles
76      Belgium     NULL    Charleroi        Belgium..Charleroi
61      Brazil      RJ      Rio de Janeiro   Brazil.RJ.Rio de Janeiro
67      Brazil      RJ      Rio de Janeiro   Brazil.RJ.Rio de Janeiro
34      Brazil      RJ      Rio de Janeiro   Brazil.RJ.Rio de Janeiro
31      Brazil      SP      Campinas         Brazil.SP.Campinas
88      Brazil      SP      Resende          Brazil.SP.Resende
81      Brazil      SP      Sao Paulo        Brazil.SP.Sao Paulo
21      Brazil      SP      Sao Paulo        Brazil.SP.Sao Paulo
15      Brazil      SP      Sao Paulo        Brazil.SP.Sao Paulo
...
```

You can see that when *region* was NULL, it was treated as an empty string, and as a result, you didn't get a NULL in the *CRC* column. Changing the session option in this case changed the meaning of a query. When you ran this stored procedure, SQL Server first checked for a cached plan that also had the same state of SET options. SQL Server didn't find one, so it had to generate a new plan.

Query *sys.syscacheobjects*:

```
SELECT cacheobjtype, objtype, usecounts, setopts, sql
FROM sys.syscacheobjects
WHERE sql NOT LIKE '%sys%'
  AND sql LIKE '%97216686-F90E-4D5A-9A9E-CFD9E548AE81%';
```

In the output, you find two plans for *CustCities* with two different *setopts* bitmaps:

```
cacheobjtype    objtype  usecounts  setopts  sql
-------------- -------- ---------- -------- -----------------------------
Compiled Plan  Proc     1          4347     CREATE PROC dbo.CustCities...
Compiled Plan  Proc     1          4339     CREATE PROC dbo.CustCities...
```

Turn the CONCAT_NULL_YIELDS_NULL option back ON:

```
SET CONCAT_NULL_YIELDS_NULL ON;
```

Note that regardless of whether the change in the SET option affects the query's meaning, SQL Server looks for a match in the set options state to reuse a plan. For example, run the following code to re-create the procedure *GetOrders* that I used in my previous examples:

```
IF OBJECT_ID('dbo.GetOrders', 'P') IS NOT NULL DROP PROC dbo.GetOrders;
GO
```

```
CREATE PROC dbo.GetOrders
  @odate AS DATETIME
AS

SELECT orderid, custid, empid, orderdate /* 33145F87-1109-4959-91D6-F1EC81F8428F */
FROM Sales.Orders
WHERE orderdate >= @odate;
GO
```

Run the procedure for the first time when the set option is on:

```
EXEC dbo.GetOrders '20080506';
```

Run the following code to turn the option off:

```
SET CONCAT_NULL_YIELDS_NULL OFF;
```

Run the procedure a second time when the option is off:

```
EXEC dbo.GetOrders '20080506';
```

Inspect the cached plans associated with the query:

```
SELECT cacheobjtype, objtype, usecounts, setopts, sql
FROM sys.syscacheobjects
WHERE sql NOT LIKE '%sys%'
  AND sql LIKE '%33145F87-1109-4959-91D6-F1EC81F8428F%';
```

Observe in the output that there are two plans:

```
cacheobjtype    objtype   usecounts   setopts  sql
--------------  --------  ----------  -------- ----------------------------
Compiled Plan   Proc      1           4339     CREATE PROC dbo.GetOrders...
Compiled Plan   Proc      1           4347     CREATE PROC dbo.GetOrders...
```

No concatenation is going on in the *GetOrders* procedure, so clearly the change in this set option doesn't have any impact on the behavior of the code. Still, SQL Server just compares bitmaps and creates a new plan if they are different.

Why should you care? Client interfaces and tools typically change the state of some SET options whenever you make a new connection to the database. Different client interfaces change different sets of options, yielding different execution environments. If you're using multiple database interfaces and tools to connect to the database and they have different execution environments, they won't be able to reuse each other's plans. You can easily identify the SET options that each client tool changes by running a trace while the applications connect to the database, or by running DBCC USEROPTIONS. If you see discrepancies in the execution environment, you can code explicit SET commands in all applications, which will be submitted whenever a new connection is made. This way, all applications have sessions with the same execution environment and can reuse one another's plans.

When you're done testing run the following code to set the option back on:

```
SET CONCAT_NULL_YIELDS_NULL ON;
```

As for recompiles caused by plan optimality, a classic example is refresh of distribution statistics (histograms). After SQL Server refreshes statistics, the next time you run a query with a nontrivial plan that relies on those statistics the plan will be recompiled. SQL Server makes the assumption that data distribution may have changed to the degree that a different plan might be optimal. If you know that your procedure is called with such inputs that the query would keep benefiting from the same plan even after statistics refresh, you can specify the KEEPFIXED PLAN query hint. This hint indicates to SQL Server not to perform plan optimality–related recompiles.

This section offered just a couple of examples for recompiles. There are many others. Later I'll provide a resource where you can find more.

Variable Sniffing

As I mentioned earlier, SQL Server generates a plan for a stored procedure based on the inputs provided to it upon first invocation, for better or worse. *First invocation* also refers to the first invocation after a plan was removed from cache for lack of reuse (or for any other reason). This capability is called *parameter sniffing*, meaning that when optimizing the code, the optimizer can "sniff" the values of the procedure's parameters. The optimizer "knows" the values of the input parameters, and it generates an adequate plan for those inputs. However, things are different when you refer to local variables in your queries. And for the sake of our discussion, it doesn't matter whether these are local variables of a plain batch or of a stored procedure. When optimizing the code at the batch level, the optimizer cannot sniff the content of the variables; therefore, when it optimizes the query, it must make a guess. Obviously, this can lead to poor plans if you're not aware of the problem and don't take corrective measures.

To demonstrate the problem, first insert a new order to the Orders table, specifying the CURRENT_TIMESTAMP function for the *orderdate* column:

```
INSERT INTO Sales.Orders
  (custid, empid, orderdate, requireddate, shippeddate, shipperid, freight,
  shipname, shipaddress, shipcity, shipregion, shippostalcode, shipcountry)
VALUES
  (1, 1, CURRENT_TIMESTAMP, '20100212 00:00:00.000', NULL, 1, 1,
  N'a', N'a', N'a', N'a', N'a', N'a');
```

Re-create the *GetOrders* stored procedure so that it declares a local variable and use it in the query's filter:

```
IF OBJECT_ID('dbo.GetOrders', 'P') IS NOT NULL DROP PROC dbo.GetOrders;
GO
```

```
CREATE PROC dbo.GetOrders
  @d AS INT = 0
AS

DECLARE @odate AS DATETIME;
SET @odate = DATEADD(day, -@d, CONVERT(VARCHAR(8), CURRENT_TIMESTAMP, 112));

SELECT orderid, custid, empid, orderdate
FROM Sales.Orders
WHERE orderdate >= @odate;
GO
```

The procedure defines the integer input parameter *@d* with a default value *0*. It declares a *datetime* local variable called *@odate*, which is set to today's date minus *@d* days. The stored procedure then issues a query returning all orders with an *orderdate* greater than or equal to *@odate*. Invoke the stored procedure using the default value of *@d*:

```
EXEC dbo.GetOrders;
GO
```

This generates the following output:

```
orderid      custid       empid        orderdate
-----------  -----------  -----------  -----------------------
11078        1            1            2009-03-09 04:19:01.540
```

> **Note** The output that you get will have a value in *orderdate* that reflects the CURRENT_TIMESTAMP value of when you inserted the new order.

Unlike recompiles, initial compiles take place at the batch level—not the statement level. Therefore, the optimizer didn't know what the value of *@odate* was when it optimized the query. So it used a conservative, hard-coded value that is 30 percent of the number of rows in the table. For such a low-selectivity estimation, the optimizer naturally chose a full clustered index scan, even though the query in practice is highly selective and would be much better off using the index on *orderdate*.

You can observe the optimizer's estimation and chosen plan by looking at the execution plan. The actual execution plan you get for this invocation of the stored procedure is shown in Figure 3-3.

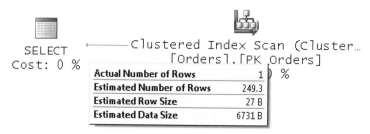

FIGURE 3-3 Execution plan showing estimated number of rows

You can see that the optimizer chose a table scan (unordered clustered index scan) because of its selectivity estimation of 30 percent (249.3 rows/831 total number of rows), although in actuality only one row was returned.

You can tackle this problem in several ways. One is to use, whenever possible, inline expressions in the query that refer to the input parameter instead of a variable. In our case, it is possible:

```
ALTER PROC dbo.GetOrders
  @d AS INT = 0
AS

SELECT orderid, custid, empid, orderdate
FROM Sales.Orders
WHERE orderdate >= DATEADD(day, -@d, CONVERT(VARCHAR(8), CURRENT_TIMESTAMP, 112));
GO
```

Run *GetOrders* again, and notice the use of the index on *orderdate* in the execution plan:

```
EXEC dbo.GetOrders;
```

The plan that you get is similar to the one shown earlier in Figure 3-1. The I/O cost here is just four logical reads.

Another way to deal with the problem is to use a stub procedure—that is, create two procedures. The first procedure accepts the original parameter, assigns the result of the calculation to a local variable, and invokes a second procedure providing it with the variable as input. The second procedure accepts an input order date passed to it and invokes the query that refers directly to the input parameter. When a plan is generated for the procedure that actually invokes the query (the second procedure), the value of the parameter will, in fact, be known at optimization time.

Run the following code to implement this solution:

```
IF OBJECT_ID('dbo.GetOrdersQuery', 'P') IS NOT NULL
  DROP PROC dbo.GetOrdersQuery;
GO

CREATE PROC dbo.GetOrdersQuery
  @odate AS DATETIME
AS

SELECT orderid, custid, empid, orderdate
FROM Sales.Orders
WHERE orderdate >= @odate;
GO

ALTER PROC dbo.GetOrders
  @d AS INT = 0
AS
```

```
DECLARE @odate AS DATETIME;
SET @odate = DATEADD(day, -@d, CONVERT(VARCHAR(8), CURRENT_TIMESTAMP, 112));

EXEC dbo.GetOrdersQuery @odate;
GO
```

Invoke the *GetOrders* procedure:

```
EXEC dbo.GetOrders;
```

You get an optimal plan for the input similar to the one shown earlier in Figure 3-1, yielding an I/O cost of only four logical reads.

Don't forget the issues I described in the previous section regarding the reuse of execution plans. The fact that you got an efficient execution plan for this input doesn't necessarily mean that you would want to reuse it in following invocations. It all depends on whether the inputs are typical or atypical. Make sure you follow the recommendations I gave earlier in case the inputs are atypical.

The stub procedure approach is a bit convoluted, however. SQL Server supports two much simpler options to tackle the variable sniffing problem—using the OPTIMIZE FOR and RECOMPILE query hints. Which of the two you use depends on whether you want to cache and reuse the plan. If you want to reuse the plan, use the OPTIMIZE FOR hint. This hint allows you to provide SQL Server with a literal that reflects the selectivity of the variable, in case the input is typical. For example, if you know that the variable will typically end up with a highly selective value, as you did in our example, you can provide the literal *'99991231'*, which reflects that:

```
ALTER PROC dbo.GetOrders
  @d AS INT = 0
AS

DECLARE @odate AS DATETIME;
SET @odate = DATEADD(day, -@d, CONVERT(VARCHAR(8), CURRENT_TIMESTAMP, 112));

SELECT orderid, custid, empid, orderdate
FROM Sales.Orders
WHERE orderdate >= @odate
OPTION(OPTIMIZE FOR(@odate = '99991231'));
GO
```

Run the stored procedure:

```
EXEC dbo.GetOrders;
```

You get an optimal plan for a highly selective *orderdate* similar to the one shown earlier in Figure 3-1, yielding an I/O cost of four logical reads.

If, on the other hand, you don't want to reuse the plan because the variable sometimes ends up with a selective value and sometimes a nonselective one, the OPTIMIZE FOR hint won't help you. Surprisingly, in such a case, the RECOMPILE query hint that I introduced earlier also resolves the variable sniffing problem. If you think about it, the variable sniffing problem has to do with SQL Server's default choice of compiling the whole batch as a unit initially. Recompiles, on the other hand, happen at the statement level. By specifying the RECOMPILE query hint (as opposed to the RECOMPILE procedure option), you explicitly request the compilation of this query to happen at the statement level. The benefit in this approach is that by the time SQL Server gets to optimize the query, the preceding statements—including the assignment of the variable—were already executed; hence the value of the variable is known at this stage. So at the cost of recompiling the statement in every invocation of the procedure, the optimization is aware of the variable's value, and this usually results in more efficient plans.

Run the following code to re-create the stored procedure with the RECOMPILE query option:

```
ALTER PROC dbo.GetOrders
  @d AS INT = 0
AS

DECLARE @odate AS DATETIME;
SET @odate = DATEADD(day, -@d, CONVERT(VARCHAR(8), CURRENT_TIMESTAMP, 112));

SELECT orderid, custid, empid, orderdate
FROM Sales.Orders
WHERE orderdate >= @odate
OPTION(RECOMPILE);
GO
```

Run the procedure with selective and nonselective values:

```
EXEC dbo.GetOrders @d = 1;
EXEC dbo.GetOrders @d = 365;
```

Examine the execution plans for the two invocations shown in Figure 3-4, and observe that both got optimal plans—the first for a selective filter and the second for a nonselective one.

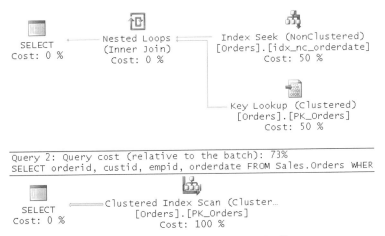

FIGURE 3-4 Execution plans for selective and nonselective filters

Note that you might face similar problems to variable sniffing when changing the values of input parameters before using them in queries. For example, say you define an input parameter called *@odate* and assign it with a default value of NULL. Before using the parameter in the query's filter, you apply the following code:

```
SET @odate = COALESCE(@odate, '19000101');
```

The query then filters orders where *orderdate* >= *@odate*. If optimization happens at the batch level, when the query is optimized the optimizer is not aware of the fact that *@odate* has undergone a change, and it optimizes the query with the original input (NULL) in mind. You will face a similar problem to the one I described with variables, and you should tackle it using similar logic.

Ironically, you may end up facing kind of an inverse problem to the variable sniffing one with parameters. As mentioned and demonstrated earlier, SQL Server does support parameter sniffing.

OPTIMIZE FOR UNKNOWN

In the previous section I described scenarios in which the optimizer doesn't sniff variable values or the correct parameter values and ends up generating an execution plan based on atypical inputs. I explained that if you knew that plan reuse was a good thing for the query, and you also knew which static values the query should be optimized for, you could use the OPTIMIZE FOR hint and provide those static values as the variable or parameter values.

Another scenario that you might face is one in which the majority of the invocations of your procedure are with typical inputs, but occasionally the procedure is invoked with atypical ones. You do know that the query would benefit from plan reuse provided that the cached plan would be the one that was optimized for the typical inputs. But the risk is that upon first invocation of the procedure—after service restart, recompile, or any other reason—the procedure will be invoked with atypical inputs, and you will end up with a cached plan that is suboptimal for the typical invocation of the stored procedure. If you have static input values that adequately represent the common case—both currently and in the future—you can use the OPTIMIZE FOR hint and specify those values. But what if there are no such static values?

SQL Server 2008 enhances the OPTIMIZE FOR hint, allowing you to indicate that you want the optimizer to optimize the query for unknown variable or parameter input values. With this option you tell SQL Server to use its existing algorithms based on statistical data to optimize the query, as opposed to attempting to sniff the inputs. For example, recall from earlier discussions that I mentioned that for a range filter the optimizer uses a selectivity estimate of 30 percent when it cannot sniff the input. By using the OPTIMIZE FOR UNKNOWN hint, you tell the optimizer that you actually want it to use such estimates even in scenarios where it could technically sniff the inputs.

You can indicate that specific parameters or variables should be assumed as unknown for optimization by using the following form:

```
<query> OPTION(OPTIMIZER FOR(@p1 UNKNOWN, @p2 UNKNWON, ...);
```

You can also indicate that all parameters and variables in the query should be assumed as unknown for optimization by using the following form:

```
<query> OPTION(OPTIMIZER FOR UNKNWON);
```

To demonstrate using this hint, run the following code, re-creating the stored procedure *GetOrders*, indicating to the optimizer to optimize the query as if the value of the *@odate* parameter is unknown:

```
IF OBJECT_ID('dbo.GetOrders', 'P') IS NOT NULL DROP PROC dbo.GetOrders;
GO

CREATE PROC dbo.GetOrders
  @odate AS DATETIME
AS

SELECT orderid, custid, empid, orderdate
FROM Sales.Orders
WHERE orderdate >= @odate
OPTION(OPTIMIZE FOR (@odate UNKNOWN));
GO
```

Suppose that in the vast majority of the invocations of the procedure, the inputs have low selectivity, but the procedure is invoked first time with a highly selective input, as follows:

```
EXEC dbo.GetOrders @odate = '20080506';
```

The execution plan for this execution is shown in Figure 3-5.

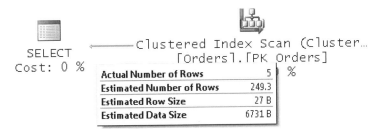

Clustered Index Scan (Cluster...	
[Orders].[PK_Orders]	
Actual Number of Rows	5
Estimated Number of Rows	249.3
Estimated Row Size	27 B
Estimated Data Size	6731 B

FIGURE 3-5 Execution plan for query with OPTIMIZE FOR UNKNOWN hint

Observe that you got a plan that is optimal for a low selectivity filter even though the input was highly selective. Also notice that the estimated number of rows shows 249.3, which is 30 percent of the number of rows in the table. That's the value that the optimizer optimized the query for. The actual number of rows returned was 5. This plan was cached, so the common subsequent invocations of the procedure that specify inputs with low selectivity can benefit from reusing this plan.

Plan Guides

SQL Server allows you to specify hints in your queries to force certain behavior. The three categories of hints are table, join, and query. Query hints are specified in an OPTION clause at the end of the query and indicate certain behavior at the whole query, or statement, level. Earlier in the chapter I covered a few query hints: OPTIMIZE FOR, RECOMPILE, and KEEPFIXED PLAN. SQL Server supports many others, and you can find details about those in SQL Server Books Online.

Before proceeding I should also mention the usual disclaimer regarding hints. You should use them with care, because a hint forces SQL Server to behave in a certain way, overriding its default behavior in that respect. Especially with performance hints such as forcing certain join ordering (FORCE ORDER), certain join algorithm ({LOOP | MERGE | HASH} JOIN), and so on, you force that part of optimization to become static. With respect to the part of optimization that you forced, you prevent dynamic cost-based optimization that would have normally taken place, and that would have taken into consideration data distribution and other changes.

Assuming that you know what you're doing and that you have your reasons to use a query hint, adding such a hint requires you to change the query's code. You need to add the OPTION clause with the relevant hint. However, changing a query's code is not always an option. For example, the code might be submitted from a third-party application, or your service-level agreements may prevent you from making revisions even if you technically could make them.

SQL Server 2008 supports a feature called *plan guides* that allows you to attach a query hint to a query without changing the query's code. A plan guide is an object in the database; as such, as soon as it is created and until it is dropped or disabled, it affects the query it is associated with.

You create a plan guide by using the *sp_create_plan_guide* stored procedure. You drop or disable a plan guide by using the *sp_control_plan_guide* procedure. SQL Server supports three types of plan guides, and you indicate the type of plan you want to create using the *sp_create_plan_guide* procedure under the *@type* parameter, whose valid values are N'OBJECT', N'SQL', and N'TEMPLATE'. You should use the type OBJECT when the statement appears in the context of a T-SQL routine such as a stored procedure. You should use the type SQL when the statement appears in the context of a stand-alone statement or batch. Finally, use the type TEMPLATE when you want to override the database's parameterization behavior for a certain class of statements. You need ALTER permission on the referenced object to create an object plan guide, and ALTER permissions on the database to create a SQL or template plan guide.

The next sections provide details about the three plan guide types.

Object Plan Guides

Use an object plan guide when the statement that you want to apply the hint to resides in a T-SQL routine. The applicable routines are: stored procedures, scalar UDFs, multi-statement table-valued UDFs, and DML triggers in the current database.

To demonstrate object plan guides, first run the following code, which re-creates the stored procedure *GetOrders* that you used in the section "Variable Sniffing" earlier:

```
IF OBJECT_ID('dbo.GetOrders', 'P') IS NOT NULL DROP PROC dbo.GetOrders;
GO

CREATE PROC dbo.GetOrders
  @d AS INT = 0
AS

DECLARE @odate AS DATETIME;
SET @odate = DATEADD(day, -@d, CONVERT(VARCHAR(8), CURRENT_TIMESTAMP, 112));

SELECT orderid, custid, empid, orderdate
FROM Sales.Orders
WHERE orderdate >= @odate;
GO
```

Remember that if there's no plan in cache, the next time the procedure is invoked SQL Server will optimize the code at the batch level. Therefore, during optimization of the query the value of the variable *@odate* will be unknown. Now invoke the procedure relying on the default value of the input parameter *@d*:

```
EXEC dbo.GetOrders;
```

The query's filter ends up being very selective, but because the optimizer wasn't aware of the value of *@odate* the optimization was for an unknown value of *@odate* (30 percent selectivity for a range filter). You get the execution plan shown in Figure 3-6, showing a full unordered clustered index scan.

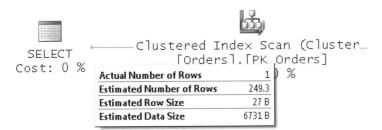

FIGURE 3-6 Execution plan without object plan guide

Suppose that you know that the value of *@odate* usually ends up being very selective, and you want to add the query hint *OPTION (OPTIMIZE FOR (@odate = '99991231'))* to the procedure's query. However, you can't—or aren't allowed to—change the procedure's code directly. You create a plan guide for the procedure's query by running the following code:

```
EXEC sp_create_plan_guide
  @name = N'PG_GetOrders_Selective',
  @stmt = N'SELECT orderid, custid, empid, orderdate
FROM Sales.Orders
WHERE orderdate >= @odate;',
  @type = N'OBJECT',
  @module_or_batch = N'dbo.GetOrders',
  @hints = N'OPTION (OPTIMIZE FOR (@odate = ''99991231''))';
```

You specify the plan guide name in the @*name* argument; the statement to which you want to add the hint in the @*stmt* argument; the type OBJECT in the @*type* argument; the name of the procedure in the @*module_or_batch* argument; and finally the hint itself in the @*hints* argument.

> **Note** Regarding object plan guides, SQL Server doesn't expect an exact match between the query in the procedure and the one you specify in the @*stmt* argument. For example, SQL Server doesn't expect an exact match in terms of use of white spaces. If SQL Server can't match the statement in the @*stmt* argument with a statement in the procedure, it generates an error such as the following:
>
> ```
> Msg 10507, Level 16, State 1, Procedure GetOrders, Line 2
> Cannot create plan guide 'PG_GetOrders_Selective' because the statement specified by
> @stmt and @module_or_batch, or by @plan_handle and @statement_start_offset, does not
> match any statement in the specified module or batch. Modify the values to match a
> statement in the module or batch.
> ```
>
> So if you don't get an error, this fact by itself is a kind of validation that SQL Server successfully managed to match your plan guide with a statement in the procedure. Unfortunately, with the other types of plan guides SQL Server is much more strict, expecting an exact match between the code that you provide when creating the guide and the code that executes against SQL Server that is supposed to use the guide.

Execute the stored procedure again:

```
EXEC dbo.GetOrders;
```

You get the execution plan shown in Figure 3-7, showing that the index on the *orderdate* column was used, as is optimal for a selective filter.

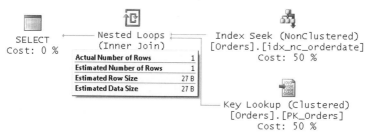

FIGURE 3-7 Execution plan with object plan guide

If you want to know whether the plan guide was used, examine the XML form of the query's execution plan. For object and SQL plan guides you should find the attributes *PlanGuideDB* and *PlanGuideName*, which are self-explanatory. You can obtain the XML plan form of a query using the SHOWPLAN_XML or STATISTICS XML set options, or the *Showplan XML* trace event. For example, run the following code to return the XML form of the query's estimated execution plan:

```
SET SHOWPLAN_XML ON;
GO
EXEC dbo.GetOrders;
GO
SET SHOWPLAN_XML OFF;
```

Within the XML plan you will find these attributes: *PlanGuideDB="InsideTSQL2008"* and *PlanGuideName="PG_GetOrders_Selective"*.

You can also query the *sys.plan_guides* view to get information about the plan guides that are stored in the current database, like so:

```
SELECT * FROM sys.plan_guides;
```

When you're done, run the following code to drop the plan guide *PG_GetOrders_Selective*:

```
EXEC sp_control_plan_guide N'DROP', N'PG_GetOrders_Selective';
```

Note that if you only want to disable the plan guide but still keep it in the database for later enabling, you should specify DISABLE instead of DROP when invoking the *sp_control_plan_guide* procedure. Later you can call the *sp_control_plan_guide* procedure again with the ENABLE option to enable the plan guide.

SQL Plan Guides

SQL plan guides are guides for statements that are submitted in the context of a stand-alone statement or batch. The statement can be submitted through any mechanism.

When creating the plan guide using the *sp_create_plan_guide* procedure, specify N'SQL' in the *@type* argument. The way you use some of the other arguments depends on the scenario. If you want the plan guide to be used only when the statement specified in the *@stmt* argument appears in the context of some batch containing multiple statements, specify the batch in the *@module_or_batch* argument. If you specify NULL for the *@module_or_batch* argument, SQL Server internally sets it to the value of *@stmt*.

> **Note** Unlike object plan guides, for SQL plan guides SQL Server requires an exact match between the text specified when creating the plan guide and the text used when submitting the code. This applies both to the batch specified in the *@module_or_batch* argument and to the statement specified in the *@stmt* argument.

The argument *@params* is applicable when the statement is parameterized. If the statement is not parameterized, specify a NULL in this argument or omit it since NULL is the default. As an example for a plan guide for a nonparameterized stand-alone query, suppose that you want to attach a plan guide to the following query, restricting its maximum degree of parallelism to 1:

```
SELECT empid, COUNT(*) AS cnt
FROM Sales.Orders
GROUP BY empid;
```

Run the following code to create the plan guide:

```
EXEC sp_create_plan_guide
  @name = N'PG_MyQuery1_MAXDOP1',
  @stmt = N'SELECT empid, COUNT(*) AS cnt
FROM Sales.Orders
GROUP BY empid;
',
  @type = N'SQL',
  @module_or_batch = NULL,
  @hints = N'OPTION (MAXDOP 1)';
```

As you can see, the *@module_or_batch* argument was set to NULL because this statement is not part of a batch with multiple statements, and the *@params* argument was set to NULL because the statement is not parameterized.

To verify that the plan guide was used, request the XML form of the execution plan by running the following code:

```
SET SHOWPLAN_XML ON;
GO
SELECT empid, COUNT(*) AS cnt
FROM Sales.Orders
GROUP BY empid;
GO
SET SHOWPLAN_XML OFF;
```

Make sure that you find the attributes *PlanGuideDB="InsideTSQL2008"* and *PlanGuideName= "PG_MyQuery1_MAXDOP1"*.

To request information about the plan guide, issue the following query:

```
SELECT *
FROM sys.plan_guides
WHERE name = 'PG_MyQuery1_MAXDOP1';
```

When you're done, run the following code to drop the plan guide:

```
EXEC sp_control_plan_guide N'DROP', N'PG_MyQuery1_MAXDOP1';
```

If the statement is parameterized either explicitly (for example, when submitted through *sp_executesql*), or implicitly internally by SQL Server, specify the parameterized form in the *@stmt* argument and the parameters declaration in the *@params* argument. For statements that are parameterized using *sp_executesql*, specify the exact form used in the *@stmt* and *@params* argument of *sp_executesql* in the corresponding *@stmt* and *@params* arguments of *sp_create_plan_guide*. For statements that get parameterized internally by SQL Server, use the *sp_get_query_template* procedure to create their parameterized form.

In the next section I'll demonstrate how to create a SQL plan guide for a parameterized query.

Template Plan Guides

Use template plan guides when you want to override the database's parameterization behavior for a certain class of statements. The database's parameterization behavior can be set to either SIMPLE (the default) or FORCED, using the database option PARAMETERIZATION. Simple parameterization means that for simple cases SQL Server internally tries to substitute constants with arguments to increase the chances for reusing previous cached plans for the same class of queries, even when the referenced constants are different. With simple parameterization, only a small class of query types are parameterized. Using forced parameterization, you increase the chances for queries to get parameterized; with few exceptions, all constants will be substituted with arguments during compilation.

Using a template plan guide you can override the database's parameterization behavior for a specified class of queries.

Because SQL Server is very strict about how it matches the text of the plan guide to the text of the query submitted to SQL Server, you should use the *sp_get_query_template* procedure to produce the text for both the query template and the parameters declaration. You specify the text of a sample query as the input parameter of the *sp_get_query_template* procedure, and you get the text of a normalized form of the query template and the parameters declaration through the procedure's output parameters. As an example, the following code demonstrates using the *sp_get_query_template* procedure to generate the text for the query template and parameters declaration for a given query:

```
DECLARE @stmt AS NVARCHAR(MAX);
DECLARE @params AS NVARCHAR(MAX);

EXEC sp_get_query_template
  @querytext = N'SELECT orderid, custid, empid, orderdate
FROM Sales.Orders
WHERE orderdate >= ''99991231'';',
  @templatetext = @stmt OUTPUT,
  @parameters   = @params OUTPUT;

SELECT @stmt AS stmt, @params AS params;
```

This generates the following output:

```
stmt
--------------------------------------------------------------------------------
select orderid , custid , empid , orderdate from Sales . Orders where orderdate > = @0
params
----------------
@0 varchar(8000)
```

To create a template plan guide for a certain class of queries, run the *sp_create_plan_guide*
procedure, specifying N'TEMPLATE' in the *@type* argument, NULL in the *@module_or_batch*
argument, the query template in the *@stmt* argument, and the parameters declaration text
in the *@params* argument.

Note that you can combine template and SQL plan guides. For example, for a certain class
of queries you can override the database's parameterization behavior by creating a template
plan guide. For the same class of queries you can create a SQL plan guide to add any query
hint that you want. The following is an example of creating both a template plan guide and a
SQL plan guide for the query template shown at the beginning of this section:

```
-- Create template plan guide to use forced parameterization
DECLARE @stmt AS NVARCHAR(MAX);
DECLARE @params AS NVARCHAR(MAX);

EXEC sp_get_query_template
  @querytext = N'SELECT orderid, custid, empid, orderdate
FROM Sales.Orders
WHERE orderdate >= ''99991231'';',
  @templatetext  = @stmt OUTPUT,
  @parameters  = @params OUTPUT;

EXEC sp_create_plan_guide
  @name = N'PG_MyQuery2_ParameterizationForced',
  @stmt = @stmt,
  @type = N'TEMPLATE',
  @module_or_batch = NULL,
  @params = @params,
  @hints = N'OPTION(PARAMETERIZATION FORCED)';

-- Create a SQL plan guide on the query template
EXEC sp_create_plan_guide
  @name = N'PG_MyQuery2_Selective',
  @stmt = @stmt,
  @type = N'SQL',
  @module_or_batch = NULL,
  @params = @params,
  @hints = N'OPTION(OPTIMIZE FOR (@0 = ''99991231''))';
```

The template plan guide overrides parameterization behavior for our query template to
forced, and the SQL plan guide adds the OPTIMIZE FOR hint to the same query template,
ensuring that it will get a plan for a selective filter.

To determine whether both plan guides are used for our query template, run the following code:

```
SET SHOWPLAN_XML ON;
GO
SELECT orderid, custid, empid, orderdate
FROM Sales.Orders
WHERE orderdate >= '20060101';
GO
SET SHOWPLAN_XML OFF;
```

You should find the following attributes in the XML plan: *TemplatePlanGuideDB="Inside TSQL2008"*, *TemplatePlanGuideName="PG_MyQuery2_ParameterizationForced"*, and *PlanGuideDB="InsideTSQL2008" PlanGuideName="PG_MyQuery2_Selective"*.

Run the following query to request information about the plan guides:

```
SELECT *
FROM sys.plan_guides
WHERE name IN('PG_MyQuery2_ParameterizationForced',
'PG_MyQuery2_Selective');
```

When you're done, run the following code to drop the plan guides:

```
EXEC sp_control_plan_guide N'DROP', N'PG_MyQuery2_ParameterizationForced';
EXEC sp_control_plan_guide N'DROP', N'PG_MyQuery2_Selective';
```

Using a Fixed XML Plan

SQL Server supports a query hint called USE PLAN that you can think of as the ultimate hint. With this hint you specify an XML value representing a complete query execution plan. SQL Server also supports creating a plan guide in which you specify an XML value representing a query execution plan as the hint. You can produce the XML form of the query plan you want in a controlled environment, and then use that XML value when creating the plan guide.

As an example, run the following code to create the stored procedure *GetOrders*, which accepts an order date as input (*@odate*) and returns all orders placed on or after the input date:

```
IF OBJECT_ID('dbo.GetOrders', 'P') IS NOT NULL DROP PROC dbo.GetOrders;
GO

CREATE PROC dbo.GetOrders
  @odate AS DATETIME
AS

SELECT orderid, custid, empid, orderdate
/* 33145F87-1109-4959-91D6-F1EC81F8428F */
FROM Sales.Orders
WHERE orderdate >= @odate;
GO
```

Once again, I specified a GUID in a comment to make it easy to track down the cached plan associated with this query.

Suppose that this procedure is usually invoked with a selective filter and you want to create a plan guide that ensures that the query uses the best plan for a selective filter. I already showed several ways to achieve this—for example, by using the OPTIMIZE FOR hint. Here I'll show an example using an XML plan representation.

First, run the procedure in a controlled environment, providing a selective value as input. Next, pull the XML form of the plan from cache by querying the dynamic management objects *sys.dm_exec_query_stats*, *sys.dm_exec_sql_text*, and *sys.dm_exec_query_plan*. Finally, create the plan guide using the *sp_create_plan_guide* procedure and specify the XML plan that you pulled from cache in the *@hint* argument. Here's the complete code to achieve this task:

```
EXEC dbo.GetOrders '99991231';
GO
DECLARE @query_plan AS NVARCHAR(MAX);
SET @query_plan = CAST(
  (SELECT query_plan
   FROM sys.dm_exec_query_stats AS QS
     CROSS APPLY sys.dm_exec_sql_text(QS.sql_handle) AS ST
     CROSS APPLY sys.dm_exec_query_plan(QS.plan_handle) AS QP
   WHERE
     SUBSTRING(ST.text, (QS.statement_start_offset/2) + 1,
       ((CASE statement_end_offset
           WHEN -1 THEN DATALENGTH(ST.text)
           ELSE QS.statement_end_offset END
             - QS.statement_start_offset)/2) + 1
       ) LIKE N'%SELECT orderid, custid, empid, orderdate
/* 33145F87-1109-4959-91D6-F1EC81F8428F */
FROM Sales.Orders
WHERE orderdate >= @odate;%'
     AND ST.text NOT LIKE '%sys%') AS NVARCHAR(MAX));

EXEC sp_create_plan_guide
  @name = N'PG_GetOrders_Selective',
  @stmt = N'SELECT orderid, custid, empid, orderdate
/* 33145F87-1109-4959-91D6-F1EC81F8428F */
FROM Sales.Orders
WHERE orderdate >= @odate;',
  @type = N'OBJECT',
  @module_or_batch = N'dbo.GetOrders',
  @hints = @query_plan;
```

I used the GUID that I planted in the code to easily identify the plan associated with my specific query, but of course, you might not have such a GUID planted in your procedure's code. You can specify any part of the query that is sufficient to identify it uniquely.

Run the following code to ensure that the plan guide is used:

```
SET SHOWPLAN_XML ON;
GO
EXEC dbo.GetOrders '20080506';
GO
SET SHOWPLAN_XML OFF;
```

You should get the following attributes: *PlanGuideDB="InsideTSQL2008"* and *PlanGuideName="PG_GetOrders_Selective"*.

Run the following code to get information about the plan guide:

```
SELECT *
FROM sys.plan_guides
WHERE name = 'PG_GetOrders_Selective';
```

SQL Server provides a table-valued function called *fn_validate_plan_guide* that validates a plan guide. You may want to validate a plan guide after a schema change in a referenced object, for example. The function accepts a plan guide ID as input, which you can obtain from the *sys.plan_guides* view. If the plan guide is valid, the function returns an empty result set; otherwise, it returns the first error that it encounters.

For example, the following code drops the index on the *orderdate* column from the Sales.Orders table and then validates the plan guide PG_GetOrders_Selective:

```
BEGIN TRAN
  DROP INDEX Sales.Orders.idx_nc_orderdate;

  SELECT plan_guide_id, msgnum, severity, state, message
  FROM sys.plan_guides
    CROSS APPLY fn_validate_plan_guide(plan_guide_id)
  WHERE name = 'PG_GetOrders_Selective';
ROLLBACK TRAN
```

Because the plan guide is invalid after the index is dropped you get the following output indicating the error:

```
plan_guide_id msgnum  severity state
------------- ------- -------- ------
65544         8712    16       0

message
--------------------------------------------------------------------
Index 'InsideTSQL2008.Sales.Orders.idx_nc_orderdate',
specified in the USE PLAN hint, does not exist.
Specify an existing index, or create an index with the specified name.
```

When you're done, run the following code to drop the plan guide:

```
EXEC sp_control_plan_guide N'DROP', N'PG_GetOrders_Selective';
```

Plan Freezing

Prior to SQL Server 2008, if you wanted to create a plan guide based on an existing plan in cache you had to first pull the complete XML plan from cache and then specify it as the hint when creating the guide. SQL Server 2008 introduces a new feature called *plan freezing* to allow you to create a plan guide directly from a plan in cache by using a stored procedure called *sp_create_plan_guide_from_handle*. The procedure accepts as arguments the name you want to assign to the plan (*@name*), the plan handle (*@plan_handle*), and the statement start offset in the parent batch (*@statement_start_offset*). Of course, you can query the dynamic management objects *sys.dm_exec_query_stats*, *sys.dm_exec_sql_text*, and *sys.dm_exec_query_plan* to pull the plan handle and statement start offset for a given query. Here's an example of plan freezing:

```
EXEC dbo.GetOrders '99991231';
GO
DECLARE @plan_handle AS VARBINARY(64), @offset AS INT, @rc AS INT;

SELECT @plan_handle = plan_handle, @offset = statement_start_offset
FROM sys.dm_exec_query_stats AS QS
  CROSS APPLY sys.dm_exec_sql_text(QS.sql_handle) AS ST
  CROSS APPLY sys.dm_exec_query_plan(QS.plan_handle) AS QP
WHERE
  SUBSTRING(ST.text, (QS.statement_start_offset/2) + 1,
    ((CASE statement_end_offset
        WHEN -1 THEN DATALENGTH(ST.text)
        ELSE QS.statement_end_offset END
          - QS.statement_start_offset)/2) + 1
        ) LIKE N'%SELECT orderid, custid, empid, orderdate
/* 33145F87-1109-4959-91D6-F1EC81F8428F */
FROM Sales.Orders
WHERE orderdate >= @odate;%'
  AND ST.text NOT LIKE '%sys%';

SET @rc = @@ROWCOUNT;

IF @rc = 1
  EXEC sp_create_plan_guide_from_handle
      @name =  N'PG_GetOrders_Selective',
      @plan_handle = @plan_handle,
      @statement_start_offset = @offset;
ELSE
  RAISERROR(
    'Number of matching plans should be 1 but is %d. Plan guide not created.',
    16, 1, @rc);
```

The code executes the stored procedure *GetOrders* in a controlled environment using a selective input. The code then pulls the plan handle and statement start offset for the procedure's query from cache by querying the aforementioned objects. The code finally executes the *sp_create_plan_guide_from_handle* procedure to create a plan guide for the query.

Run the following code to check whether the plan guide is used:

```
SET SHOWPLAN_XML ON;
GO
EXEC dbo.GetOrders '20080506';
GO
SET SHOWPLAN_XML OFF;
```

You should get the following attributes in the output: *PlanGuideDB="InsideTSQL2008"* and *PlanGuideName="PG_GetOrders_Selective"*.

Run the following query to get information about the plan guide:

```
SELECT *
FROM sys.plan_guides
WHERE name = 'PG_GetOrders_Selective';
```

When you're done experimenting with this plan guide, run the following code to drop it:

```
EXEC sp_control_plan_guide N'DROP', N'PG_GetOrders_Selective';
```

When you're done experimenting with compilations, recompilations, and reuse of execution plans, run the following code for cleanup:

```
DELETE FROM Sales.Orders WHERE orderid > 11077;
DBCC CHECKIDENT('Sales.Orders', RESEED, 11077);

IF OBJECT_ID('dbo.GetOrders') IS NOT NULL
  DROP PROC dbo.GetOrders;
IF OBJECT_ID('dbo.CustCities') IS NOT NULL
  DROP PROC dbo.CustCities;
IF OBJECT_ID('dbo.GetOrdersQuery') IS NOT NULL
  DROP PROC dbo.GetOrdersQuery;
```

More Info For more information on the subject, please refer to the white paper "Batch Compilation, Recompilation, and Plan Caching Issues in SQL Server 2005," by Arun Marathe, revised by Shu Scott, which can be accessed at *http://technet.microsoft.com/en-us/library/cc966425.aspx*. Though written originally for SQL Server 2005, most of the coverage describing SQL Server 2005 behavior is applicable to SQL Server 2008 as well.

EXECUTE AS

Stored procedures can play an important security role. You can grant users EXECUTE permissions on the stored procedure without granting them direct access to the underlying objects, thereby giving you more control over resource access. However, certain exceptions require the caller to have direct permissions on underlying objects. To avoid requiring direct permissions from the caller, all of the following must be true:

- The stored procedure and the underlying objects belong to the same owner.

- The activity is static (as opposed to using dynamic SQL).

- The activity is DML (SELECT, INSERT, UPDATE, DELETE, or MERGE), or it is an execution of another stored procedure.

If any listed item is not true, the caller will be required to have direct permissions against the underlying objects. Otherwise, the statements in the stored procedure that do not meet the requirements will fail on a security violation.

That's the default behavior in SQL Server 2008, which cannot be changed. However, you can set the security context of the stored procedure to that of another user, as if the other user were running the stored procedure. When you create the stored procedure, you can specify an EXECUTE AS clause with one of the following options:

- **CALLER (default)**   Security context of the caller
- **SELF**   Security context of the user creating or altering the stored procedure
- **OWNER**   Security context of the owner of the stored procedure
- **'user_name'**   Security context of the specified user name

Remember, all chaining rules and requirements not to have direct permissions for underlying objects still apply, but they apply to the effective user, not the calling user (unless CALLER was specified, of course).

In addition, a user that has impersonation rights can issue an independent EXECUTE AS <option> command to impersonate another entity (login or user). If this is done, it's as if the session changes its security context to that of the impersonated entity.

Parameterizing Sort Order

To practice what you've learned so far, try to provide a solution to the following task: write a stored procedure called *GetSortedShippers* that accepts a column name from the Shippers table in the InsideTSQL2008 database as one of the inputs (*@colname*), and that returns the rows from the table sorted by the input column name. Assume also that you have a sort direction as input (*@sortdir*), with the value *'A'* representing ascending order and *'D'* representing descending order. The stored procedure should be written with performance in mind—that is, it should use indexes when appropriate (for example, a clustered or nonclustered covering index on the sort column).

Here's the first suggested solution for the task:

```
USE InsideTSQL2008;
IF OBJECT_ID('dbo.GetSortedShippers', 'P') IS NOT NULL
  DROP PROC dbo.GetSortedShippers;
GO

CREATE PROC dbo.GetSortedShippers
  @colname AS sysname, @sortdir AS CHAR(1) = 'A'
AS
```

```
IF @sortdir = 'A'
  SELECT shipperid, companyname, phone
  FROM Sales.Shippers
  ORDER BY
    CASE @colname
      WHEN N'shipperid'   THEN shipperid
      WHEN N'companyname' THEN companyname
      WHEN N'phone'       THEN phone
      ELSE CAST(NULL AS SQL_VARIANT)
    END
ELSE
  SELECT shipperid, companyname, phone
  FROM Sales.Shippers
  ORDER BY
    CASE @colname
      WHEN N'shipperid'   THEN shipperid
      WHEN N'companyname' THEN companyname
      WHEN N'phone'       THEN phone
      ELSE CAST(NULL AS SQL_VARIANT)
    END DESC;
GO
```

The solution uses an IF statement to determine which of two queries to run based on the requested sort direction. The only difference between the queries is that one uses an ascending order for the sort expression and the other uses a descending order. Each query uses a single CASE expression that returns the appropriate column value based on the input column name.

> **Note** SQL Server determines the data type of the result of a CASE expression based on the data type with the highest precedence among the possible result values of the expression—not by the data type of the actual returned value. This means, for example, that if the CASE expression returns a VARCHAR(30) value in one of the THEN clauses and an INT value in another, the result of the expression will always be INT, because INT is higher in precedence than VARCHAR. If in practice the VARCHAR(30) value is returned, SQL Server will attempt to convert it. If the value is not convertible, you get a run-time error. If it is convertible, it becomes an INT, and of course might have a different sort behavior than the original value.

To avoid issues resulting from implicit type conversion in the CASE expression, I caused an implicit conversion of all possible return values to SQL_VARIANT by specifying an expression of an SQL_VARIANT type in the ELSE clause. SQL_VARIANT has a higher precedence than all other types; therefore, SQL Server sets the data type of the CASE expression to SQL_VARIANT, but it preserves the original base types within that SQL_VARIANT.

Run the following code to test the solution, requesting to sort the shippers by *shipperid* in descending order:

```
EXEC dbo.GetSortedShippers @colname = N'shipperid', @sortdir = N'D';
```

This generates the following output:

```
shipperid   companyname      phone
-----------  ---------------  ---------------
3           Shipper ZHISN    (415) 555-0138
2           Shipper ETYNR    (425) 555-0136
1           Shipper GVSUA    (503) 555-0137
```

The output is logically correct, but notice the plan generated for the stored procedure, shown in Figure 3-8.

FIGURE 3-8 Execution plan showing a table scan (unordered clustered index scan) and a sort operator

Remember that the optimizer cannot rely on the sort that the index maintains if you performed manipulation on the sort column. The plan shows an unordered clustered index scan followed by an explicit sort operation. For the problem the query was intended to solve, an optimal plan would have performed an ordered scan operation in the clustered index defined on the *shipperid* column—eliminating the need for an explicit sort operation.

Here's the second solution for the task:

```
ALTER PROC dbo.GetSortedShippers
  @colname AS sysname, @sortdir AS CHAR(1) = 'A'
AS

SELECT shipperid, companyname, phone
FROM Sales.Shippers
ORDER BY
  CASE WHEN @colname = N'shipperid'   AND @sortdir = 'A'
    THEN shipperid   END,
  CASE WHEN @colname = N'companyname' AND @sortdir = 'A'
    THEN companyname END,
  CASE WHEN @colname = N'phone'       AND @sortdir = 'A'
    THEN phone       END,
  CASE WHEN @colname = N'shipperid'   AND @sortdir = 'D'
    THEN shipperid   END DESC,
  CASE WHEN @colname = N'companyname' AND @sortdir = 'D'
    THEN companyname END DESC,
  CASE WHEN @colname = N'phone'       AND @sortdir = 'D'
    THEN phone       END DESC;
GO
```

This solution uses CASE expressions in a more sophisticated way. Each column and sort direction combination is treated with its own CASE expression. Only one of the CASE expressions yields TRUE for all rows, given the column name and sort direction that particular CASE expression is looking for. All other CASE expressions return NULL for all rows. This means that only one of the CASE expressions—the one that looks for the given column name and sort direction—affects the order of the output.

Run the following code to test the stored procedure:

```
EXEC dbo.GetSortedShippers @colname = N'shipperid', @sortdir = N'D';
```

Although this stored procedure applies an interesting logical manipulation, it doesn't change the fact that you perform manipulation on the column and don't sort by it as is. This means that you will get a similar nonoptimal plan to the one shown earlier in Figure 3-8.

Here's the third solution for the task:

```
ALTER PROC dbo.GetSortedShippers
  @colname AS sysname, @sortdir AS CHAR(1) = 'A'
AS

IF @colname NOT IN (N'shipperid', N'companyname', N'phone')
BEGIN
  RAISERROR('Possible SQL injection attempt.', 16, 1);
  RETURN;
END

DECLARE @sql AS NVARCHAR(500);

SET @sql = N'SELECT shipperid, companyname, phone
FROM Sales.Shippers
ORDER BY '
  + QUOTENAME(@colname)
  + CASE @sortdir WHEN 'D' THEN N' DESC' ELSE '' END
  + ';';

EXEC sp_executesql @sql;
GO
```

This solution simply uses dynamic SQL concatenating the input column name and sort direction to the ORDER BY clause of the query. In terms of performance the solution achieves our goal—namely, it uses an index efficiently if an appropriate one exists. To see that it does, run the following code:

```
EXEC dbo.GetSortedShippers @colname = N'shipperid', @sortdir = N'D';
```

Observe in the execution plan, shown in Figure 3-9, that the plan performs an ordered backward clustered index scan with no sort operator, which is optimal for these inputs.

Another advantage of this solution is that it's easy to maintain. The downside of this solution is that there are some negative implications to using dynamic SQL. As mentioned earlier in this chapter, SQL Server doesn't report dependency information for code invoked with dynamic SQL. Also, dynamic SQL involves security-related issues (for example, ownership chaining and SQL injection if the inputs are not validated). For details about security and other issues related to dynamic SQL, please refer to Chapter 9, "Dynamic SQL."

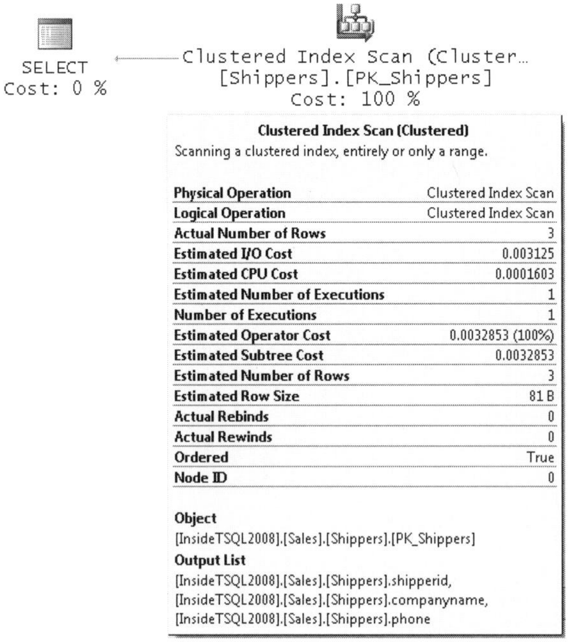

```
SELECT                    Clustered Index Scan (Cluster...
Cost: 0 %                     [Shippers].[PK_Shippers]
                                   Cost: 100 %
```

Clustered Index Scan (Clustered)	
Scanning a clustered index, entirely or only a range.	
Physical Operation	Clustered Index Scan
Logical Operation	Clustered Index Scan
Actual Number of Rows	3
Estimated I/O Cost	0.003125
Estimated CPU Cost	0.0001603
Estimated Number of Executions	1
Number of Executions	1
Estimated Operator Cost	0.0032853 (100%)
Estimated Subtree Cost	0.0032853
Estimated Number of Rows	3
Estimated Row Size	81 B
Actual Rebinds	0
Actual Rewinds	0
Ordered	True
Node ID	0

Object
[InsideTSQL2008].[Sales].[Shippers].[PK_Shippers]
Output List
[InsideTSQL2008].[Sales].[Shippers].shipperid,
[InsideTSQL2008].[Sales].[Shippers].companyname,
[InsideTSQL2008].[Sales].[Shippers].phone

FIGURE 3-9 Execution plan showing an ordered backward clustered index scan

Here's the fourth solution that I'll cover:

```
CREATE PROC dbo.GetSortedShippers_shipperid_A
AS
  SELECT shipperid, companyname, phone
  FROM Sales.Shippers
  ORDER BY shipperid;
GO
CREATE PROC dbo.GetSortedShippers_companyname_A
AS
  SELECT shipperid, companyname, phone
  FROM Sales.Shippers
  ORDER BY companyname;
GO
CREATE PROC dbo.GetSortedShippers_phone_A
AS
  SELECT shipperid, companyname, phone
  FROM Sales.Shippers
  ORDER BY phone;
GO
CREATE PROC dbo.GetSortedShippers_shipperid_D
AS
  SELECT shipperid, companyname, phone
  FROM Sales.Shippers
  ORDER BY shipperid   DESC;
GO
CREATE PROC dbo.GetSortedShippers_companyname_D
AS
```

```
  SELECT shipperid, companyname, phone
  FROM Sales.Shippers
  ORDER BY companyname DESC;
GO
CREATE PROC dbo.GetSortedShippers_phone_D
AS
  SELECT shipperid, companyname, phone
  FROM Sales.Shippers
  ORDER BY phone        DESC;
GO

ALTER PROC dbo.GetSortedShippers
  @colname AS sysname, @sortdir AS CHAR(1) = 'A'
AS

IF @colname = N'shipperid'        AND @sortdir = 'A'
  EXEC dbo.GetSortedShippers_shipperid_A;
ELSE IF @colname = N'companyname' AND @sortdir = 'A'
  EXEC dbo.GetSortedShippers_companyname_A;
ELSE IF @colname = N'phone'       AND @sortdir = 'A'
  EXEC dbo.GetSortedShippers_phone_A;
ELSE IF @colname = N'shipperid'   AND @sortdir = 'D'
  EXEC dbo.GetSortedShippers_shipperid_D;
ELSE IF @colname = N'companyname' AND @sortdir = 'D'
  EXEC dbo.GetSortedShippers_companyname_D;
ELSE IF @colname = N'phone'       AND @sortdir = 'D'
  EXEC dbo.GetSortedShippers_phone_D;
GO
```

This solution might seem awkward at first glance. You create a separate stored procedure with a single static query for each possible combination of inputs. Then, *GetSortedShippers* can act as a redirector. Simply use a series of IF/ELSE IF statements to check for each possible combination of inputs, and you explicitly invoke the appropriate stored procedure for each. Sure, it is a bit long and requires more maintenance than the previous solution, but it uses static queries that generate optimal plans. Note that each query gets its own plan and can reuse a previously cached plan for the same query.

To test the procedure, run the following code:

```
EXEC dbo.GetSortedShippers @colname = N'shipperid', @sortdir = N'D';
```

You get the optimal plan for the given inputs, similar to the plan shown earlier in Figure 3-9.

When you're done, run the following code for cleanup:

```
IF OBJECT_ID('dbo.GetSortedShippers', 'P') IS NOT NULL
  DROP PROC dbo.GetSortedShippers;
IF OBJECT_ID('dbo.GetSortedShippers_shipperid_A', 'P') IS NOT NULL
  DROP PROC dbo.GetSortedShippers_shipperid_A;
IF OBJECT_ID('dbo.GetSortedShippers_companyname_A', 'P') IS NOT NULL
  DROP PROC dbo.GetSortedShippers_companyname_A;
IF OBJECT_ID('dbo.GetSortedShippers_phone_A', 'P') IS NOT NULL
  DROP PROC dbo.GetSortedShippers_phone_A;
```

```
IF OBJECT_ID('dbo.GetSortedShippers_shipperid_D', 'P') IS NOT NULL
  DROP PROC dbo.GetSortedShippers_shipperid_D;
IF OBJECT_ID('dbo.GetSortedShippers_companyname_D', 'P') IS NOT NULL
  DROP PROC dbo.GetSortedShippers_companyname_D;
IF OBJECT_ID('dbo.GetSortedShippers_phone_D', 'P') IS NOT NULL
  DROP PROC dbo.GetSortedShippers_phone_D;
```

CLR Stored Procedures

SQL Server 2008 allows you to develop CLR stored procedures (as well as other routines) using a .NET language of your choice. The previous chapter provided background about CLR routines, gave advice on when to develop CLR routines versus T-SQL ones, and described the technicalities of how to develop CLR routines. Remember to read Appendix A for instructions on developing, building, deploying, and testing your .NET code. Here I'd just like to give a couple of examples of CLR stored procedures that apply functionality outside the reach of T-SQL code.

The first example is a CLR procedure called *GetEnvInfo*. This stored procedure collects information from environment variables and returns it in table format. The environment variables that this procedure will return include: *Machine Name*, *Processors*, *OS Version*, *CLR Version*.

Note that to collect information from environment variables, the assembly needs external access to operating system resources. By default, assemblies are created (using the CREATE ASSEMBLY command) with the most restrictive PERMISSION_SET option, SAFE, which means that they're limited to accessing database resources only. This is the recommended option to obtain maximum security and stability. The permission set options EXTERNAL_ACCESS and UNSAFE (specified in the CREATE ASSEMBLY or ALTER ASSEMBLY commands, or in the Project | Properties dialog box in Visual Studio under the Database tab) allow external access to system resources such as files, the network, environment variables, or the registry. To allow EXTERNAL_ACCESS and UNSAFE assemblies to run, you also need to set the database option TRUSTWORTHY to ON. Allowing EXTERNAL_ACCESS or UNSAFE assemblies to run represents a security risk and should be avoided. I will describe a safer alternative shortly, but first I'll demonstrate this option. To set the TRUSTWORTHY option of the CLRUtilities database to ON and to change the permission set of the CLRUtilities assembly to EXTERNAL_ACCESS, run the following code:

```
USE CLRUtilities;

-- Database option TRUSTWORTHY needs to be ON for EXTERNAL_ACCESS
ALTER DATABASE CLRUtilities SET TRUSTWORTHY ON;

-- Alter assembly with PERMISSION_SET = EXTERNAL_ACCESS
ALTER ASSEMBLY CLRUtilities
WITH PERMISSION_SET = EXTERNAL_ACCESS;
```

At this point you can run the *GetEnvInfo* stored procedure. Keep in mind, however, that UNSAFE assemblies have complete freedom and can compromise the robustness of SQL Server and the security of the system. EXTERNAL_ACCESS assemblies get the same reliability and stability protection as SAFE assemblies, but from a security perspective they're like UNSAFE assemblies.

A more secure alternative is to sign the assembly with a strong name key file or Authenticode with a certificate. This strong name (or certificate) is created inside SQL Server as an asymmetric key (or certificate) and has a corresponding login with EXTERNAL ACCESS ASSEMBLY permission (for external access assemblies) or UNSAFE ASSEMBLY permission (for unsafe assemblies). For example, suppose that you have code in the CLRUtilities assembly that needs to run with the EXTERNAL_ACCESS permission set. You can sign the assembly with a strong-named key file from the Project | Properties dialog box in Visual Studio under the *Signing* tab. Then run the following code to create an asymmetric key from the executable .dll file and a corresponding login with the EXTERNAL_ACCESS ASSEMBLY permission:

```
-- Create an asymmetric key from the signed assembly
-- Note: you have to sign the assembly using a strong name key file
USE master

CREATE ASYMMETRIC KEY CLRUtilitiesKey
  FROM EXECUTABLE FILE =
    'C:\CLRUtilities\CLRUtilities\bin\Debug\CLRUtilities.dll'

-- Create login and grant it with external access permission
CREATE LOGIN CLRUtilitiesLogin FROM ASYMMETRIC KEY CLRUtilitiesKey
GRANT EXTERNAL ACCESS ASSEMBLY TO CLRUtilitiesLogin
```

For more details about securing your assemblies, please refer to SQL Server Books Online and to the following URL: *http://msdn2.microsoft.com/en-us/library/ms345106.aspx*.

Here's the definition of the *GetEnvInfo* stored procedure using C# code:

```
// GetEnvInfo Procedure
// Returns environment info in tabular format
[SqlProcedure]
public static void GetEnvInfo()
{
    // Create a record - object representation of a row
    // Include the metadata for the SQL table
    SqlDataRecord record = new SqlDataRecord(
        new SqlMetaData("EnvProperty", SqlDbType.NVarChar, 20),
        new SqlMetaData("Value", SqlDbType.NVarChar, 256));
    // Marks the beginning of the result set to be sent back to the client
    // The record parameter is used to construct the metadata
    // for the result set
    SqlContext.Pipe.SendResultsStart(record);
    // Populate some records and send them through the pipe
    record.SetSqlString(0, @"Machine Name");
    record.SetSqlString(1, Environment.MachineName);
```

```
                SqlContext.Pipe.SendResultsRow(record);
                record.SetSqlString(0, @"Processors");
                record.SetSqlString(1, Environment.ProcessorCount.ToString());
                SqlContext.Pipe.SendResultsRow(record);
                record.SetSqlString(0, @"OS Version");
                record.SetSqlString(1, Environment.OSVersion.ToString());
                SqlContext.Pipe.SendResultsRow(record);
                record.SetSqlString(0, @"CLR Version");
                record.SetSqlString(1, Environment.Version.ToString());
                SqlContext.Pipe.SendResultsRow(record);
                // End of result set
                SqlContext.Pipe.SendResultsEnd();
            }
```

In this procedure, you can see the usage of some specific extensions to ADO.NET for usage within SQL Server CLR routines. These are defined in the *Microsoft.SqlServer.Server* namespace in the .NET Framework.

When you call a stored procedure from SQL Server, you are already connected. You don't have to open a new connection; you need access to the caller's context from the code running in the server. The caller's context is abstracted in a *SqlContext* object. Before using the *SqlContext* object, you should test whether it is available by using its *IsAvailable* property.

The procedure retrieves some environmental data from the operating system. The data can be retrieved by the properties of an *Environment* object, which can be found in the *System* namespace. But the data you get is in text format. In the CLR procedure, you can see how to generate a row set for any possible format. The routine's code stores data in a *SqlDataRecord* object, which represents a single row of data. It defines the schema for this single row by using the *SqlMetaData* objects.

SELECT statements in a T-SQL stored procedure send the results to the connected caller's "pipe." This is the most effective way of sending results to the caller. The same technique is exposed to CLR routines running in SQL Server. Results can be sent to the connected pipe using the send methods of the *SqlPipe* object. You can instantiate the *SqlPipe* object with the *Pipe* property of the *SqlContext* object.

Here's the definition of the *GetEnvInfo* stored procedure using Visual Basic code:

```
        ' GetEnvInfo Procedure
        ' Returns environment info in tabular format
        <SqlProcedure()> _
        Public Shared Sub GetEnvInfo()
            ' Create a record - object representation of a row
            ' Include the metadata for the SQL table
            Dim record As New SqlDataRecord( _
                New SqlMetaData("EnvProperty", SqlDbType.NVarChar, 20), _
                New SqlMetaData("Value", SqlDbType.NVarChar, 256))
            ' Marks the beginning of the result set to be sent back to the client
            ' The record parameter is used to construct the metadata for
            ' the result set
```

```
    SqlContext.Pipe.SendResultsStart(record)
    '' Populate some records and send them through the pipe
    record.SetSqlString(0, "Machine Name")
    record.SetSqlString(1, Environment.MachineName)
    SqlContext.Pipe.SendResultsRow(record)
    record.SetSqlString(0, "Processors")
    record.SetSqlString(1, Environment.ProcessorCount.ToString())
    SqlContext.Pipe.SendResultsRow(record)
    record.SetSqlString(0, "OS Version")
    record.SetSqlString(1, Environment.OSVersion.ToString())
    SqlContext.Pipe.SendResultsRow(record)
    record.SetSqlString(0, "CLR Version")
    record.SetSqlString(1, Environment.Version.ToString())
    SqlContext.Pipe.SendResultsRow(record)
    ' End of result set
    SqlContext.Pipe.SendResultsEnd()
End Sub
```

Run the following code to register the C# version of the *GetEnvInfo* stored procedure in the CLRUtilities database:

```
USE CLRUtilities;
IF OBJECT_ID('dbo.GetEnvInfo', 'PC') IS NOT NULL
  DROP PROC dbo.GetEnvInfo;
GO
CREATE PROCEDURE dbo.GetEnvInfo
AS EXTERNAL NAME CLRUtilities.CLRUtilities.GetEnvInfo;
```

Use the following code to register the stored procedure in case you used Visual Basic to develop it:

```
CREATE PROCEDURE dbo.GetEnvInfo
AS EXTERNAL NAME
  CLRUtilities.[CLRUtilities.CLRUtilities].GetEnvInfo;
```

Run the following code to test the *GetEnvInfo* procedure:

```
EXEC dbo.GetEnvInfo;
```

This generated the following output on my computer:

```
EnvProperty          Value
-------------------- -------------------------------------------
Machine Name         DOJO
Processors           2
OS Version           Microsoft Windows NT 6.0.6001 Service Pack 1
CLR Version          2.0.50727.3074
```

The second example for a CLR procedure creates the *GetAssemblyInfo* stored procedure, which returns information about an input assembly.

Here's the definition of the *GetAssemblyInfo* stored procedure using C# code:

```csharp
// GetAssemblyInfo Procedure
// Returns assembly info, uses Reflection
[SqlProcedure]
public static void GetAssemblyInfo(SqlString asmName)
{
    // Retrieve the clr name of the assembly
    String clrName = null;
    // Get the context
    using (SqlConnection connection =
            new SqlConnection("Context connection = true"))
    {
        connection.Open();
        using (SqlCommand command = new SqlCommand())
        {
            // Get the assembly and load it
            command.Connection = connection;
            command.CommandText =
              "SELECT clr_name FROM sys.assemblies WHERE name = @asmName";
            command.Parameters.Add("@asmName", SqlDbType.NVarChar);
            command.Parameters[0].Value = asmName;
            clrName = (String)command.ExecuteScalar();
            if (clrName == null)
            {
                throw new ArgumentException("Invalid assembly name!");
            }
            Assembly myAsm = Assembly.Load(clrName);
            // Create a record - object representation of a row
            // Include the metadata for the SQL table
            SqlDataRecord record = new SqlDataRecord(
                new SqlMetaData("Type", SqlDbType.NVarChar, 50),
                new SqlMetaData("Name", SqlDbType.NVarChar, 256));
            // Marks the beginning of the result set to be sent back
            // to the client
            // The record parameter is used to construct the metadata
            // for the result set
            SqlContext.Pipe.SendResultsStart(record);
            // Get all types in the assembly
            Type[] typesArr = myAsm.GetTypes();
            foreach (Type t in typesArr)
            {
                // Type in a SQL database should be a class or
                // a structure
                if (t.IsClass == true)
                {
                    record.SetSqlString(0, @"Class");
                }
                else
                {
                    record.SetSqlString(0, @"Structure");
                }
                record.SetSqlString(1, t.FullName);
                SqlContext.Pipe.SendResultsRow(record);
                // Find all public static methods
```

```
            MethodInfo[] miArr = t.GetMethods();
            foreach (MethodInfo mi in miArr)
            {
                if (mi.IsPublic && mi.IsStatic)
                {
                    record.SetSqlString(0, @"  Method");
                    record.SetSqlString(1, mi.Name);
                    SqlContext.Pipe.SendResultsRow(record);
                }
            }
        }
        // End of result set
        SqlContext.Pipe.SendResultsEnd();
    }
  }
}
```

A DBA could have a problem finding out exactly what part of a particular .NET assembly is loaded to the database. Fortunately, this problem can be easily mitigated. All .NET assemblies include metadata, describing all types (classes and structures) defined within it, including all public methods and properties of the types. In .NET, the *System.Reflection* namespace contains classes and interfaces that provide a managed view of loaded types.

For a very detailed overview of a .NET assembly stored in the file system, you can use the Reflector for .NET, a very sophisticated tool created by Lutz Roeder. Because it is downloadable for free from his site at *http://www.aisto.com/roeder/dotnet/*, it is very popular among .NET developers. Also, in his blog at *http://blogs.msdn.com/sqlclr/archive/2005/11/21/495438.aspx*, Miles Trochesset wrote a SQL Server CLR DDL trigger that is fired on the CREATE ASSEMBLY statement. The trigger automatically registers all CLR objects from the assembly, including UDTs, UDAs, UDFs, SPs, and triggers. I used both tools as a starting point to create my simplified version of a SQL Server CLR stored procedure. I thought that a DBA might prefer to read the assembly metadata from a stored procedure, not from an external tool (which Lutz Roeder's Reflector for .NET is). I also thought that a DBA might just want to read the metadata first, not immediately register all CLR objects from the assembly the way that Miles Trochesset's trigger does.

The *GetAssemblyInfo* procedure has to load an assembly from the *sys.assemblies* catalog view. To achieve this task, it has to execute a *SqlCommand*. *SqlCommand* needs a connection. In the *GetEnvInfo* procedure's code you saw the usage of the *SqlContext* class; now you need an explicit *SqlConnection* object. You can get the context of the caller's connection by using a new connection string option, *"Context connection = true"*.

As in the *GetEnvInfo* procedure, you want to get the results in tabular format. Again you use the *SqlDataRecord* and *SqlMetaData* objects to shape the row returned. Remember that the *SqlPipe* object gives you the best performance to return the row to the caller.

Before you can read the metadata of an assembly, you have to load it. The rest is quite easy. The *GetTypes* method of a loaded assembly can be used to retrieve a collection of all types defined in the assembly. The code retrieves this collection in an array. Then it loops through the array, and for each type it uses the *GetMethods* method to retrieve all public methods in an array of the *MethodInfo* objects. This procedure retrieves type and method names only. The *Reflection* classes allow you to get other metadata information as well—for example, the names and types of input parameters. Here's the definition of the *GetAssemblyInfo* stored procedure using Visual Basic code:

```
' GetAssemblyInfo Procedure
' Returns assembly info, uses Reflection
<SqlProcedure()> _
Public Shared Sub GetAssemblyInfo(ByVal asmName As SqlString)
    ' Retrieve the clr name of the assembly
    Dim clrName As String = Nothing
    ' Get the context
    Using connection As New SqlConnection("Context connection = true")
        connection.Open()
        Using command As New SqlCommand
            ' Get the assembly and load it
            command.Connection = connection
            command.CommandText = _
              "SELECT clr_name FROM sys.assemblies WHERE name = @asmName"
            command.Parameters.Add("@asmName", SqlDbType.NVarChar)
            command.Parameters(0).Value = asmName
            clrName = CStr(command.ExecuteScalar())
            If (clrName = Nothing) Then
                Throw New ArgumentException("Invalid assembly name!")
            End If
            Dim myAsm As Assembly = Assembly.Load(clrName)
            ' Create a record - object representation of a row
            ' Include the metadata for the SQL table
            Dim record As New SqlDataRecord( _
                New SqlMetaData("Type", SqlDbType.NVarChar, 50), _
                New SqlMetaData("Name", SqlDbType.NVarChar, 256))
            ' Marks the beginning of the result set to be sent back
            ' to the client
            ' The record parameter is used to construct the metadata
            ' for the result set
            SqlContext.Pipe.SendResultsStart(record)
            ' Get all types in the assembly
            Dim typesArr() As Type = myAsm.GetTypes()
            For Each t As Type In typesArr
                ' Type in a SQL database should be a class or a structure
                If (t.IsClass = True) Then
                    record.SetSqlString(0, "Class")
                Else
                    record.SetSqlString(0, "Structure")
                End If
                record.SetSqlString(1, t.FullName)
                SqlContext.Pipe.SendResultsRow(record)
                ' Find all public static methods
                Dim miArr() As MethodInfo = t.GetMethods
                For Each mi As MethodInfo In miArr
                    If (mi.IsPublic And mi.IsStatic) Then
                        record.SetSqlString(0, " Method")
                        record.SetSqlString(1, mi.Name)
```

```
                    SqlContext.Pipe.SendResultsRow(record)
                End If
            Next
        Next
        ' End of result set
        SqlContext.Pipe.SendResultsEnd()
    End Using
  End Using
End Sub
```

Run the following code to register the C# version of the *GetAssemblyInfo* stored procedure in the CLRUtilities database:

```
IF OBJECT_ID('dbo.GetAssemblyInfo', 'PC') IS NOT NULL
  DROP PROC dbo.GetAssemblyInfo;
GO
CREATE PROCEDURE GetAssemblyInfo
  @asmName AS sysname
AS EXTERNAL NAME CLRUtilities.CLRUtilities.GetAssemblyInfo;
```

And in case you used Visual Basic to develop the stored procedure, use the following code to register it:

```
CREATE PROCEDURE GetAssemblyInfo
  @asmName AS sysname
AS EXTERNAL NAME
  CLRUtilities.[CLRUtilities.CLRUtilities].GetAssemblyInfo;
```

Run the following code to test the *GetAssemblyInfo* procedure, providing it with the CLRUtilities assembly name as input:

```
EXEC GetAssemblyInfo N'CLRUtilities';
```

You get the following output with the assembly name and the names of all methods (routines) defined within it:

```
Type        Name
----------  ----------------------
Class       CLRUtilities
  Method    RegexIsMatch
  Method    RegexReplace
  Method    FormatDatetime
  Method    ImpCast
  Method    ExpCast
  Method    SQLSigCLR
  Method    SplitCLR
  Method    ArrSplitFillRow
  Method    GetEnvInfo
  Method    GetAssemblyInfo
  Method    trg_GenericDMLAudit
  Method    SalesRunningSum
Structure   CLRUtilities+row_item
```

You should recognize most routine names except *trg_GenericDMLAudit* and *SalesRunningSum*, which will be covered later in the book.

When you're done, run the following code for cleanup:

```
USE CLRUtilities;
IF OBJECT_ID('dbo.GetEnvInfo', 'PC') IS NOT NULL
  DROP PROC dbo.GetEnvInfo;
IF OBJECT_ID('dbo.GetAssemblyInfo', 'PC') IS NOT NULL
  DROP PROC dbo.GetAssemblyInfo;
```

Conclusion

Stored procedures are one of the most powerful tools that SQL Server provides. Understanding them well and using them wisely will result in robust, secure databases that perform well. Stored procedures give you a security layer, encapsulation, reduction in network traffic, reuse of execution plans, and much more. SQL Server 2008 supports developing CLR routines, allowing you to enhance the functionality of your database.

Chapter 4

Triggers

Itzik Ben-Gan and Dejan Sarka

Triggers are routines that fire automatically as a result of an event in the database server. Microsoft SQL Server supports data-manipulation language (DML), data-definition language (DDL) triggers, and logon triggers, which can be developed either with T-SQL or with .NET code and can fire after or instead of the triggering event. In this chapter I'll describe in detail the different types of triggers.

Triggers are first and foremost stored procedures in terms of how SQL Server treats them internally. They undergo similar processing phases to stored procedures (parsing, resolution, and optimization). However, triggers do not have an interface (input and output parameters), and you cannot invoke them explicitly. They fire automatically as a result of a statement submitted against the database server.

Triggers are part of the transaction that fired them; that is, the transaction is not considered complete until the trigger also finishes running. If you issue a ROLLBACK TRAN within the trigger's code, you effectively roll back the trigger's activity as well as all the activity of the transaction to which the trigger belongs. The rollback undoes all activity as of the outermost BEGIN TRAN statement, if one was explicitly issued. If the triggering statement was not issued in an explicit transaction, a rollback in a trigger undoes all activity issued within the trigger until the ROLLBACK TRAN statement, as well as the activity of the triggering statement.

Keep in mind that if you issue a rollback within the trigger (just as with any transaction), it's as if the activity were performed twice—done and then undone. If your trigger is intended to enforce an integrity rule and you can achieve the task by prevention rather than reaction, you should do so to get better performance. For example, if you can enforce the integrity rule with a constraint, use the constraint. If you cannot enforce it with a constraint, determine whether you can enforce it with a stored procedure that first performs validation before it determines whether to apply the change. Use triggers only if you can't enforce the rules with constraints.

Triggers allow you to automate a response to certain data modification statements or events initiated by users and applications. You can create AFTER triggers that will automatically run your code after the triggering statement or event executes, and you can create INSTEAD OF triggers that will substitute your code for the original statement. You can create both triggers for data modification statements (INSERT, UPDATE, and DELETE—but not MERGE); you can create AFTER triggers—but not INSTEAD OF triggers—for DDL activities (CREATE, ALTER, and DROP) and to respond to the establishment of a user session (LOGON event). You can develop triggers with T-SQL or with .NET code. SQL Server 2008 does not support SELECT triggers, row-level triggers, or BEFORE triggers. INSTEAD OF triggers are the closest you can get in SQL Server to BEFORE triggers.

You can use triggers to enforce complex integrity rules, to maintain denormalized data, and to do much more.

AFTER Triggers

AFTER triggers execute after the triggering statement has already taken place. You use these triggers to react to changes against the database server.

DML AFTER triggers can be created only on permanent tables. They cannot be created on views or temporary tables. You create such triggers on a specific table and for a specific DML statement or statement list, including INSERT, UPDATE, and DELETE. Note that you cannot create triggers for the MERGE statement, but INSERT, UPDATE, and DELETE triggers will fire if a MERGE statement activates the corresponding actions.

If a constraint defined on a table rejects a modification, a trigger defined on that table will not fire.

AFTER triggers are fired once per statement, not once per row. Regardless of how many rows were affected by the triggering statement (zero, one, or more than one), an AFTER trigger will fire only once.

You can create multiple AFTER triggers (both DML and DDL) on each object for each statement type. If you have multiple triggers on the same table for the same type of statement, they will fire synchronously (one after the other). SQL Server allows you to mark the trigger that will fire first and the one that will fire last by using the *sp_settriggerorder* stored procedure. The order in which triggers between the first and last are fired is undefined.

AFTER triggers are useful for automated reactive activities that you want to issue as a result of the triggering statement—for example, enforcing integrity rules that you cannot enforce with constraints, maintaining denormalized data, and so on.

The *inserted* and *deleted* Special Tables

Within DML triggers you can access the old and new image of the affected rows through special tables called *inserted* and *deleted*. The *inserted* table contains the new image of the affected rows, and *deleted* contains the old image. Naturally, *inserted* will contain rows only for INSERT and UPDATE triggers, and it will be empty for DELETE triggers. Similarly, *deleted* will contain rows only for DELETE and UPDATE triggers, and it will be empty for INSERT triggers.

The *inserted* and *deleted* tables are structured the same as the table on which the trigger was defined—that is, they have the same columns as the base table. Note that these tables are not indexed; therefore, every time you query them, you're scanning the whole thing. There are some exceptions, of course. For example, if you use the EXISTS predicate or a TOP query with no ORDER BY clause, SQL Server won't need to scan the whole table.

In SQL Server 2008, *inserted* and *deleted* point to row-versioned data in tempdb. Row versioning is a technology that supports various aspects of SQL Server, including snapshot isolation levels, triggers, online index operations, and multiple active result sets (MARS). This technology allows storing earlier versions of a row in tempdb. Regarding triggers, SQL Server stores row versions for both data changed by the triggering statement and data changed by the trigger.

Intensive trigger activity can cause performance issues. If you have a lot of trigger activity, you want to be prepared with sufficient tempdb resources. Remember that *inserted* and *deleted* are not indexed, so you might end up scanning large portions of data when querying them, causing I/O activity in tempdb. If you really need to scan *inserted* or *deleted* completely and you can obtain the data you need with a single scan (for example, a set-based join between *inserted* or *deleted* and the base table), you don't need to do much to improve performance. However, if you need to access *inserted* or *deleted* with multiple iterations—for example, if you need to treat each row individually—it would be wise to either use a cursor or to store the data in a temporary table that you can index, as in:

```
SELECT * INTO #I FROM inserted
  CREATE UNIQUE CLUSTERED INDEX idx_keycol ON #I(keycol);
```

Understanding how *inserted* and *deleted* work is key to developing robust and efficient triggers. On the other hand, misunderstanding this could lead to serious performance problems.

Identifying the Number of Affected Rows

Remember that triggers are fired once per statement, not once per affected row. This means that a trigger will fire once whether zero, one, or more than one rows were affected by the triggering statement. In most cases, if a trigger fired, but zero rows were affected, you don't want the trigger to react. If one row was affected, you can typically apply simple logic and query *inserted* or *deleted* directly, knowing that it contains only one row. For example, you can safely use an assignment SELECT like the following one to grab data from that row:

```
SELECT @var1 = col1, @var2 = col2, … FROM inserted;
```

However, you will face logical issues with such a statement if zero or multiple rows were affected. With zero affected rows, such a statement does not perform any assignment at all, so the variables will retain the values they had earlier. With multiple affected rows, this statement will perform multiple assignments—one for each row. However, the variables will have the values assigned to them in the last assignment performed. If you just assume that your triggers will fire only for single-row modifications, but they don't, you'll end up with logical bugs.

Suppose that you use a SET command to assign a value from *inserted* or *deleted* to a variable:

```
SET @var1 = (SELECT col1 FROM inserted);
```

If one row was affected, this assignment will work perfectly well. With zero affected rows, the subquery will return NULL. With multiple affected rows, this code will break, generating an error.

You need to take these things into consideration when programming triggers so that you can avoid bugs and realize good performance. You can determine a course of action based on the number of rows affected by the triggering statement. Later I'll explain how you can efficiently tell how many rows were affected.

With zero affected rows, you typically just want to return from the trigger—there's no point in wasting resources if you need not do anything. If more than zero rows were affected, the course of action you should take depends on the type of activity you want to issue from the trigger. If you can achieve the activity by using a set-based join between *inserted* or *deleted* and the base table, you can apply the same code for both single and multiple affected rows. For example, suppose that you're writing an INSERT trigger for a table called T1 that is supposed to modify an attribute called *col1* in the new rows. You can achieve this by using an UPDATE statement that is based on a join between T1 and *inserted*, like so:

```
UPDATE T1
  SET col1 = <expression>
FROM T1
  JOIN inserted AS I
    ON T1.keycol = I.keycol;
```

In SQL Server 2008 you can use the standard MERGE statement instead of the above nonstandard UPDATE statement, like so:

```
MERGE INTO T1
USING inserted AS I
  ON T1.keycol = I.keycol
WHEN MATCHED THEN
  UPDATE
    SET col1 = <expression>;
```

Either way, the purpose of the join is just to filter the new rows added to T1.

However, suppose that you need to deal with each new row individually using iterative logic. You need to retrieve values from each row individually and take some action. Remember that if only one row was affected, you can safely use an assignment SELECT to grab values from the row in *inserted* or *deleted*:

```
SELECT @var1 = col1, @var2 = col2, … FROM inserted;
```

So you can check the number of affected rows, and if it is one, use such logic. Otherwise, you need to apply iterative logic. Remember that *inserted* and *deleted* are not indexed. You can copy the data from the special table into a temporary table, index it, and then iterate through the rows in the temporary table using a loop. A more efficient solution is to use a cursor based on a query against *inserted* or *deleted*. With the latter approach you do not need to copy the data to a temporary table and index it.

To demonstrate the flow handling based on the number of affected rows, first run the following code to create the table T1:

```
SET NOCOUNT ON;
USE tempdb;
IF OBJECT_ID('dbo.T1', 'U') IS NOT NULL DROP TABLE dbo.T1;
```

```
CREATE TABLE dbo.T1
(
  keycol  INT        NOT NULL PRIMARY KEY,
  datacol VARCHAR(10) NOT NULL
);
```

Run the following code to create the trigger trg_T1_i.

```
CREATE TRIGGER trg_T1_i ON T1 FOR INSERT
AS

DECLARE @rc AS INT =
  (SELECT COUNT(*) FROM (SELECT TOP (2) * FROM inserted) AS D);

IF @rc = 0 RETURN;

DECLARE @keycol AS INT, @datacol AS VARCHAR(10);

IF @rc = 1 -- single row
BEGIN
  SELECT @keycol = keycol, @datacol = datacol FROM inserted;

  PRINT 'Handling keycol: '
    + CAST(@keycol AS VARCHAR(10))
    + ', datacol: ' + @datacol;
END
ELSE -- multi row
BEGIN

  DECLARE @C AS CURSOR;

  SET @C = CURSOR FAST_FORWARD FOR
    SELECT keycol, datacol FROM inserted;

  OPEN @C;

  FETCH NEXT FROM @C INTO @keycol, @datacol;

  WHILE @@FETCH_STATUS = 0
  BEGIN
    PRINT 'Handling keycol: '
      + CAST(@keycol AS VARCHAR(10))
      + ', datacol: ' + @datacol;

    FETCH NEXT FROM @C INTO @keycol, @datacol;
  END

END
GO
```

 Note You can use either the keyword FOR or the keyword AFTER to define an AFTER trigger.

This trigger simply prints the values provided in each new row inserted by the triggering INSERT action. It demonstrates how to deal with each row individually.

The trigger then counts the number of rows returned by a TOP (2) query against *inserted*, and stores the result in a variable called *@rc*. Possible result values are *0, 1,* and *2,* indicating that zero, one, or more rows, respectively, were affected by the action that caused the trigger to fire.

> **Note** Prior to SQL Server 2008 I simply evaluted the *@@rowcount* function within the trigger in order to tell how many rows were affected by the statement that caused the trigger to fire. However, in SQL Server 2008, when you evaluate *@@rowcount* in an INSERT, UPDATE, or DELETE trigger that was fired due to a MERGE statement, you will get the total number of rows affected by MERGE. This number includes all actions—not just the specific one that caused the trigger to fire. Since you cannot rule out running the MERGE statement in your system, you can't rely on *@@rowcount* within a trigger in SQL Server 2008. Instead, you should query *inserted* or *deleted* as I demonstrated.

If zero rows were affected, the trigger returns. If one row was affected, the code uses an assignment SELECT to grab the values from the row inserted into local variables. If multiple rows were affected, the code uses a cursor to iterate through the multiple rows in *inserted*. In each iteration, the code prints the values from the current row and fetches the values from the next row.

To test the trigger, first run the following code, which inserts zero rows:

```
INSERT INTO dbo.T1 SELECT 1, 'A' WHERE 1 = 0;
```

As expected, you get no output from the trigger.

Next, insert a single row:

```
INSERT INTO dbo.T1 SELECT 1, 'A';
```

You get the following output:

```
Handling keycol: 1, datacol: A
```

Finally, insert multiple rows:

```
INSERT INTO dbo.T1 VALUES
  (2, 'B'), (3, 'C'), (4, 'D');
```

You get the following output:

```
Handling keycol: 4, datacol: D
Handling keycol: 3, datacol: C
Handling keycol: 2, datacol: B
```

When you're done, run the following code for cleanup:

```
IF OBJECT_ID('dbo.T1', 'U') IS NOT NULL DROP TABLE dbo.T1;
```

Identifying the Type of Trigger

In some cases you may prefer to create one trigger for multiple action types but you still want to be able to identify the type of action that fired the trigger.

To identify the type of action that fired the trigger, you can inspect *inserted* and *deleted*. Of course, if zero rows were affected, both tables will be empty, but in such a case you'd typically rather do nothing. If at least one row was affected, you can check which table contains rows to determine the type of change. As a result of an INSERT action, you will find rows only in *inserted*; for a DELETE action, you will find rows only in *deleted*; for an UPDATE action, you will find rows in both tables. Remember also that a MERGE statement may cause multiple trigger types to be fired.

To demonstrate this, first create the table T1 by running the following code:

```
IF OBJECT_ID('dbo.T1', 'U') IS NOT NULL DROP TABLE dbo.T1;

CREATE TABLE dbo.T1
(
  keycol  INT          NOT NULL PRIMARY KEY,
  datacol VARCHAR(10) NOT NULL
);
```

Run the following code to create the trigger trg_T1_iud:

```
CREATE TRIGGER trg_T1_iud ON dbo.T1 FOR INSERT, UPDATE, DELETE
AS

DECLARE @i AS INT =
  (SELECT COUNT(*) FROM (SELECT TOP (1) * FROM inserted) AS I);
DECLARE @d AS INT =
  (SELECT COUNT(*) FROM (SELECT TOP (1) * FROM deleted) AS D);

IF @i = 1 AND @d = 1
  PRINT 'UPDATE of at least one row identified';
ELSE IF @i = 1 AND @d = 0
  PRINT 'INSERT of at least one row identified';
ELSE IF @i = 0 AND @d = 1
  PRINT 'DELETE of at least one row identified';
ELSE
  PRINT 'No rows affected';
GO
```

The trigger's code declares the variables $@i$ and stores within it the value *1* if at least one row appears in *inserted* and *0* otherwise. Similarly, the trigger declares the variables $@d$ and stores within it the value *1* if at least one row appears in *deleted* and *0* otherwise. The trigger then inspects the values of $@i$ and $@d$ to determine which action caused it to fire. If both variables are equal to *1*, an UPDATE action that affected at least one row caused the current instance of the trigger to fire. If $@i$ is equal to *1* and $@d$ is equal to *0*, an INSERT action that affected at least one row caused the trigger to fire. If $@i$ is equal to *0* and $@d$ is equal to *1*, a DELETE action that affected at least one row caused the trigger to fire. If both variables are equal to *0*, it cannot be determined which action caused the trigger to fire. But typically you do not want to apply any activity when both *inserted* and *deleted* are empty.

To test the trigger, run the following INSERT statement that inserts zero rows:

```
INSERT INTO T1 SELECT 1, 'A' WHERE 1 = 0;
```

You get the following output:

```
No rows affected
```

Insert one row:

```
INSERT INTO T1 SELECT 1, 'A';
```

You get the following output:

```
INSERT of at least one row identified
```

Issue an UPDATE statement:

```
UPDATE T1 SET datacol = 'AA' WHERE keycol = 1;
```

You get the following output:

```
UPDATE of at least one row identified
```

Finally, issue a DELETE statement:

```
DELETE FROM T1 WHERE keycol = 1;
```

You will get the output:

```
DELETE of at least one row identified
```

When you're done, run the following code for cleanup:

```
IF OBJECT_ID('dbo.T1', 'U') IS NOT NULL DROP TABLE dbo.T1;
```

Not Firing Triggers for Specific Statements

There's no built-in way to suppress a trigger for a particular statement. You can only disable a trigger completely using an ALTER TABLE DISABLE TRIGGER command. If you want to prevent a trigger from firing for a particular statement, you have to develop your own programmatic solution. You need to somehow signal the trigger that you don't want it to run its code.

One way to achieve this is by creating a temporary table with a particular name (for example, a GUID) in the calling batch. Remember that a local temporary table is visible only to the creating session, in the calling level, and all levels inner to it. The trigger can first check whether a temporary table with that particular name exists and, if it does, return. Otherwise, the code can continue running normally. Back in the calling batch, you can drop the temporary table when you don't want to prevent the trigger from running its code anymore.

To demonstrate this solution, first run the following code, which creates the table T1:

```
USE tempdb;
IF OBJECT_ID('dbo.T1', 'U') IS NOT NULL DROP TABLE dbo.T1;
CREATE TABLE dbo.T1(col1 INT);
```

Next, run the following code to create the trigger trg_T1_i:

```
CREATE TRIGGER trg_T1_i ON dbo.T1 FOR INSERT
AS

IF OBJECT_ID('tempdb..#do_not_fire_trg_T1_i') IS NOT NULL RETURN;

PRINT 'trg_T1_i in action...';
GO
```

The trigger uses the OBJECT_ID function to determine whether a temporary table called #do_not_fire_trg_T1_i exists. If the table does exist, it returns. If the table doesn't exist, the code continues running normally.

> **Note** Remember that temporary tables are created in tempdb. Make sure that when using the OBJECT_ID function to determine whether a temporary table exists, you database-qualify the object name. If you are connected to another database and invoke the function without the tempdb prefix, you'll always get a NULL back.

If you don't want to prevent the trigger's code from running, just submit your usual modifications. For example, run the following INSERT statement:

```
INSERT INTO dbo.T1 VALUES(1);
```

You will get the output:

```
trg_T1_i in action...
```

This output tells you that the trigger's code ran fully.

If you want to prevent the trigger's code from running in full, signal it by creating the temporary table with the expected name:

```
-- Setting signal
CREATE TABLE #do_not_fire_trg_T1_i(col1 INT);
INSERT INTO T1 VALUES(2);
-- Clearing signal
DROP TABLE #do_not_fire_trg_T1_i;
```

This solution works, but it does have an impact on tempdb's activity.

Another solution that you can implement uses the session's *context_info*. Logically, *context_info* is a VARBINARY(128) variable owned by the session. At any point in the session, you can change it by using the SET CONTEXT_INFO command or query it by using the CONTEXT_INFO function.

You can rely on the session's *context_info* to communicate between different levels of code—in our case, between the calling batch and the trigger. Think of *context_info* as a global session variable. For example, a batch can store a specific GUID in a section of the session's *context_info* when it wants to send a signal to the trigger. The trigger will look for that particular GUID to determine whether or not to continue running the code.

To generate the GUID that you will use as your signal, you can use the NEWID function, as in:

```
SELECT CAST(NEWID() AS BINARY(16));
```

The GUID is converted to a binary value because you want to store it in the session's *context_info*, which is binary. You invoke this code that generates a new GUID only once per trigger, and then specify that GUID explicitly in your trigger's code. When I invoked this code, I got the value *0x7EDBCEC5E165E749BF1261A655F52C48*. I will use this GUID in my examples. Of course, you should use the one you get. If you're using the session's *context_info* for multiple tasks (for example, to send signals to multiple different triggers), make sure that you dedicate a different section within it for each task. Whenever you set the value of *context_info*, make sure that you don't overwrite it completely. Rather, just substitute the relevant section within it dedicated to the task at hand.

For encapsulation purposes, I'll create three stored procedures: one that sets the signal, one that clears it, and one that returns it. Eventually I didn't create them as special procedures.

In our example, let's assume that we dedicate the first 16 bytes of the *context_info* (starting at position 1) for our trigger's signal.

Run the following code to create the *TrgSignal_Set* stored procedure, which sets the signal:

```
IF OBJECT_ID('dbo.TrgSignal_Set', 'P') IS NOT NULL
  DROP PROC dbo.TrgSignal_Set;
GO
CREATE PROC dbo.TrgSignal_Set
  @guid AS BINARY(16),
  @pos  AS INT
AS

DECLARE @ci AS VARBINARY(128);
SET @ci =
  ISNULL(SUBSTRING(CONTEXT_INFO(), 1, @pos-1),
         CAST(REPLICATE(0x00, @pos-1) AS VARBINARY(128)))
  + @guid +
  ISNULL(SUBSTRING(CONTEXT_INFO(), @pos+16, 128-16-@pos+1), 0x);
SET CONTEXT_INFO @ci;
GO
```

The stored procedure accepts two inputs: *@guid* is the 16-byte GUID used as the signal, and *@pos* is the starting position (byte number) in which you want to store the signal in *context_info* (in our case, 1). Notice that the procedure doesn't overwrite the whole value stored in *context_info*—just the relevant 16 bytes. It achieves this by querying the CONTEXT_INFO function. The code extracts the surrounding sections from the existing *context_info*, concatenates the signal between the preceding and following sections, and then stores the concatenated string back in the session's *context_info*.

In a similar manner, the following *TrgSignal_Clear* stored procedure clears the signal from the section dedicated to it by zeroing the relevant bits:

```
IF OBJECT_ID('dbo.TrgSignal_Clear', 'P') IS NOT NULL
  DROP PROC dbo.TrgSignal_Clear;
GO
CREATE PROC dbo.TrgSignal_Clear
  @pos  AS INT
AS

DECLARE @ci AS VARBINARY(128);
SET @ci =
  ISNULL(SUBSTRING(CONTEXT_INFO(), 1, @pos-1),
         CAST(REPLICATE(0x00, @pos-1) AS VARBINARY(128)))
  + CAST(REPLICATE(0x00, 16) AS VARBINARY(128)) +
  ISNULL(SUBSTRING(CONTEXT_INFO(), @pos+16, 128-16-@pos+1), 0x);
SET CONTEXT_INFO @ci;
GO
```

And finally, the following *TrgSignal_Get* stored procedure returns the signal by querying the CONTEXT_INFO function:

```
IF OBJECT_ID('dbo.TrgSignal_Get', 'P') IS NOT NULL
  DROP PROC dbo.TrgSignal_Get;
GO
CREATE PROC dbo.TrgSignal_Get
  @guid AS BINARY(16) OUTPUT,
  @pos  AS INT
AS

SET @guid = SUBSTRING(CONTEXT_INFO(), @pos, 16);
GO
```

Now you can alter the trg_T1_i trigger to look for the signal in the session's *context_info* instead of using the temporary table technique:

```
ALTER TRIGGER trg_T1_i ON dbo.T1 FOR INSERT
AS

DECLARE @signal AS BINARY(16);
EXEC dbo.TrgSignal_Get
  @guid = @signal OUTPUT,
  @pos  = 1;
```

```
IF @signal = 0x7EDBCEC5E165E749BF1261A655F52C48 RETURN;

PRINT 'trg_T1_i in action...';
GO
```

To test the trigger, first issue an INSERT statement without setting the signal:

```
INSERT INTO dbo.T1 VALUES(1);
```

The trigger's code runs in full, and you get the following output:

```
trg_T1_i in action...
```

To prevent the trigger's code from firing, set the signal:

```
EXEC dbo.TrgSignal_Set
  @guid = 0x7EDBCEC5E165E749BF1261A655F52C48,
  @pos = 1;
```

Now issue an INSERT statement:

```
INSERT INTO T1 VALUES(2);
```

You get no output, which indicates that the trigger got the signal and aborted.

When you want to clear the signal, issue the following code:

```
EXEC dbo.TrgSignal_Clear @pos = 1;
```

Now that the signal is cleared, issue an INSERT statement:

```
INSERT INTO T1 VALUES(3);
```

The trigger's code runs in full again, producing the following output:

```
trg_T1_i in action...
```

When you're done, run the following code for cleanup:

```
USE tempdb;
IF OBJECT_ID('dbo.T1' , 'U') IS NOT NULL
  DROP TABLE dbo.T1;
IF OBJECT_ID('dbo.TrgSignal_Set', 'P') IS NOT NULL
  DROP PROC dbo.TrgSignal_Set;
IF OBJECT_ID('dbo.TrgSignal_Clear', 'P') IS NOT NULL
  DROP PROC dbo.TrgSignal_Clear;
IF OBJECT_ID('dbo.TrgSignal_Get', 'P') IS NOT NULL
  DROP PROC dbo.TrgSignal_Get;
```

Nesting and Recursion

SQL Server supports both nesting and recursion of triggers. Nesting of triggers takes place when a statement issued from one trigger causes another trigger to fire. Recursion takes place when a trigger ends up triggering itself, either directly or through a series of other triggers.

Nesting of triggers is controlled at the server level via the *'nested triggers'* server configuration option and is turned on by default. Recursion of triggers is controlled at the database level via the RECURSIVE_TRIGGERS database option and is turned off by default. Suppose that you want to allow trigger recursion in a database called HR. You would use the following code:

```
ALTER DATABASE HR SET RECURSIVE_TRIGGERS ON;
```

Recursion in general needs a termination check to stop the recursion from going on forever. With triggers, of course, recursion won't go on forever because SQL Server has a hard-coded limit of 32 nesting levels of routines. However, when you reach that limit, the attempt to fire the 33rd trigger instance will break and all activity will be rolled back. Remember that triggers also fire for zero affected rows. If within the trigger you issue a modification that fires itself recursively, and you have no termination check, the trigger will continue firing recursively until it breaks the nesting limit. In short, make sure that you introduce a recursion termination check where you first verify whether you really need to issue a modification.

For example, suppose that you have a table called dbo.Employees in the HR database. You want to write a trigger that will, upon a deletion of employees, delete direct subordinates of the deleted employees. You want the trigger to fire recursively so that all subordinates of the deleted employees in all levels will be deleted. The code for such a trigger involves a simple join between *deleted* and the Employees table. As the recursion termination check, you can abort the trigger as soon as you cannot find any rows in *deleted*. The result of this approach is that as soon as the previous invocation of the trigger deletes no employees, the trigger aborts and recursion stops. Here's an example of what such a trigger might look like:

```
CREATE TRIGGER trg_Employees_d ON dbo.Employees FOR DELETE
AS

IF NOT EXISTS(SELECT * FROM deleted) RETURN; -- recursion termination check

DELETE E
FROM dbo.Employees AS E
  JOIN deleted AS M
    ON E.mgrid = M.empid;
GO
```

Remember that if a constraint defined on the table rejects a modification, the trigger will not have a chance to fire. This would be the case for this trigger if you had a self-referencing foreign key defined on the *mgrid* column pointing to the *empid* column. Such a foreign key will reject any attempt to delete an employee who has subordinates, and the trigger will not have a chance to fire. To allow the trigger to fire, you would have to remove or disable the foreign key. But then you would need to enforce referential integrity with your own code—for example, by using other triggers. There are simple ways to handle the task while still enforcing referential integrity with constraints, such as by using a recursive query within the trigger. I used this example only for illustration purposes.

UPDATE and COLUMNS_UPDATED

When writing a trigger for an UPDATE statement, you sometimes want to react to the change only if certain columns were modified. For example, if you want to reject an attempt to modify a primary key value, you want to react only if the primary key column was specified as the target column in the SET clause of the triggering UPDATE statement. SQL Server gives you two tools that allow you to identify whether certain columns were modified—the UPDATE predicate and the COLUMNS_UPDATED function.

The UPDATE predicate accepts a column name as input and returns TRUE if the input column was specified in the SET clause of the triggering UPDATE statement. For example, to check whether a column called *empid* was modified, you would use the following:

```
IF UPDATE(empid) …
```

The UPDATE predicate returns TRUE for any column if you use it in an INSERT trigger.

The COLUMNS_UPDATED function returns a binary string with a bit for each column. You typically use it when you need to inspect multiple columns and you don't want to specify the UPDATE predicate many times. A bit representing a column will be turned on (1) if the column was modified and off (0) if it wasn't. The bytes within the string are organized from left to right—that is, the leftmost byte represents the first 8 columns (columns with ordinal positions 1 through 8), the second byte from the left represents the next 8 columns (columns with ordinal positions 9 through 16), and so on. Within each byte, the bits are organized from right to left—that is, the rightmost bit in the leftmost byte represents the first column, the second bit from the right represents the second column, and so on.

This organization of the bits might seem strange, but in practice, it makes a lot of sense. To check whether a certain column was modified, you need to use the bitwise AND (&) operator between the bitmap returned by COLUMNS_UPDATED and your own bitmask, which contains only the relevant bits turned on. However, bitwise operators in SQL Server require integer inputs (or inputs that can be implicitly converted to integers). COLUMNS_UPDATED might be longer than eight bytes (the size of the largest supported integer—BIGINT). In that case, you would need to extract portions of the return value of COLUMNS_UPDATED using the SUBSTRING function. And for the SUBSTRING function, you specify an offset from the left of the input string. Thus, it's convenient that the bytes are organized from left to right.

For example, suppose that you want to isolate the byte containing the bit that represents a column with an ordinal position @i. The byte number (from the left) holding the relevant bit is this: *(@i – 1) / 8 + 1*. To extract that byte, you would use the following expression:

```
SUBSTRING(COLUMNS_UPDATED(),(@i - 1) / 8 + 1, 1)
```

As for the mask that you need to prepare for checking whether a certain bit is turned on, you generate it by raising 2 to the power that is one less than the bit position within the byte ($2^{bitpos-1}$). The expression calculating the bit position from the right within the byte (*bitpos*) for a column with an ordinal position $@i$ is the following: $(@i - 1) \% 8 + 1$. So the expression generating the mask would be this: $POWER(2, (@i - 1) \% 8)$. To check whether that bit is actually turned on, you perform a bitwise AND (&) operation between the relevant byte and your mask. If the result is greater than zero, that bit is turned on. Here's the full test:

```
IF SUBSTRING(COLUMNS_UPDATED(),(@i - 1) / 8 + 1, 1) & POWER(2,(@i-1) % 8) > 0
```

As a more tangible example, run the following code to create a table called T1 with 100 columns in addition to the key column, and query that table:

```
USE tempdb;
IF OBJECT_ID('dbo.T1', 'U') IS NOT NULL DROP TABLE dbo.T1;
GO

DECLARE @cmd AS NVARCHAR(4000), @i AS INT;

SET @cmd =
  N'CREATE TABLE dbo.T1(keycol INT NOT NULL IDENTITY PRIMARY KEY';

SET @i = 1;
WHILE @i <= 100
BEGIN
  SET @cmd =
    @cmd + N',col' + CAST(@i AS nvarchar(10)) +
    N' INT NOT NULL DEFAULT 0';
  SET @i = @i + 1;
END

SET @cmd = @cmd + N');'

EXEC sp_executesql @cmd;

INSERT INTO dbo.T1 DEFAULT VALUES;

SELECT * FROM T1;
```

This produces the following output, shown here in abbreviated form:

keycol	col1	col2	col3	...	col198	col199	col100
1	0	0	0		0	0	0

Suppose that you need to write an UPDATE trigger that identifies which columns were modified (or more accurately, which columns were specified as the target for the modification in the SET clause of the UPDATE statement). For the sake of our example, our trigger simply returns the set of modified columns to show that it could identify them. Run the following code to create the trg_T1_u_identify_updated_columns trigger, which achieves this task:

```
CREATE TRIGGER trg_T1_u_identify_updated_columns ON dbo.T1 FOR UPDATE
AS
SET NOCOUNT ON;
```

```
DECLARE @parent_object_id AS INT =
  (SELECT parent_object_id
   FROM sys.objects
   WHERE object_id = @@PROCID);

WITH UpdatedColumns(column_id) AS
(
  SELECT n
  FROM dbo.Nums
  WHERE n <=
    -- count of columns in trigger's parent table
    (SELECT COUNT(*)
     FROM sys.columns
     WHERE object_id = @parent_object_id)
    -- bit corresponding to nth column is turned on
    AND (SUBSTRING(COLUMNS_UPDATED(),(n - 1) / 8 + 1, 1))
        & POWER(2, (n - 1) % 8) > 0
)
SELECT C.name AS updated_column
FROM sys.columns AS C
  JOIN UpdatedColumns AS U
    ON C.column_id = U.column_id
WHERE object_id = @parent_object_id
ORDER BY U.column_id;
GO
```

The trigger stores the object ID of the parent table in a variable called *@parent_object_id*. The trigger then defines a CTE called *UpdatedColumns* that represents the set of column IDs of the columns that were modified. The CTE code uses the auxiliary table Nums that I described in Chapter 2, "User-Defined Functions." Recall that Nums contains a sequence of consecutive integers starting with 1. The CTE code returns from Nums all numbers that are smaller than or equal to the maximum column ID in the trigger's parent table, and that represent IDs of columns that were modified. Finally, the outer query joins *UpdatedColumns* with *sys.columns* to return the names of the modified columns.

To test the trigger, issue the following UPDATE statement:

```
UPDATE dbo.T1
  SET col4 = 2, col8 = 2, col90 = 2, col6 = 2
WHERE keycol = 1;
```

When you're done, run the following code for cleanup:

```
IF OBJECT_ID('dbo.T1', 'U') IS NOT NULL DROP TABLE dbo.T1;
```

Auditing Example

SQL Server 2008 introduces a feature called SQL Server Audit that provides built-in auditing capabilities based on another new feature called Extended Events. These technologies are covered in Chapter 15, "Tracking Access and Changes to Data." But if you need to develop an auditing solution that is supported on earlier versions of SQL Server as well—or for whatever reason you can't or prefer not to use SQL Server Audit—you can develop your own auditing solution by using triggers.

In the previous example, in which I discussed the COLUMNS_UPDATED function, I provided a technique to identify which columns appeared as the target for the modification in the SET clause of the triggering UPDATE statement. You might want to use that technique for auditing. However, you might want to audit actual changes in column values and not just the fact that a column was a target of a modification. To demonstrate the technique that will allow you to achieve such auditing, first run the following code creating the tables T1 and T1_Audit:

```
SET NOCOUNT ON;
USE tempdb;

IF OBJECT_ID('dbo.T1', 'U') IS NOT NULL DROP TABLE dbo.T1;
IF OBJECT_ID('dbo.T1Audit', 'U') IS NOT NULL DROP TABLE dbo.T1Audit;

CREATE TABLE dbo.T1
(
  keycol INT NOT NULL PRIMARY KEY,
  intcol INT NULL,
  varcharcol VARCHAR(10) NULL
);

CREATE TABLE dbo.T1Audit
(
  lsn     INT       NOT NULL IDENTITY PRIMARY KEY, -- log serial number
  keycol  INT       NOT NULL,
  colname sysname   NOT NULL,
  oldval  SQL_VARIANT NULL,
  newval  SQL_VARIANT NULL
);
```

Run the following code to create the trigger trg_T1_U_Audit, which records audit information about updates against T1 in T1Audit:

```
CREATE TRIGGER trg_T1_u_audit ON dbo.T1 FOR UPDATE
AS

-- If 0 affected rows, do nothing
IF NOT EXISTS(SELECT * FROM inserted) RETURN;

INSERT INTO dbo.T1Audit(keycol, colname, oldval, newval)
  SELECT *
  FROM (SELECT I.keycol, colname,
          CASE colname
            WHEN N'intcol' THEN CAST(D.intcol AS SQL_VARIANT)
            WHEN N'varcharcol' THEN CAST(D.varcharcol AS SQL_VARIANT)
          END AS oldval,
          CASE colname
            WHEN N'intcol' THEN CAST(I.intcol AS SQL_VARIANT)
            WHEN N'varcharcol' THEN CAST(I.varcharcol AS SQL_VARIANT)
          END AS newval
```

```
          FROM inserted AS I
            JOIN deleted AS D
              ON I.keycol = D.keycol
            CROSS JOIN
              (SELECT N'intcol' AS colname
               UNION ALL SELECT N'varcharcol') AS C) AS D
  WHERE oldval <> newval
    OR (oldval IS NULL AND newval IS NOT NULL)
    OR (oldval IS NOT NULL AND newval IS NULL);
GO
```

The trigger's code first checks whether zero rows were affected by the triggering UPDATE statement. If that is the case, it aborts. There's nothing to audit if nothing changed.

The code then uses a query that joins *inserted* and *deleted* by matching their *keycol* values. The query uses an unpivoting technique to rotate each column value from both *inserted* and *deleted* to its own row.

The query filters only rows where the new value is different than the old value, taking NULLs into consideration as well. An INSERT statement inserts the result of the query into the audit table.

To test the audit trigger, first insert a few rows to T1:

```
INSERT INTO dbo.T1(keycol, intcol, varcharcol) VALUES
  (1, 10, 'A'), (2, 20, 'B'), (3, 30, 'C');
```

Then issue the following UPDATE:

```
UPDATE dbo.T1
  SET varcharcol = varcharcol + 'X',
      intcol = 40 - intcol
WHERE keycol < 3;
```

Query the table T1:

```
SELECT * FROM dbo.T1;
```

This generates the following output:

```
keycol       intcol      varcharcol
----------- ----------- ----------
1            30          AX
2            20          BX
3            30          C
```

Query the table T1Audit:

```
SELECT * FROM dbo.T1Audit;
```

This generates the following output:

```
lsn  keycol  colname      oldval  newval
----  -------  -----------  -------  -------
1    2       varcharcol   B       BX
2    1       intcol       10      30
3    1       varcharcol   A       AX
```

As you can see, only column values that actually changed were audited.

> **Tip** Suppose that your trigger performs an integrity check and issues a rollback if the integrity rule is violated. And suppose that you still want to audit the attempt even though you're rolling it back. Of course, a rollback issued after the auditing activity will also roll back the auditing activity. On the other hand, if the rollback is issued before the auditing activity, *inserted* and *deleted* will be empty after the rollback, and you'll be left with no data to audit.
>
> You can use table variables to help resolve this situation. Table variables—like any variables—are not affected by a rollback because they are not considered part of an external transaction. Upon detection of the integrity rule violation, copy the contents of *inserted* and *deleted* into your own table variables; issue the rollback; and then, in a new transaction within the trigger, audit that data.

When you're done, run the following code for cleanup:

```
IF OBJECT_ID('dbo.T1', 'U') IS NOT NULL DROP TABLE dbo.T1;
IF OBJECT_ID('dbo.T1Audit', 'U') IS NOT NULL DROP TABLE dbo.T1Audit;
```

INSTEAD OF Triggers

INSTEAD OF triggers fire instead of the original modification that was issued against the target object. The concept is a bit tricky: these are not BEFORE triggers that fire before the original statement actually runs; rather, they run instead of it. The original statement never reaches the target object. Rather, the trigger's code replaces it. If the trigger is supposed to apply some integrity check and the modification passes the check, you will need to write your own code that "resubmits" the original activity. You can do so by querying the *inserted* or *deleted* table. Note that in an INSTEAD OF trigger, *inserted* and *deleted* hold the data that was supposed to be changed, as opposed to holding the data that actually changed.

If you don't take any course of action in an INSTEAD OF trigger, the original change simply evaporates. If you're fond of practical jokes, create an INSTEAD OF INSERT, UPDATE, DELETE trigger on some table where the trigger doesn't perform any activity. The trigger's body still needs some code within it to be valid, so declare a variable or issue any other statement that has no visibility. Now wait. It can be really perplexing for people who try to issue a modification against the table when their attempt has no effect whatsoever on the data. Of course, I must add the caution: *Do not do this in production*. You can do this as a puzzle to test your colleagues—create a table with such a trigger and ask them to figure out why changes do not have any effect.

Unlike AFTER triggers, INSTEAD OF triggers can be created on views, not just tables. You can create only one such trigger for each statement type on each object.

INSTEAD OF triggers do not support direct recursion. A simple form of direct recursion is when some trigger trg1_insteadof issues an action that would cause trg1_insteadof to fire again. A more complicated form of direct recursion is when some INSTEAD OF trigger trg1_ insteadof issues an action that causes some AFTER trigger trg2_after to fire. The second trigger issues an action that would cause trg1_insteadof to fire again. Note that SQL Server 2008 can silently fail to fire the trigger recursively for some forms of direct recursion of INSTEAD OF triggers, OR it can produce an error on other forms of recursion.

INSTEAD OF triggers do support indirect recursion. Indirect recursion happens when some INSTEAD OF trigger trg1_insteadof issues an action that causes another INSTEAD OF trigger trg2_insteadof to fire. The second trigger issues an action that causes the first trigger trg1_ insteadof to fire again.

One of the nice things about INSTEAD OF triggers is that they fire before constraints are checked. This means that you can identify activities that would normally fail on a constraint violation and replace them with code that will not fail. For example, a multirow insert that attempts to introduce a duplicate key would normally be rolled back completely because the whole insert is considered a transaction. If you want to allow the rows that do not introduce duplicate keys to be inserted, and you can't change the source code, you can create an INSTEAD OF trigger to insert into the table only rows from *inserted* with distinct keys not already in the table. Another option is to specify the IGNORE_DUP_KEY option when creating the index.

INSTEAD OF triggers can also be used to circumvent limitations of modifications against views. I described those limitations in Chapter 1, "Views." For example, you're not allowed to update a column in a view that is a result of a calculation. With an INSTEAD OF trigger, you can reverse-engineer such a modification and issue a modification to the underlying table.

The following sections demonstrate a few scenarios where INSTEAD OF triggers can come in handy.

Per-Row Triggers

Suppose that you have a table with an AFTER trigger that works well only for single-row modifications and breaks for multirow ones. You need to support multirow modifications, but you're not allowed to modify the trigger's code. Maybe the code was developed by a third party with the ENCRYPTION option and you don't have access to the source code. Or maybe the trigger was created by another developer and you're not allowed to change it.

To demonstrate an example for a trigger that would work well only for single-row modifications, first run the following code, which creates the table T1:

```
USE tempdb;
IF OBJECT_ID('dbo.T1', 'U') IS NOT NULL DROP TABLE dbo.T1;

CREATE TABLE dbo.T1
(
  keycol  INT NOT NULL PRIMARY KEY,
  datacol INT NOT NULL
);
```

Run the following code to create an AFTER INSERT trigger called trg_T1_i on T1:

```
CREATE TRIGGER trg_T1_i ON T1 AFTER INSERT
AS

DECLARE @msg AS VARCHAR(100);
SET @msg = 'Key: '
  + CAST((SELECT keycol FROM inserted) AS VARCHAR(10)) + ' inserted.';
PRINT @msg;
GO
```

The trigger constructs a message with the *keycol* value of the row that was inserted and prints it. It uses a subquery to fetch the *keycol* value from *inserted*.

If you insert a single row to the table, the trigger works well:

```
INSERT INTO dbo.T1(keycol, datacol) VALUES(1, 10);
```

You get the following output:

```
Key: 1 inserted.
```

However, when you issue a multirow insert, the trigger fails:

```
INSERT INTO dbo.T1(keycol, datacol) VALUES
  (2, 20), (3, 30), (4, 40);
```

The trigger produces the following error:

```
Server: Msg 512, Level 16, State 1, Procedure trg_T1_i, Line 7
Subquery returned more than 1 value. This is not permitted when the subquery follows =, !=,
<, <= , >, >= or when the subquery is used as an expression.
The statement has been terminated.
```

The error was generated because a subquery that was used where a scalar value was expected produced multiple values. Assuming that you're not allowed to alter the trigger's code, you can tackle the problem by creating an INSTEAD OF INSERT trigger. You can use the technique I showed earlier to iterate through the rows in *inserted* to collect the values from each row and issue a single row insert for each source row against the target table.

Each insert causes a different instance of the AFTER trigger to fire, but it fires for one row at a time. Run the following code to create such an INSTEAD OF trigger:

```
CREATE TRIGGER trg_T1_ioi_perrow ON dbo.T1 INSTEAD OF INSERT
AS

DECLARE @rc AS INT =
  (SELECT COUNT(*) FROM (SELECT TOP (2) * FROM inserted) AS D);

IF @rc = 0 RETURN;

IF @rc = 1
  INSERT INTO dbo.T1 SELECT * FROM inserted;
ELSE
BEGIN
  DECLARE @keycol AS INT, @datacol AS INT;
  DECLARE @Cinserted CURSOR;

  SET @Cinserted = CURSOR FAST_FORWARD FOR
    SELECT keycol, datacol FROM inserted;

  OPEN @Cinserted;

  FETCH NEXT FROM @Cinserted INTO @keycol, @datacol;
  WHILE @@fetch_status = 0
  BEGIN
    INSERT INTO dbo.T1(keycol, datacol) VALUES(@keycol, @datacol);
    FETCH NEXT FROM @Cinserted INTO @keycol, @datacol;
  END
END
GO
```

The trigger's code uses the technique I described earlier to apply a course of action that depends on the number of affected rows, only this time using a cursor to iterate through the rows in *inserted*. If zero rows were affected, the trigger exits. If one row was affected, the trigger inserts the row from *inserted* into T1, causing the AFTER trigger to fire for that row. If multiple rows were affected, the trigger uses a cursor to iterate through the rows in *inserted* one at a time, collecting the values from the current row in each iteration, and it then inserts a row to T1 with those values. As a result, the AFTER trigger fires once for each row.

To test the trigger, first issue the following INSERT statement, which inserts a single row to T1:

```
INSERT INTO dbo.T1(keycol, datacol) VALUES(5, 50);
```

You get the following output:

```
Key: 5 inserted.
```

Try inserting multiple rows using a single INSERT statement:

```
INSERT INTO dbo.T1(keycol, datacol) VALUES
  (6, 60), (7, 70), (8, 80);
```

The statement runs successfully, producing the following output:

```
Key: 6 inserted.
Key: 7 inserted.
Key: 8 inserted.
```

When you're done, run the following code for cleanup:

```
IF OBJECT_ID('dbo.T1', 'U') IS NOT NULL DROP TABLE dbo.T1;
```

Used with Views

The following example demonstrates how to use an INSTEAD OF TRIGGER to support UPDATE statements against a view that would have not been supported otherwise.

Suppose that you have a table with order details and a view that aggregates order detail quantities per order. Run the following code to create the OrderDetails table, populate it with sample data, and create the OrderTotals view, which calculates the sum of the quantity for each order:

```
USE tempdb;
IF OBJECT_ID('dbo.OrderTotals', 'V') IS NOT NULL
  DROP VIEW dbo.OrderTotals;
IF OBJECT_ID('dbo.OrderDetails', 'U') IS NOT NULL
  DROP TABLE dbo.OrderDetails;
GO

CREATE TABLE dbo.OrderDetails
(
  oid  INT NOT NULL,
  pid INT NOT NULL,
  qty INT NOT NULL,
  PRIMARY KEY(oid, pid)
);

INSERT INTO dbo.OrderDetails(oid, pid, qty) VALUES
  (10248, 1, 10),
  (10248, 2, 20),
  (10248, 3, 30),
  (10249, 1,  5),
  (10249, 2, 10),
  (10249, 3, 15),
  (10250, 1, 20),
  (10250, 2, 20),
  (10250, 3, 20);
GO

CREATE VIEW dbo.OrderTotals
AS

SELECT oid, SUM(qty) AS totalqty
FROM dbo.OrderDetails
GROUP BY oid;
GO
```

Suppose that you want to allow updating the *totalqty* column and distribute the new value between the order details of the affected order by the same proportions that they had before the update. The following trigger achieves this task:

```
CREATE TRIGGER trg_OrderTotals_iou ON dbo.OrderTotals INSTEAD OF UPDATE
AS

IF NOT EXISTS(SELECT * FROM inserted) RETURN;

IF UPDATE(oid)
BEGIN
  RAISERROR('Updates to the OrderID column are not allowed.', 16, 1);
  ROLLBACK TRAN;
  RETURN;
END;

WITH UPD_CTE AS
(
  SELECT qty, ROUND(1.*OD.qty / D.totalqty * I.totalqty, 0) AS newqty
  FROM dbo.OrderDetails AS OD
    JOIN inserted AS I
      ON OD.oid = I.oid
    JOIN deleted AS D
      ON I.oid = D.oid
)
UPDATE UPD_CTE
  SET qty = newqty;
GO
```

The trigger's code exits if no rows were updated. It then checks whether there was an attempt to update the order ID (*oid* column). If there was such an attempt, the trigger generates an error and rolls back the activity. The trigger then creates a common table expression (CTE) that joins *inserted*, *deleted*, and the OrderDetails table. The *deleted* view holds the value of *totalqty* before the update, and *inserted* holds the value after the update. The OrderDetails table is added to the join to gain access to the original quantity of each order detail row, and it also ends up being the actual target of the modification. The CTE's query calculates the portion each order detail row should get based on the original proportions (original quantity / original total quantity × new total quantity, rounded). The outer UPDATE statement updates the *qty* column in OrderDetails with the newly calculated quantity.

Run the following code to examine the contents of the table and the view before applying an update:

```
SELECT oid, pid, qty FROM dbo.OrderDetails;
SELECT oid, totalqty FROM dbo.OrderTotals;
```

This generates the following output:

```
oid          pid          qty
-----------  -----------  -----------
10248        1            10
10248        2            20
```

```
10248        3            30
10249        1            5
10249        2            10
10249        3            15
10250        1            20
10250        2            20
10250        3            20


oid          totalqty
-----------  -----------
10248        60
10249        30
10250        60
```

Issue the following UPDATE statement, which doubles the total quantity of all orders:

```
UPDATE dbo.OrderTotals
  SET totalqty = totalqty * 2;
```

Query the table and view again after the change:

```
SELECT oid, pid, qty FROM dbo.OrderDetails;
SELECT oid, totalqty FROM dbo.OrderTotals;
```

This generates the following output:

```
oid          pid          qty
-----------  -----------  -----------
10248        1            20
10248        2            40
10248        3            60
10249        1            10
10249        2            20
10249        3            30
10250        1            40
10250        2            40
10250        3            40


oid          totalqty
-----------  -----------
10248        120
10249        60
10250        120
```

When you're done, run the following code for cleanup:

```
IF OBJECT_ID('dbo.OrderTotals', 'V') IS NOT NULL
  DROP VIEW dbo.OrderTotals;
IF OBJECT_ID('dbo.OrderDetails', 'U') IS NOT NULL
  DROP TABLE dbo.OrderDetails;
```

Automatic Handling of Sequences

Suppose that you maintain your own custom sequence instead of relying on the IDENTITY column property to generate numbers that will be used as keys in a table called T1. You achieve this by holding a value in a table called Sequence; the value represents the last assigned sequence value. Whenever you need a new sequence value, you increment the value in the Sequence table and use it as the new key in T1.

Run the following code to create the table T1:

```
SET NOCOUNT ON;
USE tempdb;

IF OBJECT_ID('dbo.T1', 'U') IS NOT NULL DROP TABLE dbo.T1;
CREATE TABLE dbo.T1
(
  keycol  INT NOT NULL PRIMARY KEY,
  datacol VARCHAR(10) NOT NULL
);
```

Then run the following code to create and initialize the Sequence table:

```
IF OBJECT_ID('dbo.Sequence', 'U') IS NOT NULL
  DROP TABLE dbo.Sequence;
GO
CREATE TABLE dbo.Sequence(val INT NOT NULL);
INSERT INTO dbo.Sequence VALUES(0);
```

When you need a new sequence value, you can issue the following code:

```
DECLARE @key AS INT;
UPDATE dbo.Sequence SET @key = val = val + 1;
```

This code declares a local variable called *@key*, issues a specialized UPDATE statement that increments the *val* column value by one, and stores the result in the variable *@key*. You're effectively both updating and selecting the sequence value at the same time in an atomic operation. Suppose that you want to automate the process of assigning keys to new rows using a trigger, and you also want to support multirow inserts. An AFTER trigger is not a good choice because the primary key will reject an attempt to insert multiple rows where the key values are not specified.

Remember that an INSTEAD OF trigger is fired instead of the original modification; therefore, such a trigger will allow a multirow insert where the keys weren't specified. All rows will get the default value *0*, and the trigger can generate a different key for each row. The trigger then inserts rows into T1 with newly generated keys, while the rest of the columns (only *datacol* in our case) can be grabbed from *inserted*.

Here's the code of the INSTEAD OF trigger that will achieve the task—generating new keys and inserting them along with the other attributes from the original INSERT statement:

```
CREATE TRIGGER trg_T1_ioi_assign_key ON dbo.T1 INSTEAD OF INSERT
AS

DECLARE
  @rc  AS INT = (SELECT COUNT(*) FROM inserted),
  @key AS INT;

IF @rc = 0 RETURN; -- if 0 affected rows, exit

-- Update sequence
UPDATE dbo.Sequence SET @key = val, val = val + @rc;

INSERT INTO dbo.T1(keycol, datacol)
  SELECT @key + ROW_NUMBER() OVER(ORDER BY (SELECT 0)), datacol
  FROM inserted;
GO
```

The trigger's code first checks whether zero rows were loaded. If that's the case, it exits. The code then uses an UPDATE statement to assign the current value of the sequence to the variable @key and increment the sequence value by the number of affected rows—that is, it acquires a whole block of sequence values in one shot. Next, the trigger issues an INSERT statement that loads all rows from *inserted* into T1, generating new key values by adding a row number value to @key. The ORDER BY clause of the ROW_NUMBER function has no effect on the assignment order of the row numbers. The value of the constant will be the same in all rows anyway. The reason for using this ORDER BY clause is that it's not optional in the ROW_NUMBER function. Of course, if you want to assign keys based on some specific order, specify the relevant attribute in the ORDER BY clause.

To test the trigger, issue the following INSERT statement:

```
INSERT INTO dbo.T1(datacol)
  VALUES('G'),('U'),('I'),('N'),('N'),('E'),('S'),('S');
```

Query T1:

```
SELECT keycol, datacol FROM dbo.T1;
```

This generates the following output:

```
keycol       datacol
-----------  ----------
1            G
2            U
3            I
4            N
5            N
6            E
7            S
8            S
```

When you're done, run the following code for cleanup:

```
IF OBJECT_ID('dbo.T1', 'U') IS NOT NULL DROP TABLE dbo.T1;
IF OBJECT_ID('dbo.Sequence', 'U') IS NOT NULL DROP TABLE dbo.Sequence;
```

DDL Triggers

DDL triggers allow you to respond to DDL events issued against the database server. You can use these triggers to roll back schema changes that don't meet rules that you want to enforce, audit schema changes, or react to a schema change in a form that makes sense for your environment.

> **Note** SQL Server supports only AFTER triggers for DDL. If you want a trigger to reject the schema change that caused it to fire you must issue a ROLLBACK TRAN command in the trigger.

You can create DDL triggers either at the database level or at the server (instance) level. You can create those for particular DDL statements (for example, CREATE TABLE) or for statement groups (for example, DDL_DATABASE_LEVEL_EVENTS). Please consult SQL Server Books Online for the gory details about the hierarchy of statements and statement groups for which you can define DDL triggers.

Within the trigger, you can get information about the event that fired it via the EVENTDATA function. This function returns an XML value with the event information. For different types of statements, you will get different information from the EVENTDATA function. For example, here's the XML value returned by the EVENTDATA function for a CREATE TABLE statement:

```
<EVENT_INSTANCE>
  <EventType>CREATE_TABLE</EventType>
  <PostTime>2009-03-21T18:38:59.710</PostTime>
  <SPID>51</SPID>
  <ServerName>DOJO\SQL08</ServerName>
  <LoginName>DOJO\Gandalf</LoginName>
  <UserName>dbo</UserName>
  <DatabaseName>testdb</DatabaseName>
  <SchemaName>dbo</SchemaName>
  <ObjectName>T1</ObjectName>
  <ObjectType>TABLE</ObjectType>
  <TSQLCommand>
    <SetOptions ANSI_NULLS="ON" ANSI_NULL_DEFAULT="ON" ANSI_PADDING="ON" QUOTED_
IDENTIFIER="ON" ENCRYPTED="FALSE" />
    <CommandText>CREATE TABLE dbo.T1(col1 INT NOT NULL PRIMARY KEY);
</CommandText>
  </TSQLCommand>
</EVENT_INSTANCE>
```

As you can see, you get a lot of useful information about the event, including the event type, when it was posted, the server process ID of the session, the instance name, the login name, the user name, the database name, the schema name of the object, the object name, the object type, the state of SET options, and even the actual T-SQL statement that caused the trigger to fire.

You can query the event information from the XML value by using XQuery. To extract a particular attribute from the XML value, you use the following XQuery expression: *xml_value.value('(<path_to_element>)[1]',<sql_type>)*. *xml_value* can be a direct reference to the EVENTDATA*()* function or a variable to which you assigned the XML value returned by the function, and *<path_to_element>* is the path to the attribute you want to extract. That's about all you need to know about XML and XQuery to grab the attributes out of the XML value. All the rest is just code that implements the logic you want your trigger to apply.

In the following sections, I will provide examples of both database-level DDL triggers and server-level ones. I will provide examples for enforcing a DDL policy and auditing DDL events in case you decide to implement such tasks yourself with DDL triggers. But as I mentioned earlier, SQL Server 2008 has a new feature called SQL Server Audit that you can use to implement an audit solution. Also, SQL Server 2008 supports a new feature called Policy-Based Management that allows you to define policies from SQL Server Management Studio (SSMS). Some of those policies—specifically the ones that use an evaluation mode called On change: prevent—are implemented behind the scenes with DDL triggers.

Database-Level Triggers

Database-level DDL triggers allow you to react to database-level events, such as creating, altering, or dropping objects. Here's the syntax for the header of a database-level DDL trigger:

```
CREATE TRIGGER <trigger name>
  ON DATABASE
  FOR <one or more statements or statement groups>
```

You must be connected to the target database when creating the trigger.

In my examples, I will use a database called testdb, which you create by running the following code:

```
USE master;
IF DB_ID('testdb') IS NULL CREATE DATABASE testdb;
GO
USE testdb;
```

Suppose that you want to enforce a company policy in the testdb database that says that when you create a table you must define a primary key. You create the following trigger to achieve this task:

```
IF EXISTS(SELECT * FROM sys.triggers
          WHERE parent_class = 0 AND name = 'trg_create_table_with_pk')
  DROP TRIGGER trg_create_table_with_pk ON DATABASE;
GO
```

```
CREATE TRIGGER trg_create_table_with_pk ON DATABASE FOR CREATE_TABLE
AS

DECLARE @eventdata AS XML, @objectname AS NVARCHAR(257),
  @msg AS NVARCHAR(500);

SET @eventdata = EVENTDATA();
SET @objectname =
  + QUOTENAME(@eventdata.value('(/EVENT_INSTANCE/SchemaName)[1]', 'sysname'))
  + N'.' +
  QUOTENAME(@eventdata.value('(/EVENT_INSTANCE/ObjectName)[1]', 'sysname'));

IF COALESCE(
    OBJECTPROPERTY(OBJECT_ID(@objectname), 'TableHasPrimaryKey'),
    0) = 0
BEGIN
  SET @msg = N'Table ' + @objectname + ' does not contain a primary key.'
    + CHAR(10) + N'Table creation rolled back.';
  RAISERROR(@msg, 16, 1);
  ROLLBACK;
  RETURN;
END
GO
```

The trigger is naturally created for CREATE_TABLE statements. The trigger's code first
assigns the return XML value from the EVENTDATA function to a local variable called
@eventdata. The code then extracts the event attributes *SchemaName* and *ObjectName*,
using XQuery expressions, and it constructs a schema-qualified table name in the
@objectname variable. Finally, the code uses the OBJECTPROPERTY function to check
whether the table contains a primary key. If it doesn't, the code generates an error message
and rolls back the table creation.

To test the trigger, first try to create a table without a primary key:

```
IF OBJECT_ID('dbo.T', 'U') IS NOT NULL DROP TABLE dbo.T;
GO
CREATE TABLE dbo.T(col1 INT NOT NULL);
```

You get the following error:

```
Server: Msg 50000, Level 16, State 1, Procedure trg_create_table_with_pk, Line 19
Table [dbo].[T] does not contain a primary key.
Table creation rolled back.
Server: Msg 3609, Level 16, State 1, Line 1
The transaction ended in the trigger. The batch has been aborted.
```

Then try to create a table with a primary key. Your code will run successfully:

```
CREATE TABLE dbo.T(col1 INT NOT NULL PRIMARY KEY);
```

As I mentioned earlier, DDL triggers is one of the mechanisms in SQL Server 2008 that can
be used to audit DDL events. The trigger's implementation is straightforward: use XQuery

expressions to query the individual event attributes that you want to audit and insert them into the audit table. That's all there is to it. As an example, run the following code to create the AuditDDLEvents table and the trg_audit_ddl_events trigger:

```
IF OBJECT_ID('dbo.AuditDDLEvents', 'U') IS NOT NULL
  DROP TABLE dbo.AuditDDLEvents;
GO
CREATE TABLE dbo.AuditDDLEvents
(
  lsn              INT      NOT NULL IDENTITY,
  posttime         DATETIME NOT NULL,
  eventtype        sysname  NOT NULL,
  loginname        sysname  NOT NULL,
  schemaname       sysname  NOT NULL,
  objectname       sysname  NOT NULL,
  targetobjectname sysname  NULL,
  eventdata        XML      NOT NULL,
  CONSTRAINT PK_AuditDDLEvents PRIMARY KEY(lsn)
);
GO


IF EXISTS(SELECT * FROM sys.triggers
          WHERE parent_class = 0 AND name = 'trg_audit_ddl_events')
  DROP TRIGGER trg_audit_ddl_events  ON DATABASE;
GO
CREATE TRIGGER trg_audit_ddl_events ON DATABASE FOR DDL_DATABASE_LEVEL_EVENTS
AS

DECLARE @eventdata AS XML;
SET @eventdata = EVENTDATA();

INSERT INTO dbo.AuditDDLEvents(
  posttime, eventtype, loginname, schemaname,
  objectname, targetobjectname, eventdata)
  VALUES(
    @eventdata.value('(/EVENT_INSTANCE/PostTime)[1]',         'VARCHAR(23)'),
    @eventdata.value('(/EVENT_INSTANCE/EventType)[1]',        'sysname'),
    @eventdata.value('(/EVENT_INSTANCE/LoginName)[1]',        'sysname'),
    @eventdata.value('(/EVENT_INSTANCE/SchemaName)[1]',       'sysname'),
    @eventdata.value('(/EVENT_INSTANCE/ObjectName)[1]',       'sysname'),
    @eventdata.value('(/EVENT_INSTANCE/TargetObjectName)[1]', 'sysname'),
    @eventdata);
GO
```

The trigger is so simple that all it has is an assignment of the EVENTDATA value to a local XML variable and a single INSERT statement that inserts the event attributes into the audit table. Note that it also inserts the full XML value in case you want to query attributes that were not extracted individually.

To test the trigger, issue the following DDL events:

```
IF OBJECT_ID('dbo.T1', 'U') IS NOT NULL DROP TABLE dbo.T1;
CREATE TABLE dbo.T1(col1 INT NOT NULL PRIMARY KEY);
```

```
ALTER TABLE dbo.T1 ADD col2 INT NULL;
ALTER TABLE dbo.T1 ALTER COLUMN col2 INT NOT NULL;
CREATE NONCLUSTERED INDEX idx1 ON dbo.T1(col2);
```

Then query the audit table:

```
SELECT * FROM dbo.AuditDDLEvents;
```

This generates the following output, shown here in two parts because of page-width restrictions:

```
lsn   posttime                  eventtype       loginname       schemaname
----  ----------------------    -------------   -------------   -----------
1     2009-03-21 19:36:40.937   CREATE_TABLE    DOJO\Gandalf    dbo
2     2009-03-21 19:36:41.013   ALTER_TABLE     DOJO\Gandalf    dbo
3     2009-03-21 19:36:41.013   ALTER_TABLE     DOJO\Gandalf    dbo
4     2009-03-21 19:36:41.013   CREATE_INDEX    DOJO\Gandalf    dbo

lsn   objectname   targetobjectname   eventdata
----  -----------  -----------------  -------------------------------------------
1     T1           NULL               <EVENT_INSTANCE><EventType>CREATE_TABLE...
2     T1           NULL               <EVENT_INSTANCE><EventType>ALTER_TABLE<...
3     T1           NULL               <EVENT_INSTANCE><EventType>ALTER_TABLE<...
4     idx1         T1                 <EVENT_INSTANCE><EventType>CREATE_INDEX...
```

Of course, you will get different values in *posttime* and *loginname* attributes.

Suppose that you come to work one morning and realize that schema changes took place against a table called T1. You realize this after users keep calling you complaining that the application breaks. You ask around to see whether someone applied a schema change to T1 in the last 24 hours, but naturally everyone is silent, choosing to avoid self-incrimination. Fortunately (for you), you can query the audit table. You can even use an XQuery expression to extract event attributes that were not recorded individually. Here's the query that you would use:

```
SELECT posttime, eventtype, loginname,
  eventdata.value('(/EVENT_INSTANCE/TSQLCommand/CommandText)[1]', 'NVARCHAR(MAX)')
    AS tsqlcommand
FROM dbo.AuditDDLEvents
WHERE schemaname = N'dbo' AND N'T1' IN(objectname, targetobjectname)
  AND posttime > CURRENT_TIMESTAMP - 1
ORDER BY posttime;
```

This generates the following output, shown here in abbreviated form:

```
posttime                  eventtype       loginname       tsqlcommand
----------------------    -------------   -------------   ------------------------
2009-03-21 19:36:40.937   CREATE_TABLE    DOJO\Gandalf    CREATE TABLE dbo.T1(c...
2009-03-21 19:36:41.013   ALTER_TABLE     DOJO\Gandalf    ALTER TABLE dbo.T1 AD...
2009-03-21 19:36:41.013   ALTER_TABLE     DOJO\Gandalf    ALTER TABLE dbo.T1 AL...
2009-03-21 19:36:41.013   CREATE_INDEX    DOJO\Gandalf    CREATE NONCLUSTERED I...
```

Now you know exactly which schema changes took place and who submitted them—in some cases, you see that it was you who applied the change and that you suffered from a slight case of amnesia.

Caution XML quoting of certain characters creates a security problem. Hackers can inject XML elements through object names or even character strings in the statement that fires the trigger. For example, if you create a table called [>], the XML value returned by the EVENTDATA() function will have the object name: >, and the command text *CREATE TABLE [>](c int);*.

In the next example I'll demonstrate a DDL trigger defined for an event that is new in SQL Server 2008. In SQL Server 2005 you could define DDL triggers on events that were triggered by the formal DDL statements CREATE, ALTER, and DROP. However, stored procedures that performed DDL-like activities but didn't use formal DDL syntax were not covered by DDL triggers. SQL Server 2008 changes things in the sense that it introduces new events to cover stored procedure that perform DDL-like activities. You can find the full set of events that SQL Server 2008 supports in SQL Server Books Online. An example of a new event in SQL Server 2008 that is fired by a DDL-like stored procedure is the RENAME event, which fires when you execute the *sp_rename* procedure to rename an object or a column. Run the following code to create a trigger for the RENAME event that prints the source and target entity details:

```
IF EXISTS(SELECT * FROM sys.triggers
          WHERE parent_class = 0 AND name = 'trg_rename')
  DROP TRIGGER trg_rename  ON DATABASE;
GO
CREATE TRIGGER trg_rename ON DATABASE FOR RENAME
AS

DECLARE @eventdata AS XML = EVENTDATA();

DECLARE
  @SchemaName       AS SYSNAME =
    @eventdata.value('(/EVENT_INSTANCE/SchemaName)[1]', 'sysname'),
  @TargetObjectName AS SYSNAME =
    @eventdata.value('(/EVENT_INSTANCE/TargetObjectName)[1]', 'sysname'),
  @ObjectName       AS SYSNAME =
    @eventdata.value('(/EVENT_INSTANCE/ObjectName)[1]', 'sysname'),
  @NewObjectName    AS SYSNAME =
    @eventdata.value('(/EVENT_INSTANCE/NewObjectName)[1]', 'sysname');

DECLARE @msg AS NVARCHAR(1000) = N'RENAME event occurred.
SchemaName       : ' + @SchemaName + N'
TargetObjectName: ' + @TargetObjectName + N'
ObjectName       : ' + @ObjectName + N'
NewObjectName    : ' + @NewObjectName;

PRINT @msg;
GO
```

Run the following code to test the trigger:

```
IF OBJECT_ID('dbo.T1', 'U') IS NOT NULL DROP TABLE dbo.T1;
CREATE TABLE dbo.T1(col1 INT PRIMARY KEY);
EXEC sp_rename 'dbo.T1.col1', 'col2', 'COLUMN';
```

This generates the following output:

```
RENAME event occurred.
SchemaName       : dbo
TargetObjectName: T1
ObjectName       : col1
NewObjectName    : col2
```

When you're done, run the following code for cleanup:

```
USE testdb;

IF EXISTS(SELECT * FROM sys.triggers
          WHERE parent_class = 0 AND name = 'trg_create_table_with_pk')
  DROP TRIGGER trg_create_table_with_pk  ON DATABASE;

IF EXISTS(SELECT * FROM sys.triggers
          WHERE parent_class = 0 AND name = 'trg_audit_ddl_events')
  DROP TRIGGER trg_audit_ddl_events  ON DATABASE;

IF EXISTS(SELECT * FROM sys.triggers
          WHERE parent_class = 0 AND name = 'trg_rename')
  DROP TRIGGER trg_rename  ON DATABASE;

IF OBJECT_ID('dbo.AuditDDLEvents', 'U') IS NOT NULL
  DROP TABLE dbo.AuditDDLEvents;

IF OBJECT_ID('dbo.T1', 'U') IS NOT NULL DROP TABLE dbo.T1;

IF OBJECT_ID('dbo.T', 'U') IS NOT NULL DROP TABLE dbo.T;
```

Server-Level Triggers

Server-level DDL triggers can be defined for server-level events. Examples of such events are creation of databases, changes to logins, and so on. You develop server-level triggers in a similar manner to developing database-level ones. In the trigger's header, you specify the following: ON ALL SERVER instead of ON DATABASE.

For example, suppose that you want to audit CREATE, ALTER, and DROP statements for logins. Run the following code to create the AuditDDLLogins table and the trg_audit_ddl_logins trigger:

```
USE master;

IF OBJECT_ID('dbo.AuditDDLLogins', 'U') IS NOT NULL
  DROP TABLE dbo.AuditDDLLogins;

CREATE TABLE dbo.AuditDDLLogins
(
  lsn              INT      NOT NULL IDENTITY,
  posttime         DATETIME NOT NULL,
  eventtype        sysname  NOT NULL,
  loginname        sysname  NOT NULL,
```

```
  objectname       sysname  NOT NULL,
  logintype        sysname  NOT NULL,
  eventdata        XML      NOT NULL,
  CONSTRAINT PK_AuditDDLLogins PRIMARY KEY(lsn)
);
GO

IF EXISTS(SELECT * FROM sys.server_triggers
            WHERE name = 'trg_audit_ddl_logins')
  DROP TRIGGER trg_audit_ddl_logins ON ALL SERVER;
GO
CREATE TRIGGER trg_audit_ddl_logins ON ALL SERVER
  FOR DDL_LOGIN_EVENTS
AS
DECLARE @eventdata AS XML = EVENTDATA();

INSERT INTO master.dbo.AuditDDLLogins(
  posttime, eventtype, loginname,
  objectname, logintype, eventdata)
  VALUES(
    @eventdata.value('(/EVENT_INSTANCE/PostTime)[1]',   'VARCHAR(23)'),
    @eventdata.value('(/EVENT_INSTANCE/EventType)[1]',  'sysname'),
    @eventdata.value('(/EVENT_INSTANCE/LoginName)[1]',  'sysname'),
    @eventdata.value('(/EVENT_INSTANCE/ObjectName)[1]', 'sysname'),
    @eventdata.value('(/EVENT_INSTANCE/LoginType)[1]',  'sysname'),
    @eventdata);
GO
```

This audit trigger's code is almost identical to the audit trigger you created earlier; it just has different event attributes, which are relevant to login-related DDL events.

> **Caution** Note that this trigger suffers from the same security problem as before with characters that XML must quote. Try, for example, to create a login called *[l<gin]*, and you will find that the login name that appears in the audit table is *l<gin*.

To test the trigger, issue the following login-related statements for creating, altering, and dropping a login:

```
CREATE LOGIN login1 WITH PASSWORD = '6BAAA5FA-A8D4-469D-9713-3FFC6745513F';
ALTER LOGIN login1 WITH PASSWORD = 'E8A0D5A6-D7B7-4710-B06E-80558E08C8E0';
DROP LOGIN login1;
```

Next, query the audit table:

```
SELECT * FROM master.dbo.AuditDDLLogins;
```

This generates the following code:

```
lsn  posttime                 eventtype     loginname       objectname  logintype   eventdata
----  -----------------------  ------------  --------------  ----------  ----------  ---------
1     2009-03-22 08:16:28.520  CREATE_LOGIN  DOJO\Gandalf    login1      SQL Login   XML value
2     2009-03-22 08:16:28.660  ALTER_LOGIN   DOJO\Gandalf    login1      SQL Login   XML value
3     2009-03-22 08:16:29.173  DROP_LOGIN    DOJO\Gandalf    login1      SQL Login   XML value
```

When you're done, run the following code for cleanup:

```
IF EXISTS(SELECT * FROM sys.server_triggers
          WHERE name = 'trg_audit_ddl_logins')
  DROP TRIGGER trg_audit_ddl_logins ON ALL SERVER;

IF OBJECT_ID('dbo.AuditDDLLogins', 'U') IS NOT NULL
  DROP TABLE dbo.AuditDDLLogins;
```

Logon Triggers

Logon triggers allow you to react with procedural code when a user establishes a session against SQL Server. If in certain circumstances you want to reject the session, issue a ROLLBACK from the trigger's code. Similar to DDL triggers, also in logon triggers you can obtain information about the event by querying the XML value returned from the EVENTDATA function. The XML value contains the following information: the event type (LOGON), post time, server process ID (spid), server name, login name, login type, security identification number (SID), client host name, and an indication of whether the connection is pooled.

Note that logon triggers fire right before the session is actually established; therefore, all messages produced by the trigger's code, such as error messages or output of PRINT statements, are directed to the error log.

For example, assuming that your test SQL Server instance is defined with Mixed Mode Authentication, run the following code to create a SQL Server login called user1 and grant it with VIEW SERVER STATE permission:

```
USE master;

CREATE LOGIN user1
  WITH PASSWORD = '9500A9BA-E173-4A27-BA4A-B36DCD925877',
       CHECK_EXPIRATION = ON;

GRANT VIEW SERVER STATE TO user1;
```

Of course, if your instance is defined with Windows Authentication mode, you can run a similar test with a Windows account.

The task at hand is to create a logon trigger that rejects an attempt to establish a session if all of the following are true:

- The login name is user1.
- The login already has an open session.
- The time is peak time (>= 11:45, < 14:16).
- The new session is nonpooled.

Run the following code to create a trigger that achieves this task:

```
CREATE TRIGGER trg_logon_con_limit ON ALL SERVER
  WITH EXECUTE AS 'user1'
  FOR LOGON
AS
BEGIN
IF ORIGINAL_LOGIN()= 'user1'
    AND (SELECT COUNT(*)
         FROM sys.dm_exec_sessions
         WHERE is_user_process = 1
           AND original_login_name = 'user1') > 1
    AND CAST(SYSDATETIME() AS TIME) >= '11:45'
    AND CAST(SYSDATETIME() AS TIME) <  '14:16'
    AND EVENTDATA().value('(/EVENT_INSTANCE/IsPooled)[1]', 'INT') = 0
  ROLLBACK;
END;
GO
```

If you attempt to log on with user1 during peak time, SQL Server will reject your logon attempt.

When you're done, run the following code for cleanup:

```
DROP TRIGGER trg_logon_con_limit ON ALL SERVER;
DROP LOGIN user1;
```

CLR Triggers

As it does with other types of routines, SQL Server 2008 allows you to use a .NET language of your choice to develop common language runtime (CLR) triggers. This capability is especially useful when you want your routines to perform activity for which T-SQL is weak, such as complex calculations, procedural logic, or access to external resources. In this section, I will provide an example for a CLR trigger.

As an example, you will be provided with a DML trigger that audits the contents of the *inserted* and *deleted* tables to the Microsoft Windows application event log. Auditing to the Windows event log gives you similar functionality as auditing to a table variable—you still have the audited information, even if the transaction is later rolled back.

When I was first thinking about an example for a CLR trigger, I wanted to create a trigger that would send an e-mail message. But then I realized this would be a bad example. Remember that a trigger is part of the transaction, and resources are locked during the transaction. Depending on the action issued and isolation level used, locks can be held until the end of the transaction. Sending e-mail can take a while. Also, if you want to send an e-mail from a trigger, you should also be prepared for a variety of problems—for example, an SMTP or MAPI server could be stopped. The local event log should always be available or otherwise full, and writing to it is faster than sending e-mail. Keep in mind though, that writing to the local event log may still cause performance problems.

Note the importance of the previous paragraph. Because a trigger is part of a transaction, you should be very careful with the code you issue from the trigger; it should always run as fast as possible. I prefer to have only Transact-SQL statements in the body of a trigger. This way you have more control and you can test the performance more easily. Imagine that a performance bottleneck exists somewhere in the CLR trigger code, and you are a DBA with minimal CLR programming knowledge, or you simply don't have access to the code. There is not much that you can do.

Possible performance problems are not the only drawback of auditing in the local event log. The event log can get full, and the auditing trigger would not be able to write to it in such a case, so it would roll back the transaction. You can manually clear the log, but until the log is cleared you won't be able to modify the data. Another possibility would be that the trigger would clear the log, but then what's the purpose of auditing, if you simply recycle the previously audited information? I tried to mitigate this problem by limiting the auditing info to the first 200 characters only. Even this solution doesn't make much sense, because you could simply use the T-SQL command RAISERROR ... WITH LOG, which can accomplish the same task easily—the errors logged with RAISERROR are currently limited to 440 bytes. Writing to the event log, whether you use RAISERROR or CLR code, needs permissions of quite a high level. Also, as mentioned earlier, in SQL Server 2008 you can use the built-in SQL Server Audit feature to implement an audit solution. SQL Server Audit supports writing to the Windows Application event log as a target.

In short, my advice is to avoid developing triggers with CLR code. Still, I wanted to provide an example for a CLR trigger to demonstrate the technicalities involved, and to discuss the drawbacks of doing so.

The trigger writes to a resource external to the database. In Chapter 3, I explained how to set up the environment to allow external access to assemblies, and the security and stability issues involved. Make sure you go over that section first if you haven't done so already. To allow the trigger that is described in this section to run, you have two options:

- The less secure and therefore less recommended option is to set the TRUSTWORTHY option of the database to ON, and to create (or alter) the assembly with the EXTERNAL_ACCESS permission set (UNSAFE would be needed to write to a remote machine event log):

```
-- Database option TRUSTWORTHY needs to be ON for EXTERNAL_ACCESS
ALTER DATABASE CLRUtilities SET TRUSTWORTHY ON;
-- Alter assembly with PERMISSION_SET = EXTERNAL_ACCESS
USE CLRUtilities;
ALTER ASSEMBLY CLRUtilities
WITH PERMISSION_SET = EXTERNAL_ACCESS;
```

- As mentioned in Chapter 3, the more secure option is to sign the assembly with a strong name key file. Then run the following code to create an asymmetric key from the executable .dll file and a corresponding login with the EXTERNAL ACCESS (or UNSAFE) ASSEMBLY permission:

```
USE master;
CREATE ASYMMETRIC KEY CLRUtilitiesKey
  FROM EXECUTABLE FILE =
    'C:\CLRUtilities\CLRUtilities\bin\Debug\CLRUtilities.dll';
-- Create login and grant it with external permission level
CREATE LOGIN CLRUtilitiesLogin FROM ASYMMETRIC KEY CLRUtilitiesKey
GRANT EXTERNAL ACCESS ASSEMBLY TO CLRUtilitiesLogin;
```

CLR code inside SQL Server is always invoked in the context of the process account. If you would like to use the calling user's identity instead for your CLR code that performs an action outside SQL Server, you have to obtain an impersonation token through the *WindowsIdentity* property of the *SqlContext* object. The *WindowsIdentity* property returns a *WindowsIdentity* object instance. It represents the Windows (OS) identity of the caller (or null if the client was authenticated using SQL Server Authentication). To be able to access this property, an assembly has to be marked with the EXTERNAL_ACCESS or UNSAFE permission set.

You should be aware of all implications of setting the permission set for the assembly to EXTERNAL_ACCESS or UNSAFE and setting the database option TRUSTWORTHY to ON. Going deeper with security would be outside the scope of this book, but just be aware: the UNSAFE permission set allows assemblies unrestricted access to resources, both within and outside SQL Server, and also calling unmanaged code. From the example in this section, you can learn the technicalities of creating CLR triggers, but you can also get an impression of the implications of using CLR code inside a database imprudently.

Remember that Appendix A provides the instructions required to develop, build, deploy, and test your .NET code. Here you will be provided with the trigger's code, including explanations, and instructions to register the trigger in the database and test it.

Here's the C# code that defines the trg_GenericDMLAudit trigger:

```
// trg_GenericDMLAudit Trigger
// Generic trigger for auditing DML statements
// trigger will write first 200 characters from all columns
// in an XML format to App Event Log
[SqlTrigger(Name = @"trg_GenericDMLAudit", Target = "T1",
  Event = "FOR INSERT, UPDATE, DELETE")]
public static void trg_GenericDMLAudit()
{
  // Get the trigger context to get info about the action type
  SqlTriggerContext triggContext = SqlContext.TriggerContext;
  // Prepare the command and pipe objects
  SqlCommand command;
  SqlPipe pipe = SqlContext.Pipe;

  // Check type of action
  switch (triggContext.TriggerAction)
  {
```

```
case TriggerAction.Insert:
  // Retrieve the connection that the trigger is using
  using (SqlConnection connection
    = new SqlConnection(@"context connection=true"))
  {
    connection.Open();
    // Collect all columns into an XML type, cast it
    // to nvarchar and select only a substring from it
    // Info from Inserted
    command = new SqlCommand(
      @"SELECT 'New data: '
          + REPLACE(
              SUBSTRING(CAST(a.InsertedContents AS NVARCHAR(MAX))
                ,1,200),
              CHAR(39), CHAR(39)+CHAR(39)) AS InsertedContents200
        FROM (SELECT * FROM Inserted FOR XML AUTO, TYPE)
          AS a(InsertedContents);",
        connection);
    // Store info collected to a string variable
    string msg;
    msg = (string)command.ExecuteScalar();
    // Write the audit info to the event log
    EventLogEntryType entry = new EventLogEntryType();
    entry = EventLogEntryType.SuccessAudit;
    // Note: if the following line would use
    // Environment.MachineName instead of "." to refer to
    // the local machine event log, the assembly would need
    // the UNSAFE permission set
    EventLog ev = new EventLog(@"Application",
      ".", @"GenericDMLAudit Trigger");
    ev.WriteEntry(msg, entry);
    // send the audit info to the user
    pipe.Send(msg);
  }
  break;
case TriggerAction.Update:
  // Retrieve the connection that the trigger is using
  using (SqlConnection connection
    = new SqlConnection(@"context connection=true"))
  {
    connection.Open();
    // Collect all columns into an XML type,
    // cast it to nvarchar and select only a substring from it
    // Info from Deleted
    command = new SqlCommand(
      @"SELECT 'Old data: '
          + REPLACE(
              SUBSTRING(CAST(a.DeletedContents AS NVARCHAR(MAX))
                ,1,200),
              CHAR(39), CHAR(39)+CHAR(39)) AS DeletedContents200
        FROM (SELECT * FROM Deleted FOR XML AUTO, TYPE)
          AS a(DeletedContents);",
        connection);
    // Store info collected to a string variable
    string msg;
    msg = (string)command.ExecuteScalar();
```

```
          // Info from Inserted
          command.CommandText =
            @"SELECT ' // New data: '
                + REPLACE(
                    SUBSTRING(CAST(a.InsertedContents AS NVARCHAR(MAX))
                        ,1,200),
                    CHAR(39), CHAR(39)+CHAR(39)) AS InsertedContents200
              FROM (SELECT * FROM Inserted FOR XML AUTO, TYPE)
                AS a(InsertedContents);";
          msg = msg + (string)command.ExecuteScalar();
          // Write the audit info to the event log
          EventLogEntryType entry = new EventLogEntryType();
          entry = EventLogEntryType.SuccessAudit;
          EventLog ev = new EventLog(@"Application",
            ".", @"GenericDMLAudit Trigger");
          ev.WriteEntry(msg, entry);
          // send the audit info to the user
          pipe.Send(msg);
        }
        break;
      case TriggerAction.Delete:
        // Retrieve the connection that the trigger is using
        using (SqlConnection connection
          = new SqlConnection(@"context connection=true"))
        {
          connection.Open();
          // Collect all columns into an XML type,
          // cast it to nvarchar and select only a substring from it
          // Info from Deleted
          command = new SqlCommand(
            @"SELECT 'Old data: '
                + REPLACE(
                    SUBSTRING(CAST(a. DeletedContents AS NVARCHAR(MAX))
                        ,1,200),
                    CHAR(39), CHAR(39)+CHAR(39)) AS DeletedContents200
              FROM (SELECT * FROM Deleted FOR XML AUTO, TYPE)
                    AS a(DeletedContents);",
              connection);
          // Store info collected to a string variable
          string msg;
          msg = (string)command.ExecuteScalar();
          // Write the audit info to the event log
          EventLogEntryType entry = new EventLogEntryType();
          entry = EventLogEntryType.SuccessAudit;
          EventLog ev = new EventLog(@"Application",
            ".", @"GenericDMLAudit Trigger");
          ev.WriteEntry(msg, entry);
          // send the audit info to the user
          pipe.Send(msg);
        }
        break;
      default:
        // Just to be sure - this part should never fire
        pipe.Send(@"Nothing happened");
        break;
    }
  }
}
```

Note that the header of the trigger contains the attribute *Target = "T1"*. This attribute specifies the table on which you want to define the trigger. It is required only when deploying the trigger automatically from Microsoft Visual Studio. The trigger is written as a generic trigger that can be attached to any table. You can remove this attribute and use manual registration of the trigger to attach it to any table you like.

Using the *SqlContext* object, you can get the context of the current caller. The trigger's code uses a context connection, which should be familiar to you by now from the coverage of CLR stored procedures in the previous chapter. This is good enough for stored procedures, but inside a trigger you need a context in a much finer-grained level. You can gain the required context via the *SqlContext.TriggerContext* object (*SqlTriggerContext* class). This object provides context information about the trigger. This information includes the type of the DML action that caused the trigger to fire and which columns were modified if an UPDATE statement was issued. If this is a DDL trigger, you can get information about the event that fired the trigger from an XML *EventData* structure.

The trigger uses the *EventLogEntryType* enumeration and *EventLog* class from the *System. Diagnostics* namespace. It is also important that the trigger uses "." to refer to the current machine (remember that you want to write the auditing information to the local machine's event log). If it used the *Environment* class from the *System* namespace to get the current machine name (*Environment.MachineName*), the assembly would need the UNSAFE permission set. I have to thank Nicole Calinoiu, an extremely knowledgeable and friendly Visual Developer – Security MVP from Montreal, for pointing out this detail to me.

A small trick is used in the T-SQL part of the code embedded in the trigger (in the *CommandText* property of the *SqlCommand* object). If you want to create a generic trigger that can be used with any table, you don't want to specify an explicit column list from *inserted* or *deleted*. Also, you need to collect information from all columns of all possible data types to generate a result string, because you write messages to the event log as strings. So the trigger's code uses SELECT * to get all the columns no matter what the structure of the table is, although generally using SELECT * is a bad practice. It also uses the FOR XML clause to convert all information to XML in the inner SELECT (in the derived table). You can use the FOR XML clause in the derived table because it returns a table result. This is achieved by using the TYPE directive of the FOR XML clause. You get back a table with a single column of the XML data type; without the TYPE directive, you would get the result in textual form. The code converts the value of the XML type column to the NVARCHAR type in the outer query and writes the first 200 characters to the event log.

Here's the Visual Basic code that defines the trg_GenericDMLAudit trigger:

```
' Generic trigger for auditing DML statements
' trigger will write first 200 characters from all columns
' in an XML format to App Event Log
<SqlTrigger(Name:="trg_GenericDMLAudit", Target:="T1", _
  Event:="FOR INSERT, UPDATE, DELETE")> _
```

```
Public Shared Sub trg_GenericDMLAudit()
  ' Get the trigger context to get info about the action type
  Dim triggContext As SqlTriggerContext = SqlContext.TriggerContext
  ' Prepare the command and pipe objects
  Dim command As SqlCommand
  Dim pipe As SqlPipe = SqlContext.Pipe

  ' Check type of action
  Select Case triggContext.TriggerAction
    Case TriggerAction.Insert
      ' Retrieve the connection that the trigger is using
      Using connection _
        As New SqlConnection("Context connection = true")
        connection.Open()
        ' Collect all columns into an XML type,
        ' cast it to nvarchar and select only a substring from it
        ' Info from Inserted
        command = New SqlCommand( _
          "SELECT 'New data: ' + REPLACE(" & _
          "SUBSTRING(CAST(a.InsertedContents AS NVARCHAR(MAX)" & _
          "),1,200), CHAR(39), CHAR(39)+CHAR(39)) AS InsertedContents200 " & _
          "FROM (SELECT * FROM Inserted FOR XML AUTO, TYPE) " & _
          "AS a(InsertedContents);", _
           connection)
        ' Store info collected to a string variable
        Dim msg As String
        msg = CStr(command.ExecuteScalar())
        ' Write the audit info to the event log
        Dim entry As EventLogEntryType
        entry = EventLogEntryType.SuccessAudit
        ' Note: if the following line would use
        ' Environment.MachineName instead of "." to refer to
        ' the local machine event log, the assembly would need
        ' the UNSAFE permission set
        Dim ev As New EventLog("Application", _
          ".", "GenericDMLAudit Trigger")
        ev.WriteEntry(msg, entry)
        ' send the audit info to the user
        pipe.Send(msg)
      End Using
    Case TriggerAction.Update
      ' Retrieve the connection that the trigger is using
      Using connection _
        As New SqlConnection("Context connection = true")
        connection.Open()
        ' Collect all columns into an XML type,
        ' cast it to nvarchar and select only a substring from it
        ' Info from Deleted
        command = New SqlCommand( _
          "SELECT 'Old data: ' + REPLACE(" & _
          "SUBSTRING(CAST(a.DeletedContents AS NVARCHAR(MAX)" & _
          "),1,200), CHAR(39), CHAR(39)+CHAR(39)) AS DeletedContents200 " & _
          "FROM (SELECT * FROM Deleted FOR XML AUTO, TYPE) " & _
          "AS a(DeletedContents);", _
           connection)
```

```
        ' Store info collected to a string variable
        Dim msg As String
        msg = CStr(command.ExecuteScalar())
        ' Info from Inserted
        command.CommandText = _
          "SELECT ' // New data: ' + REPLACE(" & _
          "SUBSTRING(CAST(a.InsertedContents AS NVARCHAR(MAX)" & _
          "),1,200), CHAR(39), CHAR(39)+CHAR(39)) AS InsertedContents200 " & _
          "FROM (SELECT * FROM Inserted FOR XML AUTO, TYPE) " & _
          "AS a(InsertedContents);"
        msg = msg + CStr(command.ExecuteScalar())
        ' Write the audit info to the event log
        Dim entry As EventLogEntryType
        entry = EventLogEntryType.SuccessAudit
        Dim ev As New EventLog("Application", _
          ".", "GenericDMLAudit Trigger")
        ev.WriteEntry(msg, entry)
        ' send the audit info to the user
        pipe.Send(msg)
      End Using
    Case TriggerAction.Delete
      ' Retrieve the connection that the trigger is using
      Using connection _
        As New SqlConnection("Context connection = true")
        connection.Open()
        ' Collect all columns into an XML type,
        ' cast it to nvarchar and select only a substring from it
        ' Info from Deleted
        command = New SqlCommand( _
          "SELECT 'Old data: ' + REPLACE(" & _
          "SUBSTRING(CAST(a.DeletedContents AS NVARCHAR(MAX)" & _
          "),1,200), CHAR(39), CHAR(39)+CHAR(39)) AS DeletedContents200 " & _
          "FROM (SELECT * FROM Deleted FOR XML AUTO, TYPE) " & _
          "AS a(DeletedContents);", _
            connection)
        ' Store info collected to a string variable
        Dim msg As String
        msg = CStr(command.ExecuteScalar())
        ' Write the audit info to the event log
        Dim entry As EventLogEntryType
        entry = EventLogEntryType.SuccessAudit
        Dim ev As New EventLog("Application", _
          ".", "GenericDMLAudit Trigger")
        ev.WriteEntry(msg, entry)
        ' send the audit info to the user
        pipe.Send(msg)
      End Using
    Case Else
      ' Just to be sure - this part should never fire
      pipe.Send("Nothing happened")
  End Select
End Sub
```

Run the following code to create a test table called T1:

```
USE ClrUtilities;

IF OBJECT_ID('dbo.T1', 'U') IS NOT NULL DROP TABLE dbo.T1;

CREATE TABLE dbo.T1
(
  keycol  INT         NOT NULL PRIMARY KEY,
  datacol VARCHAR(10) NOT NULL
);
```

Use the following code to register the C# version of the trigger in the database and attach it to the table T1:

```
CREATE TRIGGER trg_T1_iud_GenericDMLAudit
 ON dbo.T1 FOR INSERT, UPDATE, DELETE
AS
EXTERNAL NAME CLRUtilities.CLRUtilities.trg_GenericDMLAudit;
```

Use the following code to register the trigger if you used Visual Basic to develop it:

```
CREATE TRIGGER trg_T1_iud_GenericDMLAudit
 ON dbo.T1 FOR INSERT, UPDATE, DELETE
AS
EXTERNAL NAME
  CLRUtilities.[CLRUtilities.CLRUtilities].trg_GenericDMLAudit;
```

Issue the following modifications against T1:

```
INSERT INTO dbo.T1(keycol, datacol) VALUES(1, N'A');
UPDATE dbo.T1 SET datacol = N'B' WHERE keycol = 1;
DELETE FROM dbo.T1 WHERE keycol = 1;
```

The trigger will produce the following output:

```
New data: <Inserted keycol="1" datacol="A"/>
Old data: <Deleted keycol="1" datacol="A"/> // New data: <Inserted keycol="1" datacol="B"/>
Old data: <Deleted keycol="1" datacol="B"/>
```

> **Tip** You can clear the root namespace in a Visual Basic project. This way the T-SQL code required to create/alter assemblies and register routines would be the same for Visual Basic and C# assemblies. To clear the root namespace, in Visual Studio select the Project | Properties menu item, click the Application tab, and clear the Root Namespace text box.

If you examine the Windows application log, you will find that the changes were audited there as well, as shown in Figure 4-1.

If you don't see the events in the Windows application log, make sure that it's not full or that you allow it to be recycled.

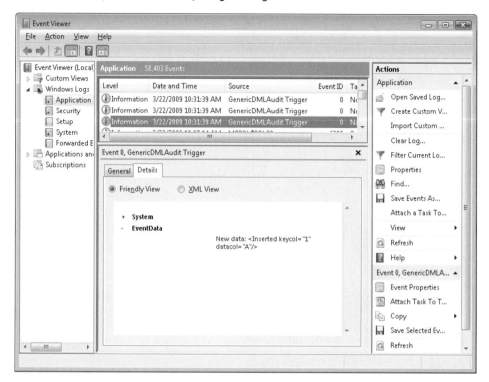

FIGURE 4-1 Application log

When you're done, run the following code for cleanup:

```
IF OBJECT_ID('dbo.T1', 'U') IS NOT NULL DROP TABLE dbo.T1;
```

Conclusion

Triggers allow you to automate processes. Process automation means less manual work and fewer chances to make mistakes and errors. You can use triggers to enforce complex integrity checks, audit changes, maintain denormalized data, and much more. SQL Server 2008 allows you to create triggers for DML statements, DDL and DDL-like statements, and logon events. You can use either T-SQL or .NET as your coding language.

Anyone can program triggers, but not everyone can program triggers efficiently. To program triggers efficiently, you need to understand the aspects of working with the *inserted* and *deleted* tables, the architecture of the product, the row versioning technology, and potential bottlenecks in the system.

Chapter 5
Transactions and Concurrency

Itzik Ben-Gan

This chapter covers various aspects of concurrency that you need to consider when developing code for SQL Server. It covers transactions, locking, blocking, isolation levels, and deadlocks. It also covers the new LOCK_ESCALATION option of ALTER TABLE, which gives you better control over how lock escalation behaves.

> **Note** In this chapter I cover features that are directly related to transactions and concurrency. Some other new features in SQL Server 2008 may have an impact on concurrency, especially if they improve the performance of certain activities and as a result finish sooner and release locks more quickly. In cases where I felt that a certain new feature is more closely related to a main topic that is covered elsewhere, I covered it there. For example, I covered improvements in minimally logged operations and the new MERGE statement in the prequel to this book: *T-SQL Querying*.

Transactions allow you to define a unit of activity that will be considered *atomic*—all or nothing. The data will be considered *consistent* at the beginning of the transaction and at the end. Locks are obtained to *isolate* data resources, preventing other processes from performing incompatible activities against those resources. You can control the degree of isolation of your transaction by specifying an *isolation level*. I will describe isolation levels in more detail later in the chapter. The database's transaction log guarantees that a committed transaction recorded within it is *durable*—that is, the change will reach the database. The aforementioned aspects of transactions are known as *ACID* (Atomicity, Consistency, Isolation, and Durability).

One aspect of database programming that determines whether a project rises or falls is the application's treatment of concurrency—multiple processes interacting with the same data. You have to understand the vision of the designers of the database product in terms of concurrency to develop well-behaving applications. You need to understand which concurrency models the product supports—and which it uses by default—so that you know how to override the default if it's not suitable for your system.

For example, by default Oracle uses an optimistic concurrency model, where writers never block readers unless the reader requests that behavior explicitly. This functionality is supported because the product is able to construct an earlier consistent (committed) version of the data. Microsoft SQL Server uses by default a pessimistic concurrency model based on locking and blocking. In the pessimistic concurrency model, SQL Server maintains only one image of each row. An uncommitted change applied by a process to a row renders an inconsistent state of the row. Unless you enable the optimistic model, under which SQL Server stores older committed versions of modified rows, another process attempting to read the row cannot obtain an earlier consistent version. Rather, it can either wait for the other process to commit, or it can request the inconsistent state of the row (commonly referred to as a *dirty read*).

Fortunately, SQL Server 2008 supports both the pessimistic and optimistic concurrency models, allowing you to choose the one that best suits your system. SQL Server 2008 also supports a choice of transaction isolation levels for each concurrency model.

What Are Transactions?

Transactions allow you to define the boundaries of activity that will be considered atomic. You do so by enclosing the statements that you want to participate in the transaction in a BEGIN TRAN/COMMIT TRAN block. Note that in SQL Server the default behavior is to consider a statement that does not appear in an explicit transaction block to be its own transaction—as if you enclosed that statement alone in a BEGIN TRAN/COMMIT TRAN block.

Whenever you submit a change to the database, SQL Server first checks whether the pages that need to be affected already reside in cache. If they do, the pages are modified in cache. If they don't, they're first loaded from disk into the cache and modified there. SQL Server records the changes in the database's transaction log. Once in a while, a process called *checkpoint* flushes changed pages ("dirty pages") from cache to the data portion of the database on disk. However, SQL Server will flush only changed pages for which the change was already recorded in the transaction log.

This architecture allows SQL Server to maintain transactions. If a transaction is rolled back—either explicitly or as a result of a failure—SQL Server has in the transaction log all the information it needs to undo the changes that were not committed. SQL Server might also use the information from the transaction log for roll-forward *recovery* capabilities, not just rollback operations. During a roll-forward recovery phase, SQL Server replays committed transactions that were recorded in the transaction log but have not yet been applied to the data portion of the database. This activity takes place, for example, when SQL Server starts up. For every database, SQL Server looks for the last checkpoint recorded in the transaction log. All transactions that were committed after the last checkpoint was recorded will be rolled forward (which is known as the *redo* phase). All open transactions for which a COMMIT TRAN was not recorded in the transaction log will be rolled back (which is known as the *undo* phase). SQL Server 2008 brings the database online as soon as the redo phase—which takes place first—finishes. This feature is known as *fast recovery*.

To demonstrate the different aspects of working with transactions in this chapter, I'll use the tables T1 and T2, which you create and populate in the testdb database by running the following code:

```
SET NOCOUNT ON;
IF DB_ID('testdb') IS NULL CREATE DATABASE testdb;
GO
USE testdb;
GO
IF OBJECT_ID('dbo.T1', 'U') IS NOT NULL DROP TABLE dbo.T1;
IF OBJECT_ID('dbo.T2', 'U') IS NOT NULL DROP TABLE dbo.T2;
GO

CREATE TABLE dbo.T1
(
  keycol INT       NOT NULL PRIMARY KEY,
  col1   INT       NOT NULL,
  col2   VARCHAR(50) NOT NULL
);

INSERT INTO dbo.T1(keycol, col1, col2) VALUES
  (1, 101, 'A'),
  (2, 102, 'B'),
  (3, 103, 'C');

CREATE TABLE dbo.T2
(
  keycol INT       NOT NULL PRIMARY KEY,
  col1   INT       NOT NULL,
  col2   VARCHAR(50) NOT NULL
);

INSERT INTO dbo.T2(keycol, col1, col2) VALUES
  (1, 201, 'X'),
  (2, 202, 'Y'),
  (3, 203, 'Z');
```

As a basic example, the following code issues two INSERT statements in a single transaction:

```
BEGIN TRAN
  INSERT INTO dbo.T1(keycol, col1, col2) VALUES(4, 101, 'C');
  INSERT INTO dbo.T2(keycol, col1, col2) VALUES(4, 201, 'X');
COMMIT TRAN
```

You enclose the two statements in a single transaction if you want the whole unit to be atomic—either both must succeed or both must fail. If your server fails for some reason, and only the first INSERT statement is recorded in the transaction log, the recovery process will roll back the partial transaction. On the other hand, if the transaction is recorded in the transaction log in full but not yet flushed to the data portion of the database (committed after the last checkpoint), the recovery process will redo it.

Note that SQL Server doesn't automatically roll back a transaction as a result of any failure. For example, constraint violations or lock timeout expirations usually leave a transaction open by default. You can write error-handling code to determine whether you want to explicitly roll the transaction back or commit it. If you want all errors to cause a rollback of a transaction, set the XACT_ABORT session option to ON. In most cases the XACT_ABORT option is OFF by default, but in a trigger it's ON by default. Note that when error handling is used, the XACT_ABORT option has a different effect. I'll discuss error handling in the next chapter.

Locking and Blocking

Locks provide the *isolation* aspect of transactions. They are acquired on data resources to prevent data inconsistency problems. SQL Server allows you to control the level of consistency you get from your data by setting the isolation level of your session or query. I'll cover isolation levels later in the chapter. In this section, I'll focus on locks.

Locks can be obtained on resources at different granularity levels of data. The smallest granularity of data is the row level. If a row of a heap is locked (a *heap* is a table without a clustered index), the locked resource is a *row identifier (RID)*. If a row in an index is locked, the locked resource is a *key*. A lock can also be obtained on a page, an extent, a partition, a table, and on other types of resources as well. SQL Server automatically chooses which resource type to lock. In your queries, you can specify a table hint where you mention the resource type that you want to be locked (ROWLOCK, PAGLOCK, TABLOCK). SQL Server might choose not to adhere to your request if it doesn't have enough resources to satisfy it or if your request conflicts with other locks.

Lock *modes* determine how resources can be accessed by concurrent transactions. That is, if a process is granted a certain lock mode on a resource, another process attempting to acquire an incompatible lock mode on the same resource will be blocked. When you modify data, your transaction needs to acquire an *exclusive* (X) lock on the resource. If granted, the transaction will keep the exclusive lock until it is committed or rolled back. When you read data, by default (in the default isolation level) your transaction will need to acquire a *shared* (S) lock on the resource. If a shared lock is granted, your transaction will keep it only until the resource has been read.

Exclusive locks are incompatible with all lock modes. Similarly, all lock modes are incompatible with exclusive locks. That is, if one process holds a lock of any mode on a resource, another process cannot obtain an exclusive lock on that resource. Similarly, if one process holds an exclusive lock on a resource, another process cannot obtain a lock of any mode on that resource—thus the mode name *exclusive*. Shared locks, on the other hand, can be obtained while other processes hold shared locks on the same resource—thus the mode name *shared*.

SQL Server also supports other lock modes. An *update* (U) lock is used on resources that can be updated. Only one process at a time can hold an update lock on a resource. You can use an update lock to prevent deadlocks that can take place when processes are reading, locking (and maintaining the locks), and later updating the resource.

When SQL Server intends to acquire a lock on a resource, it first requests *Intent* locks on resources higher in the lock hierarchy (row → page → table). This lock mode is used to "signal" the intent to lock a resource lower in the lock hierarchy, and to simplify the lock incompatibility detection between different levels of granularity. For example, suppose your process requests to lock a row exclusively. SQL Server will first request *intent exclusive* (IX) locks at the table and page levels. Assume your process obtained all locks it requested. If another process attempts to acquire an incompatible lock on the same row, page, or table, SQL Server will detect the conflict immediately, thanks to the intent locks.

Schema locks are acquired by processes that either change or depend on the schema of an object. A *schema modification* (Sch-M) lock is obtained when a data-definition-language (DDL) activity takes place against an object, and it blocks all activities against the object issued by other processes. *Schema stability* (Sch-S) locks are used when SQL Server compiles queries to block other processes from performing schema changes against the object.

Bulk update (BU) locks are used to allow multiple sessions to bulk load data into a table, while blocking processes from performing activities against the table other than bulk loads.

Finally, *key-range* locks protect ranges of rows. These are used by the serializable isolation level. I'll elaborate on this lock mode later in the chapter when discussing isolation levels.

For your convenience, Table 5-1 has a summary adapted from SQL Server Books Online of lock compatibilities between some different lock modes.

TABLE 5-1 Lock Compatibility

	Granted Mode					
Requested Mode	**IS**	**S**	**U**	**IX**	**SIX**	**X**
Intent shared (IS)	Yes	Yes	Yes	Yes	Yes	No
Shared (S)	Yes	Yes	Yes	No	No	No
Update (U)	Yes	Yes	No	No	No	No
Intent exclusive (IX)	Yes	No	No	Yes	No	No
Shared with intent exclusive (SIX)	Yes	No	No	No	No	No
Exclusive (X)	No	No	No	No	No	No

As it does with lock resource types, SQL Server determines lock modes automatically. You can use a table hint to request that SQL Server use a specific lock mode (for example, XLOCK or UPDLOCK). If you wish to disable row- or page-level locking (or both), you can set the relevant index options ALLOW_ROW_LOCKS and ALLOW_PAGE_LOCKS to OFF when using the CREATE INDEX and ALTER INDEX statements.

To demonstrate a blocking scenario, open three connections. Call them connections 1, 2, and 3.

Run the following code in connection 1 to open a transaction and update a row in table T1:

```
SET NOCOUNT ON;
USE testdb;
GO
BEGIN TRAN
  UPDATE dbo.T1 SET col2 = 'BB' WHERE keycol = 2;
```

The UPDATE transaction was granted with an exclusive lock, and the change was applied. Exclusive locks are held until the end of a transaction, and because this transaction remains open, the process preserves the lock.

Run the following code in connection 2 to attempt to select all rows from T1:

```
SET NOCOUNT ON;
USE testdb;
GO
SELECT keycol, col1, col2 FROM dbo.T1;
```

Connection 2 needs a shared lock to read the data, but it cannot obtain one because an exclusive lock is held by connection 1 on one of the rows. Connection 2 is blocked. By default, SQL Server does not set any lock timeout, so if connection 1 does not release the lock, connection 2 just keeps waiting.

To troubleshoot blocking scenarios, SQL Server 2008 gives you an array of dynamic management views (DMVs) and functions (DMFs). For example, the *sys.dm_tran_locks* view gives you information about locks. Run the following query in connection 3:

```
SET NOCOUNT ON;
USE testdb;
GO
-- Lock info
SELECT
  request_session_id          AS spid,
  resource_type               AS restype,
  resource_database_id        AS dbid,
  resource_description        AS res,
  resource_associated_entity_id AS resid,
  request_mode                AS mode,
  request_status              AS status
FROM sys.dm_tran_locks;
```

This generates the following output:

spid	restype	dbid	res	resid	mode	status
55	DATABASE	12		0	S	GRANT
54	DATABASE	12		0	S	GRANT
53	DATABASE	12		0	S	GRANT
51	DATABASE	12		0	S	GRANT
54	PAGE	12	1:153	72057594039173120	IS	GRANT
53	PAGE	12	1:153	72057594039173120	IX	GRANT

54	OBJECT	12		277576027	IS	GRANT
53	OBJECT	12		277576027	IX	GRANT
53	KEY	12	(020068e8b274)	72057594039173120	X	GRANT
54	KEY	12	(020068e8b274)	72057594039173120	S	WAIT

You can observe that processes 53 and 54 are in conflict (of course, you might get different server process IDs). Process 53 was granted an exclusive key lock, whereas process 54 is waiting for a shared lock on the same resource (last row in the output).

Query the *sys.dm_exec_connections* view to obtain information about the connections involved in the conflict (*connect_time, last_read, last_write, most_recent_sql_handle*, and so on):

```
SELECT * FROM sys.dm_exec_connections
WHERE session_id IN(53, 54);
```

SQL Server 2008 supports multiple active result sets (MARS), where a single session can have multiple active connections running asynchronously. Therefore, SQL Server 2008 separates them into two views: *sys.dm_exec_sessions* for sessions and *sys.dm_exec_connections* for each connection. Query the *sys.dm_exec_sessions* view to obtain information about the sessions involved in the conflict (*login_time, host_name, program_name, login_name, last_request_start_time, last_request_end_time*, state of set options, *transaction_isolation_level*, and so on):

```
SELECT * FROM sys.dm_exec_sessions
WHERE session_id IN(53, 54);
```

SQL Server 2008 also provides you with the *sys.dm_exec_requests* view, which gives you information about currently executing requests. For a blocked session, the *blocking_session_id* attribute of the view will give you the session ID of the blocking session. Query the view to obtain information about blocked requests (blocked *session_id, blocking_session_id, wait_type, wait_time, wait_resource*, state of set options, and so on):

```
SELECT * FROM sys.dm_exec_requests
WHERE blocking_session_id > 0;
```

The *sys.dm_exec_connections* view contains a binary handle that you can provide to the function *sys.dm_exec_sql_text* to get the code text of the last request. For example, to get the code text for sessions 53 and 54, issue the following query:

```
SELECT session_id, text
FROM sys.dm_exec_connections
  CROSS APPLY sys.dm_exec_sql_text(most_recent_sql_handle) AS ST
WHERE session_id IN(53, 54);
```

This generates the following output:

```
session_id  text
----------- --------------------------------------------------
53          BEGIN TRAN
              UPDATE dbo.T1 SET col2 = 'BB' WHERE keycol = 2;
54          SELECT keycol, col1, col2 FROM dbo.T1;
```

Other dynamic management objects give you valuable concurrency-related information as well as information about other aspects of the product. Please refer to SQL Server Books Online for details.

> **Tip** You can download a poster showing the key system views in SQL Server 2008 and the relationships between them from the following URL: *http://www.microsoft.com/downloads/ details.aspx?FamilyID=531c53e7-8a2a-4375-8f2f-5d799aa67b5c&displaylang=en*.

Back to our blocking scenario—remember that by default a blocked session will wait for the blocking session to relinquish the resource, with no time limit. If you want to set a limit for waiting, use the LOCK_TIMEOUT session setting, specifying a value in milliseconds. If the timeout value you specified in LOCK_TIMEOUT expires and your session did not get the desired lock, SQL Server will generate error 1222.

> **Note** When a lock timeout expires and SQL Server generates the error 1222, you know what caused the error. SQL Server terminates the activity, and it tells you why. On the other hand, if you set a client timeout value (for example, *command timeout*), the client initiates the termination of the activity, and it doesn't care why the activity did not finish in the allotted time. In such a case, you can't determine the reason for the error. It might be blocking, it might just be a slow-running query, or it could be something else.

As an example of setting a lock timeout, first cancel the executing query in connection 2, which should still be waiting. The transaction in connection 1 is still open, holding an exclusive lock on a row in T1. Then run the following code in connection 2, which sets the lock timeout value to five seconds and then queries T1:

```
SET LOCK_TIMEOUT 5000;
SELECT keycol, col1, col2 FROM dbo.T1;
```

After five seconds, you will get the following error:

```
Msg 1222, Level 16, State 51, Line 2
Lock request time out period exceeded.
```

To reset the lock timeout setting to its default (no timeout, or wait forever), set the LOCK_TIMEOUT value to –1:

```
SET LOCK_TIMEOUT -1;
```

To terminate the transaction in connection 1 without committing the change, issue a rollback:

```
ROLLBACK TRAN;
```

If transactions are kept open for a long time, they might be keeping locks and preventing access to the data from other processes. To improve concurrency, you should try to keep your transactions as short as possible.

Lock Escalation

SQL Server maintains a memory block for each lock. If there is no limit on the number of locks that a single transaction can acquire, SQL Server could potentially suffer from memory starvation. Therefore, when SQL Server deems a transaction as holding too many locks, it attempts to escalate the many fine-grained locks to a more coarse-grained locks. Prior to SQL Server 2008, locking could only be escalated directly to the table level. In SQL Server 2008, you can specify escalation to the partition level, or you can disable it altogether. By default the first lock escalation attempt occurs when a single transaction acquires 5,000 locks against the same table (or partition if you specified partition-level escalation). If conflicting locks are held by another transaction, the attempt fails, in which case SQL Server keeps attempting to achieve lock escalation after each additional 1,250 acquired locks. The goal of lock escalation is to reduce lock overhead, but of course it results in reduced concurrency, because SQL Server ends up locking more data than is logically needed.

> **Tip** When you set the database option to READ_ONLY, SQL Server does not bother to acquire shared locks for SELECT queries. It knows that changes cannot be applied to the database, meaning that SELECT queries can never be in conflict with any other activity. This means that queries produce less overhead and you get better performance. In systems where you only read data from the database—for example, data warehouses—consider setting the database update option to READ_ONLY. You can set the database to READ_WRITE just before invoking the extract, transform, and load (ETL) process that periodically loads changes to the data warehouse. When the ETL process finishes, set the database mode back to READ_ONLY. You can automate the changes to the database option as part of the ETL process.

As mentioned, SQL Server 2008 allows you to control the lock escalation granularity. This is achieved with a new table option called LOCK_ESCALATION that can be set to one of three values:

- **TABLE (default)**   This setting specifies the same behavior as in previous versions of SQL Server. When lock escalation takes place, it will go to the table level.

- **AUTO**   This option specifies that if the table is partitioned, locking granularity will go to the partition level. If the table is not partitioned, lock escalation goes to the table level.

- **DISABLE**   This option disables lock escalation and should be used with care.

To demonstrate the new capability, I'll compare the behavior of default lock escalation with disabled escalation. Run the following code to create a table called TestEscalation, populate it with 100,000 rows, and create a unique clustered index using the column *col1* as the key:

```
IF OBJECT_ID('dbo.TestEscalation', 'U') IS NOT NULL
  DROP TABLE dbo.TestEscalation;
GO
```

```
SELECT n AS col1, CAST('a' AS CHAR(200)) AS filler
INTO dbo.TestEscalation
FROM dbo.Nums
WHERE n <= 100000;

CREATE UNIQUE CLUSTERED INDEX idx1 ON dbo.TestEscalation(col1);
```

To demonstrate default escalation to the table level, the following code opens a transaction, deletes 20,000 rows, counts the number of locks associated with the session by querying the view *sys.dm_tran_locks*, and rolls back the transaction:

```
BEGIN TRAN

  DELETE FROM dbo.TestEscalation WHERE col1 <= 20000;

  SELECT COUNT(*)
  FROM sys.dm_tran_locks
  WHERE request_session_id = @@SPID;

ROLLBACK
```

Because the default value of the LOCK_ESCALATION option is TABLE, and the DELETE statement attempted to acquire more than 5,000 locks, SQL Server escalated the multiple fine-grained locks to a single table-level one. Hence the query reports a count of only one lock.

Next, run the following code to disable lock escalation and run the transaction again:

```
ALTER TABLE dbo.TestEscalation SET (LOCK_ESCALATION = DISABLE);

BEGIN TRAN

  DELETE FROM dbo.TestEscalation WHERE col1 <= 20000;

  SELECT COUNT(*)
  FROM sys.dm_tran_locks
  WHERE request_session_id = @@SPID;

ROLLBACK
```

This time escalation was disabled; therefore, SQL Server did not escalate the fine-grained locks. When I ran this code on my system, the query reported 20,528 locks.

Isolation Levels

Isolation levels allow you to control the consistency level that you will get when manipulating data, bearing in mind that multiple processes might be running concurrently. SQL Server 2008 gives you four isolation levels based on locking and blocking that implement a pessimistic concurrency model (*read uncommitted, read committed, repeatable read*, and *serializable*) and two isolation levels based on row versioning that implement an optimistic model (*snapshot* and *read committed snapshot*).

The different isolation levels control the level of consistency that you will get when manipulating data mainly by controlling the way readers behave. Isolation levels that are based on locking allow you to improve consistency at the cost of worsening concurrency, and vice versa. Technically, such isolation levels improve consistency by increasing the duration of locks. Of course, the other side of the coin is that processes will need to wait longer. With isolation levels based on row versioning, you improve both the consistency and the concurrency of readers at the cost of more expensive modifications and overhead on tempdb. When data is deleted or updated, SQL Server copies the committed version of the row prior to the change to the *version store* in tempdb so that readers can get the consistent version they expect without waiting.

Your choice of isolation level determines which of the following types of consistency-related problems can or cannot happen:

- **Dirty reads**   A read of uncommitted data. One process changes data but does not commit the change before another process reads the same data. The second process ends up reading an inconsistent state of the data.

- **Lost updates**   One process reads data, makes some calculations based on the data, and later updates the data based on those calculations. If two processes first read the data and later update it based on what they read, one process might overwrite the other's update.

- **Nonrepeatable reads (also known as inconsistent analysis)**   In two separate reads within the same transaction, the process gets different values when reading the same resource. This can happen if a second process changed the data between the reads made by the first process.

- **Phantoms**   In two separate reads within the same transaction using the same query filter, the second read returns rows that were not part of the first read. This can happen if a second process inserts new rows that satisfy the first transaction's query filter in between its two reads. Those new rows are known as *phantom reads*.

Several times already in this chapter I referred to pessimistic versus optimistic concurrency models. Perhaps it's time to define those clearly. In a pessimistic concurrency model, you lock a resource to guarantee that you will be able to perform an action you're planning later. Between the time you lock the resource and the time you perform the action later, no one can perform an incompatible action against the data. Obviously, this mode has the potential to hurt concurrency.

In an optimistic model, you don't lock the resource. Rather, you have the means to identify whether an incompatible action took place in between your activities. This model can potentially improve concurrency.

In the following sections, I'll describe the different isolation levels supported by SQL Server 2008 and which concurrency problems each does or doesn't allow.

SQL Server allows you to set the isolation level either at the session level or at the query level. You set the isolation level at the session level by issuing the following statement:

```
SET TRANSACTION ISOLATION LEVEL <isolation level>;
```

In this statement, *<isolation level>* can be one of the following: READ UNCOMMITTED, READ COMMITTED, REPEATABLE READ, SERIALIZABLE, or SNAPSHOT.

Or you can set the isolation level of a query by using a table hint (READUNCOMMITTED, READCOMMITTED, REPEATABLEREAD, or SERIALIZABLE). The hint NOLOCK is equivalent to READUNCOMMITTED, and the hint HOLDLOCK is equivalent to REPEATABLEREAD.

> **Tip** SQL Server also provides you with a table hint called READPAST. This hint causes your process to skip locked rows rather than being blocked or getting dirty reads. Make sure, though, that it makes sense for your application to use this hint. SQL Server 2008 supports this hint both with queries that retrieve data and ones that modify data.

SQL Server's default isolation level is read committed.

Read Uncommitted

When working with the read uncommitted isolation level, readers do not request shared locks. Thus, they're never in conflict with sessions that modify data. That is, they can read data that is locked exclusively, and they do not interfere with processes that modify data. Of course, at this level readers might get uncommitted changes. In other words, dirty reads can happen, as well as all other concurrency-related problems I described earlier. Read uncommitted is the worst isolation level in terms of consistency but the best in terms of concurrency.

To demonstrate a dirty read, first issue the following UPDATE statement to change the value of *T1.col2* to the string *'Version 1'* in the row where *keycol* is equal to 2:

```
UPDATE dbo.T1 SET col2 = 'Version 1' WHERE keycol = 2;
```

Open two connections and call them connection 1 and connection 2. From connection 1, issue the following code, which updates *col2* to *'Version 2'* within a transaction and retrieves the modified column values, keeping the transaction open:

```
BEGIN TRAN
  UPDATE dbo.T1 SET col2 = 'Version 2' WHERE keycol = 2;
  SELECT col2 FROM dbo.T1 WHERE keycol = 2;
```

You get *'Version 2'* as the output, showing you the new state of the value your own transaction changed.

From connection 2, set the session's isolation level to read uncommitted, and read the data:

```
SET TRANSACTION ISOLATION LEVEL READ UNCOMMITTED;
SELECT col2 FROM dbo.T1 WHERE keycol = 2;
```

Even though another transaction changed the data and had not committed yet, you are able to see the uncommitted change—you get the output *'Version 2'*. Note that the modifying transaction still maintains an exclusive lock on the data, but if a process that reads the data doesn't request a shared lock, it cannot get a refusal.

From connection 1, issue a rollback:

```
ROLLBACK TRAN
```

If at this point you read the *col2* value from the row where *keycol* is equal to *2*, you will get *'Version 1'* back. You realize that *'Version 2'* was never committed and that processes working with the read uncommitted isolation level might have relied on a state of the data that was never "approved."

Note that other differences exist in addition to the difference between read uncommitted and other isolation levels in terms of locking behavior. When you choose to work under the read uncommitted isolation level SQL Server assumes—whether you agree with this assumption or not—that in general the consistency of your requests is a lower priority than their performance. Thus, when the storage engine has multiple options to process a request from the relational engine, it tends to opt for the one with a potential for better performance, even at the cost of sacrificing consistency.

For example, consider a query execution plan with an Index Scan or Clustered Index Scan operator with the property *Ordered: False*. Such an operator means that as far as the relational engine is concerned, the data residing in the leaf level of the index needs to be scanned, but the order in which the data is returned doesn't matter. The storage engine has two ways to process the request: either with an allocation order scan (a scan done in file order based on IAM pages) or with an index order scan (a scan done in index key order by following the index leaf-level linked list). The former approach tends to yield better performance because it is not affected by logical scan fragmentation; however, it is more prone to yield inconsistent data.

If an allocation order scan takes place, and page splits occur during the scan because of inserts or updates made by other transactions, the scan can yield the same row multiple times or skip rows. Reading the same row multiple times can happen if a page that was already read by the scan splits, and rows from that page move to a new page that is allocated in a point that the scan did not reach yet. The rows that moved to the new page are then read again when that page is reached. Similarly, if a page that the scan didn't yet reach splits, and a new page is allocated in a point that the scan already passed, the rows that moved to the new page because of the split won't be read at all.

An index order scan is safer in the sense that splits that happen during the scan won't cause such problems. If a page splits, the new page is logically placed right after the page that split by adjusting the linked list. This means that if a page that is logically behind the scan point splits, the scan won't reread the rows that moved. If a page that is logically ahead of the scan point splits, the scan ends up reading both pages and doesn't skip any rows.

The storage engine is well aware of the difference between the approaches. Under the read uncommitted isolation level it will opt for an allocation order scan for the sake of improved performance, even in cases where this choice can result in the aforementioned problems. In any higher isolation level, the storage engine opts for an index order scan unless it knows that splits cannot happen during the scan (for example, when using the TABLOCK hint or when the filegroup or database is marked as READ_ONLY). Unfortunately the execution plan doesn't indicate which option the storage engine ended up choosing in practice. All you see in the plan is an Index Scan (or Clustered Index Scan) with the property *Ordered: False*. You have to be aware of this behavior, and consider well the implications of using the read uncommitted isolation level. As a reminder, the NOLOCK table hint is just a synonym to the READUNCOMMITTED hint.

Read Committed

Read committed is the default isolation level of SQL Server. In this isolation level, processes request a shared lock to read data and release it as soon as the data has been read— not when the statement or the transaction finishes. This means that dirty reads cannot happen—the only changes you can read are those that have been committed. However, all other concurrency-related problems can happen with this isolation level.

To demonstrate the fact that a dirty read will not occur when working with the read committed isolation level, first run the following code in connection 1, changing the value of *col2* from *'Version 1'* to *'Version 2'*:

```
BEGIN TRAN
  UPDATE dbo.T1 SET col2 = 'Version 2' WHERE keycol = 2;
  SELECT col2 FROM dbo.T1 WHERE keycol = 2;
```

You get the output *'Version 2'*, because you can read your own changes, of course.

Now try to read the data from connection 2, working in the read committed isolation level. You will be blocked:

```
SET TRANSACTION ISOLATION LEVEL READ COMMITTED;
SELECT col2 FROM dbo.T1 WHERE keycol = 2;
```

Commit the change in connection 1:

```
COMMIT TRAN
```

Connection 1 releases the exclusive lock, and connection two gets *'Version 2'* back, which is the committed state of the value after the change.

Under the read committed isolation level, page splits cannot cause read consistency problems such as reading the same row multiple times or skipping rows. As mentioned before, when processing an Index Scan (or Clustered Index Scan) with the property *Ordered: False*, the storage engine has two choices. If an allocation order scan can cause consistency problems and the transaction isolation level is read committed, then the storage engine will use an index order scan.

Note, however, that page splits are not the only potential cause of rows moving around during a scan. Index key changes cause a row to move in the B-tree, and as a result of the movement, an index order scan can end up reading the same row multiple times or skipping rows. It's important to remember that under read committed a shared lock is obtained only for the duration of the read of the resource—not for the duration of the statement. Hence, once the resource is read, the lock is released and another transaction can change the row. If a row's index key is changed after the index order scan has already read it, and the row is moved to a point in the B-tree ahead of the scan, the scan will read the row again when it reaches the row's new position. Similarly, if an index key is changed in a row that the scan has not yet reached, and the row is moved to a point in the B-tree that the scan has already passed, the scan will not reach that row at all.

For cleanup, change the value back to *'Version 1'*:

```
UPDATE dbo.T1 SET col2 = 'Version 1' WHERE keycol = 2;
```

Repeatable Read

Processes working with the repeatable read isolation level also request a shared lock when reading data, meaning that dirty reads cannot occur at this level. But unlike with read committed, at the repeatable read level transactions keep shared locks until they are terminated. You are guaranteed to get repeatable reads (consistent analysis) because no other process is able to obtain an exclusive lock in between your reads.

Lost updates cannot happen at this level as well. If two processes that read data preserve shared locks until the end of the transaction, an attempt to modify that data by both will cause a deadlock, because each requests an exclusive lock that will be blocked by the other. When SQL Server detects a deadlock, it chooses a victim—typically, the process that performed less work—and rolls the victim's transaction back. The victim process will get the infamous error 1205 and can reissue the transaction. Although lost updates cannot happen in repeatable read, phantoms are still possible.

Note that using the repeatable read isolation is not the only way to prevent lost updates. You can work under the read committed isolation level and specify UPDLOCK in situations that can potentially result in lost updates. Only one transaction can hold an update lock against the same resource at any given moment, so as soon as one read obtains such a lock, the other read has to wait. Thus the lost update is prevented without resorting to deadlocks.

To demonstrate a case in which you get consistent analysis when working at the repeatable read level, run the following code from connection 1:

```
SET TRANSACTION ISOLATION LEVEL REPEATABLE READ;
BEGIN TRAN
  SELECT col2 FROM dbo.T1 WHERE keycol = 2;
```

You get the output *'Version 1'*, and the process keeps a shared lock on the data because the transaction is still open.

If you attempt to modify the data from connection 2, you will be blocked:

```
UPDATE dbo.T1 SET col2 = 'Version 2' WHERE keycol = 2;
```

Read the data again in connection 1, and then commit:

```
 SELECT col2 FROM dbo.T1 WHERE keycol = 2;
COMMIT TRAN
```

You still get *'Version 1'* back, meaning you got a repeatable read even though another process attempted to change the data in between your reads. When the transaction committed, the shared lock was released, and connection 2 could obtain the exclusive lock it needed to update the data.

As explained earlier, under the read uncommitted and read committed isolation levels, you may experience read consistency problems—such as reading the same row multiple times or skipping rows in an index order scan—that result from an index key change. Under the repeatable read isolation level, a read acquires a shared lock on the resource and releases it only at the end of the transaction. Once a row is read it is locked; another transaction cannot change its key during the scan. Therefore, the scan cannot read the same row multiple times. However, a row that was not yet reached by the scan is not locked yet. If the index key of such a row is changed, and the row is moved to a point in the B-tree that the scan has already passed, the scan will not reach that row at all. Therefore, skipping rows can happen under repeatable read.

For cleanup, change the value back to *'Version 1'*:

```
UPDATE dbo.T1 SET col2 = 'Version 1' WHERE keycol = 2;
```

Serializable

The serializable isolation level is similar to repeatable read, with an additional facet: active transactions acquire key-range locks (placed on indexes) based on query filters. This applies not only to readers, but also to writers. Obtaining a key-range lock is as if you logically lock all data that meets the query's filter. You not only lock whatever data was physically found when you accessed it, but you also lock data that does not exist yet that would happen to meet your query's filter. This level adds the prevention of phantoms to the list of problems repeatable read handles.

Note that if there's no index on the filtered column, SQL Server has to lock the whole table to prevent phantoms. Missing indexes can have a big impact on the concurrency of the system. Therefore, pay extra attention to index design when working with the serializable isolation level.

To demonstrate the prevention of phantoms with the serializable isolation level, first create an index on *T1.col1*:

```
CREATE INDEX idx_col1 ON dbo.T1(col1);
```

Then run the following code from connection 1:

```
SET TRANSACTION ISOLATION LEVEL SERIALIZABLE;
BEGIN TRAN
  SELECT *
  FROM dbo.T1
  WHERE col1 = 102;
```

This query retrieves all rows where *col1 = 102* (currently, there's only one such row in the table) and obtains an exclusive key-range lock in the index *idx_col1* based on the filter.

Next, from connection 2, attempt to introduce a phantom row—a row that meets the filter of the query submitted by connection 1:

```
INSERT INTO dbo.T1(keycol, col1, col2) VALUES(5, 102, 'D');
```

You will be blocked.

Back in connection 1, run the following code to read the qualifying rows again and commit the transaction:

```
  SELECT *
  FROM dbo.T1
  WHERE col1 = 102;
COMMIT TRAN;
```

You get the same row as before and no new rows, meaning you didn't get a phantom read. Now that the transaction has been committed, the key-range lock is released, and the transaction in connection 2 manages to insert the row. If you make a similar attempt in any other isolation level that is locking-based (as opposed to row versioning-based), the insert will be accepted, allowing a phantom read.

Under the serializable isolation level, you will not encounter read consistency problems from index key changes. Under this isolation level, key-range locks are obtained to lock all rows that satisfy the query filter, and readers keep their shared locks until the end of a transaction. As a result, a row that satisfies the query filter cannot be modified during a scan, regardless of whether it is behind or ahead of the scan point. This means that under the serializable isolation level, a scan can neither return the same row multiple times nor skip rows.

Before you continue, run the following code to drop the index on T1:

```
DROP INDEX dbo.T1.idx_col1;
```

Also, set all connections to work under the default read committed isolation level:

```
SET TRANSACTION ISOLATION LEVEL READ COMMITTED;
```

Row Versioning–Based Isolation Levels

SQL Server 2008 supports a *row versioning* technology that allows it to maintain older images (versions) of rows that resulted from committed transactions by using linked lists in tempdb. A source row can point to a linked list in tempdb, potentially containing multiple consistent versions of the row that were available in previous points in time, from newest to oldest.

The row versioning technology supports different aspects of the product, including two isolation levels, which I'll describe here; constructing the *inserted* and *deleted* tables in triggers, as described in the previous chapter; online index operations; and multiple active result sets (MARS).

The two isolation levels that rely on row versioning are *snapshot* and *read committed snapshot*. In both isolation levels, a process does not request shared locks when reading data and is never in conflict with other processes modifying data. When reading data, if a requested row is locked, SQL Server uses the row versioning store to return an older consistent state of the row. Both of the snapshot-related isolation levels provide an optimistic concurrency model.

In both row versioning–based isolation levels, the read consistency problems described earlier—a query reads the same row multiple times or skips rows—cannot happen.

The following sections describe the two isolation levels.

Snapshot

The snapshot isolation level is similar to the serializable isolation level in terms of the logical problems that can or cannot arise, but it's based on row versioning instead of on locking and blocking.

When a process reads data during a transaction running under the snapshot isolation level, the process will get the latest consistent version of the data that was available when the *transaction* started. A transaction is technically considered to have started when the first statement within the transaction is issued. Whenever a transaction modifies a row while the snapshot isolation level is enabled in the database, SQL Server needs to store a consistent version of the row before the modification, regardless of whether the modifying transaction is running at the snapshot isolation. While the transaction that modified the data is open, another process working under snapshot isolation might request the older consistent version of the row.

Note that DELETE and UPDATE statements (and MERGE statements issuing DELETE and UPDATE actions) need to store the previous committed version of the modified rows in the version store. INSERT statements (and MERGE statements issuing an INSERT action) don't need to store the inserted rows in the version store because there was no older version. However, the new rows will internally store versioning information in a few extra bytes that are normally not added to rows when row versioning–based isolations are not enabled.

Working with the snapshot isolation level has a performance impact for all transactions that delete or update data even when no transactions are actually working at the snapshot isolation level. Therefore, SQL Server requires you to turn on a database option to allow working with the snapshot isolation level in the database:

```
ALTER DATABASE testdb SET ALLOW_SNAPSHOT_ISOLATION ON;
```

If this option is turned off, the snapshot isolation level is not allowed in the database and row versions are not recorded in tempdb for snapshot isolation purposes.

To demonstrate working with the snapshot isolation level, run the following code from connection 1 (making sure you first set the database option just shown):

```
SET NOCOUNT ON;
USE testdb;
GO
BEGIN TRAN
  UPDATE dbo.T1 SET col2 = 'Version 2' WHERE keycol = 2;
  SELECT col2 FROM dbo.T1 WHERE keycol = 2;
```

The value of *col2* is changed from *'Version 1'* to *'Version 2'*. Notice that I did not request to change the session's isolation level to snapshot. Rather, the session works in the default read committed isolation level. However, because you turned on the database option that allows the snapshot isolation level, this transaction had to store the state of the row before the change (*col2 = 'Version 1'*) in tempdb.

You can examine the row versions that SQL Server currently maintains in the version store by querying the *sys.dm_tran_version_store* view:

```
SELECT * FROM sys.dm_tran_version_store;
```

Currently, you will find one row in the version store.

Next, run the following code in connection 2, which sets the session's isolation level to snapshot, opens a transaction, and reads the contents of T1:

```
SET NOCOUNT ON;
USE testdb;
GO
SET TRANSACTION ISOLATION LEVEL SNAPSHOT;
BEGIN TRAN
  SELECT col2 FROM dbo.T1 WHERE keycol = 2;
```

You will get the output *'Version 1'*, which was the most recent consistent state of the data when the transaction started (that is, when the first statement in the transaction was issued). Of course, SQL Server acquired that version of the row from the version store.

Now commit the transaction in connection 1:

```
COMMIT TRAN
SELECT col2 FROM dbo.T1 WHERE keycol = 2;
```

The current committed state of the value is now *'Version 2'*. However, the snapshot isolation level is still in effect for the open transaction in connection 2. Remember that when reading data you're supposed to get the latest consistent version when the transaction started. Therefore, the row cannot be removed yet from the version store.

Issue the following query in connection 2:

```
SELECT col2 FROM dbo.T1 WHERE keycol = 2;
```

You will still get the value *'Version 1'*.

Note that if another process opens a transaction and modifies data, another version of the row (the one with the value *'Version 2'*) will be added to the linked list in tempdb in front of the existing one. When connection 1 reads the data again, it ends up traversing a longer linked list. This means that the longer transactions working under snapshot isolation remain open, the longer the linked lists in tempdb grow, and readers end up traversing longer linked lists.

A cleanup process runs about every minute to remove unneeded row versions from the linked lists. However, it only removes a contiguous section within the linked list starting at the tail of the list (that is, the oldest version). This means that long-running transactions might prevent the cleaning of intermediate versions following the oldest one even if they are no longer needed. This cleanup architecture is similar to the cleanup architecture of records in the transaction log.

Bearing the row versioning architecture in mind, you should try to minimize the length of your transaction when working with the snapshot isolation level. Also, you should understand that the snapshot isolation level is not suitable to all environments, but only to environments that mostly read and insert data, and occasionally delete and update data.

At this point, commit the transaction in connection 2 and reread the data:

```
COMMIT TRAN
SELECT col2 FROM dbo.T1 WHERE keycol = 2;
```

You will get the latest committed value *'Version 2'*.

Conflict Detection   Snapshot isolation also provides update-conflict detection capabilities. Remember that the snapshot isolation level is equivalent to serializable in terms of preventing update conflicts, but snapshot uses an optimistic concurrency model. When you read data, you don't acquire any locks. You might want to access data and perform calculations based on the data you accessed for a later update in the same transaction. If between the time you first accessed the data and the time you attempted to modify it another process modified that data, SQL Server will detect the update conflict and abort your transaction. If appropriate, you can reissue the transaction using error-handling code, which will rely on the new state of the data.

As an example of update-conflict detection in action, issue the following code in connection 1:

```
-- Connection 1, Step 1
SET NOCOUNT ON;
USE testdb;
GO
SET TRANSACTION ISOLATION LEVEL SNAPSHOT;
BEGIN TRAN
  SELECT col2 FROM dbo.T1 WHERE keycol = 2;
```

Under the snapshot isolation level, you opened a transaction and queried the data, getting back the value *'Version 2'*. Suppose that you now perform calculations based on the input and then want to modify the data. You issue the following code (still in connection 1), changing the value to *'Version 3'* and committing the transaction:

```
-- Connection 1, Step 2
  UPDATE dbo.T1 SET col2 = 'Version 3' WHERE keycol = 2;
COMMIT
```

The code completed successfully because there was no update conflict—no other process modified the data between the time you read it and updated it.

Now, still in connection 1, open a new transaction and query the data:

```
-- Connection 1, Step 3
BEGIN TRAN
  SELECT col2 FROM dbo.T1 WHERE keycol = 2;
```

You will get back the value *'Version 3'*. In connection 2, update this value, changing it to *'Version 4'*:

```
-- Connection 2, Step 1
SET NOCOUNT ON;
USE testdb;
GO
UPDATE dbo.T1 SET col2 = 'Version 4' WHERE keycol = 2;
```

Back in connection 1, imagine that you have used the *col2* value in a calculation and determined that you should update the value to *'Version 5'*:

```
-- Connection 1, Step 4
  UPDATE dbo.T1 SET col2 = 'Version 5' WHERE keycol = 2;
```

SQL Server detects that someone modified the data between your read and write, terminates your transaction, and produces the following error, which notifies you of the update conflict:

```
Msg 3960, Level 16, State 2, Line 1
Snapshot isolation transaction aborted due to update conflict. You cannot use snapshot
    isolation to access table 'dbo.T1' directly or indirectly in database 'testdb' to update,
    delete, or insert the row that has been modified or deleted by another transaction.
    Retry the transaction or change the isolation level for the update/delete statement.
```

You can write error-handling code that will reissue the transaction in the event that it fails after an update conflict. In the next chapter, you can find coverage of error handling with examples of the treatment of update conflicts.

Note that the snapshot isolation level is not suitable for modification-intensive environments with the potential for many update conflicts. Rather, it is recommended for environments that mainly read data and insert data, with occasional deletes and updates, and infrequent update conflicts.

For cleanup, change the value of *T1.col2* in the row where *keycol = 2* back to *'Version 1'*:

```
UPDATE dbo.T1 SET col2 = 'Version 1' WHERE keycol = 2;
```

At this point, close all connections.

Read Committed Snapshot

Read committed snapshot is a row versioning–based implementation of the read committed isolation level that can be used on a per-database basis. The database option READ_ COMMITTED_SNAPSHOT controls which version of read committed is used. As soon as you set this database option to ON, all sessions working at the read committed level (default) will actually be working at the read committed snapshot level. This is a database global behavioral change that you get just by setting the database option to ON, making it very easy to use because no code changes are required.

The read committed snapshot isolation level differs from the snapshot isolation level in two ways. The first difference is that readers get the latest consistent version of data that was available when the *statement* started, as opposed to when the transaction started. The second difference is that this isolation level does not detect update conflicts, just like read committed.

This isolation level is especially useful for applications that you migrate from platforms that support obtaining earlier consistent versions of data, such as when an application migrates from Oracle to SQL Server. Readers don't need to wait when data has been modified but not committed, and you don't sacrifice the consistency of your reads as you do with the read uncommitted isolation level.

To look at the read committed snapshot isolation level, first turn on the database option in the testdb database:

```
ALTER DATABASE testdb SET READ_COMMITTED_SNAPSHOT ON;
```

Open two new connections, and issue the following code from connection 1:

```
SET NOCOUNT ON;
USE testdb;
GO
BEGIN TRAN
  UPDATE dbo.T1 SET col2 = 'Version 2' WHERE keycol = 2;
  SELECT col2 FROM dbo.T1 WHERE keycol = 2;
```

The default isolation level is read committed as always, but that level is now functioning in its new (snapshot) implementation. The code opened a new transaction, modified the value of *T1.col2* in the row where *keycol = 2* from *'Version 1'* to *'Version 2'*, and queried it. Before the value was modified, SQL Server stored the row with *'Version 1'* in the version store in case another session later requests it.

Query the data in connection 2:

```
SET NOCOUNT ON;
USE testdb;
GO
BEGIN TRAN
  SELECT col2 FROM dbo.T1 WHERE keycol = 2;
```

You will get back the value *'Version 1'*. This is the latest consistent state of the data that was available when the SELECT statement started.

Commit the transaction in connection 1:

```
COMMIT TRAN
```

At this point, the latest consistent version of the data is *'Version 2'*. In connection 2, issue the following query:

```
 SELECT col2 FROM dbo.T1 WHERE keycol = 2;
COMMIT TRAN
```

You will get back the value *'Version 2'*. Had you worked with the snapshot isolation level, you would have gotten back *'Version 1'*.

> **Tip** If you want to request a shared lock while working with the read committed snapshot isolation level, you can do so by specifying the READCOMMITTEDLOCK table hint. Using this hint, a reader will be blocked when requesting a shared lock on a resource that is under modification (exclusively locked). This hint allows readers to work at a similar level to read committed while at read committed snapshot level.

At this point, close all connections.

Restore the testdb database to its default settings:

```
ALTER DATABASE testdb SET ALLOW_SNAPSHOT_ISOLATION OFF;
ALTER DATABASE testdb SET READ_COMMITTED_SNAPSHOT OFF;
```

For your convenience, Table 5-2 provides a summary of all isolation levels, the problems that each allows or prevents, the supported concurrency model, and whether the isolation detects update conflicts for you.

TABLE 5-2 Summary of Isolation Levels

Isolation	Dirty Reads	Lost Updates	Nonrepeatable Reads	Phantoms	Concurrency Model	Update Conflict Detection
Read Uncommitted	Yes	Yes	Yes	Yes	Pessimistic	No
Read Committed	No	Yes	Yes	Yes	Pessimistic	No
Repeatable Read	No	No	No	Yes	Pessimistic	No
Serializable	No	No	No	No	Pessimistic	No
Snapshot	No	No	No	No	Optimistic	Yes
Read Committed Snapshot	No	Yes	Yes	Yes	Optimistic	No

Savepoints

SQL Server does not support a true sense of nested transactions, nor does it support the concept of autonomous transactions yet. When you issue a ROLLBACK TRAN command within a transaction, SQL Server rolls back all activity performed as of the outermost BEGIN TRAN. If you issue a BEGIN TRAN statement within an existing transaction, you don't really open a new transaction. Rather, SQL Server simply increments an internal counter that you can query via the @@TRANCOUNT function. A COMMIT TRAN statement decrements the counter by one, and only the outermost COMMIT TRAN, which decrements the counter to zero, really commits the transaction. SQL Server will limit the number of levels you can open with BEGIN TRAN statements to 32.

SQL Server supports savepoints, which allow you to undo some partial activity within a transaction. To do so, you need to mark a savepoint by issuing a *SAVE TRAN <savepoint name>* statement and later issue a *ROLLBACK TRAN <savepoint name>* to undo the activity that was performed as of that savepoint.

As an example, remember that in the previous chapter I demonstrated how you can maintain your own custom sequence (autonumbering mechanism). I demonstrated a solution that maintains a blocking sequence. That is, when a transaction modifies the sequence value to increment it, it acquires an exclusive lock and keeps it until the transaction terminates. Other transactions attempting to increment the sequence value will be blocked—in other words, the blocking sequence queues requests for new sequence values. That's exactly what you want to establish in cases where you want to prevent gaps in the sequence—for example, when you use the sequence to generate invoice IDs.

In some cases, however, you won't care about gaps in the sequence and simply want to generate unique values—for example, to maintain keys across tables that would not overlap. In these cases, you're after a sequence generator that will not block. You want the sequence value to be locked for a fraction of time so that you can increment it and prevent multiple processes from acquiring the same sequence value. But you don't want it to be locked for the duration of the whole transaction.

You can achieve such a sequence by creating a sequence table with an IDENTITY column like this:

```
USE tempdb;
IF OBJECT_ID('dbo.Sequence', 'U') IS NOT NULL DROP TABLE dbo.Sequence;
CREATE TABLE dbo.Sequence(val INT IDENTITY);
```

Remember that an IDENTITY value increment is not considered part of an external transaction. That is, if within a transaction you insert a row into a table with an IDENTITY column, the identity increment is not rolled back if the transaction rolls back. Furthermore, the identity resource is not locked past the individual increment. To obtain a new sequence value, you simply insert a row into the Sequence table and return the value from the SCOPE_IDENTITY function or using the OUTPUT clause.

However, keep in mind that the sequence table will keep on growing larger and larger. From time to time, you will probably want to empty it. If you empty it with a DELETE statement, the activity will be fully logged; therefore, it will take a while. During the deletion, SQL Server most likely will escalate the fine-grained exclusive locks to a single exclusive table lock. This means that during the operation, processes cannot obtain new sequence values.

The recommended way to empty a large table is to use the fast TRUNCATE TABLE command, which is minimally logged. However, if you issue the TRUNCATE TABLE command, the IDENTITY seed will be reset, which is not a good thing. If you wanted to, you could have the cleanup process use the TRUNCATE TABLE command and then reseed the identity value. The process would do the following: lock the table, save the current identity value in a variable, truncate the table, reseed the identity value to the previously saved value plus 1, and then commit the transaction.

However, if you'd rather not use any cleanup process, you have another option. You can use savepoints to get around this issue. Run the following code to create the stored procedure *GetSequence*, which solves the problem:

```
IF OBJECT_ID('dbo.GetSequence', 'P') IS NOT NULL
  DROP PROC dbo.GetSequence;
GO
CREATE PROC dbo.GetSequence
  @val AS INT OUTPUT
AS
BEGIN TRAN
  SAVE TRAN S1;
  INSERT INTO dbo.Sequence DEFAULT VALUES;
  SET @val = SCOPE_IDENTITY()
  ROLLBACK TRAN S1;
COMMIT TRAN
GO
```

The stored procedure's code issues a BEGIN TRAN statement so that it can define a savepoint. The code defines the savepoint S1 and inserts a row into the Sequence table, generating a new IDENTITY value. The code continues by assigning the newly generated IDENTITY value (via the SCOPE_IDENTITY function) to the output parameter *@val*. The code then issues a rollback to the savepoint S1. The rollback will not affect an external transaction if one was open when the procedure was invoked, because it reverts to the savepoint. The code finally issues a COMMIT TRAN statement that doesn't have any changes to commit, but just terminates the BEGIN TRAN statement.

Whenever you need to get a new sequence value, invoke the *GetSequence* procedure, which returns the output parameter's value to a local variable like so:

```
DECLARE @key AS INT;
EXEC dbo.GetSequence @val = @key OUTPUT;
SELECT @key;
```

As you can see, savepoints can come in handy.

Deadlocks

Deadlocks occur when two or more processes block each other such that they enter a blocking chain that cannot be resolved without the system's intervention. Without intervention, processes involved in a deadlock have to wait indefinitely for one another to relinquish their locks.

SQL Server automatically detects deadlock situations and resolves them by terminating the transaction that did less work. The transaction that was chosen as the deadlock victim receives error 1205. You can trap such an error with error-handling code and determine a course of action. Error handling with deadlock examples is described in the next chapter.

SQL Server gives you a tool to control precedence between sessions in terms of which will be chosen as the deadlock victim. You can set the DEADLOCK_PRIORITY session option to one of 21 possible integer values in the range –10 through 10. Alternatively, you can specify the options LOW (equivalent to –5), NORMAL (default, equivalent to 0), or HIGH (equivalent to 5). Precedence in terms of choosing the deadlock victim is based first on deadlock priorities, and then by the amount of work.

Some deadlock scenarios are desirable—or more accurately, by design. For example, by using the repeatable read isolation level you prevent lost updates by creating a deadlock instead. Of course, you can use other techniques to avoid lost updates—for example, as mentioned earlier, you can have readers specify the UPDLOCK hint when reading data. But generally speaking, you might expect some deadlocks to occur to have the benefit of providing some consistency. However, I have to say that in my experience, most deadlocks I've seen are undesired ones caused by lack of sufficient indexes, unnecessarily long-running transactions, and so on. By understanding the concurrency architecture of the product you might be able to reduce undesired deadlocks, but it's very hard to avoid them altogether. So you still need to maintain error-handling code that deals with those—for example, by retrying the transaction.

In the following sections, I'll provide deadlock examples and suggest ways to troubleshoot and avoid them.

Simple Deadlock Example

Let's start with a simple and classic deadlock example. I apologize if you've seen such examples a thousand times already. I promise to be more exciting in subsequent examples. Here I just want to make sure that the fundamentals are covered, so bear with me.

Open two new connections, and call them connections 1 and 2. Issue the following code from connection 1:

```
SET NOCOUNT ON;
USE testdb;
GO
BEGIN TRAN
  UPDATE dbo.T1 SET col1 = col1 + 1 WHERE keycol = 2;
```

The code opened a new transaction and modified a row in T1. To achieve the modification, the transaction obtained an exclusive lock on the row. Because the transaction remains open, it keeps the exclusive lock on the row.

Issue the following code from connection 2, which updates a row in T2 within a transaction and keeps the transaction open, preserving the exclusive lock on the row:

```
SET NOCOUNT ON;
USE testdb;
GO
BEGIN TRAN
  UPDATE dbo.T2 SET col1 = col1 + 1 WHERE keycol = 2;
```

Issue the following code from connection 1, which attempts to read data from T2:

```
 SELECT col1 FROM dbo.T2 WHERE keycol = 2;
COMMIT TRAN
```

The SELECT query is blocked because it attempts to acquire a shared lock on the row in T2 that is locked exclusively by the other transaction. This is a normal blocking situation—it's not a deadlock yet. Connection 2 might terminate the transaction at some point, releasing the lock on the resource that connection 1 needs.

Next, issue the following code from connection 2, attempting to query the data from T1:

```
 SELECT col1 FROM dbo.T1 WHERE keycol = 2;
COMMIT TRAN
```

At this point, the two processes enter a deadlock, because each is waiting for the other to release its locks. SQL Server intervenes, terminating the transaction in one of the connections (connection 1 in my case) and producing the following error:

```
Msg 1205, Level 13, State 51, Line 1
Transaction (Process ID 53) was deadlocked on lock resources with another process
    and has been chosen as the deadlock victim. Rerun the transaction.
```

I find it a bit amusing that SQL Server uses the terminology "has been chosen" to notify a process of the failure. In my mind, being chosen is usually associated with positive things.

Connection 1 has now obtained the lock it waited for. It reads the data and commits.

This particular deadlock can be avoided if you swap the order in which you access the tables in one of the transactions, assuming that this swap does not break the application's logic. If both transactions access the tables in the same order, such a deadlock will not happen. You can make it a practice when developing transactions to access tables in a particular order (for example, by table name order), as long as this makes sense to the application and doesn't break its logic. This way you can reduce the frequency of deadlocks.

Deadlock Caused by Missing Indexes

Another example for a deadlock demonstrates the most common cause for deadlocks that I've stumbled into in production systems—lack of sufficient indexes. Processes might end up being in conflict with each other even when they need mutually exclusive resources. This can happen when you're lacking indexes on filtered columns. SQL Server has to scan all rows if there's no index on the filtered columns. Thus a conflict can occur when one process holds a lock on a row while another scans all rows to check whether they qualify to the filter instead of seeking the desired row directly through an index.

For example, currently there are no indexes on *T1.col1* and *T1.col2*. Run the following code in connection 1, which opens a transaction, modifies a row in T1 where *col1 = 101*, and keeps the transaction open, thus preserving an exclusive lock on the row:

```
BEGIN TRAN
  UPDATE dbo.T1 SET col2 = col2 + 'A' WHERE col1 = 101;
```

Similarly, run the following code in connection 2, which opens a transaction, modifies a row in T2 where *col1 = 203*, and keeps the transaction open, thus preserving an exclusive lock on the row:

```
BEGIN TRAN
  UPDATE dbo.T2 SET col2 = col2 + 'B' WHERE col1 = 203;
```

Now, in connection 1, try to query a row from T2 that is not locked by connection 2:

```
 SELECT col2 FROM dbo.T2 WHERE col1 = 201;
COMMIT TRAN
```

Because there's no index on *col1*, SQL Server must scan all rows and acquire shared locks to see whether they qualify to the query's filter. However, your transaction cannot obtain a shared lock on the row that is exclusively locked by connection 2; thus, it is blocked.

A similar blocking scenario takes place if, from connection 2, you now try to query a row that is not locked from T1:

```
SELECT col2 FROM dbo.T1 WHERE col1 = 103;
COMMIT TRAN
```

Of course, a deadlock occurs, and one of the processes is "chosen" as the deadlock victim (connection 2 in this case), and you receive the following error:

```
Msg 1205, Level 13, State 51, Line 1
Transaction (Process ID 54) was deadlocked on lock resources with another process and has
been chosen as the deadlock victim. Rerun the transaction.
```

SQL Server gives you several tools to troubleshoot deadlocks. You can start SQL Server's service with the trace flags 1204 and 1222, causing deadlocks to report information in SQL Server's error log (for details, please refer to *http://msdn.microsoft.com/en-us/library/ ms178104.aspx*). Another powerful tool for troubleshooting deadlocks is running traces while the deadlock occurs. If you can reproduce the deadlock by invoking some specific activity from the application, you can run the trace in a controlled manner. Start the trace right before you invoke the specific activity, and stop it right after the deadlock occurs. If you cannot reproduce the deadlock manually or predict when it will take place, you will have to keep the trace running in the background, which of course has a cost.

The trace should include the following events:

- **SQL:StmtStarting**   This event is recorded for each start event of a statement in a batch. If your statements are issued from stored procedures or triggers, use the *SP:StmtStarting* event. Make sure you trace a *Starting* event and not a *Completed* event because the statement that will be terminated will not complete. On the other hand, a *Starting* event will be traced even for statements that are terminated.

- **Lock:Timeout**   This event is produced when a session requests a lock and cannot obtain it. It helps you see which statements were blocked.

- **Lock:Deadlock Chain**   This event is produced for each process involved in the deadlock chain. It allows you to identify the process IDs of the processes involved in the deadlock and focus on their activities in the trace.

- **Lock:Deadlock**   This event simply indicates when the deadlock took place.

- **Deadlock Graph**   This event generates an XML value with the deadlock information. If you choose this event, you can specify on the trace's Event Extraction Settings tab that you want to save deadlock XML events separately—you can direct these deadlock graphs to a single file or to distinct files.

For example, when I traced the deadlock I described in this section I got the trace data shown in Figure 5-1.

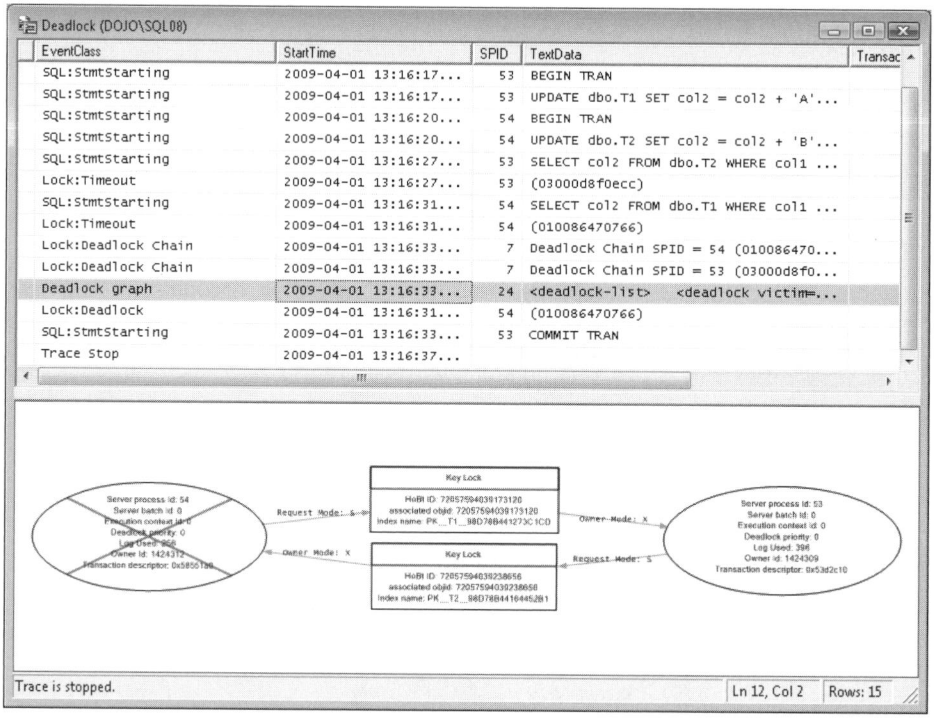

FIGURE 5-1 Deadlock trace

By looking at the *TextData* attribute of the *Lock:Deadlock Chain* event, you can identify the IDs of the processes and transactions involved in the deadlock and focus on them. Also, the *Deadlock Graph* event gives you a graphical view of the deadlock. You can follow the series of *SQL:StmtStarting* events for statements belonging to the processes involved in the deadlock. The *Lock:Timeout* events allow you to identify which statements were blocked. Analyzing this trace should lead you to the conclusion that, logically, the processes should not be in conflict and that your tables might be missing indexes on the filtered columns. If you examine the indexes on the tables, you can confirm your suspicions. To prevent such deadlocks in the future, create the following indexes:

```
CREATE INDEX idx_col1 ON dbo.T1(col1);
CREATE INDEX idx_col1 ON dbo.T2(col1);
```

Now retry the series of activities.

Note With such tiny tables as in our example, SQL Server will typically choose to scan the whole table even when indexes do exist on the filtered columns. Of course, in larger production tables SQL Server will typically use indexes for queries that are selective enough.

When you retry the activities, because our tables are so tiny, specify an index hint to make sure that SQL Server will use the index.

Start by issuing the following code from connection 1 to open a transaction and update a row in T1:

```
BEGIN TRAN
  UPDATE dbo.T1 SET col2 = col2 + 'A' WHERE col1 = 101;
```

Issue the following code from connection 2 to open a transaction, and update a row in T2:

```
BEGIN TRAN
  UPDATE dbo.T2 SET col2 = col2 + 'B' WHERE col1 = 203;
```

Go back to connection 1, and query a row that is not locked by connection 2 from T2 (and, in our case, remember to specify an index hint):

```
 SELECT col2 FROM dbo.T2 WITH (index = idx_col1) WHERE col1 = 201;
COMMIT TRAN
```

The row was obtained through the index created on *T2.col1*, and there was no conflict. The query ran successfully, and the transaction committed.

Connection 2 can now query the row from T1:

```
 SELECT col2 FROM dbo.T1 WITH (index = idx_col1) WHERE col1 = 103;
COMMIT TRAN
```

The query ran successfully, and the transaction committed.

By creating indexes on the filtered columns, you were able to avoid a deadlock. Of course, a deadlock can still happen if processes will block each other in cases where both attempt to access the same resources. In such cases, if possible, you might want to consider applying the approach I suggested in the previous section—namely, revising the order in which you access the tables in one of the transactions. Also, longer transactions increase the potential for deadlocks because locks are held longer. Therefore it's recommended to keep transactions as short as possible.

Make sure that you don't drop the index on T1 because it is used in the following section's example.

Deadlock with a Single Table

Many programmers think that deadlocks can take place only when multiple tables are involved. Keep in mind that a table can have multiple indexes, meaning that multiple resources can still be involved even when multiple processes interact with a single table.

Before I demonstrate such a scenario, let's first run the following UPDATE statement to make sure that *T1.col1* is set to 102 where *keycol = 2*:

```
UPDATE dbo.T1 SET col1 = 102, col2 = 'B' WHERE keycol = 2;
```

To generate a deadlock, first run the following code in connection 1:

```
SET NOCOUNT ON;
USE testdb;

WHILE 1 = 1
  UPDATE dbo.T1 SET col1 = 203 - col1 WHERE keycol = 2;
```

An endless loop invokes, in each iteration, an UPDATE statement against T1, alternating the value of *col1* between 102 and 101 in the row where *keycol = 2*.

Next, issue the following code from connection 2:

```
SET NOCOUNT ON;
USE testdb;

DECLARE @i AS VARCHAR(10);
WHILE 1 = 1
  SET @i = (SELECT col2 FROM dbo.T1 WITH (index = idx_col1)
            WHERE col1 = 102);
```

Again, I used an index hint here just because the T1 table is so tiny and SQL Server might decide not to use the index in such a case. This code also invokes an endless loop, where in each iteration, it issues a SELECT statement against T1 that returns the value of *col2* where *col1 = 102*.

After a few seconds, a deadlock should occur, and the transaction in connection 2 will be terminated. And this is to show that a deadlock can in fact take place even though the processes involved interact with a single table. See if you can figure out the cause of the deadlock.

The chain of events that lead to the deadlock is illustrated in Figure 5-2.

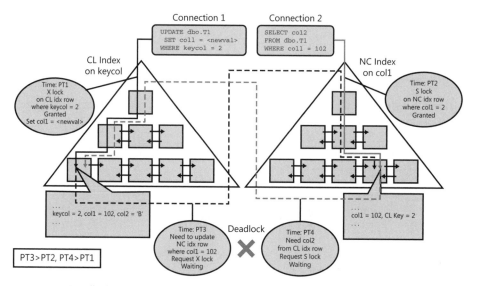

FIGURE 5-2 Deadlock with a single table

Currently, the table T1 has a clustered index defined on *keycol* and a nonclustered one defined on *col1*. With both endless loops running concurrently, there are bound to be occasions where both UPDATE and SELECT statements start running more or less at the same point in time (*PT1* ≈ *PT2*). The UPDATE transaction obtains an exclusive lock in the clustered index on the row where *keycol* = 2. It modifies the value of *col1* from 102 to 103. Then at point in time PT3 (where *PT3* > *PT2*), it attempts to obtain an exclusive lock on the row in the nonclustered index where *col1* = *102* to modify the column value there as well.

Before the UPDATE transaction manages to obtain the lock on the row in the nonclustered index (attempt at point in time PT3), the SELECT transaction obtained a shared lock on that row (at point in time PT2). The SELECT transaction then (at point in time PT4, where *PT4* > *PT1*) attempts to obtain a shared lock on the clustered index row that is currently locked by the UPDATE transaction. The SELECT transaction needs the row from the clustered index in order to return the *col2* value from that row. And you've got yourself a deadlock!

Now that you've figured out this deadlock, try to think of ways to avoid it. For example, obviously if you drop the nonclustered index from T1, such a deadlock will not occur, but such a solution can hardly be considered reasonable. You'll end up with slow queries and other types of deadlocks, such as the ones I described in the previous section. A more viable solution is to create a covering index for the SELECT query that includes *col2*. Such an index satisfies the SELECT query without the need to look up the full data row from the clustered index, thus avoiding the deadlock.

When you're done, run the following code for cleanup:

```
USE testdb;

IF OBJECT_ID('dbo.T1', 'U') IS NOT NULL DROP TABLE dbo.T1;
IF OBJECT_ID('dbo.T2', 'U') IS NOT NULL DROP TABLE dbo.T2;
```

Conclusion

This chapter covered various aspects of transactions and concurrency that you need to consider when developing applications that interact with SQL Server. It covered transactions, locks and blocking, isolation levels, and deadlocks.

You have a lot to consider when developing applications for multiple concurrent users working with SQL Server. You need to understand the concurrency models supported by SQL Server and implement the one that is most appropriate for your system. SQL Server 2008 supports isolation levels that are based on locking and blocking as well as isolation levels that are based on row versioning, providing you with different concurrency models to choose from.

SQL Server 2008 introduces the ability to control lock escalation via the LOCK_ESCALATION table option. Besides the table-level escalation that was supported in the past, you can now set the escalation granularity to the partition level, or even disable it altogether.

Chapter 6
Error Handling

Itzik Ben-Gan

When you develop T-SQL code, you need to take into consideration situations in which your code might fail. SQL Server provides you with tools to handle errors and take corrective measures. The area of error handling with T-SQL was improved dramatically only recently. SQL Server 2005 introduced the TRY/CATCH constructs, which was a big leap forward. Even though some important aspects of error handling in T-SQL are still missing, SQL Server 2008 did not add any improvements in this area. I hope that the next major release of SQL Server will add more features and improvements in this area.

To help you appreciate the benefits of using the TRY/CATCH construct I'll first describe the problematic nature of handling errors without it. Then, most of the chapter will be dedicated to handling errors in T-SQL with TRY/CATCH.

Error Handling without the TRY/CATCH Construct

Error handling in T-SQL without the TRY/CATCH construct has several limitations. It is nonstructured, awkward, and not capable of trapping all errors.

The main tool you have is the *@@ERROR* function, which returns an integer representing the way the last statement terminated (with 0 usually indicating success and a non-zero error code indicating lack of success). You have to assign the value of *@@ERROR* to your own local variable immediately after each suspect statement. Otherwise, you'd lose that value because it will be overridden by the statement that follows the suspect one. Then you have to switch between the possible error codes and determine a course of action. You have to either provide error-handling code after each suspect statement or label an error-handling block and pass control to it using a GOTO command. Either way, the result is typically nonstructured code that is very hard to maintain.

Even worse, if you don't use the TRY/CATCH construct, there are many errors that you simply can't trap, even ones that are not considered severe. Some errors simply terminate your batch and don't give the error-handling code a chance to run, so you have to deal with those at the caller. Examples of errors that terminate your batch include conversion errors and deadlocks.

You can perform a simple test to check whether an error terminates the batch. Simply print something immediately after the statement that generates the error. Then check whether output was generated. For example, the following code does invoke the PRINT statement after a divide-by-zero error is generated:

```
SELECT 1/0;
PRINT 'Still here...';
```

This tells you that a divide-by-zero error doesn't terminate the batch. On the other hand, the following code doesn't invoke the PRINT statement after the conversion error is generated, telling you that a conversion error terminates the batch:

```
SELECT 'A' + 1;
PRINT 'Still here...';
```

Similarly, resolution or compilation errors terminate the batch—for example, referring to a nonexisting object:

```
SELECT * FROM NonExistingObject;
PRINT 'Still here...';
```

Another tricky part about error handling without the TRY/CATCH construct is dealing with volatile functions, such as @@ERROR and @@ROWCOUNT, that change their values after each statement that is run. The @@ERROR function gives you an integer representing the way the last statement terminated. The @@ROWCOUNT function gives you the number of rows affected by the last statement. In many cases, you needed both for error handling. However, if you used separate SET statements to assign the function result values to your own variables (as shown in the following code), the second SET statement would not assign the correct value to @rc.

```
<suspect_statement>
SET @err = @@ERROR;
SET @rc = @@ROWCOUNT;
```

What you end up getting in @rc is the number of rows affected by the first assignment (namely 0), instead of the number of rows affected by the suspect statement. To trap both function result values, you should use a single assignment SELECT statement:

```
SELECT @err = @@ERROR, @rc = @@ROWCOUNT;
```

Here's a small example of how to trap both values immediately after a suspect query:

```
SET NOCOUNT ON;
USE InsideTSQL2008;

DECLARE @custid AS INT, @err AS INT, @rc AS INT;
SET @custid = 1;

SELECT orderid, custid, empid, orderdate
FROM Sales.Orders
WHERE custid = @custid;

SELECT @err = @@ERROR, @rc = @@ROWCOUNT;
-- error handling code goes here
SELECT @err AS error_number, @rc AS row_count;
```

Suppose that the suspect code appears within a stored procedure and you want the caller of the procedure to deal with the error. If the error is not a batch-aborting error (and not at the very end of the procedure), you have to pass the *@@ERROR* and *@@ROWCOUNT* values through the return status/output parameters of the procedure. Otherwise, you have to capture the values of the functions immediately after the procedure call. For example, the following *GetCustomerOrders* procedure returns orders for a given customer ID and date range:

```
IF OBJECT_ID('dbo.GetCustomerOrders', 'P') IS NOT NULL
  DROP PROC dbo.GetCustomerOrders;
GO

CREATE PROC dbo.GetCustomerOrders
  @custid   AS INT,
  @fromdate AS DATETIME = '19000101',
  @todate   AS DATETIME = '99991231 23:59:59.997',
  @numrows  AS INT OUTPUT
AS

DECLARE @err AS INT;

SELECT orderid, custid, empid, orderdate
FROM Sales.Orders
WHERE custid = @custid
  AND orderdate >= @fromdate
  AND orderdate < @todate;

SELECT @numrows = @@ROWCOUNT, @err = @@ERROR;

RETURN @err;
GO
```

For errors that are not batch-aborting ones, the procedure returns the *@@ERROR* value as the return status, and it returns the *@@ROWCOUNT* value through an output parameter called *@numrows*. Listing 6-1 has code that invokes the stored procedure and applies error handling.

LISTING 6-1 Handling errors in the *GetCustomerOrders* procedure

```
SET LOCK_TIMEOUT 5000;
DECLARE @err AS INT, @rc AS INT;

EXEC @err = dbo.GetCustomerOrders
  @custid   = 1, -- Also try with 999
  @fromdate = '20070101',
  @todate   = '20080101',
  @numrows  = @rc OUTPUT;

SELECT -- For batch-aborting errors
  @err = COALESCE(@err, @@ERROR),
  @rc  = COALESCE(@rc, @@ROWCOUNT);
```

```
SELECT @err AS error_number, @rc AS row_count;

IF @err = 0 AND @rc > 0 BEGIN
  PRINT 'Processing Successful';
  RETURN;
END

IF @err = 0 AND @rc = 0 BEGIN
  PRINT 'No rows were selected.';
  RETURN;
END

IF @err = 1222
BEGIN
  PRINT 'Handling lock time out expired error.';
  RETURN;
END

-- other errors
-- IF @err = ...

BEGIN
  PRINT 'Unhandled error detected.';
  RETURN;
END
```

Right after the procedure call, the code in Listing 6-1 captures the values of *@@ERROR* and *@@ROWCOUNT* in the variables *@err* and *@rc*, respectively, in case the error was a batch-aborting one. If the query completes without errors and returns rows, the first IF statement will print the message *'Processing Successful'* and exit. If the query completes without errors and returns no rows, the second IF statement will print the message *'No rows were selected.'* and exit. The PRINT statement represents the section of code where you might want to take care of a no-rows situation. If an error takes place, the code switches between the possible errors using a series of IF statements. To test the code, run it for the first time. You will get back three orders for the requested customer in the requested date range, and you will identify a successful run—that is, *@@ERROR* was *0* and *@@ROWCOUNT* was *3 (>0)*.

Next, open a new connection and run the following code to lock the Orders table:

```
USE InsideTSQL2008;

BEGIN TRAN
  SELECT * FROM Sales.Orders WITH (TABLOCKX);
```

Now go back to the original connection, and run the code in Listing 6-1 again. After about five seconds, a lock timeout expiration error will be generated, and you will get the following output:

```
Msg 1222, Level 16, State 56, Procedure GetCustomerOrders, Line 13
Lock request time out period exceeded.
error_number   row_count
------------   -----------
1222           0
```

Handling lock time out expired error.

When you're done, issue a rollback in the second connection to terminate the transaction:

```
ROLLBACK TRAN
```

There are other limitations to error handling without the TRY/CATCH construct. In addition to the error number you get from the *@@ERROR* function, no other information is available about the error—not the message, not the severity, not the state, not the procedure name where the error happened, and so on.

Error Handling with the TRY/CATCH Construct

Before the introduction of the TRY/CATCH construct you had no choice but to use the unstructured and problematic error handling approach described in the previous section. But in SQL Server versions 2005 and 2008, you can implement much more robust error-handling solutions. The rest of the chapter focuses on implementing error handling using TRY/CATCH.

TRY/CATCH

SQL Server 2008 supports the TRY/CATCH construct. To use it, you place the suspect code in a BEGIN TRY/END TRY block, followed by a BEGIN CATCH/END CATCH block. When an error is encountered in the TRY block, the error is "trapped," and control is passed to the corresponding CATCH block, where you have your error-handling code. If you trap an error, no error message will be generated and sent to the caller. If you want to throw an error to the caller, you can do so using the RAISERROR command. If no error was generated in the TRY block, the CATCH block is skipped.

To demonstrate using the TRY/CATCH construct, first run the following code, which creates the database testdb and within it the Employees table:

```
IF DB_ID('testdb') IS NULL
  CREATE DATABASE testdb;
GO
USE testdb;
GO

IF OBJECT_ID('dbo.Employees', 'U') IS NOT NULL
  DROP TABLE dbo.Employees;
GO
```

```
CREATE TABLE dbo.Employees
(
  empid   INT        NOT NULL,
  empname VARCHAR(25) NOT NULL,
  mgrid   INT        NULL,
  CONSTRAINT PK_Employees PRIMARY KEY(empid),
  CONSTRAINT CHK_Employees_empid CHECK(empid > 0),
  CONSTRAINT FK_Employees_Employees
    FOREIGN KEY(mgrid) REFERENCES Employees(empid)
);
```

Run the following simple example twice:

```
BEGIN TRY
  INSERT INTO dbo.Employees(empid, empname, mgrid)
    VALUES(1, 'Emp1', NULL);
  PRINT 'INSERT succeeded.';
END TRY
BEGIN CATCH
  PRINT 'INSERT failed.';
  /* handle error here */
END CATCH
```

The first time you ran it, the INSERT statement raised no error, so the PRINT statement following it produced the output *'INSERT succeeded'*. The CATCH block was skipped in this case. The second time you ran the code, the INSERT failed on a primary key violation and control was passed to the CATCH block. The CATCH block in this case simply printed the output *'INSERT failed'*.

If an error is generated outside of a TRY block, the error bubbles up to the previous level in the calling stack (the caller). For example, suppose that *proc1* invoked *proc2* within a TRY block and that *proc2* invoked code not in a TRY block and this code generated an error. The error is passed to *proc1*, and control is passed to the CATCH block corresponding to the TRY block that invoked *proc2*. If no TRY block is found up the call stack, the error is passed to the client application.

> **Note** Resolution/compilation errors (for example, referring to an object that does not exist) are not trappable in the same level even when invoked within a TRY block. However, the previous level in the calling stack will trap such an error. So it might be a good practice to encapsulate code that might fail on such errors within a stored procedure and invoke the stored procedure in a TRY block.

Implementing error handling with the TRY/CATCH construct has many advantages over implementing error handling without this construct. With this construct the code is more structured and elegant. All errors are trappable, except for errors with a severity level of 20 and up (for example, hardware failures). And you also have a set of useful and convenient functions available in the CATCH block, replacing the problematic @@ functions. The following section describes those functions.

Error-Handling Functions

Remember that one of the most annoying limitations of error handling without the TRY/CATCH construct is the behavior of @@ functions related to error handling. You have to grab the functions explicitly and place them into your own variables immediately after every suspect statement. If you don't, you lose their values. Furthermore, the information you get back about the error itself is limited only to the error number. When you use the TRY/CATCH construct, the following functions are available in the CATCH block:

- ERROR_NUMBER()
- ERROR_MESSAGE()
- ERROR_SEVERITY()
- ERROR_STATE()
- ERROR_LINE()
- ERROR_PROCEDURE()

Their names pretty much explain their meanings. In addition to the first four, which give you all pieces of information regarding the error that was generated, you have two other functions that allow you to even get the code line number where the error took place and the procedure name (or NULL if the error did not occur in a procedure). The really great thing about these functions, beyond the fact that you get much more information, is that their values don't change throughout the CATCH block. You don't have to access them right away. Rather, you can access them anywhere you like within the CATCH block. So you'd probably prefer to use ERROR_NUMBER, of course, instead of @@*ERROR*.

> **Note** If you trap an error with a TRY/CATCH construct, the error is not thrown to the caller. If you want to throw it to the caller as well, you have to explicitly invoke a RAISERROR command. You can use the error message information returned by the functions, but you will not be allowed to throw the original error number. It will be a user error number (50000). I hope that future versions of SQL Server will allow throwing system errors and rethrowing the original error.

To demonstrate the use of these functions, run the code in Listing 6-2.

LISTING 6-2 Error-handling functions

```
PRINT 'Before TRY/CATCH block.';

BEGIN TRY

  PRINT '  Entering TRY block.';

  INSERT INTO dbo.Employees(empid, empname, mgrid)
    VALUES(2, 'Emp2', 1);
  -- Also try with empid = 0, 'A', NULL
```

```
    PRINT '    After INSERT.';

    PRINT ' Exiting TRY block.';

END TRY
BEGIN CATCH

    PRINT '  Entering CATCH block.';

    IF ERROR_NUMBER() = 2627
    BEGIN
      PRINT '    Handling PK violation...';
    END
    ELSE IF ERROR_NUMBER() = 547
    BEGIN
      PRINT '    Handling CHECK/FK constraint violation...';
    END
    ELSE IF ERROR_NUMBER() = 515
    BEGIN
      PRINT '    Handling NULL violation...';
    END
    ELSE IF ERROR_NUMBER() = 245
    BEGIN
      PRINT '    Handling conversion error...';
    END
    ELSE
    BEGIN
      PRINT '    Handling unknown error...';
    END

    PRINT '    Error Number  : ' + CAST(ERROR_NUMBER() AS VARCHAR(10));
    PRINT '    Error Message : ' + ERROR_MESSAGE();
    PRINT '    Error Severity: ' + CAST(ERROR_SEVERITY() AS VARCHAR(10));
    PRINT '    Error State   : ' + CAST(ERROR_STATE() AS VARCHAR(10));
    PRINT '    Error Line    : ' + CAST(ERROR_LINE() AS VARCHAR(10));
    PRINT '    Error Proc    : ' + ISNULL(ERROR_PROCEDURE(), 'Not within proc');

    PRINT ' Exiting CATCH block.';

END CATCH

PRINT 'After TRY/CATCH block.';
```

The code inserts a valid row into the Employees table and should not generate an error.
It prints messages in key locations of the code so that you will be able to easily figure out
from the output which sections of the code were reached. Upon encountering an error in the
TRY block, control is passed to the CATCH block. The CATCH block examines the return value
of the ERROR_NUMBER() function to determine a course of action. It then just prints the
values from the different functions to return information about the error.

> **Tip** If you intend to repeat using the same error-handling code in other places, it is advisable to encapsulate this code in a stored procedure and call that procedure from the CATCH block. What's interesting is that you don't need to pass error information to the stored procedure as input parameters. As long as the procedure is invoked within the CATCH block, it has access to all the error functions.

The first time you invoke the code in Listing 6-2, it should cause no error and produce the following output, which indicates that the CATCH block was not reached at all:

```
Before TRY/CATCH block.
  Entering TRY block.
    After INSERT.
  Exiting TRY block.
After TRY/CATCH block.
```

Next, run the code again. It causes a primary key violation error, of course, producing the following output:

```
Before TRY/CATCH block.
  Entering TRY block.
  Entering CATCH block.
    Handling PK violation...
    Error Number  : 2627
    Error Message : Violation of PRIMARY KEY constraint 'PK_Employees'.
                    Cannot insert duplicate key in object 'dbo.Employees'.
    Error Severity: 14
    Error State   : 1
    Error Line    : 7
    Error Proc    : Not within proc
  Exiting CATCH block.
After TRY/CATCH block.
```

Similarly, you can try different errors by specifying *0*, *'A'*, *NULL* in the *empid* column, as suggested in the comment following the INSERT statement.

Errors in Transactions

When you're not using the TRY/CATCH construct and an error happens in an explicit transaction, your session can end up in one of two possible transaction states: active and committable transaction, or no open transaction. When you do use TRY/CATCH, your session can end up in a third transaction state called *failed*, also informally referred to as *doomed*. In this state, the transaction is open (still holding all locks), but it is uncommittable, that is, the transaction cannot submit any code that causes writes to the transaction log. In other words, the transaction cannot modify data; rather, it can only read data. Before you apply any modification, you have to first roll back the failed transaction.

Typically, errors with a severity level of 17 and higher, but not 20 or higher, cause a transaction to enter this failed state. You can make all errors under severity 20 enter this state by setting the XACT_ABORT session option to ON. Note that as mentioned in the previous chapter, in triggers the XACT_ABORT session option is ON by default. The nice thing about the failed, or uncommittable, state is that it allows you to keep locks on resources that would have otherwise been released. You can query data to investigate the cause of the failure, and when you're ready for action, you can roll back the existing transaction and immediately start a new one. Without support for this failed state, SQL Server would have had no choice but to roll back some types of errors that can now enter a failed state—for example, deadlocks. Of course, under the failed state you should finish your investigations as quickly as possible and issue a rollback because you are holding on to the locks, preventing others from accessing the locked resources.

The following section describes how you should react to errors based on the transaction state, which you can get by querying the XACT_STATE function.

Using XACT_STATE

XACT_STATE is a function that you invoke in the CATCH block to get the current transaction state. It returns 0 for *no active transaction*, 1 for *active and committable*, and –1 for *active but uncommittable*. To demonstrate the use of this function and how to determine the transaction state, I'll use the code in Listing 6-3.

LISTING 6-3 Error handling with transaction states

```
BEGIN TRY

  BEGIN TRAN
    INSERT INTO dbo.Employees(empid, empname, mgrid)
      VALUES(3, 'Emp3', 1);
    /* other activity */
  COMMIT TRAN

  PRINT 'Code completed successfully.';

END TRY
BEGIN CATCH

  PRINT 'Error: ' + CAST(ERROR_NUMBER() AS VARCHAR(10)) + ' found.';

  IF (XACT_STATE()) = -1
  BEGIN
    PRINT 'Transaction is open but uncommittable.';
    /* ...investigate data... */
    ROLLBACK TRAN; -- can only ROLLBACK
    /* ...handle the error... */
  END
```

```
  ELSE IF (XACT_STATE()) = 1
  BEGIN
    PRINT 'Transaction is open and committable.';
    /* ...handle error... */
    COMMIT TRAN; -- or ROLLBACK
  END
  ELSE
  BEGIN
    PRINT 'No open transaction.';
    /* ...handle error... */
  END

END CATCH
```

This code inserts a row for employee 3 into the Employees table using an explicit transaction in a TRY block. The CATCH block checks the transaction state before determining a course of action. The first time you run the code in Listing 6-3, there should be no errors, because it's a valid new employee. Run the code a second time, and you will get the following output:

```
Error: 2627 found.
Transaction is open and committable.
```

Because a primary key violation is not considered a severe error, it neither completely terminates nor fails the transaction. Rather, the transaction remains open and committable. To see an example where the transaction fails, you can simply set XACT_ABORT to ON, and rerun the code in Listing 6-3:

```
SET XACT_ABORT ON;
-- run code in listing 10-3
SET XACT_ABORT OFF;
```

This time, you get the following output:

```
Error: 2627 found.
Transaction is open but uncommittable.
```

Using Savepoints

When writing error-handling code in a stored procedure, you might want to choose how to react based on whether the procedure was invoked from within an outer explicit transaction. For example, let's say that upon encountering an error in the stored procedure, you want to undo the procedure's activity only if the procedure opened the transaction. You don't want any side effects on an outer transaction. To achieve this, you use savepoints. Run the code in Listing 6-4 to create the *AddEmp* procedure, which adds a new employee into the Employees table based on user inputs.

LISTING 6-4 Creation script for the *AddEmp* stored procedure

```
IF OBJECT_ID('dbo.AddEmp', 'P') IS NOT NULL DROP PROC dbo.AddEmp;
GO

CREATE PROC dbo.AddEmp
  @empid AS INT, @empname AS VARCHAR(25), @mgrid AS INT
AS

-- Save tran count aside
DECLARE @tc AS INT;
SET @tc = @@TRANCOUNT;

-- If tran was already active, create a savepoint
IF @tc > 0
  SAVE TRAN S1;
-- If tran was not active, open a new one
ELSE
  BEGIN TRAN

BEGIN TRY;
  -- Modify data
  INSERT INTO dbo.Employees(empid, empname, mgrid)
    VALUES(@empid, @empname, @mgrid);
  -- If proc opened the tran, it's responsible for committing it
  IF @tc = 0
    COMMIT TRAN;

END TRY
BEGIN CATCH
    PRINT 'Error detected.';
    PRINT CASE XACT_STATE()
      WHEN 0 THEN 'No transaction is open.'
      WHEN 1 THEN 'Transaction is open and committable.'
      WHEN -1 THEN 'Transaction is open and uncommittable.'
    END;
    -- Proc opened tran
    IF @tc = 0
    BEGIN
      -- Can react differently based on tran state (XACT_STATE)
      -- In this case, say we just want to roll back
      IF XACT_STATE() <> 0
      BEGIN
        PRINT 'Rollback of tran opened by proc.';
        ROLLBACK TRAN
      END
    END
    -- Proc didn't open tran
    ELSE
    BEGIN
      IF XACT_STATE() = 1
      BEGIN
        PRINT 'Proc was invoked in an open tran.
Roll back only proc''s activity.';
        ROLLBACK TRAN S1
      END
```

```
        ELSE IF XACT_STATE() = -1
            PRINT 'Proc was invoked in an open tran, but tran is uncommittable.
  Deferring error handling to caller.'
        END

        -- Raise error so that caller will determine what to do with
        -- the failure in the proc
        DECLARE
          @ErrorMessage  NVARCHAR(400),
          @ErrorSeverity INT,
          @ErrorState    INT;
        SELECT
          @ErrorMessage  = ERROR_MESSAGE()
            + QUOTENAME(N'Original error number: '
                      + CAST(ERROR_NUMBER() AS NVARCHAR(10)), N'('),
          @ErrorSeverity = ERROR_SEVERITY(),
          @ErrorState    = ERROR_STATE();
        RAISERROR (@ErrorMessage, @ErrorSeverity, @ErrorState);
  END CATCH
  GO
```

The procedure starts by saving the value of *@@TRANCOUNT* in the local variable *@tc*. The *@tc* variable tells you whether the procedure was invoked from an outer transaction (*@tc > 0*) or not (*@tc = 0*). If invoked from an outer transaction, the procedure just marks a savepoint so that it can undo only its own activity upon failure. If no transaction is open, the procedure simply opens a new one.

The procedure then issues the INSERT statement within a TRY block and commits the transaction if the procedure opened it.

The CATCH block deals separately with a case where the procedure opened the transaction and a case where it didn't. If the former situation occurs, the code checks whether a transaction is still open (XACT_STATE() <> 0) and simply rolls it back. Of course, you might want to react differently based on the transaction state. If the latter situation occurs, the code checks whether the transaction is open and committable, and in such a case rolls it back. If it's open and uncommittable, you're not allowed to roll back a transaction to a savepoint, so the code constructs an error message and throws it to the caller.

To test the procedure, first clear the Employees table:

```
TRUNCATE TABLE dbo.Employees;
```

Next, run the following code twice, but not within an explicit transaction:

```
EXEC AddEmp @empid = 1, @empname = 'Emp1', @mgrid = NULL;
```

The first run succeeds. The second run produces the following output:

```
Error detected.
Transaction is open and committable.
Rollback of tran opened by proc.
```

```
Msg 50000, Level 14, State 1, Procedure AddEmp, Line 66
Violation of PRIMARY KEY constraint 'PK_Employees'. Cannot insert duplicate key in object
    'dbo.Employees'.(Original error number: 2627)
```

Now run it again, but this time within an explicit transaction:

```
BEGIN TRAN
  EXEC AddEmp @empid = 1, @empname = 'Emp1', @mgrid = NULL;
ROLLBACK
```

You get the following output:

```
Error detected.
Transaction is open and committable.
Proc was invoked in an open tran. Roll back only proc's activity.
Msg 50000, Level 14, State 1, Procedure AddEmp, Line 67
Violation of PRIMARY KEY constraint 'PK_Employees'. Cannot insert duplicate key in object
    'dbo.Employees'.(Original error number: 2627)
```

This time the procedure identified that it was invoked from an outer transaction, and upon error rolled back only its own activity (to the savepoint). To demonstrate a failed transaction, set XACT_ABORT ON and try again:

```
SET XACT_ABORT ON;

BEGIN TRAN
  EXEC AddEmp @empid = 1, @empname = 'Emp1', @mgrid = NULL;
ROLLBACK

SET XACT_ABORT OFF;
```

You get the following output:

```
Error detected.
Transaction is open and uncommittable.
Proc was invoked in an open tran, but tran is uncommittable. Deferring error
   handling to caller.
Msg 50000, Level 14, State 1, Procedure AddEmp, Line 67
Violation of PRIMARY KEY constraint 'PK_Employees'. Cannot insert duplicate key in object
    'dbo.Employees'.(Original error number: 2627)
```

This time the procedure identified a failed transaction opened by the caller, so it deferred the error handling to the caller.

Deadlocks and Update Conflicts

In this final section about error handling, I'll demonstrate how you can trap deadlock errors and apply retry logic for them. I'll also show examples that deal with update conflicts detected when you work with the snapshot isolation level. Here as well, as in a deadlock case, you might want to retry several times before you deem the activity a goner.

I'll use simple T1 and T2 tables, which you create and populate by running the following code:

```
USE testdb;

IF OBJECT_ID('dbo.T1', 'U') IS NOT NULL DROP TABLE dbo.T1;
IF OBJECT_ID('dbo.T2', 'U') IS NOT NULL DROP TABLE dbo.T2;

CREATE TABLE dbo.T1(col1 INT);
INSERT INTO dbo.T1 VALUES(1);

CREATE TABLE dbo.T2(col1 INT);
INSERT INTO dbo.T2 VALUES(1);
```

We will look at two processes that access tables T1 and T2. Those processes will always succeed individually, but will cause a deadlock if run concurrently, because they access T1 and T2 in opposite orders.

First, examine the code in Listing 6-5, and for now, ignore the mention of the snapshot isolation level. Focus only on the deadlock treatment here.

LISTING 6-5 Error-handling retry logic, connection 1

```
SET NOCOUNT ON;
USE testdb;
GO

-- SET TRANSACTION ISOLATION LEVEL SNAPSHOT;
SET LOCK_TIMEOUT 30000;

DECLARE @retry AS INT, @i AS INT, @j AS INT, @maxretries AS INT;
SELECT @retry = 1, @i = 0, @maxretries = 3;

WHILE @retry = 1 AND @i <= @maxretries
BEGIN
  SET @retry = 0;
  BEGIN TRY
    BEGIN TRAN
      SET @j = (SELECT SUM(col1) FROM dbo.T1);
      WAITFOR DELAY '00:00:05';
      UPDATE dbo.T1 SET col1 += 1;
      WAITFOR DELAY '00:00:05';
      SET @j = (SELECT SUM(col1) FROM dbo.T2);
    COMMIT TRAN
    PRINT 'Transaction completed successfully.';
  END TRY
  BEGIN CATCH
    -- Lock timeout
    IF ERROR_NUMBER() = 1222
    BEGIN
      PRINT 'Lock timeout detected.';
      IF XACT_STATE() <> 0 ROLLBACK;
    END
    -- Deadlock / Update conflict
```

```
      ELSE IF ERROR_NUMBER() IN (1205, 3960)
      BEGIN
        PRINT CASE ERROR_NUMBER()
                WHEN 1205 THEN 'Deadlock'
                WHEN 3960 THEN 'Update conflict'
             END + ' detected.';
        IF XACT_STATE() <> 0 ROLLBACK;
        SELECT @retry = 1, @i += 1;
        IF @i <= @maxretries
        BEGIN
          PRINT 'Retry #' + CAST(@i AS VARCHAR(10)) + '.';
          WAITFOR DELAY '00:00:05';
        END
      END
      ELSE
      BEGIN
        PRINT 'Unhandled error: ' + CAST(ERROR_NUMBER() AS VARCHAR(10))
          + ', ' + ERROR_MESSAGE();
        IF XACT_STATE() <> 0 ROLLBACK;
      END
    END CATCH
  END

  IF @i > @maxretries
    PRINT 'Failed ' + CAST(@maxretries AS VARCHAR(10)) + ' retries.';
```

The TRY block runs a SELECT against T1, waits five seconds, runs an UPDATE against T1, waits five seconds, and then issues a SELECT against T2. Observe that the code runs in a loop, with a condition based on two flags: retry required (*@retry = 1*), and number of retries is smaller than or equal to a given maximum (*@i <= @maxretries*). The *@retry* flag is initialized with 1, *@i* with 0, and *@maxretries* with 3, so of course, the code runs at least once.

The code before the TRY block sets *@retry* to 0 so that if all goes well, there won't be another retry. If an error is generated, and it's one you want to apply retry logic to (for example, deadlock, update conflict), in the CATCH block you set the *@retry* flag to 1, increment *@i*, and enter a small delay. That's basically it.

Examine the CATCH block and you will see different treatments for different errors. In case of a lock timeout error (1222), there's no point in a retry, so you simply roll back the transaction if one is open. As for deadlocks and update conflicts, you do apply retry after rolling back the existing transaction (if one is open). Run the code in Listing 6-5 (call the connection *connection 1*). The code should complete after about 10 seconds without problem, producing the following output:

```
Transaction completed successfully.
```

The code in Listing 6-6 is similar to the one in Listing 6-5, except with a reversed access order to the tables.

LISTING 6-6 Error-handling retry logic, connection 2

```
SET NOCOUNT ON;
USE testdb;
GO

SET LOCK_TIMEOUT 30000;

DECLARE @retry AS INT, @i AS INT, @j AS INT, @maxretries AS INT;
SELECT @retry = 1, @i = 0, @maxretries = 3;

WHILE @retry = 1 AND @i <= @maxretries
BEGIN
  SET @retry = 0;
  BEGIN TRY
    BEGIN TRAN
      SET @j = (SELECT SUM(col1) FROM dbo.T2);
      WAITFOR DELAY '00:00:05';
      UPDATE dbo.T2 SET col1 += 1;
      WAITFOR DELAY '00:00:05';
      SET @j = (SELECT SUM(col1) FROM dbo.T1);
    COMMIT TRAN
    PRINT 'Transaction completed successfully.';
  END TRY
  BEGIN CATCH
    -- Lock timeout
    IF ERROR_NUMBER() = 1222
    BEGIN
      PRINT 'Lock timeout detected.';
      IF XACT_STATE() <> 0 ROLLBACK;
    END
    -- Deadlock / Update conflict
    ELSE IF ERROR_NUMBER() IN (1205, 3960)
    BEGIN
      PRINT CASE ERROR_NUMBER()
              WHEN 1205 THEN 'Deadlock'
              WHEN 3960 THEN 'Update conflict'
            END + ' detected.';
      IF XACT_STATE() <> 0 ROLLBACK;
      SELECT @retry = 1, @i += 1;
      IF @i <= @maxretries
      BEGIN
        PRINT 'Retry #' + CAST(@i AS VARCHAR(10)) + '.';
        WAITFOR DELAY '00:00:05';
      END
    END
    ELSE
    BEGIN
      PRINT 'Unhandled error: ' + CAST(ERROR_NUMBER() AS VARCHAR(10))
        + ', ' + ERROR_MESSAGE();
      IF XACT_STATE() <> 0 ROLLBACK;
    END
  END CATCH
END

IF @i > @maxretries
  PRINT 'Failed ' + CAST(@maxretries AS VARCHAR(10)) + ' retries.';
```

Open a new connection (call it connection 2), and have the code from Listing 6-6 ready to run. Run the code in both connections, and try to start the second very close to the first (within five seconds). One of them will finish successfully, while the other will face a deadlock and enter retry logic. In my case, it was connection 2, which generated the following output:

```
Deadlock detected.
Retry #1.
Transaction completed successfully.
```

Naturally, once connection 2 was deadlocked and released the locks, connection 1 could finish and release its own locks. Connection 2 waited a bit, tried again, and then was successful. To demonstrate exceeding the maximum number of retries you specified, open a third connection (call it connection 3) and have the following code ready in it:

```
SET NOCOUNT ON;
USE testdb;
GO

SET LOCK_TIMEOUT 30000;
DECLARE @j AS INT;

BEGIN TRAN

  UPDATE dbo.T2 SET col1 += 1;
  UPDATE dbo.T2 SET col1 += 1;
  UPDATE dbo.T2 SET col1 += 1;

  WAITFOR DELAY '00:00:05';

  WHILE 1 = 1
  BEGIN
    SET @j = (SELECT SUM(col1) FROM dbo.T1);
    WAITFOR DELAY '00:00:01';
  END
```

This code will keep an exclusive lock on T2 as soon as the first UPDATE takes place, and then in a loop, every second, it will request a shared lock on T1 to read. If you run it concurrently with the code in connection 1, you should get repeated deadlocks in connection 1. So first run the code in connection 1, and then immediately start the code in connection 3. After about a minute, you should get the following output in connection 1:

```
Deadlock detected.
Retry #1.
Deadlock detected.
Retry #2.
Deadlock detected.
Retry #3.
Deadlock detected.
Failed 3 retries.
```

Don't forget to stop the activity in connection 3 and roll back the transaction when you're done:

```
ROLLBACK TRAN
```

Update conflicts can occur when a transaction running in the snapshot isolation level reads a row at one point in time and then tries to modify the row at a later point. If SQL Server identifies that another transaction changed the row in between those two points in time, an update conflict occurs. Your transaction might be making calculations based on values it got by first reading the data, and later using the result of the calculation to update the data. If someone modifies the data between the time you first read it and the time you modify it, your modification might not be logically valid anymore.

One feature of the snapshot isolation level is that it detects such update conflicts for you automatically. This allows you to use optimistic concurrency control. If you read and then modify a resource, and no one else modified the resource in between, the modification will work smoothly. But if someone did modify the resource in between, when you try to modify the resource SQL Server will detect the conflict and terminate your transaction, generating error 3960. Typically, you want to retry the transaction in such a case. The logic is so similar to retrying in a case of a deadlock that there's nothing really much to add. The error-handling code in Listings 6-5 and 6-6 handles deadlocks (error 1205) and update conflicts (error 3960) the same way.

To work with the snapshot isolation level, you must first enable it for the current database:

```
ALTER DATABASE testdb SET ALLOW_SNAPSHOT_ISOLATION ON;
```

Make sure you still have the code from Listing 6-5 in connection 1. Open a new connection (call it connection 4), and have the following code ready:

```
SET NOCOUNT ON;
USE testdb;

SET LOCK_TIMEOUT 30000;

WHILE 1 = 1
BEGIN
  UPDATE dbo.T1 SET col1 += 1;
  WAITFOR DELAY '00:00:01';
END
```

This code simply issues an UPDATE against T1 every second. Now run the code in connection 1, and immediately start the code in connection 4 as well. The code in connection 1 keeps reading from T1, waiting five seconds, and then writing to T1. Because connection 4 changes T1 every second, connection 1 will encounter plenty of update conflicts. Feel free to stop the execution in connection 4 from time to time to see that connection 1 at some point will finish successfully. If you just allow connection 4 to keep running, after three retries connection 1 will produce the following output:

```
Update conflict detected.
Retry #1.
Update conflict detected.
Retry #2.
```

```
Update conflict detected.
Retry #3.
Update conflict detected.
Failed 3 retries.
```

Don't forget to stop the activity in connection 4 when you're done. At this point, you can close all connections.

Conclusion

Error handling has taken a major leap forward with the introduction of the TRY/CATCH construct. When you use TRY/CATCH your error-handling code is more structured, elegant, and traps all errors except for the most severe ones. It also provides a lot of useful information via the error-related functions. When you are using TRY/CATCH, and an error happens in an explicit transaction, your session can end up in one of three different transaction states: no transaction open, open and committable, or open and uncommittable (failed). Remember that the failed state allows you to keep a transaction open, holding all locks, while you're investigating data. You then must roll back the transaction before making any change. I hope that future versions of SQL Server will add more error-handling features, such as throwing system errors, rethrowing errors, and autonomous transactions, to name a few.

More Info   You can find interesting information about error handling in SQL Server at Erland Sommarskog's Web site: *www.sommarskog.se*. Erland is a very active SQL Server MVP, and the subject of error handling is very close to his heart.

Chapter 7
Temporary Tables and Table Variables

Itzik Ben-Gan

T-SQL programming often involves the need to materialize data temporarily. *Temporary tables* are just one solution; other ways for handling an independent physical or logical materialization of a set include table variables and table expressions such as views, inline user-defined functions (UDFs), derived tables, and common table expressions (CTEs).

You might need to physically persist interim states of your data for performance reasons, or just as a staging area. Examples of such scenarios include:

- Materializing aggregated data to some level of granularity (for example, employee and month), and issuing running, sliding, and other statistical reports against that data

- Materializing a result of a query for paging purposes

- Materializing result sets of interim queries, and querying the materialized data

- Materializing the result of a query with the GROUPING SETS, CUBE and ROLLUP options, and issuing queries against that data

- Walking through the output of a cursor and saving information you read or calculate per row for further manipulation

- Pivoting data from an Open Schema environment to a more traditional form, and issuing queries against the pivoted data

- Creating a result set that contains a hierarchy with additional attributes such as materialized paths or levels, and issuing reports against the result

- Holding data that needs to be scrubbed before it can be inserted

One of the benefits of materializing data in a temporary table is that it can be more compact than the base data, with preprocessed calculations, and you can index it when it might be inefficient or impractical to index all the base data. In terms of performance, you typically benefit from materializing the data when you need to access it multiple times, but in some cases, even when all you have is a single query against the data, you benefit.

You might also need to materialize interim sets logically in virtual temporary tables (table expressions) to develop solutions in a modular approach. I'll show examples in this chapter that address this need as well. Either way, there are many cases in which using temporary tables, table variables, or table expressions can be useful.

There's a lot of confusion around choosing the appropriate type of temporary object for a given task, and there are many myths regarding the differences between temporary tables and table variables. Furthermore, temporary tables and table variables are often misused because of lack of knowledge of efficient set-based programming.

In this chapter, I will try to provide you with a clear picture of how the different temporary object types behave, in which circumstances you should use each, and whether you should use them at all. At the end of the chapter, I'll provide a summary table (Table 7-1) that contrasts and compares the different types. This table covers the factors you should take into consideration before making your choice.

Temporary Tables

SQL Server supports two types of temporary tables: local and global. For the most part, I'll focus on local temporary tables because this is the type you would typically consider in the same situations as table variables and table expressions. I'll also describe global temporary tables, but these typically have different uses than local temporary tables.

Local Temporary Tables

I'll start with some fundamentals of local temporary tables before showing examples, and I'll do the same whenever discussing a new temporary object type. When referring to temporary tables in this section, assume that the discussion pertains to local ones.

You create and manipulate a temporary table just as you would a permanent one, for the most part. I'll point out the aspects of temporary tables that are different from permanent ones, or aspects that are often misunderstood.

tempdb

Temporary tables are created in tempdb, regardless of the database context of your session. They have physical representation in tempdb, although when they're small enough and Microsoft SQL Server has enough memory to spare, their pages reside in cache. SQL Server persists the temporary table's pages on disk when there is too little free memory. Furthermore, tempdb's recovery model is SIMPLE and cannot be changed. This means that bulk operations against temporary tables can benefit from minimal logging. Also, SQL Server supports a deferred drop feature in tempdb. When the application drops a large temporary table SQL Servers defers the drop activity to a background thread, so the application can continue working immediately.

Unlike user databases, tempdb is created from scratch as a copy of the model database every time you restart SQL Server, hence there's no need for a recovery process in tempdb. This fact leads to optimizations that you can benefit from when modifying data in tempdb regardless of the object type you are working with (temp table, table variable, or even a regular table). The transaction log doesn't need to be flushed to disk and therefore transactions in tempdb are committed faster. Also, certain types of modifications against objects in tempdb (mainly INSERT and UPDATE operations on heap and LOB data) can benefit from optimized logging: because you don't need to run a redo phase from the log (roll forward transactions that were committed after the last checkpoint) only the value before the change needs to be recorded in the log—not the value after the change. Later in the chapter I'll provide more details about working with tempdb.

One reason to use a temporary table is to take the load off of a user database when you need to persist temporary data. You can also enjoy the fact that tempdb is treated differently from user databases.

> **Tip** My preferred method for checking whether an object already exists is to use the OBJECT_ID function. If the function returns NULL, the object doesn't exist. If you want to check whether a temporary table already exists, make sure you specify the tempdb database prefix; otherwise, SQL Server looks for it in the current database, doesn't find it, and always returns NULL. For example, to check whether #T1 exists, use OBJECT_ID('tempdb..#T1') and not OBJECT_ID('#T1').
>
> Also, SQL Server supports a second argument for OBJECT_ID, where you can specify the object type you're looking for (for example, 'U' for user table). The second argument's value must match the type column in *sys.objects*.

Scope and Visibility

Temporary table names are prefixed with a number symbol (#). A temporary table is owned by the creating session and visible only to it. However, SQL Server allows different sessions to create a temporary table with the same name. Internally, SQL Server adds underscores and a unique numeric suffix to the table name to distinguish between temporary tables with the same name across sessions. For example, suppose that you created a temporary table called #T1. If you query the view *sys.objects* in tempdb looking for a table with the name LIKE '#T1%', you will find a table with a name similar to the following (the suffix will vary):

#T1_____
_____00000000001E. Although this is the table's internal name, you refer to it in your code by the name you used when you created it—#T1.

Within the session, the temporary table is visible only to the creating level in the call stack and also inner levels, not to outer ones. For example, if you create a temp table in the session's outermost level, it's available anywhere within the session, across batches, and even in inner levels—for example, dynamic batch, stored procedure, and trigger. As long as you don't close the connection, you can access the temporary table. If it's created within a stored procedure, it's visible to the stored procedure and inner levels invoked by that procedure (for example, a nested procedure or a trigger). You can rely on the visibility behavior of temporary tables—for example, when you want to pass data between different levels in your session, or even just signal something to an inner level and that inner level doesn't support input parameters (for example, a trigger). However, in some cases, you can pass such information through the *context_info* feature, which is visible across the session. (See SET CONTEXT_INFO in SQL Server Books Online for details.)

When its creating level gets out of scope (terminates), a temporary table is automatically destroyed. If a temporary table was created in the outermost level, it is destroyed when the session is terminated. If it's created within a stored procedure, it is automatically dropped as soon as the stored procedure is finished.

Remember that a temporary table is not visible to levels outside of the creating one in the call stack. That's why, for example, you can't use a temporary table created in a dynamic batch in the calling batch. When the dynamic batch is out of scope, the temporary table is gone. Later in the chapter, I'll suggest alternatives to use when such a need occurs. The next part, regarding the scope, is a bit tricky. You can, in fact, create multiple temporary tables with the same name within the same session, as long as you create them in different levels—although doing so might lead to trouble. I'll elaborate on this point in the "Temporary Table Name Resolution" section later in the chapter.

The scope and visibility of a temporary table are very different than they are with both permanent tables and table variables and can be major factors in choosing one type of temporary object over another.

Transaction Context

A temporary table is an integral part of an outer transaction if it's manipulated in one (with DML or DDL). This fact has consequences for logging and locking. Logging has to support rollback operations only, not roll-forward ones. (Remember, there is no recovery process in tempdb.) As for locking, because the temporary table is visible only to the creating session, less locking is involved than with permanent tables, which can be accessed from multiple sessions.

Therefore, one of the factors you should consider when choosing a temporary object type is whether you want manipulation against it to be part of an outer transaction.

Statistics

The optimizer creates and maintains distribution statistics (column value histograms) for temporary tables and keeps track of their cardinality, much as it does for permanent ones. This capability is especially important when you index the temporary table. Distribution information is available to the optimizer when it needs to estimate selectivity, and you will get optimized plans that were generated based on this information. This is one of the main areas in which temporary tables differ from table variables in terms of performance.

Also, because statistics are maintained for temporary tables, queries against your temporary tables will be recompiled because of plan optimality reasons (recompilation threshold reached, statistics refreshed, and so on). The recompilation threshold is reached when a sufficient number of rows of a referenced table have changed since the last compilation. The recompilation threshold (RT) is based on the table type and the number of rows. For permanent tables, if $n \leq 500$, then $RT = 500$ (n = table's cardinality when a query plan is compiled). If $n > 500$, then $RT = 500 + 0.20 \times n$. For temporary tables, if $n < 6$, then $RT = 6$. If $6 \leq n \leq 500$, then $RT = 500$. If $n > 500$, then $RT = 500 + 0.20 \times n$. You realize that, for example, after inserting six rows into a temporary table, adding a seventh will trigger a recompile, whereas with permanent tables the first trigger will occur much later. If you want queries against temporary tables to use the same recompilation thresholds as against permanent ones, use the KEEP PLAN query hint.

The fact that the optimizer maintains distribution statistics for temporary tables and the aforementioned implications are the most crucial aspects of choosing a temporary object type. These factors are especially important when choosing between temporary tables and table variables, for which the optimizer doesn't create or maintain distribution statistics. Rowcount information is maintained for table variables (in *sys.partitions*) but this information is often inaccurate. Table variables themselves do not trigger recompiles because of plan optimality reasons, and recompiles are required to update the rowcount information. You can force a recompile for a query involving table variables using the RECOMPILE query hint.

You must ask yourself two main questions when considering which type of temporary object to use:

1. Does the optimizer need distribution statistics or accurate cardinality estimations to generate an efficient plan, and if so, what's the cost of using an inefficient plan when statistics are not available?

2. What's the cost of recompilations if you do use temporary tables?

In some cases the optimizer doesn't need statistics to figure out an optimal plan—for example, given a query requesting all rows from a table, a point query filtering a column on which a unique index is defined, a range query that utilizes a clustered or covering index, and so on. In such cases, regardless of the table's size, there's no benefit in having statistics because you will only suffer from the cost of recompilations. In such cases, consider using a table variable.

Also, if the table is tiny (say, a couple of pages), the alternatives are 1) using a table variable resulting in complete scans and few or no recompilations; or 2) using a temporary table resulting in index seeks and more recompilations. The advantage of seeks versus scans may be outweighed by the disadvantage of recompiles. That's another case for which you should consider using table variables.

On the other hand, if the optimizer does need statistics to generate an efficient plan and you're not dealing with tiny tables, the cost of using an inefficient plan might well be substantially higher than the cost of the recompilations involved. That's a case in which you should consider using temporary tables. In the "Table Variables" section, I'll provide examples related to these scenarios in which I'll also demonstrate execution plans.

Temporary Table Name Resolution

As I mentioned earlier, technically you're allowed to create multiple local temporary tables with the same name within the same session, as long as you create them in different levels. However, you should avoid doing this because of name-resolution considerations that might cause your code to break.

When a batch is resolved, the schema of a temporary table that is created within that batch is not available. So resolution of code that refers to the temporary table is deferred to run time. However, if a temporary table name you refer to already exists within the session (for example, it has been created by a higher level in the call stack), that table name will resolve to the existing temporary table. However, the code will always run against the innermost temporary table with the referenced name.

This resolution architecture can cause your code to break when you least expect it; this can happen when temporary tables with the same name exist in different levels with different schemas.

This part is very tricky and is probably best explained by using an example. Run the following code to create the stored procedures *proc1* and *proc2*:

```
SET NOCOUNT ON;
USE tempdb;

IF OBJECT_ID('dbo.proc1', 'P') IS NOT NULL DROP PROC dbo.proc1;
IF OBJECT_ID('dbo.proc2', 'P') IS NOT NULL DROP PROC dbo.proc2;
GO

CREATE PROC dbo.proc1
AS

CREATE TABLE #T1(col1 INT NOT NULL);
INSERT INTO #T1 VALUES(1);
SELECT * FROM #T1;

EXEC dbo.proc2;
GO

CREATE PROC dbo.proc2
AS

CREATE TABLE #T1(col1 INT NULL);
INSERT INTO #T1 VALUES(2);
SELECT * FROM #T1;
GO
```

proc1 creates a temporary table called #T1 with a single integer column, inserts a row with the value 1, returns #T1's contents, and invokes *proc2*, which also creates a temporary table called #T1 with a single integer column, inserts a row with the value 2, and returns #T1's contents. Both #T1 tables have the same schema. Now, invoke *proc1*:

```
EXEC dbo.proc1;
```

The output is what you probably expected:

```
col1
-----------
1

col1
-----------
2
```

Both procedures returned the contents of the #T1 table they created. Being oblivious to the resolution process I described earlier doesn't really affect you in this case. After all, you did get the expected result, and the code ran without errors. However, things change if you alter *proc2* in such a way that it creates #T1 with a different schema than in *proc1*:

```
ALTER PROC dbo.proc2
AS

CREATE TABLE #T1(col1 INT NULL, col2 INT NOT NULL);
INSERT INTO #T1 VALUES(2, 2);
SELECT * FROM #T1;
GO
```

Run *proc1* again:

```
EXEC dbo.proc1;
```

And notice the error you get in the output:

```
col1
-----------
1

Msg 213, Level 16, State 1, Procedure proc2, Line 5
Insert Error: Column name or number of supplied values does not match table definition.
```

Can you explain the error? Admittedly, the problem in the resolution process I described is very elusive, and you might not have realized it after the first read. Try to read the paragraph describing the resolution process again, and then see whether you can explain the error. Essentially, when *proc2* was invoked by *proc1*, a table called #T1 already existed. So even though *proc2*'s code creates a table called #T1 with two columns and inserts a row with two values, when the INSERT statement is resolved, *proc2*'s #T1 does not exist yet, but *proc1*'s does. Therefore, SQL Server reports a resolution error—you attempt to insert a row with two values to a table with one column (as if).

If you invoke *proc2 alone*, the code has no reason to fail because no other #T1 table exists in the session—and it doesn't fail:

```
EXEC dbo.proc2;
```

You get an output with the row loaded to *proc2*'s #T1:

```
col1          col2
-----------   -----------
2             2
```

The execution plan for *proc2* now resides in cache. Ironically, if you now run *proc1* again, the code will complete without errors. *proc2* will not go through a resolution process again (neither will it go through parsing or optimization); rather, SQL Server simply reuses the plan from cache:

```
EXEC dbo.proc1;
```

And now you get the output you probably expected to begin with:

```
col1
-----------
1

col1          col2
-----------   -----------
2             2
```

However, if *proc2*'s plan is removed from cache and you run *proc1*, your code will break:

```
EXEC sp_recompile 'dbo.proc2';
EXEC dbo.proc1;
```

This generates the following output:

```
Object 'dbo.proc2' was successfully marked for recompilation.
col1
-----------
1

Msg 213, Level 16, State 1, Procedure proc2, Line 5
Column name or number of supplied values does not match table definition.
```

In short, I hope that you realize it's wise to avoid naming temporary tables the same in different stored procedures/levels. A way to avoid such issues is to add a unique proc identifier to the names of temporary tables. For example, you could name the temporary table in *proc1* #T1_proc1, and in *proc2* name the temporary table #T1_proc2.

When you're done, run the following code for cleanup:

```
IF OBJECT_ID('dbo.proc1', 'P') IS NOT NULL DROP PROC dbo.proc1;
IF OBJECT_ID('dbo.proc2', 'P') IS NOT NULL DROP PROC dbo.proc2;
```

Schema Changes to Temporary Tables in Dynamic Batches

Remember that a local temporary table created in a certain level is not visible to outer levels in the call stack. Occasionally, programmers look for ways around this limitation, especially when working with dynamic execution. That is, you want to construct the schema of the temporary table dynamically and populate it based on some user input, and then access it from an outer level. Frankly, insisting on using local temporary tables in such a scenario is very problematic. The solution involves ugly code, as is the nature of dynamic SQL in general, plus recompilations resulting from schema changes and data modifications. You should consider other alternatives to provide for the original need. Still, I want to show you a way around the limitations.

Here's an initial algorithm that attempts to provide a solution for this request:

1. In the outer level, create temporary table #T with a single dummy column.

2. Within a dynamic batch, perform the following tasks:

   a. Alter #T, adding the columns you need.

   b. Alter #T, dropping the dummy column.

   c. Populate #T.

3. Back in the outer level, access #T in a new batch.

The problem with this algorithm lies in the last item within the dynamic batch. References to #T will be resolved against the outer #T's schema. Remember that when the batch is resolved, #T's new schema is not available yet. The solution is to populate #T within another dynamic batch, in a level inner to the dynamic batch that alters #T's schema. You do this by performing the following tasks:

1. In the outer level, create temporary table #T with a single dummy column.

2. Within a dynamic batch, perform the following tasks:

   a. Alter #T, adding the columns you need.

   b. Alter #T, dropping the dummy column.

   c. Open another level of dynamic execution and within it populate #T.

3. Back in the outer level, access #T in a new batch.

Here's some sample code that implements this algorithm:

```
-- Assume @column_defs and @insert were constructed dynamically
-- with appropriate safeguards against SQL injection
DECLARE @column_defs AS VARCHAR(1000), @insert AS VARCHAR(1000);
SET @column_defs = 'col1 INT, col2 DECIMAL(10, 2)';
SET @insert = 'INSERT INTO #T VALUES(10, 20.30)';
```

```
-- In the outer level, create temp table #T with a single dummy column
CREATE TABLE #T(dummycol INT);

-- Within a dynamic batch:
--     Alter #T adding the columns you need
--     Alter #T dropping the dummy column
--     Open another level of dynamic execution
--        Populate #T
EXEC('
ALTER TABLE #T ADD ' + @column_defs + ';
ALTER TABLE #T DROP COLUMN dummycol;
EXEC(''' + @insert + ''')');
GO

-- Back in the outer level, access #T in a new batch
SELECT * FROM #T;

-- Cleanup
DROP TABLE #T;
```

This generates the following output:

```
col1         col2
-----------  -----------
10           20.30
```

Caching of Temporary Objects

SQL Server 2008 supports the caching of temporary objects across repeated calls of routines. This feature is applicable to local temporary tables, table variables, and table-valued functions used within routines such as stored procedures, triggers, and user-defined functions. When the routine finishes, SQL Server keeps the catalog entry. If the object is smaller than 8 MB, SQL Server keeps one data page and one IAM page, and uses those instead of allocating new ones when the object is created again. If the object is larger than 8 MB, SQL Server uses deferred drop, and immediately returns control to the application. This feature results in reduction of contention against system catalog tables and allocation pages, and in faster creating and dropping of temporary objects.

I'll demonstrate caching of temporary objects (across repeated calls of routines) through an example. Run the following code to create a stored procedure called *TestCaching* that creates a temporary table called #T1 and populates it with a few rows:

```
SET NOCOUNT ON;
USE tempdb;

IF OBJECT_ID('dbo.TestCaching', 'P') IS NOT NULL
  DROP PROC dbo.TestCaching;
GO
CREATE PROC dbo.TestCaching
AS
```

```
CREATE TABLE #T1(n INT, filler CHAR(2000));

INSERT INTO #T1 VALUES
  (1, 'a'),
  (2, 'a'),
  (3, 'a');
GO
```

Run the following query to determine which entries representing temporary tables exist in the system catalog:

```
SELECT name FROM tempdb.sys.objects WHERE name LIKE '#%';
```

At this point there are no entries in the system catalog representing temporary tables; therefore, this query returns an empty set.

Execute the *TestCaching* procedure:

```
EXEC dbo.TestCaching;
```

The stored procedure terminated, but the temporary table was cached—or more specifically, SQL Server kept its entry in the system catalog, an IAM page, and a data page. Query *tempdb.sys.objects* again:

```
SELECT name FROM tempdb.sys.objects WHERE name LIKE '#%';
```

This time you get an entry back representing the temporary table that was cached. I got the following output (but of course you will get a different table name):

```
name
-----------
#2DE6D218
```

If the procedure's execution plan is recompiled or removed from cache, SQL Server removes the cached temporary objects that were created by the stored procedure from cache as well. SQL Server also removes cached temporary objects when tempdb has little free space.

Run the following code to mark the stored procedure for recompile, causing the associated cached temporary object to be removed from cache:

```
EXEC sp_recompile 'dbo.TestCaching';
```

Query *sys.objects*:

```
SELECT name FROM tempdb.sys.objects WHERE name LIKE '#%';
```

The query should return an empty result set. If not, try again in a few seconds, because the table is dropped in the background.

Note that in the following cases SQL Server will not cache temporary objects across procedure calls:

- When you issue a DDL statement against the temporary table after it was created "e.g., CREATE INDEX".

- When you define a named constraint.

- When you create the temporary object in a dynamic batch within the routine.

- When you create the temporary object in an ad-hoc batch (not within a routine).

I'll first demonstrate the effect of applying DDL changes post-creation of the temporary table. Run the following code to alter the procedure *TestCaching*, adding an index to the temporary table after it was created:

```
ALTER PROC dbo.TestCaching
AS

CREATE TABLE #T1(n INT, filler CHAR(2000));
CREATE UNIQUE INDEX idx1 ON #T1(n);

INSERT INTO #T1 VALUES
  (1, 'a'),
  (2, 'a'),
  (3, 'a');
GO
```

Next, run the procedure and query *sys.objects*:

```
EXEC dbo.TestCaching;
SELECT name FROM tempdb.sys.objects WHERE name LIKE '#%';
```

This returns an empty result set, indicating that the temporary table wasn't cached.

As a workaround, you can include an unnamed UNIQUE or PRIMARY KEY constraint as part of the temporary table definition. The constraint implicitly creates a unique index on the constraint keys. Run the following code to test this approach:

```
ALTER PROC dbo.TestCaching
AS

CREATE TABLE #T1(n INT, filler CHAR(2000), UNIQUE(n));

INSERT INTO #T1 VALUES
  (1, 'a'),
  (2, 'a'),
  (3, 'a');
GO

EXEC dbo.TestCaching;

SELECT name FROM tempdb.sys.objects WHERE name LIKE '#%';
```

This time the query against *sys.objects* should report one temporary table. I got the following output:

```
name
-----------
#3A4CA8FD
```

Note that you can create composite indexes implicitly without sacrificing caching by including a composite UNIQUE or PRIMARY KEY constraint in your table definition, as in UNIQUE(col1, col2, col3).

As for named constraints, you might find this restriction odd, but naming a constraint prevents SQL Server from caching your temporary objects. You just saw in the last example that when the UNIQUE constraint was not named, SQL Server cached the temporary table. Now try the same example, but this time name the constraint:

```
ALTER PROC dbo.TestCaching
AS

CREATE TABLE #T1(n INT, filler CHAR(2000), CONSTRAINT UNQ_#T1_n UNIQUE(n));

INSERT INTO #T1 VALUES
  (1, 'a'),
  (2, 'a'),
  (3, 'a');
GO

EXEC dbo.TestCaching;

SELECT name FROM tempdb.sys.objects WHERE name LIKE '#%';
```

This time the temporary object wasn't cached (again, it may take a few seconds for the temporary object that was cached previously to be removed from cache). So even though naming constraints is in general a good practice, bear in mind that if you want to benefit from caching of temporary objects, you shouldn't name them.

Global Temporary Tables

Global temporary tables differ from local ones mainly in their scope and visibility. They are accessible by all sessions, with no security limitations whatsoever. Any session can even drop the table. So when you design your application, you should factor in security and consider whether you really want temporary tables or just permanent ones. You create global temporary tables by prefixing their names with two number signs (##), and like local temporary tables, they are created in tempdb. However, because global temporary tables are accessible to all sessions, you cannot create multiple ones with the same name; neither in the same session nor across sessions. So typical scenarios for using global temporary tables are when you want to share temporary data among sessions and don't care about security.

Unlike local temporary tables, global ones persist until the creating session—not the creating level—terminates. For example, if you create such a table in a stored procedure and the stored procedure goes out of scope, the table is not destroyed. SQL Server will automatically attempt to drop the table when the creating session terminates, all statements issued against it from other sessions finish, and any locks they hold are released.

I'll walk you through a simple example to demonstrate the accessibility and termination of a global temporary table. Open two connections to SQL Server (call them Connection 1 and Connection 2). In Connection 1, create and populate the table ##T1:

```
CREATE TABLE ##T1(col1 INT);
INSERT INTO ##T1 VALUES(1);
```

In Connection 2, open a transaction and modify the table:

```
BEGIN TRAN
  UPDATE ##T1 SET col1 = col1 + 1;
```

Then close Connection 1. If not for the open transaction that still holds locks against the table, SQL Server would have dropped the table at this point. However, because Connection 2 still holds locks against the table, it's not dropped yet. Next, in Connection 2, query the table and commit the transaction:

```
  SELECT * FROM ##T1;
COMMIT
```

At this point, SQL Server drops the table because no active statements are accessing it, and no locks are held against it. If you try to query it again from any session, you will get an error saying that the table doesn't exist:

```
SELECT * FROM ##T1;
```

In one special case you might want to have a global temporary table available but not owned by any session. In this case, it will always exist, regardless of which sessions are open or closed, and eliminated only if someone explicitly drops it. To achieve this, you create the table within a procedure, and mark the stored procedure with the *startup* procedure option. SQL Server invokes a startup procedure every time it starts. Furthermore, SQL Server always maintains a reference counter greater than zero for a global temporary table created within a startup procedure. This ensures that SQL Server will not attempt to drop it automatically.

Here's some sample code that creates a startup procedure called *CreateGlobals*, which in turn creates a global temporary table called ##Globals.

```
USE master;
IF OBJECT_ID('dbo.CreateGlobals', 'P') IS NOT NULL DROP PROC dbo.CreateGlobals
GO
CREATE PROC dbo.CreateGlobals
AS
```

```
CREATE TABLE ##Globals
(
  varname sysname NOT NULL PRIMARY KEY,
  val     SQL_VARIANT NULL
);
GO

EXEC dbo.sp_procoption 'dbo.CreateGlobals', 'startup', 'true';
```

After restarting SQL Server, the global temporary table will be created automatically and persist until someone explicitly drops it. To test the procedure, restart SQL Server and then run the following code:

```
SET NOCOUNT ON;
INSERT INTO ##Globals VALUES('var1', CAST('abc' AS VARCHAR(10)));
SELECT * FROM ##Globals;
```

You probably guessed already that ##Globals is a shared global temporary table where you can logically maintain cross-session global variables. This can be useful, for example, when you need to maintain temporary counters or other "variables" that are globally accessible by all sessions. The preceding code creates a new global variable called *var1*, initializes it with the character string *'abc'*, and queries the table. Here's the output of this code:

```
varname     val
----------- -----------
var1        abc
```

When you're done, run the following code for cleanup:

```
USE master;
DROP PROC dbo.CreateGlobals;
DROP TABLE ##Globals;
```

Table Variables

Table variables are probably among the least understood T-SQL elements. Many myths and misconceptions surround them, and these are embraced even by experienced T-SQL programmers. One widespread myth is that table variables are memory-resident only, without physical representation. Another myth is that table variables are always preferable to temporary tables. In this section, I'll dispel these myths and explain the scenarios in which table variables are preferable to temporary tables as well as scenarios in which they aren't preferable. I'll do so by first going through the fundamentals of table variables, just as I did with temporary tables, and follow with tangible examples.

You create a table variable using a DECLARE statement, followed by the variable name and the table definition. You then refer to it as you do with permanent tables. Here's a very basic example:

```
DECLARE @T1 TABLE(col1 INT);
INSERT @T1 VALUES(1);
SELECT * FROM @T1;
```

Note that the table-valued parameters that were added in SQL Server 2008 are implemented internally like table variables. So the performance discussions in this section regarding table variables apply to table-valued parameters as well. Table-valued parameters were discussed earlier in the book in Chapter 3, "Stored Procedures."

Limitations

Many limitations apply to table variables but not to temporary tables. In this section, I'll describe some of them, whereas others will be described in dedicated sections.

- You cannot create explicit indexes on table variables, only PRIMARY KEY and UNIQUE constraints, which create unique indexes underneath the covers. You cannot create non-unique indexes. If you need an index on a non-unique column, you must add attributes that make the combination unique and create a PRIMARY KEY or UNIQUE constraint on the combination.

- You cannot alter the definition of a table variable once it is declared. This means that everything you need in the table definition must be included in the original DECLARE statement. This fact is limiting on one hand, but it also results in fewer recompilations. Remember that one of the triggers of recompilations is DDL changes.

- You cannot issue SELECT INTO against a table variable, rather you have to use INSERT SELECT instead. Prior to SQL Server 2008 this limitation put table variables at a disadvantage compared to temporary tables because SELECT INTO could be done as a minimally logged operation, though INSERT SELECT couldn't. SQL Server 2008 introduces improvements in minimally logged operations, including the ability to process INSERT SELECT with minimal logging. I'll demonstrate this capability later in the chapter.

- You cannot qualify a column name with a nondelimited table variable name (as in @T1.col1). This is especially an issue when referring to a table variable's column in correlated subqueries with column name ambiguity. To circumvent this limitation, you have to delimit the table variable name (as in [@T1].col1, or "@T1".col1).

- In queries that modify table variables, parallel plans will not be used. Queries that only read from table variables can be parallelized.

tempdb

To dispel what probably is the most widespread myth involving table variables, let me state that they do have physical representation in tempdb, very similar to temporary tables.

As proof, run the following code that shows which temporary tables currently exist in tempdb by querying metadata info, creating a table variable, and querying metadata info again:

```
SELECT TABLE_NAME
FROM tempdb.INFORMATION_SCHEMA.TABLES
WHERE TABLE_NAME LIKE '#%';
GO
DECLARE @T TABLE(col1 INT);

INSERT INTO @T VALUES(1);

SELECT TABLE_NAME
FROM tempdb.INFORMATION_SCHEMA.TABLES
WHERE TABLE_NAME LIKE '#%';
```

When I ran this code, the first batch returned no output, whereas the second returned #0CBAE877, which is the name of the temporary table in tempdb that represents the table variable @T. Of course, you will probably get a different name when you run this code. But the point is to show that a hidden temporary table is created behind the scenes. Just like temporary tables, a table variable's pages reside in cache when the table is small enough and when SQL Server has enough memory to spare. So the discussion about aspects of working with temporary tables with regard to tempdb applies to table variables as well.

Scope and Visibility

The scope of a table variable is well defined. It is defined as the current level, and within it the current batch only, just as with any other variable. That is, a table variable is not accessible to inner levels, and not even to other batches within the same level. In short, you can use it only within the same batch it was created. This scope is much more limited than that of a local temporary table and is typically an important factor in choosing a temporary object type.

Transaction Context

Unlike a temporary table, a table variable is not part of an outer transaction; rather, its transaction scope is limited to the statement level to support statement rollback capabilities only. If you modify a table variable and the modification statement is aborted, the changes of that particular statement will be undone. However, if the statement is part of an outer transaction that is rolled back, changes against the table variable that finished will not be undone. Table variables are unique in this respect.

You can rely on this behavior to your advantage. For example, suppose that you need to write an audit trigger that audits changes against some table. If some logical condition is met, you want to roll back the change; however, you still want to audit the attempted change. If you copy data from inserted/deleted to your audit tables, a rollback in the trigger also undoes the audit writes. If you first roll back the change and then try to audit it, deleted and inserted are empty.

To solve the problem, you first copy data from inserted/deleted to table variables, issue a rollback, and then in a new transaction within the trigger, copy the data from the table variables to your audit tables. This is the simplest way around the problem.

The unique transaction context of table variables has performance advantages over temporary tables because less logging and locking are involved.

Statistics

As I mentioned earlier, SQL Server doesn't create distribution statistics or maintain accurate cardinality information for table variables as it does for temporary tables. This is one of the main factors you should consider when choosing a type of temporary object for a given task. The downside is that you might get inefficient plans when the optimizer needs to consult histograms to determine selectivity. This is especially a problem with big tables, where you might end up with excessive I/O. The upside is that table variables, for the very same reason, involve much fewer recompilations. Before making your choice, you need to figure out which is more expensive in the particular task for which you're designating the temporary object.

To explain the statistics aspect of table variables in a more tangible way, I'll show you some queries, their execution plans, and their I/O costs.

Examine the following code, and request an estimated execution plan for it from SQL Server Management Studio (SSMS):

```
DECLARE @T TABLE
(
  col1 INT NOT NULL PRIMARY KEY,
  col2 INT NOT NULL,
  filler CHAR(200) NOT NULL DEFAULT('a'),
  UNIQUE(col2, col1)
);

INSERT INTO @T(col1, col2)
  SELECT n, (n - 1) % 10000 + 1 FROM dbo.Nums
  WHERE n <= 100000;

SELECT * FROM @T WHERE col1 = 1;
SELECT * FROM @T WHERE col1 <= 50000;

SELECT * FROM @T WHERE col2 = 1;
SELECT * FROM @T WHERE col2 <= 2;
SELECT * FROM @T WHERE col2 <= 5000;
```

You can find the code to create and populate the Nums table in Chapter 2, "User-Defined Functions."

The estimated execution plans generated for these queries are shown in Figure 7-1.

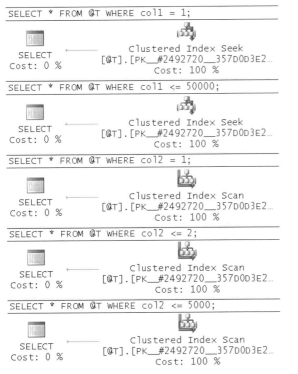

FIGURE 7-1 Estimated execution plans for queries against a table variable

The code creates a table variable called *@T* with two columns. The values in *col1* are unique, and each value in *col2* appears 10 times. The code creates two unique indexes underneath the covers: one on *col1*, and one on *(col2, col1)*.

The first important thing to notice in the estimated plans is the number of rows the optimizer estimates to be returned from each operator—one in all five cases, even when looking for a non-unique value or ranges. You realize that unless you filter a unique column, the optimizer simply cannot estimate the selectivity of queries for lack of statistics. So it assumes one row. This hard-coded assumption is based on the fact that SQL Server assumes that you use table variables only with small sets of data.

As for the efficiency of the plans, the first two queries get a good plan (seek, followed by a partial scan in the second query). But that's because you have a clustered index on the filtered column, and the optimizer doesn't need statistics to figure out what the optimal plan is in this case. However, with the third and fourth queries you get a table scan (an unordered clustered index scan) even though both queries are very selective and would benefit from using the index on *(col2, col1)*, followed by a small number of lookups. The fifth query would benefit from a table scan because it has low selectivity. Fortunately, it got an adequate plan, but that's by chance. To analyze I/O costs, run the code after turning on the SET STATISTICS IO option. The amount of I/O involved with each of the last three queries is 2,713 reads, which is equivalent to the number of pages consumed by the table.

Next, go through the same analysis process with the following code, which uses a temporary table instead of a table variable:

```
SELECT n AS col1, (n - 1) % 10000 + 1 AS col2,
  CAST('a' AS CHAR(200)) AS filler
INTO #T
FROM dbo.Nums
WHERE n <= 100000;

ALTER TABLE #T ADD PRIMARY KEY(col1);
CREATE UNIQUE INDEX idx_col2_col1 ON #T(col2, col1);
GO

SELECT * FROM #T WHERE col1 = 1;
SELECT * FROM #T WHERE col1 <= 50000;

SELECT * FROM #T WHERE col2 = 1;
SELECT * FROM #T WHERE col2 <= 2;
SELECT * FROM #T WHERE col2 <= 5000;
```

The estimated execution plans generated for these queries are shown in Figures 7-2 and 7-3.

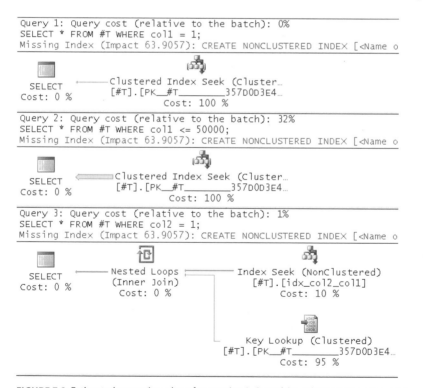

FIGURE 7-2 Estimated execution plans for queries 1, 2, and 3 against a temporary table

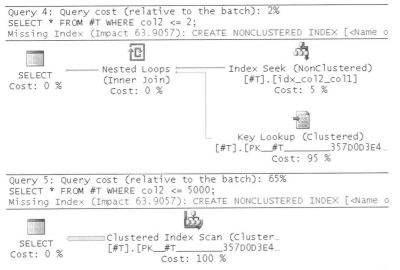

```
Query 4: Query cost (relative to the batch): 2%
SELECT * FROM #T WHERE col2 <= 2;
Missing Index (Impact 63.9057): CREATE NONCLUSTERED INDEX [<Name o
```

```
Query 5: Query cost (relative to the batch): 65%
SELECT * FROM #T WHERE col2 <= 5000;
Missing Index (Impact 63.9057): CREATE NONCLUSTERED INDEX [<Name o
```

FIGURE 7-3 Estimated execution plans for queries 4 and 5 against a temporary table

As an aside, in case you're curious about the Missing Index messages, SSMS 2008 reports this information in the graphical execution plan. Both SQL Server 2005 and SQL Server 2008 may enter a phase in optimization where they report missing index info. In both versions this information is available in the XML form of the execution plan. The new feature in SSMS 2008 is that it exposes this info graphically with the green-colored messages, whereas SSMS 2005 didn't.

Now that statistics are available, the optimizer can make educated estimations. You can see that the estimated number of rows returned from each operator is more reasonable. You can also see that high-selectivity queries 3 and 4 use the index on *(col2, col1)*, and the low-selectivity query 5 does a table scan, as it should.

STATISTICS IO reports dramatically reduced I/O costs for queries 3 and 4. These are 32 and 62 reads, respectively, against the temporary table versus 2,713 for each of these queries against the table variable.

When you're done, drop #T for cleanup:

```
DROP TABLE #T;
```

Minimally Logged Inserts

As mentioned earlier, you can use SELECT INTO with temporary tables but not with table variables. With table variables you have to use INSERT SELECT instead. Prior to SQL Server 2008, INSERT SELECT involved more logging than SELECT INTO. This was true even with the reduced logging that happens with inserts against objects in tempdb. SQL Server 2008 adds the INSERT SELECT statement to the list of insertion methods that can be performed in a minimally logged mode, just like SELECT INTO.

I'll demonstrate this capability through an example. I'll insert data into the temporary object using SELECT INTO and INSERT SELECT in both SQL Server 2005 and SQL Server 2008. To figure out the amount of logging involved with the operation, I'll query the undocumented *fn_dblog* function before and after the operation, and calculate the differences in terms of number of log records, and total record lengths, like so:

```
CHECKPOINT;
GO

DECLARE @numrecords AS INT, @size AS BIGINT;

SELECT
  @numrecords = COUNT(*),
  @size       = COALESCE(SUM([Log Record Length]), 0)
FROM fn_dblog(NULL, NULL) AS D;

-- <operation>

SELECT
  COUNT(*) - @numrecords AS numrecords,
  CAST((COALESCE(SUM([Log Record Length]), 0) - @size)
    / 1024. / 1024. AS NUMERIC(12, 2)) AS size_mb
FROM fn_dblog(NULL, NULL) AS D;
```

The first test is with the SELECT INTO statement that is processed with minimal logging in both SQL Server 2005 and SQL Server 2008, provided that the recovery model of the database is not set to FULL. As a reminder, tempdb's recovery model is SIMPLE and cannot be changed. Here's the code I used for this test:

```
USE tempdb;
CHECKPOINT;
GO

DECLARE @numrecords AS INT, @size AS BIGINT;

SELECT
  @numrecords = COUNT(*),
  @size       = COALESCE(SUM([Log Record Length]), 0)
FROM fn_dblog(NULL, NULL) AS D;

SELECT n, CAST('a' AS CHAR(2000)) AS filler
INTO #TestLogging
FROM dbo.Nums
WHERE n <= 100000;

SELECT
  COUNT(*) - @numrecords AS numrecords,
  CAST((COALESCE(SUM([Log Record Length]), 0) - @size)
    / 1024. / 1024. AS NUMERIC(12, 2)) AS size_mb
FROM fn_dblog(NULL, NULL) AS D;
GO

DROP TABLE #TestLogging;
```

As you can see, the operation is a SELECT INTO statement populating the temporary table #TestLogging with 100,000 rows by querying the Nums table. The output I got in SQL Server 2005 and SQL Server 2008 was similar:

```
numrecords  size_mb
----------- --------
9560        0.63
```

The number of log records is far lower than the number of rows inserted because only changes in allocation bitmaps (GAM, SGAM, PFS, IAM) were recorded in the log. Also, the total size recorded in the log is very small.

Next, I used the following code to test an INSERT SELECT against a table variable populating it with the same sample data used in the SELECT INTO test:

```
USE tempdb;
CHECKPOINT;
GO

DECLARE @numrecords AS INT, @size AS BIGINT;

SELECT
  @numrecords = COUNT(*),
  @size       = COALESCE(SUM([Log Record Length]), 0)
FROM fn_dblog(NULL, NULL) AS D;

DECLARE @TestLogging AS TABLE(n INT, filler CHAR(2000));

INSERT INTO @TestLogging(n, filler)
  SELECT n, CAST('a' AS CHAR(2000))
  FROM dbo.Nums
  WHERE n <= 100000;

SELECT
  COUNT(*) - @numrecords AS numrecords,
  CAST((COALESCE(SUM([Log Record Length]), 0) - @size)
    / 1024. / 1024. AS NUMERIC(12, 2)) AS size_mb
FROM fn_dblog(NULL, NULL) AS D;
GO
```

Here's the output I got in SQL Server 2005, indicating more logging activity than the corresponding SELECT INTO method:

```
numrecords  size_mb
----------- --------
184394      12.92
```

In SQL Server 2008 the output of the INSERT SELECT method was similar to the output I got for the corresponding SELECT INTO test, indicating minimal logging in both cases:

```
numrecords  size_mb
----------- --------
9539        0.63
```

This improvement in SQL Server 2008 means that temporary tables don't have an advantage over table variables in terms of amount of logging of SELECT INTO versus INSERT SELECT.

tempdb Considerations

Remember that temporary tables and table variables are physically stored in tempdb. SQL Server also stores data in tempdb for many implicit activities that take place behind the scenes. Examples for such activities include: spooling data as part of an execution plan of a query, sorting, hashing, and maintaining row versions. You realize that tempdb can become a bottleneck, and you should give it focused tuning attention so that it will accommodate the workload against your server.

Here are some important points you should consider when tuning tempdb:

- In systems where tempdb is heavily used (explicitly or implicitly), consider placing tempdb on its own disk array, and not on the same drives where other databases are located. Also, stripe the data portion to multiple drives to increase I/O throughput. The more spindles, the better. Ideally, use RAID 10 for the data portion and RAID 1 for the log.

- Every time you restart SQL Server, tempdb is re-created, and its size reverts to the effective defined size. If you made no changes to the original size configuration after installing SQL Server, tempdb's size will default to 8 MB and its growth increment will default to 10 percent. In most production environments, these values might not be practical. Whenever a process needs to store data in tempdb and tempdb is full, SQL Server will initiate an autogrow operation. The process will have to wait for the space to be allocated. Also, when the database is small, 10 percent is a very small unit. The small fragments will most probably be allocated in different places on disk, resulting in a high level of file-system fragmentation. And if that's not enough, remember that every time SQL Server restarts, tempdb's size will revert to its defined size (8 MB). This means that the whole process will start again, where tempdb will keep on autogrowing until it reaches a size appropriate to your environment's workload. Until it reaches that point, processes will suffer as they wait while tempdb autogrows.

- You can figure out the appropriate size for tempdb by observing its actual size after a period of activity without restarts. You then alter the database and change the SIZE parameter of tempdb's files so that tempdb's size will be appropriate. Whenever SQL Server is restarted, tempdb will just start out at the defined size. If you do this, there won't be a need for autogrowth until tempdb gets full, which should occur only with irregular and excessive tempdb activity.

- Remember that logically tempdb is re-created whenever SQL Server restarts. Like any other new database, tempdb is created as a copy of the model database. This means that if you create permanent objects in tempdb (permanent tables, user-defined types, database users, and so on), they're erased in the next restart. If you need objects to exist in tempdb after restarts, you have two options. One is to create them in model. They will appear in tempdb after a restart. However, this option will also affect new user databases you create. Another option is to encapsulate code that creates all objects in a startup procedure. (See information on startup procedures earlier in the chapter in the "Global Temporary Tables" section.) Remember that a startup procedure is invoked whenever SQL Server is restarted. Essentially the objects will be re-created every time upon restart, but this will be invisible to users.

■ With regard to temporary tables, obviously dealing with very large volumes of data can cause performance problems. However, you might face performance problems with tempdb even when working with small temporary tables. When many concurrent sessions create temporary tables, SQL Server might experience latch contention on allocation bitmaps when it tries to allocate pages. In the last couple of versions of SQL Server this problem was reduced substantially because of improvements in the engine— caching of temporary objects across routine calls—and improvements in the proportional fill algorithm SQL Server uses. Still, the problem may occur. The recommended practices to mitigate the problem are to use multiple data files for tempdb (as a general rule of thumb, one file per each CPU core), and to meet the requirements described earlier that would allow caching of temporary objects across routine calls.

> **More Info** You can find more details about tempdb in papers found at the following URLs: *http://technet.microsoft.com/en-us/library/cc966545.aspx* and *http://technet.microsoft.com/en-us/library/cc966425.aspx*. Even though the papers were originally written for SQL Server 2005, most of the content describing SQL Server 2005 behavior is applicable for SQL Server 2008 as well.

Table Expressions

In this chapter's opening paragraphs, I mentioned that there might be cases in which you need "logical" temporary tables—that is, only virtual materialization of interim sets, as opposed to physical materialization in temporary tables and table variables. Table expressions give you this capability. These include derived tables, CTEs, views, and inline table-valued UDFs. Here I'll point out the scenarios in which these are preferable to other temporary objects and provide an example.

You should use table expressions in cases where you need a temporary object mainly for simplification—for example, when developing a solution in a modular approach, a step at a time. Also, use table expressions when you need to access the temporary object only once or a very small number of times and you don't need to index interim result sets. SQL Server doesn't physically materialize a table expression. The optimizer merges the outer query with the inner one, and it generates one plan for the query accessing the underlying tables directly. So I'm mainly talking about simplification, and I show such examples throughout the book. But even beyond simplification, in some cases you will be able to improve performance of solutions by using table expressions. There might be cases where the optimizer will generate a better plan for your query compared to alternative queries.

In terms of scope and visibility, derived tables and CTEs are available only to the current statement, whereas views and inline UDFs are available globally to users that have permissions to access them.

As an example of using a table expression to solve a problem, suppose you want to return from the Sales.Orders table in the InsideTSQL2008 database, the row with the highest *orderid* for each employee. Here's a solution that uses a CTE:

```
USE InsideTSQL2008;

WITH EmpMax AS
(
  SELECT empid, MAX(orderid) AS maxoid
  FROM Sales.Orders
  GROUP BY empid
)
SELECT O.orderid, O.empid, O.custid, O.orderdate
FROM Sales.Orders AS O
  JOIN EmpMax AS EM
    ON O.orderid = EM.maxoid;
```

This generates the following output:

```
orderid      empid        custid       orderdate
-----------  -----------  -----------  -----------------------
11077        1            65           2008-05-06 00:00:00.000
11073        2            58           2008-05-05 00:00:00.000
11063        3            37           2008-04-30 00:00:00.000
11076        4            9            2008-05-06 00:00:00.000
11043        5            74           2008-04-22 00:00:00.000
11045        6            10           2008-04-23 00:00:00.000
11074        7            73           2008-05-06 00:00:00.000
11075        8            68           2008-05-06 00:00:00.000
11058        9            6            2008-04-29 00:00:00.000
```

Comparison Summary

Table 7-1 contains a summary of the functionality and behavior of the different object types. Note that I don't include global temporary tables because typically you use those for different purposes than the other types of temporary objects. You might find this table handy as a reference when you need to choose the appropriate temporary object type for a given task.

TABLE 7-1 **Comparison Summary**

Functionality/Object Type	Local Temp Table	Table Variable	Table Expression
Scope/Visibility	Current and inner levels	Local Batch	Derived Table/CTE: Current statement View/Inline UDF: Global
Physical representation in tempdb	Yes	Yes	No
Part of outer transaction/ affected by outer transaction rollback	Yes	No	N/A
Logging and locking	To support transaction rollback	To support statement rollback	N/A
Statistics/recompilations/ efficient plans	Yes	No	N/A
Table size	Any	Typically recommended for small tables	Any

Summary Exercises

This section will introduce three scenarios in which you need to work with temporary objects. Based on the knowledge you've acquired in this chapter, you need to implement a solution with the appropriate temporary object type.

The scenarios involve querying Customers and Orders tables. To test the logical correctness of your solutions, use the Sales.Customers and Sales.Orders tables in the InsideTSQL2008 sample database. To test the performance of your solutions, use the tables that you create and populate in tempdb by running the code in Listing 7-1.

LISTING 7-1 Code that creates large tables for summary exercises

```
SET NOCOUNT ON;
USE tempdb;

IF SCHEMA_ID('Sales') IS NULL EXEC('CREATE SCHEMA Sales');
IF OBJECT_ID('Sales.Customers', 'U') IS NOT NULL DROP TABLE Sales.Customers;
IF OBJECT_ID('Sales.Orders', 'U') IS NOT NULL DROP TABLE Sales.Orders;
GO

SELECT n AS custid
INTO Sales.Customers
FROM dbo.Nums
WHERE n <= 10000;
```

```
ALTER TABLE Sales.Customers ADD PRIMARY KEY(custid);

SELECT n AS orderid,
  DATEADD(day, ABS(CHECKSUM(NEWID())) % (4*365), '20060101') AS orderdate,
  1 + ABS(CHECKSUM(NEWID())) % 10000 AS custid,
  1 + ABS(CHECKSUM(NEWID())) % 40     AS empid,
  CAST('a' AS CHAR(200)) AS filler
INTO Sales.Orders
FROM dbo.Nums
WHERE n <= 1000000;

ALTER TABLE Sales.Orders ADD PRIMARY KEY(orderid);
CREATE INDEX idx_cid_eid ON Sales.Orders(custid, empid);
```

Comparing Periods

The first exercise involves multiple references to the same intermediate result set of a query. The task is to query the Orders table, and return for each order year the number of orders placed that year, and the difference from the number of orders placed in the previous year. Here's the desired output when you run your solution against InsideTSQL2008:

```
orderyear   numorders   diff
----------- ----------- -----------
2006        152         NULL
2007        408         256
2008        270         -138
```

You could use a table expression representing yearly counts of orders, and join two instances of the table expression to match to each current year the previous year, so that you can calculate the difference. Here's an example for implementing such an approach using a CTE:

```
SET STATISTICS IO ON;

WITH YearlyCounts AS
(
  SELECT YEAR(orderdate) AS orderyear, COUNT(*) AS numorders
  FROM Sales.Orders
  GROUP BY YEAR(orderdate)
)
SELECT C.orderyear, C.numorders, C.numorders - P.numorders AS diff
FROM YearlyCounts AS C
  LEFT OUTER JOIN YearlyCounts AS P
    ON C.orderyear = P.orderyear + 1;
```

Remember that a table expression is nothing but a reflection of the underlying tables. When you query two occurrences of the *YearlyCounts* CTE, both get expanded behind the scenes. All the work of scanning the data and aggregating it happens twice. You can see this clearly in the query's execution plan shown in Figure 7-4.

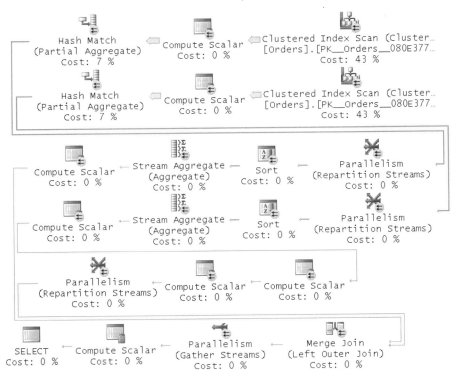

FIGURE 7-4 Execution plan for a solution to the "comparing periods" exercise (using table expressions)

Scanning the base data from the clustered index involves 28,807 reads. Because the data was scanned twice, STATISTICS IO reports 57,614 reads. As you can realize, scanning and aggregating the base data twice is unnecessary. This is a scenario where you should consider using a temporary table or a table variable. When choosing between the two, remember that one of the things to consider is the size of the intermediate result set that will be stored in the temporary object. Because the intermediate result set here will have only one row per year, obviously it's going to be very tiny, and it will probably require only one or two pages. In this case, it makes sense to use a table variable and benefit from the fact that it will not cause plan optimality related recompiles.

Here's the solution using a table variable:

```
DECLARE @YearlyCounts AS TABLE
(
  orderyear INT PRIMARY KEY,
  numorders INT
);

INSERT INTO @YearlyCounts(orderyear, numorders)
  SELECT YEAR(orderdate) AS orderyear, COUNT(*) AS numorders
  FROM Sales.Orders
  GROUP BY YEAR(orderdate);
```

```
SELECT C.orderyear, C.numorders, C.numorders - P.numorders AS diff
FROM @YearlyCounts AS C
  LEFT OUTER JOIN @YearlyCounts AS P
    ON C.orderyear = P.orderyear + 1;
```

The work that includes scanning the base data and aggregating it happens only once and the tiny result is stored in a table variable. Then the last query joins two instances of the tiny table variable to produce the desired output. The execution plan for this solution is shown in Figure 7-5.

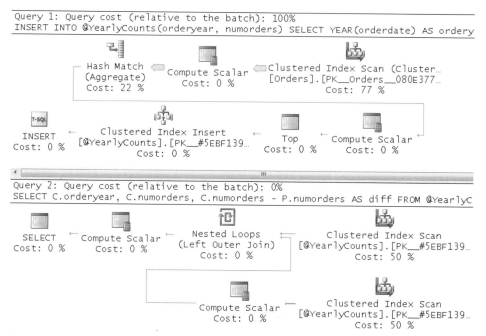

FIGURE 7-5 Execution plan for a solution to the "comparing periods" exercise (using table variables)

Because the base data from the clustered index on the Orders table was scanned only once, STATISTICS IO reports only about half the number of reads (28,621) compared to the previous solution. It also reports a very small number of reads (11) from the table variable.

Recent Orders

The task in the second exercise is to query the Orders table, and return for each customer the orders with the most recent order date for the customer. Here's the desired output when you run your solution against InsideTSQL2008, shown in abbreviated form:

orderid	orderdate	custid	empid
11044	2008-04-23 00:00:00.000	91	4
11005	2008-04-07 00:00:00.000	90	2
11066	2008-05-01 00:00:00.000	89	7
10935	2008-03-09 00:00:00.000	88	4

11025	2008-04-15 00:00:00.000	87	6
11046	2008-04-23 00:00:00.000	86	8
10739	2007-11-12 00:00:00.000	85	3
10850	2008-01-23 00:00:00.000	84	1
10994	2008-04-02 00:00:00.000	83	2
10822	2008-01-08 00:00:00.000	82	6

...

There are many ways to solve this problem, some of which I'll present here. But most solutions benefit from the following index on *custid, orderdate* as the keys and *empid, orderid* as included columns:

```
CREATE INDEX idx_cid_od_i_eid_oid ON Sales.Orders(custid, orderdate)
  INCLUDE(empid, orderid);
```

The first solution I'll present is one where I use a CTE to calculate the maximum order date per customer, and then in the outer query join the Orders table with the CTE to return the orders with the maximum order date for each customer, like so:

```
WITH CustMax AS
(
  SELECT custid, MAX(orderdate) AS mx
  FROM Sales.Orders
  GROUP BY custid
)
SELECT O.orderid, O.orderdate, O.custid, O.empid
FROM Sales.Orders AS O
  JOIN CustMax AS M
    ON O.custid = M.custid
    AND O.orderdate = M.mx;
```

Here the fact that a table expression is not materialized—rather its definition gets expanded—is an advantage. You might expect SQL Server to scan the data twice—once to process the inner reference to the Orders table in the CTE query, and another for the outer reference to the Orders table. But the optimizer figured out a way to handle this query by scanning the data only once, which is truly admirable. Figure 7-6 shows the execution plan the optimizer produced for this query.

FIGURE 7-6 Execution plan for a solution to the "recent orders" exercise (using a CTE and join)

The Index Seek operator against the index you just created seeks the last entry in the leaf of the index, and then starts scanning the leaf level backward. The Segment operator segments the rows by customer, and the Top operator filters only the rows with the maximum order date per customer. This is a very efficient plan that requires scanning the index you created earlier only once, in order. STATISTICS IO reports 3,231 reads, which is close to the number of pages in the leaf of the index.

You realize that if you implement a similar solution, except using a temporary table instead of the table expression, the data will have to be scanned more than once—one time to produce the aggregated information you store in the temporary table, and another time to process the outer reference to Orders representing the base data that you join with the temporary table. Here's an implementation of this approach:

```
CREATE TABLE #CustMax
(
  custid INT      NOT NULL PRIMARY KEY,
  mx      DATETIME NOT NULL
);

INSERT INTO #CustMax(custid, mx)
  SELECT custid, MAX(orderdate) AS mx
  FROM Sales.Orders
  GROUP BY custid;

SELECT O.orderid, O.orderdate, O.custid, O.empid
FROM Sales.Orders AS O
  JOIN #CustMax AS M
    ON O.custid = M.custid
    AND O.orderdate = M.mx;

DROP TABLE #CustMax;
```

The execution plan for this solution is shown in Figure 7-7.

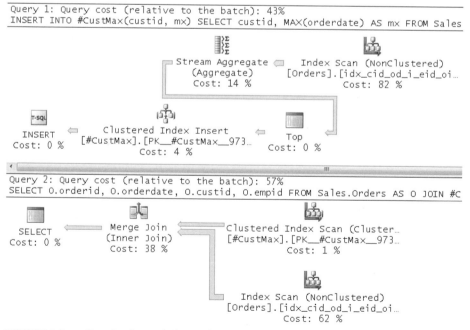
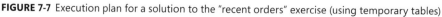

FIGURE 7-7 Execution plan for a solution to the "recent orders" exercise (using temporary tables)

The first plan is for the population of the temporary table, and here you can see the first scan of the index you created earlier, plus aggregation of the data, and storing the result in the temp table's clustered index. The second plan is for the join query, showing that the base data from the index on Orders is scanned again, as well as the data from the temporary table, and the two inputs are joined using a merge join algorithm. STATISTICS IO reports twice 3,231 logical reads against Orders for the first plan, plus 3,231 logical reads against Orders and 28 logical reads against the temporary table for the second plan.

Clearly, in this case, the approach using the table expression was more efficient. By the way, this problem has other solutions using table expressions. For example, the following solution uses the CROSS APPLY operator and a derived table:

```
SELECT A.*
FROM Sales.Customers AS C
  CROSS APPLY (SELECT TOP (1) WITH TIES orderid, orderdate, custid, empid
               FROM Sales.Orders AS O
               WHERE O.custid = C.custid
               ORDER BY orderdate DESC) AS A;
```

Figure 7-8 shows the execution plan for this query.

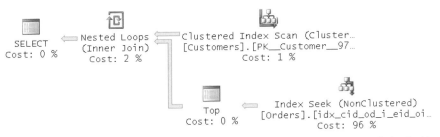

FIGURE 7-8 Execution plan for a solution to the "recent orders" exercise (using a derived table and APPLY)

As you can see, the plan scans the clustered index on the Customers table, and for each customer, uses a seek operation against the nonclustered index on Orders to pull the orders that were placed by the current customer in its maximum order date. With a low density of customers—as in our case—this plan is less efficient than the one shown in Figure 7-7 for the previous solution based on a CTE. STATISTICS IO reports 31,931 reads from Orders, and those are random reads unlike the sequential ones you got from the plan in Figure 7-7. The solution based on the APPLY operator excels particularly when the density of customers is very high, and the number of seek operations is therefore accordingly small.

Finally, another solution based on table expressions that you might want to consider is one that assigns ranks to orders partitioned by customer—ordered by order date descending—and then filter only the rows with a rank value equal to 1. For a partitioned ranking calculation, the optimizer will only use an index and avoid sorting if the key columns have the same sorting direction in the index as they do in the ranking calculation's OVER clause. Create a nonclustered index with *orderdate* descending like so:

```
CREATE INDEX idx_cid_od_i_eid_oidD ON Sales.Orders(custid, orderdate DESC)
  INCLUDE(empid, orderid);
```

Then you will get an efficient plan from the following solution:

```
WITH OrderRanks AS
(
  SELECT orderid, orderdate, custid, empid,
    RANK() OVER(PARTITION BY custid ORDER BY orderdate DESC) AS rnk
  FROM Sales.Orders
)
SELECT *
FROM OrderRanks
WHERE rnk = 1;
```

The plan is shown in Figure 7-9.

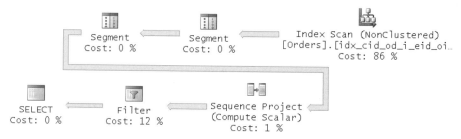

FIGURE 7-9 Execution plan for a solution to the "recent orders" exercise (using ranks and a CTE)

The efficiency of the plan is quite similar to the one shown earlier in Figure 7-7. Here as well the nonclustered index is scanned once in order. STATISTICS IO reports 3,231 logical reads as expected. This plan, like the one shown in Figure 7-7, excels when the density of customers is low.

When you're done, run the following code for cleanup:

```
DROP INDEX Sales.Orders.idx_cid_od_i_eid_oid;
DROP INDEX Sales.Orders.idx_cid_od_i_eid_oidD;
```

Relational Division

For the last summary exercise, you're given the following task: you need to determine which customers have orders handled by the same set of employees. The result set should contain one row for each customer, with two columns: the customer ID and a value that identifies the group of employees that handled orders for the customer. The latter is expressed as the minimum customer ID out of all customers that share the same group of employees. That is, if customers A, B, and D were handled by one group of employees (for example, 3, 7, 9), and customers C and

E by a different group (for example, 3 and 7), the result set would contain {(A, A), (B, A), (D, A), (C, C), (E, C)}. It will be convenient to use NULL instead of the minimum customer ID to identify the group of no employees for customers without orders. Following is the desired result against the InsideTSQL2008 database, shown here in abbreviated form:

```
custid       grp
-----------  -----------
22           NULL
57           NULL
1            1
2            2
78           2
3            3
81           3
4            4
5            5
34           5
...
```

You can observe, for example, that customers 2 and 78 were handled by the same group of employees, because for both customers, *grp* is 2. Remember that you should use the sample tables in the InsideTSQL2008 database only to check the accuracy of your result. For performance estimations, use the tables you created earlier in tempdb by running the code in Listing 7-1. Like before, also with this problem the performance measures I will mention were measured against the tables in tempdb.

The first solution doesn't make any use of temporary objects; rather, it implements a classic relational division approach applying reverse logic with subqueries:

```
SELECT custid,
    CASE WHEN EXISTS(SELECT * FROM Sales.Orders AS O
                     WHERE O.custid = C1.custid)
      THEN COALESCE(
        (SELECT MIN(C2.custid)
           FROM Sales.Customers AS C2
           WHERE C2.custid < C1.custid
             AND NOT EXISTS
               (SELECT * FROM Sales.Orders AS O1
                 WHERE O1.custid = C1.custid
                   AND NOT EXISTS
                     (SELECT * FROM Sales.Orders AS O2
                       WHERE O2.custid = C2.custid
                         AND O2.empid = O1.empid))
             AND NOT EXISTS
               (SELECT * FROM Sales.Orders AS O2
                 WHERE O2.custid = C2.custid
                   AND NOT EXISTS
                     (SELECT * FROM Sales.Orders AS O1
                       WHERE O1.custid = C1.custid
                         AND O1.empid = O2.empid))),
        custid) END AS grp
FROM Sales.Customers AS C1
ORDER BY grp, custid;
```

The query invokes a CASE expression for every customer from the Customers table (C1). The CASE expression invokes the COALESCE function for customers who placed orders, and returns NULL for customers who placed no orders. If the customer placed orders, COALESCE will substitute a NULL returned by the input expression with the current *custid*. The input expression will return the result of the following:

- Return the minimum *custid* from a second instance of Customers (C2)

- Where *C2.custid* (*cust2*) is smaller than *C1.custid* (*cust1*)

- And you cannot find an employee in *cust1*'s orders that does not appear in *cust2*'s orders

- And you cannot find an employee in *cust2*'s orders that does not appear in *cust1*'s orders

Logically, you could do without filtering *cust2* < *cust1*, but this expression is used to avoid wasting resources. Anyway, you need to return the minimum *custid* out of the ones with the same employee list. If customer A has the same employee group as customer B, both will end up with a *grp* value of A. For customer B, there's a point in comparing it to customer A (smaller ID), but for customer A there's no point in comparing it to customer B (higher ID). Naturally, the minimum *custid* with a given employee group will not have the same employee group as any customers with smaller IDs. In such a case, the expression will return NULL, and the outer COALESCE will substitute the NULL with the current *custid*. As for the rest, it's a classical phrasing of relational division with reverse logic.

This solution is expensive because of the excessive scan count, which has to do with the large number of invocations of the correlated subqueries. To give you a sense, this solution ran over an hour before I gave up waiting for it to finish and stopped it. Most standard set-based solutions you can come up with for this problem that don't use temporary objects will typically be expensive.

If you devise a solution in which you generate an interim set that can benefit from an index, you might want to consider using temporary tables. For example, you can materialize the distinct list of *custid*, *empid* values; index the temporary table; and continue from there. The materialized data would substantially reduce the number of rows in the set you'll query. Still, you won't be dealing with a tiny set, and most probably your solution will access the table multiple times. You want efficient plans to be generated based on distribution statistics and accurate cardinality information. All this should lead you to use a local temporary table and not a table variable.

Here's a solution that first creates the suggested local temporary table, indexes it, and then queries it:

```
SELECT DISTINCT custid, empid
INTO #CustsEmps
FROM Sales.Orders;
```

```
CREATE UNIQUE CLUSTERED INDEX idx_cid_eid
  ON #CustsEmps(custid, empid);
GO

WITH Agg AS
(
  SELECT custid,
    MIN(empid) AS MN,
    MAX(empid) AS MX,
    COUNT(*)   AS CN,
    SUM(empid) AS SM,
    CHECKSUM_AGG(empid) AS CS
  FROM #CustsEmps
  GROUP BY custid
),
AggJoin AS
(
  SELECT A1.custid AS cust1, A2.custid AS cust2, A1.CN
  FROM Agg AS A1
    JOIN Agg AS A2
      ON  A2.custid <= A1.custid
      AND A2.MN = A1.MN
      AND A2.MX = A1.MX
      AND A2.CN = A1.CN
      AND A2.SM = A1.SM
      AND A2.CS = A1.CS
),
CustGrp AS
(
  SELECT cust1, MIN(cust2) AS grp
  FROM AggJoin AS AJ
  WHERE CN = (SELECT COUNT(*)
              FROM #CustsEmps AS C1
                JOIN #CustsEmps AS C2
                  ON C1.custid = AJ.cust1
                  AND C2.custid = AJ.cust2
                  AND C2.empid = C1.empid)
  GROUP BY cust1
)
SELECT custid, grp
FROM Sales.Customers AS C
  LEFT OUTER JOIN CustGrp AS G
    ON C.custid = G.cust1
ORDER BY grp, custid;
GO

DROP TABLE #CustsEmps;
```

I also used CTEs here to build the solution in a modular approach. The first CTE (*Agg*) groups the data from the temporary table by *custid*, and returns several aggregates based on *empid* for each customer (MIN, MAX, COUNT, SUM, CHECKSUM_AGG).

The second CTE (*AggJoin*) joins two instances of *Agg* (*A1* and *A2*)—matching each customer in *A1* to all customers in *A2* with a lower *custid* that have the same values for all the aggregates.

The purpose of comparing aggregates is to identify pairs of customers that *potentially* share the same group of employees. The reasoning behind the use of less than or equal to (<=) in the filter is similar to the one in the previous solution. That is, comparing groups of employees between customers when *A2.custid (cust2)* is greater than *A1.custid (cust1)* is superfluous.

The third CTE, (*CustGrp*), filters from *AggJoin* only pairs of customers that actually share the same group of employees, by verifying that the count of matching employees in both groups is identical to the total count of employees in each group by itself. The query aggregates the filtered rows by *cust1*, returning the minimum *cust2* for each *cust1*. At this point, *CustGrp* contains the correct *grp* value for each customer.

Finally, the outer query performs a left outer join that adds customers without orders.

This solution runs for eight seconds. Note that you could use a CTE with the set of distinct *custid, empid* combinations instead of the temporary table #CustEmps. This way, you could avoid using temporary tables altogether. I tested such a solution and it ran for about 12 seconds—50 percent more than the solution that utilizes a temporary table. The advantage in the temporary table approach was that you could index it.

Considering the fastest solution we had so far—the one utilizing a temporary table—is this really the best you can get? Apparently not. You can use the FOR XML PATH option to concatenate all distinct *empid* values per customer. You can then group the data by the concatenated string, and return for each customer the minimum *custid* within the group using the OVER clause. The fast and nifty concatenation technique was originally devised by Michael Rys and Eugene Kogan. The PATH mode provides an easier way to mix elements and attributes than the EXPLICIT directive. Here's the complete solution:

```
WITH CustGroups AS
(
  SELECT custid,
    (SELECT CAST(empid AS VARCHAR(10)) + ';' AS [text()]
     FROM (SELECT DISTINCT empid
           FROM dbo.Orders AS O
           WHERE O.custid = C.custid) AS D
     ORDER BY empid
     FOR XML PATH('')) AS CustEmps
  FROM dbo.Customers AS C
)
SELECT custid,
  CASE WHEN CustEmps IS NULL THEN NULL
    ELSE MIN(custid) OVER(PARTITION BY CustEmps) END AS grp
FROM CustGroups
ORDER BY grp, custid;
```

The solution is short and slick, doesn't use temporary tables at all, and runs for six seconds!

Conclusion

I hope this chapter helped you realize the significant differences between the various types of temporary objects supported by SQL Server. I had to dispel a few widespread myths, especially with regard to table variables. Remember that it's typically advisable to use table variables for small tables and to compare table variables against temporary tables for the most critical queries. You realize that there's a time and place for each type and that no one type is always preferable to the others. I gave you a summary table with the aspects and functionality of each type, which should help you make the right choices based on your needs. Also, remember to pay special attention to tempdb, which can become a bottleneck in your system, especially when working extensively with temporary tables.

Chapter 8

Cursors

Itzik Ben-Gan

A cursor is a programmatic construct in T-SQL. It represents a result set of a query that you can iterate through one row at a time, possibly in a predetermined order. Programmers who are used to procedural programming but are not yet experienced with SQL tend to use cursors a lot because using cursors feels like an extension of what they already know. However, you should be aware of the implications of using cursors. Using cursors is not in accord with the relational model, which deals with whole sets, as opposed to dealing with individual rows. By using cursors, you pretty much go against the model. Also, in terms of the work done by the Microsoft SQL Server engine, the processing of each cursor row incurs an overhead cost that is not applicable when processing set-based code (queries). For these reasons, it is generally recommended to avoid using cursors for the most part. Still, even after you become well versed in T-SQL and gain knowledge and experience in query tuning, you realize that a certain minority of problems are best solved with cursors. This chapter explores the differences between cursor-based and set-based solutions to querying problems, and it focuses on types of problems that for now are best solved with cursors—at least as far as performance is concerned.

Some of the problems covered in this chapter were covered in *T-SQL Querying*—the prequel to this book—where I focused on set-based solutions. In this chapter I'll mainly focus on the cursor-based solutions to those problems.

Using Cursors

Support for cursors in T-SQL hasn't changed for quite a few versions of SQL Server now. I'll assume that you have sufficient technical knowledge of the various cursor types and know the syntax for declaring and using them. If you don't, you can find a lot of information about cursors in SQL Server Books Online. My focus is to explain the differences between cursor-based and set-based solutions to querying problems, and to present the cases in which using cursors does make sense.

So why should you avoid using cursors for the most part?

Cursors conflict with the main premise of the relational model. Using cursors, you apply procedural logic and iterate through individual rows, as opposed to applying set-based logic, where you handle whole sets of rows. With cursors, you end up writing a lot of code with iterations, where you mainly focus on *how* to deal with data. When you apply set-based logic, you typically write substantially less code, as you focus on *what* you want and not how to get it.

You need to be able to recognize the cases in which a problem is procedural/iterative in nature—where you truly need to process one row at a time. In these cases, you should consider using a cursor. For example, suppose you need to invoke a stored procedure for each row in a table, using column values as arguments. If the procedure's logic can be written as a table-valued function, you can use the APPLY operator in a query to invoke the function for each row of the table. But if the procedure's logic cannot be written as a table-valued function, using a cursor to invoke the procedure for each row of the table is a viable option.

Cursors also have a lot of overhead involved with the row-by-row manipulation and are typically substantially slower than set-based code. I demonstrate the use of set-based solutions throughout the book. You need to be able to measure and estimate the cursor overhead and identify the few scenarios where cursors will yield better performance than set-based code. In some cases, data distribution will determine whether a cursor or a set-based solution will yield better performance.

Cursors have another very important aspect—they can request and assume ordered data as input, whereas queries can accept only a relational input, which by definition cannot assume a particular order. This difference is important in identifying scenarios in which cursors might actually be faster—such as problems that can benefit from ordered access to the data. An example of such a problem is running aggregations. The I/O cost involved with the cursor activity plus the cursor overhead might end up being lower than a set-based solution that performs substantially more I/O.

ANSI recognizes the practical need for calculations that are based on some logical order and provides some standards for addressing this need. In the ANSI SQL standard you can find several query constructs that rely on logical ordering—for example, the OVER(ORDER BY ...) clause, which includes the calculation order for ranking and aggregate functions, or the SEARCH clause defined with recursive CTEs, which determines the order of traversal of trees. Note, however, that supporting a calculation based on logical ordering doesn't contradict the relational model. The model deals with relations (sets) and operations on relations. Both the input and the output of operations or calculations must be sets. As long as this rule is preserved, having operations or calculations that use logical ordering as part of their definition is not a contradiction with the model. With cursors it's different in the sense that you actually force order in the data, and therefore contradict the model.

SQL Server 2008 lacks full support for window functions and window specifications compared to the ANSI SQL standard. It supports the window partition (PARTITION BY) and order (ORDER BY) clauses with four ranking functions (ROW_NUMBER, RANK, DENSE_RANK, and NTILE). These functions are handled by SQL Server's engine very efficiently compared to alternative solutions using cursors. As for the OVER clause for aggregate functions, SQL Server 2008 supports only a window partition clause, but not the window order and frame (ROWS, RANGE) clauses. The lack of support for window order and frame clauses is the main obstacle to efficient set-based queries for running aggregates and similar calculations. For such calculations, cursor-based solutions are currently more efficient. I'll demonstrate this in the section "Running Aggregations" later in this chapter. The SEARCH clause for recursive common table expressions (CTEs) has not been implemented in SQL Server 2008.

Matching problems are another kind of problem in which cursor solutions are faster than set-based solutions—I'll also demonstrate this use of cursors. With matching problems, I haven't found set-based solutions that perform nearly as well as cursor solutions.

Of course, from time to time you should revisit problems for which cursor solutions perform better then set-based ones. You might come up with a new set-based approach, and you might be able to benefit from enhancements in SQL Server.

Cursor Overhead

In this chapter's introduction, I talked about the benefits that set-based solutions have over cursor-based ones. I mentioned both logical and performance benefits. For the most part, efficiently written set-based solutions will outperform cursor-based solutions for two reasons.

First, you empower the optimizer to do what it's so good at—generating multiple valid execution plans and choosing the most efficient one. When you apply a cursor-based solution, you're basically forcing the optimizer to go with a rigid plan that doesn't leave much room for optimization—at least not as much room as with set-based solutions.

Second, the processing of each cursor row involves overhead that is not applicable when processing set-based code. You can run some simple tests to witness and measure this overhead—for example, by comparing the costs of scanning a table by using a simple query and by using a cursor. If you express the cost of scanning n rows with a query as n, you can express the cost of scanning the same number of rows with a cursor as $n + n \times o$, where o represents the overhead, or extra cost, associated with the processing of a single cursor row. You can eliminate the actual disk I/O cost by running the code twice. (The first run will load the data to cache.) To eliminate the time it takes to generate the output, you should run your code with the Discard results after execution option in SQL Server Management Studio (SSMS) is turned on. The difference in performance between the set-based code and the cursor code will then be the cursor's overhead.

I will now demonstrate how to compare scanning the same amount of data with set-based code versus with a cursor. Run the following code to generate a table called T1, with a million rows, each containing slightly more than 200 bytes:

```
SET NOCOUNT ON;
USE tempdb;
IF OBJECT_ID('dbo.T1', 'U') IS NOT NULL DROP TABLE dbo.T1;
GO

SELECT n AS keycol, CAST('a' AS CHAR(200)) AS filler
INTO dbo.T1
FROM dbo.Nums
WHERE n <= 1000000;

CREATE UNIQUE CLUSTERED INDEX idx_keycol ON dbo.T1(keycol);
```

You can find the code to create and populate the Nums table in Chapter 2, "User-Defined Functions."

Turn on the Discard results after execution option in SSMS (under Query | Query Options | Results | Grid Or Text). Now run the following code to issue a checkpoint to ensure that all dirty pages are flushed from cache to disk, and then clear the cache:

```
CHECKPOINT;
DBCC DROPCLEANBUFFERS;
```

Run the following set-based code twice—the first run measures performance against a cold cache, and the second measures it against a warm cache:

```
SELECT keycol, filler FROM dbo.T1;
```

On my system, this query ran for 10 seconds against a cold cache and 1 second against a warm cache. Clear the cache again, and then run the cursor code twice:

```
DECLARE @keycol AS INT, @filler AS CHAR(200);
DECLARE C CURSOR FAST_FORWARD FOR SELECT keycol, filler FROM dbo.T1;
OPEN C;
FETCH NEXT FROM C INTO @keycol, @filler;
WHILE @@fetch_status = 0
BEGIN
  -- Process data here
  FETCH NEXT FROM C INTO @keycol, @filler;
END
CLOSE C;
DEALLOCATE C;
```

This code ran for 25 seconds against a cold cache and 19 seconds against a warm cache. Considering the warm cache example, in which no physical I/O is involved, the cursor code ran almost 20 times longer than the set-based code, and notice that I used a FAST_FORWARD cursor, which is a FORWARD_ONLY, READ_ONLY cursor with performance optimization enabled. Both solutions scanned the same amount of data. In addition to the performance overhead, you also have the development and maintenance overhead of your code. This is a very basic example involving little code; in production environments with more complex code, the problem is, of course, much worse.

> **Tip** SQL Server allows you to declare a cursor variable, assign it with a cursor definition, and manipulate the cursor through the variable. Because variables are local to the batch, SQL Server automatically closes and deallocates the cursor after the batch expires, even if you don't specify the CLOSE and DEALLOCATE commands explicitly. Here's the code you would use to substitute the cursor from the previous example with a cursor variable:
>
> ```
> DECLARE @C AS CURSOR, @keycol AS INT, @filler AS CHAR(200);
> SET @C = CURSOR FAST_FORWARD FOR SELECT keycol, filler FROM dbo.T1;
> OPEN @C;
> FETCH NEXT FROM @C INTO @keycol, @filler;
> ```

```
WHILE @@fetch_status = 0
BEGIN
  -- Process data here
  FETCH NEXT FROM @C INTO @keycol, @filler;
END
```

Still, even when using cursor variables it is good practice to close and deallocate your cursors explicitly to free up the resources as soon as you are done with the cursor. You might end up adding code to the same batch in the future.

Dealing with Each Row Individually

Remember that cursors can be useful when the problem is a procedural one, and you must deal with each row individually. I provided examples of such scenarios earlier. Here I want to show an alternative to cursors that programmers may use to apply iterative logic, and compare its performance with the cursor code I just demonstrated in the previous section. Remember that the cursor code that scanned a million rows took approximately 25 seconds to complete against a cold cache and 19 seconds against a warm cache. In terms of I/O cost, the cursor solution scanned the data once, and because the data resides in approximately 25,000 pages, the I/O cost was about 25,000 reads. Another common technique to iterate through a table's rows is to loop through the keys and use a set-based query for each row. To test the performance of such a solution, make sure the Discard results after execution option in SSMS is still turned on. Then run the code in Listing 8-1.

LISTING 8-1 Code to iterate through rows without a cursor

```
DECLARE @keycol AS INT, @filler AS CHAR(200);

SELECT TOP (1) @keycol = keycol, @filler = filler
FROM dbo.T1
ORDER BY keycol;

WHILE @@rowcount = 1
BEGIN
  -- Process data here

  -- Get next row
  SELECT TOP (1) @keycol = keycol, @filler = filler
  FROM dbo.T1
  WHERE keycol > @keycol
  ORDER BY keycol;
END
```

You use a TOP (1) query to grab the first row based on key order. Within a loop, when a row is found in the previous iteration, you process the data and request the next row (the row with the next key). This code ran for about 25 seconds against a cold cache and 17 seconds against a warm cache—similar to the cursor code. However, keep in mind that I created a clustered index on *keycol* to improve performance by accessing the desired row in each iteration with minimal I/O. You can see the plan for this code in Figure 8-1.

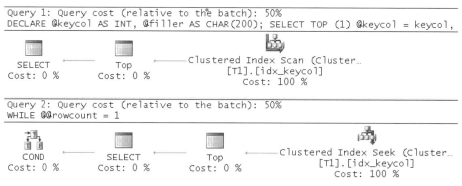

```
Query 1: Query cost (relative to the batch): 50%
DECLARE @keycol AS INT, @filler AS CHAR(200); SELECT TOP (1) @keycol = keycol,
```

```
   SELECT      ←      Top      ←          Clustered Index Scan (Cluster...
  Cost: 0 %         Cost: 0 %                  [T1].[idx_keycol]
                                                 Cost: 100 %
```

```
Query 2: Query cost (relative to the batch): 50%
WHILE @@rowcount = 1
```

```
    COND     ←     SELECT    ←      Top    ←          Clustered Index Seek (Cluster...
  Cost: 0 %       Cost: 0 %       Cost: 0 %                  [T1].[idx_keycol]
                                                               Cost: 100 %
```

FIGURE 8-1 Execution plan for the code in Listing 8-1

Even with the index in place, this approach involves a very high I/O cost compared to the cursor approach. The plan in Figure 8-1 performs a seek operation in the index for each row in the table. With the number of rows in our table the index has three levels. This means that the approach shown in Listing 8-1 involves 3 reads per row, amounting in a total of 3,000,000 reads for 1,000,000 rows. That's compared to about 25,000 reads that the cursor approach involves because it simply scans the data once.

Without that index, matters are even worse for the approach shown in Listing 8-1. The code would run substantially slower because each invocation of the query would need to rescan large portions of data. The cursor solution would still perform the same because it would still scan the data only once.

Note that a cursor solution based on sorted data would also benefit from an index and would run substantially slower without one because it would need to sort the data after scanning it. With large tables and no index on the sort columns, the sort operation can be expensive because sorting in terms of complexity is $O(n \log n)$, whereas scanning is only $O(n)$.

Before you proceed, make sure you turn off the "Discard results after execution" option in SSMS.

Order-Based Access

In the introduction, I mentioned that cursors have the potential to yield better performance than set-based code when the problem is inherently order-based. In this section, I'll show some examples. Where relevant, I'll discuss query constructs that ANSI introduces to allow for "cleaner" code that performs well without the use of cursors. However, some of these ANSI constructs are not implemented in SQL Server 2008.

Custom Aggregates

In *T-SQL Querying*, I discussed custom aggregates by describing problems that require you to aggregate data even though SQL Server doesn't provide such aggregates as built-in functions—for example, product of elements, string concatenation, and so on. I described four classes of solutions and demonstrated three of them: pivoting, which is limited to a small number of elements in a group; CLR user-defined aggregates (UDAs), which require you to write in a .NET language and enable CLR support in SQL Server; and specialized solutions, which can be very fast but require you to reinvent the wheel, so to speak, and are not as natural as some of the other solutions. Another approach to solving custom aggregate problems is using cursors. This approach is not very fast; nevertheless, it is straightforward, generic, and not limited to situations in which you have a small number of elements in a group. To see a demonstration of a cursor-based solution for custom aggregates, run the following code to create and populate the Groups table:

```
USE tempdb;
IF OBJECT_ID('dbo.Groups', 'U') IS NOT NULL DROP TABLE dbo.Groups;

CREATE TABLE dbo.Groups
(
  groupid  VARCHAR(10) NOT NULL,
  memberid INT         NOT NULL,
  string   VARCHAR(10) NOT NULL,
  val      INT         NOT NULL,
  PRIMARY KEY (groupid, memberid)
);
GO

INSERT INTO dbo.Groups(groupid, memberid, string, val) VALUES
  ('a', 3, 'stra1',  6),
  ('a', 9, 'stra2',  7),
  ('b', 2, 'strb1',  3),
  ('b', 4, 'strb2',  7),
  ('b', 5, 'strb3',  3),
  ('b', 9, 'strb4', 11),
  ('c', 3, 'strc1',  8),
  ('c', 7, 'strc2', 10),
  ('c', 9, 'strc3', 12);
```

The following code shows a cursor-based solution that calculates the aggregate product of the *val* column for each group represented by the *groupid* column:

```
DECLARE
  @Result AS TABLE(groupid VARCHAR(10), product BIGINT);
DECLARE
  @groupid AS VARCHAR(10), @prvgroupid AS VARCHAR(10),
  @val AS INT, @product AS BIGINT;

DECLARE C CURSOR FAST_FORWARD FOR
  SELECT groupid, val FROM dbo.Groups ORDER BY groupid;
```

```
OPEN C;

FETCH NEXT FROM C INTO @groupid, @val;
SELECT @prvgroupid = @groupid, @product = 1;

WHILE @@fetch_status = 0
BEGIN
  IF @groupid <> @prvgroupid
  BEGIN
    INSERT INTO @Result VALUES(@prvgroupid, @product);
    SELECT @prvgroupid = @groupid, @product = 1;
  END

  SET @product = @product * @val;

  FETCH NEXT FROM C INTO @groupid, @val;
END

IF @prvgroupid IS NOT NULL
  INSERT INTO @Result VALUES(@prvgroupid, @product);

CLOSE C;

DEALLOCATE C;

SELECT groupid, product FROM @Result;
```

This generates the following output:

```
groupid    product
---------- --------------------
a          42
b          693
c          960
```

The algorithm is straightforward: scan the data in *groupid* order; while traversing the rows in the group, keep multiplying by *val*; and whenever the *groupid* value changes, store the result of the product for the previous group aside in a table variable. When the loop exits, you still hold the aggregate product for the last group, so store it in the table variable as well unless the input was empty. Finally, return the aggregate products of all groups as output. Note that if you need to apply the aggregate within the group in a certain order, this option is supported by the cursor solution. For example, if you're implementing a string concatenation aggregate, you can control the order of concatenation by adding the ordering attributes to the ORDER BY list right after the grouping attributes.

Running Aggregations

The previous problem, which discussed custom aggregates, used a cursor-based solution that scanned the data only once, but so did the pivoting solution, the UDA solution, and some of the specialized set-based solutions. If you consider that cursors incur more overhead than set-based solutions that scan the same amount of data, you can see that the cursor-based solutions are bound to be slower. On the other hand, set-based solutions for running aggregation problems (also known as *running totals*) in SQL Server 2008 involve rescanning portions of the data multiple times, whereas the cursor-based solutions scan the data only once.

I covered set-based solutions to running aggregations in *T-SQL Querying*. Here, I'll demonstrate cursor-based solutions. Run the following code, which creates and populates the Sales table in the CLRUtilities database:

```
SET NOCOUNT ON;
IF DB_ID('CLRUtilities') IS NULL CREATE DATABASE CLRUtilities;
GO
USE CLRUtilities;

IF OBJECT_ID('dbo.Sales', 'U') IS NOT NULL DROP TABLE dbo.Sales;

CREATE TABLE dbo.Sales
(
  empid INT       NOT NULL,               -- partitioning column
  dt    DATETIME NOT NULL,                -- ordering column
  qty   INT       NOT NULL DEFAULT (1),   -- measure 1
  val   MONEY     NOT NULL DEFAULT (1.00), -- measure 2
  CONSTRAINT PK_Sales PRIMARY KEY(empid, dt)
);
GO

DECLARE
  @num_partitions     AS INT,
  @rows_per_partition AS INT,
  @start_dt           AS DATETIME;

SET @num_partitions     = 10000;
SET @rows_per_partition = 10;
SET @start_dt = '20090101';

TRUNCATE TABLE dbo.Sales;

INSERT INTO dbo.Sales WITH (TABLOCK) (empid, dt)
  SELECT NP.n AS empid, DATEADD(day, RPP.n - 1, @start_dt) AS dt
  FROM dbo.Nums AS NP
    CROSS JOIN dbo.Nums AS RPP
WHERE NP.n <= @num_partitions
  AND RPP.n <= @rows_per_partition;
```

Each row in the table holds the sales quantity and value for a given employee and date. The table is initially populated with 100,000 rows, representing 10,000 partitions (employees), with 10 rows in each partition. To run performance tests with a different number of partitions and rows per partition, simply rerun this code after assigning the desired values to the variables *@num_partitions* and *@rows_per_partition*, respectively.

As an example of a running aggregate problem, suppose that you need to calculate the running total of *qty* for each employee and date. That is, for each employee and date you need to return the current quantity and also the total quantity from the beginning of the employee's activity until the current date.

The common set-based solutions for this task that are supported by SQL Server 2008 use either subqueries or joins. Here's an example using a subquery:

```
SELECT empid, dt, qty,
  (SELECT SUM(S2.qty)
   FROM dbo.Sales AS S2
   WHERE S2.empid = S1.empid
     AND S2.dt <= S1.dt) AS sumqty
FROM dbo.Sales AS S1;
```

For each row from the outer instance of the Sales table (S1), a subquery calculates the sum of quantities of all rows from a second instance of Sales (S2), that have the same employee ID as in the outer row, and a date that is smaller than or equal to the one in the outer row.

This query generates the following output, shown here in abbreviated form:

```
empid       dt                        qty          sumqty
----------- ------------------------- -----------  --------------------
1           2009-01-01 00:00:00.000   1            1
1           2009-01-02 00:00:00.000   1            2
1           2009-01-03 00:00:00.000   1            3
1           2009-01-04 00:00:00.000   1            4
1           2009-01-05 00:00:00.000   1            5
1           2009-01-06 00:00:00.000   1            6
1           2009-01-07 00:00:00.000   1            7
1           2009-01-08 00:00:00.000   1            8
1           2009-01-09 00:00:00.000   1            9
1           2009-01-10 00:00:00.000   1            10
2           2009-01-01 00:00:00.000   1            1
2           2009-01-02 00:00:00.000   1            2
2           2009-01-03 00:00:00.000   1            3
2           2009-01-04 00:00:00.000   1            4
2           2009-01-05 00:00:00.000   1            5
2           2009-01-06 00:00:00.000   1            6
2           2009-01-07 00:00:00.000   1            7
2           2009-01-08 00:00:00.000   1            8
2           2009-01-09 00:00:00.000   1            9
2           2009-01-10 00:00:00.000   1            10
...
```

The cursor-based solution is straightforward. In fact, it's similar to calculating custom aggregates except for a simple difference: the code calculating custom aggregates sets aside in a table variable only the final aggregate for each group, whereas the code calculating running aggregations sets aside the running aggregate value for each row. Here's the cursor-based solution for our task:

```
DECLARE @Result AS TABLE
(
  empid  INT,
  dt     DATETIME,
  qty    INT,
  sumqty BIGINT
);
```

```
DECLARE
  @empid    AS INT,
  @prvempid AS INT,
  @dt       AS DATETIME,
  @qty      AS INT,
  @sumqty   AS BIGINT;

DECLARE C CURSOR FAST_FORWARD FOR
  SELECT empid, dt, qty
  FROM dbo.Sales
  ORDER BY empid, dt;

OPEN C;

FETCH NEXT FROM C INTO @empid, @dt, @qty;

SELECT @prvempid = @empid, @sumqty = 0;

WHILE @@fetch_status = 0
BEGIN
  IF @empid <> @prvempid
    SELECT @prvempid = @empid, @sumqty = 0;

  SET @sumqty = @sumqty + @qty;

  INSERT INTO @Result VALUES(@empid, @dt, @qty, @sumqty);

  FETCH NEXT FROM C INTO @empid, @dt, @qty;
END

CLOSE C;

DEALLOCATE C;

SELECT * FROM @Result;
```

Provided that a covering index is in place defined with the cursor ordering columns as the index keys and the measure you're aggregating as an included column, the cursor solution scans the data only once without the need for sorting. If you have p partitions with an average of r rows per partition, and a relatively uniform distribution of rows per partition, you can express the cost of this solution as $p \times r + p \times r \times o$, where o, as before, represents the cursor overhead. Therefore, the complexity of this solution is linearly proportional to the number of partitions and linearly proportional to the partition size.

Assuming you have the aforementioned index in place, the cost of the set-based solution can be expressed as $p \times r + p \times (r + r^2)/2$. With respect to the number of partitions, the complexity of the set-based solution is linear, but with respect to the partition size, it's quadratic, or $O(n^2)$. If the partition size grows by a factor of f, the cost increases by almost f^2. Without the aforementioned index in place, of course, things are even worse.

When the partition size is small, the set-based solution will typically be faster than the cursor solution. That's when the cursor's overhead exceeds the set-based solution's extra work of scanning more data. However, as the partition size increases, the cursor solution's cost grows linearly while the set-based solution's cost grows much more rapidly—quadratically, and at some point the cursor solution becomes faster. Tests that I've done show that up to a partition size of about 500 rows the set-based solution tends to perform better, whereas beyond 500 rows the cursor solution performs better. I'll provide actual benchmark results later in this section.

So now you can see that in certain cases a T-SQL cursor-based solution can be faster than a set-based solution. If you are willing to consider an iterative approach based on cursors, you should consider a CLR-based solution. Using a CLR procedure, you can use a data reader to iterate through the records one at a time, then pipe the rows in the result back to the caller. Think of a .NET data reader as a faster cursor than the T-SQL one. You still pay some overhead to manipulate each row, but the overhead is much lower than that of the T-SQL cursor.

Here's the definition of a CLR stored procedure called *SalesRunningSum* that implements our task in C#:

```csharp
using System;
using System.Data;
using System.Data.SqlClient;
using System.Data.SqlTypes;
using Microsoft.SqlServer.Server;

public partial class StoredProcedures
{
  [Microsoft.SqlServer.Server.SqlProcedure]
  public static void SalesRunningSum()
  {
    using (SqlConnection conn = new SqlConnection("context connection=true;"))
    {
      SqlCommand comm = new SqlCommand();
      comm.Connection = conn;
      comm.CommandText = "" +
          "SELECT empid, dt, qty " +
          "FROM dbo.Sales " +
          "ORDER BY empid, dt;";

      SqlMetaData[] columns = new SqlMetaData[4];
      columns[0] = new SqlMetaData("empid", SqlDbType.Int);
      columns[1] = new SqlMetaData("dt", SqlDbType.DateTime);
      columns[2] = new SqlMetaData("qty", SqlDbType.Int);
      columns[3] = new SqlMetaData("sumqty", SqlDbType.BigInt);

      SqlDataRecord record = new SqlDataRecord(columns);

      SqlContext.Pipe.SendResultsStart(record);

      conn.Open();

      SqlDataReader reader = comm.ExecuteReader();

      SqlInt32 prvempid = 0;
      SqlInt64 sumqty = 0;
```

```
    while (reader.Read())
    {
      SqlInt32 empid = reader.GetSqlInt32(0);
      SqlInt32 qty = reader.GetSqlInt32(2);

      if (empid == prvempid)
      {
        sumqty += qty;
      }
      else
      {
        sumqty = qty;
      }

      prvempid = empid;

      record.SetSqlInt32(0, reader.GetSqlInt32(0));
      record.SetSqlDateTime(1, reader.GetSqlDateTime(1));
      record.SetSqlInt32(2, qty);
      record.SetSqlInt64(3, sumqty);

      SqlContext.Pipe.SendResultsRow(record);
    }

    SqlContext.Pipe.SendResultsEnd();
  }
 }
};
```

And here's the definition of the procedure using Microsoft Visual Basic:

```
Imports System
Imports System.Data
Imports System.Data.SqlClient
Imports System.Data.SqlTypes
Imports Microsoft.SqlServer.Server

Partial Public Class StoredProcedures
  <Microsoft.SqlServer.Server.SqlProcedure()> _
  Public Shared Sub SalesRunningSum()

    Using conn As New SqlConnection("context connection=true")
      Dim comm As New SqlCommand
      comm.Connection = conn
      comm.CommandText = "" & _
          "SELECT empid, dt, qty " & _
          "FROM dbo.Sales " & _
          "ORDER BY empid, dt;"

      Dim columns() As SqlMetaData = New SqlMetaData(3) {}
      columns(0) = New SqlMetaData("empid", SqlDbType.Int)
      columns(1) = New SqlMetaData("dt", SqlDbType.DateTime)
      columns(2) = New SqlMetaData("qty", SqlDbType.Int)
      columns(3) = New SqlMetaData("sumqty", SqlDbType.BigInt)

      Dim record As New SqlDataRecord(columns)
```

```
        SqlContext.Pipe.SendResultsStart(record)

        conn.Open()

        Dim reader As SqlDataReader = comm.ExecuteReader

        Dim prvempid As SqlInt32 = 0
        Dim sumqty As SqlInt64 = 0

        While (reader.Read())
          Dim empid As SqlInt32 = reader.GetSqlInt32(0)
          Dim qty As SqlInt32 = reader.GetSqlInt32(2)

          If (empid = prvempid) Then
            sumqty = sumqty + qty
          Else
            sumqty = qty
          End If

          prvempid = empid

          record.SetSqlInt32(0, reader.GetSqlInt32(0))
          record.SetSqlDateTime(1, reader.GetSqlDateTime(1))
          record.SetSqlInt32(2, qty)
          record.SetSqlInt64(3, sumqty)

          SqlContext.Pipe.SendResultsRow(record)
        End While

        SqlContext.Pipe.SendResultsEnd()
      End Using

    End Sub
End Class
```

For this example, I tailored code that was originally provided by Adam Machanic in this blog post: *http://sqlblog.com/blogs/adam_machanic/archive/2006/07/12/running-sums-yet-again-sqlclr-saves-the-day.aspx.*

The code defining the procedure is pretty straightforward, and in essence it implements very similar logic to the T-SQL cursor solution I provided earlier. As for deploying the solution, remember that instructions are provided in Appendix A. If you deployed the assembly as instructed in Appendix A, the database CLRUtilities should already contain the procedure *SalesRunningSum.* Run the following code to execute the procedure:

```
EXEC dbo.SalesRunningSum;
```

Like the T-SQL cursor-based solution, the CLR-based solution also has linear complexity with respect to both the number of partitions and the partition size—except that the former is about five times slower.

I ran a benchmark to compare the different solutions and to show how they scale. Because all solutions scale linearly with respect to changes in number of partitions, I used a constant number of partitions. However, I did use varying partition sizes to show the different manner in which the solutions scale. The results of the benchmark are shown in Figure 8-2.

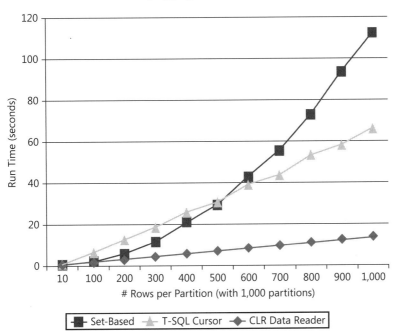

FIGURE 8-2 Benchmark for running aggregations

You can clearly see that the set-based solution is faster than the T-SQL cursor-based solution up to a partition size of about 500 rows, and slower beyond that point. As for the CLR-based solution, you can see that it's about five times faster than the T-SQL cursor-based one. The set-based solution is faster than the CLR-based solution up to a partition size of about 15, and slower beyond that point. I find the results quite fascinating, even though you could argue that they merely confirm the obvious.

This is one of the problems that ANSI SQL already provided an answer for in the form of query constructs; however, SQL Server has not yet implemented it. According to ANSI SQL, you would write the following solution:

```
SELECT empid, dt, qty,
  SUM(qty) OVER(PARTITION BY empid
               ORDER BY dt
               ROWS BETWEEN UNBOUNDED PRECEDING
                        AND CURRENT ROW) AS sumqty
FROM dbo.Sales;
```

As mentioned earlier, SQL Server 2008 already has the infrastructure to support the OVER clause. It currently implements it with both the PARTITION BY and ORDER BY clauses for ranking functions, but only with the PARTITION BY clause for aggregate functions. I hope that future versions of SQL Server will enhance the support for the OVER clause and provide a more complete implementation of the standard's feature set. Queries such as the one just shown have the potential to run substantially faster than any of the existing solutions. Better support for window specifications would also prevent developers from having to sacrifice performance if they require benefits specific to T-SQL solutions, such as dependency tracking.

Maximum Concurrent Sessions

The Maximum Concurrent Sessions problem is yet another example of calculations that can benefit from processing the data in an ordered fashion. You record data for user sessions against different applications in a table called Sessions. Run the code in Listing 8-2 to create and populate the Sessions table.

LISTING 8-2 Creating and populating the Sessions table

```
USE tempdb;
IF OBJECT_ID('dbo.Sessions', 'U') IS NOT NULL DROP TABLE dbo.Sessions;

CREATE TABLE dbo.Sessions
(
  keycol    INT        NOT NULL IDENTITY,
  app       VARCHAR(10) NOT NULL,
  usr       VARCHAR(10) NOT NULL,
  host      VARCHAR(10) NOT NULL,
  starttime DATETIME    NOT NULL,
  endtime   DATETIME    NOT NULL,
  CONSTRAINT PK_Sessions PRIMARY KEY(keycol),
  CHECK(endtime > starttime)
);
GO

INSERT INTO dbo.Sessions VALUES
  ('app1', 'user1', 'host1', '20090212 08:30', '20090212 10:30'),
  ('app1', 'user2', 'host1', '20090212 08:30', '20090212 08:45'),
  ('app1', 'user3', 'host2', '20090212 09:00', '20090212 09:30'),
  ('app1', 'user4', 'host2', '20090212 09:15', '20090212 10:30'),
  ('app1', 'user5', 'host3', '20090212 09:15', '20090212 09:30'),
  ('app1', 'user6', 'host3', '20090212 10:30', '20090212 14:30'),
  ('app1', 'user7', 'host4', '20090212 10:45', '20090212 11:30'),
  ('app1', 'user8', 'host4', '20090212 11:00', '20090212 12:30'),
  ('app2', 'user8', 'host1', '20090212 08:30', '20090212 08:45'),
  ('app2', 'user7', 'host1', '20090212 09:00', '20090212 09:30'),
  ('app2', 'user6', 'host2', '20090212 11:45', '20090212 12:00'),
  ('app2', 'user5', 'host2', '20090212 12:30', '20090212 14:00'),
  ('app2', 'user4', 'host3', '20090212 12:45', '20090212 13:30'),
  ('app2', 'user3', 'host3', '20090212 13:00', '20090212 14:00'),
  ('app2', 'user2', 'host4', '20090212 14:00', '20090212 16:30'),
  ('app2', 'user1', 'host4', '20090212 15:30', '20090212 17:00');

CREATE INDEX idx_nc_app_st_et ON dbo.Sessions(app, starttime, endtime);
```

The request is to calculate, for each application, the maximum number of sessions that were open at the same point in time. Such types of calculations are required to determine the cost of a type of service license that charges by the maximum number of concurrent sessions.

Try to develop a set-based solution that works; then try to optimize it; and then try to evaluate its algorithmic complexity. Later I'll discuss a cursor-based solution and show a benchmark that compares the set-based solution with the cursor-based solution.

One way to solve the problem is to generate an auxiliary table with all possible points in time during the covered period, use a subquery to count the number of active sessions during each such point in time, create a derived table/CTE from the result table, and then group the rows from the derived table by application, requesting the maximum count of concurrent sessions for each application. Such a solution is extremely inefficient. Assuming you create the optimal index for it—one on (*app, starttime, endtime*)—the total number of rows you end up scanning just in the leaf level of the index is huge. It's at minimum the number of rows in the auxiliary table multiplied by the average number of active sessions at any point in time. To give you a sense of the enormousness of the task, if you need to perform the calculations for a month's worth of activity, the number of rows in the auxiliary table will be: 31 (days) × 24 (hours) × 60 (minutes) × 60 (seconds) × 300 (units within a second). Now multiply the result of this calculation by the average number of active sessions at any given point in time (let's use 20 as an example), and you get 16,070,400,000. That's assuming that you use the DATETIME data type. If you use the DATETIME2 data type, which has an accuracy of 100 nanoseconds, the number is 26,784,000,000,000.

Of course there's room for optimization. There are periods in which the number of concurrent sessions doesn't change, so why calculate the counts for those? The count changes only when a new session starts (increased by 1) or an existing session ends (decreased by 1). Furthermore, because a start of a session increases the count and an end of a session decreases it, a start event of one of the sessions is bound to be the point at which you will find the maximum you're looking for.

In short, you can simply use as your auxiliary table a derived table or CTE that returns all start times of sessions per application. From there, all you need to do is follow logic similar to that mentioned earlier. Here's the optimized set-based solution:

```
SELECT app, MAX(concurrent) AS mx
FROM (SELECT app,
        (SELECT COUNT(*)
         FROM dbo.Sessions AS S
         WHERE T.app = S.app
           AND T.ts >= S.starttime
           AND T.ts < S.endtime) AS concurrent
      FROM (SELECT app, starttime AS ts FROM dbo.Sessions) AS T) AS C
GROUP BY app;
```

This generates the following output:

```
app          mx
----------   -----------
app1         4
app2         3
```

Notice that instead of using a BETWEEN predicate to determine whether a session was active at a certain point in time (*ts*), I used *ts >= starttime AND ts < endtime*. If a session ends at the *ts* point in time, I don't want to consider it as active.

The execution plan for this query is shown in Figure 8-3. Note that I captured this plan after populating the Sales table with a more realistic volume of data. With very little data you might get a different plan.

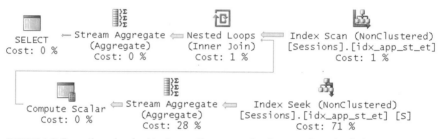

FIGURE 8-3 Execution plan for Maximum Concurrent Sessions, set-based solution

First, the index I created on (*app, starttime, endtime*) is scanned. The number of rows returned will be the same as the number of rows in the table. For each *app, starttime* (call it *ts*) returned, a Nested Loops operator initiates activity that calculates the count of active sessions (by a seek within the index, followed by a partial scan to count active sessions). The number of pages read in each iteration of the Nested Loops operator is the number of levels in the index plus at least the number of pages consumed by the rows representing active sessions. To make my point, I'll focus on the number of rows scanned at the leaf level because this number varies based on active sessions. Of course, to do adequate performance estimations, you should take page counts (logical reads) as well as many other factors into consideration. If you have *n* rows in the table, and there are *c* concurrent sessions on average at any given point in time when a session starts, you're looking at the following at least: $n \times c$ rows scanned in total at the leaf level, beyond the pages scanned by the seek operations that got you to the leaf.

You now need to figure out how this solution scales when the data volume increases. Typically, such reports are required periodically—for example, once a month, for the most recent month. With the recommended index in place, the performance shouldn't change as long as the traffic doesn't increase for a month's worth of activity. But suppose that you anticipate traffic increase by a factor of *f*. If traffic increases by a factor of *f*, both total rows and number of active sessions at a given time grow by that factor; so in total, the number of rows scanned at the leaf level becomes at least $(n \times f)(c \times f) = n \times c \times f^2$. You see, as the traffic grows, the cost doesn't increase linearly; rather, it increases in a quadratic manner.

Next, let's talk about a cursor-based solution. The power of a cursor-based solution is that it can scan data in order. Relying on the fact that each session represents two events—one that increases the count of active sessions, and one that decreases the count—I'll declare a cursor for the following query:

```
SELECT app, starttime AS ts, 1 AS event_type FROM dbo.Sessions
UNION ALL
SELECT app, endtime, -1 FROM dbo.Sessions
ORDER BY app, ts, event_type;
```

This query returns the following for each session start or end event: the application (*app*), the timestamp (*ts*); an event type (*event_type*) of +1 for a session start event or –1 for a session end event. The events are sorted by *app*, *ts*, and *event_type*. The reason for sorting by *app*, *ts* is obvious. The reason for adding *event_type* to the sort is to guarantee that if a session ends at the same time another session starts, you will take the end event into consideration first (because sessions are considered to have ended at their end time). Other than that, the cursor code is straightforward—simply scan the data in order and keep adding up the +1s and –1s for each application. With every new row scanned, check whether the cumulative value to that point is greater than the current maximum for that application, which you store in a variable. If it is, store it as the new maximum. When you're done with an application, insert a row containing the application ID and maximum into a table variable. That's about it. The following code has the complete cursor solution:

```
DECLARE
    @app AS VARCHAR(10), @prevapp AS VARCHAR (10), @ts AS datetime,
    @event_type AS INT, @concurrent AS INT, @mx AS INT;

DECLARE @Result AS TABLE(app VARCHAR(10), mx INT);

DECLARE C CURSOR FAST_FORWARD FOR
    SELECT app, starttime AS ts, 1 AS event_type FROM dbo.Sessions
    UNION ALL
    SELECT app, endtime, -1 FROM dbo.Sessions
    ORDER BY app, ts, event_type;

OPEN C;

FETCH NEXT FROM C INTO @app, @ts, @event_type;
SELECT @prevapp = @app, @concurrent = 0, @mx = 0;

WHILE @@fetch_status = 0
BEGIN
  IF @app <> @prevapp
  BEGIN
    INSERT INTO @Result VALUES(@prevapp, @mx);
    SELECT @prevapp = @app, @concurrent = 0, @mx = 0;
  END

  SET @concurrent = @concurrent + @event_type;
  IF @concurrent > @mx SET @mx = @concurrent;
```

```
    FETCH NEXT FROM C INTO @app, @ts, @event_type;
END

IF @prevapp IS NOT NULL
   INSERT INTO @Result VALUES(@prevapp, @mx);

CLOSE C;

DEALLOCATE C;

SELECT * FROM @Result;
```

The cursor solution scans the leaf of the index only twice. You can represent its cost as $2 \times n + 2 \times n \times o$, where o is the cursor overhead involved with each single row manipulation. Also, if the traffic grows by a factor of f, the performance degrades linearly to $2 \times n \times f + 2 \times n \times f \times o$. You realize that unless you're dealing with a very small input set, the cursor solution has the potential to perform much faster, and as proof, you can use the following code to conduct a benchmark test:

```
SET NOCOUNT ON;
USE tempdb;

IF OBJECT_ID('dbo.Sessions', 'U') IS NOT NULL DROP TABLE dbo.Sessions
GO

DECLARE @numrows AS INT;
SET @numrows = 10000;
-- Test with 10K - 100K

SELECT
  IDENTITY(int, 1, 1) AS keycol,
  D.*,
  DATEADD(
    second,
    1 + ABS(CHECKSUM(NEWID())) % (20*60),
    starttime) AS endtime
INTO dbo.Sessions
FROM
(
  SELECT
    'app' + CAST(1 + ABS(CHECKSUM(NEWID())) % 10 AS VARCHAR(10)) AS app,
    'user1' AS usr,
    'host1' AS host,
    DATEADD(
      second,
      1 + ABS(CHECKSUM(NEWID())) % (30*24*60*60),
      '20090101') AS starttime
  FROM dbo.Nums
  WHERE n <= @numrows
) AS D;

ALTER TABLE dbo.Sessions ADD PRIMARY KEY(keycol);
CREATE INDEX idx_app_st_et ON dbo.Sessions(app, starttime, endtime);
```

```
CHECKPOINT;
DBCC FREEPROCCACHE WITH NO_INFOMSGS;
DBCC DROPCLEANBUFFERS WITH NO_INFOMSGS;

DECLARE @dt1 AS DATETIME, @dt2 AS DATETIME,
  @dt3 AS DATETIME, @dt4 AS DATETIME;
SET @dt1 = GETDATE();

-- Set-Based Solution
SELECT app, MAX(concurrent) AS mx
FROM (SELECT app,
        (SELECT COUNT(*)
          FROM dbo.Sessions AS S
          WHERE T.app = S.app
            AND T.ts >= S.starttime
            AND T.ts < S.endtime) AS concurrent
      FROM (SELECT app, starttime AS ts FROM dbo.Sessions) AS T) AS C
GROUP BY app;

SET @dt2 = GETDATE();

DBCC FREEPROCCACHE WITH NO_INFOMSGS;
DBCC DROPCLEANBUFFERS WITH NO_INFOMSGS;

SET @dt3 = GETDATE();

-- Cursor-Based Solution
DECLARE
  @app AS VARCHAR(10), @prevapp AS VARCHAR (10), @ts AS datetime,
  @event_type AS INT, @concurrent AS INT, @mx AS INT;

DECLARE @Result TABLE(app VARCHAR(10), mx INT);

DECLARE C CURSOR FAST_FORWARD FOR
  SELECT app, starttime AS ts, 1 AS event_type FROM dbo.Sessions
  UNION ALL
  SELECT app, endtime, -1 FROM dbo.Sessions
  ORDER BY app, ts, event_type;

OPEN C;

FETCH NEXT FROM C INTO @app, @ts, @event_type;
SELECT @prevapp = @app, @concurrent = 0, @mx = 0;

WHILE @@FETCH_STATUS = 0
BEGIN
  IF @app <> @prevapp
  BEGIN
    INSERT INTO @Result VALUES(@prevapp, @mx);
    SELECT @prevapp = @app, @concurrent = 0, @mx = 0;
  END

  SET @concurrent = @concurrent + @event_type;
  IF @concurrent > @mx SET @mx = @concurrent;

  FETCH NEXT FROM C INTO @app, @ts, @event_type;
END
```

```
IF @prevapp IS NOT NULL
  INSERT INTO @Result VALUES(@prevapp, @mx);

CLOSE C;

DEALLOCATE C;

SELECT * FROM @Result;

SET @dt4 = GETDATE();

PRINT CAST(@numrows AS VARCHAR(10)) + ' rows, set-based: '
  + CAST(DATEDIFF(ms, @dt1, @dt2) / 1000. AS VARCHAR(30))
  + ', cursor: '
  + CAST(DATEDIFF(ms, @dt3, @dt4) / 1000. AS VARCHAR(30))
  + ' (sec)';
```

Change the value of the *@numrows* variable to determine the number of rows in the table. I ran this code with numbers varying from 10,000 through 100,000 in steps of 10,000. Figure 8-4 shows a graphical depiction of the benchmark test I ran.

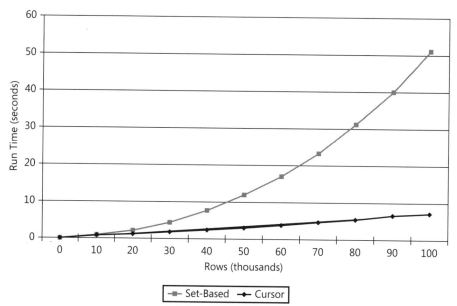

FIGURE 8-4 Benchmark for Maximum Concurrent Sessions solutions

Again, you can see a nicely shaped parabola in the set-based solution's graph, and now you know how to explain it: remember—if traffic increases by a factor of *f*, the number of leaf-level rows inspected by the set-based query grows by a factor of f^2. In other words, the algorithmic complexity of the set-based solution is $O(n^2)$.

> **Tip** It might seem that all the cases in which I show cursor code that performs better than set-based code have to do with problems where cursor code has a complexity of $O(n)$ and set-based code has a complexity of $O(n^2)$, where n is the number of rows in the table. These are just convenient problems to demonstrate performance differences. However, you might face problems for which the solutions have different complexities. The important point is to be able to estimate complexity and performance. If you want to learn more about algorithmic complexity, see Chapter 5 in the book *T-SQL Querying*.

Interestingly, this is yet another type of problem where a more complete implementation of the OVER clause would have allowed for a set-based solution to perform substantially faster than the cursor one. Here's what the set-based solution would have looked like if SQL Server supported ORDER BY and ROWS in the OVER clause for aggregations:

```
SELECT app, MAX(concurrent) AS mx
FROM (SELECT app, SUM(event_type)
        OVER(PARTITION BY app
             ORDER BY ts, event_type
             ROWS BETWEEN UNBOUNDED PRECEDING
                      AND CURRENT ROW) AS concurrent
      FROM (SELECT app, starttime AS ts, 1 AS event_type FROM dbo.Sessions
            UNION ALL
            SELECT app, endtime, -1 FROM dbo.Sessions) AS D1) AS D2
GROUP BY app;
```

Before I proceed to the next class of problems, I'd like to stress the importance of using good sample data in your benchmarks. Sometimes programmers simply duplicate data from a small table many times to generate larger sets of sample data. If you simply duplicate the small sample data that I provided in Listing 8-2 (16 rows) many times, you will not increase the number of distinct timestamps accordingly. The optimizer may realize that the number of distinct timestamps is small and therefore won't bother to perform the work involved in counting active sessions more than once per distinct timestamp. The results that you will get when measuring performance won't give you a true indication of cost for production environments where, obviously, you have almost no duplicates in the data.

To demonstrate the problem, first rerun the code in Listing 8-2 to repopulate the Sessions table with 16 rows. Next, populate the table with 10,000 duplicates of each row:

```
INSERT INTO dbo.Sessions
  SELECT app, usr, host, starttime, endtime
  FROM dbo.Sessions
    JOIN dbo.Nums
      ON n <= 10000;
```

Rerun the solution query, and examine the execution plan shown in Figure 8-5.

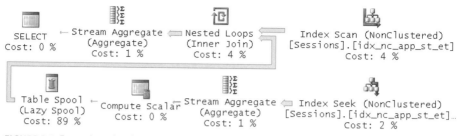

FIGURE 8-5 Execution plan for revised Maximum Concurrent Sessions solution, large data set with high density

If you have a keen eye, you will find interesting differences between this plan and the previous one, even though the query remained the same and only the data density changed. This plan executes the Index Seek and Stream Aggregate operations here only 14 times— once for each unique *app, ts* value, and not once for each row in the table as might happen in production. You can see this in the tooltip box for the operators in the *Number of Executions* measure. The distinct results are stored in a temporary table (Table Spool operator). This plan reuses (rewinds)—instead of recalculating (rebinding)—row counts that were already calculated for a given *app, ts*. Again, you see how a bad choice of sample data can yield a result that is not representative of your production environment. Using this sample data and being oblivious to the discrepancy might lead you to believe that this set-based solution scales linearly. But of course, if you use more realistic sample data, such as the data I used in my benchmark, you won't fall into that trap. I used random calculations for the start times within the month and added a random value of up to 20 minutes for the end time, assuming that this represents the average session duration in my production environment.

Matching Problems

The algorithms for the solutions that I have discussed so far, both set-based and cursor-based, had simple to moderate complexity levels. This section covers a class of problems that are algorithmically much more complex, known as *matching problems*. In a matching problem, you have a specific set of items of different values and volumes and one container of a given size, and you must find the subset of items with the greatest possible value that will fit into the container. I have yet to find reasonable set-based solutions that are nearly as good as cursor-based solutions, both in terms of performance and simplicity.

I'll introduce a couple of simple variations of the problem. You're given the tables Events and Rooms, which you create and populate by running the following code:

```
USE tempdb;
IF OBJECT_ID('dbo.Events', 'U') IS NOT NULL DROP TABLE dbo.Events;
IF OBJECT_ID('dbo.Rooms', 'U') IS NOT NULL DROP TABLE dbo.Rooms;
GO

CREATE TABLE dbo.Rooms
```

```
(
  roomid VARCHAR(10) NOT NULL PRIMARY KEY,
  seats INT NOT NULL
);

INSERT INTO dbo.Rooms(roomid, seats) VALUES
  ('C001', 2000),
  ('B101', 1500),
  ('B102', 100),
  ('R103', 40),
  ('R104', 40),
  ('B201', 1000),
  ('R202', 100),
  ('R203', 50),
  ('B301', 600),
  ('R302', 55),
  ('R303', 55);

CREATE TABLE dbo.Events
(
  eventid INT NOT NULL PRIMARY KEY,
  eventdesc VARCHAR(25) NOT NULL,
  attendees INT NOT NULL
);

INSERT INTO dbo.Events(eventid, eventdesc, attendees) VALUES
  (1, 'Adv T-SQL Seminar', 203),
  (2, 'Logic Seminar',      48),
  (3, 'DBA Seminar',       212),
  (4, 'XML Seminar',        98),
  (5, 'Security Seminar',  892),
  (6, 'Modeling Seminar',   48);

CREATE UNIQUE INDEX idx_att_eid_edesc
  ON dbo.Events(attendees, eventid, eventdesc);
CREATE UNIQUE INDEX idx_seats_rid
  ON dbo.Rooms(seats, roomid);
```

The Events table holds information for seminars that you're supposed to run on a given date. Typically, you will need to keep track of events on many dates, but our task here will be one that we would have to perform separately for each day of scheduled events. Assume that this data represents one day's worth of events; for simplicity's sake, I didn't include a date column because all its values would be the same. The Rooms table holds room capacity information. To start with a simple task, assume that you have reserved a conference center with the guarantee that enough rooms will be available to host all your seminars. You now need to match events to rooms with as few empty seats as possible, because the cost of renting a room is determined by the room's seating capacity, not by the number of seminar attendees.

A naïve algorithm that you can apply is somewhat similar to a merge join algorithm that the optimizer uses to process joins. Figure 8-6 has a graphical depiction of it, which you might find handy when following the verbal description of the algorithm. The following code implements this algorithm:

```
DECLARE
  @roomid AS VARCHAR(10), @seats AS INT,
  @eventid AS INT, @attendees AS INT;

DECLARE @Result AS TABLE(roomid  VARCHAR(10), eventid INT);

DECLARE CRooms CURSOR FAST_FORWARD FOR
  SELECT roomid, seats FROM dbo.Rooms
  ORDER BY seats, roomid;
DECLARE CEvents CURSOR FAST_FORWARD FOR
  SELECT eventid, attendees FROM dbo.Events
  ORDER BY attendees, eventid;

OPEN CRooms;
OPEN CEvents;

FETCH NEXT FROM CEvents INTO @eventid, @attendees;
WHILE @@FETCH_STATUS = 0
BEGIN
  FETCH NEXT FROM CRooms INTO @roomid, @seats;

  WHILE @@FETCH_STATUS = 0 AND @seats < @attendees
    FETCH NEXT FROM CRooms INTO @roomid, @seats;

  IF @@FETCH_STATUS = 0
    INSERT INTO @Result(roomid, eventid) VALUES(@roomid, @eventid);
  ELSE
  BEGIN
    RAISERROR('Not enough rooms for events.', 16, 1);
    BREAK;
  END

  FETCH NEXT FROM CEvents INTO @eventid, @attendees;
END

CLOSE CRooms;
CLOSE CEvents;

DEALLOCATE CRooms;
DEALLOCATE CEvents;

SELECT roomid, eventid FROM @Result;
```

Here's a description of the algorithm as it's implemented with cursors:

1. Declare two cursors, one on the list of rooms (*CRooms*) sorted by increasing capacity (number of seats), and one on the list of events (*CEvents*) sorted by increasing number of attendees.

2. Fetch the first (smallest) event from the *CEvents* cursor.

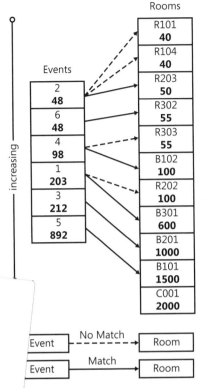

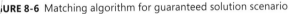

FIGURE 8-6 Matching algorithm for guaranteed solution scenario

3. While the fetch returned an actual event that needs a room:

    3.1 Fetch the smallest unrented room from *CRooms*. If no room was available, or if the room you fetched is too small for the event, fetch the next smallest room from *CRooms*, and continue fetching as long as you keep fetching actual rooms and they are too small for the event. You will either find a big enough room, or you will run out of rooms without finding one.

    3.2 If you did not run out of rooms, and the last fetch yielded a room and the number of seats in that room is smaller than the number of attendees in the current event:

        3.2.1 If you found a big enough room, schedule the current event in that room. If you did not, you must have run out of rooms, so generate an error saying that there are not enough rooms to host all the events, and break out of the loop.

        3.2.2 Fetch another event.

4. Return the room/event pairs you stored aside.

Notice that you scan both rooms and events in order, never backing up; you merge matching pairs until you either run out of events to find rooms for or you run out of rooms to accommodate events. In the latter case, you run out of rooms, generating an error, because the algorithm used was guaranteed to find a solution if one existed.

Next, let's complicate the problem by assuming that even if there aren't enough rooms for all events, you still want to schedule something. This will be the case if you remove rooms with a number of seats greater than 600:

```
DELETE FROM dbo.Rooms WHERE seats > 600;
```

Assume you need to come up with a *greedy* algorithm that finds seats for the highest possible number of attendees (to increase revenue) and for that number of attendees, involves the lowest cost. The algorithm I used for this case is graphically illustrated in Figure 8-7 and implemented with cursors using the following code:

```
DECLARE
  @roomid AS VARCHAR(10), @seats AS INT,
  @eventid AS INT, @attendees AS INT;

DECLARE @Events AS TABLE(eventid INT, attendees INT);
DECLARE @Result AS TABLE(roomid  VARCHAR(10), eventid INT);

-- Step 1: Descending
DECLARE CRoomsDesc CURSOR FAST_FORWARD FOR
  SELECT roomid, seats FROM dbo.Rooms
  ORDER BY seats DESC, roomid DESC;
DECLARE CEventsDesc CURSOR FAST_FORWARD FOR
  SELECT eventid, attendees FROM dbo.Events
  ORDER BY attendees DESC, eventid DESC;

OPEN CRoomsDesc;
OPEN CEventsDesc;

FETCH NEXT FROM CRoomsDesc INTO @roomid, @seats;
WHILE @@FETCH_STATUS = 0
BEGIN
  FETCH NEXT FROM CEventsDesc INTO @eventid, @attendees;

  WHILE @@FETCH_STATUS = 0 AND @seats < @attendees
    FETCH NEXT FROM CEventsDesc INTO @eventid, @attendees;

  IF @@FETCH_STATUS = 0
    INSERT INTO @Events(eventid, attendees)
      VALUES(@eventid, @attendees);
  ELSE
    BREAK;

  FETCH NEXT FROM CRoomsDesc INTO @roomid, @seats;
END

CLOSE CRoomsDesc;
CLOSE CEventsDesc;
```

```
DEALLOCATE CRoomsDesc;
DEALLOCATE CEventsDesc;

-- Step 2: Ascending
DECLARE CRooms CURSOR FAST_FORWARD FOR
  SELECT roomid, seats FROM Rooms
  ORDER BY seats, roomid;
DECLARE CEvents CURSOR FAST_FORWARD FOR
  SELECT eventid, attendees FROM @Events
  ORDER BY attendees, eventid;

OPEN CRooms;
OPEN CEvents;

FETCH NEXT FROM CEvents INTO @eventid, @attendees;
WHILE @@FETCH_STATUS = 0
BEGIN
  FETCH NEXT FROM CRooms INTO @roomid, @seats;

  WHILE @@FETCH_STATUS = 0 AND @seats < @attendees
    FETCH NEXT FROM CRooms INTO @roomid, @seats;

  IF @@FETCH_STATUS = 0
    INSERT INTO @Result(roomid, eventid) VALUES(@roomid, @eventid);
  ELSE
  BEGIN
    RAISERROR('Not enough rooms for events.', 16, 1);
    BREAK;
  END

  FETCH NEXT FROM CEvents INTO @eventid, @attendees;
END

CLOSE CRooms;
CLOSE CEvents;

DEALLOCATE CRooms;
DEALLOCATE CEvents;

SELECT roomid, eventid FROM @Result;
```

The algorithm has two phases:

1. Use logic similar to the previous algorithm to match events to rooms, but scan both in descending order to assure the largest events can find rooms. Store the *eventids* that found a room in a table variable (*@Events*). At this point, you have the list of events you can fit that produce the highest revenue, but you also have the least efficient room utilization, meaning the highest possible costs. However, the purpose of the first step was merely to figure out the most profitable events that you can accommodate.

2. The next step is identical to the algorithm in the previous problem with one small revision: declare the *CEvents* cursor against the *@Events* table variable and not against the real Events table. By doing this, you end up with the most efficient room utilization for this set of events.

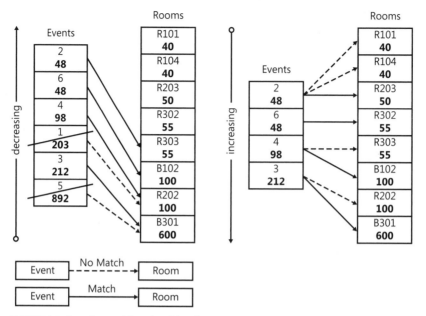

FIGURE 8-7 Greedy matching algorithm for nonguaranteed solution scenario

I'd like to thank my good friend, Fernando G. Guerrero, who suggested ways to improve and optimize the algorithms for this class of problems.

If you're up for challenges, try to look for ways to solve these problems with set-based solutions. Also, try to think of solutions when adding another layer of complexity. Suppose each event has a revenue value stored with it that does not necessarily correspond to the number of attendees. Each room has a cost stored with it that does not necessarily correspond to its capacity. Again, you have no guarantee that there will be enough rooms to host all events. The challenge is to find the most profitable solution.

Conclusion

Throughout this book, I try to stress the advantages set-based solutions have over cursor-based ones. I show many examples of tuned set-based solutions that outperform the cursor alternatives. In this chapter, I explained why that's the case for most types of problems. Nevertheless, I tried giving you the tools to identify the classes of problems that are exceptions—where currently SQL Server 2008 doesn't provide a better solution than using cursors. Some of the problems would have better set-based answers if SQL Server implemented additional ANSI constructs, whereas others don't even have proper answers in the ANSI standard yet. The point is that there's a time and place for cursors if they are used wisely and if a set-based means of solving the problem cannot be found.

Chapter 9
Dynamic SQL

Itzik Ben-Gan

Dynamic SQL (code that is executed dynamically), like cursors and temporary tables, is an area of T-SQL that should be used with care and caution. It has the potential to be used in an unsafe way and could lead to serious security breaches and code that performs badly and is difficult to maintain. On the other hand, when used wisely, dynamic SQL can help you achieve things that would be difficult to achieve any other way. And in some cases it is the only way you can provide good performance.

> **Note** I'll discuss some of the potential security breaches involved with dynamic SQL later in the chapter under the section "SQL Injection." SQL injection is a hacking technique that is used to "plant" malicious code through strings that are later parsed and executed by SQL Server. I strongly recommend that you research the subject thoroughly before using dynamic SQL in both production and test or development environments. A lot of information about the subject is available on the Internet and in other resources. You can access a short but excellent article about SQL injection in SQL Server Books Online at *http://msdn.microsoft.com/en-us/library/ms161953.aspx.*

Dynamic SQL is typically required when you must construct sections of your code based on user input. This is exactly why it is so dangerous; it is like allowing customers in a store to use the cash register themselves to ring up their own purchases and make their own change. Using dynamic SQL—where you concatenate your code strings based on user inputs— amounts to letting users write your code, and it is extremely difficult to do it safely. I've made the effort to demonstrate some techniques to protect against security breaches involved with SQL injection; but even if you let security experts review your code, they will tell you that it's almost impossible to protect against SQL injection attempts when incorporating user input in your code. Static code can have some dynamic elements, but only when the dynamic part is an expression that returns a scalar value. For example, you can incorporate an input parameter for a filter expression in a static query. In other words, parameterization, when handled correctly, encapsulates and type-checks the user inputs.

Microsoft SQL Server provides you with two commands that invoke code strings that you construct dynamically—EXEC (short for EXECUTE) and *sp_executesql*.

> **Note** The EXEC command has two uses: one to invoke a stored procedure: *EXEC <procedure name and arguments>*, and the other to invoke dynamic code: *EXEC(<string>)*. When discussing EXEC in this chapter, I'll be referring to the latter use unless explicitly stated otherwise.

As a rule, *sp_executesql* is preferable because it has an interface (input/output parameters) and EXEC doesn't. With *sp_executesql*, you are more likely to reuse execution plans because you can more easily generate a query string that you invoke repeatedly—the same query string with different input values as arguments in each invocation. Also, with *sp_executesql* you can write safer code, as I will explain later in the chapter. Still, EXEC is more flexible in certain cases, which I will describe in this chapter. So remember that unless you have a compelling reason to use EXEC, stick with using *sp_executesql*.

Before I delve into EXEC, *sp_executesql*, and their characteristics and applications, I'd like to briefly mention some important aspects of working with dynamic SQL in general:

- By default, dynamic SQL requires the user executing the code to have direct permissions to execute it even if the code is within a stored procedure. That is, if you provide a user with EXECUTE permissions on a routine and the routine invokes dynamic code, the user is still required to have direct permissions to run the code that is invoked dynamically. You can circumvent this requirement by impersonating another user, and this way allow the code to run under any security context that you like, and that context will apply to all activities. This is achieved by using the EXECUTE AS clause, which I discussed in Chapter 3, "Stored Procedures."

- Dynamic SQL operates in a batch that is separate from the calling batch. This means that the dynamic batch is parsed, resolved, and optimized as a separate unit. This aspect of dynamic SQL can be a drawback because you end up with another unit of compilation. But when used wisely, it can actually be beneficial to you. I'll demonstrate how you can take advantage of this behavior later in the chapter.

- Environmental settings of the calling batch—such as the database context, session options, and the like—are in effect for all inner levels in the call stack (dynamic batch, stored procedure call, and so on). For example, if you change the database context of a calling batch with the USE *<database_name>* command, the new database context is in effect for a dynamic batch. However, changes made to environmental settings within a dynamic batch are not in effect for outer levels after the dynamic batch expires. I'll demonstrate this behavior later in the chapter.

- Much like environmental settings, a local temporary table created in a calling batch is visible to inner levels, including a dynamic batch. However, a local temporary table created in an inner level is not visible to outer levels. As soon as the creating level expires, the local temporary table is automatically destroyed. For details about this behavior, please refer to Chapter 7, "Temporary Tables and Table Variables."

- Unlike environmental settings and temporary tables, a local variable is visible only to the batch where it was declared. It is not visible to inner levels. I'll also demonstrate this behavior later in the chapter.

So without further ado, let's delve into EXEC, *sp_executesql*, and the uses of dynamic SQL.

EXEC

The EXEC command (short for EXECUTE) has two uses: to execute a stored procedure and to execute a dynamic batch. The latter gets a character string within parentheses as an input and invokes that character string as code. In the following section, I'll describe EXEC(*<string>*).

Simple EXEC Examples

I'll start with a couple of simple examples demonstrating the use of EXEC. Suppose that you have a separate Orders table for each year, and the table is named OrdersYYYY, where YYYY represents the year. For reasons beyond your control, you can't create a partitioned view across these tables. You need to write code that queries the table representing the current year. For the code samples to actually work, first run the following code to create an Orders table for the current year in the tempdb database for test purposes:

```
USE tempdb;

DECLARE @year AS CHAR(4) = CAST(YEAR(CURRENT_TIMESTAMP) AS CHAR(4));
EXEC('IF OBJECT_ID(''dbo.Orders' + @year + ''', ''U'') IS NOT NULL
  DROP TABLE dbo.Orders' + @year + ';
CREATE TABLE dbo.Orders' + @year + '(orderid INT PRIMARY KEY);');
```

If the current year is 2009, the code that is constructed and executed dynamically looks like this:

```
IF OBJECT_ID('dbo.Orders2009', 'U') IS NOT NULL
  DROP TABLE dbo.Orders2009;
CREATE TABLE dbo.Orders2009(orderid INT PRIMARY KEY);
```

Similarly, to query the table representing the current year you would use the following code:

```
DECLARE @year AS CHAR(4) = CAST(YEAR(CURRENT_TIMESTAMP) AS CHAR(4));
EXEC('SELECT orderid FROM dbo.Orders' + @year + ';');
```

I constructed the code within the parentheses of the EXEC command, but note that only a string variable, a string literal, or a concatenation of string variables and/or string literals are allowed within the parentheses. You're not allowed to invoke functions or use a CASE expression. For example, the following code, which attempts to invoke the CAST function within the parentheses, fails:

```
EXEC('SELECT orderid FROM dbo.Orders'
     + CAST(YEAR(CURRENT_TIMESTAMP) AS CHAR(4)) + ';');
```

This code produces the following error:

```
Msg 102, Level 15, State 1, Line 2
Incorrect syntax near 'CAST'.
```

So it's a good practice to always construct the code in a variable, where such limitations don't apply, and then provide the variable name as input to the EXEC command, as shown here:

```
DECLARE @sql AS VARCHAR(500) =
  'SELECT orderid FROM dbo.Orders'
    + CAST(YEAR(CURRENT_TIMESTAMP) AS CHAR(4)) + ';';
EXEC(@sql);
```

This code executes successfully.

EXEC Has No Interface

As I mentioned earlier, EXEC(<*string*>) has no interface. Its only input is a character string with the code that you want to invoke. Remember that a dynamic batch has no access to local variables defined in the calling batch. For example, the following code attempts to access a variable defined in the calling batch and fails:

```
USE InsideTSQL2008;

DECLARE @lastname AS NVARCHAR(40) = N'Davis';
DECLARE @sql AS NVARCHAR(500) =
  N'SELECT empid, firstname, lastname
FROM HR.Employees
WHERE lastname = @lastname;';
EXEC(@sql);
```

This code produces the following error:

```
Msg 137, Level 15, State 2, Line 3
Must declare the scalar variable "@lastname".
```

Using EXEC, if you want to access the variable, you have to concatenate its contents to the code string you're constructing:

```
DECLARE @lastname AS NVARCHAR(40) = N'Davis';
DECLARE @sql AS NVARCHAR(500) =
  N'SELECT empid, firstname, lastname
FROM HR.Employees
WHERE lastname = ' + QUOTENAME(@lastname, N'''') + N';';
EXEC(@sql);
```

Concatenating the contents of a variable to a code string imposes a security risk (SQL injection). You can take some measures to protect against SQL injection, such as limiting the size of the code string you're constructing, using the QUOTENAME function to quote your strings, and others; however, it's very hard if not impossible to completely eliminate the exposure. Of course, in practice you don't need dynamic SQL at all in such a situation. You could simply use static code and refer to @*lastname* in the filter, as in:

```
DECLARE @lastname AS NVARCHAR(40) = N'Davis';

SELECT empid, firstname, lastname
FROM HR.Employees
WHERE lastname = @lastname;
```

I've used this simple example just for demonstration purposes. Imagine that other sections of the code are constructed dynamically and cannot be used in a static query.

Concatenating the contents of a variable has its performance drawbacks. SQL Server may end up creating a new ad hoc execution plan for each unique query string even though the query pattern is the same. To demonstrate this, run the following code invoking the same dynamic batch twice, with a different value in the variable in each invocation:

```
-- Run with Davis
DECLARE @lastname AS NVARCHAR(40) = N'Davis';
DECLARE @sql AS NVARCHAR(500) =
  N'SELECT empid, firstname, lastname
/* 65353E43-7E73-4094-84AC-D632ABB0FF7F */
FROM HR.Employees
WHERE lastname = ' + QUOTENAME(@lastname, N'''') + N';';
EXEC(@sql);
GO

-- Run with King
DECLARE @lastname AS NVARCHAR(40) = N'King';
DECLARE @sql AS NVARCHAR(500) =
  N'SELECT empid, firstname, lastname
/* 65353E43-7E73-4094-84AC-D632ABB0FF7F */
FROM HR.Employees
WHERE lastname = ' + QUOTENAME(@lastname, N'''') + N';';
EXEC(@sql);
GO
```

I planted a GUID as a comment in the code so that it would be easy to track down the associated plans in cache. Run the following code to query the plans in cache:

```
SELECT cacheobjtype, objtype, usecounts, sql
FROM sys.syscacheobjects
WHERE sql LIKE N'%65353E43-7E73-4094-84AC-D632ABB0FF7F%'
  AND sql NOT LIKE N'%sys%';
```

This generates the following output:

```
cacheobjtype    objtype   usecounts  sql
--------------  --------  ---------- -----------------------------------
Compiled Plan   Adhoc     1          SELECT ... WHERE lastname = 'Davis';
Compiled Plan   Adhoc     1          SELECT ... WHERE lastname = 'King';
```

A separate ad hoc plan was created for each unique input. If you invoke the code again with an input that was already specified, the corresponding plan can be reused. But with many unique inputs, you can end up flooding the cache with ad hoc plans. Note that in certain cases SQL Server may automatically parameterize your code, but still, chances for efficient plan reuse are better when you explicitly parameterize your code with *sp_executesql*, as I will demonstrate later in the chapter.

In addition to supporting no input parameters in the dynamic batch, EXEC doesn't support output parameters. If you want to return the scalar result of a calculation that you stored in a variable in the dynamic batch to the caller, you can't do this through a parameter. You could, if you wanted, return the value of the variable as a result set by using a query, like so:

```
DECLARE @sql AS VARCHAR(500) =
  'DECLARE @result AS INT = 42;
SELECT @result AS result;';
EXEC(@sql);
```

But then you would face some challenges trying to return the value to a variable in the calling batch. To achieve this, you must first insert the output to a target table using the INSERT EXEC syntax, and then retrieve the value from the table into the variable, as in:

```
DECLARE @sql AS VARCHAR(500) =
  'DECLARE @result AS INT = 42;
SELECT @result AS result;';

DECLARE @myresult AS INT;
CREATE TABLE #T(result INT);
INSERT INTO #T(result) EXEC(@sql);
SET @myresult = (SELECT result FROM #T);
SELECT @myresult AS result;
DROP TABLE #T;
```

Remember that if you create a temporary table in a calling batch, it is visible to an inner dynamic batch. So you could also create a temporary table first, and insert the value into the temporary table within the dynamic batch using a plain INSERT statement:

```
DECLARE @sql AS VARCHAR(500) =
  'DECLARE @result AS INT = 42;
INSERT INTO #T(result) VALUES(@result);'

DECLARE @myresult AS INT;
CREATE TABLE #T(result INT);
EXEC(@sql);
SET @myresult = (SELECT result FROM #T);
SELECT @myresult AS result;
DROP TABLE #T;
```

As you can imagine, passing scalar values from one batch to another through tables involves I/O and therefore isn't the most efficient way to handle this need.

Another option is to use the session context, which is a VARBINARY(128) value owned by the session, and can be changed and queried from anywhere in the session. You set its value by using the SET CONTEXT_INFO command, and retrieve its value by querying the CONTEXT_INFO function. You can designate a certain segment of your session context for passing an argument between batches. For example, suppose you want to designate the first four bytes of the session context to pass an integer argument. You can overwrite only the designated four bytes by concatenating your value to bytes 5 and on of the session context. Here's an example of storing the constant value 42 in the first 4 bytes of the session context while preserving the rest of the information that was there:

```
DECLARE @ci AS VARBINARY(128) =
  CAST(42 AS BINARY(4)) + COALESCE(SUBSTRING(CONTEXT_INFO(), 5, 124), 0x);

SET CONTEXT_INFO @ci;
```

And here's how you would query the value:

```
DECLARE @myval AS INT =
  CAST(SUBSTRING(CONTEXT_INFO(), 1, 4) AS INT);

SELECT @myval AS val;
```

Based on this technique, you can store the value of a variable in a dynamic batch in a segment of your session context and then retrieve it from the session context in the outer batch, like so:

```
DECLARE @sql AS VARCHAR(500) =
  'DECLARE @result AS INT = 42;
DECLARE @ci AS VARBINARY(128) =
  CAST(@result AS BINARY(4))
        + COALESCE(SUBSTRING(CONTEXT_INFO(), 5, 124), 0x);

SET CONTEXT_INFO @ci;';
EXEC(@sql);

DECLARE @myresult AS INT =
  CAST(SUBSTRING(CONTEXT_INFO(), 1, 4) AS INT);

SELECT @myresult AS result;
```

In short, the fact that EXEC has no interface leads to inefficient and cumbersome code.

Concatenating Variables

In SQL Server 2008 you can store a dynamic batch of code in a local variable of large object type and then invoke it as code with EXEC or *sp_executesql*. Such support was introduced for the first time in SQL Server 2005. In older versions of SQL Server you couldn't define local variables longer than 8,000 bytes. This could pose a problem if you needed to construct large dynamic batches. Even though technically *sp_executesql*'s input code string was of an NTEXT data type, you typically wanted to construct the code string in a local variable. However, you couldn't declare a local variable with a large object type, so practically speaking, query strings executed with *sp_executesql* were limited to the largest supported length of a Unicode character string (NVARCHAR), which was 4,000 characters. EXEC, on the other hand, supported a regular character (VARCHAR) input code string, allowing up to 8,000 characters. Furthermore, EXEC supports a special functionality that allows you to concatenate multiple variables within the parentheses, each up to the maximum supported size of 8,000 characters, like so:

```
DECLARE
  @sql1 AS VARCHAR(8000),
  @sql2 AS VARCHAR(8000),
  @sql3 AS VARCHAR(8000);

SET @sql1 = <part 1>;
SET @sql2 = <part 2>;
SET @sql3 = <part 3>;

EXEC(@sql1 + @sql2 + @sql3);
```

However, this technique is very awkward, and it requires some acrobatics to construct code strings longer than 8,000 characters. In SQL Server 2008, this technique is not needed because you can provide the EXEC command with a variable defined as VARCHAR(MAX) or NVARCHAR(MAX) as input. The input string can be up to 2 gigabytes (GB) in size, which is the maximum supported size for large objects in SQL Server 2008. For example, the following code generates a large batch with more than 8,000 characters and executes it:

```
DECLARE @sql AS VARCHAR(MAX) =
  'PRINT ''This output was generated by'
    + REPLICATE(CAST('.' AS VARCHAR(MAX)), 100000) + ''''
    + CHAR(13) + CHAR(10)
    + 'PRINT ''a long batch.''';
EXEC(@sql);

SELECT LEN(@sql) AS batch_length;
```

This code generates the following output, shown here in abbreviated form:

```
This output was generated by...
a long batch.
batch_length
-------------------
100059
```

As you can see, the LEN function reports a batch length of 100,059 characters.

EXEC AT

SQL Server 2008 supports the EXEC AT syntax, which allows you to invoke dynamic pass-through code against a linked server. In certain cases this feature is preferable to the alternative method of submitting pass-through code against linked servers using the OPENQUERY table function. OPENQUERY has several limitations: the input query string must be static—it can't be a variable—and it can't accept input arguments. Furthermore, you invoke OPENQUERY in the FROM clause of an outer query, so the function must represent a table. This requirement is very limiting when you just want to invoke executable code against the target server; for example, DDL statements. Similar limitations apply to the OPENROWSET table function. For details about the OPENQUERY and OPENROWSET functions, please refer to SQL Server Books Online.

All these limitations are addressed by the EXEC AT command. To see the capabilities of the EXEC AT command, from a SQL Server 2008 instance, create a linked server to another SQL Server instance to which you have access, for example, a local instance of SQL Server Express. I will use a linked server called Dojo in my examples:

```
EXEC sp_addlinkedserver [Dojo], 'SQL Server';
```

The following example shows how you can use input parameters in the input string:

```
EXEC
(
 'SELECT productid, productname, unitprice
FROM InsideTSQL2008.Production.Products
WHERE ProductID = ?;', 3
) AT [Dojo];
```

I'm assuming in this example that the InsideTSQL2008 database exists in the target server, and permissions were set to allow access to the target linked server.

EXEC invokes a query against Dojo, which returns the product details of a specified product ID (3 in this case):

```
productid  productname     unitprice
---------- --------------- ----------
3          Product IMEHJ   10.00
```

The question mark is replaced with the specified input value. The input value doesn't have to be a constant; it can be a variable:

```
DECLARE @pid AS INT;
SET @pid = 3;
EXEC
(
 'SELECT productid, productname, unitprice
FROM InsideTSQL2008.Production.Products
WHERE ProductID = ?;', @pid
) AT [Dojo];
```

In fact, even the input code string can be a variable, which you construct dynamically:

```
DECLARE @sql AS NVARCHAR(500), @pid AS INT;

SET @sql =
 'SELECT productid, productname, unitprice
```

```
FROM InsideTSQL2008.Production.Products
WHERE ProductID = ?;'
SET @pid = 3;

EXEC(@sql, @pid) AT [Dojo];
```

Furthermore, EXEC doesn't have to return a table result. The following example creates a table called T1 in tempdb at Dojo:

```
EXEC
(
 'USE tempdb;
IF OBJECT_ID(''dbo.T1'', ''U'') IS NOT NULL
  DROP TABLE dbo.T1;
CREATE TABLE dbo.T1
(
  keycol INT NOT NULL PRIMARY KEY,
  datacol VARCHAR(10) NOT NULL
);'
) AT [Dojo];
```

Remember that the AT clause allows you to invoke pass-through code at a specified linked server. The pass-through code is in the target server's dialect, and the target server type is not limited to SQL Server. It can be any OLEDB or ODBC provider supported as a linked server.

To demonstrate the use of EXEC AT against a non–SQL Server provider, first Use Microsoft Access 2007 to create a blank Access database called Database1 in the folder C:\temp. Then, execute the following code, which creates and configures a linked server called AccessDatabase1 against the Access database you created:

```
-- Create a linked server to an Access database
EXEC sp_addlinkedserver
    @server = 'AccessDatabase1',
    @provider = 'Microsoft.ACE.OLEDB.12.0',
    @srvproduct = 'OLE DB Provider for ACE',
    @datasrc = 'C:\temp\Database1.accdb';
```

For security reasons, use the *sp_droplinkedsrvlogin* stored procedure to remove the default self-mapping added for all local logins. Use the *sp_addlinkedsrvlogin* stored procedure to map local logins to a security account on the remote server, like so:

```
-- Remove default self-mapping added for all local logins
EXEC sp_droplinkedsrvlogin 'AccessDatabase1', NULL;
-- Add login mappings
EXEC sp_addlinkedsrvlogin
  'AccessDatabase1', 'false', '<specify_local_login_name_here>', Admin, NULL;
GO
```

Use the *sp_serveroption* stored procedure to allow remote procedure calls (RPCs) against the linked server, like so:

```
-- Allow RPC out
EXEC sp_serveroption 'AccessDatabase1', 'rpc out', true;
```

Note By enabling RPC, you're increasing the attackable surface area of the target server. I'm turning this setting on for the AccessDatabase1 linked server so that the code samples that I'll be demonstrating will work. For details about enabling RPC, please refer to the section "Security for Remote Servers" in SQL Server Books Online at *http://msdn.microsoft.com/en-us/library/ms175030.aspx.*

The following code demonstrates running a DDL statement that creates a table called Orders in the Access database using the EXEC AT syntax:

```
EXEC('CREATE TABLE Orders
(
  orderid   INT  NOT NULL PRIMARY KEY,
  orderdate DATE NOT NULL,
  empid     INT  NOT NULL
)') AT AccessDatabase1;
```

You can then populate the table with data from SQL Server by running an INSERT statement against the linked server, like so:

```
INSERT INTO AccessDatabase1...Orders
  SELECT orderid, orderdate, empid
  FROM InsideTSQL2008.Sales.Orders;
```

The following code invokes a TRANSFORM query against the linked server. The query pivots monthly counts of orders per year, including a filter on the *empid* column based on an input parameter:

```
EXEC
(
 'TRANSFORM Count(*) AS cnt
  SELECT YEAR(orderdate) AS orderyear
  FROM Orders
  WHERE empid = ?
  GROUP BY YEAR(orderdate)
  PIVOT MONTH(orderdate);', 3
) AT AccessDatabase1;
```

This generates the following output:

```
orderyear 1     2     3     4     5     6     7     8     9     10    11    12
--------- ----  ----  ----  ----  ----  ----  ----  ----  ----  ----  ----  ----
2006      NULL  NULL  NULL  NULL  NULL  NULL  4     2     1     3     4     4
2007      7     9     3     5     5     6     2     4     4     7     8     11
2008      10    6     12    10    NULL  NULL  NULL  NULL  NULL  NULL  NULL  NULL
```

If you'll allow me to digress a bit, this reminds me of one of Steve Kass's intriguing tricks for overcoming the fact that pivoting in SQL Server is not dynamic. Steve is the technical editor of this book and is well versed in the principles of logic. Steve once suggested creating a linked server to an Access database, which in turn has a linked table pointing to a SQL Server table. You then issue a TRANSFORM pass-through query against the linked server, which queries your SQL Server table using full dynamic pivoting capabilities. I thought this was quite nifty and original!

When you're done, remember to drop the T1 table and the linked servers created in this section:

```
EXEC
(
 'USE tempdb;
IF OBJECT_ID(''dbo.T1'', ''U'') IS NOT NULL
  DROP TABLE dbo.T1;'
) AT [Dojo];
EXEC sp_droplinkedsrvlogin 'AccessDatabase1', '<specify_local_login_name_here>';
EXEC sp_dropserver AccessDatabase1;
EXEC sp_dropserver Dojo;
```

sp_executesql

The *sp_executesql* command was introduced in SQL Server later than the EXEC command, mainly to provide better support for reusing execution plans. In this section, I'll describe *sp_executesql* and its advantages over EXEC.

The *sp_executesql* Interface

The *sp_executesql* command is more flexible than EXEC(*<string>*) because it has an interface, which supports both input and output parameters. This capability allows you to create query strings with arguments that can reuse execution plans more efficiently than EXEC. The components of *sp_executesql* are very similar to those of a stored procedure, with the difference being that you construct the code dynamically. Those components include: a batch of code, parameter declaration section, and a parameter assignment section. The syntax for using *sp_executesql* is as follows:

```
EXEC sp_executesql
  @stmt = <statement>, -- similar to proc's body
  @params = <params>,  -- similar to proc's params declaration
  <params assignment>  -- like in a procedure call
```

The *@stmt* parameter is the input dynamic batch, which can refer to input and output parameters. This section is similar to a stored procedure's body except that *@stmt* can be constructed dynamically, whereas a stored procedure's body is static. In fact, you might want to invoke *sp_executesql* from a stored procedure's code, whereby you construct the dynamic batch based on user inputs to the stored procedure. The *@params* parameter is similar to the header of a stored procedure, where you define input/output parameters. In fact, the syntax for *@params* is identical to that of a stored procedure's declaration section. You can even define default values to the parameters just as you can with a stored procedure. The *@params* string can also be constructed dynamically. Finally, the *<params assignment>* section is similar to the EXEC part of invoking a stored procedure, in which you assign values to the input/output parameters.

To demonstrate that *sp_executesql* plan management is superior to that of EXEC, I'll use the same example I showed earlier when discussing EXEC:

```
USE InsideTSQL2008;
GO
DECLARE @mylastname AS NVARCHAR(40) = N'Davis';
DECLARE @sql AS NVARCHAR(500) =
  N'SELECT empid, firstname, lastname
FROM HR.Employees
WHERE lastname = @lastname';

EXEC sp_executesql
  @stmt = @sql,
  @params = N'@lastname AS NVARCHAR(40)',
  @lastname = @mylastname;
```

Notice that now, instead of concatenating the contents of *@mylastname*, this code defines an input parameter called *@lastname*. The code defines *@lastname* as a Unicode character string input in the *@params* section, and it assigns the contents of *@mylastname* from the calling batch to *@lastname* in the *<params assignment>* section.

Run the following code invoking the dynamic batch twice, each with a different last name input:

```
-- Run with Davis
DECLARE @mylastname AS NVARCHAR(40) = N'Davis';
DECLARE @sql AS NVARCHAR(500) =
  N'SELECT empid, firstname, lastname
/* A2E6C9ED-E75A-42F7-BD22-EB671798B0DC */
FROM HR.Employees
WHERE lastname = @lastname';

EXEC sp_executesql
  @stmt = @sql,
  @params = N'@lastname AS NVARCHAR(40)',
  @lastname = @mylastname;
GO

-- Run with King
DECLARE @mylastname AS NVARCHAR(40) = N'King';
DECLARE @sql AS NVARCHAR(500) =
  N'SELECT empid, firstname, lastname
/* A2E6C9ED-E75A-42F7-BD22-EB671798B0DC */
FROM HR.Employees
WHERE lastname = @lastname';

EXEC sp_executesql
  @stmt = @sql,
  @params = N'@lastname AS NVARCHAR(40)',
  @lastname = @mylastname;
GO
```

Here I also planted a GUID so that it would be easy to track down the associated plans in cache. Run the following code to query the cached objects:

```
SELECT cacheobjtype, objtype, usecounts, sql
FROM sys.syscacheobjects
WHERE sql LIKE N'%A2E6C9ED-E75A-42F7-BD22-EB671798B0DC%'
  AND sql NOT LIKE N'%sys%';
```

This generates the following output:

```
cacheobjtype    objtype    usecounts   sql
--------------  ---------  ----------  -------------------------------
Compiled Plan   Prepared   2           ... WHERE lastname = @lastname
```

Notice in the output that only one prepared plan was created and that it was reused two times. As a reminder, EXEC created two separate ad hoc plans in the same scenario. Now imagine production environments in which the same query pattern is invoked thousands or tens of thousands of times a day, or even more.

Another powerful capability of *sp_executesql* related to its support for an interface is that it lets you use output parameters to return values to a variable defined in the calling batch. This capability avoids the need to return data through tables, and it results in more efficient code and fewer recompilations. The syntax for defining and using output parameters is identical to that of stored procedures. Namely, you need to declare the parameter specifying the OUTPUT clause and also specify the OUTPUT clause when assigning the parameter with a pointer to a variable defined in the calling batch. For example, the following simple code sample demonstrates how to return a value from the dynamic batch, through the output parameter *@result* to the outer batch's variable *@myresult*:

```
DECLARE @sql AS NVARCHAR(500), @myresult AS INT

SET @sql = N'SET @result = 42;';

EXEC sp_executesql
  @stmt   = @sql,
  @params = N'@result AS INT OUTPUT',
  @result = @myresult OUTPUT;

SELECT @myresult;
```

This code returns the output 42.

You can use *sp_executesql*'s output parameters in many interesting ways. For example, here's a nifty trick I learned from Ron Talmage, who is a SQL Server MVP, a mentor, and a founder of Solid Quality Mentors. Suppose that you have a character string stored in a variable called *@s* that holds hexadecimal digits that represent a binary string. You want to convert the character string to a real binary value and store it in a variable called *@b*. In SQL Server 2008 the task is quite simple to address as I will demonstrate shortly, but prior to SQL Server 2008 the task was actually much trickier than it seems. If you used simple conversions, you got the binary representation of each character, which is not really what you're after. However, as Ron figured out, you could use *sp_executesql*'s output parameter to assign the string as if it were a binary value to a binary parameter, as demonstrated by the following code:

```
DECLARE @sql AS NVARCHAR(MAX),
  @b AS VARBINARY(MAX), @s AS NVARCHAR(MAX);
SET @s = N'0x4775696E6E657373';

IF @s NOT LIKE N'0x%' OR @s LIKE N'0x%[^0-9a-fA-F]%'
BEGIN
  RAISERROR('Possible SQL injection attempt.', 16, 1);
  RETURN;
END

SET @sql = N'SET @o = ' + @s + N';';
EXEC sp_executesql
  @stmt = @sql,
  @params = N'@o AS VARBINARY(MAX) OUTPUT',
  @o = @b OUTPUT;

SELECT @b;
```

This code first checked for a possible SQL injection attempt (the input string must be a valid binary string). The code then converted the character string (*'0x4775696E6E657373'* in this example) to the binary value *0x4775696E6E657373*. Unfortunately, you could not use this technique to convert a binary value to a character string. Prior to SQL Server 2008 you could use a scalar user-defined function (UDF) called *fn_varbintohexstr* to achieve this:

```
DECLARE @sql AS NVARCHAR(MAX),
  @b AS VARBINARY(MAX), @s AS VARCHAR(MAX);
SET @b = 0x4775696E6E657373;
SET @s = sys.fn_varbintohexstr(@b);
SELECT @s;
```

> **Note** The *fn_varbintohexstr* function is undocumented and unsupported.

This code converted the binary value *0x4775696E6E657373* to the character string *'0x4775696E6E657373'*.

SQL Server 2008 introduces a new feature that makes such conversions very easy to handle. The CONVERT function now supports the third argument (style) when converting from a character string to a binary value or the other way around. Style 0 is the default, representing the pre-2008 behavior. Styles 1 and 2 introduce new functionality where the hex digits are preserved, but the type is converted. When converting from binary to character, use style 1 if you want the result string to include the prefix 0x, and style 2 otherwise. For example, run the following code to demonstrate both styles:

```
SELECT
  CONVERT(VARCHAR(20), 0x4775696E6E657373, 1) AS bin_to_prefixed_char,
  CONVERT(VARCHAR(20), 0x4775696E6E657373, 2) AS bin_to_nonprefixed_char;
```

This generates the following output:

```
bin_to_prefixed_char bin_to_nonprefixed_char
-------------------- -----------------------
0x4775696E6E657373   4775696E6E657373
```

When converting from character to binary, use style 1 when the source string contains the 0x prefix, and style 2 when it doesn't. For example, run the following code:

```
SELECT
  CONVERT(VARBINARY(10), '0x4775696E6E657373', 1) AS prefixed_char_to_bin,
  CONVERT(VARBINARY(10),   '4775696E6E657373', 2) AS nonprefixed_char_to_bin;
```

This generates the following output:

```
prefixed_char_to_bin   nonprefixed_char_to_bin
---------------------- -----------------------
0x4775696E6E657373     0x4775696E6E657373
```

Statement Limit

As I mentioned earlier, legacy versions of SQL Server did not support defining local variables of a large object type. You could not store a Unicode string longer than 4,000 characters (8,000 bytes) in a local variable that you fed to *sp_executesql* as input. So EXEC had an advantage over *sp_executesql* in this respect because it supported concatenating multiple variables, each up to the maximum supported size. In SQL Server 2008 you can define local variables of a large object type, so this is no longer an issue. Use the NVARCHAR(MAX) type for *sp_executesql*, and you can construct a batch that is up to 2 GB in size. Earlier I demonstrated using EXEC to execute a long batch. Here's code that accomplishes the same thing using *sp_executesql*:

```
DECLARE @sql AS NVARCHAR(MAX) =
  N'PRINT ''This output was generated by'
    + REPLICATE(CAST(N'.' AS NVARCHAR(MAX)), 100000) + ''''
    + NCHAR(13) + NCHAR(10)
    + N'PRINT ''a long batch.''';
EXEC sp_executesql @sql;

SELECT LEN(@sql) AS batch_length;
```

This generates the following output, shown here in abbreviated form:

```
This output was generated by...
a long batch.
batch_length
--------------------
100059
```

Environmental Settings

As I mentioned in this chapter's opening section, environmental settings (such as database context and SET options) that are set in a calling batch are in effect for a dynamic batch, but not the other way around. To demonstrate this aspect of environmental settings, the following code sets the database context of a calling batch to InsideTSQL2008; it invokes a dynamic batch, which changes the database context to an input database name (tempdb in this case); and finally, it outputs the database context of the outer batch after the dynamic batch is invoked:

```
USE InsideTSQL2008;
DECLARE @db AS NVARCHAR(258) = QUOTENAME(N'tempdb');
EXEC(N'USE ' + @db + ';');
SELECT DB_NAME();
```

Because a change in database context in the inner batch has no effect on an outer batch, the output is InsideTSQL2008 and not tempdb. On the other hand, environmental changes in the dynamic batch are in effect for the dynamic batch itself. Therefore, the following code returns the output tempdb:

```
USE InsideTSQL2008;
DECLARE @db AS NVARCHAR(258) = QUOTENAME(N'tempdb');
EXEC(N'USE ' + @db + N'; SELECT DB_NAME();');
```

Similarly, such changes are in effect for levels inner to the dynamic batch, such as a nested level of dynamic SQL:

```
USE InsideTSQL2008;
DECLARE @db AS NVARCHAR(258) = QUOTENAME(N'tempdb');
EXEC(N'USE ' + @db + N'; EXEC(''SELECT DB_NAME();'');');
```

The output of this code is also tempdb.

Uses of Dynamic SQL

Now that the fundamentals of dynamic SQL, EXEC, and *sp_executesql* have been covered, this section will demonstrate several ways to apply dynamic SQL.

Dynamic Maintenance Activities

One use of dynamic SQL is to construct code dynamically for automated maintenance activities such as performing index defragmentation, backups, and the like. You need to query metadata and environmental information and use it to construct the code.

Caution Be aware that metadata should be carefully checked for potential SQL injection attempts (for example, through maliciously named objects).

A classic scenario for automated maintenance code that is constructed dynamically is index defragmentation. You inspect fragmentation information by querying the *sys.dm_db_index_physical_stats* function. You then rebuild or reorganize indexes with a higher level of fragmentation than a certain threshold that you determine as high enough to justify defragmentation. The following code, which is adapted from SQL Server Books Online, demonstrates how to achieve this:

```
-- Ensure a USE <databasename> statement has been executed first.
SET NOCOUNT ON;
DECLARE @objectid int;
DECLARE @indexid int;
DECLARE @partitioncount bigint;
DECLARE @schemaname nvarchar(130);
DECLARE @objectname nvarchar(130);
DECLARE @indexname nvarchar(130);
DECLARE @partitionnum bigint;
DECLARE @partitions bigint;
DECLARE @frag float;
DECLARE @command nvarchar(4000);
-- Conditionally select tables and indexes from the
-- sys.dm_db_index_physical_stats function and convert object and index IDs to names.
SELECT
    object_id AS objectid,
    index_id AS indexid,
    partition_number AS partitionnum,
    avg_fragmentation_in_percent AS frag
INTO #work_to_do
FROM sys.dm_db_index_physical_stats (DB_ID(), NULL, NULL , NULL, 'LIMITED')
WHERE avg_fragmentation_in_percent > 10.0 AND index_id > 0;

-- Declare the cursor for the list of partitions to be processed.
DECLARE partitions CURSOR FOR SELECT * FROM #work_to_do;

-- Open the cursor.
OPEN partitions;

-- Loop through the partitions.
WHILE (1=1)
    BEGIN;
        FETCH NEXT
            FROM partitions
            INTO @objectid, @indexid, @partitionnum, @frag;
        IF @@FETCH_STATUS < 0 BREAK;
        SELECT @objectname = QUOTENAME(o.name), @schemaname = QUOTENAME(s.name)
        FROM sys.objects AS o
        JOIN sys.schemas as s ON s.schema_id = o.schema_id
        WHERE o.object_id = @objectid;
        SELECT @indexname = QUOTENAME(name)
        FROM sys.indexes
        WHERE  object_id = @objectid AND index_id = @indexid;
        SELECT @partitioncount = count (*)
        FROM sys.partitions
        WHERE object_id = @objectid AND index_id = @indexid;
```

```
-- 30 is an arbitrary decision point at which to switch between reorganizing
-- and rebuilding.
      IF @frag < 30.0
          SET @command = N'ALTER INDEX ' + @indexname + N' ON ' + @schemaname + N'.'
            + @objectname + N' REORGANIZE';
      IF @frag >= 30.0
          SET @command = N'ALTER INDEX ' + @indexname + N' ON ' + @schemaname + N'.'
            + @objectname + N' REBUILD';
      IF @partitioncount > 1
          SET @command = @command + N' PARTITION='
            + CAST(@partitionnum AS nvarchar(10));
      EXEC (@command);
      PRINT N'Executed: ' + @command;
   END;

-- Close and deallocate the cursor.
CLOSE partitions;
DEALLOCATE partitions;

-- Drop the temporary table.
DROP TABLE #work_to_do;
GO
```

> **Note** This code uses EXEC and not *sp_executesql*. Remember that *sp_executesql* is mainly beneficial for better reuse of execution plans and when you need an interface. Because the maintenance activities invoked dynamically here don't involve querying, plan reuse is not really an issue. Also, there's no need for an interface in this activity.

This code defragments indexes in the current database that have a fragmentation level (expressed in code as *avg_fragmentation_in_percent*) greater than 10 percent. If the fragmentation level is greater than 10 percent and less than 30 percent, this code constructs and invokes an index reorganize operation. If the fragmentation level is greater than or equal to 30 percent, it invokes a full index rebuild operation. These are arbitrary numbers that were chosen for demonstration purposes. You should use your own thresholds based on the performance of the queries and the maintenance window that you have available.

Storing Computations

The support that *sp_executesql* has for output parameters allows you to create very interesting applications. For example, a customer of mine who develops software for salary calculations once asked me to evaluate T-SQL expression strings dynamically. The company had a table that contained several inputs for a calculation in several columns, and they had a T-SQL expression that referred to those inputs in another column. Each row represented the salary computation of a particular employee, and the row could contain a salary computation that was different from other rows based on the employee's contract.

To provide for this need, you can create a trigger on the table for INSERT and UPDATE statements. The trigger will read the input arguments and the computation from the inserted table for each row, run *sp_executesql* to return the result of the computation through an output parameter to a local variable defined in the trigger, and use an UPDATE statement to store the result in a result column in the table. Taking this approach would make the table resemble a Microsoft Office Excel spreadsheet.

Here I'll represent the problem in more generic terms. To demonstrate the technique, first run the following code to create the Computations table:

```
USE tempdb;

IF OBJECT_ID('dbo.Computations', 'U') IS NOT NULL
  DROP TABLE dbo.Computations;

CREATE TABLE dbo.Computations
(
  keycol      INT           NOT NULL IDENTITY PRIMARY KEY,
  arg1        INT           NULL,
  arg2        INT           NULL,
  arg3        INT           NULL,
  computation VARCHAR(4000) NOT NULL,
  result      INT           NULL,
  CONSTRAINT CHK_Computations_SQL_Injection
    CHECK (REPLACE(computation,'@arg','') NOT LIKE '%[^0-9.+/* -]%')
);
```

The columns *arg1, arg2,* and *arg3* will hold the input arguments for the computation. The *computation* column will hold T-SQL expressions that refer to the inputs using an @ symbol in front of each argument (for example, *@arg1* would stand for the value in *arg1*). Examples of expressions are as follows: '*@arg1* + *@arg2* + *@arg3*', '*@arg1* * *@arg2* – *@arg3*', ' 2. * *@arg2* / *@arg1*', or any other valid T-SQL expression that yields a scalar value as a result. A CHECK constraint is defined on the *computation* column to protect against SQL injection attempts. The constraint allows only arguments (*@arg*), digits, dots, and basic arithmetic operations; you may want to revise the constraint based on your needs, but bear in mind that the more you "relax" the constraint, the greater is the risk that SQL injection attempts will succeed. The trigger should evaluate the expression from each modified row and store the result value in the result column.

Run the following code to create the *trg_Computations_iu_calc_result* trigger:

```
CREATE TRIGGER trg_Computations_iu_calc_result
  ON dbo.Computations FOR INSERT, UPDATE
AS

DECLARE @rc AS INT =
  (SELECT COUNT(*) FROM (SELECT TOP (2) * FROM inserted) AS D);

-- If no rows affected, return
IF @rc = 0 RETURN;

-- If none of the columns: arg1, arg2, arg3, computation
-- were updated, return
```

```
IF COLUMNS_UPDATED() & 30 /* 00011110 binary */ = 0 RETURN;

-- Not allowed to update result
IF    EXISTS(SELECT * FROM inserted)
  AND EXISTS(SELECT * FROM deleted)
  AND UPDATE(result)
BEGIN
  RAISERROR('Not allowed to update result.', 16, 1);
  ROLLBACK;
  RETURN;
END

DECLARE
  @key        AS INT,             -- keycol
  @in_arg1    AS INT,             -- arg1
  @in_arg2    AS INT,             -- arg2
  @in_arg3    AS INT,             -- arg3
  @out_result AS INT,             -- result of computation
  @comp       AS NVARCHAR(4000),  -- computation
  @params     AS NVARCHAR(100);   -- parameter's list for sp_executesql

-- If only one row was affected, don't use a cursor
IF @rc = 1
BEGIN
  -- Grab values from inserted
  SELECT @key = keycol, @in_arg1 = arg1, @in_arg2 = arg2,
    @in_arg3 = arg3, @comp = N'SET @result = ' + computation
  FROM inserted;

  -- Generate a string with the in/out parameters
  SET @params = N'@result INT output, @arg1 INT, @arg2 INT, @arg3 INT';

  -- Calculate computation and store the result in @out_result
  EXEC sp_executesql
    @comp,
    @params,
    @result = @out_result OUTPUT,
    @arg1   = @in_arg1,
    @arg2   = @in_arg2,
    @arg3   = @in_arg3;

  -- Update the result column in the row with the current key
  UPDATE dbo.Computations
    SET result = @out_result
  WHERE keycol = @key;
END
-- If only multiple rows were affected, use a cursor
ELSE
BEGIN
  -- Loop through all keys in inserted
  DECLARE CInserted CURSOR FAST_FORWARD FOR
    SELECT keycol, arg1, arg2, arg3, N'SET @result = ' + computation
    FROM inserted;

  OPEN CInserted;
```

```
      -- Get first row from inserted
      FETCH NEXT FROM CInserted
        INTO @key, @in_arg1, @in_arg2, @in_arg3, @comp ;

      WHILE @@fetch_status = 0
      BEGIN

        -- Generate a string with the in/out parameters
        SET @params = N'@result INT output, @arg1 INT, @arg2 INT, @arg3 INT';

        -- Calculate computation and store the result in @out_result
        EXEC sp_executesql
          @comp,
          @params,
          @result = @out_result OUTPUT,
          @arg1   = @in_arg1,
          @arg2   = @in_arg2,
          @arg3   = @in_arg3;

        -- Update the result column in the row with the current key
        UPDATE dbo.Computations
          SET result = @out_result
        WHERE keycol = @key;

        -- Get next row from inserted
        FETCH NEXT FROM CInserted
          INTO @key, @in_arg1, @in_arg2, @in_arg3, @comp;
      END

    CLOSE CInserted;
    DEALLOCATE CInserted;
  END
  GO
```

The trigger first evaluates the number of rows that were affected by the firing statement
(INSERT, UPDATE, or MERGE). If zero rows were modified, the trigger simply terminates. It
has nothing to do in such a case. The trigger then checks whether one of the four relevant
columns (*arg1, arg2, arg3, computation*) was modified, using the COLUMNS_UPDATED()
function. I described this function in more detail in Chapter 4, "Triggers." This function
returns a bitmap with a representative bit for each column. For an UPDATE statement, the bit
is turned on if the corresponding column was specified in the SET clause, and it's turned off
if the corresponding column wasn't specified in the SET clause. For an INSERT statement, all
column bits are turned on. If none of the relevant columns were modified, the trigger simply
terminates. It has no reason to reevaluate the computation if neither the inputs nor the
computation changed. If the statement that fired the trigger was an UPDATE statement (or
a MERGE statement containing an UPDATE action), and the column *result* was modified, the
trigger generates an error message and rolls back the update.

The trigger defines local variables to host the input arguments, the computation, and the
result value. Each row must be handled separately, so a cursor is needed if there is more than
one row.

For each modified row, the trigger reads the inputs and the computation into its local variables. Notice that the trigger adds a prefix to the computation: *N'SET @result = '* + *computation*. This is a very important trick that allows you to return the result of the computation back to the trigger's local variable (*@out_result*) through an output parameter (*@result*). After reading the inputs and the computation from the current row into the trigger's local variables, the code invokes *sp_executesql* to evaluate the expression and store it in *@out_result* through the output parameter *@result*:

```
EXEC sp_executesql
  @comp,
  @params,
  @result = @out_result OUTPUT,
  @arg1   = @in_arg1,
  @arg2   = @in_arg2,
  @arg3   = @in_arg3;
```

Now that the result is stored in the *@result* variable, the trigger updates the corresponding row in the Computations table with the result value.

To test the trigger, issue the following INSERT statements and query the Computations table:

```
INSERT INTO dbo.Computations(arg1, arg2, arg3, computation) VALUES
  (1, 2, 3, '@arg1 + @arg2 + @arg3'),
  (4, 5, 6, '@arg1 * @arg2 - @arg3'),
  (7, 8, DEFAULT, '2. * @arg2 / @arg1');

SELECT * FROM dbo.Computations;
```

This generates the following output:

```
keycol  arg1  arg2  arg3  computation            result
------- ----- ----- ----- ---------------------- -------
1       1     2     3     @arg1 + @arg2 + @arg3  6
2       4     5     6     @arg1 * @arg2 - @arg3  14
3       7     8     NULL  2. * @arg2 / @arg1     2
```

Next, issue an UPDATE statement that changes the *arg1* values in all rows, and then query the table again:

```
UPDATE dbo.Computations SET arg1 *= 2;
SELECT * FROM dbo.Computations;
```

This generates the following output:

```
keycol  arg1  arg2  arg3  computation            result
------- ----- ----- ----- ---------------------- -------
1       2     2     3     @arg1 + @arg2 + @arg3  7
2       8     5     6     @arg1 * @arg2 - @arg3  34
3       14    8     NULL  2. * @arg2 / @arg1     1
```

Observe that the change is reflected correctly in the *result* column.

Bear in mind that dynamic SQL is used to run code that is constructed, among other things, from the *computation* column values. I added a CHECK constraint to guard against common strings used in SQL injection; but as I mentioned earlier, it's almost impossible to guarantee that all cases are covered. There are alternatives to this solution that do not use dynamic SQL. For strings with limited complexity, this can be done in a UDF written by Steve Kass, as shown at *http://www.users.drew.edu/skass/sql/infix.sql.txt.* A CLR function could also be used to evaluate the expression. If the expression result is given by a UDF, this example can be much less complex, because the result can be defined as a persisted computed column, and no trigger will be required. It will also not be a security risk from dynamic SQL. Allowing complete flexibility to include SQL expressions in the calculation string is a priority that competes with security, because validation that a string represents only an expression can be done with a T-SQL parser.

Dynamic Filters

Another important use of dynamic SQL is supporting applications that allow users to choose dynamic filters, which is very typical of many Web applications. You can achieve this by using dynamic SQL, but of course you should consider seriously the risk of SQL injection in your solutions.

Note that static query solutions are available for dynamic filtering; however, these typically produce very inefficient plans that result in slow-running queries. By using dynamic SQL wisely, you can get efficient plans, and if you define the inputs as parameters, you can even get efficient reuse of execution plans and a secure solution.

In my examples, for simplicity's sake I'll demonstrate dynamic filters based on equality operators. Of course, you can apply more complex filtering logic with other operators. At the end of this chapter I'll provide a pointer where you can find more information about dynamic filtering and other subjects related to dynamic SQL.

Suppose that you're given a task to write a stored procedure that returns orders from the Orders table, providing optional filters on various order attributes. You create and populate the Orders table by running the following code:

```
SET NOCOUNT ON;
USE tempdb;

IF OBJECT_ID('dbo.GetOrders', 'P') IS NOT NULL DROP PROC dbo.GetOrders;
IF OBJECT_ID('dbo.Orders', 'U') IS NOT NULL DROP TABLE dbo.Orders;
GO

CREATE TABLE dbo.Orders
(
  orderid   INT     NOT NULL,
  custid    INT     NOT NULL,
  empid     INT     NOT NULL,
```

```
  orderdate DATETIME  NOT NULL,
  filler    CHAR(200) NOT NULL DEFAULT('a'),
  CONSTRAINT PK_Orders PRIMARY KEY NONCLUSTERED(orderid)
);

CREATE CLUSTERED INDEX idx_orderdate ON dbo.Orders(orderdate);
CREATE INDEX idx_custid ON dbo.Orders(custid);
CREATE INDEX idx_empid ON dbo.Orders(empid);

INSERT INTO dbo.Orders(orderid, custid, empid, orderdate)
  SELECT orderid, custid, empid, orderdate
  FROM InsideTSQL2008.Sales.Orders;
```

Write a stored procedure that queries and filters orders based on user inputs. The stored procedure should have a parameter for each of the order attributes: *orderid, custid, empid,* and *orderdate*. All parameters should have a default value NULL. If a parameter was assigned with a value, your stored procedure should filter the rows in which the corresponding column is equal to the parameter's value; otherwise (parameter is NULL), the parameter should simply be ignored. Note that all four columns in the Orders table were defined as NOT NULL, so you can rely on this fact in your solutions.

Static Solution Using IS NULL

Here's one common solution that uses static code:

```
CREATE PROC dbo.GetOrders
  @orderid   AS INT      = NULL,
  @custid    AS INT      = NULL,
  @empid     AS INT      = NULL,
  @orderdate AS DATETIME = NULL
WITH RECOMPILE
AS

SELECT orderid, custid, empid, orderdate, filler
FROM dbo.Orders
WHERE (orderid   = @orderid   OR @orderid   IS NULL)
  AND (custid    = @custid    OR @custid    IS NULL)
  AND (empid     = @empid     OR @empid     IS NULL)
  AND (orderdate = @orderdate OR @orderdate IS NULL);
GO
```

I created the stored procedure with the RECOMPILE option to generate a new execution plan whenever the code is run. Without the RECOMPILE option, regardless of the inputs, the stored procedure would reuse the cached execution plan generated for the first invocation, which is not a good idea in this case.

The main trick here is to use the following expression for each input:

```
(<col> = <@parameter> OR <@parameter> IS NULL)
```

If a value is specified for <@*parameter*>, then <@*parameter*> IS NULL is false, and the expression is equivalent to <*col*> = <@*parameter*> alone. If a value is not specified for <@*parameter*>, it will be NULL, and <@parameter> IS NULL will be true, making the whole expression true.

The problem with this implementation is that it produces inefficient plans. The optimizer doesn't have the capability to create different branches of a plan, where each branch represents a completely different course of action based on whether a parameter contains a known value or a NULL. Remember that the stored procedure was created with the RECOMPILE option, meaning that for each invocation of the stored procedure the optimizer generated a plan that it perceived as adequate for the given inputs. Still, the plans that the optimizer generated were inefficient. Run the following code, which invokes the stored procedure with different arguments:

```
EXEC dbo.GetOrders @orderid   = 10248;
EXEC dbo.GetOrders @orderdate = '20070101';
EXEC dbo.GetOrders @custid    = 3;
EXEC dbo.GetOrders @empid     = 5;
```

Of course, you can specify more than one argument. The optimizer generates the plans shown in Figure 9-1 for the preceding invocations of the procedure.

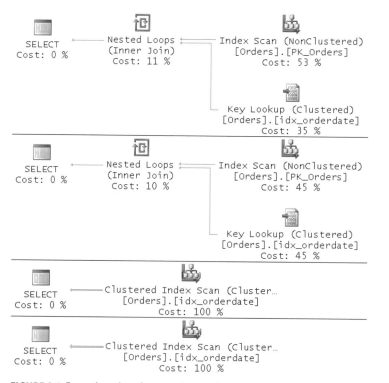

FIGURE 9-1 Execution plans for stored procedure *GetOrders*, static solution using IS NULL

For the first invocation of the stored procedure, where the *orderid* column is being filtered, you would expect the plan to show an Index Seek operation in the index *PK_Orders*, followed by a lookup. For the second invocation of the stored procedure, where the *orderdate* column is being filtered, you would expect to see an Index Seek operation within the index *idx_orderdate*. But that's not what you get; rather, you see inefficient plans. The first two plans perform a full scan of the index *PK_Orders* followed by lookups for the qualifying rows. The last two plans simply perform full scans of the clustered index. If you run this code against a much larger test table, you'll see a high I/O cost due to the index scans.

Static Solution Using COALESCE

Here's another common implementation of dynamic filters using static code:

```
ALTER PROC dbo.GetOrders
   @orderid   AS INT      = NULL,
   @custid    AS INT      = NULL,
   @empid     AS INT      = NULL,
   @orderdate AS DATETIME = NULL
WITH RECOMPILE
AS

SELECT orderid, custid, empid, orderdate, filler
FROM dbo.Orders
WHERE orderid   = COALESCE(@orderid, orderid)
  AND custid    = COALESCE(@custid, custid)
  AND empid     = COALESCE(@empid, empid)
  AND orderdate = COALESCE(@orderdate, orderdate);
GO
```

The trick here is to use the following expression for each parameter:

```
<col> = COALESCE(<@parameter>, <col>)
```

If a value is specified, COALESCE returns that value. If a value isn't specified, COALESCE returns *<col>*, in which case the expression *<col> = COALESCE(<@parameter>, <col>)* will be true, provided that the column was defined as not allowing NULLs. Note that if the column allows NULLs, this expression won't do the job. Rows with NULLs in that column will always be filtered out, even when *<@parameter>* is NULL.

If you rerun the test code, which invokes the stored procedure four times, you will see that with this solution you also get inefficient plans, as shown in Figure 9-2.

In this case, all invocations of the stored procedure ended up getting a plan that does a full clustered index scan.

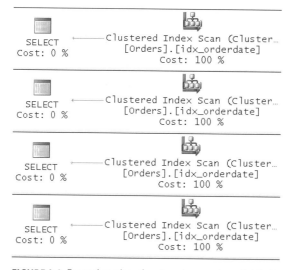

FIGURE 9-2 Execution plans for stored procedure *GetOrders*, static solution using COALESCE

Using the RECOMPILE Statement Option

In SQL Server 2008 RTM, if you specified the RECOMPILE statement hint (as opposed to the procedure option) with either of the two static solutions that I just presented, you got efficient plans. Here's how the code would look like using the first static solution I showed:

```
ALTER PROC dbo.GetOrders
  @orderid   AS INT      = NULL,
  @custid    AS INT      = NULL,
  @empid     AS INT      = NULL,
  @orderdate AS DATETIME = NULL
AS

SELECT orderid, custid, empid, orderdate, filler
FROM dbo.Orders
WHERE (orderid   = @orderid   OR @orderid   IS NULL)
  AND (custid    = @custid    OR @custid    IS NULL)
  AND (empid     = @empid     OR @empid     IS NULL)
  AND (orderdate = @orderdate OR @orderdate IS NULL)
OPTION (RECOMPILE);
GO
```

Apparently the RECOMPILE statement hint was enhanced in SQL Server 2008 RTM. When this option was specified, the optimizer didn't attempt to produce a reusable plan that would fit any value in the input parameters. It knew that the plan was not going to be reused. The result was that when you specified this hint in either of the two static solutions I showed to dynamic filtering, you got efficient plans. Unfortunately, a bug in the enhanced RECOMPILE statement option was discovered by SQL Server MVP Tony Rogerson. When the procedure was called concurrently by multiple sessions, one call could end up using another's arguments. You can find details about this bug here: *https://connect.microsoft.com/ SQLServer/feedback/ViewFeedback.aspx?FeedbackID=386810*. Microsoft fixed this bug in SQL Server 2008 Service Pack 1 by reverting to the behavior of the RECOMPILE statement hint as it was in SQL Server 2005. Unfortunately, what this means is that you will again get inefficient plans for the aforementioned static solutions to dynamic filtering.

Using an Inline Table UDF

Interestingly, as discovered by Marcello Poletti (Marc), the two static solutions I showed earlier produce good plans if you implement the query in an inline table UDF and not within a stored procedure. The reason for getting good plans is that an inline UDF is a table expression, which is expanded when queried. That is, the references to arguments in the function's query are substituted with the constants that are passed to it. This way the optimizer can ignore the parts of the filter that are logically inapplicable. Here's the definition of the function:

```
IF OBJECT_ID('dbo.fn_GetOrders', 'IF') IS NOT NULL
  DROP FUNCTION dbo.fn_GetOrders;
GO
CREATE FUNCTION dbo.fn_GetOrders
(
  @orderid   AS INT      = NULL,
  @custid    AS INT      = NULL,
  @empid     AS INT      = NULL,
  @orderdate AS DATETIME = NULL
) RETURNS TABLE
AS
RETURN
  SELECT orderid, custid, empid, orderdate, filler
  FROM dbo.Orders
  WHERE (orderid   = @orderid   OR @orderid   IS NULL)
    AND (custid    = @custid    OR @custid    IS NULL)
    AND (empid     = @empid     OR @empid     IS NULL)
    AND (orderdate = @orderdate OR @orderdate IS NULL);
GO
```

Run the following code to test the function:

```
SELECT * FROM dbo.fn_GetOrders(10248, NULL , NULL, NULL);
SELECT * FROM dbo.fn_GetOrders(NULL , NULL, NULL, '20070101');
SELECT * FROM dbo.fn_GetOrders(NULL , 3 , NULL, NULL);
SELECT * FROM dbo.fn_GetOrders(NULL , NULL , 5, NULL);
```

As you can see in Figures 9-3 and 9-4, the execution plans produced for these queries are efficient ones.

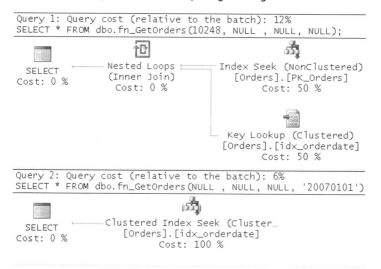

FIGURE 9-3 Execution plans for inline UDF, Query 1 and Query 2

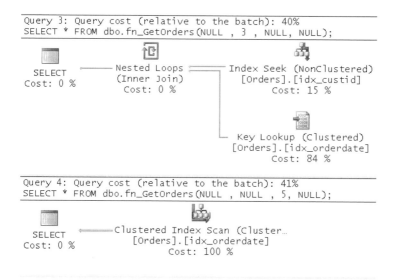

FIGURE 9-4 Execution plans for inline UDF, Query 3 and Query 4

Be aware, though, that if you invoke the inline function from a stored procedure and pass the function the stored procedure's parameters as inputs, you're back to square one in terms of the performance problem. After expansion of the function, the query will still contain references to parameters, and the optimizer will try to come up with a plan that would work for any input. To test this approach, alter the procedure to invoke the function:

```
ALTER PROC dbo.GetOrders
    @orderid   AS INT      = NULL,
    @custid    AS INT      = NULL,
    @empid     AS INT      = NULL,
    @orderdate AS DATETIME = NULL
```

```
WITH RECOMPILE
AS

SELECT * FROM dbo.fn_GetOrders(@orderid, @custid , @empid, @orderdate);
GO
```

Run the code provided earlier to test the procedure. You will get the same inefficient plans that where shown earlier in Figure 9-1.

Static Solution Based on Multiple Procedures

There is another static solution that is probably rather obvious, but I will mention it here for the sake of completeness. You could, of course, create a separate procedure for each possible combination of parameters, like so:

```
IF OBJECT_ID('dbo.GetOrders0', 'P') IS NOT NULL DROP PROC dbo.GetOrders0;
IF OBJECT_ID('dbo.GetOrders1', 'P') IS NOT NULL DROP PROC dbo.GetOrders1;
IF OBJECT_ID('dbo.GetOrders2', 'P') IS NOT NULL DROP PROC dbo.GetOrders2;

/* ... other procedures ... */

IF OBJECT_ID('dbo.GetOrders15', 'P') IS NOT NULL DROP PROC dbo.GetOrders15;
GO

CREATE PROC dbo.GetOrders0
AS
SELECT orderid, custid, empid, orderdate, filler
FROM dbo.Orders;
GO

CREATE PROC dbo.GetOrders1
  @orderdate AS DATETIME
AS
SELECT orderid, custid, empid, orderdate, filler
FROM dbo.Orders
WHERE orderdate = @orderdate;
GO

CREATE PROC dbo.GetOrders2
  @empid AS INT
AS
SELECT orderid, custid, empid, orderdate, filler
FROM dbo.Orders
WHERE empid = @empid;
GO

/* ... other procedures ... */

CREATE PROC dbo.GetOrders15
  @orderid   AS INT,
  @custid    AS INT,
  @empid     AS INT,
  @orderdate AS DATETIME
AS
SELECT orderid, custid, empid, orderdate, filler
```

```
FROM dbo.Orders
WHERE orderid   = @orderid
  AND custid    = @custid
  AND empid     = @empid
  AND orderdate = @orderdate;
GO
```

The original *GetOrders* procedure serves as nothing more than a redirector to the correct procedure based on the input, like so:

```
ALTER PROC dbo.GetOrders
  @orderid   AS INT      = NULL,
  @custid    AS INT      = NULL,
  @empid     AS INT      = NULL,
  @orderdate AS DATETIME = NULL
AS

IF      @orderid   IS     NULL
    AND @custid    IS     NULL
    AND @empid     IS     NULL
    AND @orderdate IS     NULL

  EXEC dbo.GetOrders0;

ELSE IF @orderid   IS     NULL
    AND @custid    IS     NULL
    AND @empid     IS     NULL
    AND @orderdate IS NOT NULL
  EXEC dbo.GetOrders1
    @orderdate = @orderdate;

ELSE IF @orderid   IS     NULL
    AND @custid    IS     NULL
    AND @empid     IS NOT NULL
    AND @orderdate IS     NULL
  EXEC dbo.GetOrders2
    @empid     = @empid;

/* ... other procedures ... */

ELSE IF @orderid   IS NOT NULL
    AND @custid    IS NOT NULL
    AND @empid     IS NOT NULL
    AND @orderdate IS NOT NULL
  EXEC dbo.GetOrders15
    @orderid   = @orderid,
    @custid    = @custid,
    @empid     = @empid,
    @orderdate = @orderdate;
GO
```

Naturally you will get beautiful plans, because each procedure has only the relevant part in the filter. Subsequent invocations of each procedure can also reuse a previously cached plan. So in terms of performance, this solution is pretty good. Because the solution relies on static code, there's no exposure to SQL injection. However, this solution is a nightmare in terms of maintenance.

Solution Based on Dynamic SQL

By using dynamic SQL, you address two problems. First, you get efficient plans. Second, the dynamic batch can reuse execution plans when given the same combination of arguments. Also, by using input parameters in the dynamic batch, you can completely eliminate the exposure to SQL injection. The following code shows a stored procedure implementation that uses dynamic SQL:

```
ALTER PROC dbo.GetOrders
  @orderid   AS INT      = NULL,
  @custid    AS INT      = NULL,
  @empid     AS INT      = NULL,
  @orderdate AS DATETIME = NULL
AS

DECLARE @sql AS NVARCHAR(1000);

SET @sql =
    N'SELECT orderid, custid, empid, orderdate, filler'
  + N' /* 27702431-107C-478C-8157-6DFCECC148DD */'
  + N' FROM dbo.Orders'
  + N' WHERE 1 = 1'
  + CASE WHEN @orderid IS NOT NULL THEN
      N' AND orderid = @oid' ELSE N'' END
  + CASE WHEN @custid IS NOT NULL THEN
      N' AND custid = @cid' ELSE N'' END
  + CASE WHEN @empid IS NOT NULL THEN
      N' AND empid = @eid' ELSE N'' END
  + CASE WHEN @orderdate IS NOT NULL THEN
      N' AND orderdate = @dt' ELSE N'' END;

EXEC sp_executesql
  @stmt = @sql,
  @params = N'@oid AS INT, @cid AS INT, @eid AS INT, @dt AS DATETIME',
  @oid = @orderid,
  @cid = @custid,
  @eid = @empid,
  @dt  = @orderdate;
GO
```

You can see that an expression involving a filter on a certain column is concatenated only if a value was specified in the corresponding parameter. The expression 1=1 prevents you from needing to determine dynamically whether to specify a WHERE clause at all when no input is specified. This expression has no effect on performance because the optimizer realizes that it always evaluates to TRUE and is therefore neutral. Notice that the procedure was not created with the RECOMPILE option. It's not needed here because the dynamic batch will naturally reuse a plan when given the same list of arguments. It does this because the query string that will be constructed is the same. You can easily observe the efficient plan reuse here by querying *sys.syscacheobjects*.

Run the test code, which invokes the stored procedure four times, and observe the desired efficient plans shown in Figures 9-5 and 9-6.

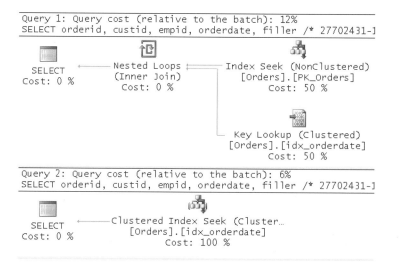

FIGURE 9-5 Execution plans for solution-based on dynamic SQL, Query 1 and Query 2

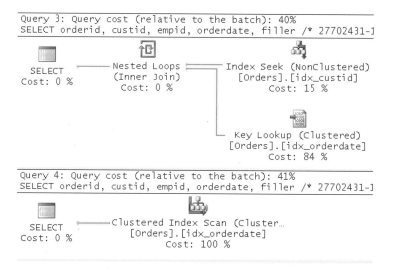

FIGURE 9-6 Execution plans for solution-based on dynamic SQL, Query 3 and Query 4

Run the test code again so that each procedure reuses the previously cached plan. Next, run the following code to analyze plan reuse behavior:

```
SELECT cacheobjtype, objtype, usecounts, sql
FROM sys.syscacheobjects
WHERE sql LIKE '%27702431-107C-478C-8157-6DFCECC148DD%'
  AND sql NOT LIKE '%sys%';
```

You get the following output, shown here in abbreviated form:

```
cacheobjtype    objtype    usecounts  sql
--------------  ---------  ---------  ------------------------------------
Compiled Plan   Prepared   2          ... WHERE 1 = 1 AND orderdate = @dt
Compiled Plan   Prepared   2          ... WHERE 1 = 1 AND empid = @eid
Compiled Plan   Prepared   2          ... WHERE 1 = 1 AND custid = @cid
Compiled Plan   Proc       8          CREATE PROC dbo.GetOrders...
Compiled Plan   Prepared   2          ... WHERE 1 = 1 AND orderid = @oid
```

Observe that the procedure got a plan that was reused eight times, but in this case the procedure is nothing but a shell for the dynamic SQL batch. The dynamic SQL batch got four parameterized plans—one for each unique string that was executed; in other words, one for each unique combination of parameters. And as you can see, each such plan was used twice. Each plan is different and is optimal for the given inputs. Multiple invocations with the same argument list will efficiently reuse previously cached parameterized execution plans.

When you're done, run the following code for cleanup:

```
IF OBJECT_ID('dbo.GetOrders', 'P') IS NOT NULL DROP PROC dbo.GetOrders;
IF OBJECT_ID('dbo.Orders', 'U') IS NOT NULL DROP TABLE dbo.Orders;
IF OBJECT_ID('dbo.fn_GetOrders', 'IF') IS NOT NULL DROP FUNCTION dbo.fn_GetOrders;
IF OBJECT_ID('dbo.GetOrders0', 'P') IS NOT NULL DROP PROC dbo.GetOrders0;
IF OBJECT_ID('dbo.GetOrders1', 'P') IS NOT NULL DROP PROC dbo.GetOrders1;
IF OBJECT_ID('dbo.GetOrders2', 'P') IS NOT NULL DROP PROC dbo.GetOrders2;
/* ... other procedures ... */
IF OBJECT_ID('dbo.GetOrders15', 'P') IS NOT NULL DROP PROC dbo.GetOrders15;
```

Dynamic PIVOT/UNPIVOT

Pivot queries rotate data from a state of rows to columns, and unpivot queries rotate data from a state of columns to rows. I covered pivoting and unpivoting techniques in *T-SQL Querying*. Static pivot and unpivot queries cannot handle an unknown number of elements that must be rotated. I'll show you how to deal with an unknown number of elements by using dynamic SQL.

Dynamic PIVOT

In my examples, I'll use the Sales.Orders table from the InsideTSQL2008 database. The following static PIVOT query returns total freight values by shipper and shipping country (for brevity I listed only three of the existing countries):

```
USE InsideTSQL2008;

WITH PivotInput AS
(
  SELECT shipperid, shipcountry, freight
  FROM Sales.Orders
)
```

```
SELECT *
FROM PivotInput
  PIVOT(SUM(freight) FOR shipcountry IN
    ([Argentina],[Austria],[Belgium]/* other countries */)) AS P;
```

This generates the following output:

```
shipperid  Argentina  Austria  Belgium
---------- ---------- -------- --------
3          55.54      2107.10  279.73
1          131.97     2218.57  269.00
2          411.07     3065.83  731.41
```

When using a static query, you have to know in advance which items you want to rotate. Suppose that you need to write a solution that handles all shipping countries that exist in the table. The list of distinct countries may change because of changes in the Orders table. Therefore, you need to construct the query string dynamically by querying the distinct shipping countries that appear in the data and use dynamic SQL to execute the batch of code you constructed, like so:

```
DECLARE
  @cols AS NVARCHAR(MAX),
  @sql  AS NVARCHAR(MAX);

-- Construct the column list for the IN clause
-- e.g., [Argentina],[Austria],[Belgium]
SET @cols = STUFF(
  (SELECT N',' + QUOTENAME(shipcountry) AS [text()]
   FROM (SELECT DISTINCT shipcountry FROM Sales.Orders) AS D
   ORDER BY shipcountry
   FOR XML PATH(''), TYPE).value('.[1]', 'VARCHAR(MAX)'),
  1, 1, N'');

-- Check @cols for possible SQL injection attempt
-- Use when example is extended to concatenating strings
-- (not required in this particular example
--  since concatenated elements are integers)
IF   UPPER(@cols) LIKE UPPER(N'%0x%')
  OR UPPER(@cols) LIKE UPPER(N'%;%')
  OR UPPER(@cols) LIKE UPPER(N'%''%')
  OR UPPER(@cols) LIKE UPPER(N'%--%')
  OR UPPER(@cols) LIKE UPPER(N'%/*%*/%')
  OR UPPER(@cols) LIKE UPPER(N'%EXEC%')
  OR UPPER(@cols) LIKE UPPER(N'%xp_[_]%')
  OR UPPER(@cols) LIKE UPPER(N'%sp_[_]%')
  OR UPPER(@cols) LIKE UPPER(N'%SELECT%')
  OR UPPER(@cols) LIKE UPPER(N'%INSERT%')
  OR UPPER(@cols) LIKE UPPER(N'%UPDATE%')
  OR UPPER(@cols) LIKE UPPER(N'%DELETE%')
  OR UPPER(@cols) LIKE UPPER(N'%TRUNCATE%')
  OR UPPER(@cols) LIKE UPPER(N'%CREATE%')
  OR UPPER(@cols) LIKE UPPER(N'%ALTER%')
  OR UPPER(@cols) LIKE UPPER(N'%DROP%')
  -- look for other possible strings used in SQL injection here
```

```
BEGIN
  RAISERROR('Possible SQL injection attempt.', 16, 1);
  RETURN;
END

-- Construct the full T-SQL statement
-- and execute dynamically
SET @sql = N'WITH PivotInput AS
(
  SELECT shipperid, shipcountry, freight
  FROM Sales.Orders
)
SELECT *
FROM PivotInput
  PIVOT(SUM(freight) FOR shipcountry IN
    (' + @cols + N')) AS P;';

EXEC sp_executesql @sql;
```

> **Caution** Note that whenever constructing code from user input—be it direct user input, or data from a table (like in our case)—such code is susceptible to SQL injection attacks. I added validation of the string generated in *@cols*. Still, remember that sophisticated hackers will always find ways to circumvent your validations, so never assume that your code is completely safe.

I described the technique to concatenate strings using the FOR XML PATH option in Chapter 2, "User-Defined Functions."

Generalizing Dynamic Pivoting

Assume that you're given the task of writing a stored procedure that produces a dynamic pivot in the database you are connected to. The stored procedure accepts the following parameters (all Unicode character strings): *@query*, *@on_rows*, *@on_cols*, *@agg_func*, and *@agg_col*. Based on the inputs, you're supposed to construct a PIVOT query string and execute it dynamically. Here's the description of the input parameters:

@query   Query or table/view name given to the PIVOT operator as input

@on_rows   Column/expression list that will be used as the grouping columns

@on_cols   Column or expression to be pivoted; the distinct values from this column will become the target column names

@agg_func   Aggregate function (MIN, MAX, SUM, COUNT, and so on)

@agg_col   Column/expression given to the aggregate function as input

If you're still confused regarding the requirements and the meaning of each input, skip the solution in Listing 9-1. Instead, examine the invocation examples and the outputs that follow the listing and the explanation of the solution. Then try to provide your own solution before looking at this one.

> ⚠️ **Important** Note that the solution in Listing 9-1 follows bad programming practices and is insecure. I'll use this solution to discuss flaws in its implementation and then suggest a more robust and secure alternative.

Listing 9-1 shows a suggested solution for the task.

LISTING 9-1 Creation script for the *sp_pivot* stored procedure

```
USE master;
IF OBJECT_ID('dbo.sp_pivot', 'P') IS NOT NULL DROP PROC dbo.sp_pivot;
GO

CREATE PROC dbo.sp_pivot
  @query    AS NVARCHAR(MAX),   -- The query, or a table/view name.
  @on_rows  AS NVARCHAR(MAX),   -- The columns that will be regular rows.
  @on_cols  AS NVARCHAR(MAX),   -- The columns that are to be pivoted.
  @agg_func AS NVARCHAR(257) = N'MAX', -- Aggregate function.
  @agg_col  AS NVARCHAR(MAX),   -- Column to aggregate.
  @debug    AS BIT = 1          -- Statement will be printed if 1.
AS


-- Input validation
IF @query IS NULL OR @on_rows IS NULL OR @on_cols IS NULL
   OR @agg_func IS NULL OR @agg_col IS NULL
BEGIN
  RAISERROR('Invalid input parameters.', 16, 1);
  RETURN;
END

BEGIN TRY
  DECLARE
    @sql     AS NVARCHAR(MAX),
    @cols    AS NVARCHAR(MAX),
    @newline AS NVARCHAR(2);

  SET @newline = NCHAR(13) + NCHAR(10);

  -- If input is a valid table or view
  -- construct a SELECT statement against it
  IF COALESCE(OBJECT_ID(@query, N'U'),
              OBJECT_ID(@query, N'V')) IS NOT NULL
    SET @query = N'SELECT * FROM ' + @query;

  -- Make the query a derived table
  SET @query = N'(' + @query + N') AS Query';

  -- Handle * input in @agg_col
  IF @agg_col = N'*' SET @agg_col = N'1';

  -- Construct column list
  SET @sql =
    N'SET @result = '                                   + @newline +
```

```
      N'  STUFF('                                    + @newline +
      N'    (SELECT N'','' +  QUOTENAME('
          + 'CAST(pivot_col AS sysname)' +
          + ') AS [text()]'                          + @newline +
      N'      FROM (SELECT DISTINCT('
          + @on_cols + N') AS pivot_col'             + @newline +
      N'            FROM' + @query + N') AS DistinctCols'   + @newline +
      N'      ORDER BY pivot_col'                    + @newline +
      N'      FOR XML PATH(''''), TYPE)'
          + N'.value(''.[1]'', ''VARCHAR(MAX)'')'    + @newline +
      N'    ,1, 1, N'''');'

  IF @debug = 1 PRINT @sql;

  EXEC sp_executesql
    @stmt   = @sql,
    @params = N'@result AS NVARCHAR(MAX) OUTPUT',
    @result = @cols OUTPUT;

  -- Create the PIVOT query
  SET @sql =
    N'SELECT *'                                      + @newline +
    N'FROM (SELECT '
            + @on_rows
            + N', ' + @on_cols + N' AS pivot_col'
            + N', ' + @agg_col + N' AS agg_col'      + @newline +
      N'      FROM ' + @query + N')' +
            + N' AS PivotInput'                      + @newline +
      N'  PIVOT(' + @agg_func + N'(agg_col)'         + @newline +
      N'    FOR pivot_col IN(' + @cols + N')) AS PivotOutput;'

  IF @debug = 1 PRINT @sql;

  EXEC sp_executesql @sql;

END TRY
BEGIN CATCH
  DECLARE
    @error_message  AS NVARCHAR(2047),
    @error_severity AS INT,
    @error_state    AS INT;

  SET @error_message  = ERROR_MESSAGE();
  SET @error_severity = ERROR_SEVERITY();
  SET @error_state    = ERROR_STATE();

  RAISERROR(@error_message, @error_severity, @error_state);

  RETURN;
END CATCH
GO
```

I'm using this exercise both to explain how to achieve dynamic pivoting and to discuss bad programming practices and security flaws. I'll start by discussing the logic behind the code, and then I'll describe the bad programming practices and flaws and present a more robust and secure solution.

- The stored procedure is created as a special procedure in master to allow it to be run in any database. Remember that dynamic execution is invoked in the context of the current database. This means that the stored procedure's code will effectively run in the context of the current database, interacting with local user objects.

- The code checks whether the input parameter *@query* names a valid table or view. If it does, the code constructs a SELECT statement against the object, storing the statement back in *@query*. If *@query* doesn't equal an existing table or view name, the code treats it as a query.

- The code then makes the query a derived table by adding surrounding parentheses and a derived table alias (*AS Query*). The result string is stored back in *@query*. This derived table will be used both to determine the distinct values that need to be pivoted (from the column/expression stored in the *@on_cols* input parameter) and as the input table expression for the PIVOT operator.

- Because the PIVOT operator doesn't support * as an input for the aggregate function—for example, COUNT(*)—the code substitutes a * input in *@agg_col* with the constant *1*.

- The code continues by constructing a dynamic query string within the *@sql* variable. This string has code that constructs the column list that will later serve as the PIVOT's IN clause. The column list is constructed by a FOR XML PATH query. The query concatenates the distinct list of values from the column/expression stored in the *@on_cols* input parameter. The concatenation query string (stored in *@sql*) is invoked dynamically. The dynamic code returns the column list through the output parameter *@cols*.

- The next section of code constructs the actual PIVOT query string in the *@sql* variable. It constructs an outer query against the derived table (aliased as Query), which is currently stored in *@query*. The outer query creates another derived table called PivotInput. The SELECT list in the outer query includes the following items:

  - The grouping column/expression list stored in *@on_rows*, which is the part that the PIVOT operator will use in its implicit grouping activity

  - The column/expression to be pivoted (currently stored in *@on_cols*), aliased as *pivot_col*

  - The column that will be used as the aggregate function's input (currently stored in *@agg_col*), aliased as *agg_col*

- The PIVOT operator works on the derived table PivotInput. Within PIVOT's parentheses, the code embeds the following items: the aggregate function (*@agg_func*) with the aggregate column as its input (*agg_col*), and the column list (*@cols*) within the parentheses of the IN clause. The outermost query simply uses a SELECT * to grab all columns returned from the PIVOT operation.

- Finally, the PIVOT query constructed in the *@sql* variable is invoked dynamically.

The *sp_pivot* stored procedure is extremely flexible, though this flexibility comes at a high security cost, which I'll describe later. To demonstrate its flexibility, I'll provide three examples of invoking it with different inputs. Make sure you study and understand all the inputs carefully.

The following code produces the count of orders per employee and order year, pivoted by order month:

```
EXEC InsideTSQL2008.dbo.sp_pivot
   @query    = N'Sales.Orders',
   @on_rows  = N'empid, YEAR(orderdate) AS orderyear',
   @on_cols  = N'MONTH(OrderDate)',
   @agg_func = N'COUNT',
   @agg_col  = N'*';
```

This generates the following output:

empid	orderyear	1	2	3	4	5	6	7	8	9	10	11	12
1	2006	0	0	0	0	0	0	1	5	5	2	4	9
2	2006	0	0	0	0	0	0	1	2	5	2	2	4
3	2006	0	0	0	0	0	0	4	2	1	3	4	4
4	2006	0	0	0	0	0	0	7	5	3	8	5	3
5	2006	0	0	0	0	0	0	3	0	1	2	2	3
6	2006	0	0	0	0	0	0	2	4	3	0	3	3
7	2006	0	0	0	0	0	0	0	1	2	5	3	0
8	2006	0	0	0	0	0	0	2	6	3	2	2	4
9	2006	0	0	0	0	0	0	2	0	0	2	0	1
1	2007	3	2	5	1	5	4	7	3	8	7	3	7
2	2007	4	1	4	3	3	4	3	1	7	1	5	5
3	2007	7	9	3	5	5	6	2	4	4	7	8	11
4	2007	8	6	4	8	5	5	6	11	5	7	6	10
5	2007	0	0	3	0	2	2	1	3	2	3	1	1
6	2007	2	2	2	4	2	2	2	2	1	4	5	5
7	2007	3	1	2	6	5	1	5	3	5	1	1	3
8	2007	5	8	6	2	4	3	6	5	3	7	2	3
9	2007	1	0	1	2	1	3	1	1	2	1	3	3
1	2008	9	9	11	8	5	0	0	0	0	0	0	0
2	2008	7	3	9	18	2	0	0	0	0	0	0	0
3	2008	10	6	12	10	0	0	0	0	0	0	0	0
4	2008	6	14	12	10	2	0	0	0	0	0	0	0
5	2008	4	6	2	1	0	0	0	0	0	0	0	0
6	2008	3	4	7	5	0	0	0	0	0	0	0	0
7	2008	4	6	4	9	2	0	0	0	0	0	0	0
8	2008	7	2	10	9	3	0	0	0	0	0	0	0
9	2008	5	4	6	4	0	0	0	0	0	0	0	0

The following code produces the sum of the value (*qty* * *unitprice*) per employee, pivoted by order year:

```
EXEC InsideTSQL2008.dbo.sp_pivot
  @query    = N'
SELECT O.orderid, empid, orderdate, qty, unitprice
FROM Sales.Orders AS O
  JOIN Sales.OrderDetails AS OD
    ON OD.orderid = O.orderid',
  @on_rows  = N'empid',
  @on_cols  = N'YEAR(OrderDate)',
  @agg_func = N'SUM',
  @agg_col  = N'qty*unitprice';
```

This generates the following output:

```
empid  2006       2007        2008
------ ---------- ----------- ---------
3      19231.80   111788.61   82030.89
6      17731.10   45992.00    14475.00
9      11365.70   29577.55    42020.75
7      18104.80   66689.14    56502.05
1      38789.00   97533.58    65821.13
4      53114.80   139477.70   57594.95
2      22834.70   74958.60    79955.96
5      21965.20   32595.05    21007.50
8      23161.40   59776.52    50363.11
```

The following code produces the count of orders per employee pivoted by shipper ID and order year:

```
EXEC InsideTSQL2008.dbo.sp_pivot
  @query    = N'
SELECT empid, shipperid, YEAR(orderdate) AS orderyear
FROM Sales.Orders',
  @on_rows  = N'empid',
  @on_cols  =
N'CAST(shipperid AS VARCHAR(10)) + ''_''
        + CAST(orderyear AS VARCHAR(4))',
  @agg_func = N'COUNT',
  @agg_col  = N'*';
```

This generates the following output:

empid	1_2006	1_2007	1_2008	2_2006	2_2007	2_2008	3_2006	3_2007	3_2008
3	4	22	10	6	24	15	8	25	13
6	7	12	4	7	11	7	1	10	8
9	2	5	3	0	8	11	3	6	5
7	1	14	5	3	12	9	7	10	11
1	6	16	16	8	20	16	12	19	10
4	9	23	14	13	35	22	9	23	8
2	5	19	11	8	11	17	3	11	11
5	3	6	5	3	7	5	5	5	3
8	1	16	10	8	25	15	10	13	6

The implementation of the stored procedure *sp_pivot* suffers from bad programming practices and security flaws. As I mentioned earlier in the chapter, Microsoft strongly advises against using the *sp_* prefix for user-defined procedure names. On one hand, creating this procedure as a special procedure allows flexibility; on the other hand, by doing so you're relying on behavior that is not supported. It is advisable to forgo the flexibility obtained by creating the procedure with the *sp_* prefix and create it as a regular user-defined stored procedure in the user databases where you need it.

The code defines most input parameters with a virtually unlimited size (using the MAX specifier) and doesn't have any input validation. Because the stored procedure invokes dynamic execution based on user input strings, it's very important to limit the sizes of the inputs and to check those for potential SQL injection attacks. With the existing implementation it's very easy for hackers to inject code that will do damage in your system. As an example for injecting malicious code through user inputs, consider the following invocation of the stored procedure:

```
EXEC InsideTSQL2008.dbo.sp_pivot
  @query     = N'Sales.Orders',
  @on_rows   = N'1 AS dummy_col ) DummyTable;
PRINT ''SQL injection...
This could have been a DROP TABLE or xp_cmdshell command!'';
SELECT * FROM (SELECT empid',
  @on_cols   = N'MONTH(orderdate)',
  @agg_func  = N'COUNT',
  @agg_col   = N'*';
```

The query string generated by the stored procedure looks like this:

```
SELECT *
FROM (SELECT 1 AS dummy_col ) DummyTable;
PRINT 'SQL injection...
This could have been a DROP TABLE or xp_cmdshell command!';
SELECT * FROM (SELECT empid, MONTH(orderdate) AS pivot_col, 1 AS agg_col
      FROM (SELECT * FROM Sales.Orders) AS Query) AS PivotInput
  PIVOT(COUNT(agg_col)
    FOR pivot_col IN([1],[2],[3],[4],[5],[6],[7],[8],[9],[10],[11],[12])) AS PivotOutput;
```

When this code is executed, the injected PRINT statement executes without any problem. I used a harmless PRINT statement just to demonstrate that code can be easily injected here, but obviously the malicious code could be any valid T-SQL code; for example, a DROP TABLE statement, invocation of *xp_cmdshell*, and so on. In short, it is vital here to take protective measures against SQL injection attempts, as I will demonstrate shortly.

Before I present the revised solution, get rid of the existing *sp_pivot* implementation:

```
USE master;
IF OBJECT_ID('dbo.sp_pivot', 'P') IS NOT NULL DROP PROC dbo.sp_pivot;
```

Then run the following code to create the *usp_pivot* stored procedure in the InsideTSQL2008 database:

```
USE InsideTSQL2008;
IF OBJECT_ID('dbo.usp_pivot', 'P') IS NOT NULL DROP PROC dbo.usp_pivot;
GO

CREATE PROC dbo.usp_pivot
  @schema_name AS sysname      = N'dbo', -- schema of table/view
  @object_name AS sysname      = NULL,   -- name of table/view
  @on_rows     AS sysname      = NULL,   -- group by column
  @on_cols     AS sysname      = NULL,   -- rotation column
  @agg_func    AS NVARCHAR(12) = N'MAX', -- aggregate function
  @agg_col     AS sysname      = NULL,   -- aggregate column
  @debug       AS BIT = 1               -- debug flag
AS

DECLARE
  @object  AS NVARCHAR(600),
  @sql     AS NVARCHAR(MAX),
  @cols    AS NVARCHAR(MAX),
  @newline AS NVARCHAR(2),
  @msg     AS NVARCHAR(500);

SET @newline = NCHAR(13) + NCHAR(10);
SET @object  = QUOTENAME(@schema_name) + N'.' + QUOTENAME(@object_name);

-- Check for missing input
IF   @schema_name IS NULL
  OR @object_name IS NULL
  OR @on_rows     IS NULL
  OR @on_cols     IS NULL
  OR @agg_func    IS NULL
  OR @agg_col     IS NULL
BEGIN
  SET @msg = N'Missing input parameters: '
    + CASE WHEN @schema_name IS NULL THEN N'@schema_name;' ELSE N'' END
    + CASE WHEN @object_name IS NULL THEN N'@object_name;' ELSE N'' END
    + CASE WHEN @on_rows     IS NULL THEN N'@on_rows;'     ELSE N'' END
    + CASE WHEN @on_cols     IS NULL THEN N'@on_cols;'     ELSE N'' END
    + CASE WHEN @agg_func    IS NULL THEN N'@agg_func;'    ELSE N'' END
    + CASE WHEN @agg_col     IS NULL THEN N'@agg_col;'     ELSE N'' END
  RAISERROR(@msg, 16, 1);
  RETURN;
END

-- Allow only existing table or view name as input object
IF COALESCE(OBJECT_ID(@object, N'U'),
            OBJECT_ID(@object, N'V')) IS NULL
BEGIN
  SET @msg = N'%s is not an existing table or view in the database.';
  RAISERROR(@msg, 16, 1, @object);
  RETURN;
END
```

```
-- Verify that column names specified in @on_rows, @on_cols, @agg_col exist
IF  COLUMNPROPERTY(OBJECT_ID(@object), @on_rows, 'ColumnId') IS NULL
  OR COLUMNPROPERTY(OBJECT_ID(@object), @on_cols, 'ColumnId') IS NULL
  OR COLUMNPROPERTY(OBJECT_ID(@object), @agg_col, 'ColumnId') IS NULL
BEGIN
  SET @msg = N'%s, %s and %s must'
    + N' be existing column names in %s.';
  RAISERROR(@msg, 16, 1, @on_rows, @on_cols, @agg_col, @object);
  RETURN;
END

-- Verify that @agg_func is in a known list of functions
-- Add to list as needed and adjust @agg_func size accordingly
IF @agg_func NOT IN
  (N'AVG', N'COUNT', N'COUNT_BIG', N'SUM', N'MIN', N'MAX',
   N'STDEV', N'STDEVP', N'VAR', N'VARP')
BEGIN
  SET @msg = N'%s is an unsupported aggregate function.';
  RAISERROR(@msg, 16, 1, @agg_func);
  RETURN;
END

BEGIN TRY

  -- Construct column list
  SET @sql =
    N'SET @result = '                                + @newline +
    N'  STUFF('                                      + @newline +
    N'    (SELECT N'','' +  QUOTENAME('
          + 'CAST(pivot_col AS sysname)' +
          + ') AS [text()]'                          + @newline +
    N'    FROM (SELECT DISTINCT('
          + QUOTENAME(@on_cols) + N') AS pivot_col'  + @newline +
    N'          FROM' + @object + N') AS DistinctCols' + @newline +
    N'    ORDER BY pivot_col'                        + @newline +
    N'    FOR XML PATH(''''), TYPE)'
          + N'.value(''.[1]'', ''VARCHAR(MAX)'')'    + @newline +
    N'    ,1, 1, N'''');'

  IF @debug = 1 PRINT @sql;

  EXEC sp_executesql
    @stmt   = @sql,
    @params = N'@result AS NVARCHAR(MAX) OUTPUT',
    @result = @cols OUTPUT;

  -- Check @cols for possible SQL injection attempt
  IF  UPPER(@cols) LIKE UPPER(N'%0x%')
    OR UPPER(@cols) LIKE UPPER(N'%;%')
    OR UPPER(@cols) LIKE UPPER(N'%''%')
    OR UPPER(@cols) LIKE UPPER(N'%--%')
    OR UPPER(@cols) LIKE UPPER(N'%/*%*/%')
    OR UPPER(@cols) LIKE UPPER(N'%EXEC%')
    OR UPPER(@cols) LIKE UPPER(N'%xp[_]%')
    OR UPPER(@cols) LIKE UPPER(N'%sp[_]%')
```

```
       OR UPPER(@cols) LIKE UPPER(N'%SELECT%')
       OR UPPER(@cols) LIKE UPPER(N'%INSERT%')
       OR UPPER(@cols) LIKE UPPER(N'%UPDATE%')
       OR UPPER(@cols) LIKE UPPER(N'%DELETE%')
       OR UPPER(@cols) LIKE UPPER(N'%TRUNCATE%')
       OR UPPER(@cols) LIKE UPPER(N'%CREATE%')
       OR UPPER(@cols) LIKE UPPER(N'%ALTER%')
       OR UPPER(@cols) LIKE UPPER(N'%DROP%')
       -- look for other possible strings used in SQL injection here
    BEGIN
      SET @msg = N'Possible SQL injection attempt.';
      RAISERROR(@msg, 16, 1);
      RETURN;
    END

    -- Create the PIVOT query
    SET @sql =
      N'SELECT *'                                            + @newline +
      N'FROM (SELECT '
              + QUOTENAME(@on_rows)
              + N', ' + QUOTENAME(@on_cols) + N' AS pivot_col'
              + N', ' + QUOTENAME(@agg_col) + N' AS agg_col' + @newline +
      N'      FROM ' + @object + N')' +
              + N' AS PivotInput'                            + @newline +
      N'  PIVOT(' + @agg_func + N'(agg_col)'                 + @newline +
      N'    FOR pivot_col IN(' + @cols + N')) AS PivotOutput;'

    IF @debug = 1 PRINT @sql;

    EXEC sp_executesql @sql;
  END TRY
  BEGIN CATCH
    DECLARE
      @error_message  AS NVARCHAR(2047),
      @error_severity AS INT,
      @error_state    AS INT;

    SET @error_message  = ERROR_MESSAGE();
    SET @error_severity = ERROR_SEVERITY();
    SET @error_state    = ERROR_STATE();

    RAISERROR(@error_message, @error_severity, @error_state);

    RETURN;
  END CATCH
GO
```

This implementation of the stored procedure follows good programming practices and addresses the security flaws mentioned earlier. Keep in mind, however, that when constructing code based on user inputs and stored data/metadata, it is extremely difficult (if at all possible) to achieve complete protection against SQL injection.

The stored procedure *usp_pivot* is created as a user-defined procedure in the InsideTSQL2008 database with the *usp_* prefix. This means that it isn't as flexible as the previous implementation in the sense that it interacts only with tables and views from InsideTSQL2008. Note that you can create a view in InsideTSQL2008 that queries objects from other databases, and provide this view as input to the stored procedure.

The *usp_pivot* stored procedure's code takes several measures to try and prevent SQL injection attempts:

- The sizes of the input parameters are limited.

- Instead of allowing any query as input, the stored procedure accepts only a valid table or view name that exists in the database. Similarly, instead of allowing any T-SQL expression for the arguments @*on_rows*, @*on_cols*, and @*agg_col*, the stored procedure accepts only valid column names that exist in the input table/view. Note that you can create a view with any query that you like and serve it as input to the stored procedure.

- The code uses QUOTENAME where relevant to quote object and column names with square brackets.

- The stored procedure's code inspects the @*cols* variable for possible code strings injected to it through data stored in the rotation column values that are being concatenated.

The code also performs input validation to verify that all parameters were supplied, that the table/view and column names exist, and that the aggregate function appears in the list of functions that you want to support.

The *usp_pivot* stored procedure might seem much less flexible than *sp_pivot*, but remember that you can always create a view to prepare the data for *usp_pivot*. For example, consider the following code used earlier to return the sum of the value *qty * unitprice* for each employee, pivoted by order year:

```
EXEC InsideTSQL2008.dbo.sp_pivot
  @query   = N'
SELECT O.orderid, empid, orderdate, qty, unitprice
FROM Sales.Orders AS O
  JOIN Sales.OrderDetails AS OD
    ON OD.orderid = O.orderid',
  @on_rows = N'empid',
  @on_cols = N'YEAR(OrderDate)',
  @agg_func = N'SUM',
  @agg_col = N'qty*unitprice';
```

You can achieve the same result with *usp_pivot* by first creating a view that prepares the data:

```
USE InsideTSQL2008;
IF OBJECT_ID('dbo.ViewForPivot', 'V') IS NOT NULL
  DROP VIEW dbo.ViewForPivot;
GO

CREATE VIEW dbo.ViewForPivot
AS
```

```
SELECT
  o.orderid      AS orderid,
  empid          AS empid,
  YEAR(orderdate) AS orderyear,
  qty * unitprice AS val
FROM Sales.Orders AS O
  JOIN Sales.OrderDetails AS OD
    ON OD.orderid = O.orderid;
GO
```

Then invoke *usp_pivot*, as in:

```
EXEC dbo.usp_pivot
  @object_name = N'ViewForPivot',
  @on_rows  = N'empid',
  @on_cols  = N'orderyear',
  @agg_func = N'SUM',
  @agg_col  = N'val';
```

When you think about it, that's a small price to pay compared to compromising the security of your system.

When you're done, run the following code for cleanup:

```
USE InsideTSQL2008;
IF OBJECT_ID('dbo.ViewForPivot', 'U') IS NOT NULL
  DROP VIEW dbo.ViewForPivot;
IF OBJECT_ID('dbo.usp_pivot', 'P') IS NOT NULL
  DROP PROC dbo.usp_pivot;
```

Dynamic UNPIVOT

In a similar manner, you can support dynamic unpivoting. To see how the technique works, first run the following code, which creates and populates the CustOrders table with pivoted total yearly order values per customer.

```
USE InsideTSQL2008;
IF OBJECT_ID('dbo.CustOrders', 'U') IS NOT NULL
  DROP TABLE dbo.CustOrders;
GO

CREATE TABLE dbo.CustOrders
(
  custid    INT           NOT NULL,
  [2006]    NUMERIC(12, 2) NULL,
  [2007]    NUMERIC(12, 2) NULL,
  [2008]    NUMERIC(12, 2) NULL,
  CONSTRAINT PK_CustOrders PRIMARY KEY(custid)
);

WITH PivotInput AS
(
  SELECT custid, YEAR(orderdate) AS orderyear, val
  FROM Sales.OrderValues
)
```

```
INSERT INTO dbo.CustOrders(custid, [2006], [2007], [2008])
SELECT custid, [2006], [2007], [2008]
FROM PivotInput
  PIVOT(SUM(val) FOR orderyear IN([2006],[2007],[2008])) AS P;
GO
```

Here's the static query that unpivots the rows in such a way that the result will contain a row for each customer and year:

```
SELECT custid, orderyear, val
FROM dbo.CustOrders
  UNPIVOT(val FOR orderyear IN([2006],[2007],[2008])) AS U;
```

This generates the following output, shown here in abbreviated form:

```
custid  orderyear  val
-------  ----------  -------------
1       2007        2022.50
1       2008        2250.50
2       2006        88.80
2       2007        799.75
2       2008        514.40
3       2006        403.20
3       2007        5960.78
3       2008        660.00
4       2006        1379.00
4       2007        6406.90
4       2008        5604.75
5       2006        4324.40
5       2007        13849.02
5       2008        6754.16
...
```

To make the solution dynamic, you use code similar to the pivoting code shown earlier:

```
DECLARE
  @cols AS NVARCHAR(MAX),
  @sql  AS NVARCHAR(MAX);

-- Construct the column list for the IN clause
-- e.g., [2006],[2007],[2008]
SET @cols = STUFF(
  (SELECT N','+ QUOTENAME(name) AS [text()]
    FROM (SELECT name
          FROM sys.columns
          WHERE object_id = OBJECT_ID(N'dbo.CustOrders')
            AND name NOT IN(N'custid')) AS D
    ORDER BY name
    FOR XML PATH(''), TYPE).value('.[1]','VARCHAR(MAX)'),
  1, 1, N'');

-- Construct the full T-SQL statement
-- and execute dynamically
```

```
SET @sql = N'SELECT custid, orderyear, val
FROM dbo.CustOrders
  UNPIVOT(val FOR orderyear IN(' + @cols + N')) AS U;';

EXEC sp_executesql @sql;
```

Here, instead of querying the attribute list from the data table, you query the column list from the sys.columns view.

SQL Injection

One of the greatest security risks and causes of great damage to computerized systems is a hacking technique called SQL injection. By using SQL injection, hackers inject their own malicious code into statements you execute dynamically on your SQL Servers, often from accounts with elevated privileges. An attacker can launch a SQL injection attack when you construct code by concatenating strings. I'll explain and demonstrate SQL injection techniques by presenting examples of both client-based attacks and server-based attacks. I'll then explain what measures you can take to block some of the attacks. But bear in mind that sophisticated attackers have very innovative minds; if you construct code that concatenates strings based on user input or stored data or metadata, it's almost impossible to block SQL injection attacks altogether. In this section I'll demonstrate a couple of simple examples for SQL injection attacks and provide a few suggestions regarding protective measures that you can take. This section is by no means complete. As I mentioned earlier, you can find a lot of information about the subject on the Internet and in other resources, and I also pointed out an excellent article on the subject that appears in SQL Server Books Online.

SQL Injection: Code Constructed Dynamically at Client

Suppose that you provide a login screen in your client Microsoft Visual Basic application that is designed to collect a username and password in two input text boxes (call them *InputUserName* and *InputPass*). You construct a query that verifies this information against a Users table, which you have in your database to determine whether to allow or reject the login attempt. Run the following code to create the Users table and populate it with two sample users:

```
USE tempdb;
IF OBJECT_ID('dbo.Users', 'U') IS NOT NULL DROP TABLE Users;

CREATE TABLE dbo.Users
(
  username VARCHAR(30) NOT NULL PRIMARY KEY,
  pass     VARCHAR(16) NOT NULL
);

INSERT INTO Users(username, pass) VALUES('user1', '123');
INSERT INTO Users(username, pass) VALUES('user2', '456');
```

Suppose that you're using the following Visual Basic code at the client application to construct a query and verify the user credentials:

```
sql = "SELECT COUNT(*) AS cnt FROM dbo.Users WHERE username = '" _
  & InputUserName & "' AND pass = '" & InputPass & "';"
```

Suppose that *user1* enters the following information in the input boxes:

```
InputUserName = "user1"
InputPass     = "123"
```

Your code constructs the following query, and executing it returns a count of 1:

```
SELECT COUNT(*) AS cnt FROM dbo.Users WHERE username = 'user1' AND pass = '123';
```

Your code checks whether the count is greater than 0. If it is, as is the case here, you allow the user to log in, and if it is 0, you reject the login attempt. A hacker versed in SQL injection will very likely try to enter the following inputs:

```
InputUserName = "' OR 1 = 1 --"
InputPass = ""
```

Your Visual Basic code then constructs the following query:

```
SELECT COUNT(*) AS cnt FROM dbo.Users WHERE username = '' OR 1 = 1 --' AND pass = '';
```

The trick here is that the hacker closed the quote you opened in front of the user name, added the expression 1=1—which will become part of the filter expression—and then added the two dashes (--) to make the rest of the original code (which is now invalid SQL) into a comment so that it won't generate an error. This query will always return a count greater than 0, thereby allowing the hacker to log in without having the right credentials. Note that if you use a member of the sysadmin role or another privileged user to connect to SQL Server and invoke this query, a hacker will be able to do a lot of damage in your system. In addition to gaining the ability to log in, a hacker can inject additional code beyond the original query—for example, *"' OR 1 = 1 DROP DATABASE <db_name> --" or "' OR 1 = 1 EXEC master. dbo.xp_cmdshell "format d:" --"*.

> **Note** Note that in SQL Server 2008, *xp_cmdshell* is disabled by default for security reasons. If you enable it, bear in mind that you increase SQL Server's attackable surface area.

SQL Injection: Code Constructed Dynamically at Server

This section will introduce an example for a SQL injection attack that exploits code constructed dynamically at the server. Consider the very common technique of passing SQL Server a dynamic list of arguments using a single input string with a comma-separated list of values. For example, the following stored procedure accepts such an input array with order IDs called @*orders,* and it returns the *orderid* (integer) and *shipcountry* (character) for matching orders:

```
USE InsideTSQL2008;
IF OBJECT_ID('dbo.GetOrders', 'P') IS NOT NULL DROP PROC dbo.GetOrders;
GO

CREATE PROC dbo.GetOrders
  @orders AS VARCHAR(1000)
AS

DECLARE @sql AS NVARCHAR(1100);

SET @sql = N'SELECT orderid, shipcountry
FROM Sales.Orders
WHERE orderid IN(' + @orders + ');';

EXEC sp_executesql @sql;
GO
```

The procedure constructs the query string dynamically, concatenating the input array of orders in the parentheses of the IN predicate. The user enters a string with a list of orders and gets back the *orderid* and *custid* of the input orders. For example, run the following code:

```
EXEC dbo.GetOrders '10248,10249,10250';
```

This generates the following output:

```
orderid      shipcountry
-----------  ---------------
10248        France
10249        Germany
10250        Brazil
```

A hacker will know how to communicate with SQL Server by testing various code strings to check whether you constructed the code dynamically. If the code wasn't developed with security in mind, the application probably doesn't hide error messages generated by SQL Server from the user. By default, such error messages will simply show up in the browser. Imagine that you're the hacker. You will first test whether the code is constructed dynamically by specifying two dashes in the input box. Here is the stored procedure call that is submitted by the client to SQL Server:

```
EXEC dbo.GetOrders ' --';
```

And here is the code that is executed by the stored procedure at the server:

```
SELECT orderid, shipcountry
FROM Sales.Orders
WHERE orderid IN( --);
```

You get the following error message:

```
Msg 102, Level 15, State 1, Line 3
Incorrect syntax near '('.
```

The error tells you that there are unclosed parentheses, indicating dynamic code that concatenates the input after an opening parenthesis. That's actually what you (the hacker) wanted to see, and at this point you already know that the server is yours.

Next, you want to examine the format of the output of the stored procedure, so you specify '-1) --' as the input. Here's the code executed by the stored procedure:

```
SELECT orderid, shipcountry
FROM Sales.Orders
WHERE orderid IN(-1) --);
```

You get an empty set back:

```
orderid      shipcountry
-----------  ---------------
```

But you can see that the output contains an integer column and a character one. Now you use a UNION ALL operator to return table information from the database instead of order information, as shown in the following code:

```
EXEC dbo.GetOrders '-1)
UNION ALL
SELECT object_id, QUOTENAME(SCHEMA_NAME(schema_id)) + ''.'' + QUOTENAME(name)
FROM sys.objects --';
```

The stored procedure executes the following code:

```
SELECT orderid, shipcountry
FROM Sales.Orders
WHERE orderid IN(-1)
UNION ALL
SELECT object_id, QUOTENAME(SCHEMA_NAME(schema_id)) + '.' + QUOTENAME(name)
FROM sys.objects --);
```

It is important to look at this code to realize how easy it is for a hacker to obtain information from your database that you did not intend to expose. For example, running this code in the InsideTSQL2008 database produces the following output, shown here in abbreviated form:

```
orderid      shipcountry
-----------  ------------------------------
...
149575571    [HR].[Employees]
165575628    [HR].[PK_Employees]
181575685    [HR].[FK_Employees_Employees]
197575742    [HR].[CHK_birthdate]
213575799    [Production].[Suppliers]
229575856    [Production].[PK_Suppliers]
```

```
245575913    [Production].[Categories]
261575970    [Production].[PK_Categories]
277576027    [Production].[Products]
293576084    [Production].[PK_Products]
309576141    [Production].[DFT_Products_unitprice]
325576198    [Production].[DFT_Products_discontinued]
341576255    [Production].[FK_Products_Categories]
357576312    [Production].[FK_Products_Suppliers]
373576369    [Production].[CHK_Products_unitprice]
389576426    [Sales].[Customers]
405576483    [Sales].[PK_Customers]
421576540    [Sales].[Shippers]
437576597    [Sales].[PK_Shippers]
453576654    [Sales].[Orders]
469576711    [Sales].[PK_Orders]
485576768    [Sales].[DFT_Orders_freight]
501576825    [Sales].[FK_Orders_Customers]
517576882    [Sales].[FK_Orders_Employees]
533576939    [Sales].[FK_Orders_Shippers]
549576996    [Sales].[OrderDetails]
565577053    [Sales].[PK_OrderDetails]
581577110    [Sales].[DFT_OrderDetails_unitprice]
597577167    [Sales].[DFT_OrderDetails_qty]
613577224    [Sales].[DFT_OrderDetails_discount]
629577281    [Sales].[FK_OrderDetails_Orders]
645577338    [Sales].[FK_OrderDetails_Products]
661577395    [Sales].[CHK_discount]
677577452    [Sales].[CHK_qty]
693577509    [Sales].[CHK_unitprice]
709577566    [Sales].[OrderValues]
725577623    [Sales].[OrderTotalsByYear]
741577680    [Sales].[CustOrders]
773577794    [dbo].[GetOrders]
...
```

Suppose that you're interested in customer information. You have the object ID of the Customers table, so now you use UNION ALL to return column information by using the following code:

```
EXEC dbo.GetOrders '-1)
UNION ALL
SELECT column_id, name
FROM sys.columns
WHERE object_id = 389576426 --';
```

The following code is executed at the server:

```
SELECT orderid, shipcountry
FROM Sales.Orders
WHERE orderid IN(-1)
UNION ALL
SELECT column_id, name
FROM sys.columns
WHERE object_id = 389576426 --);
```

This generates the following output:

```
orderid      shipcountry
-----------  -----------------
1            custid
2            companyname
3            contactname
4            contacttitle
5            address
6            city
7            region
8            postalcode
9            country
10           phone
11           fax
```

Now that you have the full column list from the Customers table, you use the following code to request customer data by concatenating the customer attributes you need under the character column:

```
EXEC dbo.GetOrders '-1)
UNION ALL
SELECT custid, companyname + '';'' + phone
FROM Sales.Customers --';
```

The following code is executed at the server:

```
SELECT orderid, shipcountry
FROM Sales.Orders
WHERE orderid IN(-1)
UNION ALL
SELECT custid, companyname + ';' + phone
FROM Sales.Customers --);
```

This generates the following output, shown here in abbreviated form:

```
orderid      shipcountry
-----------  ------------------------------------
1            Customer NRZBB;030-3456789
2            Customer MLTDN;(5) 789-0123
3            Customer KBUDE;(5) 123-4567
4            Customer HFBZG;(171) 456-7890
5            Customer HGVLZ;0921-67 89 01
6            Customer XHXJV;0621-67890
7            Customer QXVLA;67.89.01.23
8            Customer QUHWH;(91) 345 67 89
9            Customer RTXGC;23.45.67.89
10           Customer EEALV;(604) 901-2345
11           Customer UBHAU;(171) 789-0123
12           Customer PSNMQ;(1) 890-1234
13           Customer VMLOG;(5) 456-7890
14           Customer WNMAF;0452-678901
15           Customer JUWXK;(11) 012-3456
...
```

Imagine—you get customer IDs, company names, and phone numbers, and you could request more information!

Now the real "fun" begins as you inject changes and destructive commands—for example, suppose you executed the procedure with the following parameter (don't run it):

```
EXEC GetOrders '-1);
UPDATE Sales.Customers
  SET phone = ''9999999''
WHERE custid = 1; --';
```

The code that would run behind the scenes looks like this (don't run it):

```
SELECT orderid, shipcountry
FROM Sales.Orders
WHERE orderid IN(-1);
UPDATE Sales.Customers
  SET phone = '9999999'
WHERE custid = 1; --);
```

To experiment and observe which code strings the stored procedure generates based on various inputs, use a version with a *PRINT @sql* command instead of *EXEC sp_executesql @sql*.

Protecting Against SQL Injection

Following are examples for measures you can take to provide some level of protection (though not complete) for your environment against SQL injection attacks:

- To reduce the surface area for attack, do not enable functionality that is not needed, such as *xp_cmdshell*, the SQL Server Agent service, and so on.

- Provide minimal permissions to the executing user. For example, in the login scenario I presented, there's no reason to connect to the database using a powerful user. Create a user that has access only to the Users table and has no other permissions. This will prevent hackers from modifying data, but they might still be able to read it. In SQL Server 2008, you can impersonate users, so the new credentials will even apply to code invoked dynamically at the server. This opens a whole window of opportunities for hackers. Dynamic SQL can now run under impersonated user credentials and not even require direct permissions from the user executing the stored procedure.

- Inspect user input thoroughly and use stored procedures. For example, the input to the *GetOrders* stored procedure should contain only digits and commas. If you inspect the input and find that it contains other characters, don't run the code. Instead, send an alert to notify an administrator of a potential SQL injection attempt:

```
IF @orders LIKE '%[^0-9,]%'
BEGIN
  -- Raise an error
```

```
  -- Send an alert
  RETURN;
END
```

If other characters are allowed, use pattern matching to check whether common SQL injection constructs—such as a single quote, two dashes, EXEC, *sp_*, *xp_*, UNION, and so on—exist in the input. Note, however, that this technique is not bulletproof because so many attacks are possible.

■ Limit the length of the inputs when possible. For example, a user name or password should not be hundreds or thousands of characters long. Such limitations are an effortless way to prevent many SQL injection attempts. Note, though, that some hacking techniques rely on truncation of the inputs; for example, if you set a variable defined as NVARCHAR(128) with a value that is longer than 128 characters, SQL Server will truncate the input beyond the 128th character. Such techniques and ways to block them are described in the article on SQL injection article in SQL Server Books Online.

■ Use stored procedures. Stored procedures help by encapsulating input, type-checking it (good for integers and date inputs), allowing permissions settings, and so on.

■ Avoid using dynamic SQL when possible. Static code is safe, especially if you write it yourself giving attention to security issues. For example, I discussed techniques to split an array of elements into multiple rows using a static query in Chapter 2. You can create a function that accepts an array and invokes a static query that splits it into elements, returning a table with the different elements in separate rows. You can then use this function, joining its result table with the data table to return the order attributes. Such an implementation not only prevents SQL injection attacks, but it also reuses the same execution plan for multiple invocations of the code. The current implementation of the stored procedure will produce a different execution plan for each unique input. Imagine the performance effect of invoking such a stored procedure thousands of times a day. You can use thousands of plans or one plan. I provided the static function implementation in Chapter 2. Also be careful with CLR routines, which could have dynamic SQL hidden in them.

■ When you need to quote inputs, don't do it explicitly. Rather, use the QUOTENAME function for this purpose, or to be even safer, replace CHAR(39) with CHAR(39)+CHAR(39). QUOTENAME has some limitations, which you can read about in the SQL Injection article in SQL Server Books Online. The function will double each explicit quote that a hacker specifies, practically ensuring that the input is treated as an input string argument and not as part of your code. To demonstrate this, I'll use PRINT to return the code string that is generated. In practice, there will be an EXEC or *sp_executesql* invocation. The following code doesn't use the QUOTENAME function to quote the input value:

```
DECLARE @lastname AS NVARCHAR(40), @sql AS NVARCHAR(200);
SET @lastname = N'Davis';
SET @sql = N'SELECT * FROM HR.Employees WHERE lastname = N'''
  + @lastname + ''';';
PRINT @sql;
```

With innocent input such as Davis, this code produces the following query:

```
SELECT * FROM HR.Employees WHERE lastname = N'Davis';
```

But a hacker can easily inject code, like so:

```
DECLARE @lastname AS NVARCHAR(40), @sql AS NVARCHAR(200);
SET @lastname = N''' DROP TABLE HR.Employees --';
SET @sql = N'SELECT * FROM HR.Employees WHERE lastname = N'''
  + @lastname + ''';';
PRINT @sql;
```

And that code injection produces the following code:

```
SELECT * FROM HR.Employees WHERE lastname = N'' DROP TABLE HR.Employees --';
```

Now use QUOTENAME instead of explicitly adding single quotes to the last name:

```
DECLARE @lastname AS NVARCHAR(40), @sql AS NVARCHAR(200);
SET @lastname = N''' DROP TABLE HR.Employees --';
SET @sql = N'SELECT * FROM HR.Employees WHERE lastname = N'
  + QUOTENAME(@lastname, '''') + ';';
PRINT @sql;
```

By doing this, you get the following harmless query:

```
SELECT * FROM HR.Employees WHERE lastname = N''' DROP TABLE HR.Employees --';
```

Here I tried to make a point regarding user input strings you concatenate to your code. Of course your code would be much safer if you do not concatenate the last name at all; rather, use *sp_executesql* with an input parameter defined for last name:

```
DECLARE @entered_lastname AS NVARCHAR(40), @sql AS NVARCHAR(200);
-- user input
SET @entered_lastname = N''' DROP TABLE HR.Employees --';

SET @sql = N'SELECT * FROM HR.Employees WHERE lastname = @lastname;'

EXEC sp_executesql
  @stmt = @sql,
  @params = N'@lastname AS NVARCHAR(40)',
  @lastname = @entered_lastname;
```

Or even better, don't use dynamic SQL at all in such cases—use static SQL:

```
DECLARE @lastname AS NVARCHAR(40);
-- user input
SET @lastname = N''' DROP TABLE dbo.Employees --';

SELECT * FROM HR.Employees WHERE lastname = @lastname;
```

Conclusion

By now, you probably have realized that dynamic SQL holds within it great power and, at the same time, great risk. By using dynamic SQL wisely, you can get great performance benefits and flexible solutions. Using it unwisely often leads to lengthy, inefficient code that is open to attacks that can cause damage in your system.

For more information about many of the subjects discussed in this chapter including dynamic SQL in general, dynamic search conditions, dynamic pivoting, arrays and lists, and others, you can find excellent articles written by SQL Server MVP Erland Sommarskog on his Web site: *http://www.sommarskog.se/*.

Chapter 10
Working with Date and Time

Itzik Ben-Gan

When you need to store facts in your database, often those facts include date- and time-related attributes, such as order date, birth date, update timestamp, and so on. Dealing with date and time data can sometimes be challenging because of language-related issues, tricky querying logic, and other reasons.

This chapter focuses on working with date and time data. I'll describe the date and time data types supported by SQL Server 2008, most of which are new. I'll discuss built-in functions that operate on date and time data, and different aspects of date and time manipulation. I'll also go over a few querying problems related to date and time data.

I'd like to thank several people from whom I originally learned some of the techniques that I will present in this chapter: Steve Kass, Aaron Bertrand, Peter Larsson, Craig Pessano, and probably others.

Date and Time Data Types

SQL Server 2008 supports six data types designed specifically to store date and time data: DATETIME, SMALLDATETIME, DATE, TIME, DATETIME2, and DATETIMEOFFSET. The last four were introduced in SQL Server 2008. Table 10-1 provides information about the six data types, including their storage requirements, supported date range, precision, and recommended entry format for literals.

TABLE 10-1 Date and Time Data Types

Data Type	Storage (bytes)	Date Range	Precision	Recommended Entry Format and Example
DATETIME	8	January 1, 1753 through December 31, 9999	3 1/3 milliseconds	'YYYYMMDD hh:mm:ss.nnn' '20090212 12:30:15.123'
SMALLDATETIME	4	January 1, 1900 through June 6, 2079	1 minute	'YYYYMMDD hh:mm' '20090212 12:30'
DATE	3	January 1, 0001 through December 31, 9999	1 day	'YYYYMMDD' '20090212'

Data Type	Storage (bytes)	Date Range	Precision	Recommended Entry Format and Example
TIME(*p*)	3 to 5		100 nanoseconds	'hh:mm:ss.nnnnnnn' '12:30:15.1234567'
DATETIME2(*p*)	6 to 8	January 1, 0001 through December 31, 9999	100 nanoseconds	'YYYY-MM-DD hh:mm:ss.nnnnnnn' '2009-02-12 12:30:15.1234567'
DATETIMEOFFSET(*p*)	8 to 10	January 1, 0001 through December 31, 9999	100 nanoseconds	'YYYY-MM-DD hh:mm:ss.nnnnnnn [+|-]hh:mm' '2009-02-12 12:30:15.1234567 +02:00'

Typically it is recommended that you use the smallest type that serves your needs because this means less storage, which in turn usually means faster queries. For example, prior to SQL Server 2008, your default choice should be SMALLDATETIME, as long as it covers the range of dates and the accuracy that you need to support. You should only consider the DATETIME data type if SMALLDATETIME doesn't meet these requirements. In SQL Server 2008, observe that the types TIME(*p*), DATETIME2(*p*), and DATETIMEOFFSET(*p*) have varying storage sizes. This is because these types allow you to define a fractional second precision (*p*) as an integer in the range 0 through 7, with 0 representing a whole second, and 7 (the default if *p* is not specified) representing 100 nanoseconds. The difference in terms of storage requirements between the two extreme precisions is three bytes. If you don't really need 100-nanosecond precision, why pay for the extra storage? For example, if you need one-millisecond precision, specify 3 as the fractional second precision—that is, DATETIME2(3); if you need one-second precision, specify 0 in the parentheses.

SQL Server 2008 introduces several significant improvements with the new date and time data types. As you can see in Table 10-1, the earliest date supported by the older DATETIME data type is January 1, 1753, whereas the new types that contain a date component (DATE, DATETIME2, DATETIMEOFFSET) support dates starting with January 1 of the year 1.

> **Note** SQL Server uses the proleptic Gregorian calendar to extend support for dates that precede those that are supported by the Gregorian calendar, which was introduced in 1583. For details see *http://en.wikipedia.org/wiki/Proleptic_Gregorian_calendar.*

You might wonder why the earliest date supported by the DATETIME data type is January 1, 1753—technically, the data type could support earlier dates. This limitation is related to the shift from the Julian to Gregorian calendar. For details, see the sidebar "Why Is 1753 the Earliest Date for DATETIME?"

Why Is 1753 the Earliest Date for DATETIME?

By Tibor Karaszi, SQL Server MVP

Good question. There are historical reasons for this limitation. In what we sometimes refer to as the "Western world," two calendars have been used in modern times: the Julian calendar and the Gregorian calendar. These calendars were a number of days apart (depending on which century you looked at), so when a culture that used the Julian calendar moved to the Gregorian calendar, it removed between 10 and 13 days. Great Britain made this shift in 1752. (In that year, September 2, 1752, was followed by September 14, 1752.)

An educated guess as to why Sybase SQL Server—the predecessor of Microsoft SQL Server—selected 1753 as the earliest date is that if you were to store a date earlier than 1753, you would also have to know which country was using which calendar and also how to handle this 10- to 13-day jump. So Sybase decided to not allow dates earlier than 1753. Note, too, that other countries made the shift later than 1752. Turkey, for instance, did it in 1927.

Being Swedish, I find it amusing that Sweden had the weirdest implementation. Sweden originally planned to skip every February 29, leap day, over a period of 40 years (from 1700 to 1740) so that Sweden would be in sync with the Gregorian calendar after 1740 (but meanwhile not in sync with anyone else). However, in 1704 and 1708 the leap day wasn't skipped for some reason, so in 1712 (which was a leap year), Sweden inserted yet one more extra day (imagine being born on February 30!) and then made the shift over a day, in 1753, in a similar manner to everyone else.

For more information, refer to "The ultimate guide to the datetime datatypes" published on my Web site at *http://www.karaszi.com/SQLServer/info_datetime.asp*.

In terms of precision, the older DATETIME data type supports a rather peculiar precision of 3 1/3 milliseconds. I'll elaborate on problems that stem from this precision later in the chapter. The new types that have a time component (TIME, DATETIME2, DATETIMEOFFSET) support a precision of 100 nanoseconds.

The new DATE and TIME data types finally provide a separation between date and time. I'll elaborate on the problems stemming from the need to work only with dates or only with times prior to SQL Server 2008 later in the chapter.

SQL Server 2008 introduces support for a time zone component for date and time data in the new data type DATETIMEOFFSET. Unfortunately, however, we don't have built-in support for a daylight savings component yet.

Date and Time Manipulation

Date and time manipulation can be quite challenging. What's the correct way to express date and time literals? How do you identify the weekday of a date in a language-neutral manner? How do you separate date and time prior to SQL Server 2008? The following sections provide some answers to these questions.

Date and Time Functions

The list of date and time functions supported by SQL Server is short, but the functions are handy. These functions perform correct date and time calculations and take into account leap years (to some extent) and other calendar details. Therefore, it's advisable to use them whenever possible and avoid using your own manipulations. SQL Server 2008 introduces several new functions related to date and time data, and it provides enhancements to the existing date and time functions for the new types and the increased precision they provide.

I'll describe the list of functions briefly in the next section, and make use of them in subsequent sections.

Functions Supported Prior to SQL Server 2008

The following date- and time-related functions were supported prior to SQL Server 2008: DATEADD, DATEDIFF, DATEPART, DAY, MONTH, YEAR, DATENAME, GETDATE, CURRENT_ TIMESTAMP, GETUTCDATE, and ISDATE. All are still supported in SQL Server 2008, with enhancements for the new data types.

DATEADD allows you to add a specified number of some date and time unit to a given date and time value. For example, the expression *DATEADD(month, 1, '20090725')* adds one month to July 25, 2009. Subtraction is achieved by adding a negative number of units.

> **Note** The DATETIME and SMALLDATETIME data types support using the plus (+) and minus (–) operators with an integer to add or subtract a number of days as an alternative to using the DATEADD function. For example, *DATEADD(day, 1, dt)* is equivalent to *dt + 1*. It is probably a bad practice to rely on this alternative because it makes the code less clear. Also, none of the new data types introduced in SQL Server 2008 supports this option.

DATEDIFF calculates the difference in a specified date part between two date and time values. For example, the expression *DATEDIFF(month, '20090725', '20090825')* calculates the difference in months between July 25, 2009 and August 25, 2009.

> **Caution** The DATEDIFF function doesn't take into consideration higher levels of granularity than the specified date part; rather, it takes into consideration only lower ones. For example, when you calculate the following difference in years between two very close values, you get *1: DATEDIFF(year, '20091231', '20100101')*. DATEDIFF ignores those part of the values that have a higher level of granularity than year. (That is, it ignores the month, day, hour, and so on.)

Using DATEPART, you can extract a specified date and time part from a date and time value, and it gives an integer result. For example, the expression *DATEPART(hour, '20090118 14:39:05.370')* extracts the hour portion of the input DATETIME value. The YEAR, MONTH, and DAY functions are abbreviations of the DATEPART function that return the year, month, and day of the month, respectively. DATENAME is similar to DATEPART, but it returns the name of the date part (or the numeral if there is no name) as a character string. For example, the expression *DATENAME(weekday, '20090118 14:39:05.370')* returns the weekday name of the input DATETIME value.

Note that some of the results that you get from expressions involving DATETIME functions are language-dependent. For example, the expression *DATENAME(weekday, '20090118 14:39:05.370')* will return 'Sunday' if the session's language is set to us_english, and 'domenica' if it is set to Italian.

GETDATE gives you the server's local date and time value, and GETUTCDATE gives you the current Coordinated Universal Time (UTC), which is calculated from the server's local time and time zone settings. The CURRENT_TIMESTAMP function is the ANSI form of GETDATE. The last three functions accept no arguments.

Finally, the ISDATE function accepts a character string as input, and returns 1 if the value can be converted to DATETIME or SMALLDATETIME and 0 if it cannot. For example, the expression *ISDATE('20090229')* returns 0, whereas the expression *ISDATE('20120229')* returns 1. Note that in SQL Server 2008 this function was not enhanced to recognize values that can be converted to one of the new date and time types, but not to one of the older ones—for example, the expression *ISDATE('20100212 10:00:00.1234567')* returns 0 even though the value can be converted to DATETIME2.

Functions Introduced in SQL Server 2008

SQL Server 2008 introduces the following new functions to support the new date- and time-related data types: SYSDATETIME, SYSUTCDATETIME, SYSDATETIMEOFFSET, SWITCHOFFSET, and TODATETIMEOFFSET.

The first three functions return the current system's date and time value. The SYSDATETIME function returns the system's local time as a DATETIME2 value. The SYSUTCDATETIME returns the system's UTC time as a DATETIME2 value. The SYSDATETIMEOFFSET function returns the system's local time as a DATETIMEOFFSET value that also includes a time zone component. Note that SQL Server 2008 doesn't provide built-in functions for the current date and current time as DATE and TIME values separately. Instead, simply cast SYSDATETIME to DATE or TIME, like so:

```
SELECT
  CAST(SYSDATETIME() AS DATE) AS [current_date],
  CAST(SYSDATETIME() AS TIME) AS [current_time];
```

Existing functions that require a datepart parameter have been enhanced to accept the following new parts: microsecond, nanosecond, TZoffset, and ISO_WEEK.

The SWITCHOFFSET function accepts a DATETIMEOFFSET value and a target time zone as input, and adjusts the input value to the target time zone. For example, the following code switches the time zone of a DATETIMEOFFSET value from Eastern Standard Time (UTC -05:00) to Pacific Standard Time (UTC -08:00):

```
DECLARE @dto AS DATETIMEOFFSET = '2009-02-12 12:30:15.1234567 -05:00';
SELECT SWITCHOFFSET(@dto, '-08:00');
```

Because the target time zone is three hours behind the source time zone, the function subtracts three hours from the source local time, returning the value '2009-02-12 09:30:15. 1234567 -08:00' as output.

When used with DATETIMEOFFSET inputs, the DATEDIFF function returns the difference between the UTC times represented by the inputs. If you're not aware of this behavior and therefore don't expect it, the result might be surprising. For example, consider the following code:

```
SELECT
  DATEDIFF(day,
    '2009-02-12 12:00:00.0000000 -05:00',
    '2009-02-12 22:00:00.0000000 -05:00') AS days;
```

Both values are on the same date locally, but the UTC times they represent fall on different dates. You can see this by switching the offsets of both values to UTC explicitly:

```
SELECT
  SWITCHOFFSET('2009-02-12 12:00:00.0000000 -05:00', '+00:00') AS val1,
  SWITCHOFFSET('2009-02-12 22:00:00.0000000 -05:00', '+00:00') AS val2;
```

This generates the following output:

```
val1                               val2
---------------------------------  ---------------------------------
2009-02-12 17:00:00.0000000 +00:00 2009-02-13 03:00:00.0000000 +00:00
```

Those who assume that DATEDIFF performs the calculation locally will be surprised to get the output 1 and not 0 from the aforementioned DATEDIFF expression.

The TODATETIMEOFFSET function accepts as inputs a DATETIME2 value (or one that can be implicitly converted to DATETIME2), and a target time zone. The function returns the local date and time with no adjustments as a DATETIMEOFFSET value in the target time zone. For example, the following code converts a DATETIME2 value to a DATETIMEOFFSET value in Pacific Standard Time:

```
DECLARE @dt2 AS DATETIME2 = '2009-02-12 12:30:15.1234567';
SELECT TODATETIMEOFFSET(@dt2, '-08:00');
```

This code generates the output: '2009-02-12 12:30:15.1234567 -08:00'.

Besides adding completely new functions, SQL Server 2008 provides enhancements to the existing date and time functions for the new types and the new date and time parts. The new supported parts are microsecond, nanosecond, TZoffset, and ISO_WEEK. The first three are self-explanatory. The last is interesting if you need to support the ISO week-numbering system. In SQL Server 2008, you simply specify the ISO_WEEK part in the DATEPART function to return the ISO week number of a given date. Prior to SQL Server 2008, you had to create your own solution. I'll first explain what the ISO week-numbering system is and demonstrate how you calculate it prior to SQL Server 2008. Then I'll demonstrate how easy it is to calculate in SQL Server 2008.

The ISO week is a week-numbering standard by which a week number is not broken if the week spans two years. Week 1 of year Y is the week (Monday through Sunday) containing January 4 of year Y. To implement the ISO week-numbering standard, you need to consider two special cases: when up to three days in January are part of the previous year's final week, and when up to three days in December are part of the following year's first week. One might argue that it's just as annoying to have the week number of January 1 be 53, or of December 30 to be 1 as the alternative. But it should be stressed that the ISO standard is a widely used international standard.

Run the following code to create the pre-2008 *ISOweek* function implementation, which appears in SQL Server Books Online:

```
IF OBJECT_ID (N'dbo.ISOweek', N'FN') IS NOT NULL
    DROP FUNCTION dbo.ISOweek;
GO
CREATE FUNCTION dbo.ISOweek (@DATE DATETIME)
RETURNS int
WITH EXECUTE AS CALLER
AS
BEGIN
    DECLARE @ISOweek int
    SET @ISOweek= DATEPART(wk,@DATE)+1
        -DATEPART(wk,CAST(DATEPART(yy,@DATE) as CHAR(4))+'0104')
--Special case: Jan 1-3 might belong to the previous year
    IF (@ISOweek=0)
        SET @ISOweek=dbo.ISOweek(CAST(DATEPART(yy,@DATE)-1
            AS CHAR(4))+'12'+ CAST(24+DATEPART(DAY,@DATE) AS CHAR(2)))+1
--Special case: Dec 29-31 might belong to the next year
    IF ((DATEPART(mm,@DATE)=12) AND
        ((DATEPART(dd,@DATE)-DATEPART(dw,@DATE))>= 28))
        SET @ISOweek=1
    RETURN(@ISOweek)
END;
GO
```

Note that you need to set DATEFIRST to 1 before invoking the function. To test the function, run the following code, which invokes it against dates at the beginning and end of a year:

```
DECLARE @DF AS INT;
SET @DF = @@DATEFIRST;
SET DATEFIRST 1;
```

```
WITH Dates AS
(
  SELECT CAST('20091227' AS DATETIME) AS dt
  UNION ALL SELECT '20091228'
  UNION ALL SELECT '20091229'
  UNION ALL SELECT '20091230'
  UNION ALL SELECT '20091231'
  UNION ALL SELECT '20100101'
  UNION ALL SELECT '20100102'
  UNION ALL SELECT '20100103'
  UNION ALL SELECT '20100104'
  UNION ALL SELECT '20100105'
  UNION ALL SELECT '20100106'
  UNION ALL SELECT '20100107'
  UNION ALL SELECT '20100108'
  UNION ALL SELECT '20100109'
  UNION ALL SELECT '20100110'
  UNION ALL SELECT '20100111'
)
SELECT dt, dbo.ISOweek(dt) AS wk, DATENAME(weekday, dt) AS wd
FROM Dates;

SET DATEFIRST @DF;
```

This generates the following output:

```
dt                      wk          wd
----------------------- ----------- -----------
2009-12-27 00:00:00.000 52          Sunday
2009-12-28 00:00:00.000 53          Monday
2009-12-29 00:00:00.000 53          Tuesday
2009-12-30 00:00:00.000 53          Wednesday
2009-12-31 00:00:00.000 53          Thursday
2010-01-01 00:00:00.000 53          Friday
2010-01-02 00:00:00.000 53          Saturday
2010-01-03 00:00:00.000 53          Sunday
2010-01-04 00:00:00.000 1           Monday
2010-01-05 00:00:00.000 1           Tuesday
2010-01-06 00:00:00.000 1           Wednesday
2010-01-07 00:00:00.000 1           Thursday
2010-01-08 00:00:00.000 1           Friday
2010-01-09 00:00:00.000 1           Saturday
2010-01-10 00:00:00.000 1           Sunday
2010-01-11 00:00:00.000 2           Monday
```

As mentioned, in SQL Server 2008 you simply use the DATEPART function with the ISO_WEEK part, like so:

```
WITH Dates AS
(
  SELECT CAST(dt AS DATE) AS dt
  FROM ( VALUES
          ('20091227'),
          ('20091228'),
          ('20091229'),
```

```
                    ('20091230'),
                    ('20091231'),
                    ('20100101'),
                    ('20100102'),
                    ('20100103'),
                    ('20100104'),
                    ('20100105'),
                    ('20100106'),
                    ('20100107'),
                    ('20100108'),
                    ('20100109'),
                    ('20100110'),
                    ('20100111')   ) AS D(dt)
)
SELECT dt, DATEPART(ISO_WEEK, dt) AS wk, DATENAME(weekday, dt) AS wd
FROM Dates;
```

Literals

Expressing date and time literals for data entry in T-SQL is a tricky business. When you need to express a literal, you typically use a character string that is implicitly convertible to the target type. If a string appears in a context where a date and time type is expected—for example, as the target value of a date and time column in an INSERT or UPDATE statement—it will be implicitly converted to the target type. Also, when expressions contain operands with different data types, normally the highest in precedence determines the data type of all operands. Date and time types have higher precedence than character strings. For example, if you compare two values—one of which is of a date and time type and the other is of a character string type—the character string gets implicitly converted to the date and time type.

To add to the confusion, there are various conventions for expressing date and time values. The value '02/12/10' means different things to different people. When this string must be converted to a date and time type, SQL Server will convert it based on the language settings of the session. The session's language is determined by the login's default language, but it can be overwritten by using the SET LANGUAGE session option. You can also control how date and time literals comprising digits and separators are interpreted by using the SET DATEFORMAT option, specifying a combination of the characters d, m, and y. For example, *mdy* means month, day, year. (By the way, SET LANGUAGE implicitly sets DATEFORMAT to match the language's convention for date formatting.)

So you have tools to control the way some date and time literals will be interpreted, but you realize that by issuing one of the aforementioned SET options, you're changing the behavior of the whole session. What if other code that will end up running in your session is supposed to be dependent on the login's default language? This consideration is especially important with international applications.

Whenever possible, I write code that is independent of any settings or switches in the system. Each of the date and time types supports several forms of language-neutral character string literals. This means that when you convert the literal character string to the target date and time type, SQL Server interprets the value the same way regardless of the effective language or DATEFORMAT setting. Table 10-2 provides the language-neutral forms supported by each of the date and time types. I strongly recommend sticking to those to avoid ambiguity.

TABLE 10-2 Date and Time Data Type Formats

Data Type	Language-Neutral Formats	Examples
DATETIME	'YYYYMMDD hh:mm:ss.nnn'	'20090212 12:30:15.123'
	'YYYY-MM-DDThh:mm:ss.nnn'	'2009-02-12T12:30:15.123'
	'YYYYMMDD'	'20090212'
SMALLDATETIME	'YYYYMMDD hh:mm'	'20090212 12:30'
	'YYYY-MM-DDThh:mm'	'2009-02-12T12:30'
	'YYYYMMDD'	'20090212'
DATE	'YYYYMMDD'	'20090212'
	'YYYY-MM-DD'	'2009-02-12'
DATETIME2	'YYYYMMDD hh:mm:ss.nnnnnnn'	'20090212 12:30:15.1234567'
	'YYYY-MM-DD hh:mm:ss.nnnnnnn'	'2009-02-12 12:30:15.1234567'
	'YYYY-MM-DDThh:mm:ss.nnnnnnn'	'2009-02-12T12:30:15.1234567'
	'YYYYMMDD'	'20090212'
	'YYYY-MM-DD'	'2009-02-12'
DATETIMEOFFSET	'YYYYMMDD hh:mm:ss.nnnnnnn [+|-]hh:mm'	'20090212 12:30:15.1234567 +02:00'
	'YYYY-MM-DD hh:mm:ss.nnnnnnn [+|-]hh:mm'	'2009-02-12 12:30:15.1234567 +02:00'
	'YYYY-MM-DDThh:mm:ss.nnnnnnn'	'2009-02-12T12:30:15.1234567'
	'YYYYMMDD'	'20090212'
	'YYYY-MM-DD'	'2009-02-12'

Important You should be extra careful with the form 'YYYY-MM-DD', which is considered an ISO standard. In SQL Server this form is language-dependent for the types DATETIME and SMALLDATETIME, and language-neutral only for the new types DATE, DATETIME2, and DATETIMEOFFSET. For example, suppose you convert the value '2010-02-12' to DATETIME or SMALLDATETIME. If your environment has an effective DATEFORMAT setting of *mdy* (for example, because the language is set to us_english), the value will be interpreted as February 12, 2010. In an environment with an effective DATEFORMAT of dmy (for example, because the language is set to British), the value will be interpreted as December 2, 2010. Make sure that you strictly stick to the forms provided in Table 10-2.

Another technique you can use to specify date and time values is to explicitly convert the character string to the target type using the T-SQL function CONVERT, specifying the optional style parameter in the function call. For example, if you want to use the British/French style with two digits for the year, specify style 3: CONVERT(DATE, '12/02/10', 3). For the full list of supported styles, please refer to SQL Server Books Online, under the subject "CONVERT function."

At some point, you may see a date or time literal such as {d '2010-02-12'}. This is an ODBC format that can be used in some APIs. I wouldn't recommend using such literals because even though they are independent of settings, they are API-dependent.

Identifying Weekday

Identifying the weekday of a given date is a much trickier problem than it might seem. Say, for example, that you are asked to return all orders from the Sales.Orders table in the InsideTSQL2008 database that were placed on a Tuesday. The DATEPART function using the weekday unit allows you to extract the weekday number (1 through 7) of a given DATETIME value. However, the weekday number that you get for a given DATETIME value will vary depending on the setting of the session option DATEFIRST, which determines the first day of the week. If you set it to 1, you instruct SQL Server to consider Monday as the first day of the week, in which case you will filter orders with the weekday 2 for Tuesday. Setting DATEFIRST to 2 means that Tuesday will be considered the first day of the week, and so on.

If the DATEFIRST session option is not set explicitly, the session will set it implicitly based on your language settings. This is yet another example where you might not want to change a setting lest you affect other code in your session that depends on the current setting. Using DATENAME to identify a certain weekday as an alternative does not solve the problem because the weekday names can also vary based on your language settings. In short, you should look for an independent way to identify a weekday—one that is not based on settings or switches in the system.

The solution lies in logic. Think of the relationship between some value f (the DATEFIRST value) and the weekday number you will get back from the DATEPART function for a given DATETIME value d. The two values have an inverse relationship. That is, if you increase f by n, d is decreased by n. For example, suppose you set the DATEFIRST value to 1, meaning that Monday is the first day of the week. Given a date that falls on a Tuesday, you will get 2 as the weekday number back from the DATEPART function. Now, increase the value of DATEFIRST by 1, setting it to 2, meaning that Tuesday is now the first day of the week. Now the weekday number that you get back from the DATEPART function will be decreased by 1—namely, you will get 1 back. Keep in mind that the system of weekday numbers is cyclic, which will add a bit of complexity to the inverse relationship calculations. An entire branch of mathematics deals only with cyclic number systems. For example, here are a few calculations based on the weekday number system:

1 + 1 = 2; 7 + 1 = 1; 7 − 1 = 6; 1 − 1 = 7

Note that you have access to the session's effective DATEFIRST value through the @@DATEFIRST function. Bearing this in mind, and the inverse relationship between the DATEFIRST setting and the weekday number you get back from the DATEPART function, here's what you can do: Add @@DATEFIRST days to the given DATETIME value. This way, you neutralize the effect of the DATEFIRST setting. For example, take the date '20130212', which happens to fall on Tuesday. Check the result of the expression after setting DATEFIRST to any value you want:

```
SELECT DATEPART(weekday, DATEADD(day, @@DATEFIRST, '20130212'));
```

You will always get 3, as if you set DATEFIRST to 7. If you want to "logically" set DATEFIRST to 1, simply subtract the constant 1 from the date:

```
SELECT DATEPART(weekday, DATEADD(day, @@DATEFIRST - 1, '20130212'));
```

If you do this, you will always get 2 for a Tuesday regardless of the DATEFIRST setting. To generalize the formula, you can get an independent weekday number for a given date and time value *dt*, as if DATEFIRST was logically set to *n*, by using the following expression:

```
DATEPART(weekday, DATEADD(day, @@DATEFIRST - n, dt))
```

Now we'll deal with the original request. To get all orders placed on a Tuesday, use the following query:

```
USE InsideTSQL2008;

SELECT orderid, orderdate,
  DATENAME(weekday, orderdate) AS weekdayname
FROM Sales.Orders
WHERE DATEPART(weekday, DATEADD(day, @@DATEFIRST - 1, orderdate)) = 2;
```

This generates the following output, shown here in abbreviated form:

```
orderid      orderdate                weekdayname
-----------  -----------------------  -----------------------------
10248        2006-07-04 00:00:00.000  Tuesday
10254        2006-07-11 00:00:00.000  Tuesday
10259        2006-07-18 00:00:00.000  Tuesday
10265        2006-07-25 00:00:00.000  Tuesday
10270        2006-08-01 00:00:00.000  Tuesday
10271        2006-08-01 00:00:00.000  Tuesday
10276        2006-08-08 00:00:00.000  Tuesday
10282        2006-08-15 00:00:00.000  Tuesday
10287        2006-08-22 00:00:00.000  Tuesday
10293        2006-08-29 00:00:00.000  Tuesday
...

(172 row(s) affected)
```

The ability to calculate an independent weekday can come in handy when dealing with other problems that involve controlling which day of the week is considered first without changing the session's DATEFIRST setting.

The question "which orders were placed on a Tuesday?" can be answered with another easy-to-generalize idea. A date is a Tuesday means that the number of days between that date and another Tuesday is divisible by 7. For this kind of problem, a reference date is a valuable and general idea. It is handy to remember that January 1, 1900, was a Monday. Bearing this in mind, to return orders that were placed on a Tuesday, filter the rows where the difference in days between a reference date that is a Tuesday (such as January 2, 1900) and the *orderdate* modulo 7 is equal to zero, like so:

```
SELECT orderid, orderdate,
  DATENAME(weekday, orderdate) AS weekdayname
FROM Sales.Orders
WHERE DATEDIFF(day, '19000102', orderdate) % 7 = 0;
```

To get a weekday number for a date and time value *dt* where you logically set the first day of the week to *n* (1 = Monday, 2 = Tuesday, and so on), use the following expression:

```
DATEDIFF(day, '1900010n', dt) % 7 + 1
```

For example, to get the current date's weekday number with the logical first day of the week set to Sunday (7), use the following expression:

```
SELECT DATEDIFF(day, '19000107', SYSDATETIME()) % 7 + 1;
```

To get the current date's weekday number with the logical first day of the week set to Monday (1), use the following expression:

```
SELECT DATEDIFF(day, '19000101', SYSDATETIME()) % 7 + 1;
```

Handling Date-only or Time-only Data Prior to SQL Server 2008

SQL Server 2008 introduces separate DATE and TIME data types for the first time. Previous versions of SQL Server only supported combined date and time types. You had to make do with the whole date plus time package, even when you needed to represent only a date or only a time. This section is dedicated to handling only dates or only times prior to SQL Server 2008.

When you need to specify only dates, you omit the time portion. When converted to a date and time type (DATETIME or SMALLDATETIME prior to SQL Server 2008), such a value will still contain a time portion, but it will represent midnight. Similarly, when a character string with only a time portion is converted in a T-SQL statement to a date and time type, SQL Server will set the date part to its base date of January 1, 1900.

If you care only about the date or only about the time, when writing T-SQL code, specify only the part you care about and allow SQL Server to assume the defaults I mentioned earlier. This will simplify manipulation of those values. For example, suppose that you want to create a DEFAULT constraint that stores the current date in a column named *dt*. If you simply use the

CURRENT_TIMESTAMP function as *dt*'s default, you will need to use range filters when looking for a particular date. Instead of using CURRENT_TIMESTAMP as the default, use an expression that sets the time part to midnight. One way to handle this task is to use the following expression:

```
CAST(CONVERT(CHAR(8), CURRENT_TIMESTAMP, 112) AS DATETIME)
```

The expression first converts the current date and time to a character string in the form 'YYYYMMDD' without the time part. When the resulting character string is converted back to DATETIME, SQL Server interprets the time to be midnight.

Similar to the last expression, use style 114 to extract only the time portion of CURRENT_TIMESTAMP, like so:

```
CAST(CONVERT(CHAR(12), CURRENT_TIMESTAMP, 114) AS DATETIME)
```

When converted back to DATETIME, SQL Server will assume the base date January 1, 1900, by default.

There are more efficient methods to set the time part to midnight or the date part to the base date using integer-based offset calculations. To set the time part to midnight, use the following expression:

```
DATEADD(day, DATEDIFF(day, '19000101', CURRENT_TIMESTAMP), '19000101')
```

The DATEDIFF function calculates the difference in terms of whole days between an anchor date at midnight and the current date and time value. Call that difference *diff*. If you add *diff* days to the anchor date, you will get the current date at midnight.

To set the date part to the base date of January 1, 1900, use the following expression:

```
DATEADD(day, DATEDIFF(day, CURRENT_TIMESTAMP, '19000101'), CURRENT_TIMESTAMP)
```

The DATEDIFF function calculates the difference in terms of whole days between the current date and time value and the base date, January 1, 1900. You will get a negative value back. Call that value *diff*. If you add *diff* days to the current date and time value, you will get the current time on the base date, January 1, 1900.

In SQL Server 2008 you don't need all these tricky manipulations. If you need only the date part of a given date and time value, simply cast the value to DATE—CAST(SYSDATETIME() AS DATE). If you need only the time part, cast the value to TIME—CAST(SYSDATETIME() AS TIME).

Examples of Date and Time Calculations

This section covers calculations such as finding the date of the first or last day in a period, the date of the last or next occurrence of a certain weekday, and so on. All calculations that I'll cover are with respect to some given date and time value. I'll use the SYSDATETIME function as the given value, but you can change SYSDATETIME to any date and time value.

First or Last Day of a Period

This section covers calculations of the first and last date in a period such as the month or year with respect to some given reference date and time value.

Earlier I provided the following expression to set the time part of a given date and time value to midnight:

```
SELECT DATEADD(day, DATEDIFF(day, '19000101', CURRENT_TIMESTAMP), '19000101');
```

You can use very similar logic to calculate the date of the first day of the month. You need to make sure that you use an anchor date that is a first day of a month, and use the *month* part instead of the *day* part, like so:

```
SELECT DATEADD(month, DATEDIFF(month, '19000101', SYSDATETIME()), '19000101');
```

This expression calculates the difference in terms of whole months between some first day of a month and the reference date. Call that difference *diff*. The expression then adds *diff* months to the anchor date, producing the date of the first day of the month corresponding to the given reference date. To return the date of the last day of the month, simply use an anchor date that is an end of a month, like so:

```
SELECT DATEADD(month, DATEDIFF(month, '18991231', SYSDATETIME()), '18991231');
```

Note that it's important to use an anchor date that is a 31st of some month, such as December, so that if the target month has 31 days the calculation works correctly.

To calculate the date of the first day of the year, use an anchor that is a first day of some year, and specify the year part, like so:

```
SELECT DATEADD(year, DATEDIFF(year, '19000101', SYSDATETIME()), '19000101');
```

To calculate the date of the last day of the year, use an anchor date that is the last day of some year:

```
SELECT DATEADD(year, DATEDIFF(year, '18991231', SYSDATETIME()), '18991231');
```

Previous or Next Weekday

This section covers calculations that return a next or previous weekday with respect to a given date and time value. I use the word *respective* to describe this sort of calculation.

Suppose that you need to calculate the latest Monday before or on a given reference date and time. The calculation needs to be *inclusive* of the reference date; that is, if the reference date is a Monday, return the reference date; otherwise, return the latest Monday before the reference date. You can use the following expression to achieve this:

```
SELECT DATEADD(
        day,
        DATEDIFF(
          day,
          '19000101', -- Base Monday date
          SYSDATETIME()) /7*7,
        '19000101'); -- Base Monday date
```

The expression calculates the difference in terms of days between some anchor date that is a Monday and the reference date. Call that difference *diff*.

> **Tip** It's convenient to use dates in the range January 1, 1900, and January 7, 1900, as anchor dates because they represent the weekdays Monday through Sunday, respectively. The day parts of the suggested anchor dates (1 through 7) are aligned with the integers used in SQL Server to represent the first day of the week; therefore, it's easy to remember which day of the week each date in the range represents.

The expression then rounds the value down to the nearest multiple of 7 by dividing *diff* by 7 using integer division, then multiplying it by 7. Call the result *floor_diff*. Note that the calculation of *floor_diff* will work correctly only when the result of DATEDIFF is nonnegative. So make sure you use an anchor date that is earlier than the reference date. The expression then adds *floor_diff* days to the anchor date, producing the latest occurrence of a Monday, inclusive. Remember that in *inclusive* I mean that if the reference date is a Monday, the calculation is supposed to return the reference date.

Here's the expression formatted in one line of code:

```
SELECT DATEADD(day, DATEDIFF(day, '19000101', SYSDATETIME()) /7*7, '19000101');
```

Similarly, to return the date of the last Tuesday, use an anchor date that is a Tuesday:

```
SELECT DATEADD(day, DATEDIFF(day, '19000102', SYSDATETIME()) /7*7, '19000102');
```

And to return the date of the last Sunday, use an anchor date that is a Sunday:

```
SELECT DATEADD(day, DATEDIFF(day, '19000107', SYSDATETIME()) /7*7, '19000107');
```

To make the calculation exclusive of the reference date—meaning that you're after the last occurrence of a weekday before the reference date (as opposed to on or before)—simply subtract a day from the reference date. For example, the following expression returns the date of the last occurrence of a Monday before the reference date:

```
SELECT DATEADD(day, DATEDIFF(day, '19000101', DATEADD(day, -1, SYSDATETIME())) /7*7,
        '19000101');
```

To return the next occurrence of a weekday in an inclusive manner (on or after the reference date), subtract a day from the reference date, and add 7 days to *floor_diff*. For example, the following expression returns the next occurrence of a Monday on or after the reference date:

```
SELECT DATEADD(day, DATEDIFF(day, '19000101', DATEADD(day, -1, SYSDATETIME())) /7*7 + 7,
    '19000101');
```

Like before, replace the anchor date if you need to handle a different weekday. For example, Tuesday:

```
SELECT DATEADD(day, DATEDIFF(day, '19000102', DATEADD(day, -1, SYSDATETIME())) /7*7 + 7,
    '19000102');
```

Or Sunday:

```
SELECT DATEADD(day, DATEDIFF(day, '19000107', DATEADD(day, -1, SYSDATETIME())) /7*7 + 7,
    '19000107');
```

To make the calculation exclusive, meaning the next occurrence of a weekday after the reference date (as opposed to on or after), simply skip the step of subtracting a day from the anchor date. For example, the following expression returns the next occurrence of a Monday after the reference date:

```
SELECT DATEADD(day, DATEDIFF(day, '19000101', SYSDATETIME()) /7*7 + 7, '19000101');
```

Next occurrence of a Tuesday, exclusive:

```
SELECT DATEADD(day, DATEDIFF(day, '19000102', SYSDATETIME()) /7*7 + 7, '19000102');
```

Next occurrence of a Sunday, exclusive:

```
SELECT DATEADD(day, DATEDIFF(day, '19000107', SYSDATETIME()) /7*7 + 7, '19000107');
```

First or Last Weekday

In this section, I'll describe calculations that return the first and last occurrences of a certain weekday in a period such as a month or year. To calculate the first occurrence of a certain weekday in a month you need to combine two types of calculations that I described earlier. One is the calculation of the first day of the month:

```
SELECT DATEADD(month, DATEDIFF(month, '19000101', SYSDATETIME()), '19000101');
```

The other is the calculation of the next occurrence of a weekday, inclusive—Monday in this example:

```
SELECT DATEADD(day, DATEDIFF(day, '19000101', DATEADD(day, -1, SYSDATETIME())) /7*7 + 7,
    '19000101');
```

The trick is to simply use the first day of the month calculation as the reference date within the next weekday occurrence calculation. For example, the following expression returns the first occurrence of a Monday in the reference month:

```
SELECT DATEADD(day, DATEDIFF(day, '19000101',
  -- first day of month
  DATEADD(month, DATEDIFF(month, '19000101', SYSDATETIME()), '19000101')
    -1) /7*7 + 7, '19000101');
```

To handle a different weekday, replace the anchor date in the part of the expression that calculates the next occurrence of a weekday—not in the part that calculates the first month day. The following expression returns the date of the first occurrence of a Tuesday in the reference month:

```
SELECT DATEADD(day, DATEDIFF(day, '19000102',
  -- first day of month
  DATEADD(month, DATEDIFF(month, '19000101', SYSDATETIME()), '19000101')
    -1) /7*7 + 7, '19000102');
```

To calculate the date of the last occurrence of a weekday in the reference month you need to combine two calculations as well. One is the calculation of the last day of the reference month:

```
SELECT DATEADD(month, DATEDIFF(month, '18991231', SYSDATETIME()), '18991231');
```

The other is the calculation of the previous occurrence of a weekday, inclusive—Monday in this example:

```
SELECT DATEADD(day, DATEDIFF(day, '19000101', SYSDATETIME()) /7*7, '19000101');
```

Simply use the last day of the month calculation as the reference date in the last weekday calculation. For example, the following expression returns the last occurrence of a Monday in the reference month:

```
SELECT DATEADD(day, DATEDIFF(day, '19000101',
  -- last day of month
  DATEADD(month, DATEDIFF(month, '18991231', SYSDATETIME()), '18991231')
  ) /7*7, '19000101');
```

To address a different weekday, substitute the anchor date in the last weekday calculation to the applicable one. For example, the following expression returns the last occurrence of a Tuesday in the reference month:

```
SELECT DATEADD(day, DATEDIFF(day, '19000102',
  -- last day of month
  DATEADD(month, DATEDIFF(month, '18991231', SYSDATETIME()), '18991231')
  ) /7*7, '19000102');
```

In a manner very similar to calculating the first and last occurrence of a weekday in the reference month, you can calculate the first and last occurrence of a weekday in the reference year. Simply substitute the first or last month day calculation with the first or last year day calculation. Following are a few examples.

First occurrence of a Monday in the reference year:

```
SELECT DATEADD(day, DATEDIFF(day, '19000101',
  -- first day of year
  DATEADD(year, DATEDIFF(year, '19000101', SYSDATETIME()), '19000101')
    -1) /7*7 + 7, '19000101');
```

First occurrence of a Tuesday in the reference year:

```
SELECT DATEADD(day, DATEDIFF(day, '19000102',
  -- first day of year
  DATEADD(year, DATEDIFF(year, '19000101', SYSDATETIME()), '19000101')
    -1) /7*7 + 7, '19000102');
```

Last occurrence of a Monday in the reference year:

```
SELECT DATEADD(day, DATEDIFF(day, '19000101',
  -- last day of year
  DATEADD(year, DATEDIFF(year, '18991231', SYSDATETIME()), '18991231')
  ) /7*7, '19000101');
```

Last occurrence of a Tuesday in the reference year:

```
SELECT DATEADD(day, DATEDIFF(day, '19000102',
  -- last day of year
  DATEADD(year, DATEDIFF(year, '18991231', SYSDATETIME()), '18991231')
  ) /7*7, '19000102');
```

Rounding Issues

Conversions between date and time values and strings are not always exact. For example, if '20100923 03:23:47.001' is converted to DATETIME, it will be rounded to the nearest three-hundredth of a second, which is a millisecond earlier than the string indicates. Similarly, when converting a string to SMALLDATETIME, DATETIME2, DATETIMEOFFSET, or TIME, the source value gets rounded to the nearest value that can be expressed in the target type. The only exception is the DATE data type. If you convert a string that contains both date and time to DATE, SQL Server simply extracts only the date portion. It doesn't round the value to the next date if it's at or past noon. As another example, if the aforementioned string is converted to SMALLDATETIME, it will be rounded to the nearest minute, almost 13 seconds later than the string indicates. Date- and time-to-string conversions are not always exact, either. When converted to a string format that includes milliseconds, DATETIME values are rounded to the nearest millisecond. Otherwise, time fields not in the destination format will be truncated.

With regard to DATETIME, be aware that values that cannot be represented exactly are rounded to the nearest DATETIME value that can be represented. This behavior is inconsistent with conversions between some other data types (for example, from DECIMAL to INT) where the value is simply truncated. (For example, 10.99 DECIMAL is converted to 10 INT). The milliseconds part of a DATETIME data type will match the pattern [0-9][0-9][037] when displayed to millisecond precision. If, for example, you specify 994 as the milliseconds part of a DATETIME value, the actual value stored will contain 993 ⅓ milliseconds, and it will appear to contain 993 milliseconds when viewed as a character string. The value 996 will be rounded to 997. The value 999 will be rounded to 000 in the next second. This can be especially tricky if you try to specify the last moment of a particular date. If you specify '20080101 23:59:59.999' SQL Server cannot exactly represent the value, and it is rounded to the nearest DATETIME value: '20080102 00:00:00.000'. That's why it's not a good idea to use a filter such as the following when looking for rows where a DATETIME column falls on a particular date:

```
USE InsideTSQL2008;

SELECT orderid, orderdate
FROM Sales.Orders
WHERE orderdate BETWEEN '20080101 00:00:00.000' AND '20080101 23:59:59.999';
```

This generates the following output:

```
orderid     orderdate
----------- ------------------------
10808       2008-01-01 00:00:00.000
10809       2008-01-01 00:00:00.000
10810       2008-01-01 00:00:00.000
10811       2008-01-02 00:00:00.000
10812       2008-01-02 00:00:00.000
```

Rows where *orderdate* is equal to '20080102 00:00:00.000' also qualify. I've seen programmers using 997 as the milliseconds portion in the upper bound, but this works correctly only with the DATETIME data type specifically. What if at some point in the future you alter the column's type to DATETIME2? You'd better use the following predicate, which works correctly with all date and time types, including when a time component is present:

```
SELECT orderid, orderdate
FROM Sales.Orders
WHERE orderdate >= '20080101'
  AND orderdate  < '20080102';
```

This predicate is a Search Argument (SARG), meaning that the optimizer can consider the potential of using an index seek operation. Although you can also write this predicate using a function to extract the date portion, the result is not a SARG, so for better performance, refrain from using a predicate such as the following:

```
SELECT orderid, orderdate
FROM Sales.Orders
WHERE DATEADD(day, DATEDIFF(day, '19000101', orderdate), '19000101') = '20080101';
```

Interestingly, in SQL Server 2008, you can cast a date and time column to DATE, and still be able to rely on index ordering, as in the following query:

```
SELECT orderid, orderdate
FROM Sales.Orders
WHERE CAST(orderdate AS DATE) = '20080101';
```

The execution plan for this query is shown in Figure 10-1.

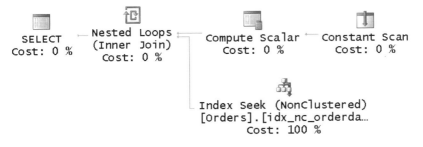

FIGURE 10-1 Execution plan for query with CAST expression

The Constant Scan and Compute Scalar operators calculate the range boundary points that are applicable to the filtered date, and then the plan applies a range filter in the index created on the *orderdate* attribute.

Date- and Time-Related Querying Problems

Now that the fundamentals of date and time have been covered, the next section will explore date- and time-related querying problems.

Age Problems

The first date- and time-related problem is to calculate the next date on which a person's age changes, based on the person's birth date and today's date. The calculation should be inclusive; that is, inclusive of today's date. This problem demonstrates how to correctly handle leap years by using date- and time-related functions. To be more specific, using the HR.Employees table in the InsideTSQL2008 database, your query needs to return the date of each employee's next birthday, as of today's date, based on the stored *birthdate* and SYSDATETIME values. If this year's birthday date has already passed, your query should return the birthday date for next year; otherwise, it should return this year's date.

> **Note** DATEADD and other date and time functions only deal with leap years to the extent that
> they never give results such as February 29, 2010. People still need to make definitions that take
> leap years into account. If the system's default behavior does not meet your needs, you need to
> make the appropriate adjustments to your expressions. The default behavior of DATEADD when
> adding a certain number of years to a date that falls on February 29 is to return a date with
> February 29 if the target year is a leap year, and February 28 if it is a common year. Most people
> born on February 29 in a leap year celebrate their birthdays on March 1 in a non-leap year (also
> for many legal purposes), and that's the approach that we will apply in our solution. For example,
> if today's date is September 26, 2009, someone born on February 29, 1972, should get back from
> your query the next birthday date March 1, 2010. If today's date is September 26, 2011, the query
> should return February 29, 2012.

Before you start working on a solution, run the following code, which adds two employees to
the Employees table:

```
INSERT INTO HR.Employees
  (lastname, firstname, birthdate, title, titleofcourtesy, hiredate,
   address, city, region, postalcode, country, phone, mgrid)
VALUES
  (N'Schaller', N'George', '19720229', N'VP', N'Ms.',
   '20020501 00:00:00.000', N'7890 - 20th Ave. E., Apt. 2A',
   N'Seattle', N'WA', N'10003', N'USA', N'(206) 555-0101', NULL),
  (N'North', N'Mary', CAST(SYSDATETIME() AS DATE), N'VP', N'Dr.',
   '20020814 00:00:00.000', N'9012 W. Capital Way',
   N'Tacoma', N'WA', N'10001', N'USA', N'(206) 555-0100', 1);
```

George Schaller was born on February 29, 1972, and Mary North was born today. Here's the
solution query:

```
WITH Args1 AS
(
  SELECT empid, firstname, lastname, birthdate,
    DATEDIFF(year, birthdate, SYSDATETIME()) AS diff,
    CAST(SYSDATETIME() AS DATE) AS today
  FROM HR.Employees
),
Args2 AS
(
  SELECT empid, firstname, lastname, birthdate, today,
    CAST(DATEADD(year, diff, birthdate) AS DATE) AS bdcur,
    CAST(DATEADD(year, diff + 1, birthdate) AS DATE) AS bdnxt
  FROM Args1
),
Args3 AS
(
  SELECT empid, firstname, lastname, birthdate, today,
    DATEADD(day, CASE WHEN DAY(birthdate) <> DAY(bdcur)
      THEN 1 ELSE 0 END, bdcur) AS bdcur,
    DATEADD(day, CASE WHEN DAY(birthdate) <> DAY(bdnxt)
      THEN 1 ELSE 0 END, bdnxt) AS bdnxt
  FROM Args2
)
```

```
SELECT empid, firstname, lastname, birthdate,
  CASE WHEN bdcur >= today THEN bdcur ELSE bdnxt END AS birthday
FROM Args3;
```

The query defining the CTE Args1 calculates for each employee the difference in years between the birth date and today's date (*diff*), and it also calculates today's date (*today*). If you highlight and run only the query defining the CTE Args1, you get the following output, shown here in abbreviated form, assuming today's date is May 6, 2009:

```
empid  firstname  lastname      birthdate               diff  today
------ ---------- ------------- ----------------------- ----- ----------
1      Sara       Davis         1958-12-08 00:00:00.000 51    2009-05-06
2      Don        Funk          1962-02-19 00:00:00.000 47    2009-05-06
3      Judy       Lew           1973-08-30 00:00:00.000 36    2009-05-06
4      Yael       Peled         1947-09-19 00:00:00.000 62    2009-05-06
5      Sven       Buck          1965-03-04 00:00:00.000 44    2009-05-06
6      Paul       Suurs         1973-07-02 00:00:00.000 36    2009-05-06
7      Russell    King          1970-05-29 00:00:00.000 39    2009-05-06
8      Maria      Cameron       1968-01-09 00:00:00.000 41    2009-05-06
9      Zoya       Dolgopyatova  1976-01-27 00:00:00.000 33    2009-05-06
10     George     Schaller      1972-02-29 00:00:00.000 37    2009-05-06
11     Mary       North         2009-05-06 00:00:00.000 0     2009-05-06
```

To calculate the date of the next birthday for a given employee, you need to add *diff* years to *birthdate*. If the result is less than *today*, you need to add another year. The query defining the CTE Args2 adds to Args1 two attributes called *bdcur* and *bdnxt*, which hold the birthday dates this year and next year, respectively. Note, however, that if *birthdate* falls on February 29, and the target date (*bdcur* or *bdnxt*) is not in a leap year, it will contain February 28 and not March 1. The query defining the CTE Args3 adjusts the dates in *bdcur* and *bdnxt* to March 1 if needed. The outer query returns *bdcur* as the nearest birthday if it is greater than or equal to today's date, and *bdnxt* otherwise. Here's the output of the solution query, again assuming today's date is May 6, 2009:

```
empid  firstname  lastname      birthdate               birthday
------ ---------- ------------- ----------------------- ----------
1      Sara       Davis         1958-12-08 00:00:00.000 2009-12-08
2      Don        Funk          1962-02-19 00:00:00.000 2010-02-19
3      Judy       Lew           1973-08-30 00:00:00.000 2009-08-30
4      Yael       Peled         1947-09-19 00:00:00.000 2009-09-19
5      Sven       Buck          1965-03-04 00:00:00.000 2010-03-04
6      Paul       Suurs         1973-07-02 00:00:00.000 2009-07-02
7      Russell    King          1970-05-29 00:00:00.000 2009-05-29
8      Maria      Cameron       1968-01-09 00:00:00.000 2010-01-09
9      Zoya       Dolgopyatova  1976-01-27 00:00:00.000 2010-01-27
10     George     Schaller      1972-02-29 00:00:00.000 2010-03-01
11     Mary       North         2009-05-06 00:00:00.000 2009-05-06
```

You can see that George Schaller's next birthday will occur next year, on March 1. Mary North's birthday is, not surprisingly, today.

A related problem is to calculate the age of a person on a given date. The following query shows one way to achieve this, demonstrating the technique using the Employees table:

```
DECLARE @targetdate AS DATE = CAST(SYSDATETIME() AS DATE);

SELECT empid, firstname, lastname, birthdate,
  DATEDIFF(year, birthdate, @targetdate)
  - CASE WHEN 100 * MONTH(@targetdate) + DAY(@targetdate)
            < 100 * MONTH(birthdate) + DAY(birthdate)
         THEN 1 ELSE 0
    END AS age
FROM HR.Employees;
```

The expression first calculates the difference in years between the employee's birth date and the target date. Call that difference *diff*. If the month plus day part of the target date is smaller than the month plus date part of the employee's birth date, the calculation subtracts one year from *diff*. Interestingly, this calculation handles leap years correctly. This code generates the following output:

```
empid  firstname  lastname      birthdate                age
------ ---------- ------------- ----------------------- ----
1      Sara       Davis         1958-12-08 00:00:00.000 50
2      Don        Funk          1962-02-19 00:00:00.000 47
3      Judy       Lew           1973-08-30 00:00:00.000 35
4      Yael       Peled         1947-09-19 00:00:00.000 61
5      Sven       Buck          1965-03-04 00:00:00.000 44
6      Paul       Suurs         1973-07-02 00:00:00.000 35
7      Russell    King          1970-05-29 00:00:00.000 38
8      Maria      Cameron       1968-01-09 00:00:00.000 41
9      Zoya       Dolgopyatova  1976-01-27 00:00:00.000 33
10     George     Schaller      1972-02-29 00:00:00.000 37
11     Mary       North         2009-05-06 00:00:00.000 0
```

Another very interesting technique to calculate age is based on integer manipulating, and is surprisingly minimalistic. The idea is to express the target date and the person's birth date as integers in the form YYYYMMDD, calling them *a* and *b*, respectively. Then the age can be simply calculated as $(a - b) / 10000$, using integer division. Here's an example of applying this logic to our Employees table:

```
DECLARE @targetdate AS DATE = CAST(SYSDATETIME() AS DATE);

SELECT empid, firstname, lastname, birthdate,
  (CAST(CONVERT(CHAR(8), @targetdate, 112) AS INT)
   - CAST(CONVERT(CHAR(8), birthdate, 112) AS INT)) / 10000 AS age
FROM HR.Employees;
```

To clean up, delete the two added employees by running the following code:

```
DELETE FROM HR.Employees WHERE empid > 9;
```

Overlaps

Many temporal querying problems require you to identify overlapping periods. Here I'll present a few such problems. In my examples, I'll use the Sessions table, which you create and populate by running the following code:

```
USE tempdb;

IF OBJECT_ID('dbo.Sessions') IS NOT NULL DROP TABLE dbo.Sessions;

CREATE TABLE dbo.Sessions
(
  id        INT          NOT NULL IDENTITY(1, 1),
  username  VARCHAR(10)  NOT NULL,
  starttime DATETIME2     NOT NULL,
  endtime   DATETIME2     NOT NULL,
  CONSTRAINT PK_Sessions PRIMARY KEY(id),
  CONSTRAINT CHK_endtime_gteq_starttime
    CHECK (endtime >= starttime)
);
GO

CREATE INDEX idx_nc_username_st_ed ON dbo.Sessions(username, starttime, endtime);
CREATE INDEX idx_nc_username_ed_st ON dbo.Sessions(username, endtime, starttime);

INSERT INTO dbo.Sessions(username, starttime, endtime) VALUES
  ('User1', '20091201 08:00', '20091201 08:30'),
  ('User1', '20091201 08:30', '20091201 09:00'),
  ('User1', '20091201 09:00', '20091201 09:30'),
  ('User1', '20091201 10:00', '20091201 11:00'),
  ('User1', '20091201 10:30', '20091201 12:00'),
  ('User1', '20091201 11:30', '20091201 12:30'),
  ('User2', '20091201 08:00', '20091201 10:30'),
  ('User2', '20091201 08:30', '20091201 10:00'),
  ('User2', '20091201 09:00', '20091201 09:30'),
  ('User2', '20091201 11:00', '20091201 11:30'),
  ('User2', '20091201 11:32', '20091201 12:00'),
  ('User2', '20091201 12:04', '20091201 12:30'),
  ('User3', '20091201 08:00', '20091201 09:00'),
  ('User3', '20091201 08:00', '20091201 08:30'),
  ('User3', '20091201 08:30', '20091201 09:00'),
  ('User3', '20091201 09:30', '20091201 09:30');
```

The Sessions table tracks user sessions against some application or service. Each row contains a key (*id*), user name (*user*), start time (*starttime*), and end time (*endtime*). The code creates indexes to speed the queries that I'll present in my solutions. I'll discuss two problems involving overlaps: identifying overlaps and grouping overlaps.

Identifying Overlaps

To illustrate how to identify overlaps, I'll suppose that you get a request to identify, for each session, all sessions (including self) with the same user that overlap. That is, per each session (call it S), you need to identify all sessions that were active at any point in time that S was active. You need to join two instances of Sessions (call them *S1* and *S2*) based on the predicate *S2.username = S1.username*, with another logical expression that checks whether the two sessions overlap. Most programmers will probably come up with the following expression, which uses OR logic to express the idea that one session begins during the other:

```
S2.starttime BETWEEN S1.starttime AND S1.endtime
OR S1.starttime BETWEEN S2.starttime AND S2.endtime
```

Here's the full query:

```
SELECT S1.username,
  S1.id AS key1, S1.starttime AS start1, S1.endtime AS end1,
  S2.id AS key2, S2.starttime AS start2, S2.endtime AS end2
FROM dbo.Sessions AS S1
  JOIN dbo.Sessions AS S2
    ON S2.username = S1.username
    AND (S2.starttime BETWEEN S1.starttime AND S1.endtime
        OR S1.starttime BETWEEN S2.starttime AND S2.endtime);
```

This generates the following output (with dates omitted for brevity because all are the same—February 12, 2009):

```
username   key1   start1   end1    key2   start2   end2
--------   ----   -------   ------   ----   -------   -----
User1      1      08:00     08:30   1      08:00    08:30
User1      1      08:00     08:30   2      08:30    09:00
User1      2      08:30     09:00   1      08:00    08:30
User1      2      08:30     09:00   2      08:30    09:00
User1      2      08:30     09:00   3      09:00    09:30
User1      3      09:00     09:30   2      08:30    09:00
User1      3      09:00     09:30   3      09:00    09:30
User1      4      10:00     11:00   4      10:00    11:00
User1      4      10:00     11:00   5      10:30    12:00
User1      5      10:30     12:00   4      10:00    11:00
User1      5      10:30     12:00   5      10:30    12:00
User1      5      10:30     12:00   6      11:30    12:30
User1      6      11:30     12:30   5      10:30    12:00
User1      6      11:30     12:30   6      11:30    12:30
User2      9      09:00     09:30   7      08:00    10:30
User2      9      09:00     09:30   8      08:30    10:00
User2      9      09:00     09:30   9      09:00    09:30
User2      8      08:30     10:00   7      08:00    10:30
User2      8      08:30     10:00   8      08:30    10:00
User2      8      08:30     10:00   9      09:00    09:30
User2      7      08:00     10:30   7      08:00    10:30
User2      7      08:00     10:30   8      08:30    10:00
User2      7      08:00     10:30   9      09:00    09:30
User2      10     11:00     11:30   10     11:00    11:30
User2      11     11:32     12:00   11     11:32    12:00
User2      12     12:04     12:30   12     12:04    12:30
User3      14     08:00     08:30   14     08:00    08:30
User3      14     08:00     08:30   13     08:00    09:00
```

```
User3    14    08:00    08:30    15    08:30    09:00
User3    13    08:00    09:00    14    08:00    08:30
User3    13    08:00    09:00    13    08:00    09:00
User3    13    08:00    09:00    15    08:30    09:00
User3    15    08:30    09:00    14    08:00    08:30
User3    15    08:30    09:00    13    08:00    09:00
User3    15    08:30    09:00    15    08:30    09:00
User3    16    09:30    09:30    16    09:30    09:30
```

Note that you can safely use an inner join here, rather than an outer join; sessions that don't overlap with any other session will still show up because they will get a self match. If you don't want to return self matches, add the expression *S1.id <> S2.id* to the join condition. Just remember that if you make this change, sessions that don't overlap with any other session will not show up—which may very well be desired behavior. If you do want such sessions to show up, make sure that you change the join type to an outer join.

You can perform logical transformation, converting the OR logic in the join condition to AND logic, and produce a shorter expression:

```
S2.endtime >= S1.starttime AND S2.starttime <= S1.endtime
```

If you think about it, for two sessions to overlap, one must end on or after the other starts, and start on or before the other ends. AND logic transformed from OR logic is usually more confusing and tricky than the source. It requires some getting used to. But converting to AND logic might be worthwhile because the optimizer can handle AND logic more efficiently. Here's the full solution query:

```
SELECT S1.username,
  S1.id AS key1, S1.starttime AS start1, S1.endtime AS end1,
  S2.id AS key2, S2.starttime AS start2, S2.endtime AS end2
FROM dbo.Sessions AS S1
  JOIN dbo.Sessions AS S2
    ON S2.username = S1.username
    AND (S2.endtime >= S1.starttime
        AND S2.starttime <= S1.endtime);
```

Grouping Overlaps

The next problem we'll look at requires you to combine, or merge, all overlapping sessions for the same user into one session group, returning the user, start time, and end time of the session group. The purpose of such a request is to determine the amount of time a user was connected, regardless of the number of simultaneous active sessions the user had. The solution to this problem would be especially helpful to service providers that allow multiple sessions at no extra charge.

You might want to tackle the problem in steps: identify starting times of session groups, identify ending times of session groups, and then match each ending time to its corresponding starting time.

To isolate starting times of session groups, you first need to come up with a logical way of identifying them. A start time *S* starts a group if no session (for the same user) starts before *S* and continues until *S* or later. With this definition of a session group start time, if you have multiple identical start times, you will get them all. By applying DISTINCT, you will get only one occurrence of each unique start time. Here's the query that translates this logic to T-SQL:

```
SELECT DISTINCT username, starttime
FROM dbo.Sessions AS O
WHERE NOT EXISTS
  (SELECT * FROM dbo.Sessions AS I
   WHERE I.username = O.username
     AND O.starttime > I.starttime
     AND O.starttime <= I.endtime);
```

This generates the following output:

```
username    starttime
----------  ----------------------
User1       2009-12-01 08:00:00.00
User1       2009-12-01 10:00:00.00
User2       2009-12-01 08:00:00.00
User2       2009-12-01 11:00:00.00
User2       2009-12-01 11:32:00.00
User2       2009-12-01 12:04:00.00
User3       2009-12-01 08:00:00.00
User3       2009-12-01 09:30:00.00
```

To identify end times of session groups, you essentially use the inverse of the previous logic. An end time *E* ends a group if there is no session (for the same user) that had already begun by time *E* but that ends after *E*. Here's the query returning the ending times of session groups:

```
SELECT DISTINCT username, endtime
FROM dbo.Sessions AS O
WHERE NOT EXISTS
  (SELECT * FROM dbo.Sessions AS I
   WHERE I.username = O.username
     AND O.endtime >= I.starttime
     AND O.endtime < I.endtime);
```

This generates the following output:

```
username    endtime
----------  ----------------------
User1       2009-12-01 09:30:00.00
User1       2009-12-01 12:30:00.00
User2       2009-12-01 10:30:00.00
User2       2009-12-01 11:30:00.00
User2       2009-12-01 12:00:00.00
User2       2009-12-01 12:30:00.00
User3       2009-12-01 09:00:00.00
User3       2009-12-01 09:30:00.00
```

Next, you need to match a session group ending time to each session group starting time. You can achieve this by adding a row number calculation to the queries that return start and end times. Then, in the outer query, associate the right end to each start by matching the user name and row number. The row number needs to be partitioned by user name and ordered by start or end time. The tricky part is that the queries that calculate start and end times use a DISTINCT clause. Remember that in terms of logical query processing, a ROW_NUMBER calculation that appears in the SELECT list is evaluated before the DISTINCT clause. But for our purposes, we need the row numbers to be assigned after removal of duplicates. To overcome this problem, use the DENSE_RANK function instead of ROW_NUMBER. Because DISTINCT eliminates duplicates, you will effectively get the row numbers that you need in terms of the result rows.

Here's the complete solution query:

```
WITH StartTimes AS
(
  SELECT DISTINCT username, starttime,
    DENSE_RANK() OVER(PARTITION BY username ORDER BY starttime) AS rownum
  FROM dbo.Sessions AS O
  WHERE NOT EXISTS
    (SELECT * FROM dbo.Sessions AS I
      WHERE I.username = O.username
        AND O.starttime > I.starttime
        AND O.starttime <= I.endtime)
),
EndTimes AS
(
  SELECT DISTINCT username, endtime,
    DENSE_RANK() OVER(PARTITION BY username ORDER BY endtime) AS rownum
  FROM dbo.Sessions AS O
  WHERE NOT EXISTS
    (SELECT * FROM dbo.Sessions AS I
      WHERE I.username = O.username
        AND O.endtime >= I.starttime
        AND O.endtime < I.endtime)
)
SELECT S.username, S.starttime, E.endtime
FROM StartTimes AS S
  JOIN EndTimes AS E
    ON S.username = E.username
    AND S.rownum = E.rownum;
```

This generates the following output:

```
username    starttime                endtime
----------  -----------------------  -----------------------
User1       2009-12-01 08:00:00.00 2009-12-01 09:30:00.00
User1       2009-12-01 10:00:00.00 2009-12-01 12:30:00.00
User2       2009-12-01 08:00:00.00 2009-12-01 10:30:00.00
User2       2009-12-01 11:00:00.00 2009-12-01 11:30:00.00
User2       2009-12-01 11:32:00.00 2009-12-01 12:00:00.00
```

```
User2     2009-12-01 12:04:00.00 2009-12-01 12:30:00.00
User3     2009-12-01 08:00:00.00 2009-12-01 09:00:00.00
User3     2009-12-01 09:30:00.00 2009-12-01 09:30:00.00
```

Grouping by the Week

The problem that I will discuss in this section involves grouping data by the week. I will rely on the techniques I described earlier to calculate an independent weekday.

When you need to aggregate data based on date and time parts, usually the grouping elements can be easily derived from the original date and time value. However, when you need to group data by the week, the task is more challenging. Suppose that you were asked to query the Sales.OrderValues view in the InsideTSQL2008 database, and return the weekly total values and count of orders. You don't need to return weeks without orders. If you use the DATEPART function with the week part, you will get back different week numbers for dates within a week that happens to span two years.

Instead of requesting the week number within the year, you can calculate a grouping factor for each order date. The grouping factor value must be the same for all orders within the same week and different from the value generated for orders placed on other weeks. An example of a grouping factor that fits these criteria is a common day within the input order date's week—for example, the week start date. Given an input order date, to return the start date of the week you simply need to subtract as many days as the input date's weekday number and add one. You can then group the data by the start date of the week, and calculate the requested aggregates. To return the end date of the week, you can add six days to the start date of the week.

Returning to our original problem, here's the complete solution query, relying on the login's definition of the first day of the week based on its language setting:

```
USE InsideTSQL2008;

WITH C AS
(
  SELECT
    DATEADD(day, -DATEPART(weekday, orderdate) + 1, orderdate) AS startweek,
    val
  FROM Sales.OrderValues
)
SELECT
  startweek,
  DATEADD(day, 6, startweek) AS endweek,
  SUM(val) AS totalvalue,
  COUNT(*) AS numorders
FROM C
GROUP BY startweek
ORDER BY startweek;
```

Assuming a us_english language, where the first day of the week is Sunday, this query generates the following output, shown here in abbreviated form:

```
startweek                endweek                  totalvalue  numorders
-----------------------  -----------------------  ----------  -----------
2006-07-02 00:00:00.000  2006-07-08 00:00:00.000  4510.06     4
2006-07-09 00:00:00.000  2006-07-15 00:00:00.000  8607.62     5
2006-07-16 00:00:00.000  2006-07-22 00:00:00.000  5372.23     6
2006-07-23 00:00:00.000  2006-07-29 00:00:00.000  7628.59     5
2006-07-30 00:00:00.000  2006-08-05 00:00:00.000  6660.68     6
2006-08-06 00:00:00.000  2006-08-12 00:00:00.000  3940.04     5
2006-08-13 00:00:00.000  2006-08-19 00:00:00.000  3791.28     6
2006-08-20 00:00:00.000  2006-08-26 00:00:00.000  6137.86     5
2006-08-27 00:00:00.000  2006-09-02 00:00:00.000  6820.42     6
2006-09-03 00:00:00.000  2006-09-09 00:00:00.000  6828.10     6
2006-09-10 00:00:00.000  2006-09-16 00:00:00.000  9020.80     5
2006-09-17 00:00:00.000  2006-09-23 00:00:00.000  4494.40     6
2006-09-24 00:00:00.000  2006-09-30 00:00:00.000  5916.50     5
2006-10-01 00:00:00.000  2006-10-07 00:00:00.000  2368.00     6
2006-10-08 00:00:00.000  2006-10-14 00:00:00.000  10732.72    5
...
```

If you don't want the query to rely on the login's language setting, but instead define the first day of the week yourself, you can use the techniques described earlier to generate a language-neutral weekday number. Here's what the query would look like if you wanted to force Sunday to be the first day of the week regardless of the login's language setting:

```
WITH C AS
(
  SELECT
    DATEADD(day,
      -DATEPART(weekday, DATEADD(day, @@DATEFIRST - 7, orderdate)) + 1,
      orderdate) AS startweek,
    val
  FROM Sales.OrderValues
)
SELECT
  startweek,
  DATEADD(day, 6, startweek) AS endweek,
  SUM(val) AS totalvalue,
  COUNT(*) AS numorders
FROM C
GROUP BY startweek
ORDER BY startweek;
```

Working Days

Calculating the number of working days between two given dates is quite a common request. Note that both inclusive and non-inclusive counts are useful. In inclusive counts, I'm referring to taking into account the start and end dates of the range. I'll be demonstrating techniques to calculate an inclusive count. In cases for which you need to consider weekends, holidays, and other special events as nonworking days, you might want to use an auxiliary table of dates. You mark each date as working or nonworking, and when requested to calculate the number of working days, you count the rows representing working days between the two given dates. You can even optimize the solution by keeping an attribute with a cumulative count of working days as of some base date. To calculate working days, simply retrieve the cumulative values of the given input dates and subtract one from another.

However, when you want to consider only weekends as nonworking days, you don't need an auxiliary table at all. Instead, here's a solution for calculating the number of working days between @s and @e, which can be local variables or input arguments of a routine:

```
DECLARE
  @s AS DATE = '20090101',
  @e AS DATE = '20091231';

SELECT
  days/7*5 + days%7
    - CASE WHEN 6 BETWEEN wd AND wd + days%7-1 THEN 1 ELSE 0 END
    - CASE WHEN 7 BETWEEN wd AND wd + days%7-1 THEN 1 ELSE 0 END
FROM (SELECT
        DATEDIFF(day, @s, @e) + 1 AS days,
        DATEPART(weekday, @s) AS wd
     ) AS D;
```

The solution is very fast because it involves no I/O. The derived table query calculates the number of days (*days*) between @s and @e, inclusive of both @s and @e, and the weekday number (*wd*) of the date @s based on the login's language setting. Of course, if you wish, you can calculate the weekday number in a language-neutral manner using the aforementioned techniques. The outer query calculates the following: the number of working days in whole weeks covered by the range (*days/7*5*) plus the number of days in the partial week, if any (*days%7*), minus 1 if the partial week contains weekday 6 and minus 1 again if the partial week contains weekday 7. For the given dates—January 1, 2009, through December 31, 2009—you get 261 working days.

Generating a Series of Dates

You might need a series of all possible dates between two input dates. Such a series could be used, for example, to populate a time dimension in Analysis Services. An auxiliary table of numbers makes the solution quite simple. I provided the code to create and populate an auxiliary table of numbers in Chapter 2, "User-Defined Functions."

Here's the code to generate the series of dates:

```
DECLARE
  @startdt AS DATE = '20090101',
  @enddt   AS DATE = '20091231';
```

```
SELECT DATEADD(day, n - 1, @startdt) AS dt
FROM dbo.Nums
WHERE n <= DATEDIFF(day, @startdt, @enddt) + 1;
```

If you don't have a Nums table and are not allowed to create new tables, you can use one of the table-valued function implementations that I showed in *Inside T-SQL Querying*. For example, I presented the following user-defined function (UDF), which accepts the desired number of rows as input and returns a sequence of numbers accordingly:

```
IF OBJECT_ID('dbo.GetNums') IS NOT NULL
  DROP FUNCTION dbo.GetNums;
GO
CREATE FUNCTION dbo.GetNums(@n AS BIGINT) RETURNS TABLE
AS
RETURN
  WITH
  L0   AS(SELECT 1 AS c UNION ALL SELECT 1),
  L1   AS(SELECT 1 AS c FROM L0 AS A CROSS JOIN L0 AS B),
  L2   AS(SELECT 1 AS c FROM L1 AS A CROSS JOIN L1 AS B),
  L3   AS(SELECT 1 AS c FROM L2 AS A CROSS JOIN L2 AS B),
  L4   AS(SELECT 1 AS c FROM L3 AS A CROSS JOIN L3 AS B),
  L5   AS(SELECT 1 AS c FROM L4 AS A CROSS JOIN L4 AS B),
  Nums AS(SELECT ROW_NUMBER() OVER(ORDER BY (SELECT 0)) AS n FROM L5)
  SELECT TOP(@n) n FROM Nums ORDER BY n;
GO
```

Once the function is created, you can use it just like you use the Nums table:

```
DECLARE
  @startdt AS DATE = '20090101',
  @enddt   AS DATE = '20091231';

SELECT DATEADD(day, n - 1, @startdt) AS dt
FROM dbo.GetNums(DATEDIFF(day, @startdt, @enddt) + 1) AS Nums;
```

Conclusion

Date and time manipulation should not be taken lightly. Many important best practices related to working with date and time will help you ensure that your code runs correctly and efficiently. In this chapter I described such best practices and also covered querying problems related to date and time data. I also covered enhancements in SQL Server 2008 like new date- and time-related data types and new and enhanced functions.

Chapter 11
CLR User-Defined Types

Dejan Sarka

Since the advent of .NET integration in SQL Server 2005, you can create CLR-based User-Defined Types (UDTs) using a .NET language of your choice. Personally, I did not see many common language runtime (CLR) UDTs in production. I guess this is because DBAs are still somehow afraid of using CLR code in a relational database management system. My intention in this chapter is to show that CLR types can be useful. However, I am not dealing with practical issues only.

The most important new feature in Microsoft SQL Server 2008 dealing with CLR UDTs is their size. In SQL Server 2005, CLR UDTs were limited to 8,000 bytes. In SQL Server 2008, you can create large objects (LOBs), up to 2 GB, using CLR UDTs. In this chapter, I am going to explain how you can create, deploy, and use a CLR UDT.

Theoretical Introduction to UDTs

Before showing you how to implement CLR UDTs, I would first like to give you some theoretical background. I want to discuss whether CLR types go beyond the relational model—whether SQL Server is becoming an object or object-relational system. This knowledge should help you decide how to implement CLR UDTs properly. A common question these days is whether SQL Server, with all this CLR (and XML) support, has become an object-relational or even an object database management system. I will explain why I think this is not the case and that instead, SQL Server is becoming a more complete relational database management system.

Domains and Relations

In object-oriented programming (OOP), the most important concept is a class used as a template for instantiating (creating) objects; objects are variables that physically live in computer memory. So what are the most important concepts in the relational world?

> **Note** My views on this subject have been largely affected by the work of Chris J. Date and Hugh Darwen in their famous book *Foundation for Object/Relational Databases: The Third Manifesto* (Addison-Wesley Professional, 1998).

Relational databases contain relations. Table 11-1 is an example of a typical Employees relation, which is physically represented in the database as a table.

TABLE 11-1 Employees Relation

employeeid: posint	name: string	city: cityenum
17	Fernando	Alicante
19	Alejandro	Bogotá
24	Herbert	Vienna
20	Douglas	Atlanta

In every row, you can find a proposition. For example, the second row represents a proposition saying that an employee with an ID of 19 is named Alejandro and lives in Bogotá, Colombia. In the table's header, you can find the predicate for this proposition: an employee with ID *employeeid* (a positive integer) is named *name* (an arbitrary string) and lives in *city* (a value from *cityenum*, an enumeration of cities). The names *posint*, *string*, and *cityenum* in the table's header are the *domains* for the predicate's variables. Domains limit the values of the propositions. Because the domain of *EmployeeID* is the set of positive integers, an employee's ID cannot be lower than zero. Within each row, the *city* must come from the city list *cityenum*. Domains constrain the universe of discourse—they constitute the things you can talk about. Relations are sets of propositions—the truths you utter about things. With domains and relations, you can describe the whole subsystem of employees. Therefore, domains and relations are necessary and sufficient to represent reality. These are the most important concepts in the relational world.

I have to emphasize the constraining role of domains. Propositions are assertions of fact, and databases are structured collections of propositions. A database represents the world correctly if it is a collection of the true propositions about the world. Data integrity is the assurance that data is consistent and in accordance with business rules. Do please note that data integrity cannot guarantee that data is correct; no constraint can guarantee that the row (19, Alejandro, Bogotá) is in the table only if Alejandro truly lives in Bogotá. Constraints help you maintain data integrity. However, you have to carefully choose the concepts on which integrity will be based. Preferably, those concepts and their nature should be few in number and agreed upon.

Let me explain concepts for data integrity with an example. Imagine that you have a domain called *spouse*. You define a constraint for using this domain in a relation: a person can have one spouse only. By defining such a constraint, you have already made a mistake, because some cultures and religions don't limit this association to a one-to-one relationship! Still, you can include many constraints for a domain. The set of operators defined on a domain already constrain what you can do with values from that domain. Whenever you try to manipulate the data, the system could check that the operands are of the correct types for the operation. For example, the system could allow a multiplication operation between the attributes *quantity* and *price* but not allow addition, which has no meaning in this context. This is an example of how a database management system could prevent meaningless operations by using specialized types for *quantity* and *price* that are more restrictive than generic number types.

As you know, relational databases are based on set theory. A relation represents a set— that is, a set of propositions. A set contains distinct members; therefore, you need a way to distinguish propositions. You need to define candidate keys, out of which you will choose one as the primary key. A key is a minimal set of attributes needed to uniquely identify any proposition. In addition, relations are associated through keys; a foreign key in one relation matches a key from another relation. Domains and keys are sufficient to implement all possible constraints. This is how the Domain-Key normal form (DKNF) is defined: a database is in Domain-Key Normal Form if every constraint in the database is a logical consequence of the definition of keys and domains. A relation in a DKNF database is free from all update anomalies. Of course, there is no simple algorithmic procedure to implement DKNF. Achieving DKNF would involve a lot of programming.

Although achieving DKNF seems to be something you should pursue, it is not an easy task. Let me give you an example of an advanced constraint that would be very hard to implement with domains and keys only. You are probably already familiar with *adjacency list* for modeling graphs, trees, and hierarchies. If you are not familiar with this model yet, please refer to *T-SQL Querying*. In short, within an adjacency list, each tuple contains its own key and a key of the parent tuple, like in a bill of materials (BOM):

BOM {partid, assemblyid, othercolumns}

Just try to imagine how you would implement a constraint that the BOM has to be antisymmetric—the assembly cannot be contained in a part it contains. Steve Kass suggested the following possible solution. Create a table named Containments, whose tuples have the form (*first_part*, *second_part*, *direction*). Apply a domain constraint that restricts (*first_part*, *second_part*) to a domain *two_parts_alphabetical*, containing all pairs of parts (*first_part*, *second_part*) where *first_part* precedes *second_part* in some well-defined ordering of *parts_domain* elements. Apply another domain constraint to *direction*, limiting it to the set of values {−1, 1}. The predicate for the table would be "(*first_part* is contained in *second_part* and *direction* = 1) OR (*second_part* is contained in *first_part* and *direction* = −1)". Two key constraints would be the foreign key constraints on *first_part* and *second_part*, and a third key constraint would be that (*first_part*, *second_part*) is the primary key of Containments. This latter key constraint, together with the domain constraint that *first_part*<*second_part* guarantees that the table does not represent both containment directions.

Although this is a very clever solution, it would not be easy to use. Many times such advanced constraints are easier to implement with other means than a relational database management system provides, such as declarative constraints and triggers.

Domains and Classes

A domain (or a data type) consists of the following:

- A name
- A set of values allowed
- A set of operators permissible on the domain's values

Note that values of a specific type can have multiple presentations. For example, a point in a plane can be represented in Cartesian or polar coordinate system. Internal representations are hidden; you deal with presentations exposed to the users. This definition does not deal with simple or complex types. It is just a definition for any type. Think of the integer type: addition, subtraction, and multiplication operations are defined on this domain, while for division, you can use integer division (DIV) only in order to get an integer as a result. To summarize, a domain has arbitrary internal complexity, its values are manipulable solely by means of the operators defined for the domain, and its internal representations are hidden.

Now let's write the definition for a class: a class is a data type of arbitrary internal complexity, whose values are manipulable solely by means of the operators defined for the type; internal representations are hidden. The essential aspects of the definition of a class and a domain are the same. Therefore, it's reasonable to think of domains like simple classes. Of course, a class in OOP can have a much richer structure and interface than a domain, and a class also encapsulates behavior. You could use such general classes for domains without running into trouble, and call this the object-relational model. Nevertheless, I prefer to think that an object-relational system is nothing more than a true relational system.

Complex Domains

Now that you know that a domain is the same thing as a class, you can ask another question: why not use arbitrary complex domains? As I pointed out, there really do not exist "complex" and "simple" domains; I am using term *complex* domain here in sense of a domain with multiple internal data members. You could implement an Employees relation in these two different ways:

- Domain *EmployeeDomain* (EmployeeID, Name, City) and relation Employees (*employee*: *EmployeeDomain*)
- Domains *PosInt, String,* and *CityEnum* and relation Employees (*EmployeeId*: *PosInt, Name*: *String, City*: *CityEnum*)

Although you are probably more familiar with the second model, nothing in the relational theory would prevent implementing the first model. The problem with the first design is that it enforces a higher level of encapsulation. An employee has no visible components. It is less open to end users. (Developers are also end users in this context.) Reading propositions from such a design is not very transparent. All possible constraints except the primary key are included in the domain. Operations allowed on *EmployeeDomain* values are not commonly known; the author of the domain has to explain them to the public. The number of operations that the creator of the domain has to define can rise substantially with the complexity. Remember, you usually don't know who the users of the domain are going to be. It is quite possible that the constraints will not be acceptable to all of them. You don't want to implement such a high level of encapsulation. Clearly, the second design is more practical to use.

You realize that simple domains are preferable for relational database design. But why do you call built-in types such as integers *simple*? Well, that's because it is simple for you to deal with values of those types. From school, you know which operations are allowed with integer types, how the operations are named, and how they should be implemented. You don't have to learn new concepts to handle integers. The producers of database management systems are implementing standard definitions. This is why you regard built-in types as simple. Even a small deviation from commonly accepted concepts, such as SQL Server's DATETIME data types, involves complexities that you have to learn and deal with. That's the main reason why the second design of a relation is preferable (the design with simple domains, where propositions are more transparent to read.

You can build constraints in many different places:

- Data types
- Database schemas (table structures), including data types, nullability, uniqueness
- Check constraints and other constraints as explicit objects
- Read-only lookup tables, which are actually check constraints using enumerations with any finite cardinality
- Assertions
- Triggers
- Stored procedures
- Data Access Layer (DAL) procedures
- Middle-tier code
- Client code
- Screen event handlers
- Code built dynamically from values in a database

To decide where to implement a constraint, you should consider how easy it is to circumvent a constraint, and how hard it is to change a constraint. Let me explain this through a couple of simple examples. Imagine you have a column City with three possible values (i.e., with domain {New York, London, Paris}). Later you need to add Moscow to the list of allowable cities. If the constraint is built into the data type, the developer of the data type has to change it, and the developer might not be available immediately. If the constraint is implemented as a check constraint, a DBA can change it; still, end users would need to contact the DBA and wait some time before the constraint is altered. If the constraint is implemented with a lookup table, any end user with permissions to write to that table can add Moscow to the list immediately. Therefore, such a constraint is quite simple to change if it is implemented in a lookup table that allows writes. However, it is easy then for an end user to circumvent it by adding a city to a table that should not be added because of business rules. As another example, imagine that a developer needs to implement different range constraints for different integer columns. The business requirements might require ranges from 0 to 100 for percents, 1 to 2 for gender, 1 to 7 for education level, and so on. Instead of adding multiple check constraints, a developer could implement a function to check ranges in the middle tier or client code, and store the ranges for specific columns in an external text file. Adding a range for an additional column could be done then with any text editor dynamically; however, anybody that has write access to the file could change the ranges inappropriately.

A domain is a suitable place to implement constraints that are not changing or are extremely important. If constraints are volatile or not agreed upon, it is not the right place for their implementation. Imagine what would happen if Microsoft suddenly decided to change the implementation of the integer data type and disallow subtraction. Of course, this change would not be in accordance with the mathematical definition of integers; nevertheless, just imagine the impact of such a change. Again, you can clearly see that domains should not be too complex. Constraints built into domains cannot be easily relaxed, and that's just not practical.

Although you should have primary keys for all tables in production, they are not required by relational database management systems. Imagine how procedures that perform data cleansing on text files before importing them to tables would look if primary keys were mandatory. It's much more practical to import the data first, cleanse it in a relational database, and then create the constraints.

In addition to logical reasons, there are also important physical reasons for not using complex domains. The most important one is performance. If your data type is performing badly, your users cannot do much about it. Deployment is another issue. Client applications must know how to deal with your data type at the client side. Programming languages know how to deal with standard types (what we called simple types). Code for your complex data type must be available to client applications; otherwise, they won't know how to manipulate the values of your domain at the client side. This means that you might face a situation where you would have to deploy the code for your domain to thousands of client computers. First-time deployment is usually not a problem; you can do it along with the application deployment, but what about upgrades?

I am not entirely against complex domains. If you're sure that your application is the sole user of a complex domain, and if constraints are that important for the business problem you are trying to solve, a complex domain might be the right design. Another adequate use of complex types is when you are sure that the knowledge and constraints are generally agreed upon. The question is, when do you know this? Well, if you invent a new format for storing some special kind of data, you can add a data type and make your format available in databases as well. Finally, you might want to invest time in developing an advanced data type to simplify further development of queries and applications. Microsoft developed various date and time data types. Because they are available in SQL Server, and because many operations are defined on them, it is now quite easy to calculate difference in days, weeks, months, or years between two dates, for example, with the DATEDIFF function. If those data types did not exist, a developer could implement dates as integers; however, the developer would then also have to write a function to calculate the difference between dates in days, weeks, months, or years between two dates. I will show you an example of creating a user-defined type in the next chapter, "Temporal Support in the Relational Model," where I am going to develop an *interval* data type that will make some temporal constraints simpler.

Why Do We Need Complex Classes?

After realizing that simple data types are preferable to complex ones inside a relational database, and equating domains and classes, you can turn the question around and ask: Why do you then need complex classes in OOP applications?

Briefly, imagine a classic factory. The factory has a warehouse with many production lines. The same item that is available openly in a warehouse (and is, by the way, maintained with set-oriented operations) changes its shape when it comes to a production line. In a warehouse, the item is stored in such a way that it can be used by any tool from any production line. While in a concrete production line, the item becomes more closed (that is, more encapsulated), and you do not want to make a mess by handling it with inappropriate tools.

Clearly, we need both designs: simple types with a lower level of encapsulation inside a database and more complex types in applications.

Finally, as I already mentioned, object-relational mapping tools typically map classes to relations, not to domains. You can now realize that this is the correct mapping in most cases, although a relation is not the same thing as a class. Anyway, if you need to apply a more encapsulated approach, you can save data for an application using a complex domain, as you sometimes have to save semi-finished products in a factory for a while. In an extreme case, you can save the state of an object (serialize it) in a binary data type column, such as VARBINARY(MAX), and thus make it unavailable to any application that does not know how to deserialize it properly.

Note that the XML data type can be adequate to store the state of objects using XML serialization in a database as well. Because the XML data type is well-known, agreed-upon, and standardized, it allows for the interchange of complex objects between systems, objects that would otherwise be available only to the applications that created them.

Language for Creating UDTs

When I was first introduced to the idea of supporting CLR UDTs inside SQL Server, I wondered why Microsoft hadn't implemented the ANSI standard CREATE DOMAIN command instead. However, I liked the idea of implementing UDTs in .NET languages, which goes beyond what CREATE DOMAIN would have provided.

Well, to implement a data type you need to implement many fine-grained methods. Nonprocedural languages, such as T-SQL, consist of larger building blocks of commands. Think about it: a UDT knows to do only things you define in its methods and properties (which are actually methods that manipulate values of data members). Now, imagine how many different methods you would have to implement just for basic operations even for a very simple type! In addition, your mutator methods should be resilient to input errors; therefore, you need to validate the input. Regular expressions, for example, are very useful for this task, and they are not implemented in T-SQL yet. Additionally, you might get into a situation when you would have to validate values against an external source, like some web service. Programming all these fine-grained details would be very awkward, if not impossible, in T-SQL.

So my conclusion is that Microsoft's implementation of CLR-based UDTs is the correct way to go. My only disappointment is that SQL Server 2008 still doesn't support operator overloading in UDTs. Such support would have raised the level of usability of UDTs significantly. Comparison, logical, and arithmetic operators are universally understood. Thus, for any UDT that should support such operators, those operators would have been directly applicable. The lack of support for operator overloading forces you to learn how operators are implemented through UDT-specific methods. It also forces you to create your own User-Defined Aggregates (UDAs) for calculations that would have otherwise been supported by built-in aggregates directly against UDTs (for example, SUM).

I've mentioned that I would use CLR types with many internal members and operations if I needed to store a semi-finished product or implement an extremely important business rule, or if I invented some specific format for storing data only. Built-in types can be useful for standard formats that don't need to support many operations. A good example is an address type—in many applications, you just need to store and read different addresses, without advanced validation. With operator overloading, implementing types such as complex numbers, which are very well known, with UDTs could have been much simpler.

Programming a UDT

After this long theoretical introduction, let's get down to business—creating a concrete UDT. You need to create a class or a structure (struct in C#, Structure in Microsoft Visual Basic in .NET code. Classes in .NET live in assemblies, and SQL Server loads the .NET code from its own databases, so you have to catalog the assembly. I'll show you how to create a complex number domain. Besides supporting basic operations (read and write), your complex numbers need to support comparisons, basic arithmetic operations, and a SUM aggregate function.

I'll use the Cartesian form of a complex number:

cn = a + bi

where *i is the square root of –1 (i.e., i * i = –1).*

Basic arithmetic operations are defined as:

1. Addition: *(a + bi) + (c + di) = (a + c) + (b + d)i*
2. Subtraction: *(a + bi) – (c + di) = (a – c) + (b – d)i*
3. Multiplication: *(a + bi) × (c + di) = (ac – bd) + (bc + ad)i*
4. Division: *(a + bi)/(c + di) = ((ac + bd) + (bc – ad)i)/(c² + d²)*

UDT Requirements

Besides supporting operations intrinsic to the data type, a UDT must also support conversions to and from character strings to facilitate data input and presentation. Microsoft requires every UDT to implement default accessor- and mutator-specific methods for this: *ToString* and *Parse*. The *ToString* method converts the UDT to a string value. The *Parse* method converts a string input to a UDT value. If you want the *Parse* method to be resilient to erroneous input, you should include in it some error-checking logic. .NET attributes define the UDT's behavior within SQL Server, and they provide information on which the deployment process in Microsoft Visual Studio relies. The most important attribute is *Microsoft.SqlServer.Server.SqlUserDefinedType*, which defines the behavior of the type itself. This attribute is required. It defines the UDT's behavior inside SQL Server (for example, by indicating the serialization format as native or user-defined), and it also helps in deployment from Visual Studio. When Visual Studio sees this attribute, it knows that it has to use the CREATE TYPE command.

The *SqlUserDefinedType* class exposes the following properties:

- **Format**   Defines how values of your UDT are stored, or serialized in binary format. *Format can be Native or UserDefined*. Native format means you rely on SQL Server to perform the serialization. Within an instance of the UDT, the individual properties are stored in order as they are defined in the UDT. With *UserDefined* serialization, you can define your own way of storing UDT values. Binary serialization influences the ordering of UDT values when sorted.

  - If you use native serialization, you can use only the following types for UDT members: *bool, byte, sbyte, short, ushort, int, uint, long, ulong, float, double, SqlByte, SqlInt16, SqlInt32, SqlInt64, SqlDateTime, SqlSingle, SqlDouble, SqlMoney*. If your UDT is a class and not a structure, you have also to specify a *StructLayout* attribute with a *LayoutKind* value of *StructLayout.LayoutKindSequential*. This attribute is used to force the members to be laid out sequentially in the order they appear in a class. You also cannot specify *MaxByteSize* property for native serialization.

❏ For user-defined serialization, you write code for serialization and deserialization in *Read* and *Write* methods of the *IBinarySerialize* interface, which your UDT has to implement. You also specify the *MaxByteSize* property with a value between 1 and 8000 or, starting with SQL Server 2008, with value –1. This property defines the size of your UDT; in SQL Server 2005, the maximum size was 8,000 bytes. In SQL Server 2008, you can use an LOB for your UDT, which raises the maximum size to 2 GB.

- **IsByteOrdered**   This is a very important property. It indicates whether or not the values of your UDT should be ordered by their serialized (binary) value. If it is set to true, you can create indexes on your UDT, use T-SQL's ORDER BY clause, compare different values of these type, and more.

- **IsFixedLength**   This property indicates whether all instances of this user-defined type have the same length.

- **MaxByteSize**   As I already mentioned, this property defines the maximum size of a value of your type.

- **Name**   This property is not used by SQL Server; it is used by Visual Studio to name the type if you deploy your type directly from Visual Studio.

- **ValidationMethodName**   Defines the name of the method used for checking values of your type. When SQL Server converts values to your type, it checks that the property values obtained by the deserialization are valid. However, SQL Server does not call this method for inserts and updates; you can call it manually in the Parse method or in any custom property or method that changes the values of UDT members.

All SQL Server data types, as opposed to .NET native types, should know how to deal with unknown values. A NULL instance of a UDT must be supported; you can choose how to represent it internally. You can represent it with a flag. All NULL instances should be represented in the same way, so it is quite useful to create a class-level (static in C#, Shared in Visual Basic), read-only variable that holds a NULL instance of your type. When you create a UDT, you have to implement the *System.Data.SqlTypes.INullable* interface and create a public static (Shared in Visual Basic, read-only *Null* property). The interface consists of a single read-only *IsNull* property, which shows whether the value is unknown. You also have to define an additional *Null* property, again showing when a value is NULL. Why are there two properties for basically the same purpose? You use the *IsNull* property on client side, in .NET code, to check whether a value is NULL. The *Null* property is used by SQL Server when IS NULL and IS NOT NULL operators are involved in a query. Although you could write a query that uses the *IsNull* property in T-SQL as well, it is more efficient to test for NULLs using the *Null* property.

Inheritance relationships are not recognized by SQL Server. You can use class hierarchies, but they are not defined in the SQL Server catalog and not used in T-SQL operations. In the CLR code, you can use class hierarchies; that is, use a base class and then define a subclass, which is your UDT. The subclass inherits all the methods of the base class. If the inherited methods are explicitly programmed in the subclass—and this means they are overridden (commonly you do this to change the behavior of the method, not just to repeat the code from the base class)—SQL Server will recognize them. If not, SQL Server does not know how to go to the base class and execute the code from the base class. But at the client side, in a .NET application that has references to the assembly with the base class and the UDT class, you can use methods from the base class without explicitly overriding them, because .NET recognizes class hierarchies. So basically you do not use inheritance when you define a UDT, unless you want to have some additional functionality only at the client side.

Native formatting is simple to implement, but it has a drawback—you can use only .NET value types in your UDT. The only really big problem is the string type, which is a reference type in .NET. If you use strings (or, of course, any other .NET reference type) in your UDT, you have to write your own serialization code.

The UDT should support XML serialization as well. It must either implement the *System.Xml .IXmlSerializable* interface, or all public fields and properties must be of types that are XML serializable. If they are not XML serializable, they must be decorated with the *XmlIgnore* attribute if overriding standard serialization is required. The complex number UDT I am going to develop does not implement an explicit XML serialization and also does not use the *XmlIgnore* attribute, so we can use XML serialization from the string representation only.

SQL Server and .NET native types do not match one-to-one. You should use .NET *SqlTypes* whenever possible because they correspond directly to SQL Server native types. The *System.Data.SqlTypes* namespace contains the classes that represent SQL Server native data types available to the assembly.

Finally, to get a list of all the requirements of a CLR user-defined data type, please refer to the "User-Defined Type Requirements" topic in SQL Server Books Online.

Creating a UDT

Visual Studio 2008 has templates (skeletons) for creating CLR objects in SQL Server 2008. Note that you have to install Service Pack 1 or later for Visual Studio 2008 to support direct deployment of CLR objects. Some editions of Visual Studio .NET 2008 don't support the SQL Server CLR objects template. If you're working with such an edition, you have to create a standard class library, write all of the requested methods and properties manually, and then deploy the objects in SQL Server using T-SQL explicitly (via the CREATE ASSEMBLY | TYPE | AGGREGATE | FUNCTION | PROCEDURE | TRIGGER commands). In my examples, I'll take the longer route so that you'll be familiar with the whole process. In addition, in production a DBA would probably not allow deployment from Visual Studio. But first let's develop a UDT in C# step by step. I'll present a code snippet in each step accompanied by explanations. Putting all code snippets together will give you a complete working UDT.

> **More Info**   The complete UDT code is available to you as part of the book's source code, which you can download from *http://www.insidetsql.com.*

To create a UDT, first create a new project in Visual Studio 2008. Assuming that you are using Visual Studio 2008 Professional edition or higher, choose the Visual C# project type, Database subtype, and SQL Server project template. If you're using a lower edition of Visual Studio, use the Class Library project template. Name the project ComplexNumberCS and name the solution just ComplexNumber (I'll add a user-defined aggregate function written in Visual C# and also both type and function written in Visual Basic to this solution later), specify the folder where you want to create your project (I'll use C:\InsideTSQL2008), confirm to create the solution. If you want to deploy the UDT from Visual Studio, also create a target database connection in your solution when the Add Database Reference window appears, or click the Cancel button in this window if you are going to work without a database reference, like me.

> **Note**   You can specify any other folder that you like, but remember your choice because you will need to refer to the physical location of the assembly later when you deploy it in SQL Server.

Now that the solution has been created, add a new User-Defined Type item (relevant to SQL Server project template). Right-click the project and select Add, User-Defined Type from the shortcut menu. Name the class *ComplexNumberCS.cs*. Feel free to examine the basic skeleton of the UDT that the IDE created. However, for our example, you'll replace the template code with what I'll provide here. If you used the Class Library project template, rename the existing class (Class1.cs) *ComplexNumberCS.cs*.

The first part of our UDT declares the namespaces used by the assembly, the class name, and the attributes used:

```
using System;
using System.Data;
using System.Data.SqlClient;
using System.Data.SqlTypes;
using Microsoft.SqlServer.Server;
using System.Text.RegularExpressions;
using System.Globalization;
```

```
[Serializable]
[SqlUserDefinedType(Format.Native,IsByteOrdered = true)]
public struct ComplexNumberCS : INullable
{
```

Note that the UDT uses native serialization and is byte ordered. You're going to use *RegularExpressions* to split and check the input. The *Globalization* namespace is needed because you want to have a culture-invariant string representation of values of your type. You can see that the type uses native formatting and is byte ordered when persisted. It also implements the *INullable* interface. Next, define the variables you need:

```
//Regular expression used to parse values of the form (a,bi)
private static readonly Regex _parser
    = new Regex(@"\A\(\s*(?<real>\-?\d+(\.\d+)?)\s*,\s*(?<img>\-?\d+
    (\.\d+)?)\s*i\s*\)\Z",
                RegexOptions.Compiled | RegexOptions.ExplicitCapture);

// Real and imaginary parts
private double _real;
private double _imaginary;

// Internal member to show whether the value is null
private bool _isnull;

// Null value returned equal for all instances
private const string NULL = "<<null complex>>";
private static readonly ComplexNumberCS NULL_INSTANCE
    = new ComplexNumberCS(true);
```

For more details on regular expressions, please refer to the .NET Framework documentation.

> **Note** The printed code is formatted to be more readable in the book; in practice the complete regular expression should appear in a single line.

In the next step, you define two constructors, one for a known value and one for an unknown value. Unlike other methods of a UDT, constructors can be overloaded.

```
// Constructor for a known value
public ComplexNumberCS(double real, double imaginary)
{
    this._real = real;
    this._imaginary = imaginary;
    this._isnull = false;
}

// Constructor for an unknown value
private ComplexNumberCS(bool isnull)
{
    this._isnull = isnull;
    this._real = this._imaginary = 0;
}
```

As mentioned earlier, you have to define a *ToString* method in your UDT to specify the default string representation. Because your type is derived from *System.Object*, which includes a *ToString* method, you must explicitly override the inherited method:

```
// Default string representation
public override string ToString()
{
    return this._isnull ? NULL : ("("
        + this._real.ToString(CultureInfo.InvariantCulture) + ","
        + this._imaginary.ToString(CultureInfo.InvariantCulture)
        + "i)");
}
```

Now you need two read-only properties to handle unknown values:

```
// Null handling
public bool IsNull
{
    get
    {
        return this._isnull;
    }
}

public static ComplexNumberCS Null
{
    get
    {
        return NULL_INSTANCE;
    }
}
```

And maybe the most important method, which will accept, check, and parse the input—the *Parse* method:

```
// Parsing input using regular expression
public static ComplexNumberCS Parse(SqlString sqlString)
{
    string value = sqlString.ToString();

    if (sqlString.IsNull || value == NULL)
        return new ComplexNumberCS(true);

    // Check whether the input value matches the regex pattern
    Match m = _parser.Match(value);

    // If the input's format is incorrect, throw an exception
    if (!m.Success)
        throw new ArgumentException(
            "Invalid format for complex number. "
            + "Format is ( n, mi ) where n and m are floating "
            + "point numbers in normal (not scientific) format "
            + "(nnnnnn.nn).");

    // If everything is OK, parse the value;
    // we will get two double type values
```

```
        return new ComplexNumberCS(double.Parse(m.Groups[1].Value,
            CultureInfo.InvariantCulture), double.Parse(m.Groups[2].Value,
            CultureInfo.InvariantCulture));
    }
```

You've implemented the basic operations. All additional knowledge that the type should have can be added through additional methods and properties. So let's start with the two properties *Real* and *Imaginary*; they will be the public properties that access and modify the real and imaginary parts of a complex number:

```
// Properties to deal with real and imaginary parts separately
public double Real
{
    get
    {
        if (this._isnull)
            throw new InvalidOperationException();
        return this._real;
    }
    set
    {
        this._real = value;
    }
}

public double Imaginary
{
    get
    {
        if (this._isnull)
            throw new InvalidOperationException();
        return this._imaginary;
    }
    set
    {
        this._imaginary = value;
    }
}
```

I want to show some more advanced attributes as well in this example. This is why I need additional property that returns the real part as an integer in the type. I am using the *Math. Floor* method, which returns the largest whole number less than or equal to the specified number:

```
// Integer representation of real part
public int RealInt
{
    get
    {
        if (this._isnull)
            throw new InvalidOperationException();
        return (int)Math.Floor(this._real);
    }
}
```

You have arrived at the last part—programming arithmetic operations. The use of *#region* and *#endregion* here allows you to collapse this section of code in the Visual Studio interface.

```
// Region with arithmetic operations
#region arithmetic operations

// Addition
public ComplexNumberCS AddCN(ComplexNumberCS c)
{
    // null checking
    if (this._isnull || c._isnull)
        return new ComplexNumberCS(true);
    // addition
    return new ComplexNumberCS(this.Real + c.Real,
        this.Imaginary + c.Imaginary);
}

// Subtraction
public ComplexNumberCS SubCN(ComplexNumberCS c)
{
    // null checking
    if (this._isnull || c._isnull)
        return new ComplexNumberCS(true);
    // subtraction
    return new ComplexNumberCS(this.Real - c.Real,
        this.Imaginary - c.Imaginary);
}

// Multiplication
public ComplexNumberCS MulCN(ComplexNumberCS c)
{
    // null checking
    if (this._isnull || c._isnull)
        return new ComplexNumberCS(true);
    // multiplication
    return new ComplexNumberCS(this.Real * c.Real - this.Imaginary * c.Imaginary,
        this.Imaginary * c.Real + this.Real * c.Imaginary);
}

// Division
public ComplexNumberCS DivCN(ComplexNumberCS c)
{
    // null checking
    if (this._isnull || c._isnull)
        return new ComplexNumberCS(true);
    // division
    return new ComplexNumberCS(
        (this.Real * c.Real + this.Imaginary * c.Imaginary)
          / (c.Real * c.Real + c.Imaginary * c.Imaginary),
        (this.Imaginary * c.Real - this.Real * c.Imaginary)
          / (c.Real * c.Real + c.Imaginary * c.Imaginary)
        );
}
#endregion
}
```

If you followed the example, stitching the code snippets one after the other, your UDT is now ready to be built. Choose the Build menu, and select the first option, Build ComplexNumberCS. You could also deploy the UDT from Visual Studio and select the deployment options via the project's Properties dialog box. But as I mentioned earlier, I'd like to show you the T-SQL commands required for this task.

Deploying the UDT Using T-SQL

The next steps deploy the new UDT in SQL Server using T-SQL code. To follow this part, use SQL Server Management Studio (SSMS). First, you need to enable the execution of CLR assemblies on the server, unless it's already enabled, and switch context to the InsideTSQL2008 database:

```
USE master;
EXEC sp_configure 'clr enabled', 1;
RECONFIGURE;
GO
USE InsideTSQL2008;
GO
```

Now you need to import the assembly to the database. To do so, use the CREATE ASSEMBLY command. The command has a PERMISSION_SET clause, which specifies a set of code access permissions that are granted to the assembly when it is accessed by SQL Server. If the clause is not specified, the SAFE level is applied by default. I recommend using SAFE because it is the most restrictive permission set. Code executed by an assembly with SAFE permissions cannot access external system resources such as files, the network, environment variables, or the registry. EXTERNAL_ACCESS allows assemblies access to some external system resources. The UNSAFE level allows unrestricted resource access, both within and outside the SQL Server instance, and calls to unmanaged code. Run the following code to import the assembly:

```
CREATE ASSEMBLY ComplexNumberCS
FROM 'C:\InsideTSQL2008\ComplexNumber\ComplexNumberCS\bin\Debug\ComplexNumberCS.dll'
WITH PERMISSION_SET = SAFE;
```

If you used a different folder for your project, you have to change the path to the assembly in the preceding command. After you catalog the assembly, you can start using your new UDT. First, you have to bind the SQL Server type to the .NET code using the CREATE TYPE command:

```
CREATE TYPE dbo.ComplexNumberCS
EXTERNAL NAME ComplexNumberCS.[ComplexNumberCS];
```

Then you can use the UDT just like any other SQL Server native type. For example, the following code creates a table with a column of the new type:

```
CREATE TABLE dbo.CNUsage
(
  id INT IDENTITY(1,1) NOT NULL,
  cn ComplexNumberCS NULL
);
```

As you can see, the *cn* column allows NULLs. Now insert two rows with values in the format (*a*, *bi*), as expected by the *Parse* method. Then insert an incorrect value to show the error that you get:

```
-- Correct values
INSERT INTO dbo.CNUsage(cn) VALUES('(2,3i)');
INSERT INTO dbo.CNUsage(cn) VALUES('(1,7i)');
GO
-- Now an incorrect value
INSERT INTO dbo.CNUsage(cn) VALUES('(1i,7)');
```

You get the following output as the result of the last INSERT:

```
Msg 6522, Level 16, State 2, Line 1
A .NET Framework error occurred during execution of user defined routine or aggregate
'ComplexNumberCS':
System.ArgumentException: Invalid format for complex number. Format is ( n, mi ) where n and
m are floating point numbers in normal (not scientific) format (nnnnnn.nn).
System.ArgumentException:
   at ComplexNumberCS.Parse(SqlString sqlString)
   .
The statement has been terminated.
```

As you can see, you get a generic SQL Server error number 6522 and the message you defined when throwing an exception in the *Parse* method. Next, issue a SELECT statement, and notice the output.

```
SELECT * FROM dbo.CNUsage;
```

```
id          cn
----------- ------------------------------------
1           0xC000000000000000C00800000000000000
2           0xBFF0000000000000C01C00000000000000
```

SSMS displays each *cn* value as a simple byte stream. SSMS is a client tool; the UDT's code isn't transferred from the server to the client—not even the code implementing the *ToString* method.

> **Note** If *CNUsage* is edited with SSMS when you right-click the table and choose the Edit Top 200 Rows command from the shortcut menu, the default string representation is shown; SSMS invokes *ToString* behind the scenes. You can easily see this for yourself by tracing the activity submitted from SSMS to SQL Server. However, if you choose Select Top 1000 Rows from the same shortcut menu, you get a byte stream from the UDT.

To get a proper string representation, you have to call *ToString* explicitly to force it to execute at the server. Or you can make the code available to the client by putting the assembly in the global assembly cache (GAC), for example. Dealing with the client side is outside the scope of this book, so I'll make calls to *ToString* and other methods explicitly:

```
SELECT id, cn.ToString() AS cn
FROM dbo.CNUsage;
```

This query generates the following output:

```
id          cn
----------- -----------
1           (2,3i)
2           (1,7i)
```

With an explicit call to *ToString*, the presentation is more readable. Ordering should follow a byte order of the serialization (because *IsByteOrdered* = *true*), starting with the first member, which in our case is the real component of the complex number. Issue the following query, which sorts the rows by *cn* and generates the output shown right after the query:

```
SELECT id, cn.ToString() AS cn
FROM dbo.CNUsage
ORDER BY cn;
```

```
id          cn
----------- -----------
2           (1,7i)
1           (2,3i)
```

You can see that the second complex number (1, 7i) is sorted before the first one (2, 3i) because its real component is smaller. If you have different ordering needs, you have to implement a user-defined serialization and use your own algorithm for the *Write* method.

> **Note** When you implement an interface, you have to implement all methods defined in the interface; hence you also have to implement the *Read* method.

Next, check whether the UDT can really accept NULLs:

```
INSERT INTO dbo.CNUsage(cn) VALUES(NULL);

SELECT id, cn.ToString() AS cn,
   cn.Real AS [Real part],
   cn.Imaginary AS [Imaginary part]
FROM dbo.CNUsage;
```

The output is:

```
id          cn          Real part              Imaginary part
----------- ----------- ---------------------- ----------------------
1           (2,3i)      2                      3
2           (1,7i)      1                      7
4           NULL        NULL                   NULL
```

The NULL is accepted and returned without any problem.

> **Note** Can you tell why the *id* column of the unknown complex number shows the value 4 and not 3? The reason is that upon an INSERT statement, the IDENTITY value increments regardless of whether the INSERT succeeded or failed, and I issued an unsuccessful insert earlier.

As you can see, I also checked the additional *Real* and *Imaginary* properties implemented in the type. Finally, you can check the four arithmetic operations. I'll do this using variables to show that a UDT works with variables just like any other data type. I'll also use an explicit conversion from a string to the UDT—again, just to show that it is possible; SQL Server 2008 supports casting and conversion of UDTs to strings and vice versa. Run the following code to test the UDT's methods for complex arithmetic:

```
-- Arithmetic operations
-- Addition
DECLARE @cn1 ComplexNumberCS, @cn2 ComplexNumberCS, @cn3 ComplexNumberCS;
SET @cn1 = CAST('(8, 5i)' AS ComplexNumberCS);
SET @cn2 = '(2, 1i)';
SET @cn3 = @cn1.AddCN(@cn2);
SELECT @cn3.ToString(), CAST(@cn3 AS VARCHAR(MAX)), @cn3.Real, @cn3.Imaginary;
GO
-- Subtraction
DECLARE @cn1 ComplexNumberCS, @cn2 ComplexNumberCS, @cn3 ComplexNumberCS;
SET @cn1 = CAST('(3, 4i)' AS ComplexNumberCS);
SET @cn2 = '(1, 2i)';
SET @cn3 = @cn1.SubCN(@cn2);
SELECT @cn3.ToString(), CAST(@cn3 AS VARCHAR(MAX)), @cn3.Real, @cn3.Imaginary;
GO
-- Multiplication
DECLARE @cn1 ComplexNumberCS, @cn2 ComplexNumberCS, @cn3 ComplexNumberCS;
SET @cn1 = CAST('(3, 2i)' AS ComplexNumberCS);
SET @cn2 = '(1, 4i)';
SET @cn3 = @cn1.MulCN(@cn2);
SELECT @cn3.ToString(), CAST(@cn3 AS VARCHAR(MAX)), @cn3.Real, @cn3.Imaginary;
GO
-- Division
DECLARE @cn1 ComplexNumberCS, @cn2 ComplexNumberCS, @cn3 ComplexNumberCS;
SET @cn1 = CAST('(10, 5i)' AS ComplexNumberCS);
SET @cn2 = '(2, 4i)';
SET @cn3 = @cn1.DivCN(@cn2);
SELECT @cn3.ToString(), CAST(@cn3 AS VARCHAR(MAX)), @cn3.Real, @cn3.Imaginary;
GO
```

However, try running the following code using the plus (+) operator and SUM aggregate function:

```
DECLARE @cn1 ComplexNumberCS, @cn2 ComplexNumberCS, @cn3 ComplexNumberCS;
SET @cn1 = CAST('(10, 5i)' AS ComplexNumberCS);
SET @cn2 = '(2, 4i)';
SET @cn3 = @cn1 + @cn2;
SELECT SUM(cn) FROM dbo.CNUsage;
```

You get the following errors:

```
Msg 403, Level 16, State 1, Line 4
Invalid operator for data type. Operator equals add, type equals ComplexNumberCS.
Msg 8117, Level 16, State 1, Line 5
Operand data type ComplexNumberCS is invalid for sum operator.
```

You can now see how useful it would have been if SQL Server 2008 supported operator overloading with CLR user-defined types. You can overcome the plus operator problem by writing your own methods, as I demonstrated earlier. However, you can't use UDTs in aggregate functions that depend on arithmetic (such as SUM and AVG)—only in functions that depend only on comparison or nullability (such as MAX and COUNT). Fortunately, SQL Server supports user-defined aggregate functions (UDAs), which must be written in a .NET language, like user-defined types. If you need an aggregate function that supports your UDT, you have to create your own.

As background for creating UDAs, please refer to *T-SQL Querying*. Let me quickly show an example. Add a new Aggregate item to the ComplexNumberCS project in Visual Studio 2008, name it ComplexNumberCS_SUM.cs, substitute its body with the following code, and rebuild the project.

```csharp
using System;
using System.Data;
using System.Data.SqlClient;
using System.Data.SqlTypes;
using Microsoft.SqlServer.Server;

[Serializable]
[SqlUserDefinedAggregate(Format.Native)]
public struct ComplexNumberCS_SUM
{
    ComplexNumberCS cn;

    public void Init()
    {
        cn = ComplexNumberCS.Parse("(0, 0i)");
    }

    public void Accumulate(ComplexNumberCS Value)
    {
        cn = cn.AddCN(Value);
    }

    public void Merge(ComplexNumberCS_SUM Group)
    {
        Accumulate(Group.Terminate());
    }

    public ComplexNumberCS Terminate()
    {
        return cn;
    }
}
```

Next, you need to update the assembly in the database. To do so, use the ALTER ASSEMBLY command. You shouldn't have any problems because you're not changing the UDT you're already using. Remember, you have to catalog the aggregate function using the CREATE AGGREGATE command:

```
-- Alter assembly to add the ComplexNumberCS_SUM UDA
ALTER ASSEMBLY ComplexNumberCS
FROM 'C:\InsideTSQL2008\ComplexNumber\ComplexNumberCS\bin\Debug\ComplexNumberCS.dll';
GO


-- Create the aggregate function
CREATE AGGREGATE dbo.ComplexNumberCS_SUM(@input ComplexNumberCS)
RETURNS ComplexNumberCS
EXTERNAL NAME ComplexNumberCS.[ComplexNumberCS_SUM];
```

And finally, use the new aggregate function to calculate the sum of all non-NULL values in the table, and you will get (3, 10i) back:

```
SELECT dbo.ComplexNumberCS_SUM(cn).ToString() AS ComplexSum
FROM CNUsage
WHERE cn IS NOT NULL;
```

You can see that CLR UDAs can be written to support CLR UDTs.

Let's play a bit more with this UDT. What if you want to create a temporary table from your table that used the UDT with SELECT INTO statement? Try it:

```
SELECT id, cn
INTO #tmp
FROM dbo.CNUsage;
```

You get error 6220, telling you the UDT does not exist in the target database, which is tempdb for temporary objects. You could deploy UDT to tempdb. However, I want to show something else. Let's repeat SELECT INTO, this time using default string representation, and the *Real*, *Imaginary*, and *RealInt* properties:

```
SELECT id, cn.ToString() AS cn,
   cn.Real AS [Real part],
   cn.Imaginary AS [Imaginary part],
   cn.RealInt AS [Real part int]
INTO #tmp
FROM dbo.CNUsage;
```

This time SELECT INTO succeeded. Now check the destination table structure:

```
USE tempdb;
EXEC sp_help #tmp;
```

Here is part of the output of the *sp_help* procedure showing column names, types, whether they are computed or not, and their length.

Column_name	Type	Computed	Length
id	int	no	4
cn	nvarchar	no	4000
Real part	float	no	8
Imaginary part	float	no	8
Real part int	int	no	4

The data types are probably the ones you expected (*int* for the *id* and *[Real part int]* columns; *float* for the *[Real part]* and *[Imaginary part]* columns), except for the *cn* column. The data type of this column is *nvarchar(4000)*, which is the default T-SQL type for strings returned from CLR code. The *ToString* representation of your UDT needs fewer characters because it consists of two .NET *double* numbers and a couple of additional characters, like parentheses, comma, the letter I, and potentially a minus sign. The approximate range for the *double* data type is $\pm 5.0 \times 10^{-324}$ to $\pm 1.7 \times 10^{308}$. Default string representation for numbers in .NET uses fixed-point notation if the exponent that would result from expressing the number in scientific notation is greater than –5 and less than the precision specifier, which is 15 by default for *double*; otherwise, scientific notation is used, which is shorter than 15 characters. Therefore, a rough calculation indicates that 40 characters are enough (I actually managed to get a maximum length of 39 characters). To achieve this, you need to inform SQL Server about your intention by using the *SqlFacet* attribute to decorate the *ToString* method. The *SqlFacet* attribute annotates the returned result of a UDT with additional information that can be used in T-SQL. I'll use the *MaxSize* property to denote that I want a maximum of 40 character–long strings from the *ToString* method:

```
// Default string representation with SqlFacet
[return:SqlFacet(MaxSize = 40)]
public override string ToString()
{
    return this._isnull ? NULL : ("("
        + this._real.ToString(CultureInfo.InvariantCulture) + ","
        + this._imaginary.ToString(CultureInfo.InvariantCulture)
        + "i)");
}
```

Redeploy the assembly, drop and re-create the #tmp table, and check its structure again. This time you should get NVARCHAR(80) for the *cn* column.

```
-- Alter assembly to check the SqlFacet attribute

-- Drop the #tmp table
USE InsideTSQL2008;
DROP TABLE #tmp;
ALTER ASSEMBLY ComplexNumberCS
FROM 'C:\InsideTSQL2008\ComplexNumber\ComplexNumberCS\bin\Debug\ComplexNumberCS.dll'
GO
-- SELECT INTO with string and other presentations
SELECT id, cn.ToString() AS cn,
  cn.Real AS [Real part],
  cn.Imaginary AS [Imaginary part],
  cn.RealInt AS [Real part int]
```

```
INTO #tmp
FROM dbo.CNUsage;
GO
-- Check the #tmp structure
USE tempdb;
EXEC sp_help #tmp;
GO
```

After you finished with testing of the *SqlFacet* attribute, drop the temporary table:

```
DROP TABLE #tmp;
GO
```

The next issue I am interested in is indexing. Because the serialized values of the *ComplexNumberCS* type are byte ordered, you can create an index on a column of this type:

```
USE InsideTSQL2008;
CREATE INDEX CNUsage_cn ON dbo.CNUsage(cn);
GO
```

Now I would like to create an index on the *Real* property:

```
CREATE INDEX CNUsage_Real ON dbo.CNUsage(cn.Real);
```

If you try this statement, you get a syntax error. This is because you can only index columns, not properties of a column. What you can do when you want to index a property is create a computed column from a property and persist and index the computed column, so long as the column definition allows the PERSISTED property and can be used as an index key. Refer to SQL Server Books Online for the requirements regarding persisting and indexing a computed column. Two limitations are relevant here: the expression must be deterministic and it must be precise. Properties that return float values are not precise. That's why I created the additional *RealInt* property, which returns an integer representation of the real part of a complex number. This property should return deterministic and precise values. Let's try to alter the table and add a persisted computed column using this property:

```
ALTER TABLE dbo.CNUsage
 ADD RealInt AS cn.RealInt PERSISTED;
```

You get error 4936, stating that the computed column is not deterministic. Although the property *RealInt* is both deterministic and precise, you have to inform SQL Server of this. You do so by using the *SqlMethod* attribute for the *get* method of the *RealInt* property:

```
// Integer representation of real part
public int RealInt
{
    [SqlMethod(IsDeterministic = true, IsPrecise = true)]
    get
    {
        if (this._isnull)
            throw new InvalidOperationException();
        return (int)Math.Floor(this._real);
    }
}
```

Redeploy the assembly and try to create a persisted computed column again. This time the ALTER TABLE statement succeeds, and you can index the column, as shown in the following code:

```
USE InsideTSQL2008;
ALTER ASSEMBLY ComplexNumberCS
FROM 'C:\InsideTSQL2008\ComplexNumber\ComplexNumberCS\bin\Debug\ComplexNumberCS.dll'
GO
ALTER TABLE dbo.CNUsage
 ADD RealInt AS cn.RealInt PERSISTED;
GO
CREATE INDEX CNUsage_RealInt ON dbo.CNUsage(RealInt);
GO
```

In case your language of preference is Visual Basic, for your convenience below is the code for the Visual Basic–based UDT, respectively. Conceptually, all the discussion about UDTs and UDAs is language-independent.

```
Imports System
Imports System.Data
Imports System.Data.SqlClient
Imports System.Data.SqlTypes
Imports Microsoft.SqlServer.Server
Imports System.Text.RegularExpressions
Imports System.Globalization


<Serializable()> _
<SqlUserDefinedType(Format.Native, IsByteOrdered:=True)> _
Public Structure ComplexNumberVB
    Implements INullable

    Private Shared ReadOnly parser As New Regex("\A\(\s*(?<real>\-?\d+(\.\d+)?)\s*,\
s*(?<img>\-?\d+(\.\d+)?)\s*i\s*\)\Z", _
    RegexOptions.Compiled Or RegexOptions.ExplicitCapture)
    Private realValue As Double
    Private imaginaryValue As Double
    Private isNullValue As Boolean
    Private Const nullValue As String = "<<null complex>>"
    Private Shared ReadOnly NULL_INSTANCE As New ComplexNumberVB(True)

    Public Sub New(ByVal real As Double, ByVal imaginary As Double)
        Me.realValue = real
        Me.imaginaryValue = imaginary
        Me.isNullValue = False
    End Sub

    Private Sub New(ByVal isnull As Boolean)
        Me.isNullValue = isnull
        Me.realValue = 0
        Me.imaginaryValue = 0
    End Sub

    Public Overrides Function ToString() As <SqlFacet(maxSize:=700)> String
        If Me.isNullValue = True Then
            Return nullValue
```

```
        Else
            Return "(" & Me.realValue.ToString(CultureInfo.InvariantCulture) _
                & "," & Me.imaginaryValue.ToString( _
                    CultureInfo.InvariantCulture) _
                & "i)"
        End If
    End Function

    Public ReadOnly Property IsNull() As Boolean Implements INullable.IsNull
        Get
            Return Me.isNullValue
        End Get
    End Property

    Public Shared ReadOnly Property Null() As ComplexNumberVB
        Get
            Return NULL_INSTANCE
        End Get
    End Property

    Public Shared Function Parse(ByVal sqlString As SqlString) _
      As ComplexNumberVB
        Dim value As String = sqlString.ToString()

        If sqlString.IsNull Or value = nullValue Then
            Return New ComplexNumberVB(True)
        End If

        Dim m As Match = parser.Match(value)

        If Not m.Success Then
            Throw New ArgumentException( _
                "Invalid format for complex number. Format is " + _
                "( n, mi ) where n and m are floating point numbers " + _
                "in normal (not scientific) format (nnnnnn.nn).")
        End If

        Return New ComplexNumberVB(Double.Parse(m.Groups(1).Value, _
          CultureInfo.InvariantCulture), _
            Double.Parse(m.Groups(2).Value, CultureInfo.InvariantCulture))
    End Function

    Public Property Real() As Double
        Get
            If Me.isNullValue Then
                Throw New InvalidOperationException()
            End If
            Return Me.realValue
        End Get
        Set(ByVal Value As Double)
            Me.realValue = Value
        End Set
    End Property
```

```
    Public Property Imaginary() As Double
        Get
            If Me.isNullValue Then
                Throw New InvalidOperationException()
            End If
            Return Me.imaginaryValue
        End Get
        Set(ByVal Value As Double)
            Me.imaginaryValue = Value
        End Set
    End Property

    Public ReadOnly Property RealInt() As Integer
        <SqlMethod(IsDeterministic:=True, IsPrecise:=True)> _
        Get
            If Me.isNullValue Then
                Throw New InvalidOperationException()
            End If
            Return CInt(Math.Floor(Me.realValue))
        End Get
    End Property

#Region "arithmetic operations"

    ' Addition
    Public Function AddCN(ByVal c As ComplexNumberVB) As ComplexNumberVB
        'Null(checking)
        If Me.isNullValue Or c.isNullValue Then
            Return New ComplexNumberVB(True)
        End If
        ' addition
        Return New ComplexNumberVB(Me.Real + c.Real, _
            Me.Imaginary + c.Imaginary)
    End Function

    ' Subtraction
    Public Function SubCN(ByVal c As ComplexNumberVB) As ComplexNumberVB
        'Null(checking)
        If Me.isNullValue Or c.isNullValue Then
            Return New ComplexNumberVB(True)
        End If
        ' subtraction
        Return New ComplexNumberVB(Me.Real - c.Real, _
            Me.Imaginary - c.Imaginary)
    End Function

    ' Multiplication
    Public Function MulCN(ByVal c As ComplexNumberVB) As ComplexNumberVB
        'Null(checking)
        If Me.isNullValue Or c.isNullValue Then
            Return New ComplexNumberVB(True)
        End If
        ' multiplication
        Return New ComplexNumberVB(Me.Real * c.Real - _
          Me.Imaginary * c.Imaginary, _
            Me.Imaginary * c.Real + Me.Real * c.Imaginary)
    End Function
```

```
    ' Division
    Public Function DivCN(ByVal c As ComplexNumberVB) As ComplexNumberVB
        'Null(checking)
        If Me.isNullValue Or c.isNullValue Then
            Return New ComplexNumberVB(True)
        End If
        'Zero checking
        If c.Real = 0 And c.Imaginary = 0 Then
            Throw New ArgumentException()
        End If
        ' division
        Return New ComplexNumberVB( _
            (Me.Real * c.Real + Me.Imaginary * c.Imaginary) _
             / (c.Real * c.Real + c.Imaginary * c.Imaginary), _
            (Me.Imaginary * c.Real - Me.Real * c.Imaginary) _
             / (c.Real * c.Real + c.Imaginary * c.Imaginary) _
        )
    End Function

#End Region

End Structure
```

And finally, here is the code for the Visual Basic–based ComplexNumberVB_SUM UDA:

```
Imports System
Imports System.Data
Imports System.Data.SqlClient
Imports System.Data.SqlTypes
Imports Microsoft.SqlServer.Server


<Serializable()> _
<Microsoft.SqlServer.Server.SqlUserDefinedAggregate(Format.Native)> _
Public Structure ComplexNumberVB_SUM

    Dim cn As ComplexNumberVB

    Public Sub Init()
        cn = ComplexNumberVB.Parse("(0, 0i)")
    End Sub

    Public Sub Accumulate(ByVal value As ComplexNumberVB)
        cn = cn.AddCN(value)
    End Sub

    Public Sub Merge(ByVal value As ComplexNumberVB_SUM)
        Accumulate(value.Terminate())
    End Sub

    Public Function Terminate() As ComplexNumberVB
        Return cn
    End Function

End Structure
```

The T-SQL commands needed to deploy the UDT and UDA in SQL Server are the same ones you used earlier, of course.

When you're done experimenting with the new UDT, run the following code for cleanup:

```
USE InsideTSQL2008;
GO
DROP TABLE dbo.CNUsage;
DROP AGGREGATE dbo.ComplexNumberCS_SUM;
DROP TYPE dbo.ComplexNumberCS;
DROP ASSEMBLY ComplexNumberCS;
DROP AGGREGATE dbo.ComplexNumberVB_SUM;
DROP TYPE dbo.ComplexNumberVB;
DROP ASSEMBLY ComplexNumberVB;
GO
```

Conclusion

Extending built-in SQL Server types with CLR user-defined types can be very useful for maintaining important constraints and building advanced knowledge in the types. This knowledge can simplify T-SQL and client code that deals with values of the UDT. However, coding a CLR UDT is not simple. In addition to prescribed methods and properties, you can implement your own. Do not forget to inform SQL Server about intended behavior of your type. You can do this by decorating the type and its methods with attributes. I have shown you how to use the *SqlUserDefinedType*, *SqlFacet*, and *SqlMethod* attributes. You'll use the knowledge from this chapter in the next chapter, where I'll show how you can use an interval CLR UDT to simplify problems with temporal data in SQL Server.

Chapter 12
Temporal Support in the Relational Model

Dejan Sarka

Databases that serve business applications should often support temporal data. For example, suppose a contract with a supplier is valid for a limited time only. It can be valid from a specific point in time onward, or it can be valid for a specific time interval—from a starting time point to an ending time point. However, I have heard many times that the relational model and relational databases can only support current data. In this chapter, I will show you that the relational model is ready for temporal data, and how to implement temporal support in Microsoft SQL Server 2008. By *temporal support*, I mean support for representing data with a limited validity time. I will call data valid from a single point in time forward *semitemporal data*, and I will call data valid for a fixed time interval *full temporal data*.

For analytical purposes, data warehouses evolved. Data warehouses support historical data. You should not confuse data warehouse (historical) data with temporal data, the subject of this chapter. In a data warehouse, historical data means just archived non-temporal data from the past; a typical data warehouse holds from 5 to 10 years of data for analytical purposes. Data warehouses are not suitable for business applications because a data warehouse typically has no constraints. To implement properly temporal data support in a production database, constraints that enforce data integrity have to be considered. I will explain what kind of constraints you might encounter when you are working with temporal data and how to implement them. To mitigate the problems, I will develop a CLR UDT that supports intervals of time. I will also explain how it would be useful if SQL Server supported two temporal relational operators—namely PACK and UNPACK—and how you can implement those two relational operators using existing T-SQL syntax. I will also show how to maintain a history of all changes. I will explain and use the proposed sixth normal form (6NF).

Temporal support in relational databases has been the subject of nearly 30 years of research. You can find proposed solutions in many books and white papers. Although there is not a single theoretical approach to temporal problems, suggested solutions do not differ much. In the theoretical part of this chapter, I am going to lean mostly on a very fundamental book about temporal problems: *Temporal Data and the Relational Model* by C. J. Date, H. Darwen, and N. A. Lorentzos (Morgan Kaufmann, 2003).

Timestamped Predicates and Propositions

In a table with temporal support, the header represents a predicate with at least one time parameter that represents when the rest of the predicate is valid—the complete predicate is therefore a *timestamped* predicate. Rows represent timestamped propositions, and the row's valid time period is expressed with one of two attributes: *since* (for semitemporal data) or *during* (for fully temporal data); the latter attribute is usually represented with two values, *from* and *to*. I will explain these attributes in an example from the InsideTSQL2008 database. Figure 12-1 shows the original and two additional timestamped versions of the Production. Suppliers table. The additional columns required for temporal support are in bold.

Suppliers		Suppliers_Since		Suppliers_From To	
PK	supplierid	PK	supplierid	PK	supplierid
	companyname		companyname		companyname
	contactname		contactname		contactname
	contacttitle		contacttitle		contacttitle
	address		address		address
	city		city		city
	region		region		region
	postalcode		postalcode		postalcode
	country		country		country
	phone		phone		phone
	fax		fax		fax
			since		**from**
					to

FIGURE 12-1 The original Suppliers table and two timestamped versions

From the original table header, you can read a predicate saying that a supplier with identification *supplierid*, named *companyname*, having contact *contactname*, and so on is currently our supplier, or is currently under contract. The Suppliers_Since table header has this predicate modified with a time parameter: a supplier with the identification *supplierid*, named *companyname*, having contact *contactname*, and so on is under contract *since* some specific point in time. In the Suppliers_FromTo table, the header has this predicate modified with an even more specific time attribute: a supplier with ID *supplierid*, named *companyname*, having contact *contactname*, and so on is (or was, or will be, depending on the current time) under contract *from* some specific point in time *to* another point in time. This predicate can be shortened: a supplier with ID *supplierid*, named *companyname*, having contact *contactname*, and so on is (or was, or will be, depending on current time point) under contract *during* some interval of time.

So far, everything seems quite simple. You add one or two columns, and you have temporal support. However, immediately a number of questions arise. As soon as you have represented validity time in the Suppliers table, you have to implement it on supplied products as well. Furthermore, a supplier can supply a product only at times when the supplier has a valid contract. Without temporal support in the Suppliers table, you need only a foreign key on the SuppliersProducts table referencing the Suppliers table to implement the restriction that a supplied product must have a valid supplier. With temporal support in the Suppliers table, the restriction is stronger: the product's supplier must exist *and* be under contract for the entire period when the product is supplied. In addition, the time points that describe *since* and *during* have to be valid points in time. For example, there might be a requirement that no time points in a database can precede the time point when the company was established.

Another problem is with the last table, the Suppliers_FromTo table. You might think that this one table is enough to represent all possible timestamped propositions. However, if you only have this table, how do you represent the current state, the current suppliers? Current suppliers should include both suppliers with a valid open-ended contract and suppliers with a time-limited contract that includes the current time point. Some authors have suggested the use of a special marker NOW for the *to* attribute of open-ended contracts. This marker would be similar to the special NULL marker, which denotes unknown values, but the expression *t* = *NOW* would always return true when evaluated at time *t*. I do not think you can you represent both time-limited and open-ended propositions—like "is or will be a supplier since time point *from*", and "was a supplier during the (closed) interval *i*" respectively—with this table. I will show that it is better to have separate tables for semitemporal and fully temporal data if you need to represent both kinds. Many more problems arise; I will explain them and solve them in this chapter.

Time Points

First, let's look at time points. So far, I've talked about time as though it consists of discrete time points; I used the term *time point* as if it represented a single, indivisible, infinitely small point in time. Of course, time is continuous. Nevertheless, in common language, we talk about time as though it consists of discrete points. We talk in days, hours, and other time units; the granularity we use depends on what we are talking about. For example, we might describe the time point of a historical event by giving the date—July 4, 1776—but the starting time for an entertainment event by giving the time to the minute—8:00 in the evening on June 26, 2009. The time points we are talking about are actually intervals of time; a day is an interval of 24 hours, an hour is an interval of 60 minutes, and so on. Describing these intervals with points is very practical and, as I mentioned, commonly used. Therefore, it makes sense to do this in the model I am going to develop.

I want to have a solution for time points that doesn't depend on the level of granularity. It should be up to the implementer to decide exactly what time points represent: years, months, days, hours, and so on. The first constraint I want to implement is that the time points used for the attributes *since*, *from*, *to*, or *during* must be limited to time points that make sense for a particular business problem. I want to have a set of possible time points from an earliest to a latest point. I do not want a supplier on a contract *since* a time point earlier than the time point when my company was established.

I mentioned word *earlier* in the previous sentence. Why am I drawing attention to the fact that I used this word? Well, it implies something: The data type I am going to use to represent time points must support ordering. It has to support operators such as greater than, less than, and, of course, equal to.

Time Points Lookup Table

I can represent different granularity of time points by representing them with integers and a lookup table that gives context to those points. Integers support total ordering. An additional column of the lookup table gives context, such as granularity level. A lookup table also defines starting and ending points. You are already familiar with the auxiliary dbo.Nums table; this is just an expansion of it with an additional column that says my time points represent dates. In addition, the first time point in the table is January 1, 2009, and the last time point in the table is May 18, 2036 (I am using 10,000 time points). The following code creates and populates the dbo.DateNums lookup table:

```
SET NOCOUNT ON;
USE InsideTSQL2008;

IF OBJECT_ID('dbo.DateNums', 'U') IS NOT NULL DROP TABLE dbo.DateNums;
CREATE TABLE dbo.DateNums
 (n INT NOT NULL PRIMARY KEY,
  d DATE NOT NULL);

DECLARE @max AS INT, @rc AS INT, @d AS DATE;
SET @max = 10000;
SET @rc = 1;
SET @d = '20090101'      -- Initial date

INSERT INTO dbo.DateNums VALUES(1, @d);
WHILE @rc * 2 <= @max
BEGIN
  INSERT INTO dbo.DateNums
  SELECT n + @rc, DATEADD(day,n + @rc - 1, @d) FROM dbo.DateNums;
  SET @rc = @rc * 2;
END

INSERT INTO dbo.DateNums
  SELECT n + @rc, DATEADD(day,n + @rc - 1, @d)
  FROM dbo.DateNums
  WHERE n + @rc <= @max;
```

Note that this solution is quite flexible; it is not limited to representing time points only. In addition to representing a different granularity of time, the lookup table can give context to any interval you want. For example, you can represent intervals of temperature with it. Of course, this solution has disadvantages as well. Without the lookup table, you do not know what exactly your interval represents; you cannot reconstruct propositions directly from the tables that include the interval. In practice, it means you have to include this lookup table in all of your queries.

Semitemporal Problems

Let's focus on the easier part first: the predicate that involves the word *since* limits time in one direction only. A supplier is under contract since a time point, without limit on the other side; the contract in this case is valid now, if the since time point is in the past, and will be valid at any time point in the future. The primary key of the Suppliers_Since table from Figure 12-1 can remain the same as it was in the original Suppliers table. A single column, *supplierid*, is enough for the primary key because you can still have a single supplier only once in the table.

To make the problem slightly more complex, I am going to add another table in addition to Suppliers_Since to the InsideTSQL2008 database. Let's say that a single product can be supplied by multiple suppliers; therefore, the relation between suppliers and products in my case is going to be many-to-many and not one-to-many, as it is in the original database. I need an intermediate SuppliersProducts_Since table. The predicate of this table says that a supplier supplies a product since a point in time. For the sake of brevity, I am using only *supplierid*, *companyname*, and *since* columns for the Suppliers_Since table. The following code creates both tables:

```
-- Create table Production.Suppliers_Since
IF OBJECT_ID('Production.Suppliers_Since', 'U') IS NOT NULL
   DROP TABLE Production.Suppliers_Since;
CREATE TABLE Production.Suppliers_Since
(
  supplierid   INT           NOT NULL,
  companyname  NVARCHAR(40)  NOT NULL,
  since        INT           NOT NULL
  CONSTRAINT PK_Suppliers_Since PRIMARY KEY(supplierid)
);
-- Create table Production.SuppliersProducts_Since
IF OBJECT_ID('Production.SuppliersProducts_Since', 'U') IS NOT NULL
   DROP TABLE Production.SuppliersProducts_Since;
CREATE TABLE Production.SuppliersProducts_Since
(
  supplierid   INT           NOT NULL,
  productid    INT           NOT NULL,
  since        INT           NOT NULL
  CONSTRAINT PK_SuppliersProducts_Since
   PRIMARY KEY(supplierid, productid)
);
```

Semitemporal Constraints

In addition to primary keys in both semitemporal tables, additional constraints are needed. Of course, *supplierid* in the SuppliersProducts_Since table has to represent a valid supplier, and *productid* in the same table has to represent a valid product. Foreign keys to the Products and Suppliers_Since tables are needed. In addition, I want to limit the *since* column in both tables to valid time points only. The DateNums lookup table contains the valid time points. The following code creates the needed foreign keys:

```
ALTER TABLE Production.Suppliers_Since
 ADD CONSTRAINT DateNums_Suppliers_Since_FK1
     FOREIGN KEY (since)
     REFERENCES dbo.DateNums (n);
ALTER TABLE Production.SuppliersProducts_Since
 ADD CONSTRAINT Suppliers_SuppliersProducts_Since_FK1
     FOREIGN KEY (supplierid)
     REFERENCES Production.Suppliers_Since (supplierid);
ALTER TABLE Production.SuppliersProducts_Since
 ADD CONSTRAINT Products_SuppliersProducts_Since_FK1
     FOREIGN KEY (productid)
     REFERENCES Production.Products (productid);
ALTER TABLE Production.SuppliersProducts_Since
 ADD CONSTRAINT DateNums_SuppliersProducts_Since_FK1
     FOREIGN KEY (since)
     REFERENCES dbo.DateNums (n);
GO
```

One constraint is still not implemented in the model I created. A supplier can supply products only after the supplier has a contract. It would be nice if this constraint could be enforced through the syntax of a foreign key constraint. Unfortunately, such an advanced foreign key constraint is not implemented in SQL Server 2008. Therefore, I will have to use triggers. The following trigger rejects any inserts or updates that create a row in the SuppliersProducts_Since table that has a *since* value less than the *since* value of the row of the corresponding supplier in the Suppliers_Since table:

```
IF OBJECT_ID (N'Production.SuppliersProducts_Since_TR1', 'TR') IS NOT NULL
    DROP TRIGGER Production.SuppliersProducts_Since_TR1;
GO
CREATE TRIGGER Production.SuppliersProducts_Since_TR1
 ON Production.SuppliersProducts_Since
AFTER INSERT, UPDATE
AS
BEGIN
IF EXISTS
 (SELECT *
    FROM inserted AS i
         INNER JOIN Production.Suppliers_Since AS s
         ON i.supplierid = s.supplierid
            AND i.since < s.since
 )
 BEGIN
  RAISERROR('Suppliers are allowed to supply products
  only after they have a contract!', 16, 1);
  ROLLBACK TRAN;
 END
END;
GO
```

Even this trigger does not catch all possible ways of introducing invalid data. You could still update the Suppliers_Since table to set the *since* column value for a supplier to a time point later than some time point in the *since* column of the SuppliersProducts_Since table for the same supplier. Therefore, an additional update trigger on the Suppliers_Since table is needed:

```
IF OBJECT_ID (N'Production.Suppliers_Since_TR1', 'TR') IS NOT NULL
    DROP TRIGGER Production.Suppliers_Since_TR1;
GO
CREATE TRIGGER Production.Suppliers_Since_TR1
 ON Production.Suppliers_Since
AFTER UPDATE
AS
BEGIN
IF EXISTS
 (SELECT *
    FROM Production.SuppliersProducts_Since AS sp
        INNER JOIN inserted AS i
         ON sp.supplierid = i.supplierid
            AND sp.since < i.since
 )
 BEGIN
  RAISERROR('Suppliers are allowed to supply products
  only after they have a contract!', 16, 1);
  ROLLBACK TRAN;
 END
END;
GO
```

Testing Semitemporal Constraints

Let's check what we've done so far. I will execute some valid and invalid inserts. The following code inserts three valid rows into the Suppliers_Since table and four valid rows into the SuppliersProducts_Since table:

```
INSERT INTO Production.Suppliers_Since
 (supplierid, companyname, since)
VALUES
 (1, N'Supplier SWRXU', 10),
 (2, N'Supplier VHQZD', 15),
 (3, N'Supplier STUAZ', 17);
INSERT INTO Production.SuppliersProducts_Since
 (supplierid, productid, since)
VALUES
 (1, 20, 10),
 (1, 21, 12),
 (2, 22, 15),
 (3, 21, 23);
GO
```

Let's try invalid inserts. First, I will try to insert a supplier into the Suppliers_Since table with a *since* value that does not represent a valid time point:

```
INSERT INTO Production.Suppliers_Since
 (supplierid, companyname, since)
VALUES
 (4, N'Supplier MXMMM', 0);
```

As you might have expected, the foreign key to the DateNums table prevents this insert. Next, let's try to insert a row into the SuppliersProducts_Since table where the supplier is supplying a product before the supplier had a contract:

```
INSERT INTO Production.SuppliersProducts_Since
  (supplierid, productid, since)
VALUES
  (1, 22, 9);
```

The trigger on SuppliersProducts_Since fires and rolls back the transaction. Finally, let's try to update the *since* column in the Suppliers_Since table for supplier 3 to a value denoting a time point after the time point in the *since* column for the same supplier in the SuppliersProducts_Since table:

```
UPDATE Production.Suppliers_Since
   SET since = 24
 WHERE supplierid = 3;
```

This time, the trigger on Suppliers_Since fires and rolls back the update.

Queries on Semitemporal Tables

There isn't much to say about querying tables with semitemporal support. Queries on these tables are similar to queries you would perform on tables without temporal support at all; just include a join to the DateNums lookup table to get the context of the time points. For example, the following query lists all suppliers from the SuppliersSince table including the effective contract date (the date represented by the *since* value) for each supplier:

```
SELECT s.supplierid, s.companyname, s.since,
       d.d AS datesince
FROM Production.Suppliers_Since AS s
 INNER JOIN dbo.DateNums AS d
  ON s.since = d.n;
```

Tables with Full Temporal Support

Semitemporal support was quite easy to implement; however, it cannot provide an infrastructure for all business questions with temporal aspects. In the example I am developing, suppliers could have a contract valid for a limited time, and the attribute *since* is not sufficient to describe such a case. Instead of *since*, you could use two attributes, *from* and *to*, to help solve these problems. However, with the two attributes *from* and *to* in the design, as shown in Figure 12-1, many new issues arise.

In this scenario, one supplier can appear multiple times in the Suppliers_FromTo table because the same supplier could be under contract for separate intervals of time. For example, you could have two tuples like this in the relation with shortened header Suppliers_FromTo(*supplierid*, *companyname*, *from*, *to*):

{2, Supplier VHQZD, d05, d07}

{2, Supplier VHQZD, d12, d27}

I am writing time points in *d??* format to indicate they are denoting days in my examples; of course, in code examples, time points are integers. You can see that *supplierid* isn't enough for the primary key. You actually get two candidate keys here: {*supplierid, from*} and {*supplierid, to*}. The candidate keys are overlapping; thus, this design violates Boyce-Codd normal form. I prefer to have my databases normalized; therefore, I cannot be satisfied with this design.

It's not easy to identify and implement the appropriate constraints. Let me list the following useful ones:

- *To* should never be less than *from*.
- Two contracts for the same supplier should not have overlapping time intervals.
- Two contracts for the same supplier should not have abutting time intervals.

You can enforce the first rule simply, with a check constraint. The other two rules say that if you have the following tuple in your relation:

{2, Supplier VHQZD, d05, d07}

the following two tuples are forbidden, the first because its interval overlaps an existing one for the same supplier, and the second because it abuts one:

{2, Supplier VHQZD, d06, d10}

{2, Supplier VHQZD, d02, d04}

They should either be rejected by the database management system or merged with the existing tuple into a single tuple, as follows:

{2, Supplier VHQZD, d02, d10}

In my simplified example, the table Suppliers_FromTo only keeps track of the fact that a supplier has a contract in a time interval. In a real case, you may have different contracts for the same supplier. You could denote this fact by adding the additional attribute *contracttype* to the table. Then you could have the following additional constraint:

- No supplier can be under two distinct contracts at the same point in time.

So far, I haven't addressed suppliers. You could represent suppliers in an additional SuppliersProducts_FromTo table. The following important constraint is an extension of the one given in the semitemporal design:

- There should be no supplies from a supplier at a point in time when the supplier is not under a contract.

A foreign key on the *supplierid* column from the SuppliersProducts_FromTo table to Suppliers_FromTo cannot implement such a constraint. You need something different from a foreign key here; you need an inclusion dependency constraint that would guarantee the following:

SuppliersProducts_FromTo(supplierid, from, to) ⊆ *Suppliers_FromTo(supplierid, from, to)*

The design with *from* and *to* attributes does not answer all questions. How do you denote an open-ended contract? With NULL in the *to* column, with a special value like NOW, or with the last time point allowed? The propositions in a non-temporal design implicitly implement "now"; the propositions are valid now. Of course, without temporal support, the propositions are also valid at any other time.

You can imagine the hard work you would have to do to implement all of the constraints and to solve the other problems mentioned. It would be nice to have a shortcut here. Don't worry—I have a shortcut prepared. The two attributes that denote time intervals, *from* and *to*, can be merged into a single attribute named *during*. A predicate that uses the word *during* is logically equivalent to a predicate that uses the two words *from* and *to*. "Supplier *s* is under contract from time point *p* to time point *q*" is equivalent to "Supplier *s* is under contract during the interval from *p* to *q*." However, with a solution that would use a multivalued *during* attribute as a delimited list of integers, for example, none of the problems would be mitigated; in fact more problems would arise because the design would violate first normal form. This single *during* attribute needs a new data type—a data type for an interval. Such a data type should help simplify solutions for the constraints and other issues I have presented.

The IntervalCID UDT

In the previous chapter of this book, you learned how to implement a CLR UDT. You are going to exploit this knowledge now. But before I start explaining the new UDT, I have to mention that there is no single, agreed-upon definition of what it means to implement the idea of an *interval* in general as a type. Some say you actually need two new types: *interval* as a length of time and *period* as an anchored duration of time. Another possibility says that all you need is *interval* as a anchored duration between a beginning time and an end time. You can see that the second definition of an interval is identical to the first definition of period.

For the current scenario, I need the second possibility. I will define my interval type so that it represents a closed period from a beginning time and an end time. I am not going to implement an additional type that would represent an unanchored length of time, although such a type would be useful in some business scenarios. I can always calculate length from the beginning and end of an interval. Nevertheless, I am not sure which path Microsoft will prefer in future versions of SQL Server. Of course, I am quite sure Microsoft will do more to support temporal data. To prevent possible future collisions with built-in data types, I decided to name my UDT neither Interval nor Period. Because I have a lookup table that gives the context to my intervals, I can actually represent much more than just time with this solution. I can represent intervals defined on any countably infinite set that, because I give context with the lookup table. Actually, in a lookup table I can represent only finitely many time points, making my set of time points automatically discrete. Therefore, I decided to name my type IntervalCID, to show that it is an **interval** on a **c**ountably **i**nfinite **d**iscrete set. I am defining it as a closed interval; this means boundaries are part of the interval. Finally, the beginning and end points of the interval are integers in my solution, and because integers support total ordering, I can make an interval type that supports ordering and is well defined and well behaved.

I'll explain my UDT gradually; however, I trust that you've already read the previous chapter, and therefore the explanation can be very brief. Let's start with namespace declarations, UDT name, and attributes for the UDT:

```
using System;
using System.Data;
using System.Data.SqlTypes;
using System.Text.RegularExpressions;
using System.Globalization;
using Microsoft.SqlServer.Server;

[Serializable]
[SqlUserDefinedType(Format.Native,
                    IsByteOrdered = true,
                    ValidationMethodName = "ValidateIntervalCID")]
public struct IntervalCID : INullable
{
```

The *SqlUserDefinedType* attribute uses the *ValidationMethodName* property. With this property, I defined the name of the method used for checking values of type IntervalCID. SQL Server checks that values are appropriate for the serialization format using this method when doing casts to the type. However, SQL Server does not call this method for inserts and updates; therefore, I will call it manually in the *Parse* method and in any custom property that changes the values of UDT members. This method will perform a simple check that the end of an interval is equal to or greater than the beginning of the interval. Next, I need a regular expression to check input strings for the *Parse* method. I am accepting strings in format (*begin:end*), where *begin* and *end* are integers. In mathematics, closed intervals are denoted with square brackets: [*begin, end*]. However, square brackets could be confusing in code because they are used to delimit identifiers in T-SQL. The next part of the code defines the regular expression and other internal variables of the type:

```
//Regular expression used to parse values of the form (intBegin,intEnd)
private static readonly Regex _parser
    = new Regex(@"\A\(\s*(?<intBegin>\-?\d+?)\s*:\s*(?<intEnd>\-?\d+?)\s*\)\Z",
                RegexOptions.Compiled | RegexOptions.ExplicitCapture);

// Beginning and end points of interval
private Int32 _begin;
private Int32 _end;

// Internal member to show whether the value is null
private bool _isnull;

// Null value returned equal for all instances
private const string NULL = "<<null interval>>";
private static readonly IntervalCID NULL_INSTANCE
    = new IntervalCID(true);
```

Then I need two constructors, one for a known value and one for NULLs:

```
// Constructor for a known value
public IntervalCID(Int32 begin, Int32 end)
{
    this._begin = begin;
    this._end = end;
    this._isnull = false;
}

// Constructor for an unknown value
private IntervalCID(bool isnull)
{
    this._isnull = isnull;
    this._begin = this._end = 0;
}
```

You already know I have to override the *ToString* method for the default representation of values of my type, and that I need two properties to handle NULLs in SQL Server and client code:

```
// Default string representation
public override string ToString()
{
    return this._isnull ? NULL : ("("
        + this._begin.ToString(CultureInfo.InvariantCulture) + ":"
        + this._end.ToString(CultureInfo.InvariantCulture)
        + ")");
}

// Null handling
public bool IsNull
{
    get
    {
        return this._isnull;
    }
}
```

```
public static IntervalCID Null
{
    get
    {
        return NULL_INSTANCE;
    }
}
```

The *Parse* method accepts a string, validates it against a regular expression, and parses it into two integers. Note that in this *Parse* method, the validation method *ValidateIntervalCID* is called to check whether *_end* is equal to or greater than *_begin*:

```
// Parsing input using regular expression
public static IntervalCID Parse(SqlString sqlString)
{
    string value = sqlString.ToString();

    if (sqlString.IsNull || value == NULL)
        return new IntervalCID(true);

    // Check whether the input value matches the regex pattern
    Match m = _parser.Match(value);

    // If the input's format is incorrect, throw an exception
    if (!m.Success)
        throw new ArgumentException(
            "Invalid format for an interval. "
            + "Format is (intBegin:intEnd).");

    // If everything is OK, parse the value;
    // we will get two Int32 type values
    IntervalCID it = new IntervalCID(Int32.Parse(m.Groups[1].Value,
        CultureInfo.InvariantCulture), Int32.Parse(m.Groups[2].Value,
        CultureInfo.InvariantCulture));
    if (!it.ValidateIntervalCID())
        throw new ArgumentException("Invalid beginning and end values.");

    return it;
}
```

It is useful to have properties for instance variables. Therefore, I am defining properties for the fields *_begin* and *_end*. I am going to name these properties *BeginInt* and *EndInt*. Because I can also set the values of *_begin* and *_end* using these two properties, I am calling the *ValidateIntervalCID* method in the *set* part of the properties. Note also that the *get* parts of the properties are marked as deterministic and precise:

```
// Beginning and end separately
public Int32 BeginInt
{
    [SqlMethod(IsDeterministic = true, IsPrecise = true)]
    get
    {
        return this._begin;
    }
```

```
        set
        {
            Int32 temp = _begin;
            _begin = value;
            if (!ValidateIntervalCID())
            {
                _begin = temp;
                throw new ArgumentException("Invalid beginning value.");
            }

        }
    }

    public Int32 EndInt
    {
        [SqlMethod(IsDeterministic = true, IsPrecise = true)]
        get
        {
            return this._end;
        }
        set
        {
            Int32 temp = _end;
            _end = value;
            if (!ValidateIntervalCID())
            {
                _end = temp;
                throw new ArgumentException("Invalid end value.");
            }

        }
    }
```

To finish this general part of the IntervalCID type, I have to code the *ValidateIntervalCID* method:

```
// Validation method
private bool ValidateIntervalCID()
{
    if (_end >= _begin)
    {
        return true;
    }
    else
    {
        return false;
    }
}
```

Up to this point, the IntervalCID type has no special knowledge built in. Of course, the validation method solves the simplest constraint—*begin* must be less than or equal to *_end*. However, the additional operators I'll explain and code in the next steps will provide some shortcuts for issues I explained earlier in this chapter.

I will define quite a few useful Boolean operators and a couple of operators that work on intervals and return an interval. These operators are known as Allen's operators, named after J. F. Allen, who defined a number of them in a 1983 research paper on temporal intervals. Let me first introduce the notation I will use. I will work on two intervals, denoted i_1 and i_2. The beginning time point of the first interval is b_1, and the end is e_1; the beginning time point of the second interval is b_2 and the end is e_2. The Boolean operators I need are defined in Table 12-1.

TABLE 12-1 Boolean Operators for the IntervalCID Type

Name	Notation	Definition
Equals	$(i_1 = i_2)$	$(b_1 = b_2)$ AND $(e_1 = e_2)$
Before	$(i_1 \text{ before } i_2)$	$(e_1 < b_2)$
After	$(i_1 \text{ after } i_2)$	$(i_2 \text{ before } i_1)$
Includes	$(i_1 \supseteq i_2)$	$(b_1 \leq b_2)$ AND $(e_1 \geq e_2)$
Properly includes	$(i_1 \supset i_2)$	$(i_1 \supseteq i_2)$ AND $(i_1 \neq i_2)$
Meets	$(i_1 \text{ meets } i_2)$	$(b2 = e1 + 1)$ OR $(b1 = e2 + 1)$
Overlaps	$(i_1 \text{ overlaps } i_2)$	$(b_1 \leq e_2)$ AND $(b_2 \leq e_1)$
Merges	$(i_1 \text{ merges } i_2)$	$(i_1 \text{ overlaps } i_2)$ OR $(i_1 \text{ meets } i_2)$
Begins	$(i_1 \text{ begins } i_2)$	$(b_1 = b_2)$ AND $(e_1 \leq e_2)$
Ends	$(i_1 \text{ ends } i_2)$	$(e_1 = e_2)$ AND $(b_1 \geq b_2)$

The following code implements those Boolean operators in my UDT:

```
public bool Equals(IntervalCID target)
{
    return ((this._begin == target._begin) & (this._end == target._end));
}

public bool Before(IntervalCID target)
{
    return (this._end < target._begin);
}

public bool After(IntervalCID target)
{
    return (this._begin > target._end);
}

public bool Includes(IntervalCID target)
{
    return ((this._begin <= target._begin) & (this._end >= target._end));
}

public bool ProperlyIncludes(IntervalCID target)
{
    return ((this.Includes(target)) & (!this.Equals(target)));
}
```

```
public bool Meets(IntervalCID target)
{
    return ((this._end + 1 == target._begin) | (this._begin == target._end + 1));
}


public bool Overlaps(IntervalCID target)
{
    return ((this._begin <= target._end) & (target._begin <= this._end));
}


public bool Merges(IntervalCID target)
{
    return (this.Meets(target) | this.Overlaps(target));
}


public bool Begins(IntervalCID target)
{
    return ((this._begin == target._begin) & (this._end <= target._end));
}


public bool Ends(IntervalCID target)
{
    return ((this._begin >= target._begin) & (this._end == target._end));
}
```

In addition to Boolean operators, I will define three operators that accept intervals as input parameters and return an interval. These operators constitute simple interval algebra. Note that those operators have the same name as relational operators you are probably already familiar with: Union, Intersect, and Minus. However, they don't behave exactly like their relational counterparts. In general, using any of the three interval operators, if the operation would result in an empty set of time points or in a set that cannot be described by one interval, then I will return NULL. A union of two intervals makes sense only if the intervals meet or overlap. An intersection makes sense only if the intervals overlap. The Minus interval operator makes sense only in some cases. For example, (3:10) Minus (5:7) returns NULL because the result cannot be described by one interval. Table 12-2 summarizes the definition of the operators of interval algebra:

TABLE 12-2 Interval Algebra Operators for the IntervalCID Type

Name	Notation	Definition
Union	(i_1 union i_2)	(Min(b_1, b_2) : Max(e_1, e_2)), when (i_1 merges i_2); NULL otherwise
Intersect	(i_1 intersect i_2)	(Max(b_1, b_2) : Min(e_1, e_2)), when (i_1 overlaps i_2); NULL otherwise
Minus	(i_1 minus i_2)	(b_1: Min(b_2 - 1, e_1)), when ($b_1 < b_2$) AND ($e_1 \leq e_2$); (Max(e_2 + 1, b_1) : e_1), when ($b_1 \geq b_2$) AND ($e_1 > e_2$); NULL otherwise

Figure 12-2 shows the interval Union operator, Figure 12-3 the interval Intersect operator, and Figure 12-4 the interval Minus operator.

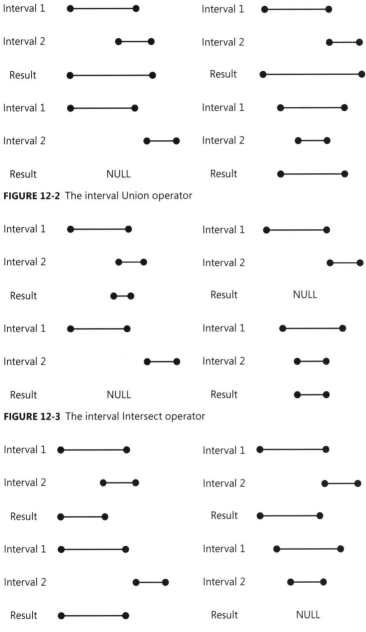

FIGURE 12-2 The interval Union operator

FIGURE 12-3 The interval Intersect operator

FIGURE 12-4 The interval Minus operator

The implementation of these interval algebra operators is the last part of my IntervalCID UDT:

```
    public IntervalCID Union(IntervalCID target)
    {
        if (this.Merges(target))
            return new IntervalCID(System.Math.Min(this.BeginInt, target.BeginInt),
                                   System.Math.Max(this.EndInt, target.EndInt));
        else
            return new IntervalCID(true);
    }

    public IntervalCID Intersect(IntervalCID target)
    {
        if (this.Overlaps(target))
            return new IntervalCID(System.Math.Max(this.BeginInt, target.BeginInt),
                                   System.Math.Min(this.EndInt, target.EndInt));
        else
            return new IntervalCID(true);
    }

    public IntervalCID Minus(IntervalCID target)
    {
        if ((this.BeginInt < target.BeginInt) & (this.EndInt <= target.EndInt))
            return new IntervalCID(this.BeginInt, System.Math.Min(target.BeginInt - 1,
this.EndInt));
        else
            if ((this.BeginInt >= target.BeginInt) & (this.EndInt > target.EndInt))
                return new IntervalCID(System.Math.Max(target.EndInt + 1, this.BeginInt),
this.EndInt);
            else
                return new IntervalCID(true);
    }
}
```

If you prefer to implement the IntervalCID type using Microsoft Visual Basic language, use the following version of the IntervalCID type:

```
Imports System
Imports System.Data
Imports System.Data.SqlTypes
Imports Microsoft.SqlServer.Server
Imports System.Text.RegularExpressions
Imports System.Globalization

<Serializable()> _
<SqlUserDefinedType(Format.Native, IsByteOrdered:=True, _
                    ValidationMethodName:="ValidateIntervalCID")> _
Public Structure IntervalCID
    Implements INullable

    Private Shared ReadOnly parser As New Regex("\A\(\s*(?<intBegin>\-?\d+?)\s*:\
s*(?<intEnd>\-?\d+?)\s*\)\Z", _
                                                RegexOptions.Compiled Or
RegexOptions.ExplicitCapture)
    Private beginValue As Integer
    Private endValue As Integer
```

```
Private isNullValue As Boolean
Private Const nullValue As String = "<<null interval>>"
Private Shared ReadOnly NULL_INSTANCE As New IntervalCID(True)

Public Sub New(ByVal _begin As Integer, ByVal _end As Integer)
    Me.beginValue = _begin
    Me.endValue = _end
    Me.isNullValue = False
End Sub

Private Sub New(ByVal isnull As Boolean)
    Me.isNullValue = isnull
    Me.beginValue = 0
    Me.endValue = 0
End Sub

Public Overrides Function ToString() As <SqlFacet(maxSize:=700)> String
    If Me.isNullValue = True Then
        Return nullValue
    Else
        Return "(" & Me.beginValue.ToString(CultureInfo.InvariantCulture) & _
               ":" & Me.endValue.ToString(CultureInfo.InvariantCulture) & ")"
    End If
End Function

Public ReadOnly Property IsNull() As Boolean Implements INullable.IsNull
    Get
        Return Me.isNullValue
    End Get
End Property

Public Shared ReadOnly Property Null() As IntervalCID
    Get
        Return NULL_INSTANCE
    End Get
End Property

Public Shared Function Parse(ByVal sqlString As SqlString) As IntervalCID
    Dim value As String = SqlString.ToString()

    If sqlString.IsNull Or value = nullValue Then
        Return New IntervalCID(True)
    End If

    Dim m As Match = parser.Match(value)

    If Not m.Success Then
        Throw New ArgumentException( _
            "Invalid format for an interval. " + _
            "Format is (intBegin:intEnd).")
    End If

    Dim it As IntervalCID
    it = New IntervalCID(Integer.Parse(m.Groups(1).Value, CultureInfo.InvariantCulture),

                         Integer.Parse(m.Groups(2).Value, CultureInfo.InvariantCulture))
```

```vb
        If Not it.ValidateIntervalCID() Then
            Throw New ArgumentException( _
                "Invalid beginning and end values.")
        Else
            Return it
        End If

End Function

Public Property BeginInt() As Integer
    <SqlMethod(IsDeterministic:=True, IsPrecise:=True)> _
    Get
        Return Me.beginValue
    End Get
    Set(ByVal Value As Integer)
        Dim temp As Integer
        temp = beginValue
        Me.beginValue = Value
        If Not ValidateIntervalCID() Then
            beginValue = temp
            Throw New ArgumentException("Invalid beginning value.")
        End If
    End Set
End Property

Public Property EndInt() As Integer
    <SqlMethod(IsDeterministic:=True, IsPrecise:=True)> _
    Get
        Return Me.endValue
    End Get
    Set(ByVal Value As Integer)
        Dim temp As Integer
        temp = endValue
        Me.endValue = Value
        If Not ValidateIntervalCID() Then
            endValue = temp
            Throw New ArgumentException("Invalid end value.")
        End If
    End Set
End Property

Private Function ValidateIntervalCID() As Boolean
    If endValue >= beginValue Then
        Return True
    Else
        Return False
    End If
End Function

Public Shadows Function Equals(ByVal target As IntervalCID) As Boolean
    Return ((Me.beginValue = target.beginValue) And (Me.endValue = target.endValue))
End Function

Public Function Before(ByVal target As IntervalCID) As Boolean
    Return (Me.endValue < target.beginValue)
End Function
```

```
Public Function After(ByVal target As IntervalCID) As Boolean
    Return (Me.beginValue > target.endValue)
End Function

Public Function Includes(ByVal target As IntervalCID) As Boolean
    Return ((Me.beginValue <= target.beginValue) And (Me.endValue >= target.endValue))
End Function

Public Function ProperlyIncludes(ByVal target As IntervalCID) As Boolean
    Return ((Me.Includes(target)) And (Not Me.Equals(target)))
End Function

Public Function Meets(ByVal target As IntervalCID) As Boolean
    Return ((Me.endValue + 1 = target.beginValue) Or (Me.beginValue = target.endValue + 1))
End Function

Public Function Overlaps(ByVal target As IntervalCID) As Boolean
    Return ((Me.beginValue <= target.endValue) And (target.beginValue <= Me.endValue))
End Function

Public Function Merges(ByVal target As IntervalCID) As Boolean
    Return (Me.Meets(target) Or Me.Overlaps(target))
End Function

Public Function Begins(ByVal target As IntervalCID) As Boolean
    Return ((Me.beginValue = target.beginValue) And (Me.endValue <= target.endValue))
End Function

Public Function Ends(ByVal target As IntervalCID) As Boolean
    Return ((Me.beginValue >= target.beginValue) And (Me.endValue = target.endValue))
End Function

Public Function Union(ByVal target As IntervalCID) As IntervalCID
    If Me.Merges(target) Then
        Return New IntervalCID(System.Math.Min(Me.BeginInt, target.BeginInt), _
                               System.Math.Max(Me.EndInt, target.EndInt))
    Else
        Return New IntervalCID(True)
    End If
End Function

Public Function Intersect(ByVal target As IntervalCID) As IntervalCID
    If Me.Overlaps(target) Then
        Return New IntervalCID(System.Math.Max(Me.BeginInt, target.BeginInt), _
                               System.Math.Min(Me.EndInt, target.EndInt))
    Else
        Return New IntervalCID(True)
    End If
End Function

Public Function Minus(ByVal target As IntervalCID) As IntervalCID
    If ((Me.BeginInt < target.BeginInt) And (Me.EndInt <= target.EndInt)) Then
        Return New IntervalCID(Me.BeginInt, System.Math.Min(target.BeginInt - 1,
Me.EndInt))
```

```
        ElseIf ((Me.BeginInt >= target.BeginInt) And (Me.EndInt > target.EndInt)) Then
            Return New IntervalCID(System.Math.Max(target.EndInt + 1, Me.BeginInt),
Me.EndInt)
        Else
            Return New IntervalCID(True)
        End If
    End Function

End Structure
```

Testing IntervalCID

It is time to test the new IntervalCID CLR UDT. Because many properties and operators are
defined, I have to perform quite a few tests. First, you have to build the CLR code; if you are
not familiar with building projects or solutions in Visual Studio from this book's previous
chapters, you can find instructions in Appendix A. Testing starts with enabling the CLR,
deploying the assembly, and creating the IntervalCID type. Note that you will have to change
the assembly name and code path in the CREATE ASSEMBLY statement to match the choices
you made when you built the assembly. In the following tests, I am testing the C# version of
the IntervalCID type.

```
USE master;
EXEC sp_configure 'clr enabled', 1;
RECONFIGURE;
GO
USE InsideTSQL2008;
GO
CREATE ASSEMBLY IntervalCIDCS
FROM 'C:\InsideTSQL2008\IntervalCID\IntervalCIDCS\bin\Debug\IntervalCIDCS.dll'
WITH PERMISSION_SET = SAFE;
GO
CREATE TYPE dbo.IntervalCID
EXTERNAL NAME IntervalCIDCS.IntervalCID;
GO
```

In the first group of tests, I want to check the assignment of values, NULLs, default string
representation, and properties that return the beginning and end of an interval. In addition,
to make the code a bit shorter, I'll check all of the Boolean operators in this part. For the sake
of brevity, I won't include here all of the code that tests improper values. I will leave this to
you; you can test more and try to create an interval using a different string than the *Parse*
method expects, or an interval with *_begin* after *_end*. Anyway, here are tests of different
representations of an interval and of Boolean operators:

```
DECLARE @i1 IntervalCID, @i2 IntervalCID, @i3 IntervalCID;
PRINT 'Testing presentation';
SET @i1 = N'(1:5)';
SELECT @i1 AS i1Bin, CAST(@i1.ToString() AS CHAR(8)) AS i1,
    @i1.BeginInt AS [Begin], @i1.EndInt AS [End];
PRINT 'Testing Equals operator';
```

```
SET @i2 = N'(1:5)';
SELECT CAST(@i1.ToString() AS CHAR(8)) AS i1,
       CAST(@i2.ToString() AS CHAR(8)) AS i2,
       @i1.Equals(@i2) AS [Equals];
PRINT 'Testing Before and After operators';
SET @i2 = N'(7:10)';
SELECT CAST(@i1.ToString() AS CHAR(8)) AS i1,
       CAST(@i2.ToString() AS CHAR(8)) AS i2,
       @i1.Before(@i2) AS [Before], @i1.After(@i2) AS [After];
PRINT 'Testing Includes and Properly Includes operators';
SET @i2 = N'(3:5)';
SELECT CAST(@i1.ToString() AS CHAR(8)) AS i1,
       CAST(@i2.ToString() AS CHAR(8)) AS i2,
       @i1.Includes(@i2) AS [i1 Includes i2],
       @i1.ProperlyIncludes(@i2) AS [i1 Properly Includes i2];
SET @i3 = N'(1:5)';
SELECT CAST(@i1.ToString() AS CHAR(8)) AS i1,
       CAST(@i3.ToString() AS CHAR(8)) AS i3,
       @i1.Includes(@i3) AS [i1 Includes i3],
       @i1.ProperlyIncludes(@i3) AS [i1 Properly Includes i3];
PRINT 'Testing Meets operator';
SET @i2 = N'(6:6)';
SELECT CAST(@i1.ToString() AS CHAR(8)) AS i1,
       CAST(@i2.ToString() AS CHAR(8)) AS i2,
       @i1.Meets(@i2) AS [Meets];
PRINT 'Testing Overlaps operator';
SET @i2 = N'(3:6)';
SELECT CAST(@i1.ToString() AS CHAR(8)) AS i1,
       CAST(@i2.ToString() AS CHAR(8)) AS i2,
       @i1.Overlaps(@i2) AS [Overlaps];
PRINT 'Testing Begins and Ends operators';
SET @i2 = N'(1:7)';
SELECT CAST(@i1.ToString() AS CHAR(8)) AS i1,
       CAST(@i2.ToString() AS CHAR(8)) AS i2,
       @i1.Begins(@i2) AS [Begins], @i1.Ends(@i2) AS [Ends];
PRINT 'Testing NULLs';
SET @i3 = NULL;
SELECT CAST(@i3.ToString() AS CHAR(8)) AS [Null Interval];
IF @i3 IS NULL
   SELECT '@i3 IS NULL' AS [IS NULL Test];
GO
```

In order to get the same results as I show below, choose Results to Text in SQL Server Management Studio. Here are the results of the previous code:

```
Testing presentation
i1Bin                   i1       Begin       End
--------------------    --------  -----------  -----------
0x800000018000000500  (1:5)     1           5


Testing Equals operator
i1       i2       Equals
--------  --------  ------
(1:5)    (1:5)    1
```

```
Testing Before and After operators
i1       i2         Before After
-------- -------- ------ -----
(1:5)    (7:10)   1      0


Testing Includes and Properly Includes operators
i1       i2         i1 Includes i2 i1 Properly Includes i2
-------- -------- -------------- -----------------------
(1:5)    (3:5)    1              1


i1       i3         i1 Includes i3 i1 Properly Includes i3
-------- -------- -------------- -----------------------
(1:5)    (1:5)    1              0


Testing Meets operator
i1       i2         Meets
-------- -------- -----
(1:5)    (6:6)    1


Testing Overlaps operator
i1       i2         Overlaps
-------- -------- --------
(1:5)    (3:6)    1


Testing Begins and Ends operators
i1       i2         Begins Ends
-------- -------- ------ -----
(1:5)    (1:7)    1      0


Testing NULLs
Null Interval
-------------
NULL


IS NULL Test
------------
@i3 IS NULL
```

The next part of the testing involves setting the beginning and end of an interval by modifying its properties:

```
DECLARE @i1 IntervalCID;
PRINT 'Original interval';
SET @i1 = N'(1:5)';
SELECT CAST(@i1.ToString() AS CHAR(8)) AS i1,
       @i1.BeginInt AS [Begin], @i1.EndInt AS [End];
PRINT 'Interval after properties modification';
SET @i1.BeginInt = 4;
SET @i1.EndInt = 10;
SELECT CAST(@i1.ToString() AS CHAR(8)) AS i1,
       @i1.BeginInt AS [Begin], @i1.EndInt AS [End];
GO
```

Here are the results:

```
Original interval
i1       Begin       End
-------- ----------- -----------
(1:5)    1           5

Interval after properties modification
i1       Begin       End
-------- ----------- -----------
(4:10)   4           10
```

Finally, I have to test whether the operators of the interval algebra work as expected. I am checking all three—Union, Intersect, and Minus—at the same time. However, I have to perform multiple checks with different intervals. I am checking interval algebra operators on intervals that overlap, that meet, that have nothing in common, and when one is properly included in the other:

```
DECLARE @i1 IntervalCID, @i2 IntervalCID;
PRINT 'Overlapping intervals';
SET @i1 = N'(4:8)';
SET @i2 = N'(6:10)';
SELECT CAST(@i1.ToString() AS CHAR(8)) AS i1,
       CAST(@i2.ToString() AS CHAR(8))AS i2,
       CAST(@i1.[Union](@i2).ToString() AS CHAR(8)) AS [i1 Union i2],
       CAST(@i1.[Intersect](@i2).ToString() AS CHAR(8)) AS [i1 Intersect i2],
       CAST(@i1.[Minus](@i2).ToString() AS CHAR(8)) AS [i1 Minus i2];
PRINT 'Intervals that meet';
SET @i1 = N'(2:3)';
SET @i2 = N'(4:8)';
SELECT CAST(@i1.ToString() AS CHAR(8)) AS i1,
       CAST(@i2.ToString() AS CHAR(8))AS i2,
       CAST(@i1.[Union](@i2).ToString() AS CHAR(8)) AS [i1 Union i2],
       CAST(@i1.[Intersect](@i2).ToString() AS CHAR(8)) AS [i1 Intersect i2],
       CAST(@i1.[Minus](@i2).ToString() AS CHAR(8)) AS [i1 Minus i2];
PRINT 'Intervals that have nothing in common';
SET @i1 = N'(2:3)';
SET @i2 = N'(6:8)';
SELECT CAST(@i1.ToString() AS CHAR(8)) AS i1,
       CAST(@i2.ToString() AS CHAR(8))AS i2,
       CAST(@i1.[Union](@i2).ToString() AS CHAR(8)) AS [i1 Union i2],
       CAST(@i1.[Intersect](@i2).ToString() AS CHAR(8)) AS [i1 Intersect i2],
       CAST(@i1.[Minus](@i2).ToString() AS CHAR(8)) AS [i1 Minus i2];
PRINT 'One interval contained in another';
SET @i1 = N'(2:10)';
SET @i2 = N'(6:8)';
SELECT CAST(@i1.ToString() AS CHAR(8)) AS i1,
       CAST(@i2.ToString() AS CHAR(8))AS i2,
       CAST(@i1.[Union](@i2).ToString() AS CHAR(8)) AS [i1 Union i2],
       CAST(@i1.[Intersect](@i2).ToString() AS CHAR(8)) AS [i1 Intersect i2],
       CAST(@i1.[Minus](@i2).ToString() AS CHAR(8)) AS [i1 Minus i2];
GO
```

The results of tests of interval algebra operators are:

```
Overlapping intervals
i1       i2       i1 Union i2 i1 Intersect i2 i1 Minus i2
-------- -------- ----------- --------------- -----------
(4:8)    (6:10)   (4:10)      (6:8)           (4:5)

Intervals that meet
i1       i2       i1 Union i2 i1 Intersect i2 i1 Minus i2
-------- -------- ----------- --------------- -----------
(2:3)    (4:8)    (2:8)       NULL            (2:3)

Intervals that have nothing in common
i1       i2       i1 Union i2 i1 Intersect i2 i1 Minus i2
-------- -------- ----------- --------------- -----------
(2:3)    (6:8)    NULL        NULL            (2:3)

One interval contained in another
i1       i2       i1 Union i2 i1 Intersect i2 i1 Minus i2
-------- -------- ----------- --------------- -----------
(2:10)   (6:8)    (2:10)      (6:8)           NULL
```

I will leave to you to perform similar tests on the Visual Basic version of the IntervalCID.
And I repeat: you can and maybe even should try many more tests with improper values.

Full Temporal Tables Using IntervalCID

It is time to revise the table with full temporal support—the Suppliers_FromTo table. Instead of using two separate *from* and *to* columns, I can use now a single *during* attribute, and create the Suppliers_During table. Of course, the *during* column's type will be my new IntervalCID data type. Similar to the way I created the SuppliersProducts_Since table in the semitemporal version, I can create a table for supplies with full temporal support, namely the SuppliersProducts_During table. Using this design, I can easily implement quite a few of the constraints I mentioned:

- *To* is never less than *from* because this constraint is implemented in the validation method of the IntervalCID data type.

- There is only one candidate key of my Suppliers_During table. This is a composite key, using the *supplierid* and *during* columns.

- The rule stating that "There should be no supplies from a supplier in time points when the supplier is not under a contract" can be implemented with triggers that aren't much more complicated than the ones I had in the semitemporal version.

I still want to have valid time points only in my *during* columns. In the semitemporal solution, I used a foreign key on the *since* column to the DateNums table. I should have a foreign key to check valid time points for each of the two properties of the IntervalCID type—the *BeginInt* and *EndInt* properties. However, SQL Server does not allow the use of CLR UDT properties for columns involved in a foreign key. Therefore, I have to create a computed column for each property and persist the two new columns. I can persist computed columns on those two properties because the *get* method of each property is marked as deterministic and precise. This design, with two added computed columns, might look complicated to you. After all, with this design I have the *from, to,* and *during* attributes. However, you should realize that I need this design because of the physical limitations of the current version of SQL Server; logically, all I need is the *during* column. The following code creates the Suppliers_During and SuppliersProducts_During tables:

```
IF OBJECT_ID('Production.Suppliers_During', 'U') IS NOT NULL
    DROP TABLE Production.Suppliers_During;
CREATE TABLE Production.Suppliers_During
(
  supplierid   INT          NOT NULL,
  during       IntervalCID  NOT NULL,
  beginint AS during.BeginInt PERSISTED,
  endint   AS during.EndInt   PERSISTED,
  CONSTRAINT PK_Suppliers_During PRIMARY KEY(supplierid, during)
);
GO
IF OBJECT_ID('Production.SuppliersProducts_During', 'U') IS NOT NULL
    DROP TABLE Production.SuppliersProducts_During;
CREATE TABLE Production.SuppliersProducts_During
(
  supplierid   INT          NOT NULL,
  productid    INT          NOT NULL,
  during       IntervalCID  NOT NULL,
  CONSTRAINT PK_SuppliersProducts_During
    PRIMARY KEY(supplierid, productid, during)
);
GO
```

In the code for creating the *during* versions of tables, you probably noticed that the Suppliers_During table does not have the *companyname* column. In addition, this table has no *beginint* and *endint* computed columns. Please also note that the foreign key in the next part of the code that checks whether *supplierid* in the SuppliersProducts_During table is a valid supplier references the Suppliers_Since table and not the Suppliers_During table. In the Suppliers_During table, *supplierid* is not unique, and you cannot reference it with a foreign key. You might think at this point that maybe I shouldn't have the Suppliers_Since table available if I have the Suppliers_During table; however, later in this chapter I will show you that I need both tables to resolve problems of temporal support I've mentioned so far. The question arises what exactly each table represents. Are the suppliers in the Suppliers_Since table only current suppliers, or all suppliers that ever were under contract? What about suppliers I already have contracted with, but where the contract begins at some time point in the future? I am going to have all suppliers that are, were, or will be under contract in this table. The Suppliers_During table is going to represent only the history, only suppliers with closed contracts. Of course, a supplier can appear in both tables; a supplier might be under contract during multiple intervals in the past, and is under contract now or will be under contract in the future. Note that in order to maintain all possibilities properly, I will have to change the Suppliers_Since table slightly. However, I am going to perform the changes later, when I am going to discuss the proposed sixth normal form. At this time, I would like to focus on problems with tables with full temporal support, with tables that include the *during* column.

Because Suppliers_Since represents all suppliers, present, past, and future, I can always get the current *companyname* column value from the Suppliers_Since table. I don't have to check whether the *during* column values in the SuppliersProducts_Since table use valid time points only because I will create a trigger that checks that the intervals in the SuppliersProducts_During table for a supplier are included in the intervals in the Suppliers_During table for the same supplier. The following code creates the foreign keys needed:

```
-- Valid time points
ALTER TABLE Production.Suppliers_During
 ADD CONSTRAINT DateNums_Suppliers_During_FK1
     FOREIGN KEY (beginint)
     REFERENCES dbo.DateNums (n);
ALTER TABLE Production.Suppliers_During
 ADD CONSTRAINT DateNums_Suppliers_During_FK2
     FOREIGN KEY (endint)
     REFERENCES dbo.DateNums (n);
GO
-- M-to-M relationship between suppliers and products
ALTER TABLE Production.SuppliersProducts_During
 ADD CONSTRAINT Suppliers_SuppliersProducts_During_FK1
     FOREIGN KEY (supplierid)
     REFERENCES Production.Suppliers_Since (supplierid);
ALTER TABLE Production.SuppliersProducts_During
 ADD CONSTRAINT Products_SuppliersProducts_During_FK1
     FOREIGN KEY (productid)
     REFERENCES Production.Products (productid);
GO
```

Next, I need a trigger on the SuppliersProducts_During table to implement the first part of the rule that a supplier can supply products only during periods when the supplier has a contract. However, because of operators I have built in the IntervalCID data type, this trigger is no more complex than its semitemporal counterpart:

```
IF OBJECT_ID (N'Production.SuppliersProducts_During_TR1','TR') IS NOT NULL
    DROP TRIGGER Production.SuppliersProducts_During_TR1;
GO
CREATE TRIGGER Production.SuppliersProducts_During_TR1
 ON Production.SuppliersProducts_During
AFTER INSERT, UPDATE
AS
BEGIN
IF EXISTS
 (SELECT *
    FROM inserted AS i
   WHERE NOT EXISTS
         (SELECT * FROM Production.Suppliers_During AS s
```

```
            WHERE s.supplierid = i.supplierid
                AND s.during.Includes(i.during) = 1)
)
BEGIN
  RAISERROR('Suppliers are allowed to supply products
            only in periods they have a contract!', 16, 1);
  ROLLBACK TRAN;
 END
END;
GO
```

Finally, I need a second trigger, a trigger on the Suppliers_During table to fully implement the rule that a supplier can supply products only during periods when the supplier has a contract. I have to prevent invalid updates of the *during* column as well as invalid deletes from this table:

```
IF OBJECT_ID (N'Production.Suppliers_During_TR1','TR') IS NOT NULL
   DROP TRIGGER Production.Suppliers_During_TR1;
GO
CREATE TRIGGER Production.Suppliers_During_TR1
 ON Production.Suppliers_During
AFTER UPDATE, DELETE
AS
BEGIN
IF EXISTS
 (SELECT *
    FROM Production.SuppliersProducts_During AS sp
   WHERE NOT EXISTS
         (SELECT * FROM Production.Suppliers_During AS s
           WHERE s.supplierid = sp.supplierid
               AND s.during.Includes(sp.during) = 1)
 )
 BEGIN
  RAISERROR('Suppliers are allowed to supply products
            only in periods they have a contract!', 16, 1);
  ROLLBACK TRAN;
 END
END;
GO
```

Testing Full Temporal Constraints

I have to check whether my constraints work as expected. Let me start again with some valid inserts:

```
INSERT INTO Production.Suppliers_During
 (supplierid, during)
VALUES
 (1, N'(2:5)'),
 (1, N'(7:8)'),
 (2, N'(1:10)');
GO
```

```
INSERT INTO Production.SuppliersProducts_During
  (supplierid, productid, during)
VALUES
  (1, 22, N'(2:5)');
GO
```

The next two statements try to insert invalid data. The first one tries to insert an invalid interval using an end point that is not a valid time point. The second one tries to insert a row for a supplier in the SuppliersProducts_During table with a supply in the period that the supplier was not under the contract; this row is rejected by the trigger:

```
INSERT INTO Production.Suppliers_During
  (supplierid, during)
VALUES
  (1, N'(1:15000)');
GO
INSERT INTO Production.SuppliersProducts_During
  (supplierid, productid, during)
VALUES
  (1, 20, N'(2:6)');
GO
```

I have to test the trigger on the Suppliers_During table as well. The following statements attempt an invalid update and an invalid delete on the Suppliers_During table. Both attempts are rolled back by a trigger:

```
UPDATE Production.Suppliers_During
   SET during = N'(3:5)'
 WHERE supplierid = 1 AND
       during = N'(2:5)';
GO
DELETE FROM Production.Suppliers_During
 WHERE supplierid = 1 AND
       during = N'(2:5)';
GO
```

Queries on Tables with Full Temporal Support

Queries on a table with full temporal support become slightly more complex. I have to give a context to two time points per row—to the beginning and end points of the *during* interval; therefore, I need two joins to the DateNums lookup table. I need another join to the Since table to get the company name. However, I can use the IntervalCID data type operators to create predicates for the WHERE clause that aren't much more complex than predicates used in queries over tables with semitemporal support. I will give a couple of examples. Let me start by selecting the contents of the Suppliers_During table:

```
SELECT sd.supplierid,
       CAST(ss.companyname AS CHAR(20)) AS companyname,
       CAST(sd.during.ToString() AS CHAR(8)) AS during,
       d1.d AS datefrom, d2.d AS dateto
```

```
FROM Production.Suppliers_During AS sd
 INNER JOIN dbo.DateNums AS d1
  ON sd.beginint = d1.n
 INNER JOIN dbo.DateNums AS d2
  ON sd.endint = d2.n
 INNER JOIN Production.Suppliers_Since AS ss
  ON sd.supplierid = ss.supplierid;
```

Results of the query:

```
supplierId  companyname          during  datefrom   dateto
----------- -------------------- -------- ---------- ----------
1           Supplier SWRXU       (2:5)    2009-01-02 2009-01-05
1           Supplier SWRXU       (7:8)    2009-01-07 2009-01-08
2           Supplier VHQZD       (1:10)   2009-01-01 2009-01-10
```

In the next example, I will find all suppliers that were under contract for a time interval fully contained within a specified interval. Here is the query:

```
DECLARE @i AS IntervalCID = N'(7:11)';
SELECT sd.supplierid,
       CAST(ss.companyname AS CHAR(20)) AS companyname,
       CAST(sd.during.ToString() AS CHAR(8)) AS during,
       d1.d AS datefrom, d2.d AS dateto
FROM Production.Suppliers_During AS sd
 INNER JOIN dbo.DateNums AS d1
  ON sd.beginint = d1.n
 INNER JOIN dbo.DateNums AS d2
  ON sd.endint = d2.n
 INNER JOIN Production.Suppliers_Since AS ss
  ON sd.supplierid = ss.supplierid
WHERE @i.Includes(sd.during) = 1;
```

And the results:

```
supplierid  companyname          during  datefrom   dateto
----------- -------------------- -------- ---------- ----------
1           Supplier SWRXU       (7:8)    2009-01-07 2009-01-08
```

In next example, I want to get suppliers that were under contract at any time point within a specified time interval. This means I have to search for rows where the *during* column overlaps the given interval:

```
DECLARE @i AS IntervalCID = N'(7:11)';
SELECT sd.supplierid,
       CAST(ss.companyname AS CHAR(20)) AS companyname,
       CAST(sd.during.ToString() AS CHAR(8)) AS during,
       d1.d AS datefrom, d2.d AS dateto
FROM Production.Suppliers_During AS sd
 INNER JOIN dbo.DateNums AS d1
  ON sd.beginint = d1.n
 INNER JOIN dbo.DateNums AS d2
  ON sd.endint = d2.n
 INNER JOIN Production.Suppliers_Since AS ss
  ON sd.supplierid = ss.supplierid
WHERE @i.Overlaps(sd.during) = 1;
```

The results are:

```
supplierid   companyname              during   datefrom     dateto
-----------  --------------------     -------  ----------   ----------
1            Supplier SWRXU           (7:8)    2009-01-07   2009-01-08
2            Supplier VHQZD           (1:10)   2009-01-01   2009-01-10
```

In final example, I need to find all the suppliers that were under contract at a specific time point, for example time point 9. This means that the specified time point has to be fully contained within the interval in the *during* column. Equivalently, the *during* interval must contain the interval consisting only of the specific time point:

```
DECLARE @i AS IntervalCID = N'(9:9)';
SELECT sd.supplierid,
       CAST(ss.companyname AS CHAR(20)) AS companyname,
       CAST(sd.during.ToString() AS CHAR(8)) AS during,
       d1.d AS datefrom, d2.d AS dateto
FROM Production.Suppliers_During AS sd
 INNER JOIN dbo.DateNums AS d1
  ON sd.beginint = d1.n
 INNER JOIN dbo.DateNums AS d2
  ON sd.endint = d2.n
 INNER JOIN Production.Suppliers_Since AS ss
  ON sd.supplierid = ss.supplierid
WHERE sd.during.Includes(@i) = 1;
```

And here is the result. Only one supplier was under contract at time point 9:

```
supplierid   companyname              during   datefrom     dateto
-----------  --------------------     -------  ----------   ----------
2            Supplier VHQZD           (1:10)   2009-01-01   2009-01-10
```

Unpack and Pack

In my tables with full temporal support, I have not yet implemented all the constraints that I mentioned I want. In this section, I'll deal with the following rules:

- Two contracts for the same supplier should have no overlapping time intervals.

- Two contracts for the same supplier should have no abutting time intervals.

- No supplier can be under two distinct contracts at the same time point.

I could solve these constraints in triggers using the operators of my IntervalCID data type. However, such triggers are not very simple, even with help of the IntervalCID data type methods. You could start with trying to implement an AFTER trigger similar to the one I implemented for the rule that a supplier can supply products only during periods when the supplier has a contract. With the help of the *Merges* operator, you might try to prevent overlapping and meeting intervals in the Suppliers_During table for a supplier with this trigger code:

```
IF OBJECT_ID (N'Production.Suppliers_During_TR2','TR') IS NOT NULL
    DROP TRIGGER Production.Suppliers_During_TR2;
GO
CREATE TRIGGER Production.Suppliers_During_TR2
 ON Production.Suppliers_During
AFTER INSERT, UPDATE
AS
BEGIN
IF EXISTS
 (SELECT *
    FROM inserted AS i
   WHERE EXISTS
         (SELECT * FROM Production.Suppliers_During AS s
           WHERE s.supplierid = i.supplierid
                 AND s.during.Merges(i.during) = 1)
 )
 BEGIN
  RAISERROR('No overlapping or meeting intervals
            for a given supplier allowed!', 16, 1);
  ROLLBACK TRAN;
 END
END;
GO
```

However, this trigger has several flaws. First, it does not allow any inserts in the Suppliers_During table at all! This is because the trigger fires after the rows are already inserted, and therefore rows from the inserted table always meet or overlap new rows in the Suppliers_Products table. You can try to avoid this flaw by changing the trigger to an INSTEAD OF trigger, which fires instead of the original statement, and thus before the target table has changed. Of course, you have to resubmit the original data modification statement in the body of the trigger. Still, this would not be a complete solution. The trigger would still reject some valid updates, like updates that shrink the *during* interval of an existing row. The shrunk interval in the *inserted* table would be included in an interval in the Products_During table for the updated rows. You can solve this problem by excluding rows from the *deleted* table from the check, by checking rows from the *inserted* table against rows from the Suppliers_Products excluding rows from the *deleted* table only. Your trigger should also reject multi-row inserts where intervals among newly inserted rows only meet or overlap for a supplier. You can accomplish this by limiting inserts and updates to a single row at a time. The following code creates such a trigger:

```
IF OBJECT_ID (N'Production.Suppliers_During_TR2','TR') IS NOT NULL
    DROP TRIGGER Production.Suppliers_During_TR2;
GO
CREATE TRIGGER Production.Suppliers_During_TR2
 ON Production.Suppliers_During
INSTEAD OF INSERT, UPDATE
AS
```

```
BEGIN
-- Disallowing multi-rows inserts and updates
IF (SELECT COUNT(*) FROM inserted) > 1
 BEGIN
  RAISERROR('Insert or update one row at a time!', 16, 1);
  ROLLBACK TRAN;
  RETURN;
 END;
-- Checking for overlapping or meeting intervals
IF EXISTS
 (SELECT *
    FROM inserted AS i
   WHERE EXISTS
         (SELECT * FROM
          (SELECT * FROM Production.Suppliers_During
           -- excluding checking against existing row for an update
           EXCEPT
           SELECT * FROM deleted) AS s
            WHERE s.supplierid = i.supplierid
                  AND s.during.Merges(i.during) = 1)
 )
 BEGIN
  RAISERROR('No overlapping or meeting intervals
             for a given supplier allowed!', 16, 1);
  ROLLBACK TRAN;
 END
ELSE
-- Resubmitting update or insert
 IF EXISTS(SELECT * FROM deleted)
  UPDATE Production.Suppliers_During
     SET during = (SELECT during FROM inserted)
   WHERE supplierid = (SELECT supplierid FROM deleted) AND
         during = (SELECT during FROM deleted);
 ELSE
  INSERT INTO Production.Suppliers_During
   (supplierid, during)
  SELECT supplierid, during
   FROM inserted;
END;
GO
```

Now let's perform some tests. The following two statements try to insert rows where the *during* interval overlaps or meets an existing interval for the same supplier:

```
-- Overlapping interval
INSERT INTO Production.Suppliers_During
 (supplierid, during)
VALUES
 (1, N'(3:6)');
GO
-- Meeting interval
INSERT INTO Production.Suppliers_During
 (supplierid, during)
VALUES
 (1, N'(6:6)');
```

Both inserts are rejected. Now, let's try a valid insert:

```
INSERT INTO Production.Suppliers_During
 (supplierid, during)
VALUES
 (2, N'(12:20)');
```

This insert succeeds. Let's try a valid update, an update that shrinks the interval in the row inserted in the previous test:

```
UPDATE Production.Suppliers_During
   SET during = N'(13:20)'
 WHERE supplierid = 2 AND
       during = N'(12:20)';
```

This update succeeds. Finally, let's delete the new row to revert the table to the state before the tests:

```
DELETE FROM Production.Suppliers_During
 WHERE supplierid = 2 AND
       during = N'(13:20)';
```

The trigger has become quite complicated. I am still not sure it works correctly in all circumstances. In addition, I would need to create yet another trigger to prevent the possibility that a supplier would be under two distinct contracts at the same time point. However, I want to show a different way to implement the three constraints mentioned in this section. I am going to introduce two relational operators called UNPACK and PACK. As you know, there are no such operators in T-SQL. I am going to show how useful it would be if they were implemented in T-SQL and, of course, how you can express them with existing operators. Before defining the operators, let's delete the trigger created in this section:

```
IF OBJECT_ID (N'Production.Suppliers_During_TR2','TR') IS NOT NULL
   DROP TRIGGER Production.Suppliers_During_TR2;
GO
```

Expanded and Collapsed Forms of Interval Sets

Any set of points in time can be represented by a collection of intervals, which I'll call an *interval set*. Look at the following three interval sets:

{(2:5), (3:7), (10:12)}

{(2:2), (3:3), (4:4), (5:5), (6:6), (7:7), (10:10), (11:11), (12:12)}

{(2:7), (10:12)}

Each set represents the same set of time points. The first set contains overlapping intervals. The second set contains only intervals exactly one time point long, or unit intervals. The third set represents the time points using the smallest possible number of intervals.

An interval set is in *expanded form* (or is *unpacked*) if it contains unit intervals only. An interval set is in *collapsed form* (or is *packed*) if it contains no intervals that overlap or meet. Any set of points in time can be represented uniquely in either form, and you can require one or the other form without losing anything. Of course, you already know I want to prevent overlapping or meeting intervals for the same suppliers or supplier and product in my Suppliers_During and SuppliersProducts_During tables; therefore, the collapsed form is required in my database.

The UNPACK Operator

I can transform a relation that has an attribute—such as *during*—of interval data type into another relation similarly to the way I rearranged sets of intervals. Without further delay, I'll define the *unpacked form* of a relation: a relation with full temporal support is *unpacked* if every value of interval type is a unit interval. To show how to implement PACK and UNPACK operators, I am going to create a new auxiliary table called Suppliers_Temp_During. I actually do not have any meeting or overlapping intervals in the Suppliers_During table, and I want it to keep it this way. Here is the code to create and populate this table:

```
CREATE TABLE Production.Suppliers_Temp_During
(
  supplierid   INT         NOT NULL,
  during       IntervalCID  NOT NULL,
  beginint AS during.BeginInt PERSISTED,
  endint   AS during.EndInt  PERSISTED,
  CONSTRAINT PK_Suppliers_Temp_During PRIMARY KEY(supplierid, during)
);
GO
INSERT INTO Production.Suppliers_Temp_During
 (supplierid, during)
VALUES
 (1, N'(2:5)'),
 (1, N'(3:7)'),
 (2, N'(10:12)');
GO
```

Table 12-3 shows the relation. Note that the *during* interval column overlaps in two rows for supplier 1.

TABLE 12-3 Suppliers_Temp_During Original Relation

supplierid	during
1	(2:5)
1	(3:7)
2	(10:12)

Table 12-4 shows the unpacked form of the relation.

TABLE 12-4 Suppliers_During Unpacked Relation

supplierid	during
1	(2:2)
1	(3:3)
1	(4:4)
1	(5:5)
1	(6:6)
1	(7:7)
2	(10:10)
2	(11:11)
2	(12:12)

Note something interesting in the unpacked form of the relation: A simple unique or primary key constraint over the *supplierid* and *during* columns enforces the rule that no supplier can be under two distinct contracts at the same time point. You can see how nice it would be if T-SQL supported the UNPACK operator. You could add a view with an unpacked version of the original relation and index it with a unique index over the *supplierid* and *during* columns. This unique index would prevent the insertion of rows that would violate the constraint mentioned.

So how can you get an unpacked form of a relation? Again, the DateNums lookup table is handy here. I can join the Suppliers_Temp_During table with DateNums using a non-equijoin, using the BETWEEN operator to find all time points between the beginning and end of an interval. From the time points, I can create unit intervals, as in the following query:

```
SELECT sd.supplierid,
       CAST(sd.during.ToString() AS CHAR(8)) AS completeduring,
       dn.n, dn.d,
       N'(' + CAST(dn.n AS NVARCHAR(10)) +
       N':' + CAST(dn.n AS NVARCHAR(10)) + N')'
        AS unpackedduring
  FROM Production.Suppliers_Temp_During AS sd
       INNER JOIN dbo.DateNums AS dn
        ON dn.n BETWEEN sd.beginint AND sd.endint
ORDER BY sd.supplierid, dn.n;
```

Here are the results of the query:

```
supplierid  completeduring n           d          unpackedduring
----------  -------------- ----------- ---------- ----------------------
1           (2:5)          2           2009-01-02 (2:2)
1           (2:5)          3           2009-01-03 (3:3)
1           (3:7)          3           2009-01-03 (3:3)
1           (3:7)          4           2009-01-04 (4:4)
1           (2:5)          4           2009-01-04 (4:4)
```

1	(2:5)	5	2009-01-05 (5:5)
1	(3:7)	5	2009-01-05 (5:5)
1	(3:7)	6	2009-01-06 (6:6)
1	(3:7)	7	2009-01-07 (7:7)
2	(10:12)	10	2009-01-10 (10:10)
2	(10:12)	11	2009-01-11 (11:11)
2	(10:12)	12	2009-01-12 (12:12)

The query uses the *beginint* and *endint* computed columns. Now I am going to use this query to create an indexed view on the Suppliers_During table. This indexed view is going to enforce the rule that no supplier can be under two distinct contracts on the same time point. SQL Server 2008 does not allow indexing a view that references methods and properties of a CLR data type directly. Again, you can see how handy it is to have these two computed columns included. Of course, the view has to be schema bound to make indexing it possible. The following code creates and indexes the view:

```
IF OBJECT_ID('Production.Suppliers_During_Unpacked', 'V') IS NOT NULL
    DROP VIEW Production.Suppliers_During_Unpacked;
GO
CREATE VIEW Production.Suppliers_During_Unpacked
WITH SCHEMABINDING
AS
SELECT sd.supplierid,
       N'(' + CAST(dn.n AS NVARCHAR(10)) +
       N':' + CAST(dn.n AS NVARCHAR(10)) + N')'
        AS unpackedduring
  FROM Production.Suppliers_During AS sd
       INNER JOIN dbo.DateNums AS dn
        ON dn.n BETWEEN beginint AND sd.endint;
GO
CREATE UNIQUE CLUSTERED INDEX Suppliers_During_Unpacked_ClIx
 ON Production.Suppliers_During_Unpacked(supplierid, unpackedduring);
GO
```

Now I'll try to insert an invalid row:

```
INSERT INTO Production.Suppliers_During
 (supplierid, during)
VALUES
 (1, N'(1:3)');
```

This row was rejected by the unique index on the view because the interval (1:3) for supplier 1 overlaps with interval (2:5) for the same supplier; if it were not rejected, supplier 1 would be under two distinct contracts in time points 2 and 3.

PACK Operator

I am going write a query on the relation from Table 12-3 in another way—the query is going to return a packed version of the relation. In the packed form of a relation, no *during*

intervals for a given supplier meet or overlap. Table 12-5 shows the packed form of the
Suppliers_Temp_During relation.

TABLE 12-5 Suppliers_Temp_During Packed Relation

supplierid	companyname	during
1	Supplier SWRXU	(2:7)
2	Supplier VHQZD	(10:12)

Note the two rules saying that two contracts for the same supplier should have no overlapping
or abutting time intervals are satisfied if you keep the relation in packed form. Therefore,
the only problem is how to keep the relation in packed form. If T-SQL supported the PACK
operator, this task would be quite simple. However, SQL Server 2008 has no such operator.
Again, I will express it with existing T-SQL operators.

Before developing the PACK operator, I have to mention explicitly something that is probably
self-evident: no matter whether you pack the original or unpacked form of a relation, you get
the packed form of the relation:

PACK(relation) = PACK(UNPACK(relation))

Therefore, I can pack the unpacked form of the relation. Intuitively, you can imagine that
packing is going to involve the GROUP BY operator. What I need to do is identify groups
of unit intervals that abut; I need a *grouping factor.* The technique for finding the grouping
factor I am going to use is explained in *Inside T-SQL Querying.* The idea is that if you subtract
the dense rank partitioned by *supplierid* from the time point *id* of the unpacked form of the
Suppliers_Temp_During relation, you get the same result for all rows that have time points in
a sequence without holes for a given supplier. Look at this query:

```
WITH UnpackedCTE AS
(
  SELECT sd.supplierid,
         CAST(sd.during.ToString() AS CHAR(8)) AS CompleteInterval,
         dn.n, dn.d,
         N'(' + CAST(dn.n AS NVARCHAR(10)) +
         N':' + CAST(dn.n AS NVARCHAR(10)) + N')'
           AS UnpackedDuring
  FROM Production.Suppliers_Temp_During AS sd
    INNER JOIN dbo.DateNums AS dn
      ON dn.n BETWEEN sd.beginint AND sd.endint
),
GroupingFactorCTE AS
(
  SELECT supplierid, n,
         DENSE_RANK() OVER (ORDER BY n) AS dr,
         n - DENSE_RANK() OVER(ORDER BY n) AS gf
  FROM UnpackedCTE
)
SELECT * FROM GroupingFactorCTE;
```

Here is the result of this query:

```
supplierid  n            dr                    gf
----------- ------------ --------------------- ---------------------
1           2            1                     1
1           3            2                     1
1           3            2                     1
1           4            3                     1
1           4            3                     1
1           5            4                     1
1           5            4                     1
1           6            5                     1
1           7            6                     1
2           10           7                     3
2           11           8                     3
2           12           9                     3
```

You can see that the grouping factor is 1 for supplier 1 for time points 2 to 7, and 3 for supplier 2 for time points 10 to 12. Now I can group by *supplierid* and grouping factor; the minimum time point per group will be the beginning and the maximum time point per group will be the ending time point of the interval of the group. The following query does the packing:

```
WITH UnpackedCTE AS
(
  SELECT sd.supplierid,
         CAST(sd.during.ToString() AS CHAR(8)) AS CompleteInterval,
         dn.n, dn.d,
         N'(' + CAST(dn.n AS NVARCHAR(10)) +
         N':' + CAST(dn.n AS NVARCHAR(10)) + N')'
           AS UnpackedDuring
  FROM Production.Suppliers_Temp_During AS sd
    INNER JOIN dbo.DateNums AS dn
      ON dn.n BETWEEN sd.beginint AND sd.endint
),
GroupingFactorCTE AS
(
  SELECT supplierid, n,
         DENSE_RANK() OVER (ORDER BY n) AS rn,
         n - DENSE_RANK() OVER(ORDER BY n) AS gf
  FROM UnpackedCTE
)
SELECT supplierid, gf,
       N'(' + CAST(MIN(n) AS NVARCHAR(10)) +
       N':' + CAST(MAX(n) AS NVARCHAR(10)) + N')'
         AS packedduring
FROM GroupingFactorCTE
GROUP BY supplierid, gf
ORDER BY supplierid, packedduring;
```

The result of this query is the packed form of the Suppliers_Temp_Products table:

```
supplierid  gf                   packedduring
----------- -------------------- -----------------------
1           1                    (2:7)
2           3                    (10:12)
```

Note that in my query, the *packedduring* column actually isn't a IntervalCID column, but a string column that mimics IntervalCID's ToString() result. To completely implement the PACK operator, you should CAST the *packedduring* column to the IntervalCID data type. Now you can create a stored procedure for inserts and updates that will keep the data always in packed form. I will leave this exercise to you; I have a couple more issues to solve.

Sixth Normal Form in Use

I have not solved two issues yet. How do I show that a contract is open-ended in a table with full temporal support? How do I denote the moving point now—in other words, how do I show which is the current version of the data for a given supplier? I am going to use an approximation of the sixth normal form (6NF), proposed by C. J. Date, to solve those two issues. Additionally, with 6NF I will also solve the problem of maintaining history for every single attribute.

Horizontal and Vertical Decompositions

C. J. Date proposed solving both problems with something he called *horizontal decomposition* of the original Suppliers table into two tables: one with semitemporal and one with full temporal support. Namely, for 6NF, I need both the Suppliers_Since and the Suppliers_During tables. In the Suppliers_Since table, I can maintain the current state. In the Suppliers_During table, I can maintain history. According to Date's proposal, the *since* table should have no rows in common with the *during* table. When a contract with a supplier finishes, I can delete the row for this supplier from the Suppliers_Since table and add it to the Suppliers_During table. The Suppliers_Since table shows the current state, which is limited to the open-ended contracts, and the Suppliers_During table shows the history—namely, all closed contracts. Therefore, the Suppliers_Since table shows current state without need for a special marker NOW.

This kind of design can work well in many business scenarios. However, many additional issues arise. When a supplier appears for the first time, the supplier has to be inserted in the Suppliers_Since table. You have to start with open-ended contracts. The Suppliers_During table maintains history; you have to move the supplier from the Suppliers_Since table to Suppliers_During table when the contract finished. The question arises what if a supplier is under a closed contract immediately. You can insert this supplier in the Suppliers_Since table, showing since which time point the supplier is under contract, and move this supplier to the Suppliers_During table when the contract ends. However, while the contract is valid, while the supplier exists in the Suppliers_Since table, your database does not represent this business scenario correctly; you have not represented when the contract ends anywhere. Probably a better design would be to include three tables: Suppliers, Suppliers_Since, and Suppliers_During. You would have all suppliers in the Suppliers table; the Suppliers_Since would represent open-ended contracts, and Suppliers_During closed contracts. Of course, then it would be appropriate to rename the *since* and *during* tables to something like Contracts_Since and Contracts_During. Nevertheless, I want to follow Date's proposed 6NF solution as closely as possible with SQL Server 2008. Therefore, I am going to continue with Suppliers_Since and Suppliers_During tables only.

As I mentioned, I have to make some compromises. The foreign key that checks whether the *supplierid* values in the SuppliersProducts_During table are valid references the Suppliers_Since table and not the Suppliers_During table. Because of that, I cannot delete a supplier from the Suppliers_Since table when the contract is over. The question now is what to do with the row in the Suppliers_Since for a given supplier when the contract with this supplier is over. As I should never delete a supplier from the Suppliers_Since table, I have to introduce a flag that marks the supplier as currently inactive instead. However, I can also represent future suppliers with open-ended contracts in the Suppliers_Since table; the *since* column value is not limited to current or past values only. Do please note that as soon as I allow the same supplier in both the *since* and *during* tables, they are not disjoint any more. In addition, they do not have the same set of attributes. Therefore, the term *horizontal decomposition* is not entirely accurate. Nevertheless, I use it because I want to discuss Date's proposed 6NF solution. In addition, in my model, the constraint that a supplier cannot have two different contracts at the same time point is not fully implemented. Because I do not have disjoint suppliers in the Suppliers_Since and Suppliers_During table, you could have a supplier under a valid contract in both tables.

To maintain history, I would ideally create a trigger that automatically adds a row to the Suppliers_During table when the inactive flag value in Suppliers_Since changes. Of course, I should similarly introduce "horizontal decomposition" and a trigger for the SuppliersProducts table; I need the SuppliersProducts_Since and the SuppliersProducts_During tables. Here is the code that adds a column *currentlyactiveflag* to the Suppliers_Since table:

```
USE InsideTSQL2008;
ALTER TABLE Production.Suppliers_Since
  ADD currentlyactiveflag BIT NOT NULL DEFAULT 1;
GO
```

I will now add two suppliers—one that was active only in the past and one that is going to become active in the future. In addition, I am adding history for the first of these into the Suppliers_During table. Both inserts are below:

```
INSERT INTO Production.Suppliers_Since
  (supplierid, companyname, since, currentlyactiveflag)
VALUES
  (4, N'Supplier NZLIF', 5, 0),
  (5, N'Supplier KEREV', 7000, 0);
INSERT INTO Production.Suppliers_During
  (supplierid, during)
VALUES
  (4, N'(5:8)');
```

Of course, in order to get currently active suppliers only, you have to select only rows where *currentlyactiveflag* equals 1:

```
SELECT s.supplierid,
       CAST(s.companyname AS CHAR(20)) AS companyname,
       s.since,
       d.d AS datesince,
       s.currentlyactiveflag
FROM Production.Suppliers_Since AS s
 INNER JOIN dbo.DateNums AS d
  ON s.since = d.n
WHERE s.currentlyactiveflag = 1;
```

And here are the results—currently active suppliers only:

```
supplierid  companyname          since      datesince  currentlyactiveflag
----------- -------------------- ---------- ---------- --------------------
1           Supplier SWRXU       10         2009-01-10 1
2           Supplier VHQZD       15         2009-01-15 1
3           Supplier STUAZ       17         2009-01-17 1
```

I am not going to create the trigger I mentioned. I am going to create another, similar trigger. Before that, I need to explain a new problem I introduced with my design. Remember that in the Suppliers_Since table, I have a *companyname* column; I did not add this column to the Suppliers_During table. It would be wrong to add a company name to the Suppliers_During table. This table shows only time intervals when the supplier was under contract; if the company name were included, this table would say that the supplier's company name has never changed in a given time interval. This is not true; a supplier can change its company name at any point in time, no matter whether the supplier has a contract at that time. Therefore, I have to maintain a history of company names separately from the history of contract validity intervals. I have to make a *vertical decomposition* of the Suppliers_During table into one table showing the intervals when a supplier was under contract, and additional tables, one for each attribute I want to maintain a history for, showing intervals when the attribute had a specific value.

I am going to show this vertical decomposition by introducing the SuppliersNames_During table. This table will maintain a history of suppliers' company names. The following code creates this table and adds a testing row to it:

```
IF OBJECT_ID(N'Production.SuppliersNames_During', 'U') IS NOT NULL
   DROP TABLE Production.SuppliersNames_During;
GO
CREATE TABLE Production.SuppliersNames_During
(
  supplierid   INT          NOT NULL,
  companyname  NVARCHAR(40) NOT NULL,
  during       IntervalCID  NOT NULL
  CONSTRAINT PK_SuppliersNames_Since PRIMARY KEY(supplierid, during)
);
```

```
ALTER TABLE Production.SuppliersNames_During
 ADD CONSTRAINT Suppliers_SuppliersNamesDuring_FK1
     FOREIGN KEY (supplierid)
     REFERENCES Production.Suppliers_Since (supplierid);
GO
INSERT INTO Production.SuppliersNames_During
 (supplierid, companyname, during)
VALUES
 (3, N'Supplier 3OLDN', N'(17:32)');
```

As I said, I'd like to have a trigger on the Suppliers_Since table that automatically adds a row to the SuppliersNames_During table when the *companyname* column changes for a supplier.

For the sake of simplicity, my trigger limits updates of supplier names to a single row at a time. The trigger does not do anything if the *companyname* column is updated to the same value. If there is already history of the name of the same supplier present, I have to check whether the end of the interval of the last historical row is greater than the current time point. I am treating this case as an error; this would mean that in the SuppliersNames_During, there is a history of the name of the supplier with validity in the future. In such a case, I am rolling back the transaction. Such a row should be deleted from the SuppliersNames_During table.

In the trigger, I have to find the interval when the updated name was valid. The end of this interval is one time point before the current time point because the new name is going to be valid from the current time point onward. Calculating the beginning time point of this interval is slightly more complicated. If I don't have a row for the supplier for whom I am updating *companyname* in the SuppliersNames_During table, this means the name is valid from the time point denoted with the *since* column in the Suppliers_Since table. In other words, if I don't have any history of a name for this supplier, the updated name was valid from the time I have data for this supplier. If I already have a history of names of the supplier, there can be a different name in the history with an end of valid time before the time point denoted with the *since* column in the Suppliers_Since table. All together, the beginning of the validity interval of the name I am updating is the latest time point calculated among the *since* value in the Suppliers_Since table and the latest *during.EndInt* value plus one in the SuppliersNames_During table for a given supplier. However, this logic does not cover all possibilities yet. What is the name of a supplier that is updated more than once at a specific time point, i.e. on the same day?

Finding the beginning and the end of the interval for the history of the name of a supplier is more complex, as the same name can be updated more than once at a time point, on the same day in my example. For the second update of the name of the same supplier, the beginning and end points of the interval of the history row in the SuppliersNames_During table must both equal the current time point. If the same row is updated twice at the same time point, then the maximal *during.EndInt* value in the SuppliersNames_During table for a given supplier must be equal to the current time point minus one. Of course, this raises another question: what if the same supplier name is updated a third time at the same time point? I cannot add another row for the same supplier with the *during* value equal to the interval from the current time point to the current time point, as this row would violate the primary key constraint of the SuppliersNames_During table. In such a case, the trigger just updates the existing row. If the same row is updated three or more times at the same time point, then the maximal *during.EndInt* value in the SuppliersNames_During table for a given supplier must be equal to the current time point. Finally, as you already know, I can also have future suppliers in the Suppliers_Since table, where the value of the *since* column is greater than the current time point. How can I find the proper interval for the history row in this case? My trigger does not maintain history for such changes. However, it does not roll back the transaction; it just sends a warning that the history of names is not maintained for future suppliers. As you can see, the trigger has to consider quite a few possibilities.

The following trigger maintains this history of names:

```
IF OBJECT_ID (N'Production.Suppliers_UpdateName_TR1','TR') IS NOT NULL
    DROP TRIGGER Production.Suppliers_UpdateName_TR1;
GO
CREATE TRIGGER Production.Suppliers_UpdateName_TR1
 ON Production.Suppliers_Since
AFTER UPDATE
AS
IF UPDATE(companyname)
BEGIN
 -- Limit to single row updates
 IF (SELECT COUNT(*) FROM inserted) > 1
  BEGIN
   RAISERROR('Update only one company name at a time!', 16, 1);
   ROLLBACK TRAN;
   RETURN;
  END;
 -- Do nothing for dummy updates
 IF ((SELECT companyname FROM inserted) =
     (SELECT companyname FROM deleted))
  RETURN;
 -- Find beginning and end time points
 DECLARE @begin int, @end int;
 -- End of during interval for the companyname
 -- equals to the time point when updated - 1
 SET @end =
  (SELECT n - 1
     FROM dbo.DateNums
    WHERE d = CAST(GETDATE() AS date));
 -- Checking whether history of names already exists
 IF EXISTS
  (SELECT *
     FROM Production.SuppliersNames_During AS s
          INNER JOIN inserted AS i
            ON s.supplierid = i.supplierid
  )
  BEGIN
   -- Checking whether there is "history" where end is in the future
   IF ((SELECT MAX(during.EndInt)
          FROM Production.SuppliersNames_During AS s
               INNER JOIN inserted AS i
                 ON s.supplierid = i.supplierid) > @end + 1)
```

```
    BEGIN
     RAISERROR('There is already history for names in the future.
                Delete inappropriate history first.', 16, 1);
     ROLLBACK TRAN;
     RETURN;
    END;
   -- Update was already done in the same time point
   -- @begin and @end must equal to current time point
   IF ((SELECT MAX(during.EndInt)
          FROM Production.SuppliersNames_During AS s
             INNER JOIN inserted AS i
               ON s.supplierid = i.supplierid) = @end) OR
      ((SELECT MAX(during.EndInt)
          FROM Production.SuppliersNames_During AS s
             INNER JOIN inserted AS i
               ON s.supplierid = i.supplierid) = @end + 1)
    BEGIN
     SET @end = @end + 1;
     SET @begin = @end;
    END
   -- "Regular" history: @begin equals MAX(end in history) + 1
   ELSE
     SET @begin = (SELECT MAX(during.EndInt) + 1
                     FROM Production.SuppliersNames_During AS s
                        INNER JOIN inserted AS i
                          ON s.supplierid = i.supplierid);
  END
-- No history of names for the supplier
ELSE
 SET @begin = (SELECT since FROM inserted);
-- Checking whether @begin > @end
-- Updates of names of future suppliers
IF (@begin > @end)
 BEGIN
  -- Just a warning
  RAISERROR('For future suppliers, history of names is not maintained.', 10, 1);
  RETURN;
 END;
-- Creating during interval as string
DECLARE @intv NVARCHAR(25);
SET @intv = N'(' + CAST(@begin AS NVARCHAR(10)) +
            N':' + CAST(@end AS NVARCHAR(10)) + N')';
-- Checking whether there is already a row for supplier name
-- with during equal to (@begin : @end)
-- Can happen for three and more updates in same time point
IF EXISTS
 (SELECT *
    FROM Production.SuppliersNames_During
   WHERE supplierid = (SELECT supplierid FROM inserted) AND
         during = CAST(@intv AS IntervalCID)
 )
  UPDATE Production.SuppliersNames_During
     SET companyname = (SELECT companyname FROM deleted)
   WHERE supplierid = (SELECT supplierid FROM inserted) AND
         during = CAST(@intv AS IntervalCID);
```

```
 -- "Regular" history
 ELSE
  INSERT INTO Production.SuppliersNames_During
   (supplierid, companyname, during)
   SELECT supplierid, companyname, @intv
     FROM deleted;
END;
GO
```

Now let's test how the trigger works. First, I am checking the current name and history of names for supplier 3:

```
SELECT supplierid,
       CAST(companyname AS CHAR(20)) AS companyname
  FROM Production.Suppliers_Since
 WHERE supplierid = 3;
SELECT supplierid,
       CAST(companyname AS CHAR(20)) AS companyname,
       CAST(during.ToString() AS CHAR(10)) AS during
  FROM Production.SuppliersNames_During;
```

Here are the results:

```
supplierid  companyname
----------- --------------------
3           Supplier STUAZ


supplierid  companyname          during
----------- -------------------- ----------
3           Supplier 3OLDN       (17:32)
```

It is time to update supplier 3's name to test the trigger. After the update, I will immediately check both Suppliers_Since and SuppliersNames_During tables with the same two SELECT statements I used above; for the sake of brevity, I have not repeated the queries:

```
UPDATE Production.Suppliers_Since
   SET companyname = N'Supplier 3NEWN'
 WHERE supplierid = 3;
```

This time I get the following results:

```
supplierid  companyname
----------- --------------------
3           Supplier 3NEWN


supplierid  companyname          during
----------- -------------------- ----------
3           Supplier 3OLDN       (17:32)
3           Supplier STUAZ       (33:196)
```

Please note that you will get a different end time point for the second row of the SuppliersNames_During table, as it depends on the date when you are executing the update of supplier 3's name. Let's now update the same name again, twice at the same time point. I am showing the UPDATE statement and the results of the two SELECT statements here:

```
UPDATE Production.Suppliers_Since
   SET companyname = N'Supplier 3NEW2'
 WHERE supplierid = 3;

supplierid  companyname
----------- --------------------
3           Supplier 3NEW2

supplierid  companyname          during
----------- -------------------- ----------
3           Supplier 3OLDN       (17:32)
3           Supplier STUAZ       (33:196)
3           Supplier 3NEWN       (197:197)
```

Note that another row was added to the history with the *during* column having an interval with beginning and end points equal to the current time point. Let's update the same supplier name for the third time and see the results:

```
UPDATE Production.Suppliers_Since
   SET companyname = N'Supplier 3NEW3'
 WHERE supplierid = 3;

supplierid  companyname
----------- --------------------
3           Supplier 3NEW3

supplierid  companyname          during
----------- -------------------- ----------
3           Supplier 3OLDN       (17:32)
3           Supplier STUAZ       (33:196)
3           Supplier 3NEW2       (197:197)
```

Note that this time there was no additional row inserted; the last row for supplier 3 was updated. It is arguable whether this is a correct approach. Is the complete history really maintained this way? It's not clear what history to maintain if someone updates the name of a supplier twice at the same time point. I decided that for multiple updates at the same time point, I am not going to maintain all intermediate states in the history table; I am maintaining only the last state before the current state. If you would like to maintain all intermediate states, you should drop the primary key from the SuppliersNames_During table, and change the trigger to insert rows for all updates at the same time point instead of updating one row only.

For a more complete testing, I am adding the code, without results, for two more possible updates. The first one updates a name for a supplier that does not have any history of names yet. The second one updates a name for a future supplier. You can execute the two updates if you want to perform this additional testing:

```
UPDATE Production.Suppliers_Since
    SET companyname = N'Supplier 2NEWN'
 WHERE supplierid = 2;
GO
UPDATE Production.Suppliers_Since
    SET companyname = N'Supplier 5NEWN'
 WHERE supplierid = 5;
```

You could create a trigger like this to maintain the history of every single non-key attribute of the semitemporal tables. Of course, you would need a similar trigger for the main During tables as well, such as for the Suppliers_During table, which maintains the history of intervals when suppliers were under a contract.

Sixth Normal Form

Consider the design shown in Figure 12-5.

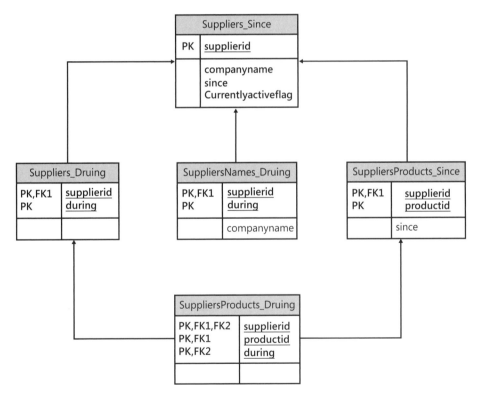

FIGURE 12-5 Proposed sixth normal form

Imagine that the functional dependencies in the picture are not foreign keys only. Imagine that the dependency between SuppliersProducts_During and Suppliers_During is value inclusion dependency. This means that such a *generalized foreign key* would check that the *supplierid* values match and that the *during* interval from the SuppliersProducts_During table is included in the *during* interval of the Suppliers_During table for a given supplier.

Such a design decomposes tables to add temporal support horizontally and vertically into irreducible components. If you join the data between any combination of tables from Figure 12-5 using a *generalized join*—a join that searches for matches in non-interval columns and intersections of intervals for overlapping columns of interval data type—you won't get any spurious rows. Therefore, with generalized constraints and operators, you don't have any trivial join dependency at all. This is exactly the definition of the sixth normal form (6NF): *A database is in 6NF if and only if it satisfies no non-trivial join dependencies at all*. Of course, SQL Server does not support generalized constraints and operators yet. However, as you've seen in this chapter, you can nearly achieve 6NF with existing possibilities. I said *nearly* because, as you'll recall, I did denormalize my actual design to have all of the constraints I wanted to have. I added the persisted computed columns *beginint* and *endint* to the Suppliers_During table. I did not implement horizontal decomposition to the *since* and *during* tables; these tables are not disjoint, as they should be in 6NF.

Finally, because this is the end of this chapter, you should clean up the Inside TSQL2008 database by dropping the objects created in this module:

```
USE InsideTSQL2008;
GO
DROP TABLE Production.Suppliers_Temp_During;
DROP VIEW Production.Suppliers_During_Unpacked;
DROP TABLE Production.SuppliersNames_During;
DROP TABLE Production.SuppliersProducts_During;
DROP TABLE Production.Suppliers_During;
DROP TYPE dbo.IntervalCID;
DROP ASSEMBLY IntervalCIDCS;
-- Note: drop the VB assembly instead of CS one
-- if you tested VB version of IntervalCID
-- DROP ASSEMBLY IntervalCIDVB;
DROP TABLE Production.SuppliersProducts_Since;
DROP TABLE Production.Suppliers_Since;
DROP TABLE dbo.DateNums;
GO
USE master;
EXEC sp_configure 'clr enabled', 0;
RECONFIGURE;
GO
```

Conclusion

It would be nice if SQL Server supported temporal data out of the box. However, you saw in this chapter that you could do a lot to maintain temporal data with the existing options. For a complete implementation of temporal data, support from the database management system would be invaluable. The proposed 6NF solution is theoretically sound, but it is hard to achieve in a real business scenario. As you could see, I had to make some compromises to the implementation.

Nonetheless, the code developed in this chapter should be useful for various scenarios. CLR helped to create the interval data type. Existing operators and other possibilities, such as triggers and indexed views, were used to maintain constraints in places where generalized relational operators and constraints would be handy. Advanced querying techniques helped to express UNPACK and PACK operators. This chapter exploited a lot of the knowledge you've learned thus far in this book.

Chapter 13
XML and XQuery

Dejan Sarka

SQL Server 2008 includes extensive support for XML. This support includes creating XML from relational data with a query and shredding XML into relational tabular format. Additionally, SQL Server 2008 has a native XML data type. You can store XML data, constrain it with XML schemas, index it with specialized XML indexes, and manipulate it using data type methods. All of T-SQL's XML data type methods accept an XQuery string as a parameter. XQuery (for XML Query Language) is the standard language used to query and manipulate XML data. The implementation of XQuery in SQL Server 2008 follows the World Wide Web Consortium (W3C) standard, and it is supplemented with extensions to support data modifications. You can find more about W3C on the Web at *http://www.w3.org/*, and news and additional resources about XQuery at *http://www.w3.org/XML/Query/*.

I will show you how you can use all of the XML features mentioned. However, I am not going to stop with the question "how"; I am going to give you a couple of ideas about why you would use XML in a relational database.

Converting Relational Data to XML and Vice Versa

I am starting with a short introduction to XML. After that, I am going to show how you can create XML as result of a query using different flavors of the FOR XML clause. You can also shred XML to relational tables using the OPENXML rowset function. Support for the FOR XML clause and OPENXML function were introduced in SQL Server 2000; support was slightly enhanced in SQL Server 2005 and SQL Server 2008.

Introduction to XML

I'll introduce basic XML through examples. I created the following XML document using the FOR XML clause; I'll show you the query later in this section.

```
<CustomersOrders>
  <Customer custid="1" companyname="Customer NRZBB">
    <Order orderid="10692" orderdate="2007-10-03T00:00:00" />
    <Order orderid="10702" orderdate="2007-10-13T00:00:00" />
    <Order orderid="10952" orderdate="2008-03-16T00:00:00" />
  </Customer>
  <Customer custid="2" companyname="Customer MLTDN">
    <Order orderid="10308" orderdate="2006-09-18T00:00:00" />
    <Order orderid="10926" orderdate="2008-03-04T00:00:00" />
  </Customer>
</CustomersOrders>
```

As you can see, XML uses *tags* to name parts of an XML document. These parts are called *elements*. Every *begin tag*, such as *<Customer>*, must have a corresponding *end tag*, in this case *</Customer>*. If an element has no nested elements, the notation can be abbreviated to a single tag that denotes the beginning and end of an element, like *<Order ... />*. Elements can be nested. Tags cannot be interleaved; the end tag of a parent element must be after the end tag of the last nested element. If every begin tag has a corresponding end tag, and if tags are nested properly, the XML document is *well-formed*.

XML documents are ordered. This does not mean they are ordered by any specific element value; it means that the position of elements matters. For example, the element with an *orderid* equal to 10702 in the preceding example is the second *Order* element under the first *Customer* element.

XML is case-sensitive Unicode text. You should never forget that XML is case sensitive. In addition, some characters in XML, such as <, which introduces a tag, are processed as markup and have special meanings. If you want to include these characters in the values of your XML document, they must be escaped using an ampersand (&), followed by a special code, followed by a semicolon (;):

- & (ampersand) must be replaced with *&*
- " (quote) must be replaced with *"*
- < (less than) must be replaced with *<*
- > (greater than) must be replaced with *>*
- ' (apostrophe) must be replaced with *'*

Alternatively, you can use the special XML *CDATA section* written as *<![CDATA[...]]>*. You can replace the three dots with any character string that does not include the string literal "]]>", and this will prevent special characters in the string from being parsed as XML markup. Processing instructions are written similarly to elements between lower than (<) and greater than (>) characters, and they start and end with a question mark (?), like *<?PItarget data?>*. The engine that processes XML—for example, the SQL Server Database Engine—receives those instructions. In addition to elements and processing instructions, XML can include *comments* in the format *<!-- This is a comment -->*. Finally, XML can have a *prolog* at the beginning of the document, denoting the XML version and encoding of the document: *<?xml version="1.0" encoding="ISO-8859-15"?>*.

In addition to XML *documents*, you can also have XML *fragments*. The only difference between a document and a fragment is that a document has a single *root* node, like <CustomersOrders> in the preceding example. If you delete this node, you get the following XML fragment:

```
<Customer custid="1" companyname="Customer NRZBB">
    <Order orderid="10692" orderdate="2007-10-03T00:00:00" />
```

```
    <Order orderid="10702" orderdate="2007-10-13T00:00:00" />
    <Order orderid="10952" orderdate="2008-03-16T00:00:00" />
  </Customer>
  <Customer custid="2" companyname="Customer MLTDN">
    <Order orderid="10308" orderdate="2006-09-18T00:00:00" />
    <Order orderid="10926" orderdate="2008-03-04T00:00:00" />
  </Customer>
```

If you delete the second customer, you get an XML document because it will have a single root node again.

As you can see from the examples so far, elements can have attributes. Attributes have their own names, and their values are enclosed in quotes. This is an *attribute-centric* presentation. However, you can write XML differently; every attribute can be a nested element of the original element. This is an *element-centric* presentation. Finally, element names do not have to be unique, as elements can be distinguished by their position; however, to distinguish between elements from different business areas, different departments or different companies, you can add namespaces. You declare namespaces used in the root element of an XML document. You can also use an alias for every single namespace. Then you prefix element names with a namespace alias. The following code is an example of element-centric XML that uses a namespace; the data is the same as in the first example of this chapter:

```
<CustomersOrders xmlns:co="InsideTSQL2008-CustomersOrders">
  <co:Customer>
    <co:custid>1</co:custid>
    <co:companyname>Customer NRZBB</co:companyname>
    <co:Order>
      <co:orderid>10692</co:orderid>
      <co:orderdate>2007-10-03T00:00:00</co:orderdate>
    </co:Order>
    <co:Order>
      <co:orderid>10702</co:orderid>
      <co:orderdate>2007-10-13T00:00:00</co:orderdate>
    </co:Order>
    <co:Order>
      <co:orderid>10952</co:orderid>
      <co:orderdate>2008-03-16T00:00:00</co:orderdate>
    </co:Order>
  </co:Customer>
  <co:Customer>
    <co:custid>2</co:custid>
    <co:companyname>Customer MLTDN</co:companyname>
    <co:Order>
      <co:orderid>10308</co:orderid>
      <co:orderdate>2006-09-18T00:00:00</co:orderdate>
    </co:Order>
    <co:Order>
      <co:orderid>10926</co:orderid>
      <co:orderdate>2008-03-04T00:00:00</co:orderdate>
    </co:Order>
  </co:Customer>
</CustomersOrders>
```

XML is very flexible. As you've seen so far, there are very few rules for a well-formed XML document. In an XML document, the actual data is mixed with metadata, such as element and attribute names. Because XML is text, it is very convenient for exchanging data between different systems and even between different platforms. However, when exchanging data, it becomes important to have the metadata fixed. If you had to import a document with customers, orders, as in the preceding examples, every couple of minutes, you'd definitely want to automate the importing process. Imagine how hard you'd have to work if the metadata changed with every new import. For example, imagine that the *Customer* element name changes to *Client*, and *Order* to *Purchase*. Or imagine that the *orderdate* attribute (or element) suddenly changes its data type from timestamp to integer. You'd quickly conclude that you should have fixed the schema for the XML documents you are importing.

Many different standards have evolved to describe the metadata of XML documents. Currently, the most widely used metadata description is with *XML Schema Description* (XSD) documents. XSD documents are XML documents that describe the metadata of other XML documents. The schema of an XSD document is predefined. The XSD standard allows you to specify element names, data types, number of occurrences of an element, some constraints, and more. The following example shows an XSD schema describing the element-centric version of customers and their orders:

```
<CustomersOrders>
  <xsd:schema targetNamespace="InsideTSQL2008-CustomersOrders" xmlns:schema="InsideTSQL2008-
CustomersOrders" xmlns:xsd="http://www.w3.org/2001/XMLSchema"
xmlns:sqltypes="http://schemas.microsoft.com/sqlserver/2004/sqltypes"
elementFormDefault="qualified">

    <xsd:import namespace="http://schemas.microsoft.com/sqlserver/2004/sqltypes"
schemaLocation="http://schemas.microsoft.com/sqlserver/2004/sqltypes/sqltypes.xsd" />
      <xsd:element name="Customer">
        <xsd:complexType>
          <xsd:sequence>
            <xsd:element name="custid" type="sqltypes:int" />
            <xsd:element name="companyname">
              <xsd:simpleType>
                <xsd:restriction base="sqltypes:nvarchar" sqltypes:localeId="1033"
sqltypes:sqlCompareOptions="IgnoreCase IgnoreKanaType IgnoreWidth" sqltypes:sqlSortId="52">
                  <xsd:maxLength value="40" />
                </xsd:restriction>
              </xsd:simpleType>
            </xsd:element>
            <xsd:element ref="schema:Order" minOccurs="0" maxOccurs="unbounded" />
          </xsd:sequence>
        </xsd:complexType>
      </xsd:element>
      <xsd:element name="Order">
        <xsd:complexType>
          <xsd:sequence>
            <xsd:element name="orderid" type="sqltypes:int" />
            <xsd:element name="orderdate" type="sqltypes:datetime" />
          </xsd:sequence>
        </xsd:complexType>
```

```
     </xsd:element>
   </xsd:schema>
</CustomersOrders>
```

In addition to XSD, SQL Server supports *XML Data Reduced* (XDR), another standard for metadata definition. Because XDR is an older and less powerful standard than XSD, I am going to focus on XSD in this chapter. In addition, XDR is deprecated, and Microsoft recommends against using it in new development work.

When you check whether a XML document complies with a schema, you *validate* the document. A document with a predefined schema is said to be a *typed* XML document.

I'll finish this brief introduction to XML by explaining another term: the XML *Document Object Model* (DOM). The DOM provides an object-oriented presentation of an XML document. XML DOM allows you to manipulate the document with properties, methods, and events. Note that the memory consumption of the XML DOM can be quite high.

Producing XML from Relational Data

I created all the XML in this chapter, including the schemas, using T-SQL. In this section, I'll explain how you can convert a query result set to XML using the FOR XML clause of the T-SQL SELECT statement. I'll explain the most useful options and directives of this clause; for a detailed description of complete syntax, please refer to SQL Server Books Online.

FOR XML RAW

The first option for creating XML from a query result is the RAW option. The XML created is quite close to the relational (tabular) presentation of the data. In RAW mode, every row from returned rowsets converts to a single element named *row*, and columns translate to the attributes of this element. Here is a simple query using the FOR XML RAW clause:

```
USE InsideTSQL2008;
SELECT Customer.custid, Customer.companyname,
       [Order].orderid, [Order].orderdate
FROM Sales.Customers AS Customer
  JOIN Sales.Orders AS [Order]
    ON Customer.custid = [Order].custid
WHERE Customer.custid <= 2
      AND [Order].orderid %2 = 0
ORDER BY Customer.custid, [Order].orderid
FOR XML RAW;
```

Note that for the sake of brevity I limited the number of customers returned to two, and that filtered only even-numbered orders (where *orderid* modulo 2 returns 0). The result of this query is:

```
<row custid="1" companyname="Customer NRZBB" orderid="10692" orderdate="2007-10-03T00:00:00" />
<row custid="1" companyname="Customer NRZBB" orderid="10702" orderdate="2007-10-13T00:00:00" />
```

```
<row custid="1" companyname="Customer NRZBB" orderid="10952" orderdate="2008-03-16T00:00:00" />
<row custid="2" companyname="Customer MLTDN" orderid="10308" orderdate="2006-09-18T00:00:00" />
<row custid="2" companyname="Customer MLTDN" orderid="10926" orderdate="2008-03-04T00:00:00" />
```

You can enhance the RAW mode by renaming the *row* element, adding a root element, including namespaces, and making the XML returned element-centric. The following query renames the *row* element and adds a root element with the ROOT directive; I will show how to make an element-centric presentation and include namespaces when I explain the AUTO option.

```
SELECT Customer.custid, Customer.companyname,
       [Order].orderid, [Order].orderdate
FROM Sales.Customers AS Customer
  JOIN Sales.Orders AS [Order]
    ON Customer.custid = [Order].custid
WHERE Customer.custid <= 2
      AND [Order].orderid %2 = 0
ORDER BY Customer.custid, [Order].orderid
FOR XML RAW('Customer'), ROOT('CustomersOrders');
```

The resulting XML of this query is:

```
<CustomersOrders>
  <Customer custid="1" companyname="Customer NRZBB" orderid="10692" orderdate="2007-10-
03T00:00:00" />
  <Customer custid="1" companyname="Customer NRZBB" orderid="10702" orderdate="2007-10-
13T00:00:00" />
  <Customer custid="1" companyname="Customer NRZBB" orderid="10952" orderdate="2008-03-
16T00:00:00" />
  <Customer custid="2" companyname="Customer MLTDN" orderid="10308" orderdate="2006-09-
18T00:00:00" />
  <Customer custid="2" companyname="Customer MLTDN" orderid="10926" orderdate="2008-03-
04T00:00:00" />
</CustomersOrders>
```

As you can see, I created a document instead of a fragment. It looks more like "real" XML; however, it does not include any additional level of nesting. The customer with *custid* equal to one is repeated three times, once for each order; it would be nicer if it appeared once only and had included orders as nested elements.

FOR XML AUTO

I find the AUTO option the most useful. It gives you nice XML documents with nested elements, and it is not complicated to use. In AUTO and RAW modes, you can use the keyword ELEMENTS to produce element-centric XML. The WITH NAMESPACES clause, preceding the SELECT part of the query, defines namespaces and aliases in the returned XML. Here is the query I used to create the chapter's second example of an XML document, which features element-centric XML with a root node and a single namespace:

```
WITH XMLNAMESPACES('InsideTSQL2008-CustomersOrders' AS co)
SELECT [co:Customer].custid AS 'co:custid',
       [co:Customer].companyname AS 'co:companyname',
```

```
        [co:Order].orderid AS 'co:orderid',
        [co:Order].orderdate AS 'co:orderdate'
FROM Sales.Customers AS [co:Customer]
  JOIN Sales.Orders AS [co:Order]
    ON [co:Customer].custid = [co:Order].custid
WHERE [co:Customer].custid <= 2
      AND [co:Order].orderid %2 = 0
ORDER BY [co:Customer].custid, [co:Order].orderid
FOR XML AUTO, ELEMENTS, ROOT('CustomersOrders');
```

The T-SQL table and column aliases in the query are used to produce element names,
prefixed with a namespace. A colon is used in XML to separate the namespace from the
element name.

Note that a proper ORDER BY clause is very important. With T-SQL SELECT, you are actually
formatting the returned XML. Without the ORDER BY clause, the order of rows returned is
unpredictable, and you can get a weird XML document with an element repeated multiple
times with just part of the nested elements every time. In the following query, I used
ORDER BY NEWID() to produce an approximately randomly ordered result:

```
SELECT Customer.custid, Customer.companyname,
       [Order].orderid, [Order].orderdate
FROM Sales.Customers AS Customer
  JOIN Sales.Orders AS [Order]
    ON Customer.custid = [Order].custid
WHERE Customer.custid <= 2
      AND [Order].orderid %2 = 0
ORDER BY NEWID()
FOR XML AUTO;
```

What I got is:

```
<Customer custid="2" companyname="Customer MLTDN">
  <Order orderid="10308" orderdate="2006-09-18T00:00:00" />
</Customer>
<Customer custid="1" companyname="Customer NRZBB">
  <Order orderid="10952" orderdate="2008-03-16T00:00:00" />
</Customer>
<Customer custid="2" companyname="Customer MLTDN">
  <Order orderid="10926" orderdate="2008-03-04T00:00:00" />
</Customer>
<Customer custid="1" companyname="Customer NRZBB">
  <Order orderid="10692" orderdate="2007-10-03T00:00:00" />
  <Order orderid="10702" orderdate="2007-10-13T00:00:00" />
</Customer>
```

Note that you might get quite different results; as I said, the exact form of XML returned is
unpredictable without a proper ORDER BY clause. It is not only the ORDER BY clause that is
important; the order of columns in the SELECT clause also influences the XML returned. SQL
Server uses column order to determine the nesting of elements. The following query uses
the correct ORDER BY clause; however, SQL Server generates the weird nesting, nesting you

probably did not want to return (*Customer* element under *Order* element) because of the wrong order of columns:

```
SELECT [Order].orderid, [Order].orderdate,
       Customer.custid, Customer.companyname
FROM Sales.Customers AS Customer
  JOIN Sales.Orders AS [Order]
    ON Customer.custid = [Order].custid
WHERE Customer.custid <= 2
      AND [Order].orderid %2 = 0
ORDER BY Customer.custid, [Order].orderid
FOR XML AUTO;
```

The result of this query is:

```
<Order orderid="10692" orderdate="2007-10-03T00:00:00">
  <Customer custid="1" companyname="Customer NRZBB" />
</Order>
<Order orderid="10702" orderdate="2007-10-13T00:00:00">
  <Customer custid="1" companyname="Customer NRZBB" />
</Order>
<Order orderid="10952" orderdate="2008-03-16T00:00:00">
  <Customer custid="1" companyname="Customer NRZBB" />
</Order>
<Order orderid="10308" orderdate="2006-09-18T00:00:00">
  <Customer custid="2" companyname="Customer MLTDN" />
</Order>
<Order orderid="10926" orderdate="2008-03-04T00:00:00">
  <Customer custid="2" companyname="Customer MLTDN" />
</Order>
```

Let me show you another example of how important it is to take care with the SELECT list. The following query is very similar to the previous one; I just replaced the *Customer.custid* column with *[Orders].custid*:

```
SELECT [Order].orderid, [Order].orderdate,
       [Order].custid, Customer.companyname
FROM Sales.Customers AS Customer
  JOIN Sales.Orders AS [Order]
    ON Customer.custid = [Order].custid
WHERE Customer.custid <= 2
      AND [Order].orderid %2 = 0
ORDER BY Customer.custid, [Order].orderid
FOR XML AUTO;
```

Without a FOR XML clause, you get the same result before and after this change. However, look at the XML generated by the second query:

```
<Order orderid="10692" orderdate="2007-10-03T00:00:00" custid="1">
  <Customer companyname="Customer NRZBB" />
</Order>
<Order orderid="10702" orderdate="2007-10-13T00:00:00" custid="1">
  <Customer companyname="Customer NRZBB" />
</Order>
```

```
<Order orderid="10952" orderdate="2008-03-16T00:00:00" custid="1">
  <Customer companyname="Customer NRZBB" />
</Order>
<Order orderid="10308" orderdate="2006-09-18T00:00:00" custid="2">
  <Customer companyname="Customer MLTDN" />
</Order>
<Order orderid="10926" orderdate="2008-03-04T00:00:00" custid="2">
  <Customer companyname="Customer MLTDN" />
</Order>
```

Can you spot the difference from the XML returned by the previous query? In this XML, *custid* is an attribute of *Order*; in the previous one, *custid* was an attribute of *Customer*.

You might be vexed by the fact that you have to be so careful with the columns you select; in a relation, the order of columns and rows is not important. Nevertheless, you have to realize that the result of your query is not a relation; it is text in XML format, and parts of your query are used for formatting the text.

In RAW and AUTO mode, you can also return the XSD schema of the document you are creating. This schema is included inside XML returned, before the actual XML data; therefore, it is called an *inline* schema. You return XSD with the XMLSCHEMA directive. This directive accepts a parameter that defines a target namespace. If you want to return XDR, use the XMLDATA directive. If you need schema only, without data, simply include a WHERE condition in your query with a predicate that no row can satisfy. I used the following query to return the schema I showed in the section "Introduction to XML" earlier in the chapter:

```
SELECT [Customer].custid AS 'custid',
       [Customer].companyname AS 'companyname',
       [Order].orderid AS 'orderid',
       [Order].orderdate AS 'orderdate'
FROM Sales.Customers AS [Customer]
  JOIN Sales.Orders AS [Order]
    ON [Customer].custid = [Order].custid
WHERE 1 = 2
FOR XML AUTO, ELEMENTS, ROOT('CustomersOrders'),
       XMLSCHEMA('InsideTSQL2008-CustomersOrders');
```

FOR XML EXPLICIT

With the last two flavors of the FOR XML clause—the EXPLICIT and PATH options—you can define the XML returned manually. With these two options, you have total control of the XML document returned. The EXPLICIT mode is included for backward compatibility only; it uses proprietary T-SQL syntax for formatting XML. The PATH mode uses standard XML XPath expressions to define the elements and attributes of the XML you are creating. I find it also easier to use than EXPLICIT mode.

SQL Server needs a specific format of the rowset returned to process the XML in EXPLICIT mode. The first two columns must be Tag and Parent integers, which provide the hierarchy information. Tag defines the level of nesting, and Parent points to the parent level. You create multiple levels with multiple SELECTs using the UNION ALL operator; the first SELECT defines the first level of nesting, the second defines the second level of nesting, and so on. Every SELECT must include all columns, of course; however, the columns that are not applicable for a specific level must have NULLs instead of a value. You define element and attribute names with column aliases of the SELECT clause in the *ElementName!TagNumber!AttributeName! Directive* format. If the *Directive* part is omitted, you are creating attribute-centric XML. You can use the *element* directive to produce element-centric XML. The following query is an example of producing XML with the EXPLICIT option:

```
SELECT 1 AS Tag,
       NULL AS Parent,
       Customer.custid AS [Customer!1!custid],
       Customer.companyname AS [Customer!1!companyname],
       NULL AS [Order!2!orderid],
       NULL AS [Order!2!orderdate]
FROM Sales.Customers AS Customer
WHERE Customer.custid <= 2
UNION ALL
SELECT 2 AS Tag,
       1 AS Parent,
       Customer.custid AS [Customer!1!custid],
       NULL AS [Customer!1!companyname],
       [Order].orderid AS [Order!2!orderid],
       [Order].orderdate AS [Order!2!orderdate]
FROM Sales.Customers AS Customer
  JOIN Sales.Orders AS [Order]
    ON Customer.custid = [Order].custid
WHERE Customer.custid <= 2
      AND [Order].orderid %2 = 0
ORDER BY [Customer!1!custid],
         [Order!2!orderid]
FOR XML EXPLICIT
```

The result is:

```
<Customer custid="1" companyname="Customer NRZBB">
  <Order orderid="10692" orderdate="2007-10-03T00:00:00" />
  <Order orderid="10702" orderdate="2007-10-13T00:00:00" />
  <Order orderid="10952" orderdate="2008-03-16T00:00:00" />
</Customer>
<Customer custid="2" companyname="Customer MLTDN">
  <Order orderid="10308" orderdate="2006-09-18T00:00:00" />
  <Order orderid="10926" orderdate="2008-03-04T00:00:00" />
</Customer>
```

FOR XML PATH

In PATH mode, column names and aliases serve as XPath expressions. XPath expressions define the path to the element in the XML generated. Path is expressed in a hierarchical way; levels are delimited with the slash (/) character. By default, every column becomes an element; if you want to generate attribute-centric XML, prefix the alias name with the at (@) character. Here is an example of a simple XPATH query:

```
SELECT Customer.custid AS [@custid],
       Customer.companyname AS [Customer/companyname]
FROM Sales.Customers AS Customer
WHERE Customer.custid <= 2
ORDER BY Customer.custid
FOR XML PATH;
```

This query produces the following XML:

```
<row custid="1">
  <Customer>
    <companyname>Customer NRZBB</companyname>
  </Customer>
</row>
<row custid="2">
  <Customer>
    <companyname>Customer MLTDN</companyname>
  </Customer>
</row>
```

As you can see, the PATH mode produced an element for each row of the resulting rowset; in other words, for each customer, the name of this element is *row*. If you want to have a different name, use the syntax FOR XML PATH('name'). In the preceding example, the *custid* column was converted to the *custid* attribute of the *row* element. This element has the nested element *Customer*, which has another nested element, *companyname*. The first level of nesting was achieved by using an XPath expression denoting the hierarchy for the *companyname* column alias, and the second level of nesting was created by SQL Server, which, as I mentioned, produces elements by default in the PATH mode.

If you specify *data()* or *text()* XPath functions in the column alias name, the result is an atomic string of values only, without any element of attribute names. The *data()* function adds a space as a delimiter between values. If you define an empty name for the *row* element with FOR XML PATH(''), you get a single atomic string of concatenated values. This makes PATH mode a good option for aggregate string concatenation across rows. The following query shows how you can use the *data()* function and an empty default element name to concatenate customer ID numbers with company names in a single string:

```
SELECT Customer.custid AS [data()],
       Customer.companyname AS [data()]
FROM Sales.Customers AS Customer
WHERE Customer.custid <= 2
ORDER BY Customer.custid
FOR XML PATH ('');
```

The result of this query is a string. Actually, it is still treated as XML; however, you can convert it to any string data type. Here is the result of the preceding query:

```
1 Customer NRZBB 2 Customer MLTDN
```

If you want to create XML with nested elements for child tables, you have to use subqueries in the SELECT part of the query in the PATH mode. Subqueries have to return a scalar value in SELECT clause. However, you know that a parent row can have multiple child rows; a customer can have multiple orders. You return a scalar value by returning XML from the subquery. Then the result is returned as a single scalar XML value. You format nested XML from the subquery with the FOR XML clause, as you format XML in outer query. Additionally, you have to use the TYPE directive of the FOR XML clause to produce a value of XML data type, and not XML as text, which cannot be consumed by the outer query. The following query shows this technique for creating the same XML that I created in the FOR XML EXPLICIT part of this section. Note the subquery with the FOR XML PATH clause and the TYPE directive.

```
SELECT Customer.custid AS [@custid],
       Customer.companyname AS [@companyname],
       (SELECT [Order].orderid AS [@orderid],
               [Order].orderdate AS [@orderdate]
        FROM Sales.Orders AS [Order]
        WHERE Customer.custid = [Order].custid
             AND [Order].orderid %2 = 0
        ORDER BY [Order].orderid
        FOR XML PATH('Order'), TYPE)
FROM Sales.Customers AS Customer
WHERE Customer.custid <= 2
ORDER BY Customer.custid
FOR XML PATH('Customer');
```

The result is, as expected, the same as the result of the query that used EXPLICIT mode to format the XML returned:

```
<Customer custid="1" companyname="Customer NRZBB">
  <Order orderid="10692" orderdate="2007-10-03T00:00:00" />
  <Order orderid="10702" orderdate="2007-10-13T00:00:00" />
  <Order orderid="10952" orderdate="2008-03-16T00:00:00" />
</Customer>
<Customer custid="2" companyname="Customer MLTDN">
  <Order orderid="10308" orderdate="2006-09-18T00:00:00" />
  <Order orderid="10926" orderdate="2008-03-04T00:00:00" />
</Customer>
```

Shredding XML to Tables

Now that I've shown you how to create XML from relational data, I want to introduce the opposite process. Converting XML to relational tables is known as *shredding* XML. You can do this by using the *nodes* method of the XML data type, which I will describe later in this chapter. Starting with SQL Server 2000, you can do this in T-SQL with the OPENXML rowset function. In this section, I will talk about this function.

The OPENXML function provides a rowset over in-memory XML documents using DOM presentation. Before parsing the DOM, you have to prepare it. To prepare the DOM presentation of XML, you have to call the system stored procedure *sp_xml_preparedocument*. After you shred the document, you have to remove the DOM presentation using the system procedure *sp_xml_removedocument*.

The OPENXML function uses the following parameters:

- An XML DOM document handle, returned by *sp_xml_preparedocument*
- An XPath expression to find the nodes you want to map to rows of a rowset returned
- A description of the rowset returned
- Mapping between XML nodes and rowset columns

The document handle is an integer. This is the simplest parameter. The XPath expression is specified as *rowpattern*, which defines how XML nodes translate to rows. The path to a node is used as a pattern; nodes below the selected node define rows of the returned rowset.

If you do not provide a description of the rowset returned, the OPENXML function returns a so-called *edge* table. Every edge in the parsed XML document tree maps to a row in the rowset; this means that this table has all possible information about the XML parsed, and you can use T-SQL statements to extract only the information you need from it. The following query shows you the edge table using an XML document very similar to the previous examples in this chapter. It extracts Customer nodes, meaning each *Customer* element; the rowpattern XPath expression is '/CustomersOrders/Customer':

```
DECLARE @DocHandle AS INT;
DECLARE @XmlDocument AS NVARCHAR(1000);
SET @XmlDocument = N'
<CustomersOrders>
  <Customer custid="1">
    <companyname>Customer NRZBB</companyname>
    <Order orderid="10692">
      <orderdate>2007-10-03T00:00:00</orderdate>
    </Order>
    <Order orderid="10702">
      <orderdate>2007-10-13T00:00:00</orderdate>
    </Order>
    <Order orderid="10952">
      <orderdate>2008-03-16T00:00:00</orderdate>
    </Order>
  </Customer>
  <Customer custid="2">
    <companyname>Customer MLTDN</companyname>
    <Order orderid="10308">
      <orderdate>2006-09-18T00:00:00</orderdate>
    </Order>
    <Order orderid="10926">
      <orderdate>2008-03-04T00:00:00</orderdate>
    </Order>
  </Customer>
</CustomersOrders>';
```

```
-- Create an internal representation
EXEC sp_xml_preparedocument @DocHandle OUTPUT, @XmlDocument
-- Show the edge table
SELECT *
FROM OPENXML (@DocHandle, '/CustomersOrders/Customer');
-- Remove the DOM
EXEC sp_xml_removedocument @DocHandle;
```

Instead of using an edge table, you can map XML elements or attributes to rows and columns by using the WITH clause of the OPENXML function. In this clause, you can specify an existing table, which is used as a template for the rowset returned, or you can define a table with syntax similar to that in the CREATE TABLE T-SQL statement.

The OPENXML function accepts an optional third parameter, called *flags*, which allows you to specify the mapping used between the XML data and the relational rowset. Value 1 means attribute-centric mapping, 2 means element-centric, and 3 means both. Maybe you already noted that the XML used for the previous query uses attributes and elements; for example, *custid* is the attribute and *companyname* is the element. I use this slightly overcomplicated XML to show you the difference between attribute-centric and element-centric mappings. The following code shreds the same XML three times to show you the difference between different mappings using the following values for the *flags* parameter: 1, 2, and 3; all three queries use the same rowset description in the WITH clause.

```
DECLARE @DocHandle AS INT;
DECLARE @XmlDocument AS NVARCHAR(1000);
SET @XmlDocument = N'
<CustomersOrders>
  <Customer custid="1">
    <companyname>Customer NRZBB</companyname>
    <Order orderid="10692">
      <orderdate>2007-10-03T00:00:00</orderdate>
    </Order>
    <Order orderid="10702">
      <orderdate>2007-10-13T00:00:00</orderdate>
    </Order>
    <Order orderid="10952">
      <orderdate>2008-03-16T00:00:00</orderdate>
    </Order>
  </Customer>
  <Customer custid="2">
    <companyname>Customer MLTDN</companyname>
    <Order orderid="10308">
      <orderdate>2006-09-18T00:00:00</orderdate>
    </Order>
    <Order orderid="10926">
      <orderdate>2008-03-04T00:00:00</orderdate>
    </Order>
  </Customer>
</CustomersOrders>';
-- Create an internal representation
EXEC sp_xml_preparedocument @DocHandle OUTPUT, @XmlDocument
```

```
-- Attribute-centric mapping
SELECT *
FROM OPENXML (@DocHandle, '/CustomersOrders/Customer',1)
     WITH (custid INT,
           companyname NVARCHAR(40));
-- Element-centric mapping
SELECT *
FROM OPENXML (@DocHandle, '/CustomersOrders/Customer',2)
     WITH (custid INT,
           companyname NVARCHAR(40));
-- Attribute- and element-centric mapping
SELECT *
FROM OPENXML (@DocHandle, '/CustomersOrders/Customer',3)
     WITH (custid INT,
           companyname NVARCHAR(40));
-- Remove the DOM
EXEC sp_xml_removedocument @DocHandle;
```

The result of the preceding three queries is below.

```
custid      companyname
----------- ----------------------------------------
1           NULL
2           NULL

custid      companyname
----------- ----------------------------------------
NULL        Customer NRZBB
NULL        Customer MLTDN

custid      companyname
----------- ----------------------------------------
1           Customer NRZBB
2           Customer MLTDN
```

As you can see, you get attributes with attribute-centric mapping, elements with element-centric mapping, and both if you combine the two mappings. The *nodes* method of the XML data type is much more efficient, and is therefore the preferred way of shredding XML documents.

The XQuery Language in SQL Server 2008

XQuery is a standard language for browsing XML instances and returning XML. It is much richer than XPath expressions, which allow you simple navigation only. With XQuery, you can navigate as with XPath; however, you can also loop over nodes, shape the returned XML instance, and much more.

For a query language, you need a query-processing engine. The SQL Server database engine processes XQuery inside T-SQL statements through XML data type methods. Not all XQuery features are supported in SQL Server. For example, XQuery user-defined functions are not supported in SQL Server because you already have T-SQL and CLR functions available. Additionally, T-SQL supports non-standard extensions to XQuery—called XML DML—that allow you to modify elements and attributes in XML data. Because an XML data type is a large object (LOB), it could be a huge performance bottleneck if the only way to modify an XML value were to replace the entire value. I will show these data modification expressions later in this chapter, when I talk about the XML data type in more detail. In this section, I introduce XQuery for data retrieval purposes only. Because I need a query processing engine to show examples, I will use variables of XML data type and use the *query* method of that type. The *query* method accepts an XQuery string as its parameter, and it returns the XML you shape in XQuery.

XQuery Basics

Let me start with an important note. XQuery is, like XML, case sensitive. Therefore, if you want to check the examples manually, you have to write the queries exactly as I wrote them. For example, if you write *Data()* instead of *data()*, you will get an error stating that there is no *Data()* function.

XQuery returns *sequences*. Sequences can include atomic values or complex values (XML nodes). Any node, such as an element, attribute, text, processing instruction, comment, or document, can be included in the sequence. Of course, you can format the sequences to get well-formed XML. The following code shows the sequences returned from a simple XML instance by three XML queries:

```
DECLARE @x AS XML;
SET @x=N'
<root>
 <a>1<c>3</c><d>4</d></a>
 <b>2</b>
</root>';
SELECT
 @x.query('*') AS Complete_Sequence,
 @x.query('data(*)') AS Complete_Data,
 @x.query('data(root/a/c)') AS Element_c_Data;
```

Here are the sequences returned:

```
Complete_Sequence                                      Complete_Data Element_c_Data
---------------------------------------------------    ------------- --------------
<root><a>1<c>3</c><d>4</d></a><b>2</b></root>          1342          3
```

The first XQuery expression uses the simplest possible path expression, which selects everything from the XML instance; the second uses the *data()* function to extract all atomic data values from the complete document; the third uses the *data()* function to extract atomic data from the element *c* only.

Every identifier in XQuery is a qualified name, or a *QName*. A QName consists of a local name and, optionally, a namespace prefix. In the preceding example, *root*, *a*, *b*, *c*, and *d* are QNames; I did not use namespace prefixes. The following standard namespaces are predefined in SQL Server:

- *xs*, which is the namespace for XML schema (the Uniform Resource Identifier, or URI, is *http://www.w3.org/2001/XMLSchema*)

- *xsi*, the XML schema instance namespace, used to associate XML Schemas with instance documents (*http://www.w3.org/2001/XMLSchema-instance*)

- *xdt*, the namespace for XPath and XQuery data types (*http://www.w3.org/2004/07/xpath-datatypes*)

- *fn*, the functions namespace (*http://www.w3.org/2004/07/xpath-functions*)

- *sqltypes*, the namespace that provides mapping for SQL Server data types (*http://schemas.microsoft.com/sqlserver/2004/sqltypes*)

- *xml*, the default XML namespace (*http://www.w3.org/XML/1998/namespace*)

You can use these namespaces in your queries without defining them again. You define your own data types in the *prolog*, which belongs at the beginning of your XQuery. You separate the prolog from the query body with a semicolon. In addition, in T-SQL, you can declare namespaces used in XQuery expressions in advance in the WITH clause of the T-SQL SELECT command. If your XML uses a single namespace, you can also declare it as the default namespace for all elements in the XQuery prolog.

You can also include comments in your XQuery expressions. The syntax for a comment is text between parentheses and colons: (: *this is a comment* :). Do not mix this with comment nodes in your XML document; this is the comment of your XQuery, and has no influence on the XML returned. The following code shows all three methods of namespace declaration and uses XQuery comments. It extracts orders for the first customer from an XML instance. I created this XML instance with a SELECT statement similar to the one I used in the "FOR XML AUTO" section earlier in the chapter.

```
DECLARE @x AS XML;
SET @x='
<CustomersOrders xmlns:co="InsideTSQL2008-CustomersOrders">
  <co:Customer co:custid="1" co:companyname="Customer NRZBB">
    <co:Order co:orderid="10692" co:orderdate="2007-10-03T00:00:00" />
    <co:Order co:orderid="10702" co:orderdate="2007-10-13T00:00:00" />
    <co:Order co:orderid="10952" co:orderdate="2008-03-16T00:00:00" />
  </co:Customer>
  <co:Customer co:custid="2" co:companyname="Customer MLTDN">
    <co:Order co:orderid="10308" co:orderdate="2006-09-18T00:00:00" />
    <co:Order co:orderid="10926" co:orderdate="2008-03-04T00:00:00" />
  </co:Customer>
</CustomersOrders>';
```

```
-- Namespace in prolog of XQuery
SELECT @x.query('
(: explicit namespace :)
declare namespace co="InsideTSQL2008-CustomersOrders";
//co:Customer[1]/*') AS [Explicit namespace];
-- Default namespace for all elements in prolog of XQuery
SELECT @x.query('
(: default namespace :)
declare default element namespace "InsideTSQL2008-CustomersOrders";
//Customer[1]/*') AS [Default element namespace];
-- Namespace defined in WITH clause of T-SQL SELECT
WITH XMLNAMESPACES('InsideTSQL2008-CustomersOrders' AS co)
SELECT @x.query('
(: namespace declared in T-SQL :)
//co:Customer[1]/*') AS [Namespace in WITH clause];
```

Here is the output (truncated):

```
Explicit namespace
-----------------------------------------------------------------------------
<co:Order xmlns:co="InsideTSQL2008-CustomersOrders" co:orderid="10692" co:orderd

Default element namespace
-----------------------------------------------------------------------------
<Order xmlns="InsideTSQL2008-CustomersOrders" xmlns:p1="InsideTSQL2008-Customers

Namespace in WITH clause
-----------------------------------------------------------------------------
<co:Order xmlns:co="InsideTSQL2008-CustomersOrders" co:orderid="10692" co:orderd
```

Note that when using the default element namespace, the namespace is not included in the resulting XML. Therefore, only the first and third queries produce identical results.

I used a relative path to find the *Customer* element. Before explaining all the different ways of navigation in XQuery, I want to give you some brief information about the most important XQuery data types and functions.

Data Types

XQuery uses about 50 predefined data types. Additionally, in the SQL Server implementation you also have the *sqltypes* namespace, which defines SQL Server types. You already know about SQL Server types. Do not worry too much about XQuery types; you'll never use most of them. I list the most important ones here. I won't go into detail about each and every one of them; the type names will give you an idea of what they are and what you can do with them.

XQuery data types are divided into node types and atomic types. The node types include *attribute, comment, element, namespace, text, processing-instruction,* and *document-node.* The most important atomic types you might use in queries are *xs:boolean, xs:string, xs:QName, xs:date, xs:time, xs:datetime, xs:float, xs:double, xs:decimal,* and *xs:integer.*

You should just take a quick overview of this much-shortened list. The important thing to understand is that XQuery has its own type system, that it has all of the commonly used types you would expect, and that you can use specific functions on specific types only. Therefore, it is time to introduce a couple of important XQuery functions.

> **More Info** For more information on XQuery, including detailed information about data types, please refer to *XQuery: The XML Query Language* (Addison-Wesley, 2004) by Michael Brundage.

Functions

Just as there are many data types, there are dozens of functions in XQuery as well. They are organized into multiple categories. I already used the *data()* function, which is a data accessor function. Some of the most useful XQuery functions supported by SQL Server are:

- **Numeric functions**   *ceiling()*, *floor()*, and *round()*
- **String functions**   *concat()*, *contains()*, *substring()*, *string-length()*, *lower-case()*, and *upper-case()*
- **Boolean and Boolean constructor functions**   *not()*, *true()*, and *false()*
- **Nodes functions**   *local-name()*, and *namespace-uri()*
- **Aggregate functions**   *count()*, *min()*, *max()*, *avg()*, and *sum()*
- **Data accessor functions**   *data()*, and *string()*
- **SQL Server extension functions**   *sql:column()*, and *sql:variable()*

You can easily conclude what a function does and what data types it supports from the function and category names. I will use some of them, such as *namespace-uri()*, later in this chapter. For a complete list of functions with detailed descriptions, please refer to SQL Server Books Online.

The following query uses the aggregate functions *count()* and *min()* to retrieve information about orders for each customer in an XML document:

```
DECLARE @x AS XML;
SET @x='
<CustomersOrders>
  <Customer custid="1" companyname="Customer NRZBB">
    <Order orderid="10692" orderdate="2007-10-03T00:00:00" />
    <Order orderid="10702" orderdate="2007-10-13T00:00:00" />
    <Order orderid="10952" orderdate="2008-03-16T00:00:00" />
  </Customer>
  <Customer custid="2" companyname="Customer MLTDN">
    <Order orderid="10308" orderdate="2006-09-18T00:00:00" />
    <Order orderid="10926" orderdate="2008-03-04T00:00:00" />
  </Customer>
</CustomersOrders>';
```

```
SELECT @x.query('
for $i in //Customer
return
    <OrdersInfo>
        { $i/@companyname }
        <NumberOfOrders>
                    { count($i/Order) }
        </NumberOfOrders>
        <LastOrder>
                    { max($i/Order/@orderid) }
            </LastOrder>
    </OrdersInfo>
');
```

As you can see, this XQuery is more complicated than previous examples. I used iterations—FLWOR expressions—and formatted the XML returned in the return part of the query. I'll discuss iterations and returning values later in this section. For now, treat this query as an example of how you can use aggregate functions in XQuery. The result of this query is:

```
<OrdersInfo companyname="Customer NRZBB">
  <NumberOfOrders>3</NumberOfOrders>
  <LastOrder>10952</LastOrder>
</OrdersInfo>
<OrdersInfo companyname="Customer MLTDN">
  <NumberOfOrders>2</NumberOfOrders>
  <LastOrder>10926</LastOrder>
</OrdersInfo>
```

Navigation

You have plenty of ways to navigate through XML document with XQuery, and this is far from a complete treatment of the topic. Basic ways are XPath expressions. XQuery allows you to specify a path absolutely or relatively from the current node. XQuery takes care of the current position in the document; it means you can refer to a path relatively, starting from the current node, where you navigated to through previous path expression. Every path consists of a sequence of steps, listed from left to right. A complete path might take the following form:

Node-name/child::element-name[@attribute-name=value]

Steps are separated with slashes; therefore, the path example I am describing has two steps. In the second step you can see in detail from which parts a step can be constructed. A step may consist of three parts:

- Axis, which specifies the direction of travel. In the example, the axis is *child::*, which specifies child nodes of the node from the previous step.

- Node test, which specifies the criterion for selecting nodes. In the example, *element-name* is the node test; it selects only nodes named *element-name*.

- Predicate, which further narrows down the search. In the example, there is one predicate: *[@attribute-name=value]*, which selects only nodes that have an attribute named *attribute-name* with value *value*, such as *[@orderid=10952]*. Note that in the predicate example, I am referring to an axis, namely the *attribute::* ; the at sign *(@)* is an abbreviation for the axis *attribute::*. This looks a bit confusing; it might help if you think of navigation in an XML document in three directions: *up* (in the hierarchy), *down* (in the hierarchy), *here* (in current node), and *right* (in the current context level, to find attributes). In Table 13-1, I identify the axis direction in the description column.

Table 13-1 describes the axes supported in SQL Server 2008.

TABLE 13-1 Axes Supported in SQL Server 2008

Axis	Abbreviation	Description
child::		Returns children of the current context node. This is the default axis; you can omit it. Direction is *down*.
descendant::		Retrieves all descendants of the context node. Direction is *down*.
self::	.	Retrieves the context node. Direction is *here*.
descendant-or-self::	//	Retrieves the context node and all its descendants. Direction is *here* and then *down*.
attribute::	@	Retrieves the specified attribute of the context node. Direction is *right*.
parent::	..	Retrieves the parent of the context node. Direction is *up*.

A *node test* follows the axis you specify. A node test can be as simple as a name test. Specifying a name means that you want nodes with that name. You can also use wildcards. An asterisk (*) means that you want any *principal node*, with any name. A principal node is the default node kind for an axis. The principal node is an attribute if the axis is *attribute::* and an element for all other axes. You can also narrow down wildcard searches. If you want all principal nodes in the namespace *prefix*, use *prefix:**. If you want all principal nodes named *local-name*, no matter which namespace they belong to, use **:local-name*.

You can also perform node kind tests, which help you query nodes that are not principal nodes. You can use the following node type tests:

- *comment()* allows you to select comment nodes.

- *node()* is true for any kind of node. Do not mix this with the asterisk (*) wildcard; * means any principal node, whereas *node()* means any node at all.

- *processing-instruction()* allows you to retrieve a processing instruction node.

- *text()* allows you to retrieve text nodes, or nodes without tags.

Predicates

Finally, I have to describe basic predicates. Basic predicates include numeric and Boolean predicates. Numeric predicates simply select nodes by position. You include them in brackets. For example, */x/y[1]* means the first *y* child element of each *x* element. You can also use parentheses to apply a numeric predicate to the entire result of a path. For example, *(/x/y)[1]* means the first element out of all nodes selected by *x/y*.

Boolean predicates select all nodes for which the predicate evaluates to true. XQuery supports logical *and* and *or* operators. However, you might be surprised by how comparison operators work. They work on both atomic values and sequences. For sequences, if one atomic value in a sequence leads to a true exit of the expression, the whole expression is evaluated to true. Look at this example:

```
DECLARE @x AS XML = N'';
SELECT @x.query('(1, 2, 3) = (2, 4)');      -- true
SELECT @x.query('(5, 6) < (2, 4)');         -- false
SELECT @x.query('(1, 2, 3) = 1');           -- true
SELECT @x.query('(1, 2, 3) != 1');          -- true
```

The first expression evaluates to true because the number 2 is in both sequences. The second evaluates to false because none of the atomic values from the first sequence is less than any of the values from the second sequence. The third expression is true because there is an atomic value in the sequence on the left that is equal to the atomic value on the right. The fourth expression is true because there is an atomic value in the sequence on the left that is not equal to the atomic value on the right. Interesting result, right? Sequence (1, 2, 3) is both equal and not equal to atomic value 1. If this confuses you, use the *value comparison operators*. (The familiar symbolic operators in the preceding example are called *general comparison operators* in XQuery.) Value comparison operators do not work on sequences. Table 13-2 lists the general comparison operators and their value comparison operator counterparts.

TABLE 13-2 General and Value Comparison Operators

General comparison operators	Value comparison operators	Description
=	*eq*	equal
!=	*ne*	not equal
<	*lt*	less than
<=	*le*	less than or equal to
>	*gt*	greater than
>=	*ge*	greater than or equal to

XQuery also supports conditional if-then-else expressions with the following syntax:

```
if (<expression1>)
then
  <expression2>
else
  <expression3>
```

Note that the *if..then..else* expression is not used to change the program flow of the XQuery query. It is more like a function that evaluates a logical expression parameter and returns one expression or another depending on the value of the logical expression. It is more like the T-SQL CASE expression than the T-SQL IF statement.

Examples of Navigation

To help you better understand how navigation works, I've included some examples. I limited the results to 80 text characters to fit on a single line.

```
-- Navigation examples
SET NOCOUNT ON;
GO
DECLARE @x AS XML;
SET @x = N'
<CustomersOrders>
  <Customer custid="1">
    <!-- Comment 111 -->
    <companyname>Customer NRZBB</companyname>
    <Order orderid="10692">
      <orderdate>2007-10-03T00:00:00</orderdate>
    </Order>
    <Order orderid="10702">
      <orderdate>2007-10-13T00:00:00</orderdate>
    </Order>
    <Order orderid="10952">
      <orderdate>2008-03-16T00:00:00</orderdate>
    </Order>
  </Customer>
  <Customer custid="2">
    <!-- Comment 222 -->
    <companyname>Customer MLTDN</companyname>
    <Order orderid="10308">
      <orderdate>2006-09-18T00:00:00</orderdate>
    </Order>
    <Order orderid="10952">
      <orderdate>2008-03-04T00:00:00</orderdate>
    </Order>
  </Customer>
</CustomersOrders>';
-- Children of CustomersOrders/Customer
-- Principal nodes only
SELECT @x.query('CustomersOrders/Customer/*')
       AS [1. Principal nodes];
```

```
-- All nodes
SELECT @x.query('CustomersOrders/Customer/node()')
        AS [2. All nodes];
-- Comment nodes only
SELECT @x.query('CustomersOrders/Customer/comment()')
        AS [3. Comment nodes];
-- Customer 2 orders
SELECT @x.query('//Customer[@custid=2]/Order')
        AS [4. Customer 2 orders];
-- All orders with orderid=10952, no matter of parents
SELECT @x.query('//../Order[@orderid=10952]')
        AS [5. Orders with orderid=10952];
-- Second Customer with at least one Order childSELECT @x.query('(/CustomersOrders/Customer/
                Order/parent::Customer)[2]')
        AS [6. 2nd Customer with at least one Order];
-- Conditional expressionS
-- Testing sql variable
DECLARE @element NVARCHAR(20);
SET @element=N'orderdate';
SELECT @x.query('
if (sql:variable("@element")="companyname") then
 CustomersOrders/Customer/companyname
else
 CustomersOrders/Customer/Order/orderdate
')
        AS [7. Order dates];
-- This if does not change the flow of XQuery
-- It returns company names for both customers
SELECT @x.query('
if (CustomersOrders/Customer[@custid=1]) then
 CustomersOrders/Customer/companyname
else
 CustomersOrders/Customer/Order/orderdate
')
        AS [8. Company names];
GO
SET NOCOUNT OFF;
GO
```

The results are:

```
1. Principal nodes
----------------------------------------------------------------------------
<companyname>Customer NRZBB</companyname><Order orderid="10692"><orderdate>2007-

2. All nodes
----------------------------------------------------------------------------
<!-- Comment 111 --><companyname>Customer NRZBB</companyname><Order orderid="106

3. Comment nodes
----------------------------------------------------------------------------
<!-- Comment 111 --><!-- Comment 222 -->

4. Customer 2 orders
----------------------------------------------------------------------------
<Order orderid="10308"><orderdate>2006-09-18T00:00:00</orderdate></Order><Order
```

```
5. Orders with orderid=10952
--------------------------------------------------------------------------------
<Order orderid="10952"><orderdate>2008-03-16T00:00:00</orderdate></Order><Order
```

```
6. Second Customer with at least one
Order---------------------------------------------------------------------------
<Customer custid="2"><!-- Comment 222 --><companyname>Customer MLTDN</companynam
```

```
7. Order dates
--------------------------------------------------------------------------------
<orderdate>2007-10-03T00:00:00</orderdate><orderdate>2007-10-13T00:00:00</orderd
```

```
8. Company names
--------------------------------------------------------------------------------
<companyname>Customer NRZBB</companyname><companyname>Customer MLTDN</companynam
```

Let me quickly describe the queries and comment on the results. First note that you are already familiar with the XML I am querying, which was created by SELECT with a FOR XML clause. I changed it a bit in order to show more examples. I changed the second order of the second customer—I changed *orderid* to *10952*, to have the same *orderid* as one of the orders of the first customer. I also added a comment node for each customer.

The first three queries select *Customer* nodes with child nodes. The first query—*SELECT @x.query('CustomersOrders/Customer/*')*—uses an asterisk to select child nodes, which means principal nodes (elements in this context) only. The second query—*SELECT @x.query('CustomersOrders/Customer/node()')*—uses the *nodes()* node type test to select child nodes, and this means all nodes are returned, including comment nodes. The third query—*SELECT @x.query('CustomersOrders/Customer/comment()')*—uses the *comment()* node type test; therefore, it returns only comment child nodes.

The fourth query—*SELECT @x.query('//Customer[@custid=2]/Order')*—uses the predicate *[@custid=2]* inside the *Customer* element, and then selects *Order* nodes in next step. This means it selects all orders for customer 2. The fifth query—*SELECT @x.query('//../Order[@ orderid=10952]')*—uses abbreviated syntax for the parent axis (two dots) and a predicate *[ordered=10952]* to find all orders with this order number, no matter the customer. The sixth query—*SELECT @x.query('(/CustomersOrders/Customer/Order/parent::Customer)[2]')*—uses the numeric predicate *[2]* to find the second node returned by the query *(/CustomersOrders /Customer/Order/parent::Customer)*. The query *(/CustomersOrders/Customer/Order /parent::Customer)* returns all Customer nodes that are children of the *CustomersOrders* node and that also have at least one Order.

The seventh query—*SELECT @x.query(' if (sql:variable("@element")="companyname") then CustomersOrders/Customer/companyname else CustomersOrders/Customer/Order/orderdate')*— uses the conditional *if..then..else* expression and the SQL Server XQuery extension *sql:variable()*. This function allows you to use SQL Server variables inside XQuery. The SQL variable *@element* is tested inside XQuery; because it is not equal to the string *"companyname"*, order dates are returned. With help of an outer T-SQL IF block, you can control program flow.

The eighth query—*SELECT @x.query('if (CustomersOrders/Customer[@custid=1]) then CustomersOrders/Customer/companyname else CustomersOrders/Customer/Order/orderdate')*—shows that the XQuery *if..then..else* expression is not a flow element like T-SQL's IF...ELSE. The logical expression in the *if..then..else* block evaluates to true because there is a *Customer* element where the *@custid* attribute equals 1. Therefore, company names are returned for both customers.

Iteration and Returning Values

The real power of XQuery lies in so-called FLWOR expressions. FLWOR is the acronym for *for*, *let*, *where*, *order by*, and *return*. A FLWOR expression is actually a for each loop. You can use it to iterate through a sequence returned by an XPath expression. Although you typically iterate through a sequence of nodes, you can use FLWOR expressions to iterate through any sequence. You can limit the nodes to be processed with a predicate, sort the nodes, and format the returned XML. The parts of a FLWOR statement are:

- **For**   With the *for clause*, you bind iterator variables to input sequences. Input sequences are either sequences of nodes or sequences of atomic values. You create atomic value sequences using literals or functions.

- **Let**   With the optional *let clause*, you assign a value to a variable for a specific iteration. The expression used for assignment can return a sequence of nodes or a sequence of atomic values.

- **Where**   With the optional *where clause*, you filter the iteration.

- **Order by**   Using the *order by clause*, you can control the order in which the elements of the input sequence are processed. You control the order based on atomic values.

- **Return**   The *return clause* is evaluated once for each iteration, and the results are returned to the client in the iteration order.

I'll use some examples to explain how to use each clause. I'll use the same sample XML variable that I used in the previous section. Note that if you want to check these examples yourself, you have to declare @x and assign a value to it in the same T-SQL batch as the example query. Here is the declaration and assignment of the sample XML variable:

```
DECLARE @x AS XML;
SET @x = N'
<CustomersOrders>
  <Customer custid="1">
    <!-- Comment 111 -->
    <companyname>Customer NRZBB</companyname>
    <Order orderid="10692">
      <orderdate>2007-10-03T00:00:00</orderdate>
    </Order>
    <Order orderid="10702">
      <orderdate>2007-10-13T00:00:00</orderdate>
    </Order>
```

```
  <Order orderid="10952">
    <orderdate>2008-03-16T00:00:00</orderdate>
  </Order>
</Customer>
<Customer custid="2">
  <!-- Comment 222 -->
  <companyname>Customer MLTDN</companyname>
  <Order orderid="10308">
    <orderdate>2006-09-18T00:00:00</orderdate>
  </Order>
  <Order orderid="10952">
    <orderdate>2008-03-04T00:00:00</orderdate>
  </Order>
</Customer>
</CustomersOrders>';
```

The first query just iterates through all *Order* nodes using an iterator variable and returns those nodes. The name of the iterator variable must start with a dollar sign ($) in XQuery. This query uses *for* and *return* clauses only:

```
SELECT @x.query('for $i in CustomersOrders/Customer/Order
                 return $i')
       AS [1. Orders];
```

The result of this query is simple—it's just the nodes I was iterating through. Of course, I could achieve this result without the FLWOR expression by simply navigating to the Order nodes with the query *@x.query('CustomersOrders/Customer/Order')*. The result is:

```
<Order orderid="10692">
  <orderdate>2007-10-03T00:00:00</orderdate>
</Order>
<Order orderid="10702">
  <orderdate>2007-10-13T00:00:00</orderdate>
</Order>
<Order orderid="10952">
  <orderdate>2008-03-16T00:00:00</orderdate>
</Order>
<Order orderid="10308">
  <orderdate>2006-09-18T00:00:00</orderdate>
</Order>
<Order orderid="10952">
  <orderdate>2008-03-04T00:00:00</orderdate>
</Order>
```

My next query uses the *where* clause to limit the *Order* nodes processed to those with an *orderid* attribute smaller than 10900.

```
SELECT @x.query('for $i in CustomersOrders/Customer/Order
                 where $i/@orderid < 10900
                 return $i')
       AS [2. Filtered orders];
```

The result is, as you might expect, filtered—only three orders are returned:

```
<Order orderid="10692">
  <orderdate>2007-10-03T00:00:00</orderdate>
</Order>
<Order orderid="10702">
  <orderdate>2007-10-13T00:00:00</orderdate>
</Order>
<Order orderid="10308">
  <orderdate>2006-09-18T00:00:00</orderdate>
</Order>
```

In next example, I introduce the *order by* clause. The expression I pass to this clause must return values of a type compatible with the *gt* XQuery operator. As you'll recall, the *gt* operator expects atomic values. I am ordering by the *orderdate* element. Although there is a single *orderdate* element per order, XQuery does not know this, and it considers *orderdate* to be a sequence, not an atomic value. In this example I use a numeric predicate to specify the first *orderdate* element of an order as the value to order by. Without this numeric predicate, I would get an error.

```
SELECT @x.query('for $i in CustomersOrders/Customer/Order
                 where $i/@orderid < 10900
                 order by ($i/orderdate)[1]
                 return $i')
       AS [3. Filtered and sorted orders];
```

The three orders returned are now sorted by *orderdate*:

```
<Order orderid="10308">
  <orderdate>2006-09-18T00:00:00</orderdate>
</Order>
<Order orderid="10692">
  <orderdate>2007-10-03T00:00:00</orderdate>
</Order>
<Order orderid="10702">
  <orderdate>2007-10-13T00:00:00</orderdate>
</Order>
```

In my next query, I'll return something other than the iterator variable combining literals with my iterator variable. I am converting the *orderid* attribute to an element by creating the element manually and extracting only the value of the attribute with the *data()* function. I am returning the *orderdate* element as well, and wrapping both in the *Order-orderid-element* element. Note the braces around the expressions that extract the value of the *orderid* element and the *orderdate* element. XQuery evaluates expressions in braces; without braces, everything would be treated as a string literal and returned as such.

```
SELECT @x.query('for $i in CustomersOrders/Customer/Order
                 where $i/@orderid < 10900
                 order by ($i/orderdate)[1]
                 return
                 <Order-orderid-element>
```

```
            <orderid>{data($i/@orderid)}</orderid>
            {$i/orderdate}
          </Order-orderid-element>')
    AS [4. Filtered, sorted and reformatted orders];
```

This is the result:

```
<Order-orderid-element>
  <orderid>10308</orderid>
  <orderdate>2006-09-18T00:00:00</orderdate>
</Order-orderid-element>
<Order-orderid-element>
  <orderid>10692</orderid>
  <orderdate>2007-10-03T00:00:00</orderdate>
</Order-orderid-element>
<Order-orderid-element>
  <orderid>10702</orderid>
  <orderdate>2007-10-13T00:00:00</orderdate>
</Order-orderid-element>
```

In previous query, I am referring to the *orderdate* element of my *$i* iterator variable twice, once in the *order by* clause and once in the *return* clause. I can spare myself some typing if I use a *let* clause to assign a name to the repeating expression. To name the expression, I have to use a variable different from *$i*. XQuery inserts the expression every time the new variable is referenced. Here is the query with the *let* clause:

```
SELECT @x.query('for $i in CustomersOrders/Customer/Order
              let $j := $i/orderdate
              where $i/@orderid < 10900
              order by ($j)[1]
              return
              <Order-orderid-element>
               <orderid>{data($i/@orderid)}</orderid>
               {$j}
              </Order-orderid-element>')
     AS [5. Filtered, sorted and reformatted orders with let clause];
```

The result of this query is exactly the same as the result of the previous query. It is actually still the same query; I just used the *let* clause to name the expression that selects the *orderdate* element and repeats in the query.

Before finishing this introduction to XQuery, let me show you a slightly more advanced example. You can use a FLWOR expression to mimic the T-SQL operator JOIN. Look at this XML variable:

```
DECLARE @co AS XML;
SET @co = N'
<CustomersOrders>
  <Customer customercustid="1" companyname="Customer NRZBB">
    <Order ordercustid="1" orderid="10692" />
    <Order ordercustid="1" orderid="10702" />
    <Order ordercustid="1" orderid="10952" />
  </Customer>
```

```
    <Customer customercustid="2" companyname="Customer MLTDN">
      <Order ordercustid="2" orderid="10308" />
      <Order ordercustid="2" orderid="10926" />
    </Customer>
</CustomersOrders>';
```

Each customer has nested orders. This is the normal way to represent one-to-many relationships in XML. However, this time I would like to get a simplified version of XML with all the information, including *Customer* element attributes, in attributes of a single *Order* element. In T-SQL, I would join the Sales.Customers and Sales.Orders table on the *custid* column, or I would create a table-valued function that would retrieve orders for a specific customer and use the APPLY operator with the Customers table on the left and my tabular function on the right. In XQuery, there is neither a JOIN nor APPLY operator. However, you can use multiple iterator variables in the *for* part of a FLWOR expression to achieve the desired result. The *Customer* element has a *customercustid* attribute; the *Order* element has an *ordercustid* attribute. I have to compare the values of those two attributes in the *where* part of my FLWOR expression. Here is the query:

```
SELECT @co.query('for $i in CustomersOrders/Customer
                  for $j in $i/Order
                  where $i/@customercustid = $j/@ordercustid
                  return
                    <Order
                      customerid = "{$i/@customercustid}"
                      companyname = "{$i/@companyname}"
                      orderid = "{$j/@orderid}"
                    />')
        AS [Join Customers - Orders];
```

I use the variable *$i* to iterate through Customer nodes, and I use *$j* to iterate through Order nodes. In the *where* part, I compare the values of the *customercustid* and *ordercustid* attributes, and return only nodes for which the values of these two attributes match. Note also that because I return all information as attributes of the *Order* element, I have to use quotations for values of attributes. The result of this query is:

```
<Order customerid="1" companyname="Customer NRZBB" orderid="10692" />
<Order customerid="1" companyname="Customer NRZBB" orderid="10702" />
<Order customerid="1" companyname="Customer NRZBB" orderid="10952" />
<Order customerid="2" companyname="Customer MLTDN" orderid="10308" />
<Order customerid="2" companyname="Customer MLTDN" orderid="10926" />
```

I need to add a final comment on this result. The XQuery standard defines the concept of an *ordering mode*. The order of iteration is fixed in *ordered* mode and not fixed in *unordered* mode. The ordering mode for all operations in SQL Server is *ordered*. Therefore, the result of the preceding query is ordered in SQL Server without the need for an *order by* clause. This is different from T-SQL queries without an ORDER BY clause.

XML Data Type

When introducing XQuery, I used the XML data type. XQuery expressions are parameters for the *query* method of the XML data type. The XML data type includes a total of five methods that accept XQuery as a parameter. These methods support querying (the *query* method), retrieving atomic values (the *value* method), existence checks (the *exists* method), modifying sections within the XML data (the *modify* method) as opposed to overwriting the whole element, and shredding XML data into multiple rows in a result set (the *nodes* method). In the following section, I'll explain why you need the XML data type inside a database, when to use it, and when not to use it. I hope you will get some good ideas of practical XML data type usage for your projects in this section. However, I'll start with a theoretical introduction to XML in the relational model.

> **More Info**   For more information on XML technologies in SQL Server 2008, please refer to *Pro SQL Server 2008 XML* (Apress, 2008) by Michael Coles.

XML Support in a Relational Database

The first question that came to my mind when SQL Server 2005 started to support a native XML data type was: Why do I need native XML support in a relational database? After pondering the idea for months, I became convinced that such support is important and beneficial. XML is the lingua franca of exchanging data among different applications and platforms. It is widely used, and almost all modern technologies support it. Databases simply have to deal with XML. Although XML could be stored as simple text, plain text representation means having no knowledge of the structure built into an XML document. You could decompose the text, store it in multiple relational tables, and use relational technologies to manipulate the data. Relational structures are quite static and not so easy to change. Think of dynamic or volatile XML structures. Storing XML data in a native XML data type solves these problems, enabling functionality attached to the type that can accommodate support for a wide variety of XML technologies.

Is the Relational Model Obsolete?

With the advent of XML and object-oriented (OO) technologies, some people wonder whether the relational model is obsolete. Many developers looking for greater programmatic flexibility feel that their choices are very limited with the relational model. The world is constantly changing, and you need technologies to support these changes. Some people think that storing everything in XML format bridges the gap between OO applications and relational databases. However, in many cases people are just reinventing the wheel.

I agree that the relational model is limiting, but it is intentionally so! The idea is simple—you need constraints to enforce data integrity. Constraints prevent chaos. When you're driving, you obey speed limits and traffic lights, which allow drivers to safely share the same roads and pass through the same intersections. When you need to store items in real life, you do so in an organized, structured fashion. A pharmacy that keeps its medicines lying around in a muddle probably won't get many appreciative customers. The XML data type is structured; however, its structure is more relaxed than relational data. Microsoft Office Excel also supports structured representation and is even more relaxed than XML. Nevertheless, we do not use Microsoft Office Excel as a database for business applications.

Are schemas really so volatile nowadays? Well, they are volatile for some business cases, but quite stable for the most part. Not being able to find a structure that suits a business problem does not mean that such a structure does not exist. I've seen an example in which a sales Orders table included a column with all order details (order lines) for the order as a single XML value. Come on, an order details schema is not volatile; it's actually so well known that it has a design pattern! I repeat: a relational schema constrains us deliberately. Consider the order details example again. When you are dealing with sales, data integrity is crucial; without it, your company can lose business.

Relational databases support many other constraints besides detailed schema. It's true that you can program them in a middle tier or in any other layer if you use a so-called XML database, but why reinvent the wheel? Why develop something that's already developed? In many cases, reinventing the wheel indicates a lack of knowledge. I've seen a system that started with an XML database without any constraints except schemas. The idea was to design a flexible system. Well, after a while the customer and the developers realized that they needed more constraints. As time passed, more and more constraints were built into the system. Eventually, the system had no flexibility, which in a sense was a good thing because it did in fact need a fixed schema. But with all the constraints built into the system, it was almost impossible for applications to use the data and for administrators to maintain the system, all of which made the system extremely expensive. Remember that data is usually used by more than one application—think of Customer Relationship Management (CRM) systems that need merged data from all possible sources and BI solutions, including reporting, OLAP cubes, and Data Mining models.

A couple of years ago I was in an Italian restaurant with some friends. Itzik wanted a pizza, but the restaurant didn't have it on the menu. The wait staff suggested the closest thing they had—tomato pie. Itzik ordered it and added, "As long as it looks like a pizza, smells like a pizza, and tastes like a pizza." Why am I recalling this event? Because if a problem needs a detailed schema and constraints, and the data must be available to many applications, I really don't care what kind of physical database you use—as long as it logically looks like the relational model, behaves like the relational model, and constrains like the relational model.

When Should You Use XML Instead of Relational Representation?

I hope that you won't think that I'm entirely opposed to having XML support inside a relational database. I can actually give many examples where it does make sense.

First, I have to admit that a schema sometimes is in fact volatile. Think about situations in which you have to support many different schemas for the same kind of event. There are many such cases within SQL Server itself. DDL triggers and extended events are a good example. There are dozens of different DDL events, and each event returns different event information—that is, data with a different schema. A conscious design choice was that DDL triggers return event information in XML format via the *EVENTDATA()* function. Event information in XML format is quite easy to manipulate. Furthermore, with this architecture, SQL Server will be able to extend support for new DDL events in future versions more easily.

Another interesting example of internal XML support in SQL Server—and proof that Microsoft is practicing what it preaches—is XML showplans. You can generate execution plan information in XML format using the SET SHOWPLAN_XML and SET STATISTICS XML statements. Think of the value for applications and tools that need execution plan information—it's easy to request and parse it now. You can even force the optimizer to use a given execution plan by providing the XML plan in a USE PLAN query hint.

Another place to use XML is to represent data that is sparse. Your data is sparse—having many unknown values—if some columns are not applicable to all rows. Standard solutions for such a problem introduce subtypes or implement an open schema model in a relational environment. However, a solution based on XML could be the easiest to implement. A solution that introduces subtypes can lead to many new tables. A solution that implements a relational open schema model can lead to complex, dynamic SQL statements. SQL Server 2008 introduces *sparse columns* and *filtered indexes*. Sparse columns provide another, non-XML solution for representing attributes that are not applicable for all rows in a table. Sparse columns have optimized storage for NULLs. If you have to index them, you can efficiently use filtered indexes to index known values only; this way, you optimize table and index storage. In addition, you can have access to all sparse columns at once through a *column set*. A column set is an XML representation of all the sparse columns that is even updateable. However, even with sparse columns, the schema is not dynamic. In addition, using sparse columns limits your solution to SQL Server 2008 only—the solution is not portable. In short, I find XML very suitable for dynamic schemas.

You could have other reasons to use an XML model. XML inherently supports hierarchical sorted data. This fact makes people wonder whether XML is more appropriate for representing hierarchical data than a relational model. A relational solution that has references among entities is cumbersome. However, a hierarchy can be represented in a relational model as an adjacency list (parent/child attributes) with a self-referencing foreign key constraint. You can then query the data using recursive common table expressions (CTEs). In SQL Server 2008, you can also represent graphs, trees, and hierarchies by using the new HIERARCHYID data type. Personally, I prefer to use the adjacency list model for representing hierarchies. It is a standard, portable solution. In addition, it is not limited to hierarchies only; you can use it to represent any kind of a graph, including trees and hierarchies. To summarize, I am not a fan of using XML for hierarchies.

What if ordering is inherent in your data? I don't find this a good enough reason to justify using XML. You can have an attribute that defines the order; otherwise, you probably haven't done your business analysis well.

Finally, another scenario for using XML representation is when you want to modify parts of the data based on its structure. I agree with using XML in such a scenario in some cases, and I'll explain and demonstrate why in the following section.

Objects in .NET applications can be persisted in one of two ways: using binary or XML serialization. Binary serialization is very encapsulated; only applications that know the structure (class) of the object and the way it is serialized can deserialize it. XML serialization is much more open. All you need to know is the XML schema, and even without it, you can browse the data. Now think of objects in a wider sense. Everything you store in a computer is a kind of object. For example, take Microsoft Visio diagrams. They can be stored in internal Visio format or as XML. If they are stored in the internal format, you can open them only with Microsoft Visio. If they are stored in XML format, you can open them even with Notepad. And if you store them using XML format in a database, you can use T-SQL queries to search and manipulate the document data. That is valuable functionality! Imagine you are searching for all Visio documents that include a specific element. If they are stored in internal format, you have to open them one by one and visually check them. If they are stored as XML documents in a file system, you can use full-text indexes and search through them. But if they are stored in a database in an XML column, you can find all documents you need with a single SELECT statement.

As another example of using XML, consider a frequently asked question: "How do you pass an array as a parameter to a stored procedure?" In SQL Server 2008, you can use table-valued parameters. Table-valued parameters were not available in previous versions of SQL Server. Another option is to pass the array of values as a comma-separated string and then use T-SQL code to separate the elements. Or you can pass the array as an XML parameter, and use the *nodes* method to shred the values into a relational presentation.

After this introduction, you should have an idea of when the XML data type is appropriate and when you should stick to the relational model. Now that I've covered the background, I can discuss the XML data type methods, and some other XML enhancements. I'll also walk you through code samples that you're likely to find useful.

XML Serialized Objects in a Database

> **Note** This section contains queries that require an active connection to the Internet. If you don't have one, you can simply read this section without running those queries yourself.

The XML data type supports the following methods:

- *value()*, which returns a scalar value for the value of an XML element or attribute
- *query()*, which returns XML
- *exist()*, which returns a BIT value that indicates whether an XML node exists
- *modify()*, which uses Microsoft extensions to XQuery, allowing you to update only part of the XML document
- *nodes()*, which can be used to shred the XML document in relational format

All of these methods accept an XQuery expression as a parameter. I am going to describe the methods through an example. In addition, I'll introduce XML indexes during the code walkthrough of the same example.

Figure 13-1 shows three simple Visio drawings: an Entity-Relationship (ER) diagram for the customer entity, an ER diagram for the product entity, and a Unified Modeling Language (UML) class diagram for the product entity.

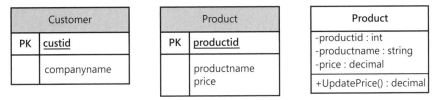

FIGURE 13-1 Visio drawings

I saved all three diagrams in the XML for Visio file format for drawings (.vdx). The XML schema definition (XSD) for Visio documents is published on MSDN in the Visio 2007 XML Reference at *http://msdn.microsoft.com/en-us/library/ms426602.aspx*. The filenames of the three diagrams are ProductER.vdx, ProductUML.vdx, and CustomerER.vdx. These files are available for download at *http://www.insidetsql.com* as part of the book's source code. I'll demonstrate how to import these files into XML column values in a table and manipulate them. To follow the demonstration, create the folder C:\InsideTSQL2008\VisioFiles and copy the .vdx files to that folder.

Use the following code to create a table with an XML column and import the Visio documents into the table:

```
USE InsideTSQL2008;
GO
CREATE TABLE dbo.VisioDocs
(
  id  INT NOT NULL,
  doc XML NOT NULL
);
GO

INSERT INTO dbo.VisioDocs (id, doc)
  SELECT 1, *
  FROM OPENROWSET(BULK 'C:\InsideTSQL2008\VisioFiles\ProductER.vdx',
    SINGLE_BLOB) AS x;
INSERT INTO dbo.VisioDocs (id, doc)
  SELECT 2, *
  FROM OPENROWSET(BULK 'C:\InsideTSQL2008\VisioFiles\ProductUML.vdx',
    SINGLE_BLOB) AS x;
INSERT INTO dbo.VisioDocs (id, doc)
  SELECT 3, *
  FROM OPENROWSET(BULK 'C:\InsideTSQL2008\VisioFiles\CustomerER.vdx',
    SINGLE_BLOB) AS x;
```

You can clearly see the advantage of loading file data using the BULK rowset provider. It is so simple!

It's time to check what you loaded:

```
SELECT id, doc FROM dbo.VisioDocs;
```

This simple SELECT statement produces the output shown in Table 13-3.

TABLE 13-3 Visio Documents Stored in an XML Column

id	doc
1	<VisioDocument xmlns="http://schemas.microsoft.co...
2	<VisioDocument xmlns="http://schemas.microsoft.co...
3	<VisioDocument xmlns="http://schemas.microsoft.co...

If you use "Results to Grid" option in SSMS, then the XML data is shown in the table as a hyperlink. SSMS can properly parse and represent XML data. If you click the hyperlink in the row having *id* 1, you get the XML data in a new window. Here's a small snippet of what you get:

```
<VisioDocument xmlns="http://schemas.microsoft.com/visio/2003/core" xmlns:vx="http://
schemas.microsoft.com/visio/2006/extension" key="0269EFD90D045A4D95F376CA56FAB87BB98119E6
509C39621E6CBF4D5A9109F19DEB3216703EFA4BD87208EBB452A892E2D15FB26D5B15453486A571908861D9"
start="190" metric="1" DocLangID="1033" buildnum="6336" version="12.0" xml:space="preserve">
```

```
<DocumentProperties>
  <Creator>Dejan Sarka</Creator>
  <Template>c:\program files (x86)\microsoft office\office12\1033\DBMODL_M.VST</Template>
  <Company>Solid Quality Mentors</Company>
  <BuildNumberCreated>805378240</BuildNumberCreated>
  <BuildNumberEdited>805378240</BuildNumberEdited>
```

You can see that the document has an internal structure, and of course the structure complies with the published XML schema I mentioned earlier.

The *value* and *query* XML Data Type Methods

You can use the XQuery language within a SELECT statement to extract portions of the XML data. For example, the following query returns the company of the creator of each document.

```
SELECT id,
  doc.value('declare namespace VI=
    "http://schemas.microsoft.com/visio/2003/core";
    (/VI:VisioDocument/VI:DocumentProperties/VI:Company)[1]',
    'NVARCHAR(50)') AS company
FROM dbo.VisioDocs;
```

The results of the query are:

```
id          company
----------- -------------------------------------------------
1           Solid Quality Mentors
2           Solid Quality Mentors
3           Unknown Company
```

I used the *value* method of the XML data type. This method returns a scalar value, so it can be specified in the SELECT list. Note that the *value* method accepts an XQuery expression as the first input parameter. The second parameter is the SQL Server data type returned. The XQuery in this example contains two parts: prolog and body. In the prolog, I declared the namespace I copied out of the XML output from the previous example. A namespace is declared with a prefix—that is, an alias I used in the body of the query. In the XQuery expression, I defined the path to the element I wanted to read. Starting from the root element (*<VisioDocument>*) and going through the second-level element (*<DocumentProperties>*), I arrived at the element I needed (*<Company>*). Notice the use of the numeric predicate *[1]*. The *value* method must return a scalar value; therefore, you have to specify the position of the element in the sequence you are browsing, even if you know that there is only one. Finally, every column in the returned result set must have a data type, so the XQuery expression converts the returned value to NVARCHAR(50).

Next, suppose you want to find all database model diagrams (ER diagrams). All documents with database models are based on the DBMODL_M.VST template, and the template is included in the *<Template>* element of the XML schema for Visio documents. You can use the *value* method in the WHERE clause like so:

```
SELECT id, 'ER DB Model' AS templatetype
FROM dbo.VisioDocs
WHERE doc.value(
  'declare namespace VI="http://schemas.microsoft.com/visio/2003/core";
  (/VI:VisioDocument/VI:DocumentProperties/VI:Template)[1]',
  'NVARCHAR(100)') LIKE N'%DBMODL_M.VST%';
```

And here are the results:

```
id          templatetype
----------- ------------
1           ER DB Model
3           ER DB Model
```

Next, the *query* method, as the name implies, is used to query XML data. You already know this method from the previous section of this chapter. It returns an instance of an untyped XML value. As an example for using the *query* method, the following code invokes a FLWOR expression to iterate through subelements of the *<DocumentSettings>* element:

```
SELECT doc.query('
  declare namespace VI="http://schemas.microsoft.com/visio/2003/core";
  for $v in /VI:VisioDocument/VI:DocumentSettings
  return $v') AS settings
FROM dbo.VisioDocs;
```

This is one of the XML documents returned by the preceding query:

```
<VI:DocumentSettings xmlns:VI="http://schemas.microsoft.com/visio/2003/core" TopPage="0"
DefaultTextStyle="3" DefaultLineStyle="3" DefaultFillStyle="3" DefaultGuideStyle="4">
  <VI:GlueSettings>9</VI:GlueSettings>
  <VI:SnapSettings>39</VI:SnapSettings>
  <VI:SnapExtensions>34</VI:SnapExtensions>
  <VI:DynamicGridEnabled>0</VI:DynamicGridEnabled>
  <VI:ProtectStyles>0</VI:ProtectStyles>
  <VI:ProtectShapes>0</VI:ProtectShapes>
  <VI:ProtectMasters>0</VI:ProtectMasters>
  <VI:ProtectBkgnds>0</VI:ProtectBkgnds>
</VI:DocumentSettings>
```

As you already know, the return clause of the FLWOR expression can be used to shape the XML value returned. For example, the following query retrieves the *<Creator>* element, returning it as an attribute called *creatorname* of an element called *<Person>*:

```
SELECT doc.query('
  declare namespace VI="http://schemas.microsoft.com/visio/2003/core";
  for $v in /VI:VisioDocument/VI:DocumentProperties
  return element Person
    {
      attribute creatorname
                 {$v/VI:Creator[1]/text()[1]}
    }')
FROM dbo.VisioDocs;
```

Here's the XML value this query returns in the first output row:

```
<Person creatorname="Dejan Sarka" />
```

XML Indexes

Suppose that you want to find all Visio documents with an unknown creator company (<*Company*> element has "Unknown Company"). You might be thinking of using the *value* method in the WHERE clause. However, remember that the XML data type is actually a LOB type. There can be up to 2 GB of data in every single column value. Scanning through the XML data sequentially is not a very efficient way of retrieving a simple scalar value. With relational data, you can create an index on a filtered column, allowing an index seek operation instead of a table scan. Similarly, you can index XML columns with specialized XML indexes. The first index you create on an XML column is the *primary XML index*. This index contains a shredded persisted representation of the XML values. For each XML value in the column, the index creates several rows of data. The number of rows in the index is approximately the number of nodes in the XML value. Such an index alone can speed up searches for a specific element using the *exist* method, which I'll describe later. After creating the primary XML index, you can create up to three other types of *secondary XML indexes*:

- **PATH**   A PATH secondary XML index is especially useful if your queries specify path expressions. It speeds up the *exist* method better than the Primary XML index. Such an index also speeds up queries that use *value* for a fully specified path.

- **VALUE**   A VALUE secondary XML index is useful if queries are value-based and the path is not fully specified or it includes a wildcard.

- **PROPERTY**   A PROPERTY secondary XML index is very useful for queries that retrieve one or more values from individual XML instances using the *value* method.

The primary XML index has to be created first. It can be created only on tables with a clustered primary key. The query you are going to use to find all unknown companies invokes the *value* method in the WHERE clause, searching for a single value. The use of the *value* method in this case is similar to using the *exist* method; therefore, a PATH secondary XML index is most appropriate. You need to create a clustered primary key, then a primary XML index, and then a secondary one:

```
ALTER TABLE dbo.VisioDocs
  ADD CONSTRAINT PK_VisioDocs PRIMARY KEY CLUSTERED (id);

CREATE PRIMARY XML INDEX idx_xml_primary ON dbo.VisioDocs(doc);

CREATE XML INDEX idx_xml_path ON VisioDocs(doc)
  USING XML INDEX idx_xml_primary
  FOR PATH;
```

Next, invoke the following three statements in a single batch, with Include Actual Execution Plan turned on in SSMS:

```
SELECT id, doc
FROM dbo.VisioDocs
WHERE doc.value(
  'declare namespace VI="http://schemas.microsoft.com/visio/2003/core";
  (/VI:VisioDocument/VI:DocumentProperties/VI:Company)[1]',
  'NVARCHAR(50)') LIKE N'Unknown%';

DROP INDEX idx_xml_primary ON dbo.VisioDocs;

SELECT id, doc
FROM dbo.VisioDocs
WHERE doc.value(
  'declare namespace VI="http://schemas.microsoft.com/visio/2003/core";
  (/VI:VisioDocument/VI:DocumentProperties/VI:Company)[1]',
  'NVARCHAR(50)') LIKE N'Unknown%';
```

Both SELECT statements are identical, retrieving documents with unknown companies. The first one uses XML indexes; the second doesn't (because it's invoked after dropping the indexes).

> **Note** When you drop the Primary XML index, all secondary XML indexes are dropped automatically.

In my example, the cost estimate for the first query was 2 percent of the whole batch, versus 98 percent for the second query. You can see that the substantial cost difference exists because the first query uses XML indexes and the second doesn't. By the way, I saved the execution plan in an XML file to use in an example later in the chapter. To save your plans, right-click the graphical presentation of the plans in SSMS and select the Show Execution Plan XML option. Then save the XML in the query window that opens. I saved this plan as C:\InsideTSQL2008\VisioFiles\VisioDocsQueries.xml. This will save the execution plan for the entire batch; you cannot save the individual plans within a batch separately from SSMS.

> **Caution** You can also save an execution plan by choosing the Save Execution Plan As option after you right-click. However, this will create a UTF-8 encoded file that you will not be able to import directly into an XML column of a table with the OPENROWSET BULK provider. Use the two-step method described here if you plan to import the saved plan into an XML column. Use the Save Execution Plan As option to save a plan with the intent to reopen it as a graphical plan in SSMS.

The modify and exists XML Data Type Methods

The XML data type is an LOB type. The amount of data stored in a column of this type can be very large. It would not be very practical to replace the complete value when all you need is just to change a small portion of it—for example, a scalar value of some subelement. SQL Server XML data type provides you with the *modify* method, similar in concept to the WRITE method that can be used in a T-SQL UPDATE statement for VARCHAR(MAX) and the other MAX types.

> **Note** You might have noticed that I'm strictly using lowercase for XML data type methods. That's because they are case sensitive, just like everything in XML.

The W3C standard doesn't support data modification with XQuery. However, SQL Server provides its own language extensions to support data modification with XQuery. SQL Server XQuery supports three DML keywords for data modification: *insert*, *delete*, and *replace value of*.

You invoke the *modify* method in an UPDATE T-SQL statement. Suppose I want to add a second company as an element after the *company* element of the first Visio document in my VisioDocs table. This is the UPDATE statement using the *modify* method:

```
UPDATE dbo.VisioDocs
  SET doc.modify('declare namespace VI=
    "http://schemas.microsoft.com/visio/2003/core";
    insert <VI:SecondCompany>Customer NRZBB</VI:SecondCompany>
    after (/VI:VisioDocument/VI:DocumentProperties/VI:Company)[1]')
WHERE id = 1;
```

Here is the resulting XML, abbreviated to show only the first few elements:

```
<VisioDocument xmlns="http://schemas.microsoft.com/visio/2003/core" xmlns:vx="http://
schemas.microsoft.com/visio/2006/extension" key="0269EFD90D045A4D95F376CA56FAB87BB98119E6
509C39621E6CBF4D5A9109F19DEB3216703EFA4BD87208EBB452A892E2D15FB26D5B15453486A571908861D9"
start="190" metric="1" DocLangID="1033" buildnum="6336" version="12.0" xml:space="preserve">
  <DocumentProperties>
    <Creator>Dejan Sarka</Creator>
    <Template>c:\program files (x86)\microsoft office\office12\1033\DBMODL_M.VST</Template>
    <Company>Solid Quality Mentors</Company>
    <SecondCompany>Customer NRZBB</SecondCompany>
    <BuildNumberCreated>805378240</BuildNumberCreated>
    <BuildNumberEdited>805378240</BuildNumberEdited>
    <PreviewPicture Size="5812">
```

As you can see, the *SecondCompany* element is properly inserted after the first *Company* element. The *insert* XQuery extension allows you to insert a node *after* a specified node, *before* a specified node, or *as first* or *as last* node on the specified level. In addition, you can use the *into* keyword just to insert a node as a direct descendant of a specified node.

Now I'll check which Visio documents in my table have the second company assigned. I will search for rows where the *SecondCompany* element is present in the XML column using the *exist* XML data type method.

```
SELECT id, doc
FROM dbo.VisioDocs
WHERE doc.exist('declare namespace VI=
    "http://schemas.microsoft.com/visio/2003/core";
    /VI:VisioDocument/VI:DocumentProperties/VI:SecondCompany') = 1;
```

This query properly returns only the document with *id* equal to 1. After checking the result, I might decide to change the second company name. I can use the *modify* XML data type method again to make the change. This time I'll need the *replace value of* XQuery DML extension:

```
UPDATE dbo.VisioDocs
  SET doc.modify('declare namespace VI=
    "http://schemas.microsoft.com/visio/2003/core";
    replace value of
    /VI:VisioDocument[1]/VI:DocumentProperties[1]/VI:SecondCompany[1]/text()[1]
    with "Customer MLTDN"')
WHERE id = 1;
```

I leave it to you to check whether the second company name is properly updated. Finally, suppose I notice that the *SecondCompany* element should never be a part of a Visio document XML file because it is not specified in the Visio XML schema. In order to delete it, I can use the *modify* method once more, this time with the *delete* XQuery DML extension:

```
UPDATE dbo.VisioDocs
  SET doc.modify('declare namespace VI=
    "http://schemas.microsoft.com/visio/2003/core";
    delete
    /VI:VisioDocument/VI:DocumentProperties/VI:SecondCompany[1]')
WHERE id = 1;
```

You might ask yourself whether it is possible to prevent such inserts, which result in an XML document that no longer complies with its schema. Of course it is possible; in SQL Server, you can validate an XML instance against a schema from an XML schema collection. I will explain this in the last section of this chapter, where I deal with dynamic relational schemas.

The nodes XML Data Type Method

The *nodes* method is useful when you want to shred an XML value into relational data. Its purpose is therefore the same as the purpose of the OPENXML rowset function I introduced at the beginning of this chapter. However, using the *nodes* method is usually much faster than preparing the DOM with a call to *sp_xml_preparedocument*, executing a SELECT..FROM OPENXMLstatement, and calling *sp_xml_removedocument*. The *nodes* method prepares DOM internally, during the execution of the T-SQL SELECT. The OPENXML approach could be faster if you prepared the DOM once and then shredded it multiple times in the same batch. Nevertheless, as a general approach I prefer using the *nodes* method instead of the OPENXML function.

The result of the *nodes* method is a result set that contains logical copies of the original XML instances. In those logical copies, the context node of every row instance is set to one of the nodes identified by the XQuery expression—meaning that you get a row for every single node from the starting point defined by the XQuery expression. The *nodes* method returns copies of the XML values, so you have to use additional methods to extract the scalar values out of them. The *nodes* method has to be invoked for every row in the table. The T-SQL APPLY operator allows you to invoke a right table expression for every row of a left table expression in the FROM part.

The following query invokes the *nodes* method in the FROM clause for each row in the base table using the CROSS APPLY operator. The XQuery expression supplied as input to the *nodes* method returns a row for each document properties node. Because there is only one *DocumentProperties* element per Visio document, you get one row for each method call, and therefore three rows in the output. You extract the values from the *nodes* method with the *value* XML data type method:

```
SELECT id,
  N.c1.value('declare namespace VI=
      "http://schemas.microsoft.com/visio/2003/core";
      (VI:Company)[1]','NVARCHAR(30)') AS Company,
  N.c1.value('declare namespace VI=
      "http://schemas.microsoft.com/visio/2003/core";
      (VI:Creator)[1]','NVARCHAR(30)') AS Creator
FROM dbo.VisioDocs
  CROSS APPLY
    doc.nodes('declare namespace VI=
      "http://schemas.microsoft.com/visio/2003/core";
      /VI:VisioDocument/VI:DocumentProperties') AS N(c1);
```

The results of the query are:

```
id          Company                         Creator
----------- ------------------------------- -----------------------------
1           Solid Quality Mentors           Dejan Sarka
2           Solid Quality Mentors           Dejan Sarka
3           Unknown Company                 Unknown Author
```

Reading the Execution Plan

As I mentioned, I saved the execution plan of the batch with two identical queries and the index dropping statement between them. Now I am going to import this plan in a SQL table and query it using the XML data type methods. This gives you another idea for using the XML data type. You can analyze execution plans with T-SQL SELECT, of course, with the help of XQuery inside XML data type methods. Use the following code to create a table for execution plans storage and to insert the execution plan saved:

```
CREATE TABLE dbo.ExecutionPlans
(
  id    INT NOT NULL,
  eplan XML NOT NULL
);
GO
INSERT INTO dbo.ExecutionPlans (id, eplan)
 SELECT 1, *
 FROM OPENROWSET(BULK 'C:\InsideTSQL2008\VisioFiles\VisioDocsQueries.xml',
   SINGLE_BLOB) AS x;
GO
```

If you execute the query *SELECT eplan FROM dbo.ExecutionPlans* in SSMS with grid results, and then click the link in the result, SSMS should display the graphical execution plan. This is a quick test to verify that the plan was saved and inserted into the table correctly.

If you analyze the XML of the execution plan, you can see that there is an */ShowPlanXML /BatchSequence/Batch/Statements/StmtSimple* element for each statement in the batch. This element has a couple of interesting attributes, such as *StatementId* and *StatementSubtreeCost*. From the *StatementSubtreeCost* attribute, I want to calculate each statement's estimated cost as a percentage of the total batch cost more precisely than SSMS shows it when displaying the plans. If you remember, SSMS estimated that when XML indexes were present, the query would take 2 percent of the total cost, and without XML indexes, 98 percent of the total cost. I am using a common table expression with the *nodes* and *value* XML data type methods to extract each statement ID and cost, and then a second common table expression to summarize statement costs over batches to get the total cost of batches. In the outer SELECT I am joining both CTEs to calculate the relative cost. Here is the query:

```
WITH StatementCostCTE AS
(SELECT id AS BatchId,
        N.c1.value('declare namespace EP=
          "http://schemas.microsoft.com/sqlserver/2004/07/showplan";
          (EP:StmtSimple/@StatementId)[1]',
          'INT') AS StatementId,
        N.c1.value('declare namespace EP=
          "http://schemas.microsoft.com/sqlserver/2004/07/showplan";
          (EP:StmtSimple/@StatementSubTreeCost)[1]',
          'DECIMAL(10,7)') AS StatementCost
 FROM dbo.ExecutionPlans CROSS APPLY
      eplan.nodes('declare namespace EP=
        "http://schemas.microsoft.com/sqlserver/2004/07/showplan";
        /EP:ShowPlanXML/EP:BatchSequence/EP:Batch/EP:Statements') AS N(c1)),
BatchCostCTE AS
(SELECT BatchId,
        SUM(StatementCost) AS BatchCost
 FROM StatementCostCTE
 GROUP BY BatchId)
SELECT B.BatchId,
```

```
      S.StatementId,
      CAST(ROUND((S.StatementCost / B.BatchCost) * 100,5)
        AS DECIMAL(8,5))
        AS RelativeCostPercent
FROM BatchCostCTE AS B
  JOIN StatementCostCTE AS S
    ON B.BatchId = S.BatchId;
```

And the output is:

```
BatchId     StatementId RelativeCostPercent
----------- ----------- -------------------
1           1           2.46988
1           2           97.53012
```

As you can see, the actual cost of the first statement was nearly 2.5 percent of the batch. This way, with XML execution plans, the XML data type and its methods, and XQuery, you can analyze query execution plans.

XML as a Stored Procedure Parameter

Suppose you want to create a stored procedure that accepts a list of names as a parameter and returns all contacts with a name that appears in the input list. Of course, you could use a delimited list and then separate the elements using T-SQL or CLR code. Alternatively, with SQL Server 2008, you could use table-valued parameters. However, using an XML input and applying the *nodes* method seems simpler to me. Here is the code implementing the stored procedure:

```
CREATE PROCEDURE dbo.GetProducts
  @inplist XML
AS
SELECT P.*
FROM Production.Products AS P
  JOIN (SELECT D1.c1.value('(./text())[1]','NVARCHAR(50)') AS NameNeeded
          FROM @inplist.nodes('/Names/NameNeeded') AS D1(c1)) AS D2
    ON P.productname = D2.NameNeeded;
```

The procedure uses the *nodes* and *value* methods to extract the elements from the input list. You create the input list in XML format by using the FOR XML clause extensions. You can create the input list using the VALUES clause for a derived table. Here is the code for invoking the procedure:

```
DECLARE @inplist AS XML;
SET @inplist=
  (SELECT * FROM
     (VALUES
        (N'Product HHYDP'),
        (N'Product RECZE')) AS D(NameNeeded)
  FOR XML RAW('Names'), ELEMENTS);
EXEC dbo.GetProducts @inplist;
```

Dynamic Relational Schema

One of the most common problems with applications that use relational databases is schema evolvement. Over time, you might need additional tables. In this case, you simply have to create them. However, you might need additional attributes for existing tables only. Imagine a retail store that starts selling a new category of products. These new products have properties for which you do not yet have columns in your Products table. Of course, they have some attributes in common with all existing products, such as name and price. The question is how to add the new attributes without having to upgrade the application. There are quite a few possibilities. I'll briefly introduce them using the Products table as an example. Before starting, I need to emphasize that I am especially interested in constraints. I prefer solutions that enable me to have declarative constraints in my database.

Relational Solutions

The first possibility is to have a single table with many additional columns of character data types, such as NVARCHAR(50), and then let your users insert into them any data they want. I really dislike this solution. The names of these additional attributes are typically meaningless. It is not easy to use declarative constraints, because you do not even have proper data types for specific data. You can create triggers for such columns, or try to solve integrity problems in your middle tier or client code.

Instead of having dozens of attributes prepared in advance, you can alter the table and add columns as needed. This way you can use proper data types, and also add declarative integrity constraints, such as foreign keys and check constraints. However, this is not a very dynamic solution. Your application must be able to create user interface forms dynamically; otherwise, you would have to upgrade the application for every single change.

In both cases, with a single table, you would probably get a very sparse table, meaning many NULLs in your data. This is a logical consequence because not all attributes are applicable for all rows. In addition, a table like this could grow very quickly. You can mitigate the size problem if you use the new SPARSE attribute for nullable columns in SQL Server 2008. Yet sparse columns solve the size problem only, and cannot help you with constraints or with dynamic forms in application.

A proper relational solution would be to implement subtypes. Besides the main Products table, you add additional tables for each product category with a one-to-one relationship to the main Products table and with attributes specific for that category. You leave the common attributes in the main table. This is a very good solution—it is in fact considered a good design. You can implement any constraint you need, and you store the data efficiently. Yet this is not a dynamic solution. When a new category arises, you have to create an additional table. Again, your application must be able to use the new table dynamically; otherwise, you would need to upgrade the application after adding a new subtype.

The so-called open schema solution is quite popular. In this solution, you have the main Products table with common attributes. Then you add an Entity-Attribute-Value (EAV) table, which has three columns: product ID, attribute name, and attribute value. This is a completely dynamic solution, and is quite simple. However, with this solution you cannot easily use declarative constraints. With a single EAV table, the attribute value column is either character or variant data type. In addition, you have to prevent the insertion of meaningless attributes, or binding attributes to products for which the attributes are meaningless. You can create an EAV table for every data type of attributes you need to solve the data type problems. You can add an additional table that holds valid combinations of products and attributes. You can add additional constraints using triggers, middle tier code, or client code. Whatever you do, your solution is not that simple anymore. Your database design does not reflect the business problem anymore; you do not design a database from logical point of view, you design it from a physical point of view. Because of this last fact, I would hardly call this solution relational. Note that I am not saying that if you use such a solution, you have to modify it. In the past, this was probably the best option you had if you needed dynamic schema. However, nowadays I prefer the solution I am going to introduce at the end of this section.

Finally, if you use SQL Server 2005 or later, you could even create your own CLR user-defined type (UDT) that would store a dynamic .NET collection. For example, you could use the Dictionary .NET collection. Then you could allow users to add elements to the dictionary object dynamically. You could build all kinds of constraints into your data type. Although I like CLR UDTs, and I used one to help solve temporal data problems in the previous chapter, I am not too keen on this solution for dynamic schema. It is not a standard solution; except for your application, every single application must learn to work with your UDT. In addition, this is not a simple solution; writing a good UDT with all kinds of constraints can be a very challenging task. Finally, it can be challenging to upgrade the UDT over time. What if constraints that are built into the type change?

Object-Oriented Solutions

Because truly relational solutions might be not flexible enough, some developers prefer to use object-oriented solutions. This means that an application creates collections—such as .NET Dictionary—dynamically, and stores them in a binary data type column in a relational database. Another possibility is to store—or in .NET jargon, to *serialize*—the collections to a file system directly, thus bypassing the RDBMS completely. I am not a fan of such solutions, of course.

As with the CLR UDT solution, there is no standard in such object-oriented solutions. Actually, CLR UDT is even a bit more standardized because some basic methods that a UDT has to implement are prescribed and well known. Only applications that know how to deserialize such objects can use the data. In addition, of course, with such a solution you are not using RDBMS features at all. You do not have any constraints on the database side, if you use a database at all.

One solution that is slightly more useful is to serialize objects not in binary format; you can serialize .NET objects in XML format as well. Then you can store this XML in a database column or as a file in a file system. With XML serialization, at least any application that can read XML can use the data. Of course, no matter which serialization you use, you are not exploiting the features of the RDBMS.

Using the XML Data Type for Dynamic Schema

For my last solution, I'll show you how to use the XML data type to make the schema dynamic, get a standard solution, and constrain values reasonably. I'll work on the Products table from the InsideTSQL2008 database.

Suppose that you need to store some specific attributes only for beverages and other attributes only for condiments. For example, you need to store the percentage of recommended daily allowance (RDA) of vitamins only for beverages, and a short description only for condiments to indicate the condiment's general character (such as sweet, spicy, or salty). You could add an XML data type column to the Products table; let's call it *additionalattributes*. Because the other product categories have no additional attributes, this column has to be nullable. I am altering the Products table to add this column:

```
ALTER TABLE Production.Products
 ADD additionalattributes XML NULL;
```

Before inserting data in the new column, I want to constrain the values of this column. For a start, I want to have a typed XML—in other words, XML validated against a schema. With an XML schema, you constrain the possible nodes, the data type of those nodes, and more. In SQL Server, you can validate XML data against an XML schema collection. This is exactly what I need here; if you could validate XML data against single schema only, you could not use XML data type for a dynamic schema solution. Validation against a collection of schemas enables support of different schemas for beverages and condiments. If you wanted to validate XML values only against a single schema, you would define only a single schema in the collection.

You create the schema collection using the CREATE XML SCHEMA COLLECTION T-SQL statement. You have to supply the XML schema as input—that is, the XSD document. Creating the schema is a task that should not be taken lightly. If you make an error in the schema, some invalid data might be accepted and some valid data might be rejected.

The easiest way that I can suggest to create robust XML schemas is to create relational tables first, and then use the XMLSCHEMA option of the FOR XML clause. Store the resulting XML value (the schema) in a variable, and provide the variable as input to the CREATE XML SCHEMA COLLECTION statement. The following code creates two auxiliary empty tables for beverages and condiments, and then uses SELECT with the FOR XML clause to create XML schema from those tables, store the schemas in a variable, and create a schema collection from that variable. Finally, after the schema collection is created, I drop the auxiliary tables.

```
-- Auxiliary tables
CREATE TABLE dbo.Beverages
(
  percentvitaminsRDA INT
);
CREATE TABLE dbo.Condiments
(
  shortdescription NVARCHAR(50)
);
GO
-- Store the Schemas in a Variable and Create the Collection
DECLARE @mySchema NVARCHAR(MAX);
SET @mySchema = N'';
SET @mySchema = @mySchema +
  (SELECT *
   FROM Beverages
   FOR XML AUTO, ELEMENTS, XMLSCHEMA('Beverages'));
SET @mySchema = @mySchema +
  (SELECT *
   FROM Condiments
   FOR XML AUTO, ELEMENTS, XMLSCHEMA('Condiments'));
SELECT CAST(@mySchema AS XML);
CREATE XML SCHEMA COLLECTION dbo.ProductsAdditionalAttributes AS @mySchema;
GO
-- Drop Tables
DROP TABLE dbo.Beverages, dbo.Condiments;
GO
```

I added a SELECT statement to show you the schema collection I am creating. Note that each schema in the collection has its own target namespace, defined in the XMLSCHEMA directive of the FOR XML clause. Therefore, here is the schema collection I created:

```
<xsd:schema xmlns:schema="Beverages" xmlns:xsd="http://www.w3.org/2001/
XMLSchema" xmlns:sqltypes="http://schemas.microsoft.com/sqlserver/2004/sqltypes"
targetNamespace="Beverages" elementFormDefault="qualified">
  <xsd:import namespace="http://schemas.microsoft.com/sqlserver/2004/sqltypes"
schemaLocation="http://schemas.microsoft.com/sqlserver/2004/sqltypes/sqltypes.xsd" />
  <xsd:element name="Beverages">
    <xsd:complexType>
      <xsd:sequence>
        <xsd:element name="percentvitaminsRDA" type="sqltypes:int" minOccurs="0" />
      </xsd:sequence>
    </xsd:complexType>
  </xsd:element>
</xsd:schema>
<xsd:schema xmlns:schema="Condiments" xmlns:xsd="http://www.w3.org/2001/
XMLSchema" xmlns:sqltypes="http://schemas.microsoft.com/sqlserver/2004/sqltypes"
targetNamespace="Condiments" elementFormDefault="qualified">
  <xsd:import namespace="http://schemas.microsoft.com/sqlserver/2004/sqltypes"
schemaLocation="http://schemas.microsoft.com/sqlserver/2004/sqltypes/sqltypes.xsd" />
  <xsd:element name="Condiments">
    <xsd:complexType>
      <xsd:sequence>
        <xsd:element name="shortdescription" minOccurs="0">
          <xsd:simpleType>
```

```
                <xsd:restriction base="sqltypes:nvarchar" sqltypes:localeId="1033"
        sqltypes:sqlCompareOptions="IgnoreCase IgnoreKanaType IgnoreWidth" sqltypes:sqlSortId="52">
                    <xsd:maxLength value="50" />
                </xsd:restriction>
              </xsd:simpleType>
            </xsd:element>
          </xsd:sequence>
        </xsd:complexType>
      </xsd:element>
    </xsd:schema>
```

You can get information about schema collections by querying the catalog views
sys.xml_schema_collections, sys.xml_schema_namespaces, sys.xml_schema_components, and
some others. However, a schema collection is stored in SQL Server in tabular format, not
in XML format. It would make sense to perform the same schema validation on the client
side as well; why would you send data to the server side if the RDBMS will reject it? You can
perform schema collection validation in .NET code as well, as long as you have the schemas.
Therefore, it makes sense to also save the schemas you create with T-SQL as files in the file
system for this purpose. In SQL Server, as I mentioned, you can browse catalog views to get
schema collection information:

```
-- Retrieve information about the schema collection
SELECT *
FROM sys.xml_schema_collections
WHERE name = 'ProductsAdditionalAttributes';
 -- Retrieve information about the namespaces in the schema collection
SELECT N.*
FROM sys.xml_schema_namespaces AS N
  JOIN sys.xml_schema_collections AS C
    ON N.xml_collection_id = C.xml_collection_id
WHERE C.name = 'ProductsAdditionalAttributes';
-- Retrieve information about the components in the schema collection
SELECT CP.*
FROM sys.xml_schema_components AS CP
  JOIN sys.xml_schema_collections AS C
    ON CP.xml_collection_id = C.xml_collection_id
WHERE C.name = 'ProductsAdditionalAttributes';
```

The next step is to alter the XML column from a well-formed state to a schema-validated one:

```
ALTER TABLE Production.Products
  ALTER COLUMN additionalattributes
  XML(dbo.ProductsAdditionalAttributes);
```

> **Note** When you change an XML column from well formed to schema-validated, all values in
> that column are validated, so the alteration can take a while.

Before using the new data type, I have to take care of one more issue. How do I prevent
binding the wrong schema to a product of a specific category? For example, how do
I prevent binding a condiments schema to a beverage? I want to have a declarative

constraint—namely, a check constraint. This is why I added namespaces to my schemas. I am going to check whether the namespace is the same as the product category name. You cannot use XML data type methods inside constraints. This is why I have to create two additional functions: one retrieves the XML namespace of the *additionalattributes* XML column; and the other retrieves the category name of a product. In the check constraint, I'll check whether the return values of both functions are equal:

```
-- Function to retrieve the namespace
CREATE FUNCTION dbo.GetNamespace(@chkcol XML)
 RETURNS NVARCHAR(15)
AS
BEGIN
 RETURN @chkcol.value('namespace-uri((/*)[1])','NVARCHAR(15)')
END;
GO
-- Function to retrieve the category name
CREATE FUNCTION dbo.GetCategoryName(@catid INT)
 RETURNS NVARCHAR(15)
AS
BEGIN
 RETURN
  (SELECT categoryname
    FROM Production.Categories
    WHERE categoryid = @catid)
END;
GO
-- Add the constraint
ALTER TABLE Production.Products ADD CONSTRAINT ck_Namespace
 CHECK (dbo.GetNamespace(additionalattributes) =
        dbo.GetCategoryName(categoryid));
```

Now insert some valid data:

```
-- Beverage
UPDATE Production.Products
   SET additionalattributes = N'
<Beverages xmlns="Beverages">
  <percentvitaminsRDA>27</percentvitaminsRDA>
</Beverages>'
WHERE productid = 1;
-- Condiment
UPDATE Production.Products
   SET additionalattributes = N'
<Condiments xmlns="Condiments">
  <shortdescription>very sweet</shortdescription>
</Condiments>'
WHERE productid = 3;
```

Finally, I have to determine whether the XML schema validation and the check constraint work. I'll try to insert some invalid data:

```
-- String instead of int
UPDATE Production.Products
   SET additionalattributes = N'
```

```
<Beverages xmlns="Beverages">
  <percentvitaminsRDA>twenty seven</percentvitaminsRDA>
</Beverages>'
WHERE productid = 1;
-- Wrong namespace
UPDATE Production.Products
  SET additionalattributes = N'
<Condiments xmlns="Condiments">
  <shortdescription>very sweet</shortdescription>
</Condiments>'
WHERE productid = 2;
-- Wrong element
UPDATE Production.Products
  SET additionalattributes = N'
<Condiments xmlns="Condiments">
  <unknownelement>very sweet</unknownelement>
</Condiments>'
WHERE productid = 3;
```

I will leave it to you to use the XML data type methods to extract scalar values of the elements of the *additionalattributes* XML column. Because this was the last example in this chapter, I suggest you use the following cleanup code to revert the InsideTSQL2008 database to original state:

```
DROP TABLE dbo.VisioDocs;
DROP TABLE dbo.ExecutionPlans;
DROP PROCEDURE dbo.GetProducts;
ALTER TABLE Production.Products
 DROP CONSTRAINT ck_Namespace;
ALTER TABLE Production.Products
 DROP COLUMN additionalattributes;
DROP XML SCHEMA COLLECTION dbo.ProductsAdditionalAttributes;
DROP FUNCTION dbo.GetNamespace;
DROP FUNCTION dbo.GetCategoryName;
```

Conclusion

I don't fear XML support in SQL Server. I actually find it very useful; of course, you must use XML in your database wisely. You should not abuse XML support to turn your relational database to something like an "XML database."

In this chapter, I explained how to create XML from your relational data with the FOR XML clause of the SELECT T-SQL statement. I also showed you the opposite process—shredding XML to tables. You can do this with the OPENXML function or the *nodes* XML data type method. I gave additional examples to show how you can use all the XML data type methods: *query*, *value*, *exist*, *nodes*, and *modify*. All XML data type methods accept XQuery as the only or one of the parameters. XQuery is a completely new query language; nevertheless, I hope that my brief introduction to XQuery in this chapter will help you browse and update XML data in SQL Server. However, most of all, I hope I managed to give you useful guidelines for where and when to use XML in SQL Server.

Chapter 14
Spatial Data

Ed Katibah and Isaac Kunen

Spatial data support is new to SQL Server 2008, bringing new data types, operators, and indexes to the database. This chapter is neither an exhaustive treatise on spatial data nor an encyclopedia of every spatial operator that Microsoft SQL Server supports. Instead, this chapter introduces core spatial concepts and provides key programming constructs necessary to successfully navigate this new feature of SQL Server 2008.

Introduction to Spatial Data

Spatial data describes the physical locations and extents of objects in the world. These representations may be points, lines, or regions. The use of such features is not limited to geospatial and mapping applications, but maps provide a convenient medium to illustrate them, as shown in Figure 14-1.

FIGURE 14-1 The University of Wisconsin–Madison Department of Computer Sciences and surroundings.

In this figure, the point labeled 1 shows the location of the University of Wisconsin–Madison Department of Computer Sciences; lines show the location and routes of highways, such as Interstate 90 and U.S. Highway 51; shaded regions show features with area, such as Lake Mendota and Lake Monona.

Because geospatial data has historically been difficult to acquire, process, and visualize, its use has typically been limited to specialists working in fields highly dependent on spatial reasoning. Non-specialists have had to content themselves with the textual proxies for spatial locations: addresses.

Today, collecting geospatial data is greatly simplified by technologies such as the Global Positioning System (GPS). At the same time, the number of software packages for the processing and visualization of spatial data has grown tremendously. With its 2008 release, SQL Server joins this trend, adding capabilities for the storage and analysis of spatial data alongside other relational data in the database.

Therefore, today non-specialists can start to derive value from treating their spatial data as spatial data. This chapter is for these readers, introducing the idiosyncrasies of spatial data and the new spatial functionality in SQL Server 2008, and highlighting some of the more common tasks users may wish to perform with spatial data.

Basic Spatial Data Concepts

Geometry and geography are surprisingly deep fields, and although we cannot afford a complete exposition on them here, a brief introduction will aid the SQL Server practitioner working with spatial data.

Vector Data and the OGC Simple Features Type Model

Spatial data comes in several flavors. The main division is between *raster* and *vector* data. Bitmap images are a form of raster data, which are composed of a regular array of data points. In the spatial context, aerial images are the most familiar raster data. Although such data can certainly be stored in SQL Server, it is not the focus of the new spatial support in SQL Server 2008.

SQL Server's new support is for vector data, which represents objects by building up collections of mathematical primitives, such as points and line segments. Rather than lying in a regular array, these primitives may lie anywhere in the working space. The distinction between vector and raster representations is shown in Figure 14-2, with vector data represented as black solid lines and the raster representation of the same regions as gray cells.

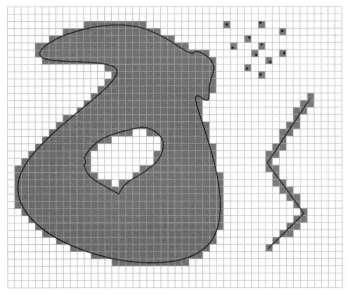

FIGURE 14-2 Raster and vector data representations of the same spatial objects

More Info An example of a large raster data system built on SQL Server is TerraServer (*http://terraserver-usa.com/*). Built to highlight the scalability of SQL Server, TerraServer currently runs on a set of SQL Server 2000 instances.

There are several common geometric object models, but in the geospatial arena, the OpenGIS model, which is a product of the Open Geospatial Consortium (OGC), predominates. SQL Server supports this system, which has the following primitives:

- **Point**   A simple position in space.

- **LineString**   A set of points with connected by straight edges. LineStrings may be open (have different start- and endpoints) or closed (have the same start- and endpoint); and may or may not be simple (non-self-intersecting). (See the section "Working on the Ellipsoid" later in the chapter for additional discussion of edges.)

- **Polygon**   A region whose boundary is defined by a set of rings (simple, closed LineStrings).

- **MultiPoint**   A collection of zero or more points.

- **MultiLineString**   A collection of zero or more LineStrings.

- **MultiPolygon**   A collection of zero or more Polygons.

- **GeometryCollection**   A collection of zero or more instances of any of these primitives.

Examples of these primitives are illustrated in Figure 14-3.

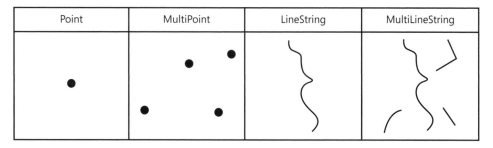

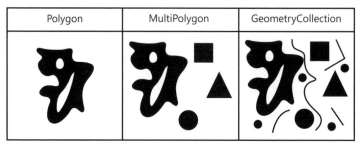

FIGURE 14-3 Open Geospatial Consortium geometry primitives

With these primitives, we can describe a wide array of objects in the world.

Planar and Geographic Coordinates

With some minor exceptions, SQL Server 2008 works only on objects in a two-dimensional space, but a two-dimensional space need not be flat. Thus, although SQL Server will work with objects in the plane, it will also work with objects on an ellipsoidal model of Earth. We call the former *planar* systems, and the latter *geographic* systems.

The choice of model affects several aspects of our work. Most fundamentally, points form the basis of our vector geometry system, and we build our other objects from them. But how do we represent points themselves? Because we're working in a two-dimensional system, we need two coordinates for each point, but the form these coordinates take varies.

In a planar coordinate system, coordinates are expressed with a *linear measure*—typically meters or feet—in each of two coordinate axes. The axes are often labeled east–west and north–south, or simply *x* and *y*, and they intersect at a zero point called the *origin*. The coordinate values tell us how far from the origin a given point is in each of these directions.

In a geographic system, coordinates are expressed with an *angular measure*—typically degrees. *Latitude* is the angle between a point and the equatorial plane, which tells us how far north or south the point lies; *longitude* is the angle east or west of the *prime meridian*. (Although the rotation of Earth gives a physical definition to the equator, the prime meridian is arbitrary and must be agreed upon.)

> **Note** Planar systems are often referred to as *Euclidean, Cartesian,* or even simply *flat*. Although we use the term *planar* throughout this chapter, these other terms are equivalent. Likewise, geographic systems are often referred to as geodetic.

Why Planar?

People have known Earth is round for more than two thousand years. So why would we ever use planar coordinates when working with Earth-oriented coordinates? Legacy. Until recently, flat maps were the computational instrument of choice for geographers. To work with a flat map, Earth—or at least a portion of it—must be flattened, or *projected* onto the plane. Once projected, however, the data can be treated as planar, which is much easier when not aided by a computer.

Today this legacy persists. Many jurisdictions mandate planar models for official work, and a vast amount of such data exists.

Planar systems also have natural application to so-called *local coordinate systems*, such as within buildings, that are not typically registered to locations on Earth.

Please see the whitepaper, Introduction to Spatial Coordinate Systems: Flat Maps for a Round Planet by Isaac Kunen (http://msdn.microsoft.com/en-us/library/cc749633.aspx) for a more detailed treatment of this subject.

When working with large-scale, Earth-oriented objects, the curvature of Earth becomes a significant factor in any computations. But on a small scale, Earth resembles a plane, and its curvature can often be ignored. *Metric* operations—meaning operations that measure, such as finding the area or length of an object—are the exception: because the formulas used with planar coordinates are fundamentally different from those used for geographic coordinates, we must be very careful to match the correct operations with the given data. Failing to do so will give us meaningless results.

SQL Server makes this differentiation simple by using two separate spatial types: the GEOGRAPHY type, which uses geographic coordinates and calculations, and the GEOMETRY type, which uses planar coordinates and calculations. You need only be careful to choose the correct type for your data. But this choice is generally straightforward: use the GEOGRAPHY type with latitude-longitude data and the GEOMETRY type with all other data.

> **Note** In keeping with the typographical conventions of this book, we write these T-SQL types in uppercase: GEOMETRY and GEOGRAPHY. However, the case-sensitivity—or not—of these types and their methods deserves some attention.
>
> - As T-SQL type identifiers, GEOMETRY and GEOGRAPHY are always case-insensitive like every T-SQL keyword.
> - The method names associated with these types, like *Parse()*, are always case-sensitive, like every CLR identifier, whether they are static methods or not.

- When used to identify the CLR class of a static method, as in *geometry::STGeomFromText()*, the identifiers GEOMETRY/geometry and GEOGRAPHY/geography are case-sensitive or case-insensitive according to the current database context. When the current database is case-sensitive, lowercase must be used to identify the CLR class of a static method.

- We've chosen to write the T-SQL types in uppercase for typographical reasons, but lowercase is the most portable choice for code.

Spatial Reference Identifiers

As you start to use spatial data in SQL Server, you'll notice that every spatial object is tagged with an SRID, or *spatial reference identifier*. These SRIDs are integers that indicate the coordinate system used for the particular spatial object.

To understand this, consider tracking the location of goods in two different warehouses. You would naturally use a planar coordinate system for this application, choosing an axis alignment and origin in each warehouse, and measuring locations in some unit, such as meters, from this point. But now two points with the same *x* and *y* coordinates may not refer to the same location. For example, each warehouse may have an object at the point (10,20), but these points do not refer to the same location; they're in separate buildings.

The SRID disambiguates these points: By assigning to each coordinate system a different SRID, we can tell in which warehouse any particular point belongs. Two coordinates with different SRIDs are not comparable.

SRIDs need not be arbitrary numbers. For Earth-oriented coordinate systems, the European Petroleum Survey Group (EPSG) established the EPSG Geodetic Parameter Dataset, which provides a standard list of SRIDs (among other data). In addition to a standard list of numbers, the EPSG repository contains the definitions of these coordinate systems, so that a user of a given SRID can determine the actual physical location for any point given the SRID.

 More Info This data set is available online at *http://www.epsg-registry.org/*. The EPSG has been absorbed into the International Association of Oil and Gas Producers (OGP), but it has left the EPSG moniker intact in reference to the Geodetic Parameter Dataset.

When SQL Server deals with planar coordinate systems (using the GEOMETRY data type), the SRID serves solely as a label; no additional semantics are implied. Although Microsoft recommends that you choose these values from the EPSG list when possible, the value can be anything in the range 0 to 999,999. When an EPSG value is not available—as in our warehouse example—you should use a value greater than 32,767 to avoid confusion with EPSG-defined values. An SRID of 0 can be used to denote an undefined coordinate system.

But, when working with geographic coordinate systems (using the GEOGRAPHY data type) the values of some computations depend on the SRID. This is because the SRID captures the size and shape of the Earth model being used. To capture this, SQL Server restricts the

SRID for geography objects to one of the 390 values taken from the EPSG repository and listed in the *sys.spatial_reference_systems* view. The most common of these is 4326, which corresponds to the World Geodetic System of 1984 (WGS 84) coordinate system. Although WGS 84 is the prevalent system in use today, it is far from the only commonly encountered system.

Standards

The main standards body involved in the geospatial arena is the Open Geospatial Consortium, or OGC (*http://www.opengeospatial.org/*). The OGC works to synchronize its specifications affecting SQL with the overlapping SQL-MM specifications. The GEOMETRY type in SQL Server 2008 is compliant with the OGC Simple Features for SQL version 1.1.0.

Because the geospatial industry has historically worked primarily with planar data, there are no standards for the behavior of geographic systems. The SQL Server team worked to make the GEOGRAPHY type as compliant with the OGC specification as possible, but both holes and conflicts still need to be resolved.

In short, if your application requires strict OGC compliance, you may have to use the GEOMETRY type. If you do not require strict compliance and are working with geographic data, the semantics of the GEOGRAPHY type will be a better match.

Working on the Ellipsoid

As suggested previously, working on the plane and working on an ellipsoid are different in some important and often surprising ways. This section highlights three increasingly eye-opening examples. Keep in mind that this is a representative collection, not a full catalog.

First, consider the definition of an edge. When working on the plane, we can form a LineString from a series of points by connecting each successive pair with a straight line. On the ellipsoid, we clearly cannot use straight lines because edges must follow the curve of the surface.

Less obvious is that this curve has multiple possible natural definitions. SQL Server uses a *great elliptic arc*—essentially a *great circle route* on the ellipsoid—to connect such points. Many other systems, including several other database systems, use this definition, but it is neither standard nor ubiquitous.

Second, consider a simple polygon on the plane defined by a single ring. (A *ring* is a simple closed LineString.) This definition is unambiguous: The ring divides the plane into two separate regions, only one of which is finite; the polygon is the finite region. Although a ring also divides an ellipsoid into two separate regions, neither can be discarded for being infinite, yielding an ambiguity. Consider a ring running around the equator: Does the polygon it defines correspond to the northern or southern hemisphere? We need not go to such extremes in search of ambiguity: a small ring could denote either a small island or a very large ocean.

> **Note**   That every closed, simple curve divides the plane into two pieces is called the *Jordan curve theorem,* and although it is seemingly obvious, is far from simple to prove. Oswald Velben was the first to provide a rigorous proof, in 1905.

To resolve this, we must take the orientation of the ring into account when working on the ellipsoid. Because a ring is defined by a series of points, we can imagine walking along the ring in the order in which the points are given. We then adopt the *left-hand rule* and interpret the resulting polygon as the region on our left as we walk along the ring. Note that the selection of left is arbitrary, and although the left-hand rule is the most common, it is again not ubiquitous. (SQL Server does not enforce this rule for the GEOMETRY type because it is not necessary, but every spatial object that SQL Server 2008 produces will conform to it.)

Finally, consider that a polygon, as defined by the OGC, consists of a single *exterior ring* and zero or more *interior rings*. The exterior ring circumscribes the region defined, and the interior rings mark holes in this region. But on the ellipsoid, this distinction loses meaning. The OGC requires methods for obtaining (a) the exterior ring and (b) the nth interior ring of any polygon. SQL Server implements these methods for the GEOMETRY type, but because they are indistinguishable, implements a single method for ring retrieval on the GEOGRAPHY type.

Data

Queries of spatial data more often rely on reference data than do queries in other common database usage scenarios. Reference data is generally static (updates may happen infrequently, if at all) and may include features such as:

- Country boundaries
- State, province, or territory boundaries
- Regional and minor political boundaries
- Property ownership (parcel) boundaries
- River and stream networks
- Lakes
- Road networks
- Points of interest (POI)

This list, by no means exhaustive, gives you the general idea. You can easily imagine other reference data for your area of interest. Before we go too much further, we should probably answer some common questions regarding data: What are the common forms of spatial data? Where can you get such data? How do you load spatial data into SQL Server 2008?

Common Forms of Data

A very common spatial data format is the *shapefile*. Created by the geospatial company ESRI and put in the public domain, shapefiles have become enormously popular. Because shapefiles are so popular, it's worth taking a moment to describe them in a little more detail.

The shapefile format is actually a set of files that together define spatial features and other related attributes. For example, the following set of files represents a single shapefile named statesp020, which you can find in the Boundary data section of the National Atlas of the United States (detailed in the "Finding Spatial Data" section of this chapter):

```
statesp020.shp
statesp020.dbf
statesp020.shx
```

As a general rule, a shapefile typically has three component files—an .shp file, a .dbf file, and a .shx file. The .shp file is a cross-platform binary containing the spatial feature definitions. The .dbf file is a standard dBase-formatted file containing column-based attribute data and definitions. The .shx file contains an index. Additionally, a .prj file is often included, which contains the coordinate system definition for the spatial data. Note that the statesp020 shapefile does not contain a .prj file; however, and this makes it more difficult to ascertain the spatial reference identifier for the associated spatial data.

Other common forms of spatial data are MapInfo TAB files (another multiple file format, akin to the shapefile format); Autodesk AutoCAD DWF, DWG, and DXF files; and the GPS Exchange Format. Additionally, simple spatial data, such as point locations, are often published in text files. The following example, from the GeoNames database, is tab-delimited, with the fourth and fifth fields containing the spatial location as single latitude and longitude values:

```
4045448 Massacre Bay   Massacre Bay   52.8266667  173.22        H  BAY  US  AK  016  0  0
0  America/Adak  2006-01-15
4045449 Maniac Hill    Maniac Hill    51.9583333  177.5097222   T  MT   US  AK  016  0  197
0  America/Adak  2006-01-15
4045451 Lunatic Lake   Lunatic Lake   51.9402778  177.4708333   H  LK   US  AK  016  0  21
0  America/Adak  2006-01-15
```

Finding Spatial Data

Many governmental agencies are making spatial data available over the Internet. Some interesting, if somewhat random, examples are:

- **Geospatial One Stop** (*http://www.geodata.gov*)   U.S. government spatial data

- **U.S. Census Bureau** (*http://www.census.gov/cgi-bin/geo/shapefiles/national-files*)   U.S. Census Bureau spatial data

- **UC Berkeley Environmental Design** (*http://dcrp.ced.berkeley.edu/research/footprint/index.php?option=com_content&task=view&id=15&Itemid=29*)   Urban and Environmental Modeler's Datakit

- **Ohio State University** (*http://ncl.sbs.ohio-state.edu/5_sdata.html*)   General spatial data sources

- **National Weather Service** (*http://www.weather.gov/gis/shapepage.htm*)   National weather data in shapefile format

- **National Atlas of the United States** (*http://nationalatlas.gov/atlasftp.html*)   Agriculture, biology, boundaries, climate, environment, geology, transportation, water, etc. spatial data in shapefile format for North America

- **Geofabrik** (*http://www.geofabrik.de/data/download.html*)   Open Street Map Data in shapefile format

- **Southern Nevada GIS** (*http://gisgate.co.clark.nv.us/gismo/Freedata.HTM*)   Clarke County, Nevada, spatial data

- **GeoNames** (*http://download.geonames.org/export/dump/*)   Points of interest for the world in a text file format

- **National Transportation Atlas Database** (*http://www.bts.gov/publications/national_transportation_atlas_database/2009/*)   Transportation data in shapefile format

Although data sources such as these can be very useful, at times you may need commercial data. Some good sources for commercial spatial data include:

- **NAVTEQ** (*http://www.navteq.com*)   Worldwide data

- **Tele Atlas** (*http://www.teleatlas.com*)   Worldwide data

- **ESRI** (*http://www.esri.com/data/esri_data/*)   Business and demographic data

- **Ordnance Survey** (*http://www.ordnancesurvey.co.uk*)   Spatial data for Great Britain

- **Pitney Bowes Business Insight** (*http://www.mapinfo.com/products/data*)   Worldwide demographic and business data

- **DTMI Spatial** (*http://www.dmtispatial.com/*)   Spatial data for Canada

Loading Spatial Data

SQL Server 2008 can ingest data from several standard formats, but much of the data available is in formats not directly supported by SQL Server. A variety of spatial data loaders are available, however. Discussion about data loaders and techniques for loading text files with spatial locations can be found in the upcoming section "Using Spatial Data to Solve Problems."

Sample Spatial Data

We have assembled a sample database, Sample_USA, for this chapter. The tables in this database are described in Table 14-1.

TABLE 14-1 **Contents of the Sample_USA Database**

Table Name	Feature Type	Description
CensusBlockGroups	Polygon	2000 U.S. Census Block Group boundaries
Counties	Polygon	U.S. county boundaries
CountiesFIPSCodes	tabular	lookup table for County FIPS codes
GeoNames	Point	GeoNames points-of-interest for the U.S.
GeoNamesFeatures	tabular	GeoNames feature class and feature codes lookup table
Highways	LineString	U.S. highways
States	Polygon	U.S. state boundaries
StatesFIPSCodes	tabular	lookup table for State FIPS codes
Zipcodes	Polygon	U.S. 5-digit ZIP codes

With the exception of the StatesFIPSCodes, CountiesFIPSCodes, and GeoNamesFeatures tables, each table contains two spatial columns: a GEOGRAPHY column (*GEOG*), and a GEOMETRY column (*GEOM*). The *GEOG* column is stored in WGS 84 coordinates (SRID = 4326). The *GEOM* column is stored in coordinates based on an Albers equal-area conic projection (and assigned an arbitrary SRID of 32768), with units in meters.

This data is the basis for many of this chapter's T-SQL examples.

> **More info** Strictly speaking, the values in the Zipcodes table are ZCTAs (ZIP code Tabulation Areas), not ZIP codes. ZCTAs are assigned by the U.S. Census Bureau, not the U.S. Postal Service, which assigns ZIP codes. For most geographic locations, they are the same. One difference you may notice is that ZCTAs are not all numeric—some end in XX or HH. The Census Bureau maintains a ZCTA FAQ page at *http://www.census.gov/geo/ZCTA/zctafaq.html#Q8*.

Getting Started with Spatial Data

As we begin to examine spatial data programming in T-SQL, we will concentrate on using those constructs that are supported for both the GEOGRAPHY and GEOMETRY data types. This will make the types interchangeable in many of the examples. For the initial discussion, we will use the GEOMETRY type.

Creating a Table with a Spatial Column

Let's start by creating a table containing a column of type GEOMETRY. We will use this table as we explain the basic properties of SQL Server Spatial:

```
USE tempdb;
GO
CREATE TABLE t1 (
  ID INT IDENTITY(1,1) PRIMARY KEY,
  NAME VARCHAR(64),
  GEOM GEOMETRY
);
```

Creating a column of type GEOGRAPHY is as simple as replacing the word GEOMETRY with GEOGRAPHY.

Well-Known Text

Before proceeding, a short discussion about well-known text (WKT) is in order. WKT and its companion format, well-known binary (WKB), are OGC-regulated formats that describe spatial objects and their locations as vectors. WKT is particularly useful because it is a text format that can be easily constructed with standard editing tools. WTK is composed of a keyword, such as POINT, LINESTRING, or POLYGON, and a list of coordinate pairs. Coordinate lists for LINESTRING and POLYGON are ordered, providing additional meaning to the spatial object. Let's take a look at some examples of WKT strings:

- *'POINT (3 4)'* — a single point
- *'LINESTRING (2 2, 5 5)'* — a simple two-point line
- *'POLYGON ((1 1, 4 1, 4 5, 1 5, 1 1))'* — a four-point polygon
- *'POLYGON ((1 1, 4 1, 4 5, 1 5, 1 1), (2 2, 2 4, 3 4, 3 2, 2 2))'* — polygon with a hole

Notice that coordinate pairs are space-separated and separated from other coordinate pairs with a comma. Polygons have the added requirement that the first and last coordinate pair (vertex) are the same, closing the polygon ring definition. Additionally, it is important to understand that WKT does not support SRID values.

Finally, WKT and WKB coordinate pairs are constructed in *x, y* order for GEOMETRY and longitude, latitude order for GEOGRAPHY.

 Important Be careful when you specify latitude and longitude values, because they don't always go in the same order. For OGC-based methods and for WKT, you must put *longitude* first to comply with industry convention. For non-OGC methods, such as *Point()*, you must put *latitude* first.

> **More Info** For more information on WKT, please see section 6.2, "Well-Known Text Representation for Geometry," in the document "OpenGIS Implementation Specification for Geographic information—Simple feature access—Part 1: Common architecture, Version 1.1.0" (OGC Reference Number: OGC 05-126). You can find this document at *http://www.opengeospatial.org/standards/sfa*.

Constructing Spatial Objects from Strings and Inserting into a Table

Now that we have a basic understanding of the spatial object string format (WKT), let's put some data into table t1:

```
INSERT INTO t1 VALUES ('Point1', geometry::Parse('POINT(3 4)'));
```

Before adding more data, notice that the *Parse()* method used in the example is not an OGC-required operator (it uses OGC WKT, however). Additionally, because this method does not provide a way to specify an SRID value, a value of 0 will be assigned to the instance by default.

Let's insert another point using a different non-OGC-required method:

```
INSERT INTO t1 VALUES ('Point2', geometry::Point(5, 3, 0));
```

This constructor does not use WKT, but instead requires the coordinates to be supplied as individual parameters.

> **Note** The methods *Parse()* and *Point()* are static GEOMETRY methods. Consequently, they require the notation :: instead of dot notation. In addition, the type name appears in lowercase to ensure compatibility with case-sensitive databases.

Now, let's put in additional line and area features using OGC-required constructors:

```
INSERT INTO t1 VALUES ('Line1', geometry::STLineFromText('LINESTRING(2 2, 5 5)',0));
INSERT INTO t1 VALUES ('Line2', geometry::STGeomFromText('LINESTRING(5 1, 6 1, 6 2, 7 2, 7 3)',0));
INSERT INTO t1 VALUES ('Area1', geometry::STPolyFromText('POLYGON ((1 1, 4 1, 4 5, 1 5, 1 1))',0));
```

Up to this point, all spatial objects have been given an SRID value of 0. Let's insert the next feature with an SRID of 1:

```
INSERT INTO t1 VALUES ('Area2', geometry::STGeomFromText('POLYGON ((5 4, 5 7, 8 7, 8 4, 5 4))',1));
```

Now query the table as follows:

```
SELECT ID, NAME, GEOM FROM t1;
```

This returns the following results:

```
ID     NAME    GEOM
--     ----    ------------------------------------------------------------------------------
1      Point1  0x0000000010C000000000000008400000000000001040
2      Point2  0x0000000010C000000000000014400000000000000840
3      Line1   0x00000000011400000000000000040000000000000040000000000000014400000000000001440
4      Line2   0x000000000104050000000000000000001440000000000000F03F000000000001840000000
000000F03F00000000000018400000000000000040000000000000001C40000000000000000400000000000001C4000
0000000000840010000000100000000010000000FFFFFFFF0000000002
5      Area1   0x000000000104050000000000000000000F03F000000000000F03F0000000000000104000000000
0000F03F000000000000010400000000000000144000000000000000F03F0000000000001440000000000000000F03F0000
00000000F03F010000000200000000010000000FFFFFFFF0000000003
6      Area2   0x00000000010405000000000000000000001440000000000000010400000000000001440000000000
00001C400000000000000204000000000000001C40000000000000020400000000000000104000000000000001440000000
0000000001040010000000200000000010000000FFFFFFFF0000000003
```

Although the *ID* and *NAME* attributes are human-readable, *GEOM*—rendered in binary—is not. To provide a more useful display of *GEOM*, we can write the query as:

```
SELECT ID, NAME, GEOM.STAsText() AS LOCATION FROM t1;
```

This query produces the following results:

```
ID     NAME    LOCATION
--     ------  -----------------------------------
1      Point1  POINT (3 4)
2      Point2  POINT (5 3)
3      Line1   LINESTRING (2 2, 5 5)
4      Line2   LINESTRING (5 1, 6 1, 6 2, 7 2, 7 3)
5      Area1   POLYGON ((1 1, 4 1, 4 5, 1 5, 1 1))
6      Area2   POLYGON ((5 4, 5 7, 8 7, 8 4, 5 4))
```

The *STAsText()* method returns the OGC WKT format of the GEOMETRY values, the same format that we used to specify GEOMETRY values earlier. But it is still difficult to understand the shapes and relative positions of these values. A simple visual representation would be more useful, and Management Studio can provide such a view. First, choose the Results to Grid option in Management Studio. Second, return the spatial column(s) directly, rather than converting them to text. So, let's perform the earlier query selecting the full table:

```
SELECT ID, NAME, GEOM FROM t1;
```

Because this query contains a spatial column and Results to Grid was chosen, a Spatial results tab appears. Click the Spatial results tab. You get the display shown in Figure 14-4.

Note several interesting things here. First, note that the following message appears above the visual display: *Some spatial objects were not displayed since their SRID is different than the SRID of the first object in the record set*. This is caused by the last spatial object—the polygon we named *Area2*—in which we intentionally set the SRID to a value different from the previous rows.

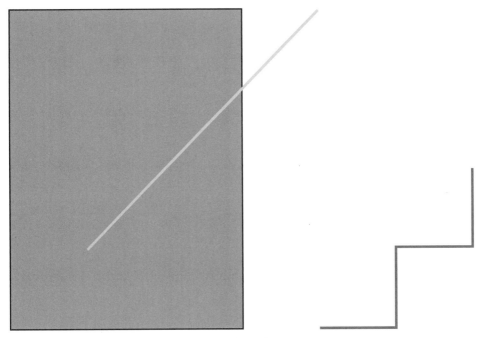

FIGURE 14-4 Display of Point, LineString, and Polygon data

Next, it is nearly impossible to see the point symbols. Later on, we will describe a trick to make the points more visible. Note that you can rest the cursor on the spatial objects for a display of their other column values.

Let's assume that the SRID of 1 assigned to *Area2* was incorrect and should be 0. Here's the T-SQL to fix that error:

```
UPDATE t1
  SET GEOM.STSrid = 0
WHERE NAME = 'Area2';
```

Note the use of the accessor property, *STSrid*, which we use to both get and set SRID values for spatial instances. Let's try the previous query again:

```
SELECT ID, NAME, GEOM FROM t1;
```

On the Spatial Results tab, we can now see the *Area2* polygon in context of the other spatial objects, as shown in Figure 14-5.

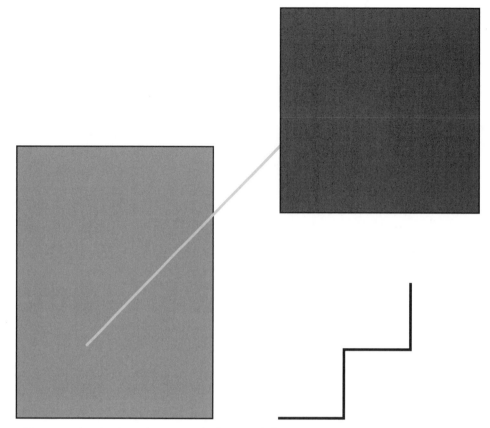

FIGURE 14-5 *Area2* polygon in context of other spatial objects

But what about the point objects? They are actually there, but Management Studio is rendering them in a very simplistic way that makes them virtually impossible to see. The trick to making them visible is to create a larger, temporary spatial object. To do this, we use a *buffer*, which we will spend more time on in a later section. For now, we will use the *STBuffer()* method to create a circular polygon, around the point objects, and we will display it along with the original points by combining two queries with UNION ALL. Please note that the Spatial results tab in Management Studio is not meant for generating pretty pictures. We are pointing out this trick because it may be valuable if you're trying to debug a query.

```
SELECT ID,NAME,GEOM FROM t1
UNION ALL
SELECT ID,NAME,GEOM.STBuffer(.1)
  FROM t1
WHERE GEOM.InstanceOf('Point')=1;
```

This is a good place to reemphasize that instance methods use the dot syntax (*instance.method* or *instance.property*) and static methods use the double-colon syntax (*datatype::method* or *datatype::property*).

Using the Spatial Results tab, we now get a much more legible display of our spatial objects, as shown in Figure 14-6.

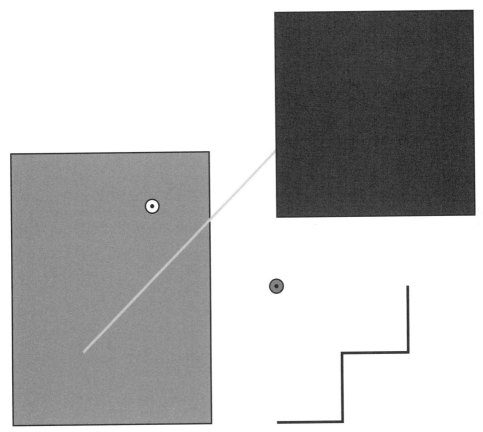

FIGURE 14-6 Using *STBuffer* to make point objects legible

Basic Object Interaction Tests

To more simply illustrate the various spatial operations, we will restrict the types of objects we operate on by splitting points, lines, and polygons into their own tables. It is not unusual to find similar partitions in real-world spatial data. These tables all have the same structure as the table t1 defined earlier in this section. Table 14-2 provides a list of the new tables.

TABLE 14-2 New Tables and Spatial Features

Table	Geometry Column	Features
Points	GEOM	*Point1, Point2, Point3, Point4, Point5*
Lines	GEOM	*Line1, Line2, Line3*
Polygons	GEOM	*Area1, Area2, Area3*

Figure 14-7 illustrates the spatial features relative to each other.

First, let's create the new tables:

```
USE tempdb;
GO
CREATE TABLE Points (
ID INT IDENTITY(1,1) PRIMARY KEY,
NAME VARCHAR(64),
GEOM GEOMETRY
);
GO
CREATE TABLE Lines (
ID INT IDENTITY(1,1) PRIMARY KEY,
NAME VARCHAR(64),
GEOM GEOMETRY
);
GO
CREATE TABLE Polygons (
ID INT IDENTITY(1,1) PRIMARY KEY,
NAME VARCHAR(64),
GEOM GEOMETRY
);
GO
```

Now, we can populate new tables with data:

```
INSERT INTO Points VALUES('Point1', geometry::Parse('POINT(3 4)'));
INSERT INTO Points VALUES('Point2', geometry::STGeomFromText('POINT(5 3)',0));
INSERT INTO Points VALUES('Point3', geometry::STGeomFromText('POINT(5 2)',0));
INSERT INTO Points VALUES('Point4', geometry::STGeomFromText('POINT(2 4.7)',0));
INSERT INTO Points VALUES('Point5', geometry::STGeomFromText('POINT(4.1 2)',0));
INSERT INTO Lines VALUES('Line1', geometry::STGeomFromText('LINESTRING(2 2, 5 5)',0));
INSERT INTO Lines VALUES('Line2', geometry::STGeomFromText('LINESTRING(5 1, 6 1, 6 2, 7 2, 7 3)',0));
INSERT INTO Lines VALUES('Line3', geometry::STGeomFromText('LINESTRING(4 7, 5 1.5)',0))
INSERT INTO Polygons VALUES('Area1', geometry::STGeomFromText('POLYGON ((1 1, 4 1, 4 5, 1
5,1 1))',0));
INSERT INTO Polygons VALUES('Area2', geometry::STGeomFromText('POLYGON ((5 4, 5 7, 8 7, 8 4,
5 4))',0));
INSERT INTO Polygons VALUES('Area3', geometry::STGeomFromText('POLYGON ((2 3, 6 3, 6 6, 2 6,
2 3))',0));
```

We can view this spatial data by executing this query:

```
SELECT GEOM.STBuffer(.1) FROM Points
UNION ALL
SELECT GEOM.STBuffer(.02) FROM Lines
UNION ALL
SELECT GEOM .STBuffer(.02) FROM Polygons;
```

Figure 14-7 provides an illustration of this new data:

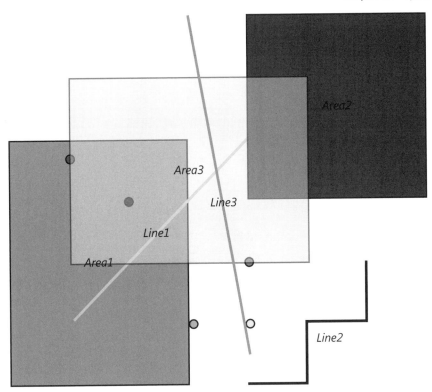

FIGURE 14-7 Relationship of spatial features with respect to each other

Let's try a few simple queries using spatial operators to perform tests on the relationships between objects. First, let's see which points intersect the polygon *Area1*:

```
DECLARE @polygon GEOMETRY;
SET @polygon = (SELECT GEOM FROM Polygons WHERE NAME = 'Area1');
SELECT NAME FROM Points WHERE @polygon.STIntersects(GEOM)=1;
```

This generates the following output:

```
NAME
-----
Point1
Point4
```

Now let's see which polygons intersect *Line1*:

```
DECLARE @line GEOMETRY;
SET @line = (SELECT GEOM FROM Lines WHERE NAME = 'Line1');
SELECT NAME FROM Polygons WHERE @line.STIntersects(GEOM)=1;
```

This generates the following output:

```
NAME
-----
Area1
Area2
Area3
```

Note that although *Line1* just touches the *Area2* polygon, the two objects still intersect each other. We can also test for the opposite of intersection, disjointness, using the *STDisjoint()* method:

```
DECLARE @line GEOMETRY;
SET @line = (SELECT GEOM FROM Lines WHERE NAME = 'Line1');
DECLARE @area GEOMETRY;
SET @area = (SELECT GEOM FROM Polygons WHERE NAME = 'Area2');
SELECT @line.STDisjoint(@area) AS Disjoint;
```

This generates the following output:

```
Disjoint
--------
0
```

The result of 0 indicates that the two spatial objects are not disjoint—they intersect:

We can ask the same question about *Line2* and *Area2*:

```
DECLARE @line GEOMETRY;
DECLARE @area GEOMETRY;
SET @line = (SELECT GEOM FROM Lines WHERE NAME = 'Line2');
SET @area = (SELECT GEOM FROM Polygons WHERE NAME = 'Area2');
SELECT @line.STDisjoint(@area) AS Disjoint;
```

This generates the following output:

```
Disjoint
--------
1
```

The result of 1 indicates that *Line2* and *Area2* are disjoint.

Basic Spatial Operations

In this section, we explore some of the basic concepts that are used in common spatial workflows:

- Intersecting spatial objects
- Unioning spatial objects
- Generalization of spatial objects
- Proximity queries
- Spatial buffers and distance-based calculations

Intersecting Spatial Objects

Let's make a new spatial object that is the intersection of polygons *Area1* and *Area3* and display well-known text for the resulting object:

```
DECLARE @area1 GEOMETRY;
DECLARE @area3 GEOMETRY;
SET @area1 = (SELECT GEOM FROM Polygons WHERE NAME = 'Area1');
SET @area3 = (SELECT GEOM FROM Polygons WHERE NAME = 'Area3');
SELECT @area1.STIntersection(@area3).STAsText() AS Well_Known_Text;
```

This generates the following output:

```
Well_Known_Text
-----------------------------------
POLYGON ((2 3, 4 3, 4 5, 2 5, 2 3))
```

Figure 14-8 illustrates the intersection of the two polygons *Area1* and *Area3*.

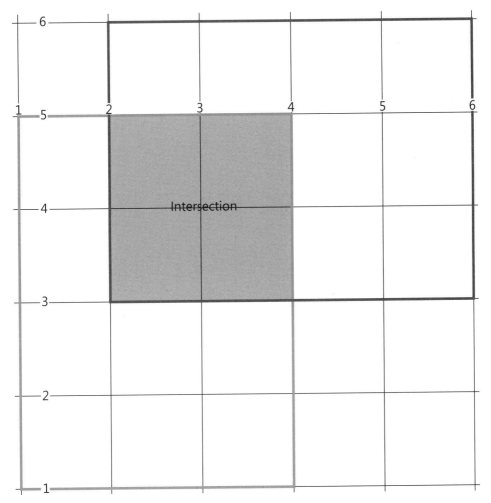

FIGURE 14-8 Intersection of polygons *Area1* and *Area3*

The result is the region that is covered by both *Area1* and *Area3*. What happens when we intersect two disjoint polygons, such as *Area1* and *Area2*, as shown in Figure 14-9?

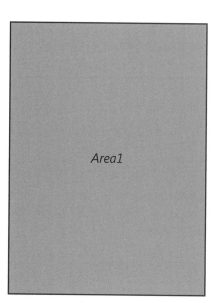

FIGURE 14-9 Illustration of the spatial relationship between disjoint features *Area1* and *Area2*.

We can perform this operation as before:

```
DECLARE @area1 GEOMETRY;
DECLARE @area2 GEOMETRY;
SET @area1 = (SELECT GEOM FROM Polygons WHERE NAME = 'Area1');
SET @area2 = (SELECT GEOM FROM Polygons WHERE NAME = 'Area2');
SELECT @area1.STIntersection(@area2).STAsText() AS Well_Known_Text;
```

This generates the following output:

```
Well_Known_Text
-----------------------
GEOMETRYCOLLECTION EMPTY
```

Intersecting disjoint objects yields an empty spatial object.

What happens when we intersect objects of different object types, such as a point located within a polygon?

```
DECLARE @area1 GEOMETRY;
DECLARE @point1 GEOMETRY;
SET @area1 = (SELECT GEOM FROM Polygons WHERE NAME = 'Area1');
SET @point1 = (SELECT GEOM FROM Points WHERE NAME = 'Point1');
SELECT @area1.STIntersection(@point1).STAsText() AS Well_Known_Text;
```

This generates the following output:

```
Well_Known_Text
---------------
POINT (3 4)
```

The result describes the region in space covered by both objects—a single point in this case.

Union of Spatial Objects

We will now see how to combine spatial objects together using the *STUnion()* method. First, we combine two objects of similar types:

```
DECLARE @point1 GEOMETRY;
DECLARE @point2 GEOMETRY;
SET @point1 = (SELECT GEOM FROM Points WHERE NAME = 'Point1');
SET @point2 = (SELECT GEOM FROM Points WHERE NAME = 'Point2');
SELECT @point1.STUnion(@point2).STAsText() AS Well_Known_Text;
```

This generates the following output:

```
Well_Known_Text
------------------------
MULTIPOINT ((3 4), (5 3))
```

The result in this case is a homogeneous collection, a MultiPoint.

We can also combine objects of different types:

```
DECLARE @point1 GEOMETRY;
DECLARE @line1 GEOMETRY;
SET @point1 = (SELECT GEOM FROM Points WHERE NAME = 'Point1')'
SET @line1 = (SELECT GEOM FROM Lines WHERE NAME = 'Line1');
SELECT @point1.STUnion(@line1).STAsText() AS Well_Known_Text;
```

This generates the following output:

```
Well_Known_Text
------------------------------------------------------
GEOMETRYCOLLECTION (POINT (3 4), LINESTRING (5 5, 2 2))
```

This time we get a heterogeneous collection, a GeometryCollection made up of a Point and a LineString.

What happens if we combine two objects, one of which lies wholly within the other? For example, if we combine *Point1* with *Area1*, we may expect another GeometryCollection:

```
DECLARE @point1 GEOMETRY;
DECLARE @area1 GEOMETRY;
DECLARE @union1 GEOMETRY;
SET @point1 = (SELECT GEOM FROM Points WHERE NAME = 'Point1');
SET @area1 = (SELECT GEOM FROM Polygons WHERE NAME = 'Area1');
SET @union1 = @area1.STUnion(@point1);
SELECT @union1.STAsText() AS Well_Known_Text;
```

This generates the following output:

```
Well_Known_Text
------------------------------------
POLYGON ((1 1, 4 1, 4 5, 1 5, 1 1))
```

As you can see, the polygon swallows the point. This will happen whenever one object in the union wholly contains the other.

Another common case is that two objects overlap, but neither wholly contains the other—what happens when we combine them? Figure 14-10 shows two such objects—*Line1* and *Area1*—before being combined.

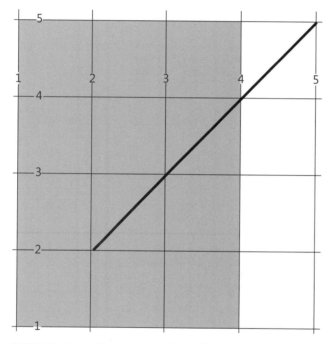

FIGURE 14-10 Position of spatial objects *Line1* and *Area1* relative to each other

We can combine them as before:

```
DECLARE @line1 GEOMETRY;
DECLARE @area1 GEOMETRY;
SET @line1 = (SELECT GEOM FROM Lines WHERE NAME = 'Line1');
SET @area1 = (SELECT GEOM FROM Polygons WHERE NAME = 'Area1');
SELECT @line1.STUnion(@area1).STAsText() AS Well_Known_Text;
```

This generates the following output:

```
Well_Known_Text
----------------------------------------------------------------------------
GEOMETRYCOLLECTION (LINESTRING (5 5,4 4),  POLYGON ((1 1,4 1,4 4,4 5,1 5,1 1)))
```

Figure 14-11 illustrates the results.

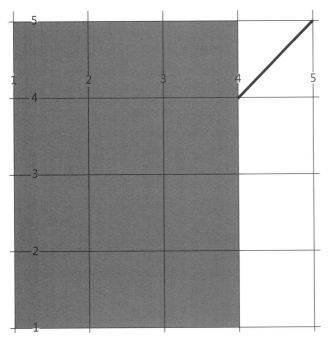

FIGURE 14-11 Union of spatial objects *Line1* and *Area1*

Notice that the result of the union operation contains a LineString clipped to the edge of the polygon.

Generalization of Spatial Objects

In the real world, spatial data is often quite detailed. Detail in vector spatial data is manifested by the number of shape points (vertex points) used to define the spatial object. We have all observed this on printed maps before. Consider San Francisco Bay. On a map showing all of North America, San Francisco Bay might appear as nothing more than a small indentation on the California coastline. On the other hand, on a map of the San Francisco Bay Area, San Francisco Bay might be highly detailed, showing local coves and other nuances in its rendition. Reducing the level of detail of a spatial object is called *cartographic generalization*, or simply *generalization*. In SQL Server 2008, the *Reduce()* method of a geometry instance returns a generalization of the instance. The degree of generalization can be controlled with the required *tolerance* parameter. Roughly speaking, the *tolerance* is the size below which details need not be preserved.

Reduce() has some other interesting characteristics: Imagine two polygons, one very thin and linear in nature and the other a small triangle. As we reduce the complexity by removing the vertex points of these polygons, they will at some point be converted into other geometric forms. The thin, linear polygon will become a LINESTRING. The small triangle will become a POINT. Let's take a look at the result of *Reduce()* on such data.

First, the T-SQL to produce the spatial data:

```
DECLARE @small_triangle GEOMETRY;
DECLARE @thin_polygon GEOMETRY;
DECLARE @jagged_line GEOMETRY;
SET @small_triangle  = geometry::STGeomFromText(
  'POLYGON((9 1,10 1,9.5 2,9 1))',0);
SET @thin_polygon = geometry::STGeomFromText(
  'POLYGON((1 2.5,19 2.5,19 3,1 3,1 2.5))',0);
SET @jagged_line = geometry::STGeomFromText(
  'LINESTRING(1 5,2 5,3 8,4 5,5 6,5 5,6 6,6 5,8 8,8 5,9 6,10 5,
    11 6,12 4,13 7,14 5,15 6,15 4,16 7,16 5,18 8,18 5,19 5)',0);
```

The following query displays these three objects:

```
SELECT @small_triangle
UNION ALL
SELECT @thin_polygon
UNION ALL
SELECT @jagged_line;
```

Figure 14-12 shows what the data looks like.

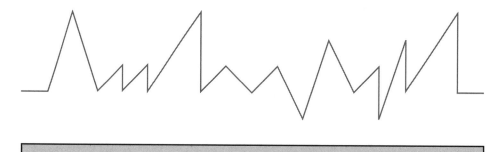

FIGURE 14-12 Illustration of data prior to generalization

Now, let's reduce the objects using a *tolerance* of 2:

```
SET @small_triangle = @small_triangle.Reduce(2);
SET @thin_polygon  = @thin_polygon.Reduce(2);
SET @jagged_line = @jagged_line.Reduce(2);
```

If we run the previous SELECT query again, we will see the results shown in Figure 14-13.

Note that the polygon *@thin_polygon* was generalized to a LineString:

```
SELECT @thin_polygon. STAsText() AS Well_Known_Text;
```

This generates the following output:

```
Well_Known_Text
---------------

LINESTRING (19 3, 1 2.5)
```

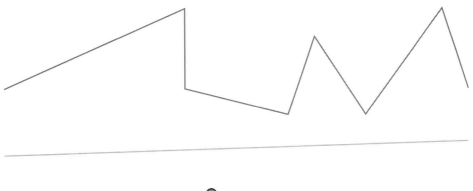

FIGURE 14-13 Data after generalization

Note also that the small triangle, *@small_triangle*, was reduced to a Point:

```
SELECT @small_triangle. STAsText() AS Well_Known_Text;
```

This generates the following output:

```
Well_Known_Text
---------------
POINT (9 1)
```

If you look carefully at the reduced versions of *@thin_polygon* and *@small_triangle*, you can see that the new objects are the result of removing vertices from the old ones. No new coordinates are created. Figure 14-14 shows the reduced *@thin_polygon* and *@small_triangle* objects overlaid on their original forms.

FIGURE 14-14 New objects created by generalization

The examples used for this discussion are extreme. If used judiciously, *Reduce()* can significantly reduce the vertex count of large spatial objects without significantly changing their shape. This can be useful for retrieving the right level of detail for a map display and for other spatial operations in which the shape of the object is important rather than the exact definition.

Proximity Queries

Queries incorporating proximity searches are powerful analysis tools, allowing us to determine which spatial objects are close to each other. We will use the spatial features in the tables Points, Lines, and Polygons for this exercise. In Figure 14-15, we have shaded the region within .4 units of *Line3* to aid the following discussion.

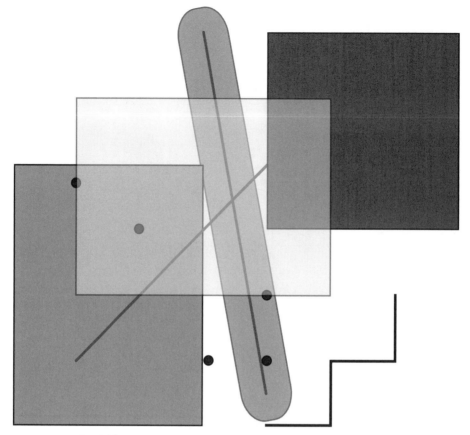

FIGURE 14-15 Spatial features augmented with a region within .4 units of *Line3*

Distance between Spatial Objects

Using the *STDistance()* method, we can determine what points are within .4 units of *Line3*:

```
DECLARE @line GEOMETRY;
SET @line = (SELECT GEOM FROM Lines WHERE NAME = 'Line3');
SELECT NAME FROM Points WHERE @line.STDistance(GEOM) <= .4;
```

This generates the following output:

```
NAME
----
Point2
Point3
```

We can perform a similar query to determine which polygons are within .4 units of *Line3:*

```
DECLARE @line GEOMETRY
SET @line = (SELECT GEOM FROM Lines WHERE NAME = 'Line3');
SELECT NAME FROM Polygons WHERE @line.STDistance(GEOM) <= .4;
```

This generates the following output:

```
NAME
----
Area1
Area3
```

We can also compute how far objects are away from each other. For instance, we can find exactly how far *Line3* is from *Point2*:

```
DECLARE @Line3 GEOMETRY =
  (SELECT GEOM FROM Lines WHERE NAME = 'Line3');
DECLARE @Point2 GEOMETRY =
  (SELECT GEOM FROM Points WHERE NAME = 'Point2');
SELECT @Point2.STDistance(@Line3) AS Distance;
```

This generates the following output:

```
Distance
-----------------
0.268328157299975
```

Distance between two points is an intuitive concept, but how is the distance between two complex objects defined, such as between a LineString and a Polygon? The distance computed is the minimum distance between the objects. The following T-SQL computes the distance between *Line3* and *Area2*:

```
DECLARE @Line3 GEOMETRY =
  (SELECT GEOM FROM Lines WHERE NAME = 'Line3');
DECLARE @Area2 GEOMETRY =
  (SELECT GEOM FROM Polygons WHERE NAME = 'Area2');
SELECT @Area2.STDistance(@Line3) AS Distance;
```

This generates the following output:

```
Distance
----------------
0.447213595499958
```

If two objects intersect, the distance between them is 0:

```
DECLARE @Line3 GEOMETRY =
  (SELECT GEOM FROM Lines WHERE NAME = 'Line3');
DECLARE @Line1 GEOMETRY =
  (SELECT GEOM FROM Lines WHERE NAME = 'Line1');
SELECT @Line1.STDistance(@Line3) AS Distance;
```

This generates the following output:

```
Distance
--------
0
```

Because the distance between two objects is 0 if and only if they intersect, we could determine whether two objects intersect using the *STDistance()* method. In general, doing so will perform worse than using the *STIntersects()* method.

Spatial Buffers

Spatial buffers are new objects created from other objects that—when combined with intersection tests—can be used for proximity testing. First, let's look deeper into buffers.

Generally, a spatial buffer is an enlargement of a spatial object by some distance, resulting in a new spatial object that includes the original object. As illustrated in Figure 14-16, when you buffer a point object, a polygon that approximates a circle is returned:

```
DECLARE @point GEOMETRY;
DECLARE @buffer GEOMETRY
SET @point = (SELECT GEOM FROM Points WHERE NAME = 'Point1');
SET @buffer = @point.STBuffer(1);
SELECT @buffer AS Buffer;
```

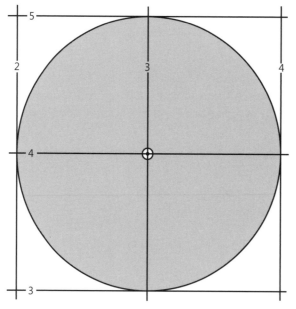

FIGURE 14-16 Point object buffer

When you buffer a polygon, you get a new polygon. As illustrated in Figure 14-17, here is *Area1* buffered by .4 units:

```
DECLARE @area GEOMETRY;
DECLARE @buffer GEOMETRY;
SET @area = (SELECT GEOM FROM Polygons WHERE NAME = 'Area1');
SELECT @buffer = @area.STBuffer(.4);
SELECT @buffer;
```

The new object consists of the original *Area1* polygon and the area around *Area1*, resulting in an enlargement of the original object.

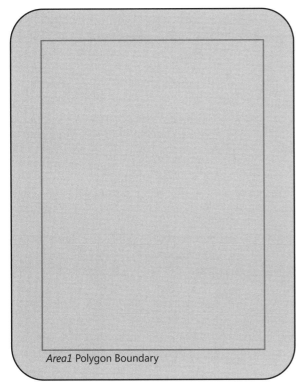

Area1 Polygon Boundary

FIGURE 14-17 Polygon object buffer

Comparing Spatial Buffers and Distance-Based Calculations to Test Proximity

Now that we've introduced distance-based proximity tests and buffers, let's perform some proximity tests using both methods.

First, let's do a proximity test to determine which points intersect a buffered polygon around *Area1*:

```
DECLARE @area GEOMETRY;
DECLARE @buffer GEOMETRY;
SET @area = (SELECT GEOM FROM Polygons WHERE NAME = 'Area1');
SET @buffer = @area.STBuffer(.4);
SELECT NAME FROM Points WHERE GEOM.STIntersects(@buffer)=1;
```

This generates the following output:

```
NAME
----
Point1
Point4
Point5
```

This query is equivalent to the following query using *STDistance()*, presented earlier:

```
DECLARE @polygon GEOMETRY;
SET @polygon = (SELECT GEOM FROM Polygons WHERE NAME = 'Area1');
SELECT NAME FROM Points WHERE @polygon.STDistance(GEOM) <= .4;
```

This generates the following output:

```
NAME
----
Point1
Point4
Point5
```

The query using *STDistance* is attractive because it uses fewer spatial methods and does not result in the creation of new spatial objects.

Let's look at a more complicated example using both techniques. What if you wanted to find those points that were within .4 units of the *Area1* boundary? Let's look at two ways to solve this, one with *STBuffer()* and one with *STDistance()*.

The first method creates a region .4 units wide, around the outside and the inside of the *Area1* polygon boundary. This is done by constructing two new buffer objects, one .4 units larger and one .4 units smaller, and taking their difference with the *STDifference()* method. The new region is intersected against the Points table:

```
DECLARE @area GEOMETRY;
DECLARE @region GEOMETRY;
DECLARE @distance FLOAT;
SET @distance = .4;
SET @area = (SELECT GEOM FROM Polygons WHERE NAME = 'Area1');
SET @region = @area.STBuffer(@distance).STDifference(@area.STBuffer(@distance * -1))
SELECT NAME
  FROM Points
    WHERE GEOM.STIntersects(@region)=1
```

This generates the following output:

```
NAME
----
Point4
Point5
```

> **Note** One of the buffer regions in the code sample above uses a negative distance value. A buffer region constructed with a negative distance value is commonly referred to as a *negative buffer*.

The second method uses the *STBoundary()* method to convert the *Area1* polygon boundary into a LineString. The *STDistance()* method is then used to find all points within .4 units of the LineString:

```
DECLARE @area GEOMETRY
DECLARE @distance FLOAT = .4
SET @area = (SELECT GEOM FROM Polygons WHERE NAME = 'Area1');
SELECT NAME
  FROM Points
    WHERE GEOM.STDistance(@area.STBoundary()) <= @distance
```

This generates the following output:

```
NAME
----
Point4
Point5
```

> **More Info** You can substitute the *STExteriorRing()* method for the *STBoundary()* method in the above example and achieve the same results.

Figure 14-18 shows the relative position of the objects in the Points table to the polygon *Area1*. The large shaded area extends .4 units from the polygon's boundary.

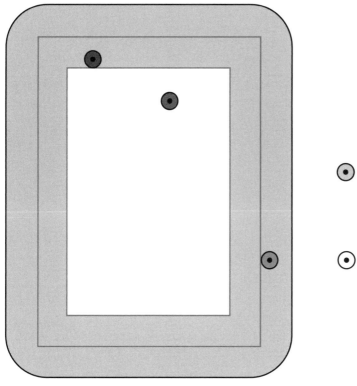

FIGURE 14-18 Points relative to the region within .4 units of *Area1*'s boundary.

These are simple spatial queries, but they emphasize the flexibility of SQL Server 2008 to solve interesting spatial problems. Additionally, they illustrate the use of the *STDistance()* method for solving queries traditionally done using buffers. Because buffers have to construct new spatial objects and *STDistance* does not, using *STDistance* can result in improved performance. Additionally, STDistance can make use of spatial indexes, further improving query performance.

The GEOGRAPHY Type

In the previous section, we concentrated on the GEOMETRY type. What changes in the previous examples are required to use the GEOGRAPHY type? Remarkably few. But those changes are significant, and we need to understand them to use the GEOGRAPHY type effectively. Consequently, we need to address four key areas:

- Spatial Reference ID (SRID) values

- Coordinate ordering for Polygons

- Coordinate systems and units of measure

- Extent of GEOGRAPHY objects

Additionally, we will need to discuss the differences in spatial index construction however we will defer that subject until the "Indexing Spatial Data" section of this chapter.

Let's start by creating a table, g1, for use with the GEOGRAPHY type. This table is quite similar to the earlier table, t1, created for use with the GEOMETRY type. The only difference is the name and type of the spatial column.

```
USE tempdb;
GO

CREATE TABLE g1 (
  ID INT IDENTITY(1,1) PRIMARY KEY,
  NAME VARCHAR(64),
  GEOG GEOGRAPHY
);
```

The Geography Type and SRIDs

The GEOGRAPHY type uses SRID values to establish a definition of Earth's surface for area, length, and distance measures. As discussed earlier in the section "Spatial Reference Identifiers," SQL Server restricts the SRID for GEOGRAPHY objects to one of 390 values listed in the *sys.spatial_reference_systems* view.

An SRID of 4326 is the default value for the GEOGRAPHY type. Let's look at some T-SQL to observe the GEOGRAPHY type default SRID behavior. We will do this by inserting a Point object into the table g1 using *Parse()*:

```
INSERT INTO g1 VALUES('Point1', geography::Parse('POINT(3 4)'));
```

Let's retrieve the SRID value for *GEOG* and verify the default SRID value:

```
SELECT GEOG.STSrid AS SRID FROM g1 WHERE NAME = 'Point1';
```

This generates the following output:

```
SRID
----
4326
```

Because *Parse()* does not take an SRID, the default SRID value of 4326 is used.

Let's take a more detailed look at SRID 4326 as defined in the *sys.spatial_reference_systems* view:

```
SELECT * FROM sys.spatial_reference_systems
  WHERE spatial_reference_id = 4326
```

Table 14-3 shows the results of the query. The results are pivoted for readability.

TABLE 14-3 **Information about SRID 4326 from sys.spatial_reference_systems**

Column	Value
spatial_reference_id	*4326*
authority_name	*EPSG*
authorized_spatial_reference_id	*4326*
well_known_text	*GEOGCS["WGS 84", DATUM["World Geodetic System 1984", ELLIPSOID["WGS 84", 6378137, 298.257223563]], PRIMEM["Greenwich", 0], UNIT["Degree", 0.0174532925199433]]*
unit_measurement	*metre*
unit_conversion_factor	*1*

The *well_known_text* for SRID 4326 provides both a description and analytic values on Earth's size and shape, which the GEOGRAPHY type uses for specific calculations. The *unit_measurement* identifies the metre (meter) as the unit of length used for geography-based measurement methods, such as *STDistance*, *STLength*, *STArea*, and *STBuffer*.

To insert the remaining spatial objects from our earlier examples, we need to change the SRID value in the *STGeomFromText()* constructors from 0 to 4326. Note that we will not insert *Area1* and *Area2* polygons into the table yet—these will be inserted and used in a future example.

```
INSERT INTO g1 VALUES ('Point2', geography::Point(3,5,4326));
INSERT INTO g1 VALUES
  ('Line1', geography::STLineFromText('LINESTRING(2 2, 5 5)',4326));
INSERT INTO g1 VALUES
  ('Line2', geography::STGeomFromText('LINESTRING(5 1, 6 1, 6 2, 7 2, 7 3)',4326));
```

The Geography Type and Coordinate Ordering

As discussed earlier, on a plane, a polygon defined by a series of rings is unambiguous. This is not true on the globe: a ring divides the globe into two pieces—an inside and an outside—but without more information, we do not know which is which. For example, consider a polygon defined by a ring around the San Francisco peninsula. Is the object a polygon covering San Francisco, or a polygon covering the entire globe *except* for San Francisco?

This ambiguity is resolved by using the ordering of each ring in the polygon. We define the inside of each ring to be the region on the left-hand side as the ring is traced. This *left-hand rule* is a common industry practice. With this new information, what happens when we attempt to insert the polygons defined for *Area1* and *Area2*?

Area1 insert without error, but the *Area2* insert fails:

```
INSERT INTO g1 VALUES
  ('Area1', geography::STPolyFromText('POLYGON ((1 1, 4 1, 4 5, 1 5, 1 1))',4326));
INSERT INTO g1 VALUES
  ('Area2', geography::STGeomFromText('POLYGON ((5 4, 5 7, 8 7, 8 4, 5 4))',4326));
```

Here is the error message:

```
Msg 6522, Level 16, State 1, Line 1
```

A .NET Framework error occurred during execution of user-defined routine or aggregate "geography":

```
Microsoft.SqlServer.Types.GLArgumentException: 24205: The specified input does not represent
a valid geography instance because it exceeds a single hemisphere. Each geography instance
must fit inside a single hemisphere. A common reason for this error is that a polygon has
the wrong ring orientation.
...
...
The statement has been terminated.
```

What happened? The ring ordering defined a polygon that covered most of the globe. Because SQL Server 2008 cannot handle objects this large it results in an error—more on this later. To correct this polygon, we simply reorder the coordinates according to the left-hand rule:

```
POLYGON ((5 4, 8 4, 8 7, 5 7, 5 4))
```

Here is the insert statement using the corrected coordinate order:

```
INSERT INTO g1 VALUES
  ('Area2', geography::STGeomFromText('POLYGON ((5 4, 8 4, 8 7, 5 7, 5 4))',4326));
```

Coordinate Systems and Units of Measure

With the GEOMETRY type, the coordinate system and the units of measure are directly related. In other words, the units along the *x* and *y* axes are the same as the units used to measure length, distance, and area. This is not true for the GEOGRAPHY type. In the GEOGRAPHY type, an ellipsoidal coordinate system is used, which has latitude and longitude components. Units of measure are defined by the *unit_of_measurement* field in the *sys.spatial_references* view for the given SRID value. Typically, these units are meters. (Out of the 390 geodetic coordinate systems defined in the *sys.spatial_references* view, only eight use a different unit of measurement.)

The Extent of Geography Objects

As the error in the earlier section specifies, "Each geography instance must fit inside a single hemisphere." But which hemisphere does this mean? No static hemisphere is used to bound objects—objects crossing from the Southern to Northern or Eastern to Western hemispheres are fine. Rather, this means that an object cannot exceed a 180-degree span. In practice, the actual geography object must be slightly less than this to be a valid. This limitation will most likely be lifted in the next major release of SQL Server.

Spatial Data Validity

A common obstacle in using spatial data within SQL Server 2008 involves invalid data. Because the SQL Server 2008 GEOMETRY type conforms to the OGC Simple Features for SQL Specification, the definition of what constitutes valid data follows the OGC's definition. The GEOGRAPHY type—not defined by OGC—adds some additional constraints. Data that is valid for the GEOMETRY type may not be valid for the GEOGRAPHY type; we have already seen this with ring orientation.

Additionally, although SQL Server provides us tools for dealing with invalid GEOMETRY data, it does not ingest invalid GEOGRAPHY data. This difference results from the fact that invalid GEOGRAPHY data is usually ambiguous as well.

Data Validity Issues with Geometry Data

The GEOMETRY data type is very tolerant of invalid spatial data. This tolerance, however, is short-lived. When OGC-based spatial methods are used on geometry data, the data must be in an OGC-valid form. It is beyond the scope of this chapter to detail all possible validity issues, but self-intersecting polygon boundaries are a common case. Let's take a look at just such a case. First, we create a new table for the invalid polygon:

```
USE tempdb;
GO
CREATE TABLE Polygons_Valid (
ID INT IDENTITY(1,1) PRIMARY KEY,
NAME VARCHAR(64),
GEOM GEOMETRY
);
```

Next, we insert an invalid polygon:

```
INSERT INTO Polygons_Valid
VALUES('Area1',
  geometry::STGeomFromText(
    'POLYGON((1 1, 1 3, 2 3, 4 1, 5 1, 5 3, 4 3, 2 1, 1 1))',0));
```

Figure 14-19 illustrates the invalid polygon.

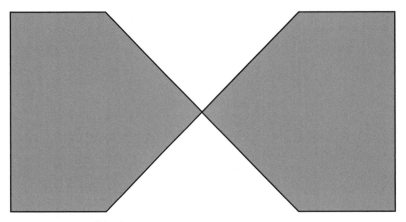

FIGURE 14-19 Invalid polygon

Here is the test to see whether this is a valid polygon:

```
DECLARE @geometry GEOMETRY;
SET @geometry = (SELECT GEOM FROM Polygons_Valid WHERE NAME = 'Area1');
SELECT @geometry.STIsValid() AS IS_VALID_GEOMETRY;
```

This generates the following output:

```
IS_VALID_GEOMETRY
-----------------
0
```

If we try to execute a spatial operation against this instance—for example, a test to see whether a point intersects it—we get an error:

```
DECLARE @point GEOMETRY;
DECLARE @polygon GEOMETRY;
SET @point = geometry::Parse('POINT(1 2)');
SET @polygon = (SELECT GEOM FROM Polygons_Valid WHERE NAME = 'Area1');
SELECT NAME FROM Polygons_Valid WHERE @polygon.STIntersects(@point)=1;
```

This generates the following error:

```
System.ArgumentException: 24144: This operation cannot be completed because the instance is
not valid. Use MakeValid to convert the instance to a valid instance. Note that MakeValid
may cause the points of a geometry instance to shift slightly.
```

As the error message recommends, try the *MakeValid()* method on this instance to see if it corrects the improper construction of this polygon. Let's see what *MakeValid()* does:

```
DECLARE @polygon GEOMETRY;
SET @polygon = (SELECT GEOM FROM Polygons_Valid WHERE NAME = 'Area1');
SELECT @polygon.MakeValid().STAsText() AS WKT;
```

This generates the following output:

```
WKT
--------------------------------------------------------------------------------
MULTIPOLYGON (((4 1, 5 1, 5 3, 4 3, 3 2, 4 1)), ((1 1, 2 1, 3 2, 2 3, 1 3, 1 1)))
```

MakeValid() takes the self-intersecting polygon and creates an OGC-compliant MultiPolygon instance.

> **Caution** You should not blindly run *MakeValid()* on invalid GEOMETRY instances. *MakeValid()* can make changes to the data which may not be desirable. For instance, if you run *MakeValid()* on the following Polygon (shown as WKT):
>
> *'POLYGON((1 1, 1 2, 2 2, 2 1, 1 1, 1 2, 2 2, 2 1, 1 1))'*
>
> *MakeValid()* will create this LineString (shown as WKT):
>
> *'LINESTRING (1 1, 2 1, 2 2, 1 2, 1 1)'*
>
> *MakeValid()* typically produces results matching the original intent for the spatial object. However, as this example shows, *MakeValid()* does not always produce the intended result, so it is prudent to use *MakeValid()* judicially.

If you plot the points that make up each polygon in the MultiPolygon returned from the *MakeValid()* operation, you will notice that the points are arranged according to the left-hand rule—the orientation required by the GEOGRAPHY type. Note, however, that if *MakeValid()* does not find an issue with a given polygon instance, it will simply return the polygon unmodified.

Measuring Length and Area

The methods for calculating the length and area of spatial objects are the same in both GEOMETRY and GEOGRAPHY: *STLength()* measures length; *STArea()* measures area. The way these methods work differs, however, as we will now investigate.

To assist in this comparison, consider the data from the section "Sample Spatial Data" near the beginning of this chapter. To recap, each table in this collection contains a column of type GEOGRAPHY named *GEOG*, and a column of type GEOMETRY named *GEOM*. The GEOMETRY column, in all cases, was derived from the GEOGRAPHY data by transforming the GEOGRAPHY data from WGS 84 coordinates into an Albers equal area coordinate system. The units of measure for both the *GEOG* and *GEOM* columns are in meters.

> **More Info** The particular Albers equal area projection chosen was designed to minimize distortion for the coterminous United States. The specific parameters used were: central meridian: –96, latitude of the origin: 20, first standard Parallel: 30, and second standard parallel: 40. This particular Albers projection is spherical and is based on the authalic (area-preserving) sphere for the WGS 84 ellipsoid (Earth radius = 6,371,007.2 meters). A false easting of 10,000,000 and a false northing of 0 were applied. The units for the resultant coordinate system are in meters.

Comparing Length Measurements between GEOMETRY and GEOGRAPHY Instances

First, we consider spatial objects that are small relative to Earth's surface. In this case, we are using a short (approximately 400-meters) road from the Highways table in the Sample_USA database:

```
USE Sample_USA;
GO

SELECT ID,
       GEOM.STLength() AS GEOM_LENGTH,
       GEOG.STLength() AS GEOG_LENGTH,
       GEOG.STLength() - GEOM.STLength() AS LENGTH_DIFFERENCE
  FROM Highways
   WHERE ID = 566;
```

Here are the results:

```
ID   GEOM_LENGTH        GEOG_LENGTH        LENGTH_DIFFERENCE
---  ----------------   ----------------   -----------------
566  412.271253468018   412.677965834253   0.406712366235695
```

The difference between the length of the geometry calculation and the geography calculation is around .4 meters.

What happens if we choose a much longer highway segment? This highway segment in the query below is Interstate 5, which travels from the Mexican to the Canadian border through the states of California, Oregon, and Washington. See More Info below for further detail.

```
SELECT ID,
       GEOM.STLength() AS GEOM_LENGTH,
       GEOG.STLength() AS GEOG_LENGTH,
       (GEOG.STLength() - GEOM.STLength()) / 1000 AS LENGTH_DIFFERENCE_KM
  FROM Highways
   WHERE ID = 378;
```

The results indicate that the measured length using the GEOGRAPHY instance is approximately 6.5 kilometers greater than that from the GEOMETRY instance:

```
ID   GEOM_LENGTH       GEOG_LENGTH         LENGTH_DIFFERENCE_KM
---  ---------------   ----------------    --------------------
378  2227919.0649429   2234410.65035147    6.49158540857723
```

It is always more accurate to make geospatial measurements using the GEOGRAPHY type than the GEOMETRY type. This is especially true as distances become greater. Still, calculations on projected coordinates using the GEOMETRY type can be quite accurate if the projection is chosen carefully.

> **More Info** The available files for this chapter contain more information about the Highways and other tables in the Sample_USA database, including a data dictionary. This will assist you in using the supplied tables to a much greater degree than presented here.

Comparing Area Measurements between GEOMETRY and GEOMETRY Instances

Now let's look at the difference between area calculations using GEOMETRY and GEOGRAPHY values for the same object. We will use the Zipcodes table as the source of a small area: the ZIP code 72445 (City of Minturn, Lawrence County, Arkansas):

```
SELECT ID,
       ZCTA,
       GEOM.STArea() AS GEOM_AREA,
       GEOG.STArea() AS GEOG_AREA,
       (GEOG.STArea() - GEOM.STArea()) AS AREA_DIFFERENCE
  FROM Zipcodes
   WHERE ZCTA = '72445';
```

This generates the following output:

```
ID     ZCTA    GEOM_AREA         GEOG_AREA         AREA_DIFFERENCE
----   -----   ---------------   ---------------   ----------------
3227   72445   5267.81079759607  5268.57512617111  0.764328575045511
```

For this polygon—which, if square, would be measure approximately 73 meters on a side—the difference between the GEOMETRY and the GEOGRAPHY area measurement is less than 1 square meter.

We can perform a similar calculation on State of Arkansas polygon, contained in the States table:

```
SELECT ID, NAME_1,
       GEOM.STArea() AS GEOM_AREA,
       GEOG.STArea() AS GEOG_AREA,
       (GEOG.STArea() - GEOM.STArea()) / (1000 * 1000) AS AREA_DIFFERENCE_KM_SQ
  FROM States
   WHERE NAME_1 = 'Arkansas';
```

This generates the following output:

```
ID   NAME_1     GEOM_AREA         GEOG_AREA         AREA_DIFFERENCE_KM_SQ
--   --------   ---------------   ---------------   ---------------------
4    Arkansas   137703845304.298  137691014780.597  -12.8305237011719
```

This is a difference of 12.83 square kilometers. This may seem large, but this is only about .0093 percent.

As with our length calculations, the GEOGRAPHY type provides the most accurate result. But with proper construction, a flat-Earth calculation using GEOMETRY can provide reasonably accurate results for objects of limited size.

It is important to note that SQL Server 2008 does not provide any projection transformation functions with the shipping version. A number of commercial software products such as Safe Software's FME *(http://www.safe.com)* provide projection transformations.

Indexing Spatial Data

The primary index structure in SQL Server is the B-tree. The B-tree is nearly ubiquitous in the database world because it very effectively handles *linearly ordered* types—those in which each value is either less than, equal to, or greater than any other. These types make up the vast majority of types in the database: integers, floating-point numbers, dates, strings, and so on.

A linear ordering generally matches the operations we perform on these types. For example, we may want to find records in which a date lies between two values. The B-tree handles these queries by decomposing dates into sorted ranges at each level of the tree, allowing fast traversals to locate the given range. All of this depends on a linear ordering of the values.

But not all types have a clear linear order. It generally does not make sense, for example, to ask whether one XML fragment is less than another: Although such an ordering could be defined—by simply treating the XML fragments as strings, for example—this ordering would not help us ask most of the common questions we have about XML. Instead, we need a different structure—the XML index—to handle XML queries.

The same holds for spatial types. Therefore, SQL Server 2008 introduces two spatial indexes that pair with the new spatial types. Proper use of these indexes is critical to achieving high performance when using spatial data. This section provides a brief introduction to these new spatial indexes.

Spatial Index Basics

Although B-trees are almost universally used for linearly-ordered types, there is much more diversity with spatial indexes. Their use, however, generally follows the same basic pattern. Let's assume we have a simple spatial query:

```
USE Sample_USA
GO

DECLARE @point GEOMETRY;
SET @point = geometry::Point(8010033.78, 3314652.47, 32768);
```

```
SELECT *
  FROM Zipcodes
  WHERE GEOM.STIntersects(@point) = 1
```

To handle this without an index, we would iterate through the rows of Zipcodes table and filter only those rows that match the spatial predicate. Evaluating spatial predicates can be expensive, and without a spatial index, it must be done for each row in the table.

When using a spatial index, these predicates are essentially split into two pieces: a *primary filter*, which is responsible for quickly excluding most rows that do not match the predicate while leaving *all* of the rows that do match the predicate; and the *secondary filter*, which works on the output of the primary filter and excludes the remaining false positives. The spatial index is used to perform the primary filter, and in many cases the secondary filter is identical to the original predicate.

SQL Server Spatial Indexes

The spatial indexes for the GEOMETRY and GEOGRAPHY types in SQL Server 2008 are very similar. We'll begin by describing the index structure used for the GEOMETRY type.

SQL Server 2008 uses a multilevel grid index. For the GEOMETRY type, this index requires the specification of a bounding box, which provides the extent of space that is to be indexed. The index structure divides this bounding region into a regular set of tiled grid cells, and each of these cells is further subdivided at lower levels of the index. SQL Server 2008 uses four levels, so if space is divided into 16 pieces at each level, it will generate 16 top-level cells, 256 second-level cells, 4096 third-level cells, and 65536 fourth-level cells. Figure 14-20 is a stylized representation of a grid index relative to a spatial object.

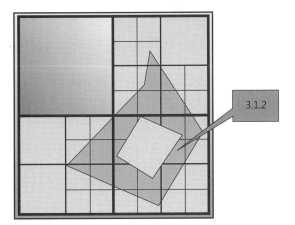

FIGURE 14-20 Grid index

Each cell in each level of the grid is given an internal identifier. These identifiers are structured so that the SQL Server engine can quickly determine whether a cell at one level either contains or is contained by another cell. In addition to these cells, an additional cell is added that covers the entire space outside of the bounding box. This allows for graceful (although inefficient) handling of objects that fall outside the bounding box.

With this strategy, any spatial object can be represented by a set of disjoint cells that cover the object. The region covered by this set of cells is a superset of that covered by the original object. Note that because the entire bounding box is covered by each level of the index, there is more than one set of such cells. For example, we could cover an object using a small number of cells at the top level of the index, by a large number of cells at the bottom level, or by some combination. Using many small cells will more closely match the object at the expense of using more cells. We'll come back to how these are chosen in a moment.

To understand how these cells are used, let us reconsider the previous query. The *STIntersects* filter can now be split into a primary and secondary filter. Although the secondary filter essentially remains the original predicate, the primary filter becomes a test to see whether *@point* and the ZIP code region have any overlapping cells. If two objects have no overlapping cells, they cannot possibly intersect, and the secondary filter need not be run. But although we have split the filter, we do not yet have an index.

When a spatial index is created on a column, SQL Server creates an internal table to contain the cells for each object in the column. In addition to a cell, each row contains a reference back to the original table. This internal table, called the spatial index, is itself indexed on the cell identifier using a standard B-tree. Given a cell, the system can now probe the spatial index to quickly find which spatial objects share the cell, and it can also quickly retrieve those spatial objects from the original table.

With this structure, we can now see how a spatial index on the *GEOM* column of the Zipcodes table would be used to answer the query above. When the query object *@point* is seen, the system determines its cells. This computation is performed once for the query. The system then probes the spatial index with each cell, retrieving the spatial objects that share the cell. After duplicate rows are eliminated, the remaining *GEOM* values (few, we hope) are tested one by one against *@point* using the expensive *STIntersects()* predicate.

Using Spatial Indexes

Before we create a spatial index, we must first ensure that the table we are indexing has a primary key. The reason for this can be seen in the procedure we outlined earlier: the spatial index needs to be able to refer back to the base table, and this is done by storing the primary key of the base table in the index. Once we have a primary key, creating a spatial index is relatively simple. For example, we can create a spatial index for the *GEOM* column of the Zipcodes table with the following command:

```
USE Sample_USA
GO
```

```
CREATE SPATIAL INDEX ZIPCODES_GEOM_IDX
  ON Zipcodes(GEOM)
    USING GEOMETRY_GRID
    WITH (
      BOUNDING_BOX = (
        XMIN= 2801277,
        YMIN= 217712,
        XMAX= 13305064,
        YMAX= 6446996),
      GRIDS = (MEDIUM, MEDIUM, MEDIUM, MEDIUM),
      CELLS_PER_OBJECT = 16
);
```

Let's pick this apart. You should recognize the start of the statement as the familiar CREATE INDEX with the addition of the keyword SPATIAL. This lets the system know that a spatial index is being created. The USING GEOMETRY GRID tells the system what kind of spatial index to use. Currently, GEOMETRY_GRID, the default for GEOMETRY columns, is the only choice for GEOMETRY columns, although this could be expanded in the future.

The WITH clause lists three parameters. For GEOMETRY, the BOUNDING_BOX is required, and sets the range to be indexed. This should be set to fully encompass the objects in the column. Failing to do so will not affect results, but it can dramatically affect performance.

To calculate the BOUNDING_BOX specification that fully encompasses the objects in a GEOMETRY column, you can use the user-defined aggregate function *GeometryEnvelopeAggregate()*, which is included in the Sample_USA database, as follows:

```
DECLARE @boundBox GEOMETRY;
SELECT @boundBox = dbo.GeometryEnvelopeAggregate(GEOM)
FROM Zipcodes;

SELECT
  FLOOR(@boundBox.STPointN(1).STX) AS MinX,
  FLOOR(@boundBox.STPointN(1).STY) AS MinY,
  CEILING(@boundBox.STPointN(3).STX) AS MaxX,
  CEILING(@boundBox.STPointN(3).STY) AS MaxY;
```

This generates the following output:

```
XMIN      YMIN     XMAX       YMAX
-------   ------   --------   -------
2801277   217712   13305064   6446996
```

This method of calculating the bounding box works because *GeometryEnvelopeAggregate* returns a rectangular polygon whose lower left-hand corner (and first point) contains the minimum *x*- and *y*-coordinate values and whose upper right-hand corner (and third point) contains the maximum *x*- and *y*-coordinate values. We use the *T-SQL FLOOR()* and *CEILING()* functions to enlarge the box slightly, truncating the minimum values and rounding the maximum values up.

Finally, the GRIDS and CELLS_PER_OBJECT clauses describe the number of divisions at each level of the index, as well as the maximum number of cells the system should use to represent each object. Setting the GRIDS values to HIGH makes a finer index; setting them to LOW makes a coarser index. Setting CELLS_PER_OBJECT to a low value forces the system to use the larger cells from higher levels of the index to represent the object, whereas setting it to a high value allows the system to more closely approximate the object with small cells. SQL Server 2008 limits CELLS_PER_OBJECT to a maximum value of 8192.

It is difficult to offer prescriptive guidance for setting these parameters—you should experiment with your data. In most cases, the GRIDS and CELLS_PER_OBJECT values shown above will provide reasonable results—in fact, they are SQL Server's default values. You can use these defaults without specifying them explicitly as follows:

```
DROP INDEX ZIPCODES_GEOM_IDX ON Zipcodes;
GO

CREATE SPATIAL INDEX ZIPCODES_GEOM_IDX
  ON Zipcodes(GEOM)
    USING GEOMETRY_GRID
    WITH (
      BOUNDING_BOX = (
        XMIN= 2801277,
        YMIN= 217712,
        XMAX= 13305064,
        YMAX= 6446996)
);
```

SQL Server 2008 allows multiple spatial indexes to be created for each spatial (GEOMETRY or GEOGRAPHY) column. This can be useful for GEOMETRY columns, with individual indexes referencing different bounding boxes.

Geography Indexes

Although there are some important differences, SQL Server's geography indexes are very similar to those for GEOMETRY. The most immediate difference is that although the GEOMETRY index must be given a bounding box, the GEOGRAPHY index does require—in fact cannot take—such a parameter. The GEOMETRY index requires this bounding box to limit the space to be indexed; the GEOGRAPHY index always indexes the entire globe.

So, a complete GEOGRAPHY index creation statement looks like this:

```
CREATE SPATIAL INDEX ZIPCODES_GEOG_IDX
      ON Zipcodes(GEOG)
USING GEOGRAPHY_GRID
WITH (
      GRIDS = (MEDIUM, MEDIUM, MEDIUM, MEDIUM),
      CELLS_PER_OBJECT = 16
);
```

The GEOMETRY grid index decomposes space into a regular set of rectangular cells; the geography grid index cannot do this directly. To obtain its gridding, the GEOGRAPHY index flattens the globe into two square regions and then grids these regions. Essentially, other than this flattening, the indexing procedures and their use are identical. So, as with the GEOMETRY indexes, the preceding syntax can be simplified if the default options are desired:

```
DROP INDEX ZIPCODES_GEOG_IDX ON Zipcodes;
GO
CREATE SPATIAL INDEX Zipcodes_GEOG_Idx
    ON Zipcodes(GEOG)
```

Query Plans

How can we tell if a spatial index is being used for a query? For simple queries, this is relatively easy. If we consider the following SELECT query, a non-indexed plan will look something like Figure 14-21.

```
DECLARE @point GEOMETRY;
SET @point = geometry::Point(8010033.78, 3314652.47, 32768);

SELECT *
  FROM Zipcodes
  WHERE GEOM.STIntersects(@point) = 1;
```

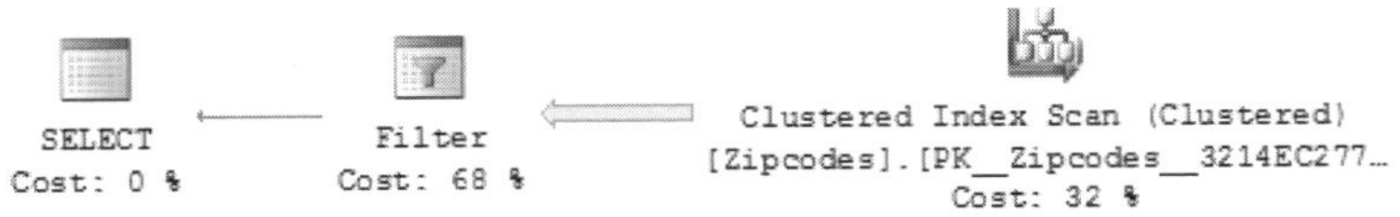

FIGURE 14-21 Non-spatially-indexed query plan

This is very straightforward: the base table is scanned and the rows matching the spatial predicate pass through the Filter operator. If the spatial index is used, we find a much more complex query plan, as shown in Figure 14-22.

This requires some additional explanation. We can roughly divide the query plan into four stages, labeled A through D in Figure 14-22:

A. The first stage computes a set of grid cells for the query object *@point*.

B. Next, the grid cells for the query object are joined with the spatial index. In a query plan, this "Clustered Index Seek (Spatial)" is your clue that a spatial index has been used. The primary keys for the matching spatial objects are extracted and duplicates are eliminated.

C. Next, the primary keys for the spatial objects are joined back to the base table to extract the spatial objects themselves, as well as any other necessary columns from the base table.

D. Finally, the secondary filter is applied to the rows that passed through the primary filter and the result of the query is assembled.

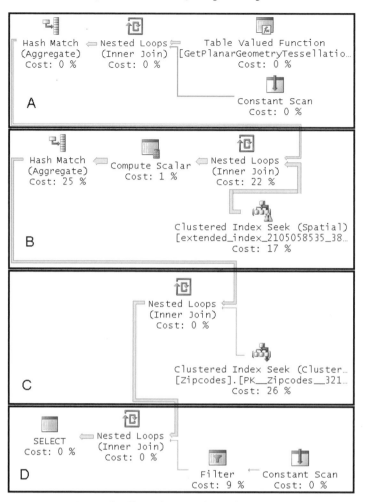

FIGURE 14-22 Query plan illustrating use of spatial index

Although this query plan is much more complex, it will usually outperform the simpler plan by a large margin. The query above finds out which of the 49,146 ZIP codes intersects a given point. We tested the two plans, and the non-indexed plan averaged 5,092 milliseconds whereas the indexed plan averaged only 4.6 milliseconds. This is not a bad return for a 9-second index build time.

Although the query optimizer tries to pick the optimal plan, you may occasionally find that the spatial index is not chosen even though the indexed plan would be better. In these cases, the spatial index can be used in an index hint just like any other index. For example, to force the use of the GEOMETRY index in our query, we would write:

```
SELECT *
  FROM Zipcodes WITH (INDEX (Zipcodes_GEOM_Idx))
    WHERE GEOM.STIntersects(@point) = 1
```

Integration with Spatial Methods

Not all spatial methods can make use of spatial indexes. For GEOMETRY, predicates of the form *method = 1* are supported by spatial indexes for these methods: *STContains*, *STEquals*, *STIntersects*, *STOverlaps*, *STTouches*, and *STWithin*. In addition, spatial indexes support predicates that test whether distances are less than (or less than or equal to) a value. For GEOGRAPHY, spatial indexes support the same predicates for those methods that exist: *STDistance*, *STEquals*, and *STIntersects*.

When querying using a literal, parameter, or variable against a table, the query processor does not care whether the method is called on the column or the parameter. In other words, all of these queries can produce indexed plans if there is an index on the spatial column:

```
SELECT *
FROM Zipcodes
WHERE GEOM.STIntersects(@point) = 1;

SELECT *
FROM Zipcodes
WHERE @point.STIntersects(GEOM) = 1;

SELECT *
FROM Zipcodes
WHERE GEOG.STDistance(@point) < 1000;

SELECT *
FROM Zipcodes
WHERE @point.STDistance(GEOG) < 1000;
```

Note that the system will not, however, produce indexed plans if the predicate is written with the test value before the equality or inequality. In other words, these queries will not produce indexed plans:

```
SELECT *
FROM Zipcodes
WHERE 1 = GEOM.STIntersects(@point);

SELECT *
FROM Zipcodes
WHERE 1000 > @point.STDistance(GEOG);
```

Using Spatial Data to Solve Problems

In this section, we will use the Sample_USA database to illustrate the use of T-SQL and spatial processing to solve the following common business problems:

- Loading spatial data
- Loading spatial data from text files

- Working with geography data validity issues

- Nearest neighbor searches

- Spatial joins

- Finding site locations within geographic regions

- Processing spatial data

- Working with geography data

- Processing the Highways table in the Sample_USA database

Loading Spatial Data

SQL Server 2008 supports three OGC-based data formats, which may be used to load spatial data:

- Well-Known Text (WKT)

- Well-Known Binary (WKB)

- Geography Markup Language (GML)

Unfortunately, very little spatial data is available in these formats. For purposes of loading commonly available spatial data, none of these formats suffices.

Each software company that supports SQL Server 2008 spatial data types provides a data loader. These include ESRI, Pitney Bowes Business Insight (MapInfo), Intergraph, Cadcorp, Autodesk, and Manifold. If you use software provided by one of these vendors, you may already have a way to load spatial data into SQL Server 2008. Other commercial software packages provide generic data loading support for SQL Server 2008; the best known of these is Safe Software's Feature Manipulation Engine (FME). With support for more than 200 spatial data formats, FME provides a flexible and powerful way to load data into either the GEOMETRY or GEOGRAPHY data type. FME has the added benefit of working as a Windows program or as an extension to SQL Server Integration Services (SSIS).

Shape2SQL

But what if you just want to load shapefiles into the database? By far the easiest and most flexible tool to use is the Shape2SQL program provided free of charge by SharpGIS (*http://www.sharpgis.net/page/Shape2SQL.aspx*). As illustrated in Figure 14-23, this program offers a single-menu panel interface from which you can load data into a SQL Server table that contains a GEOMETRY or GEOGRAPHY column and create a primary key and spatial index if desired.

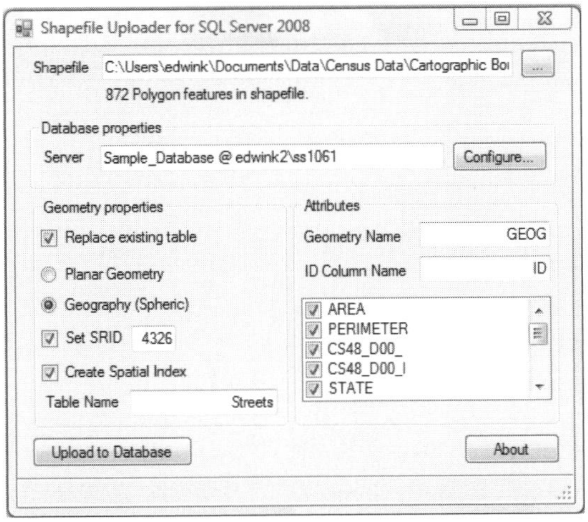

FIGURE 14-23 User interface for Shape2SQL, a spatial data-loading program

When loading data into the GEOGRAPHY data type, Shape2SQL can recombine objects split by the 180th meridian back into a single instance. For example, consider the Fiji Islands, which straddle the 180th meridian and split into two features in shapefiles when using geographic coordinates. Shape2SQL takes such features and performs a union operation, correctly reassembling the feature. Spatial features that cover the North or South Pole are not dealt with correctly, however, and are rejected when using this loader.

Note that Shape2SQL requires that a shapefile contain .shp and .shx component files. Although the .dbf file is technically optional for Shape2SQL, you will generally want to make sure that your shapefile contains this component file also.

MapPoint 2009 Add-In for SQL Server

You can also use the Import Data task in the new MapPoint Add-In for SQL Server. It is important to note that this program only supports the GEOGRAPHY type and consequently cannot load data into a column of type GEOMETRY. Import Data reorients exterior and interior polygon rings into the required order for GEOGRAPHY, but it does not correctly handle polygons, such as the Fiji Islands, that cross the 180th meridian, nor features like Antarctica that straddle either the North or South Pole. When Import Data encounters geographic features that it cannot accommodate, it skips them, providing a summary message at the end of the loading process. Figure 14-24 illustrates the user interface for the Import Data operation.

> **More Info** You can find the download page for this free add-in by searching for "Microsoft MapPoint Add-in for SQL Server" at the Microsoft Download Center: *http://www.microsoft.com/ downloads/*.

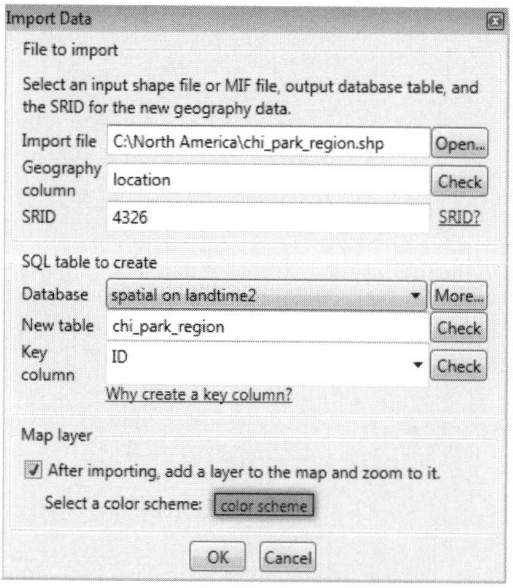

FIGURE 14-24 MapPoint Add-In for SQL Server Import Data menu

Loading Spatial Data from Text Files

Loading spatial data—specifically point locations—from text files is a common spatial business problem. A good example of such files comes from the GeoNames database (*http://www.geonames.org/*).

We consider this format: three records, tab-delimited, with CR/LF as the row terminator. Here is how our TEXT_SAMPLE.txt file content (derived from the GeoNames database) might appear in a text editor:

```
1    Massacre Bay    52.8266667    173.22
2    Maniac Hill     51.9583333    177.5097222
3    Lunatic Lake    51.9402778    177.4708333
```

First, we create a table to hold the incoming data:

```
USE tempdb
GO
CREATE TABLE Text_Sample(
  ID INT PRIMARY KEY,
  NAME VARCHAR(64),
  LATITUDE FLOAT,
  LONGITUDE FLOAT
);
GO
```

Next, we use the BULK INSERT command to load the text file data into the Sample table:

```
BULK
  INSERT Text_Sample
    FROM 'C:\temp\SAMPLE.txt'
      WITH (
        FIELDTERMINATOR = '\t',
        ROWTERMINATOR = '\n'
      );
GO
```

Here are the rows loaded into the table from BULK INSERT:

```
ID NAME          LATITUDE     LONGITUDE
-- ------------ ----------- ----------
1  Massacre Bay 52.8266667  173.22
2  Maniac Hill  51.9583333  177.5097222
3  Lunatic Lake 51.9402778  177.4708333
```

We will now add a GEOGRAPHY column to the Sample table to hold the point location data that we will construct from the LATITUDE and LONGITUDE columns:

```
ALTER TABLE Text_Sample
  ADD GEOG GEOGRAPHY NULL;
GO
```

Because the latitude and longitude are in separate table columns, it will be easiest to create points from them with *Point()* instead of with one of the OGC methods. Don't forget to supply coordinates to the *Point()* method in latitude, longitude order.

```
UPDATE Text_Sample
  SET GEOG = geography::Point(LATITUDE,LONGITUDE,4326);
GO
```

Let's take a final look at the data in the Text_Sample table:

```
SELECT ID, NAME, LATITUDE, LONGITUDE, GEOG.STAsText() AS GEOG from Text_Sample;
```

This generates the following output:

```
ID NAME          LATITUDE   LONGITUDE   GEOG
-- ------------ ---------- ----------- ----------------------
1  Massacre Bay 52.8266667 173.22       POINT(173.22 52.8267)
2  Maniac Hill  51.9583333 177.5097222 POINT(177.51 51.9583)
3  Lunatic Lake 51.9402778 177.4708333 POINT(177.471 51.9403)
```

Note that the *GEOG* column is displayed using WKT, hence the coordinate order of longitude, latitude for the point value.

Working with Geography Data Validity Issues

The GEOGRAPHY type does not allow OGC invalid data to be inserted into a table. Contrast this with the more flexible GEOMETRY type that allows a wide variety of spatial data to be loaded, even data with obvious defects. Invalid geography data often falls into one or more of the following categories:

- Polygons with incorrect orientation
- Self-intersecting polygons
- Extremely narrow polygons
- LineStrings that overlap themselves
- Spatial objects that cross the poles or 180th meridian

Why do we get invalid data in the first place?

- **Polygons with incorrect orientation**   This one is easy—many spatial data sources store exterior polygon boundaries according to the right-hand rule. Because the GEOGRAPHY type requires exterior polygon boundaries to be oriented according to the left-hand rule, this is a natural source of invalid data. It is important to note that there is no formal industry standard with regard to polygon boundary orientation. It is very common for planar polygons to be oriented according to the right-hand rule—shapefiles, for instance, almost always orient exterior polygon boundaries according to the right-hand rule. On the other hand, Oracle Spatial uses the left-hand rule for both planar and geodetic polygons. All major commercial geodetic spatial database implementations—including IBM Informix Geodetic DataBlade, IBM DB2 Geodetic Extender, Oracle Spatial, and Microsoft SQL Server 2008— orient exterior polygons using the left-hand rule.

- **Self-intersecting and extremely narrow polygons**   These two categories, although distinctly different in how they manifest themselves, are typically created during original data creation—specifically, when digitizing and assembling data. Data with these defects are rejected by the GEOGRAPHY type.

- **LineStrings that overlap themselves**   Unlike polygons, LineStrings that self-intersect at a single point are valid. LineStrings that intersect themselves at more than one location (overlapping), however, are not valid.

- **Spatial objects that cross the poles or 180th meridian**   The source of most geography data is from traditional GIS sources, such as shapefiles, among many others. Almost without exception, when these sources provide data with latitude and longitude coordinates, they do so from a planar viewpoint. The most important ramification of this surrounds the "edges" of the data. When spherical coordinates (latitude, longitude) are interpreted as planar, the data is now constrained by edges that do not naturally occur. These edges are the traditional world map boundaries at latitude ±90 degrees and longitude ±180 degrees.

Let's look at a practical example discussed earlier, the Fiji Islands. Fiji lies on the 180th meridian. When Fiji is represented as a polygon using latitude and longitude coordinates in some GIS data files, it is split into two pieces. On most maps of the world, part of Fiji appears on the left edge of the map, and another part appears on the right edge. If we attempt to load these two pieces of Fiji into the GEOGRAPHY type, we immediately encounter a problem—Fiji is interpreted as a multipart polygon with two parts intersecting along an edge. This is an invalid GEOMETRY instance according to the OGC Simple Features rules, and it is summarily rejected by the database server.

Common Workflow Patterns

There is no single right way to prepare and load data into the GEOGRAPHY type. An upcoming section, "Processing the Highways Table in the Sample_USA Database," includes one possible workflow for a specific data source. In general, however, we use a variety of tools to overcome most, if not all, issues that arise when preparing and loading commonly available spatial data.

Two tools, Safe Software's Feature Manipulation Engine 2009 (FME) and the SharpGIS Shape2SQL data loader, perform important transformations on the input data that minimize loading issues. For instance, both FME and Shape2SQL automatically reorient polygons to the left-hand rule for exterior boundaries and the right-hand rule for interior rings. Because FME is an ETL tool, it contains a plethora of other transformations to correct data inadequacies. Shape2SQL, on the other hand, is a data loader that has a basic understanding of the GEOGRAPHY type. Toward this end, Shape2SQL can automatically unify spatial objects that span the 180-degree meridian, such as the Fiji Islands, discussed previously.

But what happens if you use either FME or Shape2SQL and fail to successfully load your data? A very common workflow pattern is to load the offending data into a GEOMETRY column first. With the data in a GEOMETRY column, you can manipulate it with some standard operations prior to inserting it into a GEOGRAPHY column.

Using the GEOMETRY MakeValid Method   With the data in a GEOMETRY column, we can pass the column through the *MakeValid()* method to correct any deficiencies in the data organization. This includes fixing self-intersecting polygons and a host of other issues with the data. When invalid data is found, *MakeValid()* not only fixes the data but also reorients polygons in a manner suitable for the GEOGRAPHY type. Unfortunately, *MakeValid()* does not guarantee that valid GEOMETRY data is also valid GEOGRAPHY data. Additionally, *MakeValid()* only reorients polygons where there was a data validity issue. Before we leave this section, here is how you can update a GEOMETRY column using *MakeValid()*:

```
USE tempdb
GO
UPDATE t1
  SET GEOM = GEOM.MakeValid();
GO
```

Forcing Polygon Ring Reorientation   Because *MakeValid()* only reorients polygons that have invalid data, what if you want to force a valid GEOMETRY polygon into the ring orientation required for the GEOGRAPHY type? It turns out that when SQL Server operates on GEOMETRY data, such as an *STIntersects()*, it internally reorients a given polygon's rings according to the left-hand rule. This state just happens to be the orientation for the GEOGRAPHY type. The following T-SQL is an example of how to force SQL Server to reorient all polygon data for a GEOMETRY column. (The table t1 was created in the section "Getting Started with Spatial Data.")

```
UPDATE t1
  SET GEOM = GEOM.MakeValid().STUnion(GEOM.STStartPoint());
```

To evaluate the union of spatial objects, SQL Server deserializes each polygon and puts it into a consistent form, the polygon left-hand rule. This form represents the polygon data in a GEOGRAPHY type–friendly structure. Placing a *MakeValid()* inline completes the operation.

> **More Info** The technique for forcing polygon ring reorientation relies on an undocumented feature of SQL Server. Please use caution when using this technique.

Moving Geometry Data to Geography Data

After performing a GEOMETRY validation and a polygon reorientation, you can now attempt to move the GEOMETRY column to a GEOGRAPHY column:

```
-- Create a new table with GEOGRAPHY column
CREATE TABLE t2 (
  ID   INTEGER,
  GEOG GEOGRAPHY);
GO


-- Convert from GEOMETRY to GEOGRAPHY using Well Known Text
INSERT INTO t2
  SELECT t1.ID, geography::STGeomFromText(t1.GEOM.STAsText(),4326)
  FROM t1;
GO
```

The previous example uses Well-Known Text. The next example uses the more efficient Well-Known Binary format:

```
-- Convert from GEOMETRY to GEOGRAPHY using Well Known Binary
INSERT INTO t2
  SELECT t1.ID, geography::STGeomFromWKB(t1.GEOM.STAsBinary(),4326)
  FROM t1;
GO
```

Using *MakeValidGeographyFromGeometry*

Despite our best efforts, some data needs more touching up than the previous workflows can easily provide. New to the SQL Server Spatial Tools site at CodePlex (http://sqlspatial tools.codeplex.com/) is the function *MakeValidGeographyfromGeometry()*. This function takes an argument of type GEOMETRY and produces, in most cases, a valid geography object. There are still special cases that this function cannot resolve, but it generally works quite well. Here is how we can use this operator to move a GEOMETRY column to a GEOGRAPHY column in a new table:

```
-- Create a new table with GEOMETRY and GEOGRAPHY columns
CREATE TABLE t2 (
  NAME VARCHAR(64),
  GEOM GEOMETRY,
  GEOG GEOGRAPHY);
```

```
GO

-- Insert as a GEOMETRY with the polygon exterior ring in reverse order from
-- GEOGRAPHY's exterior ring requirement
INSERT INTO t2 VALUES
  ('Area2', geometry::STGeomFromText('POLYGON ((5 4, 5 7, 8 7, 8 4, 5 4))',4326),NULL);
GO

-- Convert from GEOMETRY to GEOGRAPHY using MakeValidGeographyFromGeometry
--  Make sure to register the dbo.MakeValidGeographyFromGeometry from the QLSpatialTools.dll
at
-- http://sqlspatialtools.codeplex.com/
-- Note that this function is already included in the Sample_USA database
UPDATE t2
  SET GEOG = dbo.MakeValidGeographyFromGeometry(GEOM);
GO
```

Finding Site Locations within Geographic Regions

For these exercises, three tables from the Sample_USA database will be used: GeoNames (containing 1,886,365 Points), Highways (containing 8,362 Lines), and Counties (containing 3,146 Polygons). The basic theme for both of the exercises will be to find subsets of the GeoNames points of interest around highways, within a specific region (Counties). Figure 14-25 illustrates the density of data. The gray background represents the county polygons, the white lines represents the network of highways, and the black dots represent the points of interest.

FIGURE 14-25 GeoNames data in King County, Washington State

Find High Schools within 2 KM of Interstate 5 in King County, Washington State

This problem is a good example of the use of a spatial buffer as opposed to using a distance method. Note how the buffered Interstate 5 LINESTRING is clipped by the King County polygon to create the final region used in the intersection test:

```
----Find all High Schools within 2 km of Interstate 5 in King County, Washington
USE Sample_USA
GO
DECLARE @i5 GEOGRAPHY;
DECLARE @kc GEOGRAPHY;
DECLARE @buf GEOGRAPHY;
SET @i5 = (
  SELECT GEOG FROM Highways
  WHERE SIGNT = 'I' AND SIGNN = '5');
SET @kc = (
  SELECT GEOG FROM Counties
  WHERE NAME_1 = 'Washington' AND NAME_2 = 'King');

SET @i5 = @i5.STIntersection(@kc); -- Clip I5 to King County
SET @buf = @i5.STBuffer(2000); -- buffer clipped I5 by 2 KM
SET @buf = @buf.STIntersection(@kc); -- Clip I5 buffer to King County
SELECT geonameid, name, feature_code
FROM GeoNames
WHERE feature_code = 'SCH'
      AND name LIKE '% High %'
      AND name NOT LIKE '% Junior %'
      AND GEOG.STIntersects(@buf) = 1
ORDER BY name;
```

This results in the following output:

```
geonameid     name                               feature_code
---------     ------------------------------     ------------
5787513       Blanchet High School               SCH
5790315       Cleveland High School              SCH
5793415       Edison High School                 SCH
5793988       Evergreen Lutheran High School     SCH
5794240       Federal Way High School            SCH
5794857       Foster High School                 SCH
5795273       Garfield High School               SCH
5795504       Glacier High School                SCH
5798335       Ingraham High School               SCH
5800987       Lincoln High School                SCH
5804101       Mount Ranier High School           SCH
5805435       ODea High School                   SCH
5807827       Rainier Beach High School          SCH
5808781       Roosevelt High School              SCH
5810300       Shorecrest High School             SCH
5810307       Shorewood High School              SCH
5813367       Thomas Jefferson high School       SCH
5814362       Tyee High School                   SCH
```

Figure 14-26 illustrates the results.

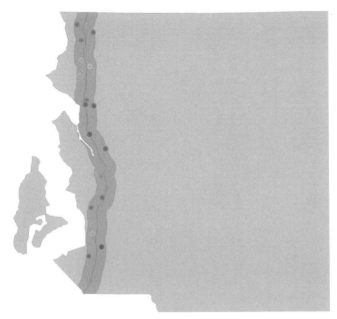

FIGURE 14-26 High Schools within 2 KM of Interstate 5 in King County, Washington State

Find Schools Within 4 KM of the Intersection of Interstate 5 and Interstate 405 in King County, Washington State

Using the previous example as a template, our first inclination might be to use a buffer to solve this problem. In this case, using *STDistance()* results in a much more efficient query:

```
--Find schools within 4 km of the intersection of Interstates 5 and 405
--in King County, Washington
DECLARE @kc    GEOGRAPHY;
DECLARE @i405 GEOGRAPHY;
DECLARE @i5    GEOGRAPHY;
DECLARE @int  GEOGRAPHY;
SET @kc = (SELECT GEOG FROM Counties WHERE NAME_1 = 'Washington' AND NAME_2 = 'King');
SET @i405 = (SELECT GEOG FROM Highways WHERE SIGNT = 'I' AND SIGNN = '405');
SET @i5 = (SELECT GEOG FROM Highways WHERE SIGNT = 'I' AND SIGNN = '5');
SET @i5 = @i5.STIntersection(@kc); -- Clip I5 to King County
SET @int = @i5.STIntersection(@i405);
SELECT geonameid, name, feature_code
  FROM GeoNames
    WHERE feature_code = 'SCH' and
          GEOG.STDistance(@int) <= 4000
          ORDER BY name;
GO
```

This results in the following output:

```
geonameid    name                                   feature_code
---------    ------------------------------         ------------
5787926      Bow Lake Elementary School             SCH
5788996      Campbell Hill Elementary School        SCH
```

5789326	Cascade View Elementary School	SCH
5790027	Chinook Middle School	SCH
5793080	Earlington School	SCH
5794857	Foster High School	SCH
5795504	Glacier High School	SCH
5802942	McMicken Heights Elementary School	SCH
5808436	Riverton Heights Elementary School	SCH
5810333	Showalter Middle School	SCH
5810745	Skyway Christian School	SCH
5813407	Thorndyke Elementary School	SCH
5814044	Tukwila Elementary School	SCH
5814362	Tyee High School	SCH
5814573	Valley View Elementary School	SCH

Figure 14-27 illustrates the results.

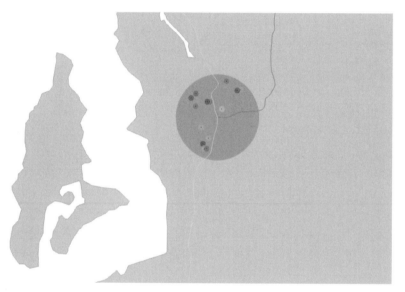

FIGURE 14-27 Schools within 4 KM of the intersection of Interstate 5 and Interstate 405 in King County, Washington State

Nearest Neighbor Searches

Nearest neighbor searches are a common spatial query. Although you can use several methods to solve this problem, we've chosen a technique using a numbers table (Nums). The numbers table approach provides iterative style processing while still making use of SQL language's more efficient set-based operations. This query also makes use of the Common Table Expression introduced in SQL Server 2005. The query produced by this technique is not a typical shape that the optimizer looks for when considering to use a spatial index, hence the use of an optimizer hint.

You can find the code to create and populate the Nums table in Chapter 2, "User-Defined Functions."

Find the Nearest GeoNames Data around a Point Location

The first example will find the nearest point of interest in the GeoNames table to a particular location in Alaska:

```
DECLARE @input GEOGRAPHY = 'POINT (-147 61)';
DECLARE @start FLOAT = 10000;
WITH NearestNeighbor AS(
  SELECT TOP 1 WITH TIES
    *, b.GEOG.STDistance(@input) AS dist
  FROM Nums n JOIN GeoNames b WITH(INDEX(geog_hhhh_16_sidx)) -- index hint
  ON b.GEOG.STDistance(@input) < @start*POWER(CAST(2 AS FLOAT),n.n)
  WHERE n <= 20
  ORDER BY n
)

SELECT TOP 1 geonameid, name, feature_code, admin1_code, dist
FROM NearestNeighbor
ORDER BY n, dist;
```

This results in the following output:

geonameid	name	feature_code	admin1_code	dist
5870476	Number One River	STM	AK	646.306152781609

In order to expand the result set to the nearest 10 points of interest instead of 1, two modifications are needed. First, both of the TOP 1 specifications must be changed to TOP 10. Second, an additional predicate must be added to the CTE's WHERE clause to ensure that the distance ranges for different values of *n* do not overlap. If they do, distinct values of *n* may produce duplicate results, and the 10 rows generated by the CTE will not correspond to 10 different points of interest.

The following query will return the 10 points of interest nearest to *@input*:

```
DECLARE @input GEOGRAPHY = 'POINT (-147 61)';
DECLARE @start FLOAT = 1000;
WITH NearestNeighbor AS(
  SELECT TOP 10 WITH TIES
    *, b.GEOG.STDistance(@input) AS dist
  FROM Nums n JOIN GeoNames b WITH(INDEX(geog_hhhh_16_sidx)) -- index hint
  ON b.GEOG.STDistance(@input) < @start*POWER(CAST(2 AS FLOAT),n.n)
  AND b.GEOG.STDistance(@input) >=
    CASE WHEN n = 1 THEN 0 ELSE @start*POWER(CAST(2 AS FLOAT),n.n-1) END
  WHERE n <= 20
  ORDER BY n
)
  SELECT TOP 10 geonameid, name, feature_code, admin1_code, dist
  FROM NearestNeighbor
  ORDER BY n, dist;
```

> **Note** Only part of this query's WHERE clause is supported by the spatial index. However, the query optimizer correctly evaluates the supported part (the "<" comparison) using the index. This restricts the number of rows for which the ">=" part must be tested, and the query performs well. Changing the value of *@start* can sometimes speed up the query if it is slower than desired.

```
geonameid    name                 feature_code  admin1_code   dist
-----------  -------------------  ------------   -----------   ----------------
5870476      Number One River     STM            AK            646.306152781609
5863866      Heather Bay          BAY            AK            842.85121182881
5865122      Jade Harbor          BAY            AK            3523.94025462351
5863873      Heather Island       ISL            AK            3729.62714753577
5861649      Emerald Cove         BAY            AK            5523.29937034676
5859736      Columbia Bay         BAY            AK            5558.74879079016
5868070      Lutris Pass          CHN            AK            5578.08228008006
5862561      Mount Freemantle     MT             AK            6089.41763362949
5873004      Round Mountain       MT             AK            6171.84197013513
5861579      Elf Point            CAPE           AK            6710.1590944647
```

> **More Info** The query filter *WHERE n <= 20* limits the search radius to $2^{20} \times @start$ meters, or about 1,000 kilometers in this case. The reason to keep *@start* small is to avoid excessively high cost in the worst-case scenario—when fewer than 10 rows are within the maximum search radius.

Find ZIP Codes around a Point Location

The previous example shows nearest neighbor queries working with point objects. Let's modify the query to use the Zipcodes table to find the distance ordered set of nearby ZIP code polygons around a point location:

```
DECLARE @input GEOGRAPHY = 'POINT (-147 61)';
DECLARE @start FLOAT = 10000;
WITH NearestNeighbor AS
(
    SELECT TOP 10 WITH TIES *, b.GEOG.STDistance(@input) AS dist
    FROM Nums n JOIN Zipcodes b WITH(INDEX(geog_hhhh_256_sidx))
    ON b.GEOG.STDistance(@input) < @start*POWER(2,n.n)
    AND b.GEOG.STDistance(@input) >=
      CASE WHEN n = 1 THEN 0 ELSE @start*POWER(2,n.n-1) END
    ORDER BY n
)
  SELECT TOP 10 ID, ZCTA, dist
  FROM NearestNeighbor
  ORDER BY n, dist;
```

This results in the following output:

```
ID          ZCTA        dist
----------- ----------  ----------------------
1642        996XX       0
1955        99686       11633.5438436035
1914        996XX       14565.4268010367
```

```
1954       99677       17449.3494959674
1908       995HH       18127.8398133392
1901       99686       25423.8744552156
1902       99686       35328.0560592605
2005       996XX       38489.6097305924
1734       99686       41477.7718586985
1919       996XX       41782.8127303003
```

Note the distance value of 0 for ID 1642. This is the ZIP code that directly intersects the
@input point value used for the query.

Increasing the search radius slows down the performance of this query as illustrated by the
following results against the Zipcode table, which contains 49,146 polygons:

```
Search Radius  Execution Time
-------------  -----------
  1000 meters     350 ms
 10000 meters     350 ms
100000 meters   23810 ms
```

A similar analysis on the GeoNames table, which contains 1,886,365 points, yields the
following results:

```
Search Radius  Execution Time
-------------  --------------
  1000 meters     147 ms
 10000 meters     163 ms
100000 meters   25660 ms
```

Although your results may vary, good performance can be achieved.

Spatial Joins

Joining tables on spatial proximity is a very common task. In this example, two tables will be
joined via spatial intersection in order to add and populate a new ZIP code column in one of
them.

Let's begin by creating the table GeoNames_CA, a subset of the GeoNames table containing
the GeoNames points-of-interest data for the state of California (110,525 rows):

```
USE Sample_USA;
GO

SELECT * INTO GeoNames_CA FROM GeoNames a
WHERE a.admin1_code = 'CA'
GO
```

In this exercise, we wish to find the ZIP code for each point of interest. As a first attempt to
do this, we join the GeoNames_CA table with the Zipcodes table on common geographic
location—the intersection of the GeoNames_CA points with the Zipcodes polygons.
(This query produces a very large result set, and you may not wish to run it.)

The following query returns a subset of the columns in the full GeoNames table plus a new column, ZCTA, that will hold the 5-digit ZIP code value:

```
SELECT g.geonameid, g.name, z.ZCTA
  FROM GeoNames_CA g
  JOIN Zipcodes z WITH(INDEX(geog_hhhh_256_sidx))
  ON z.GEOG.STIntersects(g.GEOG) = 1;
GO
```

This query produces the following results:

```
geonameid   name                        ZCTA
----------- --------------------------  --------
5284484     Bethune Park                90001
5284498     Bemmerly Park               95695
5284626     Becker Peak                 95721
5284690     Beartrap Spring             934XX
5284692     Antimony Ridge              93518
5284708     American Eagle Mine         956XX
5284710     Alaska Mine                 95960
5284714     Adams Elementary School     92116
5284716     Alpine Dam                  949XX
5284718     Albany Adult School         94706
...
...
6695788     Hidden Trails               92027
6695789     Fances Ryan Park            92027
6696626     Montessori in Redlands      92373
6696627     Legoland California         92008
6696628     Krikorian Redlands Cinema   92373
6698131     Camp Roberts                93451
6698167     Nate Harrison Homestead     92061
```

This query returns 109,176 rows. What happened to the other rows in the GeoNames_CA table? Because of the query's INNER JOIN, points of interest appear in the result set only if their *GEOG* value intersects a ZIP code polygon. If no match is found, the point of interest is not returned.

Because we will use this JOIN to update a new Zip code column in GeoNames_CA, the missing rows will not cause a problem. Although some rows will not be modified by the UPDATE, those rows represent points of interest that have no ZIP code. They will remain in the GeoNames_CA table with NULL ZIP code. To set the stage for the UPDATE, we will create a new column (ZCTA) in the GeoNames_CA table to hold the ZIP code value:

```
ALTER TABLE GeoNames_CA
  ADD ZCTA nvarchar(255) NULL.
GO
```

To populate the *GeoNames_CA* ZCTA column, we will use the same join we used in the SELECT query. When a *GeoNames_CA* point location intersects a Zipcode polygon, we will transfer the value from the *Zipcodes* ZCTA column to the *GeoNames_CA* ZCTA column. Here is the T-SQL to perform the join and execute the update:

```
UPDATE g
  SET g.ZCTA = z.ZCTA
FROM GeoNames_CA g
  JOIN dbo.Zipcodes z WITH(INDEX(geog_hhhh_256_sidx))
    ON (z.GEOG.STIntersects(g.GEOG) = 1)
GO
--Results: 109176 row(s)
```

> **Note** Some points of interest might intersect more than one ZIP code region—this could occur if two ZIP code polygons overlap, for example. The UPDATE will update these rows of *GeoNames_CA* with an arbitrary one of the matching ZIP code values.

Where (spatially) are the *GeoNames_CA* points of interest that are not inside any ZIP code polygon? We can easily select them because the ZCTA value in these rows remained NULL after the update. Here is a query that selects them, along with the California polygon from States to provide visual context:

```
SELECT GEOG FROM GeoNames_CA WHERE ZCTA IS NULL
UNION ALL
SELECT GEOG from States WHERE NAME_1 = 'California'
GO
```

In virtually all cases, the unmatched GeoNames data was on coastline features, outside of the postal mail delivery services regions (ZIP codes) (see Figure 14-28).

FIGURE 14-28 Null matches representing unjoined data

Processing Spatial Data

As a practical example illustrating how to use the new spatial features in SQL Server 2008, we have put together a set of sample spatial data, previously described. One of these samples—the Highways table—required a significant amount of preparation. We describe this process here.

Processing the Highways Table in the Sample_USA Database

The sample data set chosen for the Highways table came from the 2008 National Highway Planning Network included in the National Transportation Atlas Database from the U.S. Bureau of Transportation Statistics. You can order a free DVD of this database here: *https://www.bts.gov/pdc/user/products/src/products.xml?p=2795&c=-1*. This data set contains the local, state, and federal highways for the United States.

This data is published in the shapefile format with the highway spatial features constructed as lines. The spatial features are in WGS 84 geographic coordinates, and there are 176,191 records. The large number of records results from the detailed segmentation of routes, with each segment containing specific information relevant to the Bureau of Transportation Statistics. Consequently, logical routes are broken up into multiple records: Interstate 80, for example, is segmented into 1,427 records.

For our purposes, we want to represent each logical route as a single record. Furthermore, we only want the spatial features for interstates, U.S. highways, state routes, and county routes. Finally, we wanted to make the spatial data available as both GEOMETRY and GEOGRAPHY objects. This section only discusses the workflow for the GEOGRAPHY object creation.

The Workflow

Because we want to aggregate the multiple segments defining a given logical route into a single spatial feature, we will need two tables: one for the temporary form of the data and one for the final, processed form. The temporary table will be named HIGHWAYS_TEMP and the final table will be Highways. At this point, a couple of observations are warranted.

We have the option of loading the shapefile spatial data into either a column of type GEOGRAPHY or GEOMETRY. As we did in the section "Loading Spatial Data from Text Files," and for the reasons we gave earlier, we will insert the source data into a GEOMETRY column, then convert it to GEOGRAPHY with the CLR user-defined function *dbo.GeographyMakeValid FromGeometry()*.

We need to use two tables because the initial form of the Highways data will contain all 176,191 records. The final table will contain aggregated spatial data, which will have a significantly different structure and hence cannot be stored in the original table.

The first step is to load the shapefile data into the HIGHWAYS_TEMP table as a column of type GEOMETRY named *GEOM*. To do this we used the Shape2SQL program using the following settings:

- **Planar Geometry (GEOMETRY Data Type)**
- **Set SRID**   4326
- **Table Name**   HIGHWAYS_TEMP
- **GEOMETRY Name**   GEOM
- **ID Column Name**   ID

With the data loaded into the temporary table, the next step is to make certain that all the GEOMETRY instances represent valid data using the *MakeValid()* method:

```
UPDATE HIGHWAYS_TEMP
  SET GEOM = GEOM.MakeValid()
WHERE GEOM.STIsValid() = 0;
GO
--Result: 3 row(s) affected
```

Next, we need to add a column of type GEOGRAPHY and convert the GEOMETRY data into valid GEOGRAPHY data. The function to create valid GEOGRAPHY data is part of the SQL Server Spatial Tools distribution in CodePlex and is named *dbo.MakeValidGeographyFromGeometry()*. It takes a single argument of type GEOMETRY:

```
ALTER TABLE HIGHWAYS_TEMP
  ADD GEOG GEOGRAPHY NULL
GO
UPDATE HIGHWAYS_TEMP
  SET GEOG = dbo.MakeValidGeographyFromGeometry(GEOM)
GO
--RESULTS: 176191 row(s) affected
```

With the HIGHWAYS_TEMP table containing columns of type GEOMETRY and GEOGRAPHY, we can now create the final Highways table that will hold the highway route aggregates.

How Data Is Represented in HIGHWAYS_TEMP and Highways

A single row in HIGHWAYS_TEMP represents one stretch of road. The *GEOG* and *GEOM* columns contain equivalent LineStrings that describe the location of this road segment. In addition, other columns of the row identify one, two, or three highway routes of which the road segment is a part. The types and numbers of these highway routes are stored in non-normalized form using the six columns *SIGNT1*, *SIGNN1*, *SIGNT2*, *SIGNN2*, *SIGNT3*, and *SIGNN3*.

Interstate highways (type I) and U.S. routes (type U) are uniquely identified by their route type and route number. For state routes (route type S) and county routes (route type C), however, the (route type, route number) pair does not completely specify the route. Rows in HIGHWAYS_TEMP that represent segments of state or county routes must contain non-NULL values to indicate the county (column *CTFIPS*, needed for county routes only) and/or state (column *STFIPS*, needed for both state and county routes). Complicating the table design somewhat, only one (*CTFIPS,STFIPS*) pair appears in each row of HIGHWAYS_TEMP, and it may be needed for only some of the (route type, route number) pairs in the row.

The table Highways represents routes, not segments; routes are uniquely identified by their values on the four columns *CTFIPS*, *STFIPS*, *SIGNT*, and *SIGNN* as follows:

- Interstate *n* is represented as (NULL,NULL,'I',*n*)

- U.S. Highway *n* is represented as (NULL,NULL,'S',*n*)

- State Route *n* in state *s* is represented as (NULL,*s*,'S',*n*)

- County Route *n* in county *c*, state *s* is represented as (*c*,*s*,'C',*n*)

As you will see in the code below, as many as three route specifiers must be extracted from each row of HIGHWAYS_TEMP:

- (CTFIPS or NULL,STFIPS or NULL,SIGNT1,SIGNN1)

- (CTFIPS or NULL,STFIPS or NULL,SIGNT2,SIGNN2)

- (CTFIPS or NULL,STFIPS or NULL,SIGNT3,SIGNN3)

A specifier is valid if it contains non-NULL type and number values. For valid specifiers, CTFIPS and/or STFIPS are retained or replaced with NULL based on the route type, which appears as the *SIGNT1* (or *SIGNT2* or *SIGNT3*) value.

The Highways table contains a logical subset of the columns in the HIGHWAYS_TEMP table—the minimum necessary to be able to uniquely identify and access logical routes. The *CTFIPS* column contains the Federal Information Processing Standards (FIPS) numeric identifiers for U.S. counties. The *STFIPS* column is the equivalent for U.S. states:

```
CREATE TABLE Highways(
  ID INTEGER IDENTITY(1,1) NOT NULL,
  CTFIPS INTEGER NULL,
  STFIPS INTEGER NULL,
  SIGNT NVARCHAR(255) NOT NULL,
  SIGNN NVARCHAR(255) NOT NULL,
  GEOG GEOGRAPHY NOT NULL,
  GEOM GEOMETRY NOT NULL,
 CONSTRAINT PK_ID_HIGHWAYS PRIMARY KEY CLUSTERED (ID ASC)
 )
GO
```

The next series of operation create the route aggregates. To do this, we use the *dbo.GeographyUnionAggregate()* function from the SQL Server Spatial Tools project against the GEOGRAPHY column (*GEOG*) in the HIGHWAYS_TEMP table. To get unique route combinations to aggregate correctly (route type and route name combinations, such as Interstate 80) we use the GROUP BY operator in conjunction with a derived table. The results from the derived table are then inserted into the Highways table. For this first step, we are interested only in interstate and U.S. highways, hence the CTFIPS and STFIPS columns are not needed and are set to NULL. Additionally, since *GEOM* is declared as NOT NULL, we must supply a value for *GEOM* even though we are not describing the GEOMETRY workflow in this section. We will use an empty LineString as a placeholder:

```
DECLARE @emptyLS GEOMETRY = geometry::Parse('LINESTRING EMPTY');
INSERT INTO Highways
SELECT NULL, NULL, COL1, COL2,
       dbo.GeographyUnionAggregate(INTERMEDIATEAGG), @emptyLS
FROM
(
   SELECT SIGNT1 AS COL1, SIGNN1 AS COL2,
          dbo.GeographyUnionAggregate(GEOG) AS INTERMEDIATEAGG
    FROM HIGHWAYS_TEMP
    WHERE (SIGNT1 = 'I' OR SIGNT1 = 'U')
     AND  (GEOG IS NOT NULL)
    GROUP BY SIGNT1, SIGNN1

   UNION ALL

   SELECT SIGNT2, SIGNN2,
           dbo.GeographyUnionAggregate(GEOG)
    FROM HIGHWAYS_TEMP
    WHERE (SIGNT2 = 'I' OR SIGNT2 = 'U')
     AND  (GEOG IS NOT NULL)
    GROUP BY SIGNT2, SIGNN2

   UNION ALL

   SELECT SIGNT3, SIGNN3,
           dbo.GeographyUnionAggregate(GEOG)
    FROM HIGHWAYS_TEMP
    WHERE (SIGNT3 = 'I' OR SIGNT3 = 'U')
     AND  (GEOG IS NOT NULL)
    GROUP BY SIGNT3, SIGNN3
) AS DERIVED_TABLE
GROUP BY COL1, COL2
GO
```

To aggregate the state routes, we need to execute another pass on the HIGHWAYS_TEMP table, using another derived table. This time, we are interested in aggregating state routes, so the STFIPS values become part of the equation. We have to add this additional qualifier since state-based routes are not guaranteed to be unique. (For example, the states of California and Wyoming could both have a State Route 101.)

```
DECLARE @emptyLS GEOMETRY = geometry::Parse('LINESTRING EMPTY');
INSERT INTO Highways
SELECT NULL, COL0, COL1, COL2,
       dbo.GeographyUnionAggregate(INTERMEDIATEAGG), @emptyLS
FROM
(
   SELECT STFIPS AS COL0, SIGNT1 AS COL1, SIGNN1 AS COL2,
bo.GeographyUnionAggregate(GEOG) AS INTERMEDIATEAGG
    FROM HIGHWAYS_TEMP
    WHERE (SIGNT1 = 'S') AND (GEOG IS NOT NULL)
      GROUP BY STFIPS, SIGNT1, SIGNN1

   UNION ALL

   SELECT STFIPS, SIGNT2, SIGNN2, dbo.GeographyUnionAggregate(GEOG)
    FROM HIGHWAYS_TEMP
    WHERE (SIGNT2 = 'S') AND (GEOG IS NOT NULL)
      GROUP BY STFIPS, SIGNT2, SIGNN2

   UNION ALL

   SELECT STFIPS, SIGNT3, SIGNN3, dbo.GeographyUnionAggregate(GEOG)
    FROM HIGHWAYS_TEMP
    WHERE (SIGNT3 = 'S') AND (GEOG IS NOT NULL)
      GROUP BY STFIPS, SIGNT3, SIGNN3
) AS DERIVED_TABLE
GROUP BY COL0, COL1, COL2
GO
```

The final derived table aggregates county routes. Since county FIPS codes are only unique within a state, we have to use them in combination with the associated state FIPS codes:

```
DECLARE @emptyLS GEOMETRY = geometry::Parse('LINESTRING EMPTY');
INSERT INTO Highways
SELECT COL0, COL1, COL2, COL3,
       dbo.GeographyUnionAggregate(INTERMEDIATEAGG,0), @emptyLS
FROM
(
   SELECT CTFIPS AS COL0, STFIPS AS COL1, SIGNT1 AS COL2, SIGNN1 AS COL3,
bo.GeographyUnionAggregate(GEOG) AS INTERMEDIATEAGG
    FROM HIGHWAYS_TEMP
    WHERE (SIGNT1 = 'C') AND (GEOG IS NOT NULL)
      GROUP BY STFIPS, CTFIPS, SIGNT1, SIGNN1

   UNION ALL

   SELECT CTFIPS, STFIPS, SIGNT2, SIGNN2, dbo.GeographyUnionAggregate(GEOG)
    FROM HIGHWAYS_TEMP
    WHERE (SIGNT2 = 'C') AND (GEOG IS NOT NULL)
      GROUP BY STFIPS, CTFIPS, SIGNT2, SIGNN2

   UNION ALL
```

```
    SELECT CTFIPS, STFIPS, SIGNT3, SIGNN3, dbo.GeographyUnionAggregate(GEOG)
      FROM HIGHWAYS_TEMP
      WHERE (SIGNT3 = 'C') AND (GEOG IS NOT NULL)
        GROUP BY STFIPS, CTFIPS, SIGNT3, SIGNN3
) AS DERIVED_TABLE
GROUP BY COL1, COL0, COL2, COL3
GO
```

Populating Highways with a Single Query

Despite the non-normalized structure of HIGHWAYS_TEMP and the use of NULLs in
the route specifiers of Highways, it's nonetheless possible to populate Highways with
a single INSERT statement. Here is such a statement, which uses UNPIVOT (twice) to
normalize the data and CASE to replace *CTFIPS* and *STFIPS* with NULL when required:

```
DECLARE @emptyLS GEOGRAPHY = geography::Parse('LINESTRING EMPTY');
INSERT INTO Highways
SELECT
  CASE WHEN SIGNT = 'C' THEN CTFIPS END AS CTFIPS,
  CASE WHEN SIGNT IN ('C','S') THEN STFIPS END AS STFIPS,
  SIGNT, SIGNN,
  dbo.GeographyUnionAggregate(GEOG) AS GEOG,
  @emptyLS AS GEOM
FROM (
  SELECT
    CTFIPS, STFIPS, SIGNT1, SIGNN1, SIGNT2, SIGNN2, SIGNT3, SIGNN3, GEOG
  FROM HIGHWAYS_TEMP
) AS HT UNPIVOT (
    SIGNT FOR SignTNum IN (SIGNT1, SIGNT2, SIGNT3)
  ) S UNPIVOT (
    SIGNN FOR SignNNum IN (SIGNN1, SIGNN2, SIGNN3)
  ) as U
WHERE RIGHT(SignTNum,1) = RIGHT(SignNNum,1)
AND SIGNT IN ('I','U','C','S')
AND GEOG IS NOT NULL
GROUP BY
  CASE WHEN SIGNT = 'C' THEN CTFIPS END,
  CASE WHEN SIGNT IN ('C','S') THEN STFIPS END,
  SIGNT, SIGNN;
```

Next, we need to update the SRID value for each GEOG instance and add a constraint to
enforce this SRID:

```
-----------------------------------------------------------
--Set the SRID of each GEOGRAPHY instance to 4326 (WGS 84)
-----------------------------------------------------------
UPDATE Highways
  SET GEOG.STSrid = 4326;
GO
ALTER TABLE Highways
  ADD CONSTRAINT enforce_geog_srid CHECK (GEOG.STSrid = 4326)
GO
```

Our next step is to create the index for the *GEOG* column. The parameters for the index were chosen for the fastest results with the associated query over a broad range of grid and *cells_per_object* combinations:

```
-----------------------------------------------------------
--Create the Spatial Index on GEOG Column
-----------------------------------------------------------
CREATE SPATIAL INDEX geog_mmmm_1024_sidx
   ON Highways(GEOG)
   USING GEOGRAPHY_GRID
   WITH (
    GRIDS = (MEDIUM, MEDIUM, MEDIUM, MEDIUM),
    CELLS_PER_OBJECT = 1024,
    PAD_INDEX = ON );
GO
-----------------------------------------------------------
--Query used to test the Spatial Index on GEOG Column
DECLARE @g GEOGRAPHY
SET @g = geography::STGeomFromText('POLYGON((
    -99 40, -97 40, -97 42, -99 42, -99 40))',4326)
SET STATISTICS TIME ON
SELECT * FROM Highways WITH(INDEX(geog_mmmm_1024_sidx))
  WHERE @g.STIntersects(GEOG)=1
SET STATISTICS TIME OFF
GO
```

Extending Spatial Support with CLR Routines

That SQL Server's spatial types are exposed as CLR types opens up some powerful opportunities for extending their functionality through SQL CLR. (Chapters 3, 4, 5, and 11 contain an introduction to CLR routines and several examples.) In addition, the types expose additional interfaces for the composition and decomposition of spatial objects that greatly enhance this extensibility.

In this section, we illustrate some of these techniques with a few practical examples.

Types on the Client

SQL Server's spatial types—GEOMETRY and GEOGRAPHY—are implemented as CLR types, and contained in the Microsoft.SqlServer.Types assembly. This assembly is included as part of the Microsoft SQL Server 2008 Feature Pack (*http://www.microsoft.com/downloads/ details.aspx?FamilyId=228DE03F-3B5A-428A-923F-58A033D316E1*) and can be used on a client, and it can even be used without SQL Server itself.

Except for indexing, the spatial types have the same functionality on the client as they do within SQL Server. The types themselves have different names: the CLR type *SqlGeometry* corresponds to SQL Server's GEOMETRY; *SqlGeography* corresponds to GEOGRAPHY.

User Defined Aggregate: Union and Dissolve

Our first task is to build a union aggregate. Although both the GEOMETRY and GEOGRAPHY types expose a *STUnion* method, this method only computes the union between two instances. There is no built-in mechanism for finding the union of a set of GEOMETRY or GEOGRAPHY instances. Building one is simple. We demonstrate a GEOGRAPHY example; GEOMETRY is equally easy.

We begin our code by including two required assemblies. Microsoft.SqlServer.Types contains our spatial types; Microsoft.SqlServer.Server contains the required *SqlUserDefinedAggregate* property. We then begin our aggregate, which will have its format set to *UserDefined* and its size set to –1 to accommodate a *SqlGeography* instance:

```
using Microsoft.SqlServer.Types;
using Microsoft.SqlServer.Server;

[SqlUserDefinedAggregate(
    Format.UserDefined,
    IsInvariantToDuplicates=true,
    IsInvariantToNulls=false,
    IsInvariantToOrder=true,
    IsNullIfEmpty=true,
    MaxByteSize=-1
)]
public class UnionAgg:IBinarySerialize
{
    SqlGeography union = SqlGeography.Null;
```

Next, because this aggregate uses *UserDefined* serialization, we must provide *Read* and *Write* methods. This is fairly boilerplate:

```
    public void Read(System.IO.BinaryReader r)
    {
        union = SqlGeography.Null;
        union.Read(r);
    }

    public void Write(System.IO.BinaryWriter w)
    {
        union.Write(w);
    }
```

Finally, we provide our core aggregate methods. The logic is very simple: keep a running result by unioning each new value seen in the *Accumulate* methods. The *Merge* method simply finds the union of the running value with that of the other aggregate:

```
    public void Init()
    {
        union = SqlGeography.Null;
    }
```

```
    public void Accumulate(SqlGeography geog)
    {
        if (union.IsNull) union = geog;
        else union = union.STUnion(geog);
    }

    public void Merge(UnionAgg other)
    {
        union = union.STUnion(other.union);
    }

    public SqlGeography Terminate()
    {
        return union;
    }
}
```

We can use this aggregate on the client, but we can make better use of it if we register it and use it in the server.

Note A bug in some builds of SQL Server 2008 can prevent the automatic deployment from Visual Studio of aggregates that specify *MaxSizeBytes* = –1. If you encounter this bug, you can deploy such aggregates manually.

```
USE Spatial -- database to enable with assembly
GO

-- deploy UnionAgg
-- UnionAgg.dll has been compiled to c:\temp directory

-- drop aggregate, if it exists
IF OBJECT_ID('dbo.UnionAgg', 'AF') IS NOT NULL
        DROP AGGREGATE UnionAgg;

-- drop assembly if it exists
IF ASSEMBLYPROPERTY('UnionAgg', 'SimpleName') IS NOT NULL
        DROP ASSEMBLY UnionAgg;
GO

CREATE ASSEMBLY UnionAgg
 FROM 'c:\temp\UnionAgg.dll'
GO

CREATE AGGREGATE dbo.UnionAgg(@g GEOGRAPHY)
  RETURNS GEOGRAPHY
  EXTERNAL NAME UnionAgg.UnionAgg
GO
```

For example, once the aggregate is registered as *UnionAgg*, we can run *UnionAgg* against a GEOGRAPHY column containing points:

```
CREATE TABLE #sample_table (
 id INT IDENTITY PRIMARY KEY,
 geog GEOGRAPHY
);
```

```
-- insert three points
-- SRID defaults to 4326
INSERT INTO #sample_table VALUES('POINT(1 2)'), ('POINT(2 3)'), ('POINT(3 4)');
GO


SELECT * FROM #sample_table
GO

-- use the aggregate
DECLARE @g GEOGRAPHY
SELECT @g = dbo.UnionAgg(geog) FROM #sample_table
SELECT @g.ToString()
GO
```

This results in the following output:

```
MULTIPOINT ((3 4), (2 3), (1 2))
```

Combining this aggregate union with a standard SQL GROUP BY statement, we can perform an operation often known as a *dissolve*. Using the Counties table from the Sample_USA database (illustrated in Figure 14-29) we dissolve the 58 California counties into a single California spatial object:

```
USE Sample_USA;
GO
--California Counties query (left-hand side of Figure 14-29
SELECT NAME_2, GEOG
  FROM Counties WHERE NAME_1 = 'California';
GO
--California State aggregate (right-hand side of Figure 14-29
SELECT NAME_1, dbo.UnionAgg(GEOG)
  FROM Counties WHERE NAME_1 = 'California'
    GROUP BY NAME_1;
GO
```

FIGURE 14-29 Results of the dissolve operation

Sinks and Builders: Linear Transformations

In addition to the usual SQL CLR functionality, some special extensibility contracts are exposed for spatial objects. There are essentially three components:

- *IGeometrySink* and *IGeographySink*   These interfaces have methods that allow for a full-fidelity description of any *SqlGeometry* or *SqlGeography* instance. The exact methods are shown later in this section.

- **Populate methods**   Both *SqlGeometry* and *SqlGeography* have a *Populate* method, which takes an instance of the corresponding sink type. When the method is called, the target instance makes appropriate calls on the sink to describe itself.

- *GeometryBuilder* and *GeographyBuilder*   These classes implement the corresponding sink interface, but produce a *SqlGeometry* or *SqlGeography* instance corresponding to the series of calls made to them.

As we will see, sinks are easily chained. In our example, we will build a sink that performs an arbitrary linear transformation on a GEOMETRY instance, and chain it with a *GeometryBuilder* to create a *SqlGeometry* for the result.

First, let's look a little more closely at the sink interface. We will concentrate on the *IGeometrySink*, but the methods are essentially the same for *IGeographySink*. The interface contains six methods that must be called in a given order:

- **void SetSrid(int srid)**   This method must be called first, and sets the SRID for the instance.

- **void *BeginGeometry(OpenGisGeometryType* type)**   After setting the SRID, we must start a GEOMETRY and tell the system what its type is. *OpenGisGeometryType* is an enum containing seven values corresponding to the seven instantiable OGC types.

- **void BeginFigure(double x, double y, double? z, double? m)**   Think of a *figure* as any element that can be drawn with a single stroke of a pen. The *BeginFigure* call puts the pen down at the given location.

- **void AddLine(double x, double y, double? z, double? m)**   Once the pen is down, any number of lines can be drawn. Each call to *AddLine* adds a line from the previous point to the point given.

- **void EndFigure()**   Once the figure is complete, a call to *EndFigure* picks up the pen. In the case of a point, this call will come immediately after a *BeginFigure* call; usually it follows an *AddLine* call. If the geometry contains more figures, another *BeginFigure* may follow.

- **void EndGeometry()**   *EndGeometry* is usually the last call in the chain, finishing the geometry. Other calls may follow if a collection is being described.

It is helpful to think of *BeginGeometry* and *EndGeometry*, and *BeginFigure* and *EndFigure* as parentheses: like parentheses, they must always match.

Recall that a linear transformation is simply a matrix multiplication. We will transform a point (x,y) to (x',y') by the following rule:

$$\begin{bmatrix} x' \\ y' \end{bmatrix} = \begin{bmatrix} a & b \\ c & d \end{bmatrix} \begin{bmatrix} x \\ y \end{bmatrix}$$

So:

$$x' = ax + by$$
$$y' = cx + dy$$

Let's now begin our linear transformation sink. First, our sink's constructor will take another sink as its target. Each of the sink methods will call the target, making any changes to the data as they pass through. This construction is what allows us to chain sinks in the future. In addition, we need the four parameters that define our linear transformation:

```
using Microsoft.SqlServer.Types;

class LinearTransformationSink : IGeometrySink
{
    IGeometrySink target;
    double a, b, c, d;

    public LinearTransformationSink(IGeometrySink target,
        double a, double b, double c, double d)
    {
        this.target = target;
        this.a = a;
        this.b = b;
        this.c = c;
        this.d = d;
    }
}
```

Next, we begin implementing our actual sink methods. The *SetSrid* and *BeginGeometry* calls will make no changes, and simply pass through to the target sink:

```
    public void SetSrid(int srid)
    {
        target.SetSrid(srid);
    }

    public void BeginGeometry(OpenGisGeometryType type)
    {
        target.BeginGeometry(type);
    }
```

BeginFigure and *AddLine* perform the actual linear transformation work. We encapsulate the transformations themselves in a pair of methods so we don't have to repeat the code:

```
double TransformX(double x, double y)
{
    return a * x + b * y;
}

double TransformY(double x, double y)
{
    return c * x + d * y;
}

public void BeginFigure(double x, double y, double? z, double? m)
{
    target.BeginFigure(TransformX(x, y), TransformY(x, y), z, m);
}

public void AddLine(double x, double y, double? z, double? m)
{
    target.AddLine(TransformX(x, y), TransformY(x, y), z, m);
}
```

Finally, we can finish our sink. The *EndFigure* and *EndGeometry* calls again simply pass through to the target:

```
public void EndFigure()
{
    target.EndFigure();
}

public void EndGeometry()
{
    target.EndGeometry();
}
}
```

This concludes the *LinearTransformationSink*. But we cannot use the sink directly within SQL Server, nor is it particularly convenient to use from the CLR. To complete the example, we wrap the sink in a function that connects two sinks—our transformer and a *SqlGeometryBuilder*—into a pipeline and then runs this pipeline:

```
using Microsoft.SqlServer.Types;

public class Functions
{
    public static SqlGeometry LinearTransformation(SqlGeometry geom,
        double a, double b, double c, double d)
    {
        // build a pipeline
        SqlGeometryBuilder builder = new SqlGeometryBuilder();
```

```
        LinearTransformationSink transformer =
                new LinearTransformationSink(builder, a, b, c, d);

        // run the pipeline
        geom.Populate(transformer);

        // return the result
        return builder.ConstructedGeometry;
    }
}
```

We can use this function on the client, but we can also register it through SQL CLR and use within the server as function *LinearTransformation*:

```
USE Spatial -- database to enable with assembly
GO

-- drop function, if it exists
IF OBJECT_ID('dbo.LinearTransformation', 'FS') IS NOT NULL
        DROP FUNCTION dbo.LinearTransformation;

-- drop assembly if it exists
IF ASSEMBLYPROPERTY('transformer', 'SimpleName') IS NOT NULL
        DROP ASSEMBLY transformer;
GO

CREATE ASSEMBLY transformer
 FROM 'c:\temp\GeometryLinearTransform.dll'
GO

CREATE FUNCTION dbo.LinearTransformation(
 @g GEOMETRY,
 @a FLOAT,
 @b FLOAT,
 @c FLOAT,
 @d FLOAT
)
RETURNS GEOMETRY
AS
EXTERNAL NAME transformer.Functions.LinearTransformation;
GO
```

Here is an example of the new T-SQL function *LinearTransformation* in use:

```
DECLARE @g GEOMETRY
SET @g = 'POLYGON((0 0, 5 0, 5 5, 0 5, 0 0))'
SELECT dbo.LinearTransformation(@g, 2, 3, 4, 5).ToString() AS TransformedWKT
GO
```

This results in the following output:

```
Transformed WKT
---------------
POLYGON ((0 0, 10 20, 25 45, 15 25, 0 0))
```

Figure 14-30 illustrates the original object, *@g* (square figure), and the transformed object from the query:

```
DECLARE @g GEOMETRY;
SET @g = 'POLYGON((0 0, 5 0, 5 5, 0 5, 0 0))'
SELECT dbo.LinearTransformation(@g, 2, 3, 4, 5)
UNION ALL
SELECT @g;
```

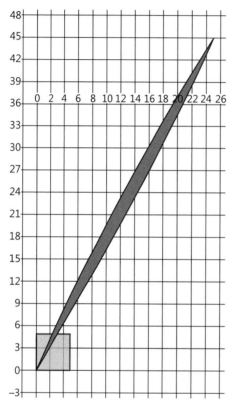

FIGURE 14-30 Illustration of the *LinearTransformation* function

Conclusion

The material presented in this chapter provide all users, including those new to spatial, the concepts and tools to successfully get started with SQL Server 2008 spatial. For more advanced users, this chapter introduces the basis for extending the spatial model with new T-SQL functions beyond the scope of the original design. As SQL Server matures and spatial type support becomes more ubiquitous, this chapter will be invaluable as an aid to fully using these important new types. A case in point, Microsoft has just released the first public beta of SQL Server 2008 R2 that includes a new Map Report Builder. Although it is relatively easy to generate your first map using this new tool, mastering the basic content of this chapter will provide a much rewarding experience.

Chapter 15
Tracking Access and Changes to Data

Greg Low

Microsoft SQL Server 2008 introduced a number of new technologies related to tracking changes to data. Although alternatives have been available for this in earlier versions of the product, tracking access to data has been more difficult in the past. SQL Server 2008 helps address this need.

Which Technology Do I Use?

We need to track access and changes to data for several reasons:

- Auditing and compliance have become very important issues in recent years. We need to be able to answer questions on who accessed which data and when they did it.

- We need to be able to support occasionally connected systems and mobile workforces.

- We need to be able to incrementally load data warehouse systems.

We can use a number of technologies to tackle this problem, depending upon the version of SQL Server that we are using.

Approaches Using Earlier SQL Server Versions

In earlier versions of SQL Server, the approaches commonly involved a mixture of:

- SQL Trace
- DML triggers
- DDL triggers
- DMVs and third-party tools

One question regularly asked in the newsgroups was "How can I create a SELECT trigger?" This was not an available option, but the question demonstrated a clear user need.

Technologies Added in SQL Server 2008

At first glance, many of the technologies added in SQL Server 2008 (change tracking, change data capture, Extended Events, and SQL Server Audit) appear to offer duplicated or overlapping capabilities; however, each has a target use case. In the first section of this chapter, I will start by providing guidance on where each of these new technologies is best used. I will then move on to describing how to implement each technology.

Extended Events

Extended Events is the name given to a new low-level (and low-impact) eventing infrastructure built directly inside the SQL Server engine. The engine is built in a generic fashion where it isn't constrained by the content of events. Event consumers are quite separate and any target can consume any event. Events are processed synchronously but can be directed to either synchronous or asynchronous targets. Predicates can be used to filter the events to minimize the amount of event data produced and actions can be defined to add additional information that needs to be collected when an event occurs.

One key advantage of this new eventing system is that it can be fully controlled through T-SQL, unlike interfaces such as SQL Trace. Another is that we can monitor processes while they are active with minimal impact on them.

Support for Event Tracing for Windows (ETW) was introduced in ADO.NET v2. The Extended Events system in SQL Server 2008 now also supports ETW as a target. This makes it possible to trace a query in detail from outside SQL Server, through the client libraries, into SQL Server, and back out again.

As an alternative to using ETW as a target, Extended Events provides the ability to send event details either synchronously or asynchronously to a file or a variety of other targets including in-memory ring buffers.

SQL Server Audit

Organizations are being forced to comply with an ever-increasing set of auditing requirements for their data. The European Union Data Protection Directive, HIPAA (the Health Insurance Portability and Accountability Act), Sarbanes-Oxley (corporation law in the United States), PCI-CISP (Payment Card Industry Cardholder Information Security Program), and many others can impact a company's data handling.

Pre-SQL Server 2008 systems typically used DML triggers to implement auditing of data changes, but it was difficult to audit access to data within the database tier.

SQL Server Audit is focused on compliance. We can use it to audit DML operations (including SELECT), DDL operations, GRANT/DENY permissions, login and logout operations, and many others. This avoids the need for many custom tools and is much easier to work with than

SQL Trace. Centralizing of logs is also possible when combining auditing with tools such as Microsoft's operation management toolset.

Auditing is implemented by hooking directly into permission checks within the engine. When a permission check occurs, a record is generated if the event is configured. The auditing infrastructure has been built over Extended Events as a private event session.

Change Tracking

Increasingly, organizations need to support occasionally connected applications or mobile workforces. Many such organizations have created custom replication schemes to deal with these scenarios.

Change tracking in SQL Server 2008 records details of which rows have changed. It is done synchronously as part of the implicit transaction when an INSERT, DELETE, MERGE, or UPDATE statement is executed. This means it can have a potential performance hit but it is the easiest of the new technologies to implement.

Tables used with change tracking must have a primary key. All SQL Server 2008 editions support change tracking and there is no dependency on SQL Server Agent. It's important to note that it can be implemented without changing the source table's schema, and this helps in integrating with existing applications.

Change tracking has relatively low disk space requirements because it only tracks details of which rows have been modified and, optionally, a bitmask that indicates which columns have been updated. Copies of the modified data are not held. The assumption is that the client application will only want the current version of the updated row that it can obtain directly from the source table.

ADO.NET Sync Services (part of the Microsoft Sync Framework) has added direct support of change tracking for SQL Server 2008.

Change Data Capture

Change data capture is the last of the technologies that will be covered in this chapter. Although on the surface it looks related to change tracking, it operates through a SQL Agent job reading the database transaction log and recording data changes into a series of change tracking tables. These tables are later cleaned up by another SQL Agent job and queried by a series of functions also provided by change data capture.

Because change data capture operates through a log reading process, it has little impact on the source application. It is not suitable for auditing because details of who made the changes are not available from the transaction log and thus can't be returned by queries on the change tables.

Change data capture is ideal for incremental population of data warehouses.

Extended Events Implementation

Before beginning an implementation of Extended Events, it is useful to spend some time exploring the most important objects provided. This can help you visualize the terminology used and also to understand the standard objects that have been delivered with the system.

If you only intend to use SQL Server Audit, you can do so without a detailed understanding of Extended Events and you may wish to skip directly to the "SQL Server Audit Implementation" section of this chapter. However, SQL Server Audit is based on Extended Events and you will have a better understanding of SQL Server Audit if you first have a better understanding of Extended Events.

We'll start with a good grounding on the major objects that make up the Extended Events feature. Later we'll look at how we use them by working through a full scenario. You'll also learn about some of the other objects while implementing the scenario. We'll finish this section with some details on managing Extended Events.

Extended Events Object Hierarchy

The most important objects are modules, packages, events, predicates, actions, maps, and targets. Details of these are mainly visible through the *sys.dm_xe_packages* and *sys.dm_xe_objects* DMVs.

Modules

The top-level container in the Extended Events system is the module. It is a representation of the executable or DLL that exposes packages. All shipped packages are contained within a single module. The following query can be executed to return a list of installed packages and the GUID of the module that exposes the package:

```
SELECT name,module_guid FROM sys.dm_xe_packages;
```

The results obtained should be similar to the following:

```
name       module_guid
---------  ------------------------------------
package0   CE79811F-1A80-40E1-8F5D-7445A3F375E7
sqlos      CE79811F-1A80-40E1-8F5D-7445A3F375E7
sqlserver  CE79811F-1A80-40E1-8F5D-7445A3F375E7
SecAudit   CE79811F-1A80-40E1-8F5D-7445A3F375E7
```

Note that the *package_guid* is identical for the four packages initially installed. These packages are all part of the sqlserver.exe module.

Packages

Packages are containers for objects and are the unit that is exposed from within a module. As seen in the previous example, four packages are shipped with SQL Server 2008. The following query can be executed to obtain further details of these packages:

```
SELECT name,capabilities,description FROM sys.dm_xe_packages;
```

This query returns the following output (wrapped for clarity):

```
name        capabilities description
---------   ------------ -------------------------------------------------
package0    256          Default package. Contains all standard types, maps,
                         compare operators, actions and targets
sqlos       NULL         Extended events for SQL Operating System
sqlserver   NULL         Extended events for Microsoft SQL Server
SecAudit    1            Security Audit Events
```

Note that the *SecAudit* and *package0* packages have different values in the *capabilities* column. The value of 1 indicates that it is a private package. The value 256 that is associated with *package0* indicates that it is a utility package. The column holds a bitmap, and you can see its possible values with the following query:

```
SELECT DISTINCT capabilities,capabilities_desc
FROM sys.dm_xe_objects;
```

It returns the following results:

```
capabilities capabilities_desc
------------ -----------------------------
NULL         NULL
1            private
256          process_whole_buffers
256          sign_extended
257          private process_whole_buffers
512          ieee754
1024         no_block
1024         synchronous
1025         private synchronous
1536         singleton synchronous
```

As an example of the bitmap nature of this column, notice that 257 represents both *private* (which as mentioned is value 1) and *process_whole_buffers* (value 256). Another important concept shown here is that the values can be package-specific.

Two rows have been returned for the value 1024. We can use the following query to see which packages use which meanings for the *capabilities* value 1024:

```
SELECT DISTINCT capabilities_desc, package_guid
FROM sys.dm_xe_objects
WHERE capabilities = 1024
ORDER BY package_guid;
```

This query returns the following results:

```
capabilities_desc package_guid
----------------- ----------------------------------
no_block          655FD93F-3364-40D5-B2BA-330F7FFB6491
no_block          BD97CC63-3F38-4922-AA93-607BD12E78B2
synchronous       60AA9FBF-673B-4553-B7ED-71DCA7F5E972
```

It is important to avoid assigning specific meanings to capability values across packages.

Events

Events are the points during SQL Server execution where SQL Server can notify us that something we have told it we are interested in has occurred. In the initial release of SQL Server 2008, 254 events were installed. You can see all of them grouped by package by running the following query:

```
SELECT dxp.[name] AS Package,
       dxo.[name] AS EventName,
       dxo.capabilities_desc AS Capabilities,
       dxo.[description] AS Description
FROM sys.dm_xe_packages AS dxp
INNER JOIN sys.dm_xe_objects AS dxo
ON dxp.[guid] = dxo.package_guid
WHERE dxo.object_type = 'event'
ORDER BY Package,EventName;
```

These events are very similar to the events you may be familiar with from SQL Server Profiler. They are not an identical set of events, but some events are common to both sets, such as *sql_statement_completed*.

Predicates

Similar to the way we can filter results in Profiler, the Extended Events system provides a set of predicates for filtering. Most important, these predicates are applied prior to any actions defined on the Event. This minimizes the number of events that the actions need to be processed for. You can execute the following query to see the available predicates:

```
SELECT dxp.[name] AS Package,
       dxo.[name] AS Predicate,
       dxo.[description] AS Description
FROM sys.dm_xe_packages AS dxp
INNER JOIN sys.dm_xe_objects AS dxo
ON dxp.[guid] = dxo.package_guid
WHERE dxo.object_type IN ('pred_compare','pred_source')
ORDER BY Package,Predicate;
```

Actions

Again, similar to the way Profiler operates, when an event occurs, a specific set of data is collected. Using the *sql_statement_completed* event as an example, we can see the columns returned by an event with a query like this:

```
SELECT column_id AS ID,
       [name] AS Name,
       [type_name] AS DataType,
       column_type AS ColumnType,
       [description] AS Description
FROM sys.dm_xe_object_columns
WHERE object_name = 'sql_statement_completed'
ORDER BY ColumnType DESC, ID;
```

The query returns the following results:

```
ID Name                   DataType    ColumnType Description
-- ---------------------- ----------- ---------- --------------------
0  ID                     uint16      readonly   Numeric ID
1  UUID                   guid_ptr    readonly   Globally Unique ID
2  VERSION                uint8       readonly   Event schema version
3  CHANNEL                etw_channel readonly   ETW Channel
4  KEYWORD                keyword_map readonly   Associated Keyword
0  source_database_id     uint16      data       NULL
1  object_id              uint32      data       NULL
2  object_type            uint16      data       NULL
3  cpu                    uint32      data       NULL
4  duration               int64       data       NULL
5  reads                  uint64      data       NULL
6  writes                 uint64      data       NULL
```

The last seven values in this list probably look the most familiar. However, if you have used Profiler in the past, you realize that there are normally other columns that you can choose to record when an event occurs.

The standard columns available via *sys.dm_xe_object_columns* aren't the only data we can collect during an event. Other data is collected via *actions*. You can see the available actions by executing the following query:

```
SELECT dxp.[name] AS Package,
       dxo.[name] AS ActionName,
       dxo.[description] AS Description,
       dxo.[type_name] AS TypeName
FROM sys.dm_xe_packages AS dxp
INNER JOIN sys.dm_xe_objects AS dxo
ON dxp.[guid] = dxo.package_guid
WHERE dxo.object_type = 'action'
ORDER BY Package,ActionName;
```

This query returns the following result (wrapped for clarity):

Package	ActionName	Description	TypeName
package0	attach_activity_id	Attach an activity ID to an event	activity_id
package0	attach_activity_id_xfer	Attach an activity ID transfer to an event	activity_id_xfer
package0	callstack	16-frame call stack	callstack
package0	collect_cpu_cycle_time	Collect the current CPU's cycle count	cpu_cycle
package0	collect_system_time	Collect the current system time with 100 microsecond precision and interrupt tick resolution	filetime
package0	debug_break	Break the process in the default debugger	null
sqlos	cpu_id	Collect current CPU ID	uint32
sqlos	node_affinity	Collect current NUMA node affinity	uint64
sqlos	scheduler_address	Collect current scheduler address	ulong_ptr
sqlos	scheduler_id	Collect current scheduler ID	uint32
sqlos	sos_context	Collect useful information related to SOS	sos_context
sqlos	system_thread_id	Collect current system thread ID	uint32
sqlos	task_address	Collect current task address	ulong_ptr
sqlos	task_elapsed_quantum	Collect current task quantum time	uint64
sqlos	task_resource_group_id	Collect current task resource group ID	uint32
sqlos	task_resource_pool_id	Collect current task resource pool ID	uint32
sqlos	task_time	Collect current task execution time	uint64
sqlos	worker_address	Collect current worker address	ulong_ptr
sqlserver	client_app_name	Collect client application name	unicode_string
sqlserver	client_hostname	Collect client hostname	unicode_string
sqlserver	client_pid	Collect client process ID	uint32
sqlserver	create_dump_all_threads	Create mini dump including all threads	null
sqlserver	create_dump_single_thread	Create mini dump for the current thread	null
sqlserver	database_context	Collect useful infomation related to the current database	database_context
sqlserver	database_id	Collect database ID	uint16
sqlserver	is_system	Collect whether current session is system	Boolean
sqlserver	nt_username	Collect NT username	unicode_string
sqlserver	plan_handle	Collect plan handle	unicode_string
sqlserver	request_id	Collect current request ID	uint32
sqlserver	session_id	Collect session ID	uint16
sqlserver	session_nt_username	Collect session's NT username	unicode_string
sqlserver	session_resource_group_id	Collect current session resource group ID	uint32
sqlserver	session_resource_pool_id	Collect current session resource pool ID	uint32
sqlserver	sql_text	Collect SQL text	unicode_string
sqlserver	transaction_id	Collect transaction ID	int64
sqlserver	tsql_stack	Collect Transact-SQL stack	unicode_string
sqlserver	username	Collect username	unicode_string

It is important to realize that not all actions are available for collection during all events and that they are processed after predicates to minimize processing overhead.

Maps

Maps are similar to enumerated values in .NET programming. They are used to provide a description of values that are stored as their numeric equivalent. You can see the available maps by executing this command:

```
SELECT dxp.[name] AS Package,
       dxo.[name] AS MapName,
       dxo.[description] AS Description
FROM sys.dm_xe_packages AS dxp
INNER JOIN sys.dm_xe_objects AS dxo
ON dxp.[guid] = dxo.package_guid
WHERE dxo.object_type = 'map'
ORDER BY Package,MapName;
```

The list returned by this query includes names such as *lock_mode* and *lock_owner_type*. Each of these has a set of defined values, which can be found in *sys.dm_xe_map_values*. As an example, the following query returns the defined values for *lock_owner_type*:

```
SELECT map_key,
       map_value
FROM sys.dm_xe_map_values
WHERE [name] = 'lock_owner_type'
ORDER BY map_key;
```

The query returns the following list:

```
map_key     map_value
----------- -----------------------------------
1           Transaction
2           Cursor
3           Session
4           SharedXactWorkspace
5           ExclusiveXactWorkspace
6           WaitForResultsNotificationObject
7           LockTableIterator
8           LastLockInfoOwner
```

If you saw the value 2 being returned for a lock owner type, you could examine this view to determine that a cursor owned the lock.

Targets

The final object that we need to be familiar with is the *target*. Event records are sent to targets. You can see the available targets by executing the following query:

```
SELECT dxp.[name] AS Package,
       dxo.[name] AS TargetName,
       dxo.[description] AS Description
```

```
FROM sys.dm_xe_packages AS dxp
INNER JOIN sys.dm_xe_objects AS dxo
ON dxp.[guid] = dxo.package_guid
WHERE dxo.object_type = 'target'
ORDER BY Package,TargetName;
```

This query returns the following list of targets (wrapped for clarity):

```
Package   TargetName                                          Description
--------  -------------------------------------------------   ------------------------------
package0  asynchronous_bucketizer                             Asynchronous bucketizing target
package0  asynchronous_file_target                            Asynchronous file target
package0  etw_classic_sync_target                             Event Tracing for Windows
                                                              (ETW) Synchronous Target
package0  pair_matching                                       Pairing target
package0  ring_buffer                                         Asynchronous ring buffer target
package0  synchronous_bucketizer                              Synchronous bucketizing target
package0  synchronous_event_counter                           Synchronous Counter target
SecAudit  asynchronous_security_audit_event_log_target        Asynchronous security audit NT
                                                              event log target
SecAudit  asynchronous_security_audit_file_target             Asynchronous security audit file
                                                              Target
SecAudit  asynchronous_security_audit_security_log_target Asynchronous security audit NT
                                                              security log target
SecAudit  synchronous_security_audit_event_log_target         Synchronous security audit NT event
                                                              log target
SecAudit  synchronous_security_audit_file_target              Synchronous security audit file
                                                              Target
SecAudit  synchronous_security_audit_security_log_target   Synchronous security audit NT
                                                              security log target
```

The two general categories of targets are synchronous and asynchronous. Rows sent to synchronous targets are sent in the context of the event that causes them to be captured. This can slow down the processing of the original code that fired the event. Asynchronous targets buffer the event rows for later processing. They have much less impact on the processing at the event time.

A few specific target types deserve particular mention.

Bucketizing targets differ from other targets in that they collect events and only output values associated with a "bucket" of events. For example, a target that counts the occurrences of an event would be considered a Bucketizing target.

The pairing—or Pair Matching—target is particularly interesting. It matches together related events. For example, a lock-acquired event could be matched with a lock-released event. Once paired, the events are usually discarded. This allows you to easily locate locks that have been acquired but not released.

The Ring Buffer target is useful for quick checks for events that don't generate too much data. The event rows are sent into a ring held in memory. This allows us to avoid being concerned about excess memory usage when buffering event rows in memory; however, the event rows will only be kept until overwritten. When configuring the Ring Buffer target, we can specify a value for *default_memory*—which is the total amount of memory to use, in KB—and the *occurrence_number*, which is the preferred number of events of each type to keep in the buffer.

Implementing a Scenario Using Extended Events

In this section, we'll look at a complete scenario from end to end using Extended Events. We're trying to locate those queries executed against the database that are taking more than 4,000 logical reads.

We need to create an EVENT SESSION using a command like the following:

```
CREATE EVENT SESSION High_Logical_Read_Queries
ON SERVER
ADD EVENT sqlserver.sql_statement_completed
  (ACTION (sqlserver.database_id,
           sqlserver.sql_text)
   WHERE reads > 4000)
ADD TARGET package0.asynchronous_file_target
  (SET filename=N'c:\temp\High_Logical_Read_Queries.xel')
WITH (MAX_DISPATCH_LATENCY = 1 SECONDS);
```

We have called our event session *High_Logical_Read_Queries* and declared that it applies at the SERVER level. This is currently the only allowable level for event sessions. To simulate an event session at the database level, we can filter a server-level session on the *database_id* column returned by the *sqlserver* package.

To be useful, the event session needs at least one event and at least one target. We have selected the *sql_statement_completed* event exposed by the *sqlserver* package. Whenever this event occurs, we need additional actions to occur, as we need more information than is collected in the standard columns. We have requested that the *database_id* and *sql_text* columns are also populated, via actions also exposed by the *sqlserver* package. To avoid excessive event records, we have specified a predicate to limit the records to those with a *reads* value higher than 4,000.

As shown earlier, there are a number of permissible targets, but for general production use, the *asynchronous_file_target* exposed by the *package0* package is likely to be the most commonly used, because it has minimal impact on the production processing. In this case we have specified that it should write to a file with an .xel extension and that the event data should be written with a maximum latency of 1 second. (Note that the syntax requires the term SECONDS without a singular option.)

We can now start our event session by executing the following command:

```
ALTER EVENT SESSION High_Logical_Read_Queries
ON SERVER STATE = START;
```

If you look in your C:\TEMP folder, you'll find that more than one file was created and that it doesn't have the name you specified. When I executed the command, the files created were:

```
High_Logical_Read_Queries_0_128835352113830000.xel
High_Logical_Read_Queries_0_128835352114230000.xem
```

The first file holds the event records. We specified the name as High_Logical_Read_Queries. xel. SQL Server has appended a file counter _0_ to this as well as a value representing the current time. The second file is used to hold metadata associated with the event records. We'll learn more about that later.

At any time, we can query the current contents of this file by executing this query:

```
SELECT *
FROM sys.fn_xe_file_target_read_file
('c:\temp\*.xel','c:\temp\*.xem',NULL,NULL);
```

This command will query any of the files produced. Alternately, you can specify the full name of both the event log file and the metadata file to read just a single file. If the folder contains a number of files and you want to start reading from a specific file, you can supply the name of the first file to read as the optional third parameter (NULL in the preceding code). If you do specify the initial file, you must also supply the fourth parameter, which is a byte offset at which to start reading within the file.

At this point we won't have any entries in our log file, so we should generate some. If we execute the following commands, we will generate some entries.

```
USE InsideTSQL2008;
GO
SELECT * FROM Production.Products;
GO
SELECT * FROM Production.Products WHERE unitprice > 10;
GO
SELECT *
FROM Production.Products AS p
CROSS JOIN Sales.OrderDetails AS od;
GO
```

If we check our log file again, we'll find that an event has been added, containing *module_guid, package_guid, object_name, event_data,* and *file_name.* A quick scan of the output would show that the column of interest to us is the *event_data* column. It contains XML data regarding the event. Note that it isn't returned as an XML column, but we can CAST it to XML via the following command:

```
SELECT CAST(event_data AS XML) AS EventLog
FROM sys.fn_xe_file_target_read_file
('c:\temp\*.xel','c:\temp\*.xem',NULL,NULL);
```

It returns the following structure (formatted for clarity):

```
<event name="sql_statement_completed" package="sqlserver"
       id="60" version="1" timestamp="2009-04-07T00:05:19.137Z">
  <data name="source_database_id">
    <value>10</value>
    <text />
  </data>
  <data name="object_id">
    <value>787488078</value>
    <text />
  </data>
  <data name="object_type">
    <value>20801</value>
    <text />
  </data>
  <data name="cpu">
    <value>218</value>
    <text />
  </data>
  <data name="duration">
    <value>4764272</value>
    <text />
  </data>
  <data name="reads">
    <value>5337</value>
    <text />
  </data>
  <data name="writes">
    <value>11</value>
    <text />
  </data>
  <action name="database_id" package="sqlserver">
    <value>10</value>
    <text />
  </action>
  <action name="sql_text" package="sqlserver">
    <value>SELECT *
FROM Production.Products AS p
CROSS JOIN Sales.OrderDetails AS od;
</value>
    <text />
  </action>
</event>
```

In this XML structure, note that the standard columns are returned along with the two additional values *database_id* and *sql_text* that were added via our ACTION clause. It's worth noting at this point that the *sql_text* column returns the entire batch that was being executed, rather than just the SQL statement involved.

If you haven't already, I'm sure that at this point you've started to realize that some skill manipulating XML is important for anyone wanting to develop advanced DBA skills in SQL

Server. We can use the preceding log query as a derived table and extract relational values directly from it via the *.value()* method of the XML data type:

```
SELECT
        EventLog.value('(/event[@name="sql_statement_completed"]/@timestamp)[1]',
                       'datetime') AS LogTime,
        EventLog.value('(/event/data[@name="reads"]/value)[1]',
                       'int') AS Reads,
        EventLog.value('(/event/action[@name="sql_text"]/value)[1]',
                       'varchar(max)') AS SQL_Text
FROM ( SELECT CAST(event_data AS XML) AS EventLog
       FROM sys.fn_xe_file_target_read_file
       ('c:\temp\*.xel','c:\temp\*.xem',NULL,NULL)
     ) AS LogRecord
ORDER BY LogTime;
```

On my system, this command returned the following output (wrapped for clarity):

```
LogTime                 Reads SQL_Text
----------------------- ----- -----------------------------------
2009-04-07 00:05:19.137 5337  SELECT *
                              FROM Production.Products AS p
                              CROSS JOIN Sales.OrderDetails AS od;
```

At this point, we have achieved our original objective of locating commands exceeding 4,000 logical reads.

Exploring Extended Events Concepts

Now that we have seen how to implement a scenario using Extended Events, it is worth spending some time further exploring some of the concepts involved. We'll look further at the *asynchronous_file_target*, then explore some management aspects of Extended Events sessions.

Asynchronous File Target

Recall that we specified MAX_DISPATCH_LATENCY in our scenario. This is an event session option that we used to make sure that our file is written relatively quickly. In practice, we probably would want the latency value to be higher to even further minimize the impact on production. Updating the file every 10 seconds (or less often) rather than every second is likely to be suitable in this case.

In addition, we can specify parameter values for each target. We can also limit the size of the file produced by specifying the *max_file_size* property (specified in MB). If not specified, the default is to fill the entire disk. If *max_file_size* is specified, you can also limit the number of files into which events will roll over via *max_rollover_files*, and you can control how much space is allocated each time the file grows via an *increment* property (also specified in MB). It is important to keep the increment value high enough to avoid unnecessary fragmentation of the file system.

Viewing Existing Sessions

Details of current sessions are exposed via another set of system views. We can start exploring these with the following query:

```
SELECT [name] AS SessionName,
       total_buffer_size AS BufferSize,
       buffer_policy_desc AS Policy,
       flag_desc AS Flags,
       create_time AS CreateTime
FROM sys.dm_xe_sessions;
```

On my system, this returned the following:

```
SessionName                 BufferSize Policy     Flags          CreateTime
--------------------------- ---------- ---------- -------------- -----------------------
system_health               4324761    drop_event flush_on_close 2009-04-06 11:42:19.930
High_Logical_Read_Queries   4324761    drop_event flush_on_close 2009-04-06 16:46:51.107
```

Note that another event session had already been created during installation. This *system_health* session will be a good example for us to explore further, and we can start exploring it by executing the following query:

```
SELECT column_name AS ColumnName,
       column_value AS Value,
       object_type AS ObjectType,
       [object_name] AS ObjectName
FROM sys.dm_xe_sessions AS s
INNER JOIN sys.dm_xe_session_object_columns AS c
ON s.address = c.event_session_address
WHERE s.[name] = 'system_health'
ORDER BY c.column_id;
```

This query returns the following results:

```
ColumnName         Value ObjectType ObjectName
------------------ ----- ---------- --------------------------------------------------
max_memory         4096  target     ring_buffer
collect_call_stack 0     event      scheduler_monitor_non_yielding_ring_buffer_recorded
occurrence_number  0     target     ring_buffer
```

We can see that this event session is used to locate non-yielding situations related to the scheduler monitor. The following query shows the events that this session is tracking:

```
SELECT a.event_name AS EventName,
       CAST(a.event_predicate AS XML) AS Predicate
FROM sys.dm_xe_sessions AS s
INNER JOIN sys.dm_xe_session_events AS a
ON s.address = a.event_session_address
WHERE s.[name] = 'system_health'
ORDER BY EventName;
```

This returns the following results (wrapped and truncated for clarity):

```
EventName                                                Predicate
-------------------------------------------------------- -------------------------------------
error_reported                                           <or><leaf><comparator
                                                         name="greater_than_equal_int64"
                                                         package="package0" /><event
                                                         name="error_reported"
                                                         package="sqlserver" field="severity" />
                                                         <value>20</value></leaf>
                                                         <or><or><or><or><or><or>
                                                         <leaf><comparator name="equal_int64"
                                                         package="package0" /><event
scheduler_monitor_non_yielding_ring_buffer_recorded NULL
wait_info                                                Predicate too large for display
wait_info_external                                       Predicate too large for display
xml_deadlock_report                                      NULL
```

We can also see the actions associated with these events by running the following query:

```
SELECT a.event_name AS EventName,
       a.action_name AS ActionName
FROM sys.dm_xe_sessions AS s
INNER JOIN sys.dm_xe_session_event_actions AS a
ON s.address = a.event_session_address
WHERE s.[name] = 'system_health'
ORDER BY EventName,ActionName;
```

This returns the following:

```
EventName           ActionName
------------------- ----------
error_reported      callstack
error_reported      session_id
error_reported      sql_text
error_reported      tsql_stack
wait_info           callstack
wait_info           session_id
wait_info           sql_text
wait_info_external  callstack
wait_info_external  session_id
wait_info_external  sql_text
```

This shows us the additional information that is being collected when these events occur. Finally, we can explore where the information for these events is being sent by executing the following command:

```
SELECT t.target_name AS TargetName,
       t.execution_count AS Executions,
       t.execution_duration_ms AS Duration,
       CAST(t.target_data AS XML) AS TargetData
FROM sys.dm_xe_sessions AS s
INNER JOIN sys.dm_xe_session_targets AS t
ON s.address = t.event_session_address
```

```
WHERE s.[name] = 'system_health'
ORDER BY TargetName;
```

This command returns the following target list (wrapped for clarity):

```
TargetName  Executions Duration TargetData
----------- ---------- -------- -----------------------------------------------
ring_buffer 0          0        <RingBufferTarget eventsPerSec="0"
                                processingTime="0" totalEventsProcessed="0"
                                eventCount="0" droppedCount="0" memoryUsed="0" />
```

We can see from this that the *system_health* event session sends output to a ring buffer target.

Managing Existing Event Sessions

An interesting target that can be used with Extended Events is the Event Tracing for Windows (ETW) target. This allows Extended Events within SQL Server to be combined with events from other Windows services. ADO.NET has included support for ETW since v2.0. Although out of scope for this book, it's worth noting that ETW support makes it possible to trace an event from outside SQL Server, through the client stack, through SQL Server, and back to the client. If the ETW target is used, the SQL Server Service account needs to be a member of two Active Directory groups: the Performance Monitor Users group and the Performance Log Users group. Assigning (or modifying) the service account via SQL Server Configuration Manager can help ensure this.

Stopping and Altering Event Sessions

We can stop our event session by executing the following command:

```
ALTER EVENT SESSION High_Logical_Read_Queries
ON SERVER STATE = STOP;
```

We can completely delete our event session by executing the following command:

```
DROP EVENT SESSION High_Logical_Read_Queries
ON SERVER;
```

Had we decided to monitor other events while our event session was running, we would not have needed to stop the session. Adding events to a running event session is permitted. We could have added transaction tracking via the following command:

```
ALTER EVENT SESSION High_Logical_Read_Queries ON SERVER
ADD EVENT sqlserver.database_transaction_begin,
ADD EVENT sqlserver.database_transaction_end;
```

It is also possible to dynamically remove events from a session via the DROP EVENT option of the same command.

SQL Server Audit Implementation

Before beginning an implementation of SQL Server Audit, it is useful to spend some time exploring the most important objects provided. This can help with visualizing the terminology used and to also understand the standard objects that have been delivered with the system.

As we did with Extended Events, we'll start with coverage of the major objects that make up SQL Server Audit. Later we'll look at how we use them, by working through a full scenario involving them. Again, we'll also learn about some of the other objects while we are implementing the scenario. We'll finish this section with some details on viewing existing audits and managing them.

Auditing Object Hierarchy

SQL Server Audit is an extension of the Extended Events infrastructure provided in SQL Server 2008. Audit objects are created as secure objects and flagged as Private (they are system objects that users may not alter). Before showing how to use SQL Server Audit, I will spend some time providing a description of the objects and terminology involved.

Audit

When I began investigating SQL Server Audit, I found the way that the term *audit* had been used was confusing. I tend to think of an audit as an action that someone performs, rather than the output of the action.

In SQL Server Audit, an *audit* is the destination for audit records, not the action of recording them. It maps to a target in the underlying Extended Events infrastructure. Audits don't contain details about what is being audited. They are the destinations for audit records.

We are provided with three destination options. We can log to a file in a proprietary binary format not intended to be read by users or administrators or to either the Security or Application Event logs in Windows. Details of the format of the log records can be seen in the SQL Server 2008 Books Online topic SQL Server Audit Records. File records are not encrypted by SQL Server. Records are limited in size, and if more data needs to be stored, multiple records are chained together with a sequence number providing the order.

Audits are created at the SQL Server instance level, not at the database level. More than one audit can be created on each instance, usually to separate events for later processing.

An important concern for any database auditing system is what happens when the server cannot write to the audit log file for some reason. Often this will happen because of a lack of disk space. SQL Server can be configured so that if an audit can't be written, the server will refuse to carry out further actions and shut down. Administrators can restart the service in single-user mode using the *–m* switch. It allows for changes to the audit configuration. A typical change would involve pointing the audit records to another file location, by creating a new audit and modifying the audit specifications that reference it. While in single-user mode, auditing is still enabled and only the shutdown action that would stop an audit is disabled. SQL Server will continue to collect audit records in a memory buffer and will attempt to flush them to an audit as soon as possible.

Creating an audit requires the ALTER ANY SERVER AUDIT permission. Users with CONTROL SERVER permission do not separately require this permission, as the CONTROL SERVER permission covers the ALTER ANY SERVER AUDIT permission.

Another important decision relates to how many audit records it is acceptable to lose on some forms of server failure. The choice made for the QUEUE_DELAY audit option (on the CREATE SERVER AUDIT command described later) determines whether a synchronous or asynchronous target is created within Extended Events. Setting the QUEUE_DELAY to zero causes a synchronous target to be selected, and all audit records are written to the audit as soon as they are generated. This can clearly have a performance impact on the production system's processing. Setting any other value indicates how long SQL Server can buffer the records (in milliseconds) before flushing them to the audit. The minimum permitted value is 1,000 (1 second), and this is the default value.

The other key configurations specified at the audit level are MAXSIZE and MAX_ROLLOVER_FILES. Note that these are options to the CREATE SERVER AUDIT command, rather than the parameters with the same names that were mentioned earlier. These determine how big the audit files can become and how many older files will be kept. Once the number of files specified in MAX_ROLLOVER_FILES has been reached, the oldest file is deleted each time a new file is created.

To avoid issues with running out of disk space for audits, SQL Server also permits you to reserve disk space at the time of creation of an audit.

Server Audit Specification

Once we have established where the audit records will be written via the audit object, we need to determine the events that will be logged. A server audit specification determines which server-level actions will be audited.

At the server level, we are only able to select action groups (predefined sets of actions), rather than individual actions. You can see the available groups by querying the *sys.dm_audit_actions* view:

```
SELECT DISTINCT a.containing_group_name AS ActionGroup
FROM sys.dm_audit_actions AS a
WHERE a.class_desc = 'SERVER'
ORDER BY ActionGroup;
```

This returns the following result:

```
ActionGroup
---------------------------------------
APPLICATION_ROLE_CHANGE_PASSWORD_GROUP
AUDIT_CHANGE_GROUP
BACKUP_RESTORE_GROUP
BROKER_LOGIN_GROUP
DATABASE_CHANGE_GROUP
DATABASE_MIRRORING_LOGIN_GROUP
DATABASE_OBJECT_ACCESS_GROUP
DATABASE_OBJECT_CHANGE_GROUP
DATABASE_OBJECT_OWNERSHIP_CHANGE_GROUP
DATABASE_OBJECT_PERMISSION_CHANGE_GROUP
DATABASE_OPERATION_GROUP
DATABASE_OWNERSHIP_CHANGE_GROUP
DATABASE_PERMISSION_CHANGE_GROUP
DATABASE_PRINCIPAL_CHANGE_GROUP
DATABASE_PRINCIPAL_IMPERSONATION_GROUP
DATABASE_ROLE_MEMBER_CHANGE_GROUP
DBCC_GROUP
FAILED_LOGIN_GROUP
FULLTEXT_GROUP
LOGIN_CHANGE_PASSWORD_GROUP
LOGOUT_GROUP
SCHEMA_OBJECT_ACCESS_GROUP
SCHEMA_OBJECT_CHANGE_GROUP
SCHEMA_OBJECT_OWNERSHIP_CHANGE_GROUP
SCHEMA_OBJECT_PERMISSION_CHANGE_GROUP
SERVER_OBJECT_CHANGE_GROUP
SERVER_OBJECT_OWNERSHIP_CHANGE_GROUP
SERVER_OBJECT_PERMISSION_CHANGE_GROUP
SERVER_OPERATION_GROUP
SERVER_PERMISSION_CHANGE_GROUP
SERVER_PRINCIPAL_CHANGE_GROUP
SERVER_PRINCIPAL_IMPERSONATION_GROUP
SERVER_ROLE_MEMBER_CHANGE_GROUP
SERVER_STATE_CHANGE_GROUP
SUCCESSFUL_LOGIN_GROUP
TRACE_CHANGE_GROUP
```

Note that this result set contains a number of database-related groups. Database-level groups at the server audit specification level apply to all databases on the instance. If you need to audit a specific database on a server, use a database audit specification instead. We can see the actions associated with any of the groups by executing a different query of the same view. For example, we might wonder what is covered by the AUDIT_CHANGE_GROUP. We can find out with the following query:

```
SELECT a.[name] AS ActionName,
       a.class_desc AS Class
FROM sys.dm_audit_actions AS a
WHERE a.covering_parent_action_name = 'AUDIT_CHANGE_GROUP'
AND a.parent_class_desc = 'SERVER'
ORDER BY ActionName;
```

It returns this result list:

```
ActionName                    Class
--------------------------    --------------------------
ALTER                         SERVER AUDIT
ALTER                         SERVER AUDIT SPECIFICATION
AUDIT SHUTDOWN ON FAILURE      SERVER AUDIT
AUDIT_CHANGE_GROUP            DATABASE
CREATE                        SERVER AUDIT
CREATE                        SERVER AUDIT SPECIFICATION
DROP                          SERVER AUDIT
DROP                          SERVER AUDIT SPECIFICATION
```

Creating or altering a server audit specification requires ALTER ANY SERVER AUDIT permission (covered by the CONTROL SERVER permission).

Database Audit Specification

Database audit specifications are also used to determine actions that will be audited. Similar to server audit specifications, you can see a fixed list of action groups by executing the following query:

```
SELECT DISTINCT a.containing_group_name AS ActionGroup
FROM sys.dm_audit_actions AS a
WHERE a.class_desc = 'DATABASE'
ORDER BY ActionGroup;
```

It returns the following list of groups:

```
ActionGroup
--------------------------------------
APPLICATION_ROLE_CHANGE_PASSWORD_GROUP
AUDIT_CHANGE_GROUP
BACKUP_RESTORE_GROUP
DATABASE_CHANGE_GROUP
DATABASE_OBJECT_ACCESS_GROUP
DATABASE_OBJECT_CHANGE_GROUP
DATABASE_OBJECT_OWNERSHIP_CHANGE_GROUP
DATABASE_OBJECT_PERMISSION_CHANGE_GROUP
DATABASE_OPERATION_GROUP
DATABASE_OWNERSHIP_CHANGE_GROUP
DATABASE_PERMISSION_CHANGE_GROUP
DATABASE_PRINCIPAL_CHANGE_GROUP
DATABASE_PRINCIPAL_IMPERSONATION_GROUP
DATABASE_ROLE_MEMBER_CHANGE_GROUP
DBCC_GROUP
SCHEMA_OBJECT_ACCESS_GROUP
SCHEMA_OBJECT_CHANGE_GROUP
SCHEMA_OBJECT_OWNERSHIP_CHANGE_GROUP
SCHEMA_OBJECT_PERMISSION_CHANGE_GROUP
```

Unlike server audit specifications, database audit specifications can also allow us to audit access and modifications to individual securables, optionally by individual principals. The following query returns the list of actions that can be individually configured:

```
SELECT a.action_id AS ID,
       a.[name] AS ActionName
FROM sys.dm_audit_actions AS a
WHERE a.class_desc = 'DATABASE'
AND a.configuration_level = 'Action'
ORDER BY ActionName;
```

It returns the following list of actions:

```
ID   ActionName
---- -----------
DL   DELETE
EX   EXECUTE
IN   INSERT
RC   RECEIVE
RF   REFERENCES
SL   SELECT
UP   UPDATE
```

These permissions can be applied to securables at different scopes. For example, we can audit actions against a table or the schema that contains it. Auditing actions at the highest scope possible will minimize the number of audit actions that need to be defined. Note that auditing at the column level is not supported.

It is possible to audit actions by a specific principal (such as a database user). To audit actions by all principals, audit the PUBLIC principal instead. We'll do this in our example scenario.

Modifying or creating database audit specifications requires the ALTER ANY DATABASE AUDIT permission (which is also covered by the CONTROL SERVER permission).

Implementing a Scenario Using Auditing

In this section, we'll implement a full end-to-end scenario using SQL Server Auditing.

Assume the following situation:

We already provide limited access to the HR.Employees table. Appropriate permissions have been associated with the table to limit the users who can access it. An organizational requirement is that all access to any table in the HR schema must be audited, as must all login attempts (successful or not) to the system and logouts. Users might be required to justify any actions they perform on tables in this schema.

When the application was run in SQL Server 2005, SQL Trace was used to capture all SQL commands executed against the database. This introduced a performance overhead on the database, and the output traces were not convenient to use. Although it was possible to filter the traces to limit them to the InsideTSQL2008 database, it was difficult to isolate access to tables in the HR schema from other database activity on the server.

The intention is to use the SQL Server Audit feature in SQL Server 2008 to replace the use of SQL Trace for this auditing. We first need to decide where the audit records will be sent. In line with the way trace files were used previously, a decision was made to again use log files rather than sending audit records to the Windows Event logs. Creating a folder C:\temp\HR_Audit (if necessary) and executing the following query will create the required server audit:

```
USE master;
GO

CREATE SERVER AUDIT InsideTSQL_HR_Audit
TO FILE (FILEPATH = 'c:\temp\HR_Audit',
        MAXSIZE = 2GB,
        MAX_ROLLOVER_FILES = 100)
WITH (QUEUE_DELAY = 0, ON_FAILURE = SHUTDOWN);
```

In this command, we have created a server audit called *InsideTSQL_HR_Audit;* determined that audit records will be sent to a file; and provided the location of the file(s), their maximum size, and maximum number of rollover files. Note that the FILEPATH needs to be the path to a folder, not a file. We have specified zero for the QUEUE_DELAY, which will cause writes to be done synchronously, and we have opted to have SQL Server shut down if writing to the audit is not possible. This could happen if we run out of disk space.

By default, objects such as server audits are created in a disabled state. This allows the auditing system to be fully configured before it begins auditing.

We can deal with the login/logout requirement by creating a server audit specification, as in the following command:

```
CREATE SERVER AUDIT SPECIFICATION Login_Logout_Audit
FOR SERVER AUDIT InsideTSQL_HR_Audit
ADD (SUCCESSFUL_LOGIN_GROUP),
ADD (FAILED_LOGIN_GROUP),
ADD (LOGOUT_GROUP)
WITH (STATE = OFF);
```

We are logging all login attempts, both successful and failed, and all logouts. Next, we need to audit access to the HR schema. We audit the schema rather than all objects in the schema by executing the following command:

```
USE InsideTSQL2008;
GO

CREATE DATABASE AUDIT SPECIFICATION HR_Schema_Audit
FOR SERVER AUDIT InsideTSQL_HR_Audit
ADD (SELECT ON SCHEMA::HR BY public),
ADD (INSERT ON SCHEMA::HR BY public),
ADD (UPDATE ON SCHEMA::HR BY public),
ADD (DELETE ON SCHEMA::HR BY public),
ADD (EXECUTE ON SCHEMA::HR BY public),
ADD (RECEIVE ON SCHEMA::HR BY public);
```

We have audited all actions that we previously discovered were individually auditable, except for REFERENCES permission. This permission isn't related to a modification or change to the objects in that schema but to objects that reference objects in the schema. For example, this might apply to a sales order raised by an employee. Creating a new sales order would cause a REFERENCES access to the HR.Employees table if there is a foreign key reference between them. In our hypothetical scenario, we have decided that we do not need to audit that situation as the list of employee identifiers is not privileged information; only the information held in the tables is privileged.

Next, we enable our audit entries by executing the following query:

```
USE master;
GO

ALTER SERVER AUDIT InsideTSQL_HR_Audit
WITH (STATE = ON);

ALTER SERVER AUDIT SPECIFICATION Login_Logout_Audit
FOR SERVER AUDIT InsideTSQL_HR_Audit
WITH (STATE = ON);

USE InsideTSQL2008;
GO

ALTER DATABASE AUDIT SPECIFICATION HR_Schema_Audit
FOR SERVER AUDIT InsideTSQL_HR_Audit
WITH (STATE = ON);
```

At this point, looking in the C:\TEMP\HR_Audit folder, I find one file has been created:

InsideTSQL_HR_Audit_F6E34C41-090A-498B-AA11-FF9CC28DEEC6_0_128836402125610000.sqlaudit.

We are able to see what's in this file by executing the following query:

```
SELECT event_time AS EventTime,
       sequence_number AS Seq,
       action_id AS ID,
       succeeded AS [S/F],
       session_id AS SessionID,
       server_principal_name AS SPrincipal
FROM sys.fn_get_audit_file('c:\temp\HR_Audit\*.sqlaudit',
                           DEFAULT,
                           DEFAULT);
```

On my test system, this returned a large number of rows already. The first row was important. Changes to the auditing system are implicitly included in any auditing performed. You'll find an entry with AUSC as the ID to show the auditing starting.

Additional information can be obtained from the *statement* column also returned by this function. We have excluded it here for brevity. For logins, this column returns details such as the session SET options in use. After leaving this running for a short time, you will quickly realize how often the SQL Server features such as Reporting Services and even SQL Server Management Studio make logins to the server.

To test our database-level auditing, execute the following command:

```
SELECT * FROM HR.Employees;
```

We can look for SELECT access in our audit file by executing the following command:

```
SELECT event_time AS EventTime,
       sequence_number AS Seq,
       action_id AS ID,
       succeeded AS [S/F],
       session_id AS SessionID,
       server_principal_name AS SPrincipal,
       [statement] AS [Statement]
FROM sys.fn_get_audit_file('c:\temp\HR_Audit\*.sqlaudit',
                    DEFAULT,
                    DEFAULT)
WHERE action_id = 'SL'
ORDER BY EventTime;
```

This query returned the following results:

```
EventTime              Seq ID S/F SessionID SPrincipal     Statement
---------------------- --- -- --- --------- -------------- ---------------------------
2009-04-08 05:29:51.12 1   SL 1   55        GREGVISTA\Greg SELECT * FROM HR.Employees;
```

Our auditing system is now producing the required results.

Exploring SQL Server Audit Concepts

In this section we'll take a look at a few other important concepts related to SQL Server Audit, based upon the audit we set up during the implementation of our scenario. In particular, we'll spend some time looking at the management of the auditing system and the interaction of auditing with database schemas.

Viewing Details of Audits

SQL Server provides a series of dynamic management views that allow us to see details of all configured audit objects. These views include:

- *sys.dm_audit_actions*
- *sys.dm_server_audit_status*
- *sys.dm_audit_class_type_map*

You saw the first view in action earlier in the "SQL Server Audit Implementation" section. The second view returns details of all configured audits and their status. This can be useful for finding out what is enabled and what isn't. The third view returns a list of securable classes.

Similarly, there is a set of system views that provide details of audits:

- *sys.server_audits*

- *sys.server_audit_specifications*

- *sys.server_audit_specification_details*

- *sys.database_audit_specifications*

- *sys.database_audit_specification_details*

Because the audits are implemented via Extended Events, we can also view their details via the Extended Events system. The following query shows details of the audit in this way:

```
SELECT p.[Name] AS PackageName,
       s.[Name] AS SessionName,
       se.event_name AS EventName,
       st.target_name AS TargetName
FROM sys.dm_xe_sessions AS s
INNER JOIN sys.dm_xe_session_events AS se
ON s.address = se.event_session_address
INNER JOIN sys.dm_xe_packages AS p
ON se.event_package_guid = p.guid
INNER JOIN sys.dm_xe_session_targets AS st
ON s.address = st.event_session_address
WHERE s.[name] <> 'system_health'
ORDER BY PackageName,SessionName,EventName,TargetName;
```

Note that we have excluded the *system_health* session described in the Extended Events section of this chapter. This query returns the following output:

```
PackageName SessionName                EventName   TargetName
----------- -------------------------- ----------- -------------------------------------
SecAudit    InsideTSQL_HR_Audit$A      audit_event synchronous_security_audit_file_target
```

You can see that the name of our server audit has been extended to create the name of an Extended Events session and because we chose a QUEUE_DELAY value of zero, a *synchronous_security_audit_file_target* has been selected.

Indirect and Parameterized Access

You might wonder whether the access to the table is audited if the table is accessed indirectly via a view or stored procedure that is part of another schema. We can easily test this by executing the following code:

```
IF OBJECT_ID('Sales.Employees','V') IS NOT NULL
  DROP VIEW Sales.Employees;
GO
```

```
CREATE VIEW Sales.Employees
AS
  SELECT * FROM HR.Employees;
GO

SELECT * FROM Sales.Employees;
```

If you rerun the code to locate SELECT access, you will notice that this entry is audited as well. This is exactly what we'd hope the system would do.

Next, we'll investigate a parameterized query executed within a stored procedure:

```
IF OBJECT_ID('Sales.EmployeesByTitle','P') IS NOT NULL
  DROP PROCEDURE Sales.EmployeesByTitle;
GO

CREATE PROCEDURE Sales.EmployeesByTitle
@TitleOfCourtesy nvarchar(25)
AS
  SELECT *
  FROM HR.Employees AS e
  WHERE e.titleofcourtesy = @TitleOfCourtesy;
GO

EXEC Sales.EmployeesByTitle 'Mrs.';
```

We again check to see that the access has been audited, and we see that it has been. However, the statement recorded is:

```
SELECT *
FROM HR.Employees AS e
WHERE e.titleofcourtesy = @TitleOfCourtesy;
```

Unfortunately, the parameterized version of the statement has been recorded, not the actual statement executed with the parameters replaced.

SQL Server Audit audits actions, not changes to data files. Change data capture is one option that might help with this.

Auditing to the Security Event Log

The Security Event log in Windows can be used as a target for SQL Server Audit. It has a reputation for being tamper-proof and can be used to centralize the storage of audit records. Microsoft System Center Operations Manager includes an Audit Collection Service (ACS) that can securely collect audit records from the Security Event logs in Windows systems and then generate reports from the consolidated data.

By default, SQL Server's service account is not permitted to write to the Security Event log in Windows. The Microsoft Knowledge Base Article at *http://support.microsoft.com/kb/921469* discusses how to use group policy to configure detailed security auditing. Basically, the service account requires SeAuditPrivilege (which can be set by the security policy snap-in (secpol.msc) to the Microsoft Management Console (MMC). This is done by adding the service account to Local Policies\User Rights Assignment\Generate Security Audits. In addition, Local Policies\Audit Policy\Audit Object Access needs both Success and Failure enabled.

An alternative to the Security Event log can be to create a share on a server (referred to by a UNC path) with permissions set so that the SQL Server service account only has permissions to write. This way you can avoid having audit records exposed to local system administrators. Most important, it causes the records to be written to another computer system. However, the performance implications of these network writes need to be considered and synchronous targets are unlikely to be suitable for such use.

Management Issues for SQL Server Audit

Like other server objects involved with database mirroring, audits need to be re-created on the mirror partner server. Otherwise, audit specifications can become orphaned because they depend on the GUIDs associated with the audit objects on the server. The SQL Server service account on the partner needs to be able to write to any file folders used for auditing, and security policy needs to be updated if the Security Event log is used as a target.

If an audit with the same GUID cannot be located (such as after a database is restored or attached), the database audit specifications will be left intact but no results will be recorded. A similar situation exists for databases restored or attached to editions of SQL Server that don't support auditing, such as SQL Server Express.

To help reconnect (or to avoid) orphaned database audit specifications, it is possible to supply an AUDIT_GUID parameter when creating an audit to ensure that it matches the original GUID.

Finally, we can remove our auditing scheme by executing the following command:

```
USE master;
GO

ALTER SERVER AUDIT InsideTSQL_HR_Audit
WITH (STATE = OFF);

DROP SERVER AUDIT InsideTSQL_HR_Audit;
GO

ALTER SERVER AUDIT SPECIFICATION Login_Logout_Audit
WITH (STATE = OFF);

DROP SERVER AUDIT SPECIFICATION Login_Logout_Audit;

USE InsideTSQL2008;
GO
```

```
ALTER DATABASE AUDIT SPECIFICATION HR_Schema_Audit
WITH (STATE = OFF);

DROP DATABASE AUDIT SPECIFICATION HR_Schema_Audit;
GO

DROP VIEW Sales.Employees;
DROP PROCEDURE Sales.EmployeesByTitle;
GO
```

Note that audit specifications need to be set to a state of OFF before they can be dropped.

Change Tracking Implementation

Unlike Extended Events and SQL Server Audit, which have a number of objects you need to be aware of before implementing anything, with change tracking it is very easy to get started. We'll jump right into a scenario and learn what we need along the way. Later, I will show you how to implement a basic solution using Microsoft Sync Services and cover some additional management aspects.

Implementing a Scenario Using Change Tracking

In the following hypothetical scenario, our organization has a small team that is responsible for employee benefits. The members of this team work directly in the field with the employees. To facilitate this, they have been provided with a small Windows Forms–based application called TeamView that has been written within the organization and which allows them to view (and potentially correct) details regarding the employees they meet with.

At present, the TeamView application connects to the SQL Server system when the employee benefit team members are in the office. Each time the application connects, it retrieves the complete list of employee details from the server. The intention is to use change tracking in SQL Server 2008 to minimize the amount of data transferred when this sync operation occurs and make it possible for the employee benefit team members to perform sync operations across the low bandwidth offered by the Internet connections on their phones, by only transferring the data that has changed.

We start by modifying the InsideTSQL2008 database to support change tracking:

```
USE InsideTSQL2008;
GO
ALTER DATABASE InsideTSQL2008
  SET ALLOW_SNAPSHOT_ISOLATION ON;

ALTER DATABASE InsideTSQL2008
  SET CHANGE_TRACKING = ON;
```

Change tracking needs to be enabled at the database level before it is enabled at the table level. Note that we have also enabled snapshot isolation on the database. Most tasks in change tracking require multiple steps and the easiest way to maintain consistency is to change the transaction isolation level for the session to snapshot. The change to snapshot isolation level needs to be enabled at the database level first. Although it is possible to use change tracking in SQL Server 2008 without snapshot isolation, doing so adds another level of complexity to the design. In general, it is recommended that you use snapshot isolation level when working with change tracking. The performance implications of this (although not necessarily large) need to be considered. We will use it for our transactions by executing the following session command:

```
SET TRANSACTION ISOLATION LEVEL SNAPSHOT;
GO
```

We can see databases that are enabled for change tracking by querying a new system view:

```
SELECT d.name AS DatabaseName,
       ctd.is_auto_cleanup_on AS AutoCleanup,
       CAST(ctd.retention_period AS varchar(10))
         + ' '
         + ctd.retention_period_units_desc  AS RetentionPeriod
FROM sys.change_tracking_databases AS ctd
INNER JOIN sys.sysdatabases AS d
ON ctd.database_id = d.dbid
ORDER BY DatabaseName;
```

It returns the following output:

```
DatabaseName    AutoCleanup RetentionPeriod
--------------  ----------- ---------------
InsideTSQL2008  1                 2 DAYS
```

From this we can see that changes to tables within the database will be held for up to two days and then automatically cleaned up. We can directly control this via the ALTER DATABASE statement. It is important that changes are kept as long as they are still needed. This will generally mean they need to be kept for a duration that is longer than the maximum time between synchronizations of any client system. The value can be set to a minimum of 1 minute. Should a situation arise where one client won't be able to sync for a longer time than is configured, you can pause the cleanup process by disabling the auto cleanup temporarily. When the auto cleanup is re-enabled, make sure that you also reestablish any required change retention time period as enabling auto cleanup resets change retention to the default value.

We enable change tracking at the table level by executing the following command:

```
ALTER TABLE HR.Employees
  ENABLE CHANGE_TRACKING;
```

Similar to the way we queried for change-tracked databases, we can query the status of change-tracked tables via another new system view:

```
SELECT OBJECT_NAME(object_id) AS TableName,
       is_track_columns_updated_on AS ColumnTracking,
       min_valid_version AS MinValidVersion,
       begin_version AS BeginVersion,
       cleanup_version AS CleanupVersion
FROM sys.change_tracking_tables
ORDER BY TableName;
```

The query returns the following result:

```
TableName ColumnTracking MinValidVersion   BeginVersion    CleanupVersion
--------- -------------- ----------------- --------------- --------------
Employees 0                   0                  0              0
```

Note that by default, tracking of changes at the column level is not provided. The assumption is that most applications will be interested in the current value of whichever rows have been modified. There are some scenarios where column tracking might be helpful. One example is that if we add an employee photo in a *varbinary(max)* column to this table, we might try to avoid downloading it each time unless it actually changes. For now, we'll concern ourselves with tracking the changes to the entire row.

Change tracking uses private tables to store details of the changes to data. We can see these by querying the *sys.internal_tables* view:

```
SELECT [name] AS TableName,
       type_desc AS TableType,
       internal_type_desc AS [Description]
FROM sys.internal_tables
ORDER BY TableName;
```

This query (on my test system) returned the following output:

```
TableName                          TableType        Description
---------------------------------- ---------------- -----------------------------
change_tracking_2105058535         INTERNAL_TABLE   CHANGE_TRACKING
filestream_tombstone_2073058421    INTERNAL_TABLE   FILESTREAM_TOMBSTONE
queue_messages_1977058079          INTERNAL_TABLE   QUEUE_MESSAGES
queue_messages_2009058193          INTERNAL_TABLE   QUEUE_MESSAGES
queue_messages_2041058307          INTERNAL_TABLE   QUEUE_MESSAGES
syscommittab                       INTERNAL_TABLE   TRACKED_COMMITTED_TRANSACTIONS
```

The two tables we are interested in for change tracking are the first and last tables in this list. The first table holds details of the changes to the HR.Employees table. One internal table is created for each user table involved in change tracking. The syscommittab table is used by change tracking to keep details of transactions that are committed involving the change-tracked tables.

The version number provided by change tracking is updated as changes occur to the tables. For example, execute the following query:

```
INSERT INTO HR.Employees
  (firstname,lastname,mgrid,title,titleofcourtesy,
   birthdate,hiredate,[address],city,country,phone)
  VALUES ('Michael','Entin',1,'','Mr.','19490101','20090401',
          '19 some lane','London','UK','n/a'),
         ('John','Chen',1,'','Mr.','19490201','20090401',
          '42 some street','London','UK','n/a'),
         ('Terry','Earls',1,'','Dr.','19490301','20090401',
          '35 some avenue','London','UK','n/a');

UPDATE HR.Employees
  SET firstname = 'Peter'
  WHERE firstname = 'Michael' AND lastname = 'Entin';
```

We have inserted three employees and then updated one of them. We can see the current change tracking version by executing the following command:

```
SELECT CHANGE_TRACKING_CURRENT_VERSION();
```

It returns the value 2. We will now make a further change by the command:

```
UPDATE HR.Employees
  SET firstname = 'Paul'
  WHERE firstname = 'Peter' AND lastname = 'Entin';
```

If we check the current version again, we can see that it now returns the value 3. This version is used in determining what rows we need to download during synchronization. At this point, imagine that our application syncs for the first time. It can get the current version and then simply select all the columns it requires directly from the table. This is where the issue of snapshot isolation suddenly becomes important. Between the time that we select the current version and the time we select the rows in the table, the rows could change. Rows could be added, deleted, or updated. A good alternative to using snapshot isolation at this step would be to select the current version while selecting the data for the rows with a command, as in the following example:

```
SELECT CHANGE_TRACKING_CURRENT_VERSION() AS CurrentVersion,
       empid, lastname, firstname, title,
       titleofcourtesy, birthdate, hiredate,
       [address], city, region, postalcode,
       country, phone, mgrid
FROM HR.Employees;
```

For this initial sync operation this is a reasonable alternative, but for later operations avoiding snapshot isolation level becomes much more complex. That's why it is recommended that you use it.

Our application now has its data and it knows that it was correct as of version 3. Let's make some more changes to the data via the following commands:

```
INSERT INTO HR.Employees
  (firstname,lastname,mgrid,title,titleofcourtesy,
   birthdate,hiredate,[address],city,country,phone)
  VALUES ('Bob','Kelly',1,'','Mr.','19490401','20090402',
          '19 some boulevarde','Los Angeles','USA','n/a');

UPDATE HR.Employees
  SET titleofcourtesy = 'Dr.'
  WHERE firstname = 'John' AND lastname = 'Chen';

DELETE FROM HR.Employees
  WHERE firstname = 'Terry' AND lastname = 'Earls';
```

We have added a new employee named Bob Kelly, updated John Chen to be Dr. John Chen, and deleted Terry Earls. Now it's time for our application to connect again. The first thing it needs to check is that the version it is currently storing (which was version 3) is at least recent enough so that the changes it needs are still present on the system. It can do this by executing the following command:

```
SELECT CHANGE_TRACKING_MIN_VALID_VERSION(OBJECT_ID(N'HR.Employees','TABLE'));
```

This command currently returns the value zero because no cleanup operations have yet occurred. This means that our application is fine to proceed with obtaining the changes. It does this through the following command:

```
SELECT c.empid, c.SYS_CHANGE_OPERATION,
       e.lastname, e.firstname, e.title,
       e.titleofcourtesy, e.birthdate, e.hiredate,
       e.[address], e.city, e.region, e.postalcode,
       e.country, e.phone, e.mgrid
FROM CHANGETABLE(CHANGES HR.Employees,3) AS c
LEFT OUTER JOIN HR.Employees AS e
ON c.empid = e.empid
ORDER BY c.empid;
```

The parameter 3 that was passed to the CHANGETABLE function was the current version of data held by our application. This command returns the following results:

```
empid SYS_CHANGE_OPERATION lastname  firstname title titleofcourtesy
----- -------------------- --------- --------- ----- ---------------
19    U                    Chen      John            Dr.
20    D                    NULL      NULL      NULL  NULL
21    I                    Kelly     Bob             Mr.
```

Note that I have removed the columns from the right-hand side of these results for clarity. It was necessary to perform a LEFT OUTER JOIN from the change table to the HR.Employees table to make sure we also returned any rows that had been deleted. We can see this in the results where the row for *empid* 20 has a D operation associated with it and no data returned for the other columns.

It is interesting to see the effect of the version number that we pass into the CHANGETABLE function. Passing the value 1 (instead of 3) returns the following results:

```
empid       SYS_CHANGE_OPERATION lastname             firstname  title    titleofcourtesy
----------- -------------------- -------------------- ---------- -------- ---------------
18          U                    Entin                Paul                Mr.
19          U                    Chen                 John                Dr.
20          D                    NULL                 NULL       NULL     NULL
21          I                    Kelly                Bob                 Mr.
```

Compare this to the results returned when passing 0 as the version:

```
empid       SYS_CHANGE_OPERATION lastname             firstname  title  titleofcourtesy
----------- -------------------- -------------------- ---------- ------ ---------------
18          I                    Entin                Paul              Mr.
19          I                    Chen                 John              Dr.
20          D                    NULL                 NULL       NULL   NULL
21          I                    Kelly                Bob               Mr.
```

Taking *empid* 18 as an example, when obtaining changes since version zero, the net effect is that *empid* 18 has just been inserted. If we obtain changes since version 1, the net effect is that *empid* 18 was updated. The CHANGETABLE function makes this calculation for us so that the client application can simply apply the changes as received. This is more efficient than a system that sends us each individual change.

At this point, you may be wondering how much space the change details are taking in the database. We can discover that by executing the following commands:

```
EXEC sp_spaceused 'sys.change_tracking_2105058535';
EXEC sp_spaceused 'sys.syscommittab';
```

You would need to use the correct change tracking table name to match your configuration but the sys.syscommittab table applies to all tables. These commands currently return the following results:

```
name                          rows    reserved        data           index_size      unused
----------------------------- ------- --------------- -------------- --------------- ------
change_tracking_2105058535 8          16 KB           8 KB           8 KB            0 KB
```

```
name                          rows    reserved        data           index_size      unused
----------------------------- ------- --------------- -------------- --------------- ------
syscommittab                  6       32 KB           8 KB           24 KB           0 KB
```

You might also wonder how we could know what the latest version number is at which each row was last modified. We can find that by using the VERSION option of the CHANGETABLE function as follows:

```
SELECT e.empid,
       c.SYS_CHANGE_VERSION,
       c.SYS_CHANGE_CONTEXT
FROM HR.Employees AS e
CROSS APPLY CHANGETABLE(VERSION HR.Employees,(empid),(e.empid)) AS c
ORDER BY e.empid;
```

It returns the following output:

empid	SYS_CHANGE_VERSION	SYS_CHANGE_CONTEXT
1	NULL	NULL
2	NULL	NULL
3	NULL	NULL
4	NULL	NULL
5	NULL	NULL
6	NULL	NULL
7	NULL	NULL
8	NULL	NULL
9	NULL	NULL
18	3	NULL
19	5	NULL
21	4	NULL

From this we can see that *empid* 18 was last modified in version 3, *empid* 19 was last modified in version 5, and *empid* 21 was last modified in version 4. No other rows have been modified since change tracking was enabled. Having access to this version detail helps in building two-way synchronization scenarios where the client system can include the row version while doing updates, similar to the way that the *rowversion* data type is often used in SQL Server when implementing optimistic concurrency. The client application knows that if the version when it last read the data does not match the current version, an update conflict has occurred if it also needs to update the row.

Also in this last result set, we can see a column named SYS_CHANGE_CONTEXT. This is an area set aside to allow us to record any other information we feel is appropriate in relation to the data changes. The downside is that it requires a change to the DML statements in the source application. As an example, execute the following code:

```
DECLARE @TrackingContext VARBINARY(128);
DECLARE @UserDetails XML;

SET @UserDetails = (SELECT USER_NAME() AS UserName
                    FOR XML RAW('User'));

SET @TrackingContext = CAST(@UserDetails AS VARBINARY(MAX));

WITH CHANGE_TRACKING_CONTEXT(@TrackingContext)
UPDATE HR.Employees
  SET titleofcourtesy = 'Mr.'
  WHERE firstname = 'John' AND lastname = 'Chen';
GO
```

We then re-execute the code we used to observe the versions and cast the column to XML as follows:

```
SELECT e.empid,
       c.SYS_CHANGE_VERSION,
       CAST(c.SYS_CHANGE_CONTEXT AS XML) AS UserDetails
FROM HR.Employees AS e
CROSS APPLY CHANGETABLE(VERSION HR.Employees,(empid),(e.empid)) AS c
ORDER BY e.empid;
```

This returns the following output:

```
empid        SYS_CHANGE_VERSION    UserDetails
-----------  --------------------  ------------------------
1            NULL                  NULL
2            NULL                  NULL
3            NULL                  NULL
4            NULL                  NULL
5            NULL                  NULL
6            NULL                  NULL
7            NULL                  NULL
8            NULL                  NULL
9            NULL                  NULL
18           3                     NULL
19           7                     <User UserName="dbo" />
21           4                     NULL
```

You can see that the CHANGE_TRACKING_CONTEXT clause can be used in queries to save and retrieve basic information about the data modification using the change table's SYS_CHANGE_CONTEXT column. However, this is limited to a VARBINARY(128) value and requires the user's application to be modified to add the context into the modification statements. Regardless, we've now satisfied the requirements of our scenario.

Change Tracking Management Issues

As we have seen, change tracking is quite straightforward to implement. However, we need to consider some issues when implementing it in a design.

Any table that is to be enabled for change tracking must have a primary key. My database purist friends would tell me that any table that doesn't have a primary key isn't really a table, but SQL Server doesn't enforce that unless you intend to implement additional technologies such as change tracking. The primary key constraint cannot be dropped while change tracking is enabled.

Change tracking doesn't work well with partitioned tables. If either table involved in an ALTER TABLE SWITCH statement has change tracking enabled, the ALTER TABLE SWITCH will fail.

Although many systems don't allow primary keys to be updated, if the primary key is changed in an UPDATE, change tracking will treat the UPDATE as a DELETE followed by an INSERT.

DDL changes need to be handled by the application. This might present a significant challenge in some environments. Dropping a column (non-primary key) is permitted, but the CHANGETABLE function might still return details about the column if column change tracking is enabled. Adding a column is also permitted but column change tracking will ignore the new column. Changes to the data type of a column are permitted but are not tracked. When change tracking for columns is enabled, a special function, CHANGE_TRACKING_IS_ COLUMN_IN_MASK, is used to determine whether a specific column has been updated.

Truncating a table does not cause each individual row DELETE to be tracked. It does, however, reset the minimum valid version for the table. Clients will then detect that they are too far out of sync and need to reload any values from the table.

Databases must be at database compatibility level 90 or higher for change tracking to be enabled. You also can't disable change tracking at the database level until it has been disabled for all tables within the database. The *sys.change_tracked_tables* system view can help with locating these tables.

Because updates to the change tracking tables are done in the context of the transaction that caused the modification, performance is impacted. SQL Server Books Online suggests that this impact is similar to having an additional non-clustered index on the table that needs to be updated as modifications occur.

Security also needs to be considered. To access changes for a table, a user needs both SELECT permission on at least the primary key of the table and also VIEW CHANGE TRACKING permission. The latter is required to avoid information leakage that could occur if only SELECT permissions were required. For example, it might be inappropriate to allow a user to have any knowledge of rows that were deleted from the table before they were given permission to view change details.

The final significant issue to consider is how to handle a restore of the database. Depending upon the time of the latest syncs, clients may or may not be affected. In most cases, a re-sync is the appropriate action.

If you have been following along with the code in this book, you might also wish to clean up the inserted data and disable change tracking with the following code:

```
DELETE FROM HR.Employees WHERE empid > 9;
DBCC CHECKIDENT('HR.Employees',RESEED,9);
ALTER TABLE HR.Employees
  DISABLE CHANGE_TRACKING;

ALTER DATABASE InsideTSQL2008
  SET CHANGE_TRACKING = OFF;

ALTER DATABASE InsideTSQL2008
  SET ALLOW_SNAPSHOT_ISOLATION OFF;
```

Microsoft Sync Framework

To round out our discussion of change tracking, it is worth spending a short while considering how it can be used from within client code. Microsoft has introduced the Sync Framework, which includes ADO.NET Sync Services. The sync adapter was introduced prior to SQL Server 2008. With SQL Server 2005, it typically detected table changes by using a series of triggers. The sync adapter has been updated to use change tracking in SQL Server 2008 when available.

In the remainder of this section, we'll work through the creation of a simple Windows Forms application that syncs with our HR.Employees table, by following these basic steps:

1. Create a new Windows Forms application in Microsoft Visual Studio 2008. I will use the C# language in this example, but very little coding is required, and the Visual Basic language is just as easy to use for this application.

2. In Solution Explorer, right-click the project object and choose *Add New Item...* then from the Add New Item dialog, choose to add a Local Database Cache. This will launch the configuration wizard for the ADO.NET sync adapter.

3. Configure a connection to the InsideTSQL2008 database. Your screen should look similar to the one shown in Figure 15-1.

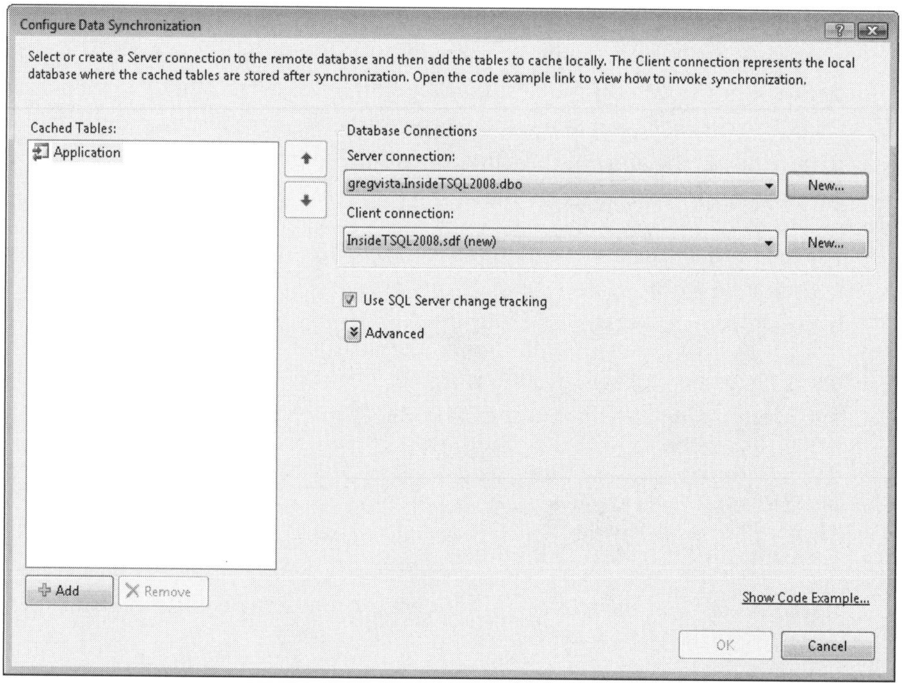

FIGURE 15-1 Configure Data Synchronization window

4. Make sure that the Use SQL Server change tracking check box is selected. If this option is not configured, the sync adapter will try to use triggers and database columns to track changes to the data. Change tracking in SQL Server 2008 makes it easy to track changes to the data without the need for triggers.

5. Click the Add button and add the HR.Employees table. Your screen should look similar to Figure 15-2.

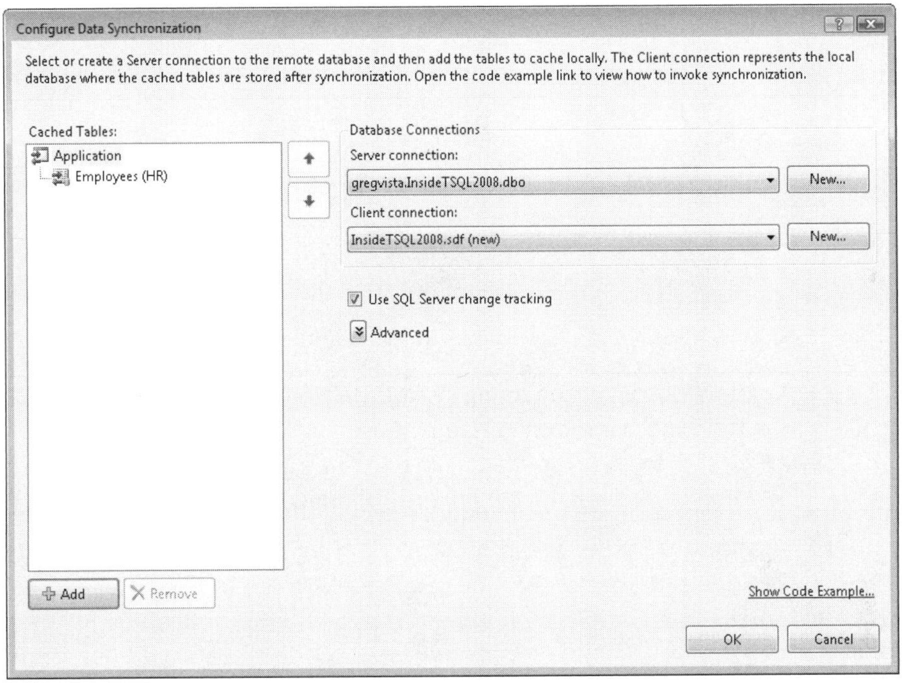

FIGURE 15-2 Adding the Employees table

6. Click Show Code Example, click Copy Code to the Clipboard, and click Close. You'll need the code later because it provides the basic synchronization code already written for us.

7. Click OK to close the Configure Data Synchronization window. At this point the sync framework creates a local SQL Server CE database, creates a schema to match the source table(s), and inserts an initial copy of the data from the source table.

8. Now you need to configure a data source in the application, so the Data Source Configuration Wizard is launched automatically for you by Visual Studio. On the Choose Your Database Objects page of the wizard, choose the HR.Employees table as shown in Figure 15-3.

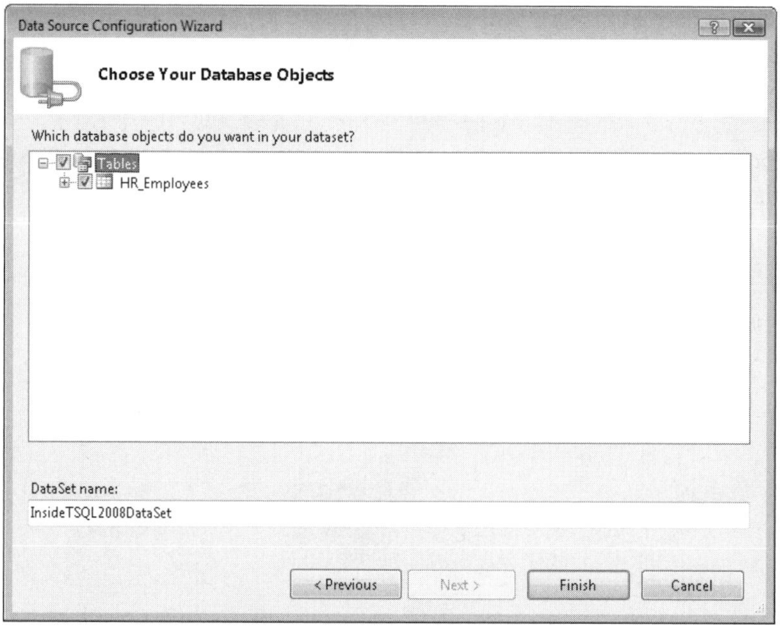

FIGURE 15-3 Data Source Configuration Wizard

9. Click Finish to close the wizard. On the Data menu, choose Show Data Sources. Drag HR_Employees from the Data Sources window onto the form.

10. As shown in Figure 15-4, choose Dock In Parent Container from the DataGridView Tasks drop-down menu on the grid that has been inserted.

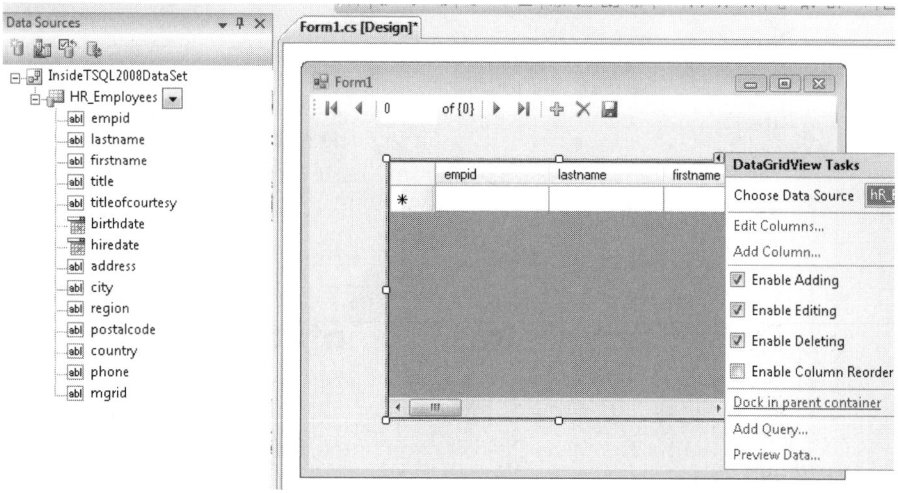

FIGURE 15-4 Dock in parent container

At this point we have built an application that will run, but cannot yet synchronize with the source database. It only has a copy of the initial data.

11. Right-click the form's toolstrip, then use the pull-down menu that appears to select Button. Double-click the new button to open a code window. Paste the code that we copied to the clipboard earlier into the body of the *toolStripbutton1_Click()* method, and also copy the single line of code from the *Form1_Load()* method to the *toolStripbutton1_Click()* method just under this method's TODO comment. Your code should look like the code in Figure 15-5.

```
}

private void Form1_Load(object sender, EventArgs e)
{
  // TODO: This line of code loads data into the 'insi
  this.hR_EmployeesTableAdapter.Fill(this.insideTSQL20

}

private void toolStripButton1_Click(object sender, Eve
{
  // Call SyncAgent.Synchronize() to initiate the sync
  // Synchronization only updates the local database,
  LocalDataCache1SyncAgent syncAgent = new LocalDataCa
  Microsoft.Synchronization.Data.SyncStatistics syncSt

  // TODO: Reload your project data source from the lo
  this.hR_EmployeesTableAdapter.Fill(this.insideTSQL20

}
```

FIGURE 15-5 Modified code

We have now created a version of the application that can also sync with the main database. The one final modification we might decide to make is to exert control over the direction of synchronization.

12. We have now completed our basic application that will utilize Change Tracking in SQL Server 2008 and can test it by pressing the F5 key or by clicking the Start Debugging button in the toolbar. (The button looks like a small green triangle.)

Change Data Capture Implementation

Change data capture is another technology that is relatively easy to get started with. The initial release of SQL Server 2008 lacks GUI tooling. Change data capture needs to be configured via T-SQL. We'll start with implementing a scenario. Later we'll consider some management aspects of change data capture. Note also that change data capture is an Enterprise edition feature.

Implementing a Scenario Using Change Data Capture

For our next hypothetical scenario, our organization has implemented a data warehouse that includes an Employee dimension table. The dimension has been implemented as a Type 1 slowly changing dimension. This means that each time data is uploaded, the rows in the dimension table have been replaced by the incoming data. It has been decided that we need to move to a Type 2 slowly changing dimension. This requires versioned rows to be stored in the dimension table when changes to the data occur. To accomplish this, we need the extract, transform, and load (ETL) process to identify rows that have changed. We will no longer extract all rows from the source if it can be avoided. Instead, we need to retrieve a rowset containing details of insertions, deletions, and updates. Change data capture should meet all these needs.

To begin our scenario, we'll create a test database and table to work with by executing the following commands:

```
USE master;
GO

CREATE DATABASE CDC;
GO

USE CDC;
GO

IF OBJECT_ID('dbo.Employees','U') IS NOT NULL
   DROP TABLE dbo.Employees;
GO

CREATE TABLE dbo.Employees
( EmployeeID int IDENTITY(1,1) PRIMARY KEY CLUSTERED,
  FullName nvarchar(50) NOT NULL,
  BadgeNumber nvarchar(20) NOT NULL);
GO

INSERT dbo.Employees (FullName, BadgeNumber)
   VALUES('John Chen','2343Q'),
        ('Terry Earls','3423B'),
        ('Michael Entin','5234Q');
GO
```

We have created a table to hold employee details and have inserted three rows into that table. We start the implementation of change data capture by enabling it at the database level. We do this by executing the following command:

```
EXEC sys.sp_cdc_enable_db;
```

Note that change data capture is configured using system-stored procedures rather than DDL statements. I do hope this situation changes in the future. Once it has been enabled at the database, we can already see some of the changes that have been made. Execute the following command:

```
SELECT uid, roles, hasdbaccess,islogin,issqluser
FROM sys.sysusers
WHERE [name] = 'cdc';

SELECT * FROM sys.schemas WHERE name = 'cdc';
```

It returns the following results:

```
uid     roles hasdbaccess islogin     issqluser
------  ----- ----------- ----------- -----------
5       NULL  1           1           1

name schema_id   principal_id
---- ----------- ------------
cdc  5           5
```

A new database user, *cdc*, and a schema, also named *cdc*, have been created. The *cdc* database user is the owner of the *cdc* schema. SQL Server has also created a database trigger. Execute the following code:

```
SELECT [name],[object_id],parent_class_desc,type_desc
FROM sys.triggers;

SELECT [object_id], type_desc
FROM sys.trigger_events;
```

It returns the following results:

```
name                object_id   parent_class_desc  type_desc
------------------  ----------- ------------------ ------------
tr_MScdc_ddl_event  357576312   DATABASE           SQL_TRIGGER

object_id   type_desc
----------- ------------
357576312   ALTER_TABLE
357576312   DROP_TABLE
357576312   ALTER_INDEX
357576312   DROP_INDEX
```

You can see from the results that a trigger named *tr_MScdc_ddl_event* has been created, and it tracks the ALTER TABLE, DROP TABLE, ALTER INDEX, and DROP INDEX events. Change data capture uses this to track DDL events related to the tables whose changes are being captured.

Enabling change data capture requires SQL Server Agent to be running. If you are following the commands in this book, you will need to ensure that SQL Server Agent is running at this point.

We now enable change data capture on our table by executing the following command:

```
EXEC sys.sp_cdc_enable_table
  @source_schema = 'dbo',
  @source_name = 'Employees',
  @supports_net_changes = 1,
  @role_name = NULL;
```

We have specified the schema and table names along with a flag to indicate that we want support for net changes. We'll explain what this means shortly. We've also indicated NULL for the *@role_name* parameter. This parameter can specify a role that a user must be a member of, in addition to having SELECT permissions for the table's columns, before the user can access details of changes on the table. This role is treated as an extra gate that users must pass through to get to the changes. In our case, we are not requiring an extra security layer. This command returns the following output:

```
Job 'cdc.CDC_capture' started successfully.
Job 'cdc.CDC_cleanup' started successfully.
```

The output provides a good clue regarding other changes that have now been made to the system. We'll find that two jobs have been created. The first job is used to capture changes from the database transaction log and record them in the change tracking tables. This job is only created if transactional replication has not already been configured. If transactional replication has previously been configured, change data capture shares the same *sp_replcmd* procedure and doesn't need to create a job to run it. This helps reduce contention in the database if both technologies are being used.

The job created in our scenario will run once every 5 seconds. Each time it runs, it will scan the logs up to 10 times, and on each scan it will process up to 500 transactions. These values can be changed by a call to the *sp_cdc_change_job* stored procedure. The changes don't take effect immediately but only after the job is restarted, which can be done by calling *sp_cdc_ stop_job* and *sp_cdc_start_job*.

A second job has also been created to clean up old data from the change tracking tables. By default, this job runs at 2:00 A.M. each day and retains changes for 72 hours (3 days). Again, these values can be changed.

You can view details of the jobs by executing the following code:

```
EXEC sys.sp_cdc_help_jobs;
```

It shows the current configuration of each of the jobs. The value 4,320 (minutes) in the retention column indicates that the retention period of the cleanup job is three days. The value in the *threshold* column is 5,000. This represents the maximum number of rows that the cleanup job will remove in a single DELETE statement, to minimize blocking within the cleanup tables.

Finally, several tables are created:

- cdc.dbo_Employee_CT is the table to hold changes from our user table.

- cdc.ddl_history holds schema changes from tables using CDC.

- cdc.index_columns indicates which columns are used for identifying rows. (Primary keys are preferred but other columns can be used instead.)

- cdc.captured_columns indicates which columns in the tables are being captured.

- cdc.change_tables indicates which tables are having their data captured.

- cdc.lsn_time_mapping is used to hold a mapping between log sequence numbers (LSNs) and the time as recorded at the server.

Let's start by making some changes to our table and then seeing the effects. Execute the following commands:

```
INSERT dbo.Employees (FullName, BadgeNumber)
  VALUES('Brian Burke','5243Z');
GO

UPDATE dbo.Employees
  SET FullName = 'Terry Earls'
  WHERE BadgeNumber = '5243Z';

DELETE dbo.Employees WHERE BadgeNumber = '5234Q';
GO
```

We can query the change table directly via:

```
SELECT __$start_lsn,
       __$operation,
       __$update_mask,
       EmployeeID, FullName
FROM cdc.dbo_Employees_CT
ORDER BY __$start_lsn;
```

It returns the following results:

```
__$start_lsn           __$operation __$update_mask EmployeeID FullName
---------------------- ------------ -------------- ---------- --------------
0x0000004D000000270004 2            0x07           4          Brian Burke
0x0000004D000000350004 3            0x02           4          Brian Burke
0x0000004D000000350004 4            0x02           4          Terry Earls
0x0000004D000000370005 1            0x07           3          Michael Entin
```

Note that four rows are returned. The first is the insert of Brian Burke (operation code 2). The second and third are both related to the update of Brian Burke's name to Terry Earls (operation codes 3 and 4). The last is related to the deletion of Michael Entin (operation code 1). The _$update_mask column is a bitmap that indicates which columns have been updated. For insert and delete operations, all columns are flagged as updated.

SQL Server gave the name dbo_Employees to our "capture instance." We could select this name ourselves when enabling change data capture at the table level, but if we don't supply a name, as the default is *<schemaname>_<tablename>*. Two capture instances can exist on a table at any time. We'll discuss the use of multiple capture instances later.

The standard way to access the changes is to use the set of functions that SQL Server also created for us when we enabled the table. The following code shows an example of this:

```
DECLARE @From_LSN binary(10);
SET @From_LSN = sys.fn_cdc_get_min_lsn('dbo_Employees');
DECLARE @To_LSN binary(10);
SET @To_LSN = sys.fn_cdc_get_max_lsn();

SELECT * FROM cdc.fn_cdc_get_all_changes_dbo_Employees
                (@From_LSN,@To_LSN,'all');
SELECT * FROM cdc.fn_cdc_get_net_changes_dbo_Employees
                (@From_LSN,@To_LSN,'all');
GO
```

In this code, we locate the first log sequence number related to our capture instance by calling the *sys.fn_cdc_get_min_lsn()* function, passing it the name of our capture instance. We locate the last LSN by calling *sys.fn_cdc_get_max_lsn()*. This provides us with a range of LSNs that we use to query the change table functions. Two functions were created. Each takes a range of LSNs and a parameter that indicates how updates should be treated. The value *all* indicates that all rows should be returned with their current values. The alternate value *all update old* indicates that both old and new data values should be returned for updates.

The other differences between the two functions are the words *all* and *net* in the names of the functions. You will see from the output that when the *all* version is selected, every change is returned. When the *net* version is selected, only the net effect of the transactions is returned. In our case, an insert of Brian Burke followed by a change of the same row to Terry Earls has the net effect of just inserting Terry Earls. The *net* functions will return a single row for each data value changed, no matter how many times they change. Supporting *net* changes requires an additional index to be built over the change table, so it adds some level of performance overhead. For our Employee dimension ETL scenario we need to capture every change to the data so we will need to use the *all* versions, but many other applications will be happy to receive only the net effect of a series of changes.

To make it easier to select the appropriate LSNs, SQL Server provides us with functions to map times to and from LSNs. It does this by querying the *cdc.lsn_time_mapping* table mentioned earlier. We can create a stored procedure to return all changes since a specified time with a command such as the following:

```
IF OBJECT_ID('dbo.Get_Employee_Data_Changes','P')
  DROP PROCEDURE dbo.Get_Employee_Data_Changes;
GO
```

```
CREATE PROCEDURE dbo.Get_Employee_Data_Changes
@FromTime datetime,
@LastTime datetime OUTPUT
AS
  DECLARE @From_LSN binary(10);
  SET @From_LSN = sys.fn_cdc_map_time_to_lsn(
    'smallest greater than or equal', @FromTime);

  DECLARE @To_LSN binary(10);
  SET @To_LSN = sys.fn_cdc_get_max_lsn();

  SET @LastTime = sys.fn_cdc_map_lsn_to_time(@To_LSN);

  SELECT * FROM cdc.fn_cdc_get_all_changes_dbo_Employees
              (@From_LSN,@To_LSN,'all');
GO
```

We could then retrieve all the changes in the past day like this:

```
DECLARE @FromTime datetime = DATEADD(DAY,-1,SYSDATETIME());
DECLARE @LastTime datetime;

EXEC dbo.Get_Employee_Data_Changes @FromTime, @LastTime OUTPUT;
```

We could build a similar procedure that took an LSN instead of a time. Our ETL process would need to remember either the latest LSN or the latest time until which it received changes and simply request everything since that value the next time.

We have now completed the basic data feed requirements of our scenario.

Change Data Capture Management Issues

Although it's easy to get started, you need to consider number of management issues when working with change data capture.

Schema Changes

First, you might wonder what happens if you change the structure of your table. Execute the following code to add a column:

```
ALTER TABLE dbo.Employees
  ADD CourtesyTitle nvarchar(20) DEFAULT ('Mr');
GO
```

If you retrieve the set of changes again, you'll find that even though every row was modified by adding a default value to this new column, no additional change records are generated. New columns are ignored. We can delete a column by executing the following code:

```
ALTER TABLE dbo.Employees
  DROP COLUMN BadgeNumber;
GO
```

The command succeeds but if we again retrieve the change records, we notice the *BadgeNumber* column is still returned and contains values. Let's generate a new data modification by executing the following command:

```
UPDATE dbo.Employees
  SET FullName = 'Test User'
  WHERE FullName = 'Terry Earls';
GO
```

When we check the data changes again, we find the *BadgeNumber* column is still present but its value is NULL for the updated row. This is helpful because it means that applications that have been written to work with the existing interface will continue to work, as long as they can deal with the NULL value. To assist with this, SQL Server also keeps a history of the DDL changes, tracked by the trigger we saw earlier. You can see the history by executing the following command:

```
EXEC sys.sp_cdc_get_ddl_history N'dbo_Employees';
```

You will note from its output that it returns details of the DDL statements that were executed and allows you to map them to which LSN they relate to.

The recommended approach for dealing with schema changes is to use a second capture instance. Applications would use the first instance until the new capture instance is created. Then they should find the lowest LSN from the new instance and request all changes less than that value from the first instance. They then stop using the old instance and switch to the next instance. After all clients stop using the old capture instance, it can be deleted, and another one can be created the next time a schema change occurs.

Performance

Given the default configuration of 5-second intervals at which up to 10 scans of up to 500 commands are processed, the theoretical limit for change data capture performance under the default would be 1,000 commands per second. These values can be changed.

Each time a log scan is performed, a row is either written or updated to a structure exposed via a DMV. We can see what is happening with log scanning by executing the following command:

```
SELECT * FROM sys.dm_cdc_log_scan_sessions;
```

This command provides a wealth of information about the process. A few columns are of particular interest, such as *empty_scan_count*, which returns the number of scans during which no changes of interest were located. An estimate of the throughput of the system could be obtained by dividing the *command_count* by the *duration*. Latency is a measure of how long it takes for change rows to be recorded in the change table after the transaction they relate to.

Keeping tables and their related change tables on different filegroups is recommended.

Security

We have previously mentioned that to view data changes, a user must have SELECT permission on all columns that are part of the capture, and the user must be a member of the role (if any) specified when enabling change data capture at the table level.

Enabling change data capture at the database level requires membership in the sysadmin fixed server role, not just database owner permissions. Enabling at the table level requires database owner permissions, not just table owner permissions.

DDL operations on a table that is enabled for change data capture can only be performed by a member of the sysadmin fixed server role, the owner of the database, or a member of the db_ddladmin fixed database role. Users who would otherwise have permissions to perform those DDL operations (because they have been directly granted such permission) will receive error 22914 when they attempt to make DDL changes.

Effects on the Source System

Enabling change data capture within a database has an effect on the transaction log similar to that of transactional replication. The ability to truncate the transaction log is delayed until the log reader has processed any relevant changes. There is also an interaction with operations that would normally be minimally logged. Even though change data capture works with all recovery models, operations (apart from index operations) that would normally be minimally logged are fully logged instead. This allows full details of the changes to be available in the transaction log for collection by the log reader.

Errors occur during the log scanning process can be viewed via the *sys.dm_cdc_errors* dynamic management view.

Change tables include data from all columns in the table, not just those columns that were modified. To minimize the size of the change tables, it is possible to include a column list when enabling Change Data Capture for a table. If not all columns are being captured, you can view the list of columns by executing the following command:

```
EXEC sys.sp_cdc_get_captured_columns 'dbo.Employees';
```

When considering the size of the tables, it is important to take into account the retention requirements to support the target applications. From data that has been retrieved, it is possible to work out whether a particular column has been modified by querying the *sys.fn_cdc_has_column_changed* function.

Standard database backups, database mirroring, and log shipping are all supported with change data capture. If a database with change data capture enabled is restored from a backup to a different server, change data capture is disabled and all related metadata is deleted unless the KEEP_CDC option is used. Databases that are detached and reattached keep their change data capture configuration. If a database with change data capture enabled is attached or restored with the KEEP_CDC option to an edition of SQL Server other than Enterprise, an error 932 occurs and the restore or attach fails.

Removing the CDC Database

If you have been following along with the code in this chapter, you might wish to clean up the changes we have made in this section on change data capture. You can do this by:

```
EXEC sys.sp_cdc_disable_db;
GO

USE master;
GO

DROP DATABASE CDC;
GO
```

Conclusion

SQL Server 2008 has introduced a wealth of new technologies to assist with tracking access and changes to data. It is important to use each technology for its intended purpose:

- Extended Events provides a low-level (and low-impact) eventing system and can integrate with Event Tracing for Windows (ETW).

- SQL Server Audit is the correct solution for auditing and compliance work.

- Change tracking is a developer-oriented solution for synchronizing occasionally connected applications.

- Change data capture is the correct solution for providing a feed of data changes when populating a data warehouse.

Chapter 16
Service Broker

Roger Wolter

In the SQL Server 2005 edition of this book, I described Service Broker as the most powerful and least understood new feature in Microsoft SQL Server 2005. In SQL Server 2008, one might argue that Service Broker still isn't well understood, but in the three intervening years, a wide variety of Service Broker applications have been built. Many of these take advantage of the reliable messaging aspects of Service Broker—reliable event distribution, distributing content to local and remote Web sites; delivering banking transactions from branch banks to the main office; delivering point-of-sale (POS) transactions from remote stores to headquarters; real-time Extract, Transform, and Load (ETL) for data warehouse applications; and so on.

A surprising number of applications use Service Broker as an asynchronous task management system. For example, a large bank rehosted their nightly batch update routines written in Visual Basic as SQL common language runtime (CLR) stored procedures that executed tasks received from a Service Broker queue. This improved their batch update time from about eight hours to a few minutes. A large content management system uses Service Broker to reliably move content through the editing and approval workflow in the approval and publishing process.

The combination of Service Broker—to manage tasks reliably and transactionally—with Database Mirroring—for data reliability—has allowed several companies to build highly reliable services with faster failover and lower cost than any other option available. A large IT organization even uses Service Broker's ability to send messages in both directions over a TCP/IP connection to provide secure paths through a one-way firewall. The large number and wide variety of Service Broker applications in production mean that Service Broker is a well-proven technology. Developers adopting a Service Broker solution no longer have to think of themselves as pioneers.

Service Broker makes SQL Server a platform for building reliable, distributed, asynchronous applications. When combined with other SQL Server features such as CLR integration and the XML data type, SQL Server is a serious platform for building data-intensive services and applications.

Service Broker is not just an application platform, however. Because of its asynchronous nature, Service Broker is also an ideal tool for making many database tasks simpler, more efficient, and more robust.

In this chapter, I'll discuss the internal details of Service Broker and how it works, and I'll provide some compelling scenarios for using Service Broker in your database applications. I'll start with the key new feature of Service Broker, the dialog conversation.

Dialog Conversations

In most messaging systems, messages are the basic unit of communication. Each message is an isolated entity, and it's up to the application logic to keep track of sent and received messages. On the other hand, most real business transactions consist of a number of related steps or operations. For example, a simple purchase order often involves a series of message exchanges between the purchaser and supplier that continue for several weeks as items are ordered, prices are negotiated, shipment dates are agreed on, order status is communicated, shipment is confirmed, billing is completed, and payment is received. Similarly, think of the number of messages exchanged during the bidding for, purchase of, and delivery of an item from an online auction site. These simple examples illustrate that many real-world business transactions take a significant amount of time and involve many related steps.

Obviously, a business transaction that takes weeks to complete can't be handled as a single database transaction. Each step of the business transaction translates to one or more database transactions. Each database transaction is related to transactions that have already occurred and transactions that will happen in the future to complete the business transaction. The application must maintain the state of the business transaction so that it knows what has happened and what remains to be done. Because this is a database application, it's logical to assume that this application state will be maintained in the database and that updates to the state will be part of the database transactions that make up the business transaction.

The Service Broker dialog conversation was designed to make managing this type of business transaction reliable and simple. As I go through the features of dialog conversations and how they are implemented, you will see how the goal of supporting this kind of business transaction influenced the design of Service Broker. Obviously, not all business transactions fit this model of a long-running exchange of data between two systems. Many business transactions have a single step and can be executed as a single database transaction. Other business transactions only flow data in one direction—for example, a point-of-sale system at a grocery store that transfers a long series of scanned items to be inserted into a database. As you'll see, dialog conversations also handle these variations well.

Conversations

Service Broker defines a conversation as a reliable, ordered, and asynchronous transfer of messages between conversation endpoints. I'll discuss conversation endpoints in more detail later, but for now think of a conversation endpoint as code that can send or receive messages. The endpoints of a conversation might be in the same database, in different databases in the same SQL Server instance, or in different databases in different SQL Server instances.

Originally two types of conversations were defined for Service Broker. A dialog conversation is a reliable, ordered, bidirectional exchange of messages between exactly two endpoints, and a monolog conversation is a reliable, ordered stream of messages from one sending endpoint to many receiving endpoints.

Monolog conversations were cut early in SQL Server 2005, but they will probably be included in a later release. Because a monolog can be implemented as a bunch of dialogs from one sending endpoint to a bunch of receiving endpoints, the dialog conversation is more important and was implemented first. Some aspects of conversations are common to both dialogs and monologs, whereas other aspects apply only to dialogs or only to monologs, so the Service Broker T-SQL statements include both DIALOG and CONVERSATION. Because SQL Server 2008 has only one type of conversation, this amounts to two words for the same thing, but because the differentiation will be necessary when monologs are implemented, both terms are used in the language. This usage might lead to some initial confusion, but in the long run, it will be necessary to make monologs work.

The three distinguishing features of Service Broker conversations are the reliable, ordered, and asynchronous delivery of messages. Because these are key concepts, I'll explain them in some detail.

Reliable

Reliable delivery of conversation messages means that Service Broker will keep trying to deliver the message in the face of pretty much any type of failure or interruption, including the following:

- The sending database is stopped and started.

- The receiving database is stopped and started.

- The network goes down.

- The network is being reconfigured.

- The sending database or receiving database is being restored from backup.

- The sending database or receiving database fails over to a disaster recovery site.

- The sending or receiving database is being moved to a different server.

This kind of reliability means Service Broker applications don't have to be written to deal with delivery issues. When a message is sent, it is delivered reliably or the conversation is put into an error state and all endpoints of the conversation are informed of the error with an error message in the endpoint queue. As you can see, Service Broker goes to great lengths to avoid declaring an error on a conversation, but in some cases a conversation can be damaged badly enough that it can't continue. The other common source of conversation errors is the lifetime of a conversation expiring. In many cases, it doesn't make sense to keep trying to deliver messages forever. If you haven't received a response from the airline reservation system and the plane has left already, you don't really care what the answer is. To accommodate this scenario, you can set a maximum lifetime on a conversation. If the conversation is still around when the lifetime expires, an error is declared and error messages are sent to both conversation endpoints.

Reliable delivery also means the message wasn't changed or intercepted along the way, so Service Broker provides a wide range of security options to give you the assurance you need that the message was delivered securely and intact. Even if all Service Broker security is turned off, Service Broker uses checksums to ensure that the message didn't change in transit.

Ordered

Service Broker provides unprecedented facilities for message ordering within a conversation. Some messaging systems will ensure that messages are delivered in order, provided that the messages are sent in a single transaction and received in a single transaction. Messages in a Service Broker conversation will be received *and processed* in the order in which they are sent, even if they are sent in multiple transactions issued by multiple applications and received in multiple transactions by multiple different applications.

To see why this is important, imagine an order-entry application that receives an order header, three order lines, and an order footer. In a messaging system that doesn't ensure ordering, your application might receive an order line before it receives the order header, or it might receive the order footer before it receives all three order lines. This means the application must be able to recognize messages arriving out of order and store them somewhere until the missing messages arrive—greatly increasing the complexity of the application.

Even if the messages are delivered in order, if your application is multithreaded for efficiency, the messages still might be processed out of order. For example, if thread one receives the order header and starts processing it and then thread two starts processing the first order line, it's very possible that the order line will be processed before the order header is completely processed. This chain of events could occur because the order header is generally more complex than the order line and thereby requiring more processing, so inserting the order line into the database will fail because the order header isn't there yet. The application can try the order line again until it works, but this is inefficient and adds to the complexity of the application. If all the messages are in a Service Broker conversation, they will be received and processed in the order in which they were sent so that the application doesn't have to deal with the complexities of processing messages out of order.

Asynchronous

Asynchronous delivery of messages effectively decouples the endpoints of a Service Broker conversation from each other. The application at one endpoint of a conversation sends a message and then goes on to process more work without knowing when or where the message will be processed. It's entirely possible that the sending application and the receiving application never run concurrently. For example, an inventory application might send out manufacturing orders as shortages develop during the day, and the manufacturing orders might be read by a planning application that runs at night. Even if the sender and receiver are running concurrently, asynchronous message delivery means that the sending application doesn't have to wait around for the receiving application to finish processing the message. It can continue with other work and rely on Service Broker to reliably deliver the message to the receiver for the receiver to process when it has time available.

Asynchronous messaging means you can link fast systems and slow systems into a single application without worrying about the slow systems holding back the fast systems. For example, your new order-entry system can send shipping instructions to your clunky old shipping system without the shipping system slowing down order entry. Virtually all big, scalable, high-performance applications make asynchronous calls to slower parts of the system. For example, the operating system performs disk I/O asynchronously, and the Web server makes asynchronous network calls. Another example is SQL Server, which performs many asynchronous operations internally.

With Service Broker, asynchronous processing is now available to database application writers. This means, for example, that if you want to write a trigger that does a significant amount of work without slowing down updates to the table, you can have the trigger send a Service Broker message to another application that does the work. You can also have one stored procedure call several other stored procedures in parallel by using asynchronous Service Broker messages to start the other stored procedures. You will see an example of this later in the chapter.

Now that you've seen what a conversation is and what it does, I'll spend the rest of this section talking about how Service Broker implements conversations. When I'm done, you will have a thorough understanding of how Service Broker works because almost all of Service Broker revolves around conversations. I'll cover programming and security separately—not because they aren't tightly tied to conversations, but because they're big enough to justify their own headings.

Messages

So far, I've talked a lot about messages without ever saying what they are. *Messages* are the information exchanged in a conversation. Messages have two parts:

- A message header, which contains information about the message, such as its source and destination, sequence number, and security credentials

- A message body, which the application uses to transport data

The Service Broker message body is a VARBINARY(MAX) data type that can contain up to 2 GB of SQL Server data in a VARBINARY(MAX) column. A Service Broker message can exist either in the database or on the wire. In the database, it is a row of a SQL Server table whose columns contain metadata about the message and the message contents. On the wire, it is binary data sent in TCP/IP packets. I won't go into detail about the wire format, but the disk format will be discussed in the upcoming "Queues" section.

The header of a Service Broker message must contain a message type. The message type is just a name for the message that makes it easier to write Service Broker programs to handle messages. To see why a message type is required, think about an application for a human resources department that sends information to an employee database. One message might be an XML document with information on one employee's benefits, another might be an employee's photograph as a JPEG file, another might be a resume created in Microsoft Office Word, and so on. Without the message type to guide you, all you know is that all the message bodies are VARBINARY(MAX). Because Service Broker ensures ordering, you might get by with knowing the first message is XML, the second is a JPEG, and so forth. However, error messages get pushed to the front of a dialog, so that is a risky strategy. Because you can rely on Service Broker to always include the message type, you can write your application to extract the message contents into the appropriate data structure depending on the message type.

Before you can use a message type in a Service Broker application, you must create the type as a database object. The message type is one of several Service Broker metadata objects that are used to enforce constraints on Service Broker dialogs. Service Broker will use only message types that are defined in the metadata for the database, so you can be confident that your application won't receive a message type you don't know about. The simplest form of a message type is just a name. The following data definition language (DDL) code snippet will create two simple message type objects:

```
CREATE MESSAGE TYPE [//microsoft.com/Inventory/AddItem];
CREATE MESSAGE TYPE [//microsoft.com/Inventory/ItemAdded];
```

The only parameter in this case is the name. Notice that the name has a URL-like format. This doesn't mean that the message type exists somewhere out on the Web. This format is used to make it easier to uniquely identify a message type. This message type adds an item in an inventory application distributed by microsoft.com. The message type name is just a string, so *AddItem* would have been perfectly legal, but in a large distributed application, it's difficult to ensure that there will never be two different message types named *AddItem*. The URL format isn't required, but it can make your life easier when you start putting together large distributed Service Broker applications.

Note Message type names are sent in messages between databases that might have been configured with very different collations. To make this work, message type names and all other Service Broker metadata sent in the message header use a binary collation. This means that the names must match exactly, character for character, with both case and accent sensitivity. The failure to adhere to this case-sensitive matching is a common source of application errors.

Although you are free to put anything you want into a Service Broker message body, you can optionally have Service Broker do some basic checking of the message body for you as messages arrive on a conversation. This checking is specified with the VALIDATION clause of the CREATE MESSAGE TYPE command:

```
CREATE MESSAGE TYPE message_type_name
   [ VALIDATION = {   NONE
                    | EMPTY
                    | WELL_FORMED_XML
                    | VALID_XML WITH SCHEMA COLLECTION
                       schema_collection_name
                   } ]
```

The NONE option, as the name implies, performs no validation, and it is the default. The EMPTY option ensures that the message body is NULL. Messages with a type but no body are useful as flags. For example, a message that reports that an action has completed successfully might not have any data to convey, so a message with a type of "Success" with no body might be appropriate. The WELL_FORMED_XML option loads the message body into an XML parser and rejects the message if parsing fails. The VALID_XML option loads the message body into the XML parser and validates the XML with the specified SCHEMA COLLECTION. (See SQL Server Books Online for a more complete explanation of what a schema collection is and how to create one.) For purposes of this chapter, it's enough to know that the message contents must be valid based on the schemas in the schema collection. Because a schema collection can contain many schemas, it is possible to use a single schema collection to validate a number of message types.

Although using one of the XML validations will ensure that your application can handle the incoming message, Service Broker loads the message body into an XML parser to validate it and then, in most cases, the application will load it into a different parser to process it. This process can be a significant resource drain if message volumes and message sizes are large, so unless you are receiving messages from an untrusted source, it might make sense to just use validation until you have your application working correctly and then turn it off when you go into production. Because validation is configured per message type, it's possible to validate only a few message types that have a higher potential to be invalid.

All Service Broker metadata can be seen in SQL Server catalog views. The view for message types is *sys.service_message_types*. If you look at that view in a user database, you will find several system-defined message types. The message types that begin with *http://schemas.microsoft.com/SQL/ServiceBroker/* are used by the Service Broker features. The other system-defined message types are used by other features such as Query Notifications and Events, which use Service Broker to deliver messages.

Contracts

Just as message types constrain the names and contents of conversation messages, a Service Broker contract constrains which message types are allowed in a conversation. A contract, as its name implies, is an agreement between the endpoints in a Service Broker conversation as to which message types can be sent and who can send them. Because the Service Broker enforces the contract, applications that process the conversation can be assured that they won't receive any message types that they aren't equipped to handle. To further ensure this agreement, once a Service Broker contract is created, the list of message types can't be changed.

A contract, like a message type, is a piece of Service Broker metadata that is used by Service Broker to enforce constraints on conversations. Each contract has a name, a list of what message types can be sent on the contract, and information that specifies which endpoint can send the approved message type. Because the endpoints of a conversation are peers once the conversation is established, the only real differentiator among endpoints is which one started the conversation. The endpoint that started the conversation is called the INITIATOR, and the opposite endpoint is called the TARGET. These labels are used to specify which endpoint can send a message type. The contract must specify the allowed sender or senders of each message type in the conversation by specifying INITIATOR, TARGET, or ANY for the message type. Put this all together and you get the following CREATE CONTRACT statement:

```
CREATE CONTRACT [//microsoft.com/Inventory/AddItemContract]
  ([//microsoft.com/Inventory/AddItem] SENT BY INITIATOR,
  [//microsoft.com/Inventory/ItemAdded] SENT BY TARGET);
```

Notice that the contract also uses a URL-like name format because it too is sent as part of the message header. The contract name uses a binary collation also, so be careful of the case when typing the name.

There's no ALTER CONTRACT statement for adding or removing message types, so you have to get the CREATE CONTRACT right. The only way to change the message type list is to drop the contract and create a new one.

The catalog view for listing contracts is *sys.service_contracts*. The view that describes how messages are related to contracts is *sys.service_contract_message_usages*. The following query generates a list of all the message types in the database, what contracts they are used in, and which endpoints send them:

```
SELECT  C.name AS Contract, M.name AS MessageType,
  CASE
    WHEN is_sent_by_initiator = 1
      AND is_sent_by_target    = 1 THEN 'ANY'
    WHEN is_sent_by_initiator = 1 THEN 'INITIATOR'
    WHEN is_sent_by_target    = 1 THEN 'TARGET'
  END AS SentBy
FROM sys.service_message_types AS M
  JOIN sys.service_contract_message_usages AS U
    ON M.message_type_id = U.message_type_id
  JOIN sys.service_contracts AS C
    ON C.service_contract_id = U.service_contract_id
ORDER BY C.name, M.name;
```

DEFAULT Message Type

If you ran the previous query, you might have noticed a message type named DEFAULT and a contract named DEFAULT that contains the DEFAULT message type. These were created as a result of customer feedback that writing a simple Service Broker application wasn't very simple. If you want to write an application that just sends and receives simple messages and you want to handle all messages the same, you can use the DEFAULT message type and contract so that you don't have to define your own. In the Service Broker Data Manipulation Language (DML) commands, if you don't specify a message type or contract, DEFAULT is used.

Queues

When I defined conversations, I said they were reliable and asynchronous, meaning that messages survive network and database failures and can be delivered even if the sender and receiver don't ever execute at the same time. Service Broker makes this happen by storing messages persistently in the database until they are successfully delivered so that the messages won't be lost. The place messages are stored while they are in transit is called a *queue*. Queues are very common in computer systems. They are used to store work that passes between tasks that run at different rates. For example, the operating system places disk commands on a disk queue, and the disk controller executes them when it has time available and then removes them from the queue. Using a queue means the operating system doesn't have to wait for the disk controller to be available to issue a disk command. It puts the command on the queue whenever it wants and then goes on to handle other tasks while the disk controller is processing the command. This kind of queue is different from a Service Broker queue because it exists only in memory. However, the principle of loose coupling—enabling the tasks that write to the queue and the tasks that read from it to each run at their own rate—applies to both.

Many large database applications use tables in the database as queues. An order-entry system, for example, might put a list of orders that need to be billed in a table in the billing database for the billing system to handle. The order-entry system only has to wait long enough to insert the order into the billing table. It doesn't have to wait for the bill to be generated. This approach not only allows the order-entry system to process orders faster, but it also allows the order-entry system to keep running when the billing system is down. Although queues are common in database applications, they are usually difficult to implement and are a frequent source of problems. If multiple processes are inserting and deleting messages, blocking can cause performance issues and deadlocks. Getting locking right is difficult—too little locking causes multiple processes to get the same message and too much locking causes deadlocks and performance problems.

At its most basic level, Service Broker is database queues done right. Service Broker queues are hidden tables that are managed by Service Broker code. Service Broker uses its own locking scheme to maximize queue performance, and queue manipulation commands built into the T-SQL language give Service Broker the tight control it needs to manage queues efficiently. This level of control is one of the primary advantages of having Service Broker built into the database. An external process couldn't get the control over query execution and locking that Service Broker uses to optimize queue operations.

Service Broker queues store messages in internal tables. Internal tables are just like normal tables except they can't be used in SQL commands because the table name is hidden. To see the name of the internal table used by a Service Broker queue, you can run this query:

```
SELECT Q.name AS QueueName, I.name AS InternalName
FROM sys.service_queues AS Q
  JOIN sys.internal_tables AS I
    ON Q.object_id = I.parent_object_id;
```

You will find, however, that trying to issue a SELECT statement against the hidden table name will fail. If you want to see the contents of a queue, you can issue a SELECT statement against the queue name. This approach works because Service Broker creates a view on the internal table with the same name as the queue name. This view is not an exact view of the internal table. Some additional columns are created through joins with the metadata tables to provide names for values that are stored as internal IDs. One of the benefits of Service Broker is that you can see what messages are available in the queue with a simple SELECT statement. If you need to run a SELECT statement on an active queue, I suggest using SELECT * FROM *<queue name>* WITH (NOLOCK), because most Service Broker actions hold locks on rows in the queue.

Queues are the only Service Broker objects that actually store data. Because of this, you can create a queue in a SQL Server schema and specify a filegroup in which you want the messages stored.

The following statement will create a Service Broker queue:

```
CREATE QUEUE dbo.InventoryQueue
  WITH ACTIVATION (
    PROCEDURE_NAME = dbo.InventoryProc,
    MAX_QUEUE_READERS = 2,
    EXECUTE AS SELF);
```

The full syntax for creating a queue is shown here:

```
CREATE QUEUE <object>
  [ WITH
    [ STATUS = { ON | OFF }  [ , ] ]
    [ RETENTION = { ON | OFF } [ , ] ]
    [ ACTIVATION (
        [ STATUS = { ON | OFF } , ]
          PROCEDURE_NAME = <procedure>,
          MAX_QUEUE_READERS = max_readers,
          EXECUTE AS { SELF | 'user_name' | OWNER }
          ) ]
  ]
    [ ON { filegroup | [ DEFAULT ] } ] ]
```

Queue names are not sent in message headers, so they are just SQL Server object names with the same collation rules as normal SQL Server objects. Queues are also contained in SQL schemas, unlike the Service Broker metadata objects, so they can be referenced with three-part names.

You can ignore the ACTIVATION options for now because I'll explain them later. The STATUS option allows you to specify whether the queue should start handling messages as soon as it's created. You might want to create queues with STATUS set to OFF to keep them from getting filled up before you're ready, but be sure to use ALTER QUEUE to turn on the queue when you want to process messages.

The RETENTION option controls whether all messages should be kept until the conversation is ended. When RETENTION is ON, all messages going both directions in a conversation are kept in the queue until the conversation ends. Turning on RETENTION might be useful if you need to back out a long-running business transaction by running compensating transactions. The messages will allow you to track what you have done so far so that you know what you have to undo. RETENTION can sometimes be useful for debugging an application also. Generally, I would advise you to use RETENTION with extreme caution. With RETENTION ON, the queue will get very big very fast and performance might degrade significantly.

The ON *<filegroup>* option tells Service Broker where to create the hidden table to store messages. Queues normally don't get too big unless RETENTION is ON or the application that receives messages is not running for a while. You might want to consider not putting queues in the DEFAULT filegroup and instead put them in their own filegroup. This will keep a sudden growth in a queue from using all the free space in one of the critical filegroups. Because a queue is built on an internal table, there is no limit to how big a queue can become other than available disk space.

A key thing to remember is that all queues have the same schema. You are not allowed to add your own columns to a queue. Although defining your own message structure in a queue might seem like an attractive option, much of Service Broker's ability to rapidly transfer and manage messages in a dialog relies on the fact that Service Broker always knows the structure of a message and a queue. For example, if only one type of message could be sent in a conversation (because a queue could only hold one message structure), message ordering would be much less effective because a single order might be sent to three or four different queues. In this case, the application would have to assemble an order from different queues with messages arriving in a different order on each queue, making the application logic much more complex.

Most of the columns in a Service Broker queue are self-explanatory and well documented in SQL Server Books Online, but a few are worth describing in a little more detail. The *status* column records the state of a message in the queue. When it is first inserted the status is 1, which means it is ready to be received. After it has been read, if RETENTION is turned on, the status is set to 0, meaning it has been received and processed by the application and the transaction has been committed. If RETENTION is not on, you won't see this status because the message is deleted as soon as it is processed. A status of 2 means the message has been received out of order, so it can't be processed until the missing messages arrive. A status of 3 means the message was sent from the end of the dialog associated with this queue and then copied into the queue because RETENTION is ON. Sent messages won't appear in the queue unless RETENTION is turned on. With RETENTION turned on, an extra copy of the sent message is inserted into the queue. This is another reason RETENTION hurts performance.

The *priority* column influences the order that messages are received. Service Broker receives messages in priority order, but in the SQL Server 2005 release, priority is always 0 and there's no way to change it. SQL Server 2008 includes a feature to assign priorities to conversations. Conversations enforce message ordering, so priority within a conversation would be meaningless because messages have to be processed in order no matter what the priority is. The *priority* column in the queue is intended to set the relative priority of conversations. In SQL Server 2005, the best way to implement priority processing is to send high-priority messages to a different queue than low-priority messages and then allow the application to process them appropriately. This approach generally entails not processing messages from the low-priority queue unless the high-priority queue is empty. However, be careful when you design this, because getting the behavior you want means dealing with starvation of the low-priority queues if there are enough high-priority messages to consume all your resources. You'll also have to make sure that processing a low-priority message doesn't keep you from seeing a high-priority message arriving.

The last two queue columns worth commenting on are *queuing_order* and *message_sequence_ number*. These columns often cause confusion because they appear to be the same thing. The *queuing_order* column is the order that the message was placed on the queue regardless of the conversation to which it belongs. The *message_sequence_number* column is the order of the message within its conversation. This is the order that gets enforced when messages are received by an application. You might see gaps in the *queuing_order* values because Service Broker might skip messages so they will be received in *message_sequence_number* order.

Service Broker queues created with the CREATE QUEUE command hold messages that are ready to be received and processed. When Service Broker needs to store messages temporarily before they reach their final destination, it puts them in the *sys.transmission_queue* view. There is one *sys.transmission_queue* in every database. The structure of the *sys.transmission_queue* is a little different from the other queues because the Service Broker needs more information to send a message over the network. If possible, Service Broker will put a sent message directly on the destination queue. This is generally possible if the destination queue is in the same SQL Server instance as the sender, but it won't be possible if the destination is in a different instance. Service Broker has an internal routine called the *classifier*, which decides what to do with messages. The classifier will put a message in the *sys.transmission_queue* in the following cases:

- The destination is in a different SQL Server instance.

- The destination queue is disabled—STATUS = OFF. The most common cause of this is a poison message on the queue. See the "Poison Messages" section later in the chapter for more information.

- The Service Broker is disabled in the database where the destination queue is. This is generally caused by a database being attached or restored without the ENABLE_BROKER option.

- The destination is unknown. Reliable, asynchronous delivery can't fail just because the destination isn't known. The message will hang around on the *sys.transmission_queue* and be reclassified periodically until the destination is configured or the conversation lifetime expires.

Queues are the key to understanding how Service Broker works. At its lowest level, Service Broker puts messages on queues, takes messages off queues, or moves messages between queues. Most Service Broker problems turn out to be caused by messages being on the wrong queue. One of the most important sources of troubleshooting information is the *transmission_status* column of the *sys.transmission_queue* view. If the message has tried to leave the queue and failed, the *transmission_status* column will indicate what went wrong.

Services

A Service Broker conversation is a reliable, ordered exchange of messages between endpoints. Service Broker names the endpoints with service names. *Service* is a very overloaded word, but in the case of Service Broker, a service is just a name for a conversation endpoint. This is important to remember because many people assume "service" refers to an executable somewhere. In Service Broker, a service is linked to a queue that is the destination for messages sent to the endpoint identified by the service name. Why not just use the queue name? The service name is a logical name used in the code, whereas a queue is a physical object. This level of indirection means that applications written using service names can be deployed in different physical configurations without needing code changes.

The service object also defines which contracts can be used to establish conversations that target the service. The service that identifies the target of a conversation determines whether it will accept the conversation. Because the list of conversations is enforced by the Service Broker infrastructure, the target application can be sure that it will not receive any unexpected message types.

Here's a simple example of a CREATE SERVICE statement:

```
CREATE SERVICE [//microsoft.com/InventoryService]
  ON QUEUE dbo.InventoryQueue
  ([//microsoft.com/Inventory/AddItemContract]);
```

Notice that services are also known across the network, so the URL format for service names is recommended. This example shows only one contract, but any number of contracts can be associated with a service. Also, any number of services can be associated with a queue.

The catalogue view that exposes services is *sys.services*. This query lists service names and the queue name that receives messages targeted at the service:

```
SELECT S.name AS [Service], Q.name AS [Queue]
FROM sys.services AS S
  JOIN sys.service_queues AS Q
  ON S.service_queue_id = Q.object_id;
```

A service can use multiple contracts and a contract can be used in multiple services; the *sys.service_contract_usages* view shows the mapping between services and contracts. The following query displays the contracts associated with each service:

```
SELECT S.name AS [Service], Q.name AS [Queue], C.name AS [Contract]
FROM sys.services AS S
  JOIN sys.service_queues AS Q
  ON S.service_queue_id = Q.object_id
  JOIN sys.service_contract_usages  AS U
  ON S.service_id = U.service_id
  JOIN sys.service_contracts AS C
  ON U.service_contract_id = C.service_contract_id;
```

The conversation endpoint that initiates the conversation does not check the contract list of the initiator service when creating a conversation. For this reason, the contract list for initiator services is generally empty. The message types and contract used by the dialog are required to begin the dialog, so requiring the contract to be in the service list is redundant. That being said, if you want to put the contracts into the initiator service's list to document the interface, it doesn't cause any harm because Service Broker will ignore them. The danger is that if the initiator service's list is wrong, you will never know it.

Beginning and Ending Dialogs

You now know about all the pieces necessary for a dialog: message types to label the messages, a contract to define which message types can be sent by each endpoint, queues to hold messages at each endpoint, and services to tie all the endpoint pieces together. In this section, I will discuss the T-SQL statements to begin and end Service Broker dialogs. The endpoint that begins the dialog is called the *initiator* and the opposite endpoint is the *target*. The T-SQL command that begins a dialog is BEGIN DIALOG CONVERSATION. The following code snippet provides an example:

```
BEGIN DIALOG CONVERSATION  @dialog
  FROM SERVICE     [//microsoft.com/ManufacturingService]
  TO SERVICE       '//microsoft.com/InventoryService'
  ON CONTRACT      [//microsoft.com/Inventory/AddItemContract]
  WITH ENCRYPTION = OFF, LIFETIME = 3600;
```

This statement begins a dialog from the *ManufacturingService* endpoint to the *InventoryService* endpoint. The *@dialog* is an output variable that returns a *uniqueidentifier*, which is used to refer to the dialog in other Service Broker DML commands. The FROM SERVICE and

TO SERVICE clauses define the endpoints of the dialog. FROM SERVICE introduces the initiator service name, and TO SERVICE introduces the target service name. The initiator service name must exist in the database where the BEGIN DIALOG command is executed. The target service name is not validated when the command is executed because in many cases it might be in another database.

> **Note** One of the more frequently asked Service Broker questions is why the initiator service name is a SQL Server name and the target service name is a string. Although in the current implementation the target service name will always be a SQL Server name, it's assumed that at some point in the future Service Broker will be talking to services that are not necessarily SQL Server services. For this reason, the target service name is a 256-character string.

The ON CONTRACT clause specifies which contract will be used by this dialog to limit which message types can be sent on the dialog and which endpoint can send each message type. If this clause is omitted, the DEFAULT contract is used. The DEFAULT contract allows only messages of the DEFAULT type to be sent by either endpoint.

The ENCRYPTION parameter might more accurately be called "encryption required." If this parameter is set to ON, the BEGIN DIALOG command will fail if dialog security is not set up—specifically, a remote service binding must be defined for the TO SERVICE name. (See the "Dialog Security" section for an explanation of dialog security.) If the ENCRYPTION parameter is set to OFF, the decision of whether to use dialog security is a deployment decision. When the service is deployed, the administrator can decide whether to use security for the dialog based on the requirements of the installation.

> **Tip** When dialog security is used, the BEGIN DIALOG command will create a key to be used for encrypting the dialog messages. This dialog must be encrypted when it is stored in the database, so if ENCRYPTION is set to ON, the database must have a master key. You can create one with this command:
>
> ```
> CREATE MASTER KEY ENCRYPTION BY PASSWORD = 'Pass.word1';
> ```

The LIFETIME parameter sets the maximum time in seconds that the dialog can remain active. If the dialog still exists when the LIFETIME expires, messages of type *http://schemas.microsoft.com/SQL/ServiceBroker/Error* are put into the queues at both endpoints of the dialog. The state of both endpoints is changed to *'Error'* so that no more messages can be sent or received on the dialog. It's important to keep in mind that the dialog still exists until both endpoints end it, so your code needs to handle error messages.

Now that you know how to begin a dialog, you'll learn how to end one. In most applications, the application at one endpoint of the dialog will know that the dialog is complete. In a purchase order application, for example, the dialog might be complete after the purchaser has received acknowledgement that the ordered item has been paid for. The endpoint that determines that the dialog is complete will end its side of the conversation with an END CONVERSATION statement:

```
END CONVERSATION @dialog;
```

This command marks the endpoint as closed, deletes any messages still on the queue, and sends a message of type *http://schemas.microsoft.com/SQL/ServiceBroker/EndDialog* to the opposite endpoint of the dialog. This message is sent with a negative sequence number so that it will be received ahead of any other messages in the queue for this dialog. When the opposite endpoint receives the *EndDialog* message, it might continue to process any messages still in the queue, but it can't send messages on the dialog because the opposite endpoint is gone. Similarly, any messages in the *sys.transmission_queue* that haven't been delivered to the opposite endpoint of the dialog are deleted when an *EndDialog* message is received. When the endpoint has processed any outstanding messages, it should do any required cleanup and then issue an END CONVERSATION command to terminate its side of the conversation. After both endpoints have ended the dialog, Service Broker will clean up the dialog state.

In some cases, one of the endpoints will decide to end the dialog because an unrecoverable error has occurred. A simple example would be a purchase order for an invalid part number. In this case, the endpoint can specify an error number and error text to let the other endpoint know what the error was. When a dialog is ended with the error option, a message of type *http://schemas.microsoft.com/SQL/ServiceBroker/Error* is sent to the opposite endpoint instead of the end conversation message. Here's an example of ending a dialog with an error:

```
END CONVERSATION @dialog WITH ERROR = 31472
  DESCRIPTION = 'Invalid Purchase Order number furnished';
```

While developing a Service Broker application, you'll see that it's not unusual to end up with a number of "orphaned" dialogs. These are dialogs that are still hanging around after the application that used them is gone. Dialogs usually end up in this state either because the application didn't call END CONVERSATION on one of the endpoints or the target wasn't configured correctly and the dialog lifetime expired before the dialog was established. You can get rid of these dialogs by ending them with cleanup code—for example:

```
END CONVERSATION @dialog WITH CLEANUP;
```

This command will unconditionally terminate the dialog without sending a message to the opposite endpoint, and it will discard any unprocessed messages. Therefore, it should be used only if you're sure the dialog is no longer in use. You can use this statement in scripts to clean up large numbers of orphaned or expired conversations. For example, the following script will clean up all conversations with endpoints in an error state in the database where the batch is executed:

```
DECLARE @handle AS UNIQUEIDENTIFIER;
DECLARE conv CURSOR FOR
  SELECT conversation_handle
  FROM sys.conversation_endpoints
  WHERE state = 'ER';
```

```
OPEN conv;
FETCH NEXT FROM conv INTO @handle;
WHILE @@FETCH_STATUS = 0
BEGIN
  END Conversation @handle WITH CLEANUP;
  FETCH NEXT FROM conv INTO @handle;
END
CLOSE conv;
DEALLOCATE conv;
```

If you remove the WHERE clause from the SELECT statement, this script will get rid of all conversations in the database. This script obviously requires administrator privileges to run and should be done only to clean up test data. It should never be done on a system with real dialogs running.

Conversation Endpoints

You have learned by now that Service Broker dialogs are reliable, persistent conversations. In this section, I'll discuss how reliability and persistence are implemented. The state that Service Broker maintains about a conversation is visible in the *sys.conversation_endpoints* view.

To ensure reliable, exactly-once-in-order delivery, Service Broker must keep track of what messages it has received from the network. Because dialog messages must be in order, Service Broker doesn't have to keep a list of all the messages it has received. It is enough to keep track of the highest numbered message received successfully on the conversation. The *receive_sequence* column is the sequence number of the next message expected on this conversation. Large Service Broker messages might be sent as a number of smaller message fragments. Each fragment is tracked and acknowledged so that the whole message doesn't have to be re-sent in the event of an error. The *receive_sequence_frag* column tracks the fragment number of the last fragment received. Note that if a fragment or message is received out of order, it is not thrown away. It is retained so that it doesn't have to be received again, but the *receive_sequence* and *receive_sequence_frag* values are not updated until all the missing fragments have been received. The *send_sequence* column tracks the sequence numbers of messages sent so that the dialog knows which sequence number to assign to the next message.

> **Note** The actual sequence number stored is not the sequence number of the last message or fragment received or sent, but rather the next sequence number expected. For example, when message 4 has been received successfully, the *receive_sequence* column will contain 5 because that is the next sequence expected. Because of this, when a message is received, its sequence number is compared to the *receive_sequence* column. If the numbers match, the message is marked as received and the *receive_sequence* is incremented. Similarly, when a message is sent, the value in the *send_sequence* column is used as its sequence number and the column is incremented after the message is sent.

The *service_id* column identifies the service associated with this conversation endpoint. You can join with the *sys.services* view to find the name of the service. The *far_service* column gives the name of the service at the opposite endpoint of this conversation. This is a name instead of an identifier because the far endpoint might be in another database. If the dialog has been successfully established and a message has been received from the opposite endpoint, the *far_broker_instance* column will be filled with the GUID taken from the *service_broker_guid* column of the *sys.databases* entry for the database where the remote endpoint is located. Together, these columns determine the two endpoints of the conversation. Notice that there is no information about the network address of either endpoint. This is to allow either endpoint to move to a different network location during the lifetime of a dialog without affecting message delivery. Moving active dialog endpoints is a very powerful feature that provides flexibility and resilience in a Service Broker network.

The *state* and *state_desc* columns of the *sys.conversation_endpoints* view display the state of the conversation endpoint. The *state* column is a two-character abbreviation for the full state description given in the *state_desc* column. The full list of possible states and their meaning is given in SQL Books Online, but I'll highlight some of the more important states here:

- **CO or CONVERSING**   This is the normal state for a conversation in progress. Both endpoints are active and talking to each other.

- **ER or ERROR**   This means the conversation has encountered an unrecoverable error. The most common error is that the conversation lifetime has expired. Remember that even though the conversation is in an error state, it will not go away until both endpoints have called END CONVERSATION.

- **DI or DISCONNECTED_INBOUND**   This means that the opposite end of the conversation has called END CONVERSATION but this endpoint hasn't. If you see many conversations in this state, the code handling this endpoint is not calling END CONVERSATION when it should.

- **CD, or CLOSED**   This means the conversation is closed completely. On the target side of a conversation, Service Broker will keep the conversation around in a CLOSED state for about half an hour to prevent replay attacks where an attacker saves and then resends a message. If the conversation endpoint entry is still there when the replayed message arrives, it will be ignored. After a half hour, the message lifetime will have expired, so a replayed message will be discarded.

One of the more confusing aspects of the *sys.conversation_endpoints* view is the *conversation_handle* and *conversation_id* columns. Both of these are GUIDs that are used to identify a conversation. The *conversation_handle* is the handle used to address the dialog in T-SQL commands such as SEND or END CONVERSATION. Each endpoint has a different handle so that Service Broker knows which endpoint you are referring to in the command. For example, if both endpoints of a dialog are in the same database, the two endpoints are in the same view. In this case, they have to be different so that Service Broker knows whether you are sending a message from the initiator to the target or from the target to the initiator. The *conversation_id* is the same for both endpoints of the conversation. It is included in each message header so that Service Broker can determine which conversation a message belongs to.

There are several more columns in the *sys.conversation_endpoints* view, but I have covered the most interesting ones here. The rest of the columns are either security-related or useful only to Microsoft Customer Support Services (CSS) or the development team trying to isolate a problem.

Conversation Groups

One of the more difficult aspects of writing asynchronous messaging applications is dealing with multiple applications or multiple threads receiving messages from a queue simultaneously. To understand why this is an issue, think about a purchase order arriving in a message queue. The purchase order is sent as multiple messages—a header message, multiple order-line messages, and a footer message. If multiple threads receive messages from the same purchase order, one or more order lines might be processed before the purchase order header. These transactions would fail because the header isn't in the database yet. Transactional messaging handles this situation because when the order-line transactions fail, the transaction rolls back and the message is put back on the queue. However, it's possible for an order line to be processed multiple times before the header is present. This is inefficient but manageable. However, if an order footer closes out the purchase order before the last order line is processed, data might be lost. Because of these problems, many messaging applications are written with only one receiving process for each queue. This approach obviously doesn't scale well, but it is often necessary to maintain consistency in the data.

The multithreaded reader problem is a bigger issue with Service Broker conversations because Service Broker ensures in-order processing of messages in a conversation. If one thread processes message 20 and another thread processes message 21 of a conversation, it's possible for 21 to complete before 20, which violates message ordering. Service Broker solves this problem through use of conversation group locking.

Every conversation is associated with a *conversation group*. When an application sends or receives messages, Service Broker locks the conversation group so that no other code can receive or send messages on the locked conversation until the transaction holding the lock completes. This means that even if your application has hundreds of queue readers active, a conversation can be accessed by only one queue reader at a time. This is a very powerful feature because it means that even when thousands of messages are being processed simultaneously, the messages for a particular conversation are processed on one thread at a time. The logic for processing a conversation can assume that a given conversation is processed sequentially, so it doesn't have to deal with the issues associated with multithreaded applications. After the transaction that is processing messages for a conversation group commits, the lock is released and the queue reader goes on to process the next message on the queue, which might be from a different conversation group. Messages in a given conversation group might be processed by many different threads during the life of the conversation group, but they are processed on only one thread at a time.

By default, there is a one-to-one correspondence between conversations and conversation groups. Each conversation group is a row in the *sys.conversation_groups* view. When a conversation endpoint is created, a GUID is generated and a row is inserted into the *sys.conversation_groups* view with the GUID in the *conversation_group_id* column. Service Broker makes the conversation endpoint part of the conversation group by using the *conversation_group_id* value as a foreign key in the *conversation_group_id* column of the *sys.conversation_endpoints* view. Obviously, any number of conversation endpoints can be made members of a conversation group by using the *conversation_group_id* foreign key. When the conversation group is locked, the lock applies to all conversation endpoints related to the conversation group. To understand why locking a group of conversations is useful, think about a typical order-entry application implemented in Service Broker. When an order is received, the order-processing logic might create dialogs to the inventory service, shipping service, credit check service, and accounts receivable service, and then send messages to all these services in the initial order transaction. These services will process the messages they received from the order service and send responses. The responses will arrive back on the order queue in a random order that is based on how long it took to process the message. If these response messages are processed by different threads, the order-processing logic will have to deal with responses being processed on different threads simultaneously. On the other hand, if all the dialogs related to a particular order are put into the same conversation group, receiving a response from any of the dialogs in the group will lock the group and ensure that other messages from dialogs in the locked conversation group are only processed by the thread that holds the lock. Thus, all the conversations in the conversation group will be single-threaded. This means that the logic that runs in a highly parallel multithreaded system can be written as a single-threaded application because Service Broker manages concurrency.

There are three ways to group conversations into a conversation group in the BEGIN DIALOG command. You can specify the conversation handle of a conversation already in the group, you can specify the conversation group ID of an existing conversation group, or you can use your own GUID to create a new conversation group. The method you choose depends on what you know at the time you begin the dialog.

For example, if you want to create dialogs from the manufacturing service to the inventory and PO services in the same conversation group, the commands would look something like this:

```
BEGIN DIALOG  @ManufacturingHandle
    FROM SERVICE    [//microsoft.com/ManufacturingService]
    TO SERVICE      '//microsoft.com/InventoryService'
    ON CONTRACT     [//microsoft.com/Inventory/AddItemContract];

BEGIN DIALOG  @POHandle
    FROM SERVICE    [//microsoft.com/ManufacturingService]
    TO SERVICE      '//microsoft.com/POService'
    ON CONTRACT     [//microsoft.com/Inventory/AddPOContract]
    WITH RELATED_CONVERSATION = @ManufacturingHandle;
```

If the order service receives an order message and wants to begin a dialog to the inventory service in the same conversation group as the incoming order dialog, it would take the conversation group ID out of the incoming message and begin the inventory dialog like this:

```
BEGIN DIALOG  @POHandle
  FROM SERVICE      [//microsoft.com/OrderService]
  TO SERVICE        '//microsoft.com/InventoryService'
  ON CONTRACT       [//microsoft.com/Inventory/CheckContract]
  WITH RELATED_CONVERSATION_GROUP = @OrderGroupID;
```

This second syntax also allows you to make up your own conversation group ID. If the conversation group specified in the RELATED_CONVERSATION_GROUP parameter doesn't exist, a conversation group with that ID will be created. This approach allows you to use an existing GUID as the conversation group identifier. For example, if the order ID in your order database is a GUID, you can use it as the conversation group for dialogs related to that order. This makes relating incoming messages to the correct order simple. Be sure that the GUID you are using is unique, however. If it isn't, you might end up with unrelated dialogs in the same conversation group.

Sending and Receiving

Now that you have learned how to configure and begin a dialog, you're ready to learn how to send and receive messages on the dialog. The T-SQL command for sending a message on a conversation is SEND, and the command for receiving a message is RECEIVE. These command names can be misleading because there might or might not be a network involved in sending and receiving messages. The SEND command puts a message on a queue, and the RECEIVE command removes a message from a queue. In some cases, the message is transferred across a network to the destination queue, but if possible, the SEND command inserts the message into the destination queue directly and the RECEIVE command deletes the message from the same queue. Arguably, these commands should have been ENQUEUE and DEQUEUE, but most messaging systems use SEND and RECEIVE so these names were adopted.

The SEND command inserts a message into a queue. If the destination queue is available and is in the same database instance where the SEND command was executed, the message is inserted directly into the destination queue. Otherwise, the message is inserted into the transmission queue in the local database. The RECEIVE command dequeues a message from the destination queue. If the RETENTION option is OFF for the queue, the RECEIVE command translates to a DELETE ... OUTPUT command that deletes the chosen rows from the queue and returns the deleted rows. If the RETENTION option is ON, the *status* column of the messages received is updated from 1 to 0 and the updated rows are returned. Because the RECEIVE is done in a database transaction, if the transaction rolls back the delete or update is undone and the messages are put back on the queue as if nothing had happened.

The SEND command needs only three parameters: the handle of the dialog to send on, the message type to use for the message, and the contents of the message. The dialog handle might come from a BEGIN DIALOG command, from a received message, or from the application state. If the supplied dialog does not exist or is in the DI, DO, ER, or CD state, the SEND will fail. One of the more common Service Broker errors is the one returned from a SEND on a closed dialog. The message type supplied must exist in the local database and must be allowed in the contract for the dialog specified. If no message type is supplied, the DEFAULT message type is used and the dialog must be using the DEFAULT contract. The message can be any SQL type that can be cast to VARBINARY(MAX). The SEND command performs an explicit CAST internally, so you can supply any compatible type. The message content can be supplied as a variable or as a literal value. Putting this all together, the SEND command looks like this:

```
SEND ON CONVERSATION @dialog
  MESSAGE TYPE [//microsoft.com/Inventory/AddItem]
  (@message_body);
```

Notice that although a message has 14 columns, the SEND command has only three parameters. The other columns are obtained from Service Broker metadata based on the *conversation_handle* parameter (@dialog, in the example above). The conversation endpoint information is used to route and secure the sent message. It is important to remember that at its lowest level, a SEND is just an INSERT command. The major difference is that SEND uses the Service Broker metadata to fill in the required routing and security information from the established conversation associated with the SEND by the *conversation_handle* parameter before the message row is inserted into the queue. The SEND command can be executed with the same tools as the INSERT command—ADO.NET, ODBC, OLE DB, Management Studio, SQL scripts, and so on. This means you can add Service Broker commands to your application without installing any new software or learning new APIs.

The syntax of the RECEIVE command is similar to the SELECT command. You specify the message columns you want to receive, the queue you want to receive from, and optionally a limited WHERE clause. Here's a typical RECEIVE command:

```
RECEIVE TOP(1)
  @message_type = message_type_name,
  @message_body = message_body,
  @dialog       = conversation_handle
FROM dbo.InventoryQueue;
```

In this case, I chose to use the TOP(1) clause to receive only a single message. This is much less efficient than receiving multiple messages with each command, but the contents of a single message can be loaded into SQL variables for use in a stored procedure or script. A RECEIVE statement in a client-side program should retrieve all available messages as a record set.

The next section of the RECEIVE statement is the list of columns to be retrieved. It has the same syntax as a column list in a basic SELECT statement. In the example, only three columns are returned. These three columns are the minimum set of columns necessary to process a message. The *message_type_name* column indicates what kind of message has been received. You must always know the message type because even if the contract limits a service to a single incoming message type, error and end dialog messages might be received and must be processed appropriately. Using the *message_type_id* column instead of the name would be a little more efficient because an internal join is eliminated. However, there is no way to control the ID assigned to a message type, so using the ID isn't recommended unless you use only system message types that have stable IDs.

The FROM clause specifies which queue to receive messages from. The RECEIVE statement finds the oldest conversation group with messages available on the queue that is not already locked by another transaction. The command then locks the conversation group and uses a DELETE or UPDATE with OUTPUT command to retrieve the messages. Even if there are messages on the queue from multiple conversation groups, only messages from a single conversation group will be returned by a RECEIVE command. This approach ensures that a RECEIVE command will lock only one conversation group at a time, which improves parallelism. It is possible—and in many cases desirable—for a single transaction to hold multiple conversation group locks, but each RECEIVE statement locks only a single conversation group. If your program has done a lot of work to restore the state for a conversation group, receiving messages from another conversation group may require throwing that state away and retrieving the state for the new conversation group. If there are more messages on the queue for the original conversation group, it will be more efficient to retrieve them while you have the state loaded. To support this, you can specify which conversation group to receive messages from:

```
RECEIVE top(1)
    @message_type = message_type_name,
    @message_body = message_body,
    @dialog       = conversation_handle
FROM dbo.InventoryQueue
WHERE conversation_group_id = @CGID;
```

If there are no messages from the specified conversation group on the queue, this statement returns no rows.

In certain, rare circumstances, it makes sense to send a message and then wait for the response from that message. This is normally a bad thing to do because it negates the advantages of asynchronous messaging. However, in some cases, the application needs to know that an action is complete before continuing. In this case, you can receive messages from a particular conversation:

```
RECEIVE top(1)
    @message_type = message_type_name,
    @message_body = message_body
FROM dbo.InventoryQueue
WHERE conversation_handle = @dialog;
```

The problem with the RECEIVE statement is that if no messages are available on the queue, it returns immediately—just like a SELECT statement that finds no records. In some cases, this is the desired behavior because if the queue is empty, the application can do other things. On the other hand, in many cases polling the queue is a waste of resources. To use resources more efficiently, Service Broker allows you to wrap the RECEIVE statement in a WAITFOR statement. The WAITFOR statement allows the RECEIVE statement to return immediately if messages are in the queue but wait until a message arrives if the queue is empty. The RECEIVE statement now looks like this:

```
WAITFOR (
  RECEIVE top(1)
     @message_type = message_type_name,
     @message_body = message_body,
     @dialog       = conversation_handle
   FROM dbo.InventoryQueue
 ), TIMEOUT 2000;
```

The TIMEOUT clause defines when the WAITFOR statement should give up and return if no messages arrive. In this case, if there are no messages after 2000 milliseconds, the statement will return no rows. If a message arrives before the timeout expires, the statement returns immediately. If the TIMEOUT clause is omitted, the statement will wait until a message arrives on the queue no matter how long it takes.

Important The RECEIVE and SEND keywords must start the RECEIVE and SEND commands. Most SQL keywords that start commands—such as SELECT, INSERT, and UPDATE—are known to the parser as terminal keywords. This means that whenever the parser sees one of these keywords, it knows that a new command is starting. SEND and RECEIVE are not marked as terminal keywords because they are not part of ANSI SQL. To ensure that the parser knows that a new command is starting, the command before SEND or RECEIVE must end with a semicolon (;).

Activation

One of the more difficult aspects of writing queued, asynchronous applications is that because messages are received from the queue to be processed, there must be an application running to receive the messages. Most asynchronous applications use one of two techniques to accomplish this:

- Implement the receiving application as a service that runs continuously. This works well if messages arrive at a pretty constant rate because there is no startup time in the receiving application—it's there whenever a message arrives—and as long as the receiving application has enough capacity to cope with the average message volume, messages are always handled eventually.

- Provide the message delivery system with an activation facility that starts the receiving application when a message arrives. This technique has the advantage that if messages arrive in bursts, the receiving application isn't running continuously when there are no messages to process. Activation can also start more than one copy of the receiving application if messages are arriving faster than a single copy of the application can process them. By starting only as many applications as required, activation supports more efficient resource utilization by the receiving application.

Service Broker supports both of these techniques, so you can choose the one that matches your application requirements. Because activation is one of the cooler features of Service Broker, it receives a lot of attention and many people believe that activation is required for Service Broker applications. The truth is that you can use a variety of methods to execute the application that receives Service Broker messages. You can run it as a Windows service or startup job. You can schedule it to run at certain times using Windows scheduler or SQL Server Agent. You can start it as a Web Services or COM component. You can even just execute it whenever you think enough messages have built up in the queue.

In SQL Server 2008, Service Broker supports two kinds of activation—internal activation and external activation.

Internal Activation

Internal activation starts a specified stored procedure to process messages on a queue. The main requirement of the stored procedure is that it read and process messages from a queue. Because there is only one named stored procedure in the queue configuration, the activation stored procedure must be able to process any message type on the queue. Activation is configured with the ACTIVATION parameter of the CREATE QUEUE or ALTER QUEUE statement. The ACTIVATION parameter is shown here:

```
[ACTIVATION (
    [ STATUS = { ON | OFF } , ]
      PROCEDURE_NAME = <procedure>,
      MAX_QUEUE_READERS = max_readers,
      EXECUTE AS { SELF | 'user_name' | OWNER }
      ) ]
]
```

The STATUS parameter turns ACTIVATION on and off. I commonly leave activation off and run the consuming stored procedure manually until I'm sure everything is working correctly and then turn activation on so I know that the procedure is running correctly before introducing activation.

Activation Procedures

The PROCEDURE_NAME parameter specifies the name of the stored procedure that will be started when messages are available for processing. The procedure specified in this parameter is started by the Service Broker logic when there are messages to process in the queue. Usually, this stored procedure should contain a loop that receives and processes messages from the queue until the queue is empty. When the queue has been empty for the length of time specified in the WAITFOR statement with the RECEIVE command (see the section on sending and receiving) the RECEIVE statement will return no messages and the stored procedure should terminate.

One of the key performance considerations with activation is how long the WAITFOR statement should wait. If you set WAITFOR to a small value, the stored procedure will terminate as soon as the queue is empty. This is appropriate if messages are delivered intermittently—SQL Event Notifications, for example—so that there's no advantage to keeping an idle stored procedure around. If events are more frequent or if the stored procedure is expensive to start, a longer WAITFOR value—maybe 20 or 30 seconds—cuts down on the overhead of starting and stopping the procedure.

If the activation stored procedure requires a lot of complex processing—XML parsing or complex calculations, for example—it often makes sense to use a CLR stored procedure to process the messages. CLR stored procedures are usually relatively expensive to start, so a longer WAITFOR value is appropriate. I have seen several cases where developers used a T-SQL stored procedure to receive messages and then called a CLR stored procedure to process each message. I assume this was done because it's easier to write Service Broker code in T-SQL, but this technique incurs the CLR startup delay for every message processed, which can reduce performance significantly. A more efficient approach is to write the activation stored procedure completely as a CLR procedure so that it is started once by activation and then receives and processes messages within the procedure until the queue is empty. Using this technique, one application was able to use VB.Net code to process more than 8,000 messages per second.

While an activation stored procedure is processing messages from a queue, the Service Broker logic monitors the number of messages arriving on the queue and the number of messages being received from the queue. If the arrival rate is higher, Service Broker starts another copy of the activation procedure to process messages faster. This continues until either the activation procedures are able to process messages fast enough to keep up with the arrival rate or until the number of procedures reaches the number specified in the MAX_QUEUE_READERS parameter. The MAX_QUEUE_READERS parameter sets an upper limit on the amount of system resources you are willing to dedicate to processing messages from a particular queue. If you set this parameter to a small value, the queue may grow very large because the activation procedures can't keep up with the number of messages arriving on the queue. If this number is set too high, a burst of arriving messages can use up most of the resources of the database and slow other applications. I generally set the MAX_QUEUE_READERS parameter to a relatively small number—maybe 10 or 15—and monitor the number of messages in the queue at peak activity times. If the number of messages grows to hundreds of messages, I increase the MAX_QUEUE_READERS until the queue stays a reasonable size most of the time. Note that this parameter takes effect immediately, so if you use ALTER QUEUE to increase it, the number of stored procedures should increase within a few minutes.

When the number of messages arriving on the queue decreases, the running copies of the activation procedures will empty the queue and some of them will terminate. This continues until the arrival rate and receive rate are in balance again. The combination of Service Broker starting more copies of the procedure when required and the procedures terminating themselves when they have no more messages to process keeps the number of running stored procedures at the optimum number to handle the current number of incoming messages.

Activation Security Context

An activation stored procedure is started by the Service Broker logic in the SQL Server process on a background thread that isn't associated with an interactive database user. This is a common source of confusion because developers will frequently develop and test a Service Broker stored procedure by running it from SQL Server Management Studio and then discover that the procedure doesn't run the same way when it is executed in the background as an activation stored procedure. The usual problem here is that the activation stored procedure executes in a different security context. The EXECUTE AS parameter of the ACTIVATION parameter defines who owns the security context for the activation stored procedure. If EXECUTE AS is set to SELF, the stored procedure will execute as if it was executed by the user running the CREATE or ALTER QUEUE statement. I use this option for sample code because a user always has enough permission to set EXECUTE AS to himself so the sample will run without problems. If the EXECUTE AS parameter is set to OWNER, the stored procedure executes as if it was run by the user who owns the queue. This is generally safe because the owner of the queue has permission to RECEIVE messages from the queue. To provide the greatest control over the security context that the stored procedure uses, you can specify a particular user in the EXECUTE AS parameter. The user executing the CREATE or ALTER QUEUE statement must have permission to impersonate the user specified in the EXECUTE AS parameter. I recommend specifying a specific user because it's much easier for administrators to understand exactly which permissions the stored procedure has.

Two issues often trip people up when they use activation stored procedures. First, they test the stored procedure using their own security credentials by running the procedure from Management Studio and then setting up the activation stored procedure to execute as a different user—so it behaves differently because the security context is different. Second, an activation stored procedure has the SQL Server permissions of the user specified in the EXECUTE AS clause but doesn't have the Windows permissions of that user because SQL Server can't impersonate the Windows user. This also results in different behavior when the procedure is run from Management Studio by a user with a particular set of Windows permissions and when the procedure is run in the background where those Windows permissions aren't used. If you need the process that receives and processes Service Broker permissions to perform Windows actions, it is generally easier and more secure to process the messages from a Windows service instead of from a stored procedure.

Using Activation

Service Broker Activation was originally developed to ensure that SQL resources were always available to process Service Broker messages when they arrived. This is still the main purpose for activation, but many users have discovered that being able to put a message on a queue to automatically cause a stored procedure to execute in a different security context, a different transaction, and even a different database has a lot of other uses. Many systems have batch tasks that run in the background after the primary task has completed. Some examples are: shipping tasks that execute after an order is placed, settling an account after a financial transaction, and writing an audit record after a critical transaction. Service Broker's reliable message processing ensures that these tasks happen reliably without impacting the primary task, and activation creates a transaction and security context for the background tasks to execute in. Service Broker can create a distributed execution environment where tasks are reliably sent to remote databases for execution by activation procedures. Taken together, Service Broker's activation capabilities can make Service Broker the core of a reliable, distributed, asynchronous job execution system.

External Activation

Although Service Broker is primarily a database feature, in several scenarios having an external application process Service Broker messages makes a lot of sense. There are many reasons why developers want to execute Windows programs or functions from SQL Server stored procedure code, but there really aren't many secure, safe, and efficient ways to do it. For example, one of the more common issues is how to execute a Web service from a stored procedure. Extended stored procedures can call Windows functions, but the Windows code runs in the SQL Server process space, so a bug in your Windows code can bring down the database. A lot of people think that CLR stored procedures are the answer, but the Windows Communications Foundation (WCF) assemblies can't be run in safe CLR procedures, so they are also high risk.

Even if you do decide that calling Windows functions directly from stored procedures will work for you, you are now using some of the most expensive processor cycles in your data center to call Web Services. In most organizations, the most sophisticated and expensive servers are dedicated to the databases, so running extraneous code in the database doesn't make much economic sense. An alternative approach that maintains the transactional reliability of a database operation without taking processor cycles away from the database engine is to put a Service Broker message on a queue for each task and then start a Windows application on another server that reads the Service Broker queue, executes the specified task, and sends the response as a Service Broker message on the same dialog. Because the reliability of the queues is handled in the database, the systems that process the messages can be relatively inexpensive processors and still provide reliable message processing. If a machine that is processing messages crashes, all the transactions that are consuming messages will roll back. The messages can then be processed by another computer.

QUEUE_ACTIVATION Event

If the resource demands for message processing on the non-database machines are fairly constant, you may want to process the messages with Windows services or even command-line processes. If, however, demand changes over time, it's more efficient to use an activation system similar to the internal activation provided by Service Broker. In SQL Server 2005 and the initial release of SQL Server 2008, Service Broker provides a SQL Server event that you can associate with a queue that will fire at the same time that internal activation would have started an additional copy of the activation stored procedure for the queue. Like all SQL Server events, the QUEUE_ACTIVATION event puts an event message on a Service Broker queue when it fires. This message is not the business message that Service Broker is delivering but a system message that indicates that the external activation service should start another copy of the activated program that processes the messages.

The following example shows how to set up the QUEUE_ACTIVATION event. First you must make sure that the queue you are going to monitor is not already set up for internal activation:

```
ALTER QUEUE [dbo].[InventoryQueue] WITH ACTIVATION ( DROP )
```

Next, create the queue and service to receive the QUEUE_ACTIVATION event messages:

```
CREATE QUEUE [ExternalActivationQueue]

CREATE SERVICE [ExternalActivationService] ON QUEUE [ExternalActivationQueue]
([http://schemas.microsoft.com/SQL/Notifications/PostEventNotification])
```

Note that this same service and queue can be used to receive activation messages from a number of Service Broker queues. The *PostEventNotification* Service Contract is system-defined so you don't have to create it. After the service to receive QUEUE_ACTIVATION events has been created, you must associate this service with the queues you want to receive activation messages from with the CREATE EVENT NOTIFICATION statement:

```
CREATE EVENT NOTIFICATION ExternalActivationEvent
 ON QUEUE [dbo].[InventoryQueue] FOR QUEUE_ACTIVATION
 TO SERVICE 'ExternalActivationService' , 'current database';
```

This example sets up the external activation event for the *InventoryQueue* that is created in the sample code later in this chapter. The QUEUE_ACTIVATION event messages will be sent to the *ExternalActivationService*. The message placed on the *ExternalActivationQueue* will look like this:

```
<EVENT_INSTANCE>
    <EventType>QUEUE_ACTIVATION</EventType>
    <PostTime>2009-01-01T17:57:33.793</PostTime>
    <SPID>22</SPID>
    <ServerName>InvServ</ServerName>
    <LoginName>Earl</LoginName>
    <UserName>dbo</UserName>
```

```
    <DatabaseName>Inventory</DatabaseName>
    <SchemaName>dbo</SchemaName>
    <ObjectName>InventoryQueue</ObjectName>
    <ObjectType>QUEUE</ObjectType>
  </EVENT_INSTANCE>
```

Notice that this message contains the server, database, schema, and queue name of the queue that needs to be serviced so the external application has all the information it needs to get to the queue that has messages waiting.

This event is all you need to build your own external activation process. Your process should open a connection to the database where the *ExternalActivationQueue* is located and start reading messages from the queue. For each message received, start a program to read messages from the queue specified in the EVENT_INSTANCE message. The external activation program should read and process messages until the queue is empty just like an activation stored procedure.

External Activation Service

Writing an external activation service isn't too difficult, but implementing robust, reliable, flexible application can be a challenge. After the SQL Server 2008 release the development team implemented a fully supported external activation service and released it in a SQL Server 2008 feature pack. It is now available for download here: *http://www.microsoft.com/downloads/details.aspx?familyid=228de03f-3b5a-428a-923f-58a033d316e1&displaylang=en*.

The Microsoft SQL Service Broker External Activator is a Windows service named Service Broker External Activator. It receives activation messages from the QUEUE_ACTIVATION event queue and starts an external process to receive Service Broker messages from the queue identified in the event message. External activation tracks the processes it has started and attempts to restart them after a failure. Just as with internal activation, the external activator assumes that the processes it starts will continue to receive and process messages until the queue is empty. The length of the WAITFOR parameter will determine how long the queue must be empty before the activation process exits. In many cases, an external process is more expensive to start than a stored procedure so you may want to consider using a longer WAITFOR time for an external activation process.

To function correctly, the external activator needs to know how to connect to and receive messages from the event queue and which external process should be started. These values are specified in the file *C:\Program Files\Service Broker\External Activator\Config\EAService .config*. Here's an example of a configuration:

```
<?xml version="1.0" encoding="utf-8"?>
<Activator
 xmlns=http://schemas.microsoft.com/sqlserver/2008/10/servicebroker/externalactivator
 xmlns:xsi=http://www.w3.org/2001/XMLSchema-instance
 xsi:schemaLocation="http://schemas.microsoft.com/sqlserver/2008/10/servicebroker/
 externalactivator EAServiceConfig.xsd" >
```

```
<NotificationServiceList>
  <NotificationService name="ExternalActivationService" id="65541" enabled="true">
    <Description>External activation sample</Description>
    <ConnectionString>
      <!-- All connection string parameters
           except User Id and Password should be specified here -->
      <Unencrypted>server=InvServ;database=Inventory;Application
Name=External Activator;Integrated Security=true;</Unencrypted>
    </ConnectionString>
  </NotificationService>
</NotificationServiceList>
<ApplicationServiceList>
  <ApplicationService name="InventoryApp" enabled="true">
    <OnNotification>
      <ServerName> InvServ </ServerName>
      <DatabaseName> Inventory </DatabaseName>
      <SchemaName>dbo</SchemaName>
      <QueueName> InventoryQueue </QueueName>
    </OnNotification>
    <LaunchInfo>
      <ImagePath>c:\ExternalActivator\InventoryApp.exe</ImagePath>
      <CmdLineArgs>/RedmondWhse</CmdLineArgs>
      <WorkDir>c:\ExternalActivator</WorkDir>
    </LaunchInfo>
    <Concurrency min="1" max="10" />
  </ApplicationService>
  <ApplicationService name="ManufacturingApp" enabled="true">
    <OnNotification>

      <ServerName>InvServ</ServerName>
      <DatabaseName>Manufacturing</DatabaseName>
      <SchemaName>dbo</SchemaName>
      <QueueName>ManufacturingyQueue</QueueName>
    </OnNotification>
    <LaunchInfo>
      <ImagePath>c:\ExternalActivator\ManufacturingApp.exe</ImagePath>
      <CmdLineArgs>/RedmondPlant</CmdLineArgs>
      <WorkDir>c:\ExternalActivator</WorkDir>
    </LaunchInfo>
    <Concurrency min="0" max="5" />
  </ApplicationService>
</ApplicationServiceList>
<LogSettings>
  <LogFilter>
  </LogFilter>
</LogSettings>
</Activator>
```

The *NotificationService* element specifies the connection to the activation event service. The service name is an attribute of the *NotificationService* element, and the *ConnectionString* element is an ADO.NET connection string for the database where the service is located. Note that for security reasons, only Windows authenticated connections are supported. Even though the *NotificationService* element is wrapped in a list, the current external activation service only supports one activation event service.

The *ApplicationServiceList* element contains an *ApplicationService* element for each queue that has a QUEUE_ACTIVATION SQL Event Notification defined. The *OnNotification* element specifies the server, database, schema, and queue names that are matched against the names in the QUEUE_ACTIVATION event to determine which queue fired the event. The *LaunchInfo* element specifies the program that gets started to process the messages on the queue that fired the activation event. The *Concurrency* element contains two attributes, *min* and *max*, that specify the minimum and maximum number of activation processes the external activator will start. If the minimum concurrency attribute is greater than 0, the specified number of processes are started as soon as the external activation service starts. This is useful if the activation process takes a while to start because there will always be a minimum number of processes available to process messages on a queue even if the queue is empty. More detailed information about setting up the external activation service is available in the SSBEA.doc document that comes with the release.

I'm not including sample code for implementing an external Service Broker activation program. There are good samples in the Service Broker samples that ship with the database release. Remember that just as with internal activation, the WAITFOR timeout value controls how long the queue must be empty before the activation process detects the empty queue status and terminates. If you set a minimum concurrency value to keep a process running all the time, you can set the WAITFOR timeout lower than you would with an internally activated procedure because at least the specified minimum number of processes will always be available to receive incoming messages.

Conversation Priority

One of the most requested features for Service Broker 2005 was the ability to set priorities to determine the order in which messages were processed by a Service Broker service. An asynchronous queued system needs to deal with the fact that not all messages are equally urgent. For example, a POS system may have hundreds of transactions queued to be sent from a store to the headquarters system at the end of the day when a clerk at the store needs to run a credit check to process a customer standing at the register. Obviously processing the credit check after all the day's work is done isn't a good experience for the customer waiting to buy groceries, so there has to be a way for a message to jump to the head of the queue.

In many messaging systems, there is a way to bump up the priority of a message so it will get processed first. In a system that uses a database table as a queue, there's a priority column in the table and the ORDER BY clause is modified to put priority to the first column in the key. This simple system won't work for Service Broker conversations because messages within a conversation must be processed in order. That means that putting a higher priority on message 5 than message 4 in a conversation won't work because message 4 must be processed before message 5. This means that in Service Broker, priorities must be assigned at the conversation level—not the individual message level.

SQL Service Broker 2005 didn't support priorities so most developers who needed to support conversation priority either created a high-priority conversation and used a WHERE clause in the RECEIVE statement to receive all the messages in the high-priority conversation first or created a high-priority queue so a queue would always be available for high-priority messages. Although both techniques are valid and may still be the best way to implement some scenarios, they are complicated to implement and generally only offer two priorities. Thus there was a need for a more capable priority feature in SQL Server 2008.

Receiving messages in priority order isn't hard. It's primarily a case of implementing the right ORDER BY clause in the statement that receives messages from the queue. SQL Server 2005 Service Broker messages had a priority column, and messages were actually returned in priority order, but there was no way to set the priority of a conversation. This was primarily a case of running out of time to implement priorities in SQL Server 2005, but there were also issues with deciding what the behavior of a conversation should be. Should priority be set by the initiator or the target? Should the priority of each conversation be set when it is created, or should priority be associated with the service contract? Do all conversations with the same service contract have the same priority, or does priority depend on who started the conversation? After a lot of thoughtful analysis, the Service Broker team came up with a priority feature for Service Broker that is simple and supports a wide variety of scenarios.

One easy way to set priority for a conversation would have been to add a priority parameter to the BEGIN DIALOG statement. The biggest problem with that approach is that the initiator has total control over the priority of the conversation. This might be acceptable if you control both ends of the conversation, but in many scenarios, the organization beginning the conversation is not the same organization that processes the messages. If that is the case, what are the chances that any of the initiators will decide that their conversations should be processed with a low priority? Another possibility would be for the target to control priorities for incoming conversations by setting the priority in the contract for the services configured for a queue. This solution also has the problem that only one end of the conversation controls the priority. In addition, contracts can't be altered once they are created, so a priority system based on contracts wouldn't have any flexibility. The final consideration is that priority is generally managed by the operations group and may change frequently as requirements change, so using the metadata or programming logic of an application to control priorities may not be practical because changes might require a software release cycle to change application code.

Broker Priority Object

The Service Broker team solved these problems by developing a *broker priority object* to control conversation priorities. When Service Broker creates a conversation, it looks through the collection of broker priority objects to find one that matches the conversation being created and assigns the priority configured for that object to the conversation. Because the priority object is a separate object with very loose coupling to the Service Broker services, you can use a broker priority object to set the priority for services that were developed by someone else without touching the application code. The broker priority object sets the priority for one endpoint of a conversation, so you can define the initiator and target priorities independently. Setting the priority of the conversation endpoints independently provides a lot of flexibility. For example, in the POS example we mentioned earlier, the store might set the priority of the credit check to the highest value available (10) so that credit check messages don't get stuck behind transaction history records, whereas the central office might give credit check conversations for larger stores a higher priority than for smaller stores. The ability to set the priority for each endpoint of the conversation independently allows for two different priority schemes to be applied to the same conversation, providing much more control than setting a single priority for the conversation would allow.

To identify a conversation to assign a priority to, Service Broker uses the local service, the remote service, and the contract that defines the conversation. These are the same three parameters that BEGIN DIALOG requires, so it's easy to see that these parameters are sufficient to identify a type of conversation. Each of these parameters can be replaced with the wildcard keyword ANY. For example, using ANY for the remote service parameter means the same priority will be used for the specified local service and contract no matter what the remote service is.

Priorities range from a low of 1 to a high of 10. If no priority is specified for a conversation, it is assigned a value of 5. The priority setting applies to both send statements and receive statements. A priority object in the initiator database controls the priority of messages sent from the initiator and messages received from the initiator queue. The priority setting in the target side controls the order of receives from the target queue and sends of messages back to the initiator. Remember that a send command to a service in the same SQL Server instance puts the message directly on the destination queue as part of the send transaction if possible so priority doesn't influence these sends. When messages go to remote SQL Server instances, the send transaction puts the message on the transmission queue and priority controls the order that these messages are sent to remote systems. A RECEIVE command will retrieve messages from the highest-priority conversation group that has messages available for processing. Within a conversation group, messages are received in conversation priority order. The messages within a conversation are still received in the exact order they were sent because priority only applies between conversations.

A description of how priority changes the RECEIVE statement processing might help. In SQL Server 2005, a RECEIVE statement would look for conversations that had messages in the queue that weren't already locked by another queue reader. Within this group of conversations, it would find the conversation that contained the message that had been the in queue the longest and lock the conversation group that contained that conversation. As long as the conversation group lock was held (the transaction wasn't committed) RECEIVE statements from that session would return messages from that group with the conversation in the group with the oldest message first and in message order within the conversation. Adding priority to this algorithm means that priority is considered before the age of the message. That is, instead of looking for the oldest unlocked message, Service Broker looks for the message from the conversation with the highest priority, locks that conversation group, and returns messages ordered by priority and conversation order. Note that this may mean that a session processes a lower-priority message even though there are higher-priority conversations with messages in the queue but in a different conversation group. If two or more conversations with the same priority contain messages, the conversation with the oldest message is chosen.

Remember that priorities only control the relative priority of conversations in a RECEIVE statement. A common mistake is to decide to increase message processing speed by setting all the conversations to priority 10. This results in the same behavior as if all the priorities were set to 1 or if no priorities were set at all. You will generally have to play with priorities a bit before you get the right processing order for your application. That's why it's a good thing that priorities are easy to change. Keep in mind that changing the priority affects new messages that are added to the queue. The priority of messages already in the queue stays the same, so if you change the priority you may have to wait a while to see the effects of your change.

Now that you understand how service broker priorities let's look at what it takes to set them up. The DDL to set up broker priority objects looks like this:

```
CREATE BROKER PRIORITY ConversationPriorityName
FOR CONVERSATION
[ SET ( [ CONTRACT_NAME = {ContractName | ANY } ]
        [ [ , ] LOCAL_SERVICE_NAME = {LocalServiceName | ANY } ]
        [ [ , ] REMOTE_SERVICE_NAME = {'RemoteServiceName' | ANY } ]
        [ [ , ] PRIORITY_LEVEL = {PriorityValue | DEFAULT } ]
      )
]
[;]
```

Like all SQL Server objects, a broker priority object has a name that you use to refer to the object: *ConversationPriorityName*. The next three parameters define which conversation endpoints this priority object refers to. The CONTRACT_NAME is pretty self-explanatory. The LOCAL_SERVICE_NAME and REMOTE_SERVICE_NAME are relative to the database where the priority object is created. From the initiator end of the conversation, local is the initiator service and remote is the target service. From the target end of the conversation, local is the target service and remote is the initiator service. This applies even if both the initiator and target are in the same database. Just as with the BEGIN DIALOG statement, the local service is the name of a service object in the local database and the remote service parameter is a string which specifies the name of a service in the remote database. The PRIORITY_LEVEL is the priority to be assigned to endpoints that match the first three parameters.

Examples

The following examples should help clarify how priorities are configured. The first example simply sets the priority of both ends of an expense submission dialog to 8. The first priority object is created in the database where the *ExpenseSubmit* service is configured. For this example, assume this is the initiator of the conversation. Notice that all three identification parameters are specified so that only conversations with the specified contract, local service, and remote service are assigned a priority of 8 by this statement.

```
CREATE BROKER PRIORITY ExpenseSubmitPriority
    FOR CONVERSATION
    SET (CONTRACT_NAME = [ExpenseSubmission],
        LOCAL_SERVICE_NAME = [ExpenseSubmit],
        REMOTE_SERVICE_NAME = N'ExpenseProcess',
        PRIORITY_LEVEL = 8);
```

The following statement creates an object to set the priority of the target end of the same conversation. It is the same as the previous statement except the local and remote service names are reversed. In this case both endpoints of the conversation are assigned a priority of 8. Although it is common for both endpoints to have the same priority, it isn't required and there are many scenarios that require different priorities for the initiator and target endpoints. For example, a target service might assign different priorities to different initiators based on relative importance or service-level agreements.

```
CREATE BROKER PRIORITY ExpenseProcessPriority
    FOR CONVERSATION
    SET (CONTRACT_NAME = [ExpenseSubmission],
        LOCAL_SERVICE_NAME = [ExpenseProcess],
        REMOTE_SERVICE_NAME = N'ExpenseSubmit',
        PRIORITY_LEVEL = 8);
```

The next example sets the priority of all conversations with a particular remote service. Because both the contract name and local service name are set to the wildcard value of ANY, the priority value applies no matter what the local service name is or what the contract name is. This might be used to assign priorities by the relative importance or urgency of conversations with a particular remote service. For example, you may decide that all conversations with the call center have higher priority because the response time impacts customer satisfaction.

```
CREATE BROKER PRIORITY SpringfieldPriority
    FOR CONVERSATION
    SET (CONTRACT_NAME = ANY,
        LOCAL_SERVICE_NAME = ANY,
        REMOTE_SERVICE_NAME = N'SpringfieldExpense',
        PRIORITY_LEVEL = 7);
```

The next statement sets the priority of all conversations that use the *ExpenseSubmission* contract no matter what the local and remote services are. This is probably the most common use case—a particular type of conversation either needs to have its messages processed first or is a background task that can afford to wait. In this example, *ExpenseSubmission* has a higher priority because there is an interactive user waiting for the results. There may be other expense-processing conversations that do things like submit the expense report for approval or send the report to the accounting system for payment. These run in the background with a lower priority so their messages will be processed after all the *ExpenseSubmission* messages.

Another reason you might want to set both the local and remote service names to ANY would be to set the priority of a conversation where both endpoints are in the same database. Because both services can take any value, the priority object matches both endpoints of the conversation so a single object can set both priorities.

```
CREATE BROKER PRIORITY ExpenseProcessPriorityAll
    FOR CONVERSATION
    SET (CONTRACT_NAME = [ExpenseSubmission],
        LOCAL_SERVICE_NAME = ANY,
        REMOTE_SERVICE_NAME = ANY,
        PRIORITY_LEVEL = 8);
```

The next example sets a priority of 9 for any conversation associated with the *ExpenseProcess* service. This would be appropriate if this service was one of the most important services in the database. Any conversations with *ExpenseProcess* as a target and any conversations that the *ExpenseProcess* service starts would have a priority of 9.

```
CREATE BROKER PRIORITY ExpensePriority
    FOR CONVERSATION
    SET (CONTRACT_NAME = ANY,
        LOCAL_SERVICE_NAME = [ExpenseProcess],
        REMOTE_SERVICE_NAME = ANY,
        PRIORITY_LEVEL = 9);
```

The final example sets the priority of any conversation with *ExpenseProcess* as the local service and *ExpenseSubmit* as the remote service to 3. When these two services communicate, the conversation has a low priority. One possible scenario would be that the *ExpenseProcess* service is in the same database as an order entry service and you want to ensure that taking orders wins over submitting expense reports.

```
CREATE BROKER PRIORITY ExpenseProcessAllContracts
    FOR CONVERSATION
    SET (CONTRACT_NAME = ANY,
        LOCAL_SERVICE_NAME = [ExpenseProcess],
        REMOTE_SERVICE_NAME = N'ExpenseSubmit',
        PRIORITY_LEVEL = 3);
```

Sample Dialog

In this section I'll present a simple Service Broker application that demonstrates how all this fits together. I'll start with an application that runs in a single database and, in subsequent sections, show how to move this application into a distributed environment.

The application to be built is an inventory application that accepts items from a manufacturing application and adds them to inventory. To simplify the code, it will be completely implemented as T-SQL stored procedures. In reality, one or more of the services would probably be either an external application connecting to the database or a CLR stored procedure.

A stored procedure called *AddItemProc* will send a message to the *InventoryService* with an XML body that contains an item to be added to the inventory. The procedure *InventoryProc* receives the message from the *InventoryQueue*, inserts a row in the Inventory table, and sends a response back to the *ManufacturingService*. The procedure *ManufacturingProc* receives the response message from the *ManufacturingQueue* and updates the State table with the response information. Figure 16-1 shows how this works.

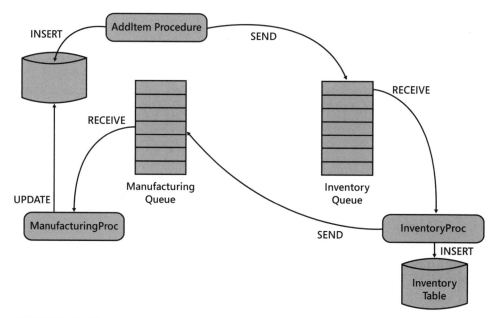

FIGURE 16-1 Add inventory sample

First, run the code in Listing 16-1 to create the Service Broker objects required to implement the Inventory service that receives and processes *AddItem* messages. Note that all the grey background code in the rest of the chapter is part of a single extended sample. Each sample assumes you have run the preceding samples.

LISTING 16-1 Inventory service metadata

```
CREATE DATABASE Inventory;
GO
USE Inventory;
GO


-------------------------------------------------------------------
-- Create the message types we will need for the conversation
-------------------------------------------------------------------


CREATE MESSAGE TYPE [//microsoft.com/Inventory/AddItem];
CREATE MESSAGE TYPE [//microsoft.com/Inventory/ItemAdded];
```

```
/*-------------------------------------------------------------------
-- Create a contract for the AddItem conversation
-------------------------------------------------------------------*/


CREATE CONTRACT [//microsoft.com/Inventory/AddItemContract]
  ([//microsoft.com/Inventory/AddItem] SENT BY INITIATOR,
   [//microsoft.com/Inventory/ItemAdded] SENT BY TARGET);
GO


/*-------------------------------------------------------------------
-- Create the procedure to service the Inventory target queue
-- Make it an empty procedure for now.  We will fill it in later
-------------------------------------------------------------------*/


CREATE PROCEDURE dbo.InventoryProc  AS
  RETURN 0;
GO


/*-------------------------------------------------------------------
-- Create the Inventory Queue which will be the target of
-- the conversations.  This is created with activation on.
-------------------------------------------------------------------*/


CREATE QUEUE dbo.InventoryQueue
  WITH ACTIVATION (
    STATUS = ON,
    PROCEDURE_NAME = dbo.InventoryProc  ,
    MAX_QUEUE_READERS = 2,
    EXECUTE AS SELF
  ) ;


/*-------------------------------------------------------------------
-- Create the Inventory Service.  Because this is the Target
-- service, the contract must be specified
-------------------------------------------------------------------*/


CREATE SERVICE [//microsoft.com/InventoryService] ON QUEUE dbo.InventoryQueue
  ([//microsoft.com/Inventory/AddItemContract]);


/*-------------------------------------------------------------------
-- Create a table to hold the inventory we're adding
-- This isn't meant to be realistic - just a way to show that the
-- service did something
-------------------------------------------------------------------*/


CREATE TABLE dbo.Inventory
(
  PartNumber   NVARCHAR(50)    Primary Key Clustered NOT NULL,
  Description  NVARCHAR (2000) NULL,
  Quantity     INT NULL,
  ReorderLevel INT NULL,
  Location     NVARCHAR(50) NULL
);
GO
```

There's nothing too exciting here. It might seem odd that the *InventoryProc* stored procedure is empty. This is done so that the name can be used to specify the activation parameters for the queue without creating the whole procedure. The other way to do this is to create the queue without activation and then use ALTER QUEUE to add activation after the stored procedure exists. The Inventory table has a few columns to illustrate how to transfer data from a message to a table, but it's obviously not a realistic inventory table. Listing 16-2 has the logic to implement the Inventory service that processes the *AddItem* messages.

LISTING 16-2 Inventory service program

```
ALTER PROCEDURE dbo.InventoryProc
AS

Declare @message_body AS xml;
Declare @response     AS xml;
Declare @message_type AS sysname;
Declare @dialog       AS uniqueidentifier ;
Declare @hDoc         AS int;
--  This procedure will  process event messages from
--  the queue until the queue is empty
WHILE (1 = 1)
BEGIN
  BEGIN TRANSACTION
  -- Receive the next available message
  WAITFOR (
    RECEIVE top(1) -- just handle one message at a time
      @message_type = message_type_name,
      @message_body = message_body,
      @dialog       = conversation_handle
    FROM dbo.InventoryQueue
    ), TIMEOUT 2000

  -- If we didn't get anything, break out of the loop
  IF (@@ROWCOUNT = 0)
  BEGIN
    ROLLBACK TRANSACTION
    BREAK;
  END

  /*-----------------------------------------------------------------
  -- Message handling logic based on the message type received
  -------------------------------------------------------------------*/

  -- Handle End Conversation messages by ending our conversation also
  IF (@message_type = 'http://schemas.microsoft.com/SQL/ServiceBroker/EndDialog')
  BEGIN
    PRINT 'End Dialog for dialog # ' + cast(@dialog as nvarchar(40));
    END CONVERSATION @dialog;
  END
    -- For error messages, just end the conversation.  In a real app, we
    -- would log the error and do any required cleanup.
  ELSE IF (@message_type = 'http://schemas.microsoft.com/SQL/ServiceBroker/Error')
```

```
    BEGIN
      PRINT 'Dialog ERROR dialog # ' + cast(@dialog as nvarchar(40));
      END CONVERSATION @dialog;
    END
     -- Handle an AddItem message
   ELSE IF (@message_type = '//microsoft.com/Inventory/AddItem')
   BEGIN
      SET @response  = N'Item added successfully'
      -- Parse the message body and add to the inventory
      BEGIN TRY
        INSERT INTO dbo.Inventory
 (PartNumber, Description, Quantity, ReorderLevel, Location)

        select itm.itm. value ('(PartNumber/text())[1]', 'nvarchar(50)')
            as PartNumber,
          itm.itm.value('(Description/text())[1]', 'nvarchar(2000)')
            as Description,
          itm.itm.value('(Quantity/text())[1]', 'int')
            as Quantity,
          itm.itm.value('(ReorderLevel/text())[1]', 'int')
            as ReorderLevel,
          itm.itm.value('(Location/text())[1]', 'nvarchar(50)')
            as Location
        from @message_body.nodes('/Item[1]') as itm(itm);

      END TRY
      BEGIN CATCH
        ROLLBACK TRANSACTION
        -- Create a new transaction to send the response
        BEGIN TRANSACTION
          SET @response  = ERROR_MESSAGE();
          -- ToDo - log the error
          -- ToDo - poison message handling
      END CATCH;
      -- Send a response message confirming the add was done
      SEND ON CONVERSATION @dialog
        MESSAGE TYPE [//microsoft.com/Inventory/ItemAdded] (@response);
      -- We handle one message at a time so we're done with this dialog
      END CONVERSATION @dialog;
   END -- If message type
   COMMIT TRANSACTION
 END -- while
 GO
```

The process flow of this procedure demonstrates the flow of almost all Service Broker services. The procedure is a continuous loop that receives a message at the top, processes the message with conditional logic based on the message type received, and then goes back to the top and receives another message. The loop continues until the @@ROWCOUNT after RECEIVE is 0, which indicates the queue is empty. Each loop iteration is a separate transaction, which means there is only one message per transaction. This is not optimal, but it makes the logic easier to follow, so I usually do this for samples. A high-performance Service Broker application would read all the messages available for a conversation group in a single RECEIVE statement and then process them all at once. If the message volume is high, you might also consider going through the loop a few times before committing the transaction. This approach makes the logic more efficient, but it also makes the processing logic much more complex.

The message processing logic is the T-SQL equivalent of a C# switch statement with separate sections for the three message types that might be found on the queue. It's important to remember that because a RECEIVE statement specifies a queue, any message type allowed on the queue might be received. This means that if two or more services are associated with the queue, the logic in the queue reader must be able to process any message allowed on any of the services.

The first two message types are *Error* and *EndDialog*. These two message types can be received by any service, so all service logic must have logic to handle them. At a minimum, the message-handling logic must contain an END CONVERSATION to close out this end of the dialog. If some cleanup is required before ending the conversation, handling these messages will include the cleanup logic in addition to ending the conversation.

The last message type is the *AddItem* message. The message body is an XML document that contains the data required to add a row to the Inventory table. The sample code processes the message with an XML Nodes query that inserts the XML data into the Inventory table. The error-handling logic is not robust, and it's there only to illustrate where real error-handling would go. In the event of an error in the insert statement—a primary key violation, perhaps— the CATCH block will roll back the transaction and put the error message into the response message. The problem with doing that is that if the error is unrecoverable—as it would be if the message contained a duplicate key—the message would be put back in the queue. When the same message is read again, it would fail again and be rolled back again. This behavior would put the stored procedure into a tight loop. A message such as this that can never be processed correctly is called a *poison message*. Transactional messaging applications must deal with poison messages. (See the "Poison Messages" section later in the chapter for details about how to deal with them.) To avoid getting into a loop, the sample unconditionally ends the conversation whether the message was processed successfully or not. This is not what you would want to do in a real application.

After inserting the message contents into the Inventory table, the response message is sent back to the *ManufacturingService* and the dialog is ended. The response message contains either a message indicating success or the error text if the insert failed. The *@dialog* variable used for the SEND and END DIALOG was obtained from the received message, so the message will be routed back to the calling dialog.

Now that a service is ready to process messages, let's implement a stored procedure to send the *AddItem* message to this service. This stored procedure will begin a dialog to the *InventoryService* and send a message on the dialog. The target service name for this dialog will be the *ManufacturingService*. Because the BEGIN DIALOG command uses the *ManufacturingService* as the target service name, the *ManufacturingService* is the initiator of the dialog and the *InventoryService* is the target. Listing 16-3 creates the queue and service for the *ManufacturingService*, and it creates the stored procedure to send the *AddItem* message.

LISTING 16-3 Dialog initiator procedure

```
/*------------------------------------------------------------------
-- Create an empty procedure for the initiator so we can use it
-- in the activation parameters when we create the queue
----------------------------------------------------------------*/

CREATE PROCEDURE dbo.ManufacturingProc  AS
  RETURN 0;
GO


/*------------------------------------------------------------------
-- Create the initiator queue.  Activation is configured
----------------------------------------------------------------*/

CREATE QUEUE dbo.ManufacturingQueue
  WITH ACTIVATION (
    STATUS = ON,
    PROCEDURE_NAME = dbo.ManufacturingProc  ,
    MAX_QUEUE_READERS = 2,
    EXECUTE AS SELF
    );


/*------------------------------------------------------------------
-- Create the Manufacturing service.  Because it is the initiator, it
-- doesn't require contracts.
----------------------------------------------------------------*/

CREATE SERVICE [//microsoft.com/ManufacturingService]
  ON QUEUE dbo.ManufacturingQueue;


/*------------------------------------------------------------------
-- Create a table to hold the state for our conversation
-- We use the conversation handle as a key instead of the
-- conversation group ID because we just have one conversation
-- in our group.
----------------------------------------------------------------*/

CREATE TABLE dbo.InventoryState
  (
    PartNumber      UNIQUEIDENTIFIER  Primary Key Clustered NOT NULL,
    Dialog          UNIQUEIDENTIFIER NULL,
    State           NVARCHAR(50) NULL
  );
GO
```

```
/*-------------------------------------------------------------------
-- Create the initiator stored procedure
-------------------------------------------------------------------*/

CREATE PROCEDURE AddItemProc
AS

DECLARE @message_body      AS xml;
DECLARE @Dialog            AS uniqueidentifier;
DECLARE @partno            AS uniqueidentifier;

--Set the part number to a new GUID so we can run
--this an unlimited number of times
SET @partno = NEWID();

-- Populate the message body
SET @message_body = '<Item>
    <PartNumber>' + CAST (@partno as NVARCHAR(50)) + '</PartNumber>
    <Description>2 cm Left Threaded machine screw</Description>
    <Quantity>5883</Quantity>
    <ReorderLevel>1000</ReorderLevel>
    <Location>Aisle 32, Rack 7, Bin 29</Location>
</Item>';

BEGIN TRANSACTION
-- Begin a dialog to the Hello World Service

BEGIN DIALOG  @Dialog
  FROM SERVICE    [//microsoft.com/ManufacturingService]
  TO SERVICE      '//microsoft.com/InventoryService'
  ON CONTRACT     [//microsoft.com/Inventory/AddItemContract]
  WITH ENCRYPTION = OFF, LIFETIME = 3600;

-- Send message
SEND ON CONVERSATION @Dialog
  MESSAGE TYPE [//microsoft.com/Inventory/AddItem] (@message_body);

-- Put a row into the state table to track this conversation
INSERT INTO dbo.InventoryState
  VALUES (@partno, @Dialog, 'Add Item Sent');
COMMIT TRANSACTION
GO
```

This service uses the message types and contract created for the *InventoryService*, so they don't have to be created again. If you create this service in another database, you must first create the message types and contract in that database.

AddItemProc is a simple procedure. It populates the message body with an XML document, begins a dialog to the *InventoryService*, and sends the message. For each message sent, a row is inserted into the InventoryState table. The InventoryState table tracks the progress of the *AddItem* messages, so a user can see the progress of the dialog.

To see whether this works, first run the following:

```
EXEC AddItemProc
```

If everything is working correctly, there should be a row in the Inventory table and a row in the InventoryState table. Because you haven't written the logic to handle the response yet, there should be a response message in the *ManufacturingQueue*. As you can see from these queries and their results, everything is indeed working correctly:

```
SELECT * FROM Inventory.dbo.[Inventory]
```

```
PartNumber      Description             Quantity  ReorderLevel Location
--------------  ----------------------  --------  ------------ --------
FB0CDFF2-A7...  2 cm Left Threaded...      5883           1000 Aisle 32...
```

```
SELECT * FROM [InventoryState]
```

```
PartNumber                            Dialog                                State
------------------------------------  ------------------------------------  ------
FB0CDFF2-A776-43BC-B7BE-52B970CD34F7  10117F26-9E74-DE11-AE90-0015B7D4AC66  Add Item Sent
```

```
SELECT CAST(message_body AS NVARCHAR(MAX)) AS msg FROM ManufacturingQueue
```

```
msg
----------------------
Item added successfully
```

You have now sent a message on a dialog, processed the message, and sent a response message. All that's left to do is process the response message. To do this, run the code in Listing 16-4 to create another simple Service Broker service with a message processing loop. The process flow will be the same as that for the inventory procedure.

LISTING 16-4 Manufacturing procedure

```
ALTER PROCEDURE dbo.ManufacturingProc
AS

DECLARE @message_body AS xml;
DECLARE @message_type AS sysname;
DECLARE @dialog       AS uniqueidentifier ;

--  This procedure will  process event messages from
--  the queue until the queue is empty

WHILE (1 = 1)
BEGIN
  BEGIN TRANSACTION

    -- Receive the next available message
    WAITFOR (
      RECEIVE top(1)
          @message_type=message_type_name,
          @message_body=message_body,
          @dialog = conversation_handle
      FROM dbo.ManufacturingQueue
      ), TIMEOUT 2000;
```

```
      -- If we didn't get anything, break out of the loop
    IF (@@ROWCOUNT = 0)
      BEGIN
        ROLLBACK TRANSACTION
        BREAK;
      END
      IF (@message_type =
        'http://schemas.microsoft.com/SQL/ServiceBroker/EndDialog')
      BEGIN
        PRINT 'End Dialog for dialog # ' + CAST(@dialog as nvarchar(40));
        END CONVERSATION @dialog;
      END
    ELSE IF (@message_type =
      'http://schemas.microsoft.com/SQL/ServiceBroker/Error')
    BEGIN
      PRINT 'Dialog ERROR dialog # ' + CAST(@dialog as nvarchar(40));
      END CONVERSATION @dialog;
    END
    ELSE IF (@message_type = '//microsoft.com/Inventory/ItemAdded')
    BEGIN
      UPDATE dbo.InventoryState  SET State = CAST(@message_body
        AS NVARCHAR(1000)) WHERE Dialog = @dialog;
    END
    COMMIT TRANSACTION
  END -- while
  GO
```

This procedure is almost identical to *InventoryProc*, with the exception of the *ItemAdded* message type handling. The logic just updates the state table with the status returned in the message body. Notice that the initiator side of the dialog is actually two different stored procedures—one that begins the dialog and sends the message, and another that handles the responses. This is a normal pattern for asynchronous services. The dialog initiator sends a message to a background service and then either goes on to do something else or goes away. When the response is received, it is handled in the background. In some cases, the response is just recorded in the database; in other cases, it might be communicated back to the user through an e-mail message or something similar.

You've now seen a simple Service Broker conversation in action. The logic might seem complex at first, but keep in mind that most Service Broker applications follow the same pattern. Once you understand it, you can apply it to a number of applications. In fact, this processing pattern is so common that it has been incorporated into a sample object model that ships with SQL Server 2008. Install the SQL Server samples, and look for the ServiceBrokerInterface sample. The sample service incorporates the message loop handling, and you just have to supply the logic to handle the messages received. In the dialog security and routing sections of this chapter, I'll move the *ManufacturingService* first to another database in the same instance to demonstrate dialog security and then to another instance to demonstrate remote communications with Service Broker.

Poison Messages

One of the advantages of transactional messaging is that if the transaction that is processing a message fails and rolls back, the message is still on the queue because the RECEIVE command is also rolled back. The application can then receive the message again, and if it processes successfully this time, the transaction will commit and the message will disappear from the queue. This is why writing transactional message processing applications is much easier than writing non-transactional message processing applications.

The downside of transactional messaging occurs when processing a message produces an error that retrying won't fix. For example, let's say that in the sample application that inserts an item into the inventory table, there is already an item with the same part number, and the part number column has a unique constraint. No matter how many times the message is processed, it will fail because the part number is a duplicate. The application will then go into a tight loop processing the message, rolling back the transaction, and then receiving the same message again. As I stated earlier, a message that can't be processed is known as a *poison message*. If left unchecked, this kind of message will cause the application to process the same message continuously and have a major negative impact on the performance of the entire database. To prevent this, if Service Broker detects five rollbacks in a row on a queue, it will disable the queue to stop the poison message. This action is a last resort, however, because the application that uses the queue will stop until the administrator ends the offending dialog and re-enables the queue.

The right way to deal with poison messages is to prevent them. If the application fails to process a message, it should roll back the transaction and then decide whether processing the same message again will be likely to succeed. If the error was something like a deadlock or a lock timeout, it is worth trying again. However, if the error is a constraint violation that won't be resolved the next time the message is processed, the conversation that contains the message should be ended and an application error should be logged. If it makes sense in the application to continue the dialog without the poison message, you can commit the receive to get rid of the poison message and go on with the dialog. The approach to handling poison messages depends on the application, the dialog, and even which message failed, so there's no single right way to handle them. There is one wrong way, which is to always roll back errors and rely on Service Broker to handle them by disabling the queue.

Dialog Security

As with any feature that sends data across the network, security is a vital part of the Service Broker infrastructure. Service Broker includes a number of security options that support the level of security appropriate to the network vulnerability and data criticality. Service Broker security must solve the unique issues presented by asynchronous messaging. Because the applications communicating over a Service Broker conversation might never be running at the same time, normal, connection-oriented network security won't provide the full range of security options required by Service Broker. This section describes how dialog security is implemented in Service Broker and how to configure it.

Dialog security isn't required if both dialog endpoints are in the same database. To configure dialog security, you'll need to move one of the endpoints of our sample application to a different database. To keep things simple, you'll move the initiator to another database in the same SQL Server instance. To set this up, create a database called Manufacturing. Create the message types and contract, as you did in Listing 16-1, and then run the two scripts that set up the initiator. The script to do this follows:

```
CREATE DATABASE Manufacturing;

GO
USE Manufacturing;
GO


-------------------------------------------------------------------
-- Create the message types we will need for the conversation
-------------------------------------------------------------------


CREATE MESSAGE TYPE [//microsoft.com/Inventory/AddItem];
CREATE MESSAGE TYPE [//microsoft.com/Inventory/ItemAdded];

/*-----------------------------------------------------------------
-- Create a contract for the AddItem conversation
-------------------------------------------------------------------*/

CREATE CONTRACT [//microsoft.com/Inventory/AddItemContract]
  ([//microsoft.com/Inventory/AddItem] SENT BY INITIATOR,
  [//microsoft.com/Inventory/ItemAdded] SENT BY TARGET);
GO

/*-----------------------------------------------------------------
-- Create an empty procedure for the initiator so we can use it
-- in the activation parameters when we create the queue
-------------------------------------------------------------------*/

CREATE PROCEDURE dbo.ManufacturingProc  AS
  RETURN 0;
GO


/*-----------------------------------------------------------------
-- Create the initiator queue.  Activation is configured
-------------------------------------------------------------------*/

CREATE QUEUE dbo.ManufacturingQueue
  WITH ACTIVATION (
    STATUS = ON,
    PROCEDURE_NAME = dbo.ManufacturingProc  ,
    MAX_QUEUE_READERS = 2,
    EXECUTE AS SELF
    );
```

```
/*------------------------------------------------------------------
-- Create the Manufacturing service.  Because it is the initiator, it
-- doesn't require contracts.
------------------------------------------------------------------*/

CREATE SERVICE [//microsoft.com/ManufacturingService]
  ON QUEUE dbo.ManufacturingQueue;

/*------------------------------------------------------------------
-- Create a table to hold the state for our conversation
-- We use the conversation handle as a key instead of the
-- conversation group ID because we just have one conversation
-- in our group.
------------------------------------------------------------------*/

CREATE TABLE dbo.InventoryState
  (
    PartNumber        UNIQUEIDENTIFIER  Primary Key Clustered NOT NULL,
    Dialog            UNIQUEIDENTIFIER NULL,
    State             NVARCHAR(50) NULL
  );
GO

/*------------------------------------------------------------------
-- Create the initiator stored procedure
------------------------------------------------------------------*/

CREATE PROCEDURE AddItemProc
AS

DECLARE @message_body      AS xml;
DECLARE @Dialog            AS uniqueidentifier;
DECLARE @partno            AS uniqueidentifier;

--Set the part number to a new GUID so we can run
--this an unlimited number of times
SET @partno = NEWID();

-- Populate the message body
SET @message_body = '<Item>
   <PartNumber>' + CAST (@partno as NVARCHAR(50)) + '</PartNumber>
   <Description>2 cm Left Threaded machine screw</Description>
   <Quantity>5883</Quantity>
   <ReorderLevel>1000</ReorderLevel>
   <Location>Aisle 32, Rack 7, Bin 29</Location>
</Item>';

BEGIN TRANSACTION
-- Begin a dialog to the Hello World Service

BEGIN DIALOG  @Dialog
   FROM SERVICE    [//microsoft.com/ManufacturingService]
   TO SERVICE      '//microsoft.com/InventoryService'
   ON CONTRACT     [//microsoft.com/Inventory/AddItemContract]
   WITH ENCRYPTION = OFF, LIFETIME = 3600;
```

```
-- Send message
SEND ON CONVERSATION @Dialog
  MESSAGE TYPE [//microsoft.com/Inventory/AddItem] (@message_body);

-- Put a row into the state table to track this conversation
INSERT INTO dbo.InventoryState
  VALUES (@partno, @Dialog, 'Add Item Sent');
COMMIT TRANSACTION
GO
ALTER PROCEDURE dbo.ManufacturingProc
AS

DECLARE @message_body AS xml;
DECLARE @message_type AS sysname;
DECLARE @dialog        AS uniqueidentifier ;

--  This procedure will  process event messages from
--  the queue until the queue is empty

WHILE (1 = 1)
BEGIN
  BEGIN TRANSACTION

  -- Receive the next available message
  WAITFOR (
    RECEIVE top(1)
        @message_type=message_type_name,
        @message_body=message_body,
        @dialog = conversation_handle
    FROM dbo.ManufacturingQueue
    ), TIMEOUT 2000;

  -- If we didn't get anything, break out of the loop
  IF (@@ROWCOUNT = 0)
    BEGIN
      ROLLBACK TRANSACTION
      BREAK;
    END
    IF (@message_type =
      'http://schemas.microsoft.com/SQL/ServiceBroker/EndDialog')
      BEGIN
        PRINT 'End Dialog for dialog # ' + CAST(@dialog as nvarchar(40));
        END CONVERSATION @dialog;
      END
    ELSE IF (@message_type =
      'http://schemas.microsoft.com/SQL/ServiceBroker/Error')
    BEGIN
      PRINT 'Dialog ERROR dialog # ' + CAST(@dialog as nvarchar(40));
      END CONVERSATION @dialog;
    END
    ELSE IF (@message_type = '//microsoft.com/Inventory/ItemAdded')
    BEGIN
      UPDATE dbo.InventoryState  SET State = CAST(@message_body
          AS NVARCHAR(1000)) WHERE Dialog = @dialog;
    END
```

```
  COMMIT TRANSACTION
END -- while
GO
```

If this all works correctly, execute *AddItemProc* in the Manufacturing database to begin a dialog and send a message to the *InventoryService*. You should find that the message never makes it to the *InventoryQueue* and instead ends up in the *sys.transmission_queue* in the Manufacturing database with a message in the *transmission_status* column that indicates a bad security context.

```
EXEC Manufacturing..AddItemProc

SELECT transmission_status FROM Manufacturing.sys.transmission_queue

An exception occurred while enqueueing a message in the target queue. Error: 916, State: 3.
The server principal <principal> is not able to access the database "Inventory" under the
current security context.
```

The security context error is caused by Service Broker impersonating the owner of the Manufacturing service to send the message. Service Broker does this because a number of users can send messages on a dialog. So the send executes in the context of the service owner to ensure consistent security behavior. SQL Server 2008 considers crossing databases with an impersonated user context a security threat. To see why this is an issue, assume that Moe is the database owner (dbo) of the Inventory database and owns the *InventoryService*. If Larry is the dbo of the Manufacturing database, he can create a user in his database for Moe's login, make this user the owner of the *ManufacturingService*, and grant himself impersonation permissions for this user. Because the Moe user in the Manufacturing database is associated with the same login as the Moe user in the Inventory database, Larry has just given himself permission to execute code in the Inventory database without Moe's knowledge or permission. Although this is a bad thing if Larry isn't a trustworthy dbo, there are valid reasons for wanting to do this. To allow cross-database permissions with an impersonated security context, the system administrator can mark the impersonating database as trustworthy. To see how this works, sign on as a system administrator and execute the following:

```
ALTER DATABASE Manufacturing SET TRUSTWORTHY ON;
```

If everything is set up correctly, the message in the *sys.transmission_queue* will be delivered and a response will be received within a minute. Check the InventoryState table in the Manufacturing database with this query to make sure it worked.

```
SELECT * FROM InventoryState
```

PartNumber	Dialog	State
E9A25A1B-4E29-4982-9B57-4B6EC11CE79A	30394488-A274-DE11-AE90-0015B7D4AC66	Item added successfully

There is now successful communication with a service in another database, but marking the Manufacturing database as trustworthy gives the Manufacturing dbo a lot of power. You wanted to allow him to access the *InventoryService* in the Inventory database, but you actually gave him the ability to access any service in any database in the instance. If Larry isn't really that trustworthy, it's possible to turn off the trustworthy flag and use dialog security to give him access to only the services he really needs. Dialog security uses public key/private key certificates for authentication, so I will start with a brief explanation of asymmetric key encryption and then show how Service Broker uses it for secure message delivery.

Asymmetric Key Authentication

Asymmetric encryption involves two keys—a public key and a private key. These two keys have a special relationship. Data encrypted with the private key can be decrypted only with the public key, and data encrypted with the public key can be decrypted only with the private key. The private key is kept tightly secured on the owner's system, and the public key is given out to systems that need to communicate with the private key owner. At first glance, it looks like a great way to secure communications. If Larry and Moe need to talk, Larry gives Moe his public key and Moe gives Larry his public key. When Larry wants to send Moe something he encrypts it with Moe's public key, confident that only Moe can decrypt it. Two issues arise with this process. First, Larry knows that only Moe can decrypt the message, but Moe doesn't know for sure that Larry sent it to him. Larry can solve this problem by signing the message with his private key so that when Moe checks the signature with Larry's public key he will know that Larry sent it. The other, more critical problem is that asymmetric key encryption and decryption are extremely slow. The processor overhead is so great that using this technique for exchanging data is impractical.

Fortunately, symmetric key encryption is relatively efficient for exchanging large messages. Symmetric key encryption is also called *shared secret* encryption because both the sender and receiver have the same key. The issue with this process is the need to reliably exchange the secret key. This issue is especially important for Service Broker because for optimal security, every conversation has its own symmetric key.

As you might have guessed, Service Broker combines these techniques for dialog security. The asymmetric key technique is used to securely exchange a symmetric key, and then the symmetric key is used to exchange data. Actually, Service Broker cuts down the asymmetric overhead even further by exchanging a symmetric key exchange key (KEK) with the asymmetric keys and then using the KEK to exchange the session keys for each dialog. The KEK is always sent in the header of the first dialog message, but it is decrypted only if the target has lost the KEK or it has changed. Each pair of Service Broker endpoints uses a different KEK for the dialogs between them. Service Broker generates a new key exchange key periodically to reduce the impact of someone using a brute-force attack to break the key.

Configuring Dialog Security

Now that you know the basics of secure data transmission and authentication with dialog security, I'll cover how to configure services to use dialog security. For mutual authentication, the initiator will need a private key and the target's public key. The target needs its private key and the initiator's public key. To provide these, Service Broker takes advantage of the support SQL Server 2008 provides for storing certificates. It's important to understand that Service Broker primarily uses a certificate as a convenient container for an asymmetric key. Service Broker never traces the issuer of the certificate. It only checks validity dates to determine a certificate's validity. For Service Broker's purposes, a self-signed certificate works just as well as a certificate from a certificate authority. To fit into the SQL Server security infrastructure, certificates need to own services and hold permissions. However, SQL Server certificates are not security principals, so they can't be assigned ownership or permissions. This means that a certificate must be associated with a user that is a security principal. The user is associated with the certificate through ownership. Certificates are not owned by schemas but are owned directly by users through the AUTHORIZATION parameter of CREATE CERTIFICATE. The other useful SQL Server 2008 feature that Service Broker takes advantage of is the user with no login. If you specify WITHOUT LOGIN in the CREATE USER statement, the user will be created without being associated with a login. This means that you can assign permissions to this user, but no external user can ever log in as this user. This arrangement helps make Service Broker applications more secure.

The BEGIN DIALOG command needs to know *which* certificates to use to secure the dialog. The private key comes from the owner of the *service* object. The public key to use comes from the user specified in the remote service binding for the service. The *Remote Service Binding* is a Service Broker object that ties a remote service name to a user who owns the public key associated with the service. The keys corresponding to these two certificates—the public key of the initiating service owner's certificate and the private key of the REMOTE SERVICE BINDING user's certificate—must be present in the target database to establish the dialog.

The private key certificate corresponding to the *remote service binding* user of the initiator must have CONTROL permission on the target service, and the public key certificate corresponding to the initiator service owner's certificate must have SEND permissions on the target service. The security header sent with the first message of a dialog contains identifiers of the two certificates used to create the security header so that the target knows which certificates to use. The certificate identifier is the combination of the issuer name and the sequence number, which should be unique. The KEK is encrypted with the public key of the *Remote Service Binding* user's certificate, and it is signed with the private key of the initiator service owner's certificate. If the target has the same certificates, it can validate the signature and decrypt the KEK. Once both endpoints have the KEK, dialogs can be established between the endpoints using the KEK to transfer the session key for the dialog without having to use the certificates until the KEK changes or is lost through a database restart. (The KEK is never written to disk for security reasons, so if either endpoint is restarted, a new KEK must be established.)

Now that you know what's needed, let's look at an example of setting up security for our sample application, as shown in Listing 16-5. This assumes you created the Manufacturing database in the cross-database example.

LISTING 16-5 Securing the *AddItem* dialog

```
/*------------------------------------------------------------------------
-- This script sets up dialog security between the initiator and target
-- of the AddItem dialog
-------------------------------------------------------------------------*/

-- First, turn off the trustworthy flag

USE master;
GO
ALTER DATABASE Manufacturing SET TRUSTWORTHY OFF;
GO


/*------------------------------------------------------------------------
-- Set up the Target Service security
-------------------------------------------------------------------------*/

USE Inventory;
GO

CREATE MASTER KEY ENCRYPTION BY PASSWORD = 'Pass.word1';

-- Create a user to represent the "Inventory" Service
CREATE USER InventoryServiceUser WITHOUT  LOGIN;

-- Grant control on the Inventory service to this user
GRANT CONTROL ON SERVICE::[//microsoft.com/InventoryService]
  TO InventoryServiceUser;

-- Make the Inventory Service user the owner of the service
ALTER AUTHORIZATION ON SERVICE::[//microsoft.com/InventoryService]
  TO InventoryServiceUser;

-- Create a Private Key Certificate associated with this user
CREATE CERTIFICATE InventoryServiceCertPriv
  AUTHORIZATION InventoryServiceUser
    WITH SUBJECT = 'ForInventoryService';

-- Dump the public key certificate to a file for use on the
-- initiating server - no private key
BACKUP CERTIFICATE InventoryServiceCertPriv
  TO FILE = 'C:\InventoryServiceCertPub'; -- Replace with a directory of your choice

/*------------------------------------------------------------------------
-- Set up the Initiator Service security
-------------------------------------------------------------------------*/

USE Manufacturing;
GO
```

```
CREATE MASTER KEY ENCRYPTION BY PASSWORD = 'Pass.word1';

-- Create a user to own the "Manufacturing" Service
CREATE USER ManufacturingServiceUser WITHOUT LOGIN;

-- Make this user the owner of the FROM service
ALTER AUTHORIZATION ON SERVICE::[//microsoft.com/ManufacturingService]
  TO ManufacturingServiceUser;

-- Create a Private Key Certificate associated with this user
CREATE CERTIFICATE ManufacturingServiceCertPriv
  AUTHORIZATION ManufacturingServiceUser
   WITH SUBJECT = 'ForManufacturingService';

-- Dump the public key certificate to a file for use on
-- the Manufacturing server
BACKUP CERTIFICATE ManufacturingServiceCertPriv
  TO FILE = 'C:\ManufacturingServiceCertPub'; -- Same directory as the previous script

-- Create a user to represent the "Inventory" Service
CREATE USER InventoryServiceUser WITHOUT LOGIN;

-- Import the cert we got from the Inventory Service owned
-- by the user we just created
CREATE CERTIFICATE InventoryServiceCertPub
  AUTHORIZATION InventoryServiceUser
   FROM FILE = 'C:\InventoryServiceCertPub';

CREATE REMOTE SERVICE BINDING ToInventoryService
  TO SERVICE '//microsoft.com/InventoryService'
   WITH USER = InventoryServiceUser;

/*-------------------------------------------------------------------
-- Finish the Target Service security setup
-------------------------------------------------------------------*/

USE Inventory;
GO

-- Create a user to represent the "Manufacturing" Service
CREATE USER ManufacturingServiceUser WITHOUT LOGIN;

-- Import the cert we got from the Manufacturing Service owned
-- by the user we just created
CREATE CERTIFICATE ManufacturingServiceCertPub
  AUTHORIZATION ManufacturingServiceUser
   FROM FILE = 'C:\ManufacturingServiceCertPub';
GRANT SEND ON SERVICE::[//microsoft.com/InventoryService]
  TO ManufacturingServiceUser ;
```

This looks like a lot of code, but in reality you've just created the four certificates used for authentication and assigned permissions to the certificate owners. Creating the public key certificates requires a certificate file exported from the private key certificate. This file is exported with the BACKUP CERTIFICATE command. If the initiator and target are located on different systems, the file must be transferred to the opposite server perhaps through a remote file share or e-mail. However, in this case, the initiator and target are in the same instance, so it is just written out and then read back in from the same file. Also notice that the trustworthy flag was set to OFF, so if this service works, it is because of dialog security.

Run the AddItemProc to ensure that security is working correctly:

```
EXEC Manufacturing..AddItemProc
```

```
SELECT * FROM Manufacturing..InventoryState
```

Setting up dialog security seems like a lot of work to avoid setting the trustworthy flag. However, another advantage of setting up dialog security to the database is that you can now detach either of these databases and attach it to a different SQL Server instance without having to change dialog security. This is what I'll do in the next section.

Routing and Distribution

In this section, I'll show you how to move the Manufacturing database to another SQL Server instance to demonstrate how to configure Service Broker routing. Although communicating between two computers is more impressive, if you have only one computer, you can use two instances of SQL Server on the same computer to set up a remote Service Broker connection. To set up a dialog initiator in another instance to test communications, detach the Manufacturing database, move the Manufacturing.mdf and Manufacturing_log.ldf files to the second instance, and attach the database to the second instance.

In the instance you have been using for the previous samples, detach the Manufacturing database with this command:

```
sp_detach_db Manufacturing
```

Move the Manufacturing.mdf and Manufacturing_log.ldf files for the Manufacturing database to the computer where the second instance is located. If you are using a second instance on the same computer, you just need to move them to the Data directory for the second instance. Attach the Manufacturing database to the second instance by executing the following command on the new instance:

```
CREATE DATABASE Manufacturing
   ON (FILENAME = 'C:\Program Files\Microsoft SQL
   Server\MSSQL.1\MSSQL\Data\Manufacturing.mdf')
   LOG ON (FILENAME = 'C:\Program Files\Microsoft SQL
   Server\MSSQL.1\MSSQL\Data\Manufacturing_log.ldf')
   FOR ATTACH
   WITH ENABLE_BROKER;
```

Note that the book formatting has wrapped the filename. Type these on a single line. Remember to include the ENABLE_BROKER option so that Service Broker will run after the attach. You must also encrypt the database master key with the new instance's service master key so that Service Broker can access its encrypted data:

```
USE Manufacturing;
GO
OPEN MASTER KEY DECRYPTION BY PASSWORD = 'Pass.word1';
ALTER MASTER KEY ADD ENCRYPTION BY SERVICE MASTER KEY;
```

If you are connecting instances on two separate computers, move the manufacturing database files to the second computer and use the same process to attach the database to the SLQ Server instance on the second computer. The only difference in the following instructions between the two instances on the same computer and the two instances on different computers is the hostname of the computers. In the examples that follow, the instance where the Inventory service is located is on a computer called mypc10 and the instance where the manufacturing service is located is called mypc11.

Adjacent Broker Protocol

Two layered protocols are involved in exchanging Service Broker messages: the dialog protocol and the adjacent broker protocol (ABP). The dialog protocol that's been already discussed maintains the reliable, persistent, stateful sessions between conversation endpoints. Messages are acknowledged and retried at this level, and dialog security is part of this protocol. Also, the dialog protocol is unaware of the transport protocol used to transfer messages on the network.

The "bits on the wire" protocol that Service Broker uses to send data over the network is called the adjacent broker protocol because it communicates between SQL Server instances connected by the network. The current ABP implementation works only on TCP/IP connections, but it is designed to be extensible to other network transports in the future. The ABP is a simple protocol designed to efficiently use the available bandwidth to transfer Service Broker messages between SQL Server instances. The ABP is so efficient that several customers have reported better performance by having the dialog initiator and target on separate computers than having them on the same computer. Of course, your results may vary. SQL Server 2008 includes some improvements to the protocol, and the new Windows 2008 TCP/IP stack does a much better job of dealing with high-bandwidth, high-latency TCP/IP connections, so upgrading Windows and SQL Server may yield better performance.

Service Broker messages from all the *sys.transmission_queues* in all the databases on a SQL Server instance are processed by a global instance of the ABP logic. The ABP logic is called a *Service Broker endpoint*. This endpoint is distinctly different from a conversation endpoint. This endpoint maintains connections to all the SQL Server instances that the local instance has dialog connections with. Only one TCP/IP connection is maintained between a given pair of instances.

To ensure fairness, messages waiting to be sent are referenced in a transmission list that is a list of all messages waiting to be sent in all the transmission queues in the instance in the order of when they were placed on the queue and their relative priority. Multiple messages to be sent to the same destination are placed into a single TCP/IP message for more efficient transfer. This process is called *boxcarring*. The format of an ABP message is a header that contains information about where the message is going and where it came from. It also includes the sequence number, fragment numbers, and when the message was sent. This header is used by the dialog protocol and the message body as a binary large object (BLOB). The first messages from the initiator contain a security header to transfer the keys and information necessary to establish dialog security. When the first message is received back from the target, the initiator knows that the target has the security information, so subsequent messages on that dialog do not include the security header.

The ABP also includes security features. ABP connections are only allowed between instances that have been authenticated and authorized to connect. Because this authentication is done on a connection-oriented session, Windows authentication is supported. Certificate-based authentication is also supported to handle connections where Windows authentication won't work, such as when the two SQL Server instances are located in different security domains. Setting up ABP authentication is covered in the next section. All messages sent over an ABP connection are signed so that any message tampering or corruption is detected. In addition, the ABP connection can be encrypted. In many cases, encryption isn't necessary because the messages are already encrypted by dialog security, but encryption at the ABP level will ensure that even messages from unsecured dialogs will be encrypted. The encryption software recognizes messages encrypted by the dialog protocol and doesn't encrypt them again, so data is not double-encrypted.

Service Broker Endpoints

In SQL Server 2008, all network connections are handled through endpoints. The types of endpoints available are T-SQL, SOAP, Database Mirroring, and Service Broker. The CREATE and ALTER ENDPOINT statements are used to configure the endpoints. The currently configured endpoints are listed in the *sys.endpoints* catalog view. A Service Broker endpoint is used to configure the port that the instance will use to listen for connections and to specify what kind of security will be used on the connection. The CREATE ENDPOINT syntax includes several protocols for connections, but currently only TCP/IP is supported by Service Broker. The command to create a basic Service Broker endpoint looks like this:

```
CREATE ENDPOINT InventoryServer
  STATE = STARTED
  AS TCP ( LISTENER_PORT = 4030 )
  FOR SERVICE_BROKER  (
    AUTHENTICATION = WINDOWS,
    ENCRYPTION = SUPPORTED);
```

The first few lines are pretty self-explanatory. The STATE = STARTED line means the endpoint will start listening for connections immediately, and the LISTENER_PORT clause means the endpoint will listen for connections on port 4030. The port you use doesn't matter as long as it is above 1024 and not already in use on your computer. If you have a tightly controlled network, your network administrator will assign port numbers for you to use. All Service Broker ABP connections must be authenticated. The WINDOWS option means a Windows authentication protocol—either NTLM or KERBEROS—will be used to authenticate the TCP/IP connections.

Other options let you specify which protocol to use. In situations where Windows authentication isn't possible, certificates can be used to authenticate the connection. The certificate authentication protocol used is the same Security Support Provider Interface (SSPI) protocol that Secure Sockets Layer (SSL) Internet connections use. I'll cover how to configure both kinds of authentication and how to control which servers you allow to connect to yours later in this section. The ENCRYPTION clause specifies whether encryption should be used on the ABP connection. The three options for this parameter are DISABLED, REQUIRED, and SUPPORTED. Table 16-1 explains how the settings for the two endpoints determine whether the connection will be encrypted.

TABLE 16-1 ENCRYPTION Settings for Two Endpoints

Endpoint 1	Endpoint 2	Encrypted
DISABLED	SUPPORTED	NO
DISABLED	DISABLED	NO
DISABLED	REQUIRED	ERROR
SUPPORTED	SUPPORTED	YES
SUPPORTED	REQUIRED	YES
REQUIRED	REQUIRED	YES

The ENCRYPTION clause also allows you to specify RC4 or AES as the encryption algorithm to use. AES is more secure than RC4, but RC4 is significantly faster.

Configuring Adjacent Broker Protocol Connections

The CREATE and ALTER ENDPOINT commands are used to configure the endpoint parameters for ABP. You must also configure permissions to determine which other instances are allowed to connect to the local instance. This is done by creating a SQL Server login in the local instance's master database to represent the remote instances and then granting that login CONNECT permission to the endpoint. When a remote instance connects to the Service Broker endpoint, the connection is authenticated using either a Windows protocol or the SSPI protocol, and the authenticated login is checked for CONNECT permission to the endpoint. If the authentication fails or the authenticated login fails, the connection is closed.

Windows Authentication   Windows authentication is generally easier to configure, so I'll start there. The Windows user that is authenticated is the service account for the instance.

Log on to the master database of the instance where the Inventory database is, and execute this script, substituting the service accounts and domains of your computers:

```
USE master
-- Create an endpoint for the inventory server
-- with Windows authentication

CREATE ENDPOINT InventoryEndpoint STATE = STARTED
  AS TCP ( LISTENER_PORT = 5523 )
    FOR SERVICE_BROKER ( AUTHENTICATION = WINDOWS );
CREATE LOGIN [MYDOMAIN\Service account of manufacturing service account] FROM Windows;

-- Grant Manufacturing instance service account connect privileges
GRANT CONNECT ON ENDPOINT::InventoryEndpoint
  TO [MYDOMAIN\service account of manufacturing instance];
```

That's all there is to configuring the Inventory instance. Next, log on to the instance where the Manufacturing database is, and execute this script:

```
USE master
-- Create an endpoint for the manufacturing server
-- with Windows authentication

CREATE ENDPOINT ManufacturingEndpoint STATE = STARTED
  AS TCP ( LISTENER_PORT = 5524 )
    FOR SERVICE_BROKER ( AUTHENTICATION = WINDOWS );

--Create a login for remote system in this instance
-- Change to your domain and server name!

CREATE LOGIN [MYDOMAIN\Service account of inventory service account] FROM Windows;

-- Grant Inventory instance service account connect privilege
GRANT CONNECT ON ENDPOINT::ManufacturingEndpoint
  TO [MYDOMAIN\Service account of manufacturing instance];
```

You can use a shortcut if you want to do some quick development or testing without going through a lot of setup. If you use the same domain user account as the service account for both SQL Server instances and configure the endpoints for Windows authentication, the connection will work because the service account for each instance is an admin in the other instance and no additional authorization is necessary.

Certificate Authentication   Certificate-based authentication for ABP endpoints uses the same SSPI authentication protocol as SSL. SSL is the encryption used for data sent between your Web browser and an https: site on the Internet. Although Service Broker uses the same connection protocol as SSL, it does not use SSL because SSL encrypts everything on the wire. Because secure Service Broker dialogs are already encrypted, re-encrypting this data would be a significant waste of resources. Like mutual SSL authentication (and dialog security), certificate authentication requires each of the two endpoints to have a private key certificate. Because SQL Server might not be connected to the Internet, or the private key certificate might not be issued by a certificate authority, the public key certificates required are also stored in the database. The way authentication works is similar to the dialog security process that's already been discussed, with some differences in the way it is configured. The following example will walk you through connecting a SQL Server instance that contains our Inventory service with another instance that contains the Manufacturing service. The setup will be the same whether the two instances are running on the same box or on different boxes. You'll start by creating the endpoint and its private key certificate in the Inventory instance. The scripts in Listings 16-6, 16-7, and 16-8 should all be run from the master database.

LISTING 16-6 Set up inventory private key

```
/*----------------------------------------------------------------------
-- Setup Certificate authenticated Endpoint
-- on the Inventory server
----------------------------------------------------------------------*/

-- Create a certificate to represent the inventory
-- server and export it to a file

USE MASTER
  CREATE MASTER KEY ENCRYPTION BY PASSWORD = 'Pass.word1';


CREATE CERTIFICATE InventoryCertPriv
  WITH SUBJECT = 'ForInventoryAuth';
BACKUP CERTIFICATE InventoryCertPriv
  TO FILE = 'C:\InventoryCertPub';
GO

-- Create a Service Broker Endpoint that uses this
-- certificate for authentication

CREATE ENDPOINT InventoryEndpoint STATE = STARTED
  AS TCP ( LISTENER_PORT = 4423 )
    FOR SERVICE_BROKER ( AUTHENTICATION = CERTIFICATE InventoryCertPriv );
```

Notice that the endpoint configuration specifies which certificate to use for the private key of the inventory endpoint. In this example, both instances were on the same server, so exporting the public key certificate to the C: drive makes sense. In a distributed environment, you would have to come up with another way to move the certificate to the opposite endpoint. A network-mapped directory, ftp, and e-mail are all viable alternatives.

Now that you have the private key of the inventory instance configured, you'll need to move to the manufacturing instance to create its private key and import the inventory public key by running the code in Listing 16-7.

LISTING 16-7 Set up manufacturing endpoint

```
/*-------------------------------------------------------------------
-- Setup Certificate authenticated Endpoint
-- on the Manufacturing server
-------------------------------------------------------------------*/

-- Create a certificate to represent the
-- manufacturing server and export it to a file
USE MASTER
 CREATE MASTER KEY ENCRYPTION BY PASSWORD = 'Pass.word1';

CREATE CERTIFICATE ManufacturingCertPriv
  WITH SUBJECT = 'ForManufacturingAuth';
BACKUP CERTIFICATE ManufacturingCertPriv
  TO FILE = 'C:\ManufacturingCertPub';
GO

-- Create a Service Broker Endpoint that uses this
-- certificate for authentication

CREATE ENDPOINT ManufacturingEndpoint
    STATE = STARTED
   AS TCP ( LISTENER_PORT = 4424 )
  FOR SERVICE_BROKER (AUTHENTICATION =
  CERTIFICATE ManufacturingCertPriv);

-- Create a user and login to represent the
-- inventory server on the manufacturing server

CREATE LOGIN InventoryProxy
  WITH PASSWORD = 'dj47dkri837&?>';
CREATE USER InventoryProxy;

-- Import the certificate exported by the inventory server

CREATE CERTIFICATE InventoryCertPub
  AUTHORIZATION InventoryProxy
    FROM FILE = 'C:\InventoryCertPub';

-- Grant connect privileges to the login that
-- represents the inventory server

GRANT CONNECT ON ENDPOINT::ManufacturingEndpoint
  TO InventoryProxy;
```

Notice that you had to create both a user and login as proxies for the inventory server. The login is necessary because it must be granted the permission to connect to the endpoint to allow the Inventory instance to connect, and the user is necessary because logins can't own certificates. It should never be necessary for anyone to log into the instance with the proxy login, so the password should be long and random for maximum security.

All that's left to do is switch back to the inventory instance to import the manufacturing public key and create the required login and user by running the code in Listing 16-8.

LISTING 16-8 Finish the inventory endpoint

```
/*-------------------------------------------------------------------
-- Finish the certificate-authenticated endpoint
-- on the Inventory server
-------------------------------------------------------------------*/

-- Create a user and login to represent the
-- manufacturing server on the inventory server

CREATE LOGIN ManufacturingProxy
  WITH PASSWORD = 'dj47dkri837&?>';
CREATE USER ManufacturingProxy;

-- Import the certificate exported by the Manufacturing server

CREATE CERTIFICATE InventoryCertPub AUTHORIZATION ManufacturingProxy
  FROM FILE = 'C:\ManufacturingCertPub';

-- Grant connect privileges to the login that
-- represents the Manufacturing server

GRANT CONNECT ON ENDPOINT::InventoryEndpoint
  TO ManufacturingProxy;
```

As you can see, setting up certificate authentication between instances is a little more complex than setting up Windows authentication. The advantage is that certificate authentication will work on any Windows security configuration, whereas Windows authentication might require Kerberos for some service accounts and might not work across domains.

Now that you have learned how to configure security for the ABP, you will learn how Service Broker dialogs determine where messages should be delivered.

Routes

A Service Broker route is just a mapping from a service to the network address where messages to that service should be sent. Service Broker routes are simple but flexible enough to support large complex networks. Execute this script in the manufacturing instance to create a route to the inventory service:

```
USE Manufacturing
GO

CREATE ROUTE Inventory_route WITH
    SERVICE_NAME = '//microsoft.com/InventoryService',
    ADDRESS =  'TCP://mypc11:44424'
GO
```

The routes configured in a database can be examined in the *sys.routes* view. The name of the route is there so that you can ALTER or DROP it. The SERVICE_NAME is the name of the service that this route provides an address for. Remember that service names use binary collation, so the name in the route must match exactly the name of the service. (Cutting and pasting is your friend here.) A common source of routing problems is having the case of the service name wrong. The ADDRESS is the network address that messages for this service should be sent to. Service Broker supports only the TCP/IP protocol, so the address should begin with TCP://. Next comes the network address, which can be a DNS name, a host name, or an IP address. The :4040 in the example indicates that Service Broker should connect to port 4040 on the remote server. This port number must match the port number configured for the Service Broker endpoint in the remote instance. If two or more instances are installed on the same remote server, you target which one gets the message with the port number. Because the port number is determined when you create the remote endpoint, there is no default port number.

It's important to remember that both the initiator and target services of a dialog need endpoints. One of the more common network configuration errors is forgetting to configure the route from the target service back to the initiator. When this happens, messages are delivered successfully from the initiator to the target but no response is returned. This leads to the strange behavior that messages are received on the target queue and processed successfully, but the messages are still on the *sys.transmission_queue* of the initiator database because the acknowledgement for the messages is not delivered to the initiator. When you see the messages in the *sys.transmission_queue* of the initiator database, you think they are not being sent. In reality, they have been delivered and processed. If you use SQL Server Profiler to monitor Service Broker message delivery, you will see the messages being delivered to the target periodically and being rejected as duplicates. If the application sends messages only in one direction, it will appear to be working but will gradually get slower because thousands of messages a minute are being re-sent by the initiator and ignored by the target. With this in mind, be sure you also log in to the Inventory database and create a route back to the Manufacturing instance:

```
CREATE ROUTE Manufacturing_route WITH
  SERVICE_NAME = '//microsoft.com/ManufacturingService',
  ADDRESS =  'TCP://mypc11:4423';
```

If you have created a route from the Manufacturing database for the *InventoryService* and in the Inventory database for the *ManufacturingService*, the distributed Service Broker configuration should be complete. Log in to the Manufacturing database, and run *AddItemProc* to test your dialog. Select from the *sys.dm_broker_connections* view to see whether a network connection was established. If it was not, check *sys.transmission_queue* for an error status and monitor the broker connection traces in SQL Server Profiler.

Broker Instance

In some cases, you might need to route a dialog to a particular database in a SQL Server instance. For example, the instance might have both a production and test version of the service in two different databases. The route to the service must be able to route the dialog to the correct database in the instance. This is done by specifying the BROKER_INSTANCE parameter in the CREATE ROUTE command. The BROKER_INSTANCE is the *service_broker_guid* column of the sys.databases table for the destination database. The following example shows a route with the BROKER_INSTANCE parameter specified:

```
CREATE ROUTE ManufacturingRoute WITH
  SERVICE_NAME = '//microsoft.com/ManufacturingService',
  BROKER_INSTANCE = 'A29EEDD3-27E3-4591-94D9-B97BAFBDB936',
  ADDRESS = 'TCP://mypc11:4423';
```

Incoming Routes

Service Broker uses routes in the database where the services are located to determine which remote instance messages should be sent to which service. When the message arrives at the remote instance, Service Broker must determine what to do with the incoming message. Service Broker uses the routes stored in the msdb database to decide what to do with incoming messages. For example, if there are three or four copies of the *InventoryService* in an instance, a route with the BROKER_INSTANCE specified can be used to route incoming messages for the *InventoryService* to the correct database. This can also lead to problems if the msdb database is attached or restored without the BROKER_ENABLED flag, so that Service Broker is disabled in msdb.

Wildcards and Special Addresses

Establishing a Service Broker conversation will fail if there is no route available for the target service. This might seem unlikely to you because if you have been following along with the examples, you have created several conversations without creating a route for the services involved. The reason this works is that there is a route called *AutoCreatedLocal* that is created when a database is created. If you look at this route in the *sys.routes* view, you will see that the *remote_service_name* and *broker_instance* columns are both NULL and the address column is LOCAL. The NULL columns are what Service Broker uses as wildcards. The wildcards mean that this route will match any service name and any broker instance. A wildcard is used as the last matching criteria so that if another route matches the service name or broker instance the more specific match will always be used. You can create your own wildcard routes by not specifying one or both of the matching parameters.

The LOCAL value for the address is one of two special addresses used in Service Broker. LOCAL means that Service Broker will look for a service in the local SQL Server instance that matches the name. If the database where the route is located has a copy of the service, that copy will be used. If that database doesn't have a copy of the service, Service Broker will look in other databases in the SQL Server instance for a matching service. If more than one copy of the service is found, a random one will be chosen. Because the *AutoCreatedLocal* route is a wildcard route with an address of LOCAL, Service Broker will check for a local service if there is no matching *remote_service_name* in the *sys.routes* view.

The other special address is TRANSPORT. If no other match is found and there is a matching route with the TRANSPORT address, Service Broker will attempt to use the name of the service as a route. For example, if the service name is TCP://mypc11:4040/Manufacturing, Service Broker will send the message to TCP://mypc11:4040. Although this might seem like a strange feature, think of an application that involves several thousand initiators connecting to a target service. Maintaining return routes for all the initiators on the target instance would be very painful. On the other hand, if each initiator uses its network address and port as the initiator service name, the target only needs to have a single wildcard route with the TRANSPORT address to route responses to all the initiators.

Load Balancing

If you define multiple routes for the same service name in a database, Service Broker will randomly pick one of them when sending the first message in a conversation. This provides a simple form of load balancing among a number of identical services. Notice that this balancing happens on a per-conversation, not per-message, basis. This makes sense if you realize that the first message of the conversation will insert a row in *sys.conversation_ endpoints* at the remote database. So, if the second message goes to a different database than the first message, Service Broker will not be able to process it because there is no conversation information in *sys.conversation_endpoints* for the conversation the message belongs to.

The issue with this type of load balancing is that it assumes all services with the same name are identical, so it doesn't matter which one you use. Depending on what the service does and how often the data used by that service changes, keeping multiple target services synchronized might be difficult. On the other hand, if the data for the service changes only rarely, replication can be used to keep the services synchronized or services can call each other with changes through a synchronization service. In other circumstances, it might make more sense for the data in the copies of the service to be partitioned. For example, one service might handle customer numbers 1 through 10000, another 10001 through 20000, and so on. In this case, the application will have to decide which copy of the service to begin the dialog with and use the broker instance in the BEGIN DIALOG command to select the appropriate one. This kind of load balancing works well if the data can be readily partitioned between services and all requests to the service know which customer number the request is for.

One possible problem to look out for is "accidental" load balancing. Whenever Service Broker finds two or more routes to a service, it will load balance dialogs among them. If you intend to have two routes, that is a good thing. However, consider a situation in which you added a route to the production version of a service and forgot to drop the route to the test version. Service Broker will send half the dialogs to test and half to production, which probably isn't what you intended. A more subtle way this happens is if you are using a LOCAL route for the service and the service exists on multiple databases in the local instance. In that case, these services will be load balanced between multiple databases in the local instance. This generally means that about half of the dialogs will end up where you intended and the other half will go to the other database. If you seem to be losing dialogs, check to see if there is another copy of the target service on the server.

To ensure that accidental load balancing doesn't happen, you should create a route for the service and specify the broker instance instead of letting it use the default route. This way you can be sure that the dialog is going where you expect it to go. This same principle applies to messages coming into the instance from outside. If only the default route is available in msdb, the incoming dialogs will be load balanced if there are multiple copies of the service in the instance. The fix here is the same—create a route for the service in msdb and use the broker instance to ensure the dialog goes where you want it to.

Routes and Database Mirroring

If the SQL Server instance you are routing messages to is actually two instances that are the primary and secondary databases of a database mirroring pair, Service Broker routing can handle this very well. The CREATE ROUTE command will accept the address of the instances that contain both the primary and secondary databases:

```
CREATE ROUTE ManufacturingMirrorRoute WITH
  SERVICE_NAME = '//microsoft.com/ManufacturingService',
  BROKER_INSTANCE = 'A29EEDD3-27E3-4591-94D9-B97BAFBDB936',
  ADDRESS =  'TCP://mypc11:4040',
  MIRROR_ADDRESS =  'TCP://mypc15:5834';
```

When Service Broker opens a connection for this route, it will connect to both instances of the mirrored pair and determine which database is the primary one. If the primary fails over and the other database becomes the primary, the Service Broker running on the new primary will notify any remote Service Brokers with conversations open that it is now the primary. The remote Service Broker will then immediately start sending the messages to the new primary database. This means that not only are no messages lost when the database fails over (because all the queues are in the database), but also that the remote applications will start sending to the new primary immediately. This arrangement provides an unprecedented degree of reliability for asynchronous distributed applications. In most cases, a failure will cause only a few seconds of hesitation and nothing will be lost.

Forwarding

When an incoming message arrives at the SQL Server instance, Service Broker looks in *sys.routes* in the msdb database for a route that matches the service name of the incoming message. If the address in the route is LOCAL, the message is put in the appropriate queue in a local database. If the address is a remote address, the message is put in a forwarding queue and sent to the remote instance specified in the address. Forwarding routes look exactly like other routes except they are created in the msdb database. The ADDRESS parameter in the CREATE ROUTE command was originally known as the "next hop address" because if forwarding is used, the address points to the next Service Broker in the forwarding chain, not the final destination.

Forwarding can be used to create complex network topologies, with messages forwarded from server to server until they reach their final destination. It is not necessary to persist messages to be forwarded because if they are lost, they will be re-sent from the message source if no acknowledgement is received. For this reason, the forwarding queues are memory queues. You can also configure the maximum size of the forwarding queues so that forwarded messages don't use too much memory. This command will turn on message forwarding and limit the forwarding queue to 50 MB of memory:

```
ALTER ENDPOINT InventoryEndpoint FOR SERVICE_BROKER
  (MESSAGE_FORWARDING = ENABLED,
  MESSAGE_FORWARD_SIZE = 50);
```

Troubleshooting

Service Broker configuration has been the most common source of problems reported on the newsgroups and forums. In this section I will point out some of the most common errors and describe a new troubleshooting tool included in the SQL Server 2008 release.

Conversation Population Explosion

One of the more common problems I hear about is an application that runs fine for a few weeks then gradually slows down until everything stops because tempdb is full or the SQL Server instance is out of memory. A little investigation will reveal that there are several million entries in the *sys.conversation_endpoints* view. Since conversation endpoints are cached in memory that is backed by storage in tempdb, enough conversation endpoint entries will exhaust memory, tempdb, or maybe both.

When you get in this state, you have two things to do: fix the cause of the problem so that new dialogs go away when they should, and get rid of the millions of dialogs that have accumulated.

One thing to be careful of here is that dialog conversations are maintained in the *sys.conversation_endpoints* view on the target side of the dialog for a half hour or so to prevent replay attacks. If they weren't kept around, it would be possible for a hacker to capture and re-send a message that restarted the dialog and processed the first message again. With the dialog in the target, the replayed message would be detected as a duplicate and ignored. After a half hour, the messages have all expired so they can't be replayed anymore. This means you should have about a half hour accumulation of conversation endpoints. If in your testing, you find out the conversations don't disappear after an hour, you have a problem.

One possible cause is that the application isn't ending both ends of the conversation. When the application using one end of the conversation completes, it should call END CONVERSATION to tell the Service Broker that it is finished. Service Broker will shut down this end of the conversation and send a message to the other endpoint to indicate that this endpoint is gone. When this happens the conversation is half closed. The endpoint that receives the end conversation message can't send any more messages because the remote end is gone but it can continue to receive and process any messages on the queue for this conversation and then call END CONVERSATION to complete the close process. Every application that receives Service Broker messages should look for and process END CONVERSATION and error messages. The minimum requirement is to call END CONVERSATION to release the local conversation endpoint so it can close. If this isn't done, the conversation will remain half closed forever.

The most frequent cause for conversations never going away is the "fire and forget" pattern that quite a few people attempt to implement with Service Broker. The general flow of this type of application is:

```
BEGIN DIALOG CONVERSATION…
SEND...
END CONVERSATION
```

This causes the initiator of the conversation to disappear before the target is created so the conversation is never completely established and the conversation endpoint never goes away. To fix this, you need to get rid of the END CONVERSATION statement in the initiator logic, end the conversation from the target, and make sure there is a service running at the initiator to receive the end dialog message and end the conversation from that end.

When you are sure your code is correctly ending conversations, you have to get rid of the excess accumulation of conversations. If you are fortunate enough to discover this problem while you're testing the application and you know that there are no messages in any queues that you need, you can get rid of all the conversations in the database with the ALTER DATABASE command:

```
ALTER DATABASE Inventory SET NEW_BROKER
```

If you're not sure that there are no conversations you need to retain, you can just get rid of the closed conversations with this batch:

```
DECLARE @handle uniqueidentifier
DECLARE conv CURSOR FOR SELECT conversation_handle FROM
    sys.conversation_endpoints
WHERE STATE = 'CLOSED'
OPEN conv
FETCH NEXT FROM conv INTO @handle
```

```
WHILE @@FETCH_STATUS = 0
  BEGIN
    END CONVERSATION @handle WITH CLEANUP
    FETCH NEXT FROM conv INTO @handle
  END
CLOSE conv
DEALLOCATE conv
```

No Reply

If the initiator and target for a dialog are different databases, you may see a case where the first message is sent successfully to the target and the target processes it successfully but no response is received. If you turn on SQL tracing and find that the first message is being sent over and over again even though it has been received and processed, a likely cause for this problem is that you have a route in the initiator database from the initiator to the target but no corresponding route in the target database from the target back to the initiator. Because the target can't send an acknowledgement message back to the initiator, the initiator keeps sending the message because it thinks the target hasn't received it. The target only processes the message once and then throws the rest of the duplicates away, so the application only sees the message once.

Poison Message Queue Disable

In the section on poison message handling you learned that Service Broker protects the queue from poison messages by disabling it if five transactions in a row involving the queue are rolled back. When you are developing an application, it's not unusual to have an error in your code that causes a transaction to roll back. If this code receives a message from a queue and rolls back the transaction it will increment the queue rollback counter. If you run this code five times, the queue will be disabled because there were five rollbacks in a row, even though you are handling poison messages correctly. If your code stops working after five tests, run this statement to see if the queue is enabled:

```
SELECT name, is_receive_enabled FROM sys.service_queues
If the queue is disabled, enable it with this statement:
ALTER QUEUE InventoryQueue WITH STATUS = ON
```

The ssbdiagnose Utility

The previous errors are just a sampling of the issues caused by incorrect configuration of the Service Broker. Because this is the source of most problems, the Service Broker developers assembled the most common errors and wrote a debugging tool to scan the configuration tables of a Service Broker application and report any configuration issues. This tool is called ssbdiagnose.exe, and it ships with SQL Server 2008.

Ssbdiagnose has two modes of operation. In the CONFIGURATION mode, it looks through the configuration for specified conversations and reports on any missing or incorrect configuration. For example, the following listing shows an analysis of all conversation types between the specified initiator service and target service:

```
C:\>ssbdiagnose -E -d Inventory CONFIGURATION FROM SERVICE //microsoft.com/InventoryService
TO SERVICE //microsoft.com/ManufacturingService
```

This command returns the following results

```
Microsoft SQL Server 10.0.1600.22
Service Broker Diagnostic Utility
D  29924 MYSERVER2         Inventory        Contract DEFAULT is not bound to service //
microsoft.com/ManufacturingService
D  29975 MYSERVER2         Inventory        User dbo does not have SEND
permission on service //microsoft.com/ManufacturingService
D  29964 MYSERVER2         Inventory        The master key was not found
3 Errors, 0 Warnings
```

In this case, the initiator service and target service were both in the Inventory database so only one database was specified. If the configuration crosses databases and computers, you must specify both database names and server names so ssbdiagnose can connect to both ends of the conversation. See SQL Server Books Online for more information.

In the RUNTIME mode, ssbdiagnose will monitor trace events to detect errors on conversations and report any configuration problems that might have caused the error. For example, the following ssbdiagnose session shows the results of creating a conversation with ENCRYPTION = ON in a database with no database master key:

```
C:\>ssbdiagnose -E RUNTIME –TIMEOUT 30 CONNECT TO -d Inventory
```

This command returns the following results

```
Microsoft SQL Server 10.0.1600.22
Service Broker Diagnostic Utility
D  29835 MYSERVER2         Inventory        Messages on conversation handle 3d12420d-22ec-
dd11-96b1-0015b7d4ac66
(conversation id 6d6a3396-1aaf-4472-a462-3a4d5073a70e)
from service //microsoft.com/ManufacturingService
to service //microsoft.com/InventoryService cannot be transmitted dues to the
following problem: The session keys for this conversation could not be
created or accessed. The database master key is required for this operation.
D  29975 InvDB   Inventory User dbo does not have SEND permission on service
 //microsoft.com/InventoryService

2 Errors, 0 Warnings
```

The RUNTIME parameter tells the utility to monitor errors in active conversations. The TIMEOUT parameter specifies how long ssbdiagnose will execute, and the CONNECT TO parameter determines which database to monitor.

The previous example used ssbdiagnose to monitor all conversations in a specified database. If you know what conversation is having problems, you can specify an ID associated with the conversation (conversation handle, conversation ID, or conversation group ID) to limit the scope of the monitoring:

```
C:\>ssbdiagnose -E -d Inventory RUNTIME -ID D97353A4-4500-4292-A6B7-A06B9E42338B -Timeout 60
```

The ssbdiagnose utility can find errors in configurations during development, during deployment, or during production. It is very lightweight so it will have minimal impact on a running system. I would recommend using it to analyze all new and existing Service Broker configurations. It will save a lot of painful troubleshooting later in the process. I have used it to find subtle errors in applications that appeared to be running fine.

Scenarios

Service Broker enables a whole new class of reliable, asynchronous database applications that could not easily be built before. With all the talk about transactional messaging, it's easy to get the impression that Service Broker is just another reliable messaging product. Although Service Broker offers unprecedented levels of reliability, availability, and performance as a transactional messaging platform, it is also extremely useful in applications that have nothing to do with networking and distribution. People often start out using Service Broker for reliable messaging and end up using it for everything from asynchronous stored procedures to batch scheduling. In this section, I'll cover a few scenarios where Service Broker provides a unique solution. This isn't meant to be en exhaustive list, but rather enough to start you thinking about how Service Broker can fit into your applications.

Reliable SOA

The latest "new thing" in software development is service-oriented architecture (SOA). Although there are as many definitions of SOA as there are vendors selling SOA tools, the basic idea is that your application consists of coarse-grained, loosely coupled services connected with messages. The message format defines the interface between services. Although most vendors use Web Services to handle the messaging, this is not absolutely required. Loosely coupled, autonomous services make assembling an application from reusable pieces a straightforward process. Services can be either new applications or legacy applications wrapped with a services layer to handle communication with other services.

The services that make up an application might be running on different systems located in different locations. Using traditional RPC-style synchronous communications to connect services is an issue because if any one of the services is down or unreachable, the application is down. For this reason, connecting services with reliable, asynchronous messaging is preferred in most SOA applications. This connection method is preferred because if one service is unavailable, the application might continue to run. This makes Service Broker an ideal candidate for an SOA infrastructure. Reliable, asynchronous messaging means that if a service is unavailable, the application can continue to run while messages for the unavailable service are reliably queued for later processing. Because messaging is tightly integrated with the database, all of SQL Server's reliability and high-availability features, such as database mirroring, apply to messages as well as data. When a database-mirrored primary database fails over to the secondary database, the messages and the data in the database fail over to a transactionally consistent state. This means the application can be up and running again in a few seconds without manual intervention and no loss of data.

The development features of SQL Server 2008 enable rich data-oriented services that are hosted in a database. Using CLR stored procedures for the processing logic and Service Broker as an asynchronous execution environment, services can be contained entirely within a database. This includes all configuration and security. The advantage of this is that by detaching and attaching a database, a service can be transferred from an overloaded server to an idle server without ending active conversations or losing any messages or transactions. Moving and even duplicating services without impact on the running application provides a great deal of flexibility in changing deployments in response to changing loads and conditions.

Asynchronous Processing

Service Broker queues and activation open up a number of possibilities for asynchronous database operations. For example, if you want to do some extensive operations in a trigger—such as creating a purchase order when an inventory update takes the on-hand quantity below the restock level—you can send a message to a Service Broker queue in the trigger and use an activation procedure to do the purchase order after the initiating transaction has completed. Because the majority of the work is done outside of the original transaction, the trigger has a minimal impact on performance of the main transaction. You could also write a stored procedure that uses Service Broker to start a number of asynchronous services in parallel and then wait for all of them to finish. The parallel service might be in the same database or spread out across a number of remote databases.

Because Service Broker ensures that messages on a dialog are processed in order, a dialog can be used to manage a multistep batch of SQL commands. If each message is a SQL statement or stored procedure to process, a service could be written that receives messages from the queue and executes the contents of the message by passing it to a SQL EXEC statement. A typical example of this is the night processing for a data warehouse. If the results of processing the statements are returned as response messages on the dialog, the initiator can collect the results of a number of batches. Statements that must be executed serially are placed in a dialog. Multiple dialogs can be started to enable parallel processing. Because Service Broker dialogs can be distributed, a single controlling database can start batches on a number of computers in a distributed environment. Reliable message delivery means the target computer doesn't have to be running or connected when the batch is started. When the connection is restored, the batch will be delivered and processed.

With a little imagination, a Service Broker user can come up with a number of uses for Service Broker's asynchronous execution capabilities. People who start using Service Broker for a specific project often end up using it for a number of other things once they discover the power of controlled asynchronous processing in a database.

Where Does Service Broker Fit?

When I talk to people about Service Broker, I inevitably get questions about how it relates to Microsoft Message Queue (MSMQ), BizTalk, or Windows Communication Foundation (WCF). This section will discuss some general guidelines for deciding whether Service Broker or one of the other messaging technologies is appropriate for your needs.

What Service Broker Is

With Service Broker, SQL Server becomes a platform for building loosely coupled, asynchronous database applications. Service Broker implements queues as first-class database objects. The queue-handling code built into the database kernel handles the locking, ordering, and multithreading issues associated with managing queues.

To support scaling out asynchronous database applications, Service Broker includes reliable, transactional messaging between SQL Server instances. Because Service Broker messaging is built into the database, it offers message integrity, performance, and reliability that most transactional messaging systems can't match. Service Broker dialogs provide ordering and delivery guarantees that no other messaging system offers.

Finally, Service Broker is not just a messaging system. Although the messaging features might be very useful, a large number of Service Broker scenarios don't require messaging at all. The ability to perform asynchronous, queued database actions is very useful, even if your database application isn't distributed.

What Service Broker Isn't

Service Broker isn't a general-purpose messaging system. Although no other transactional messaging system offers the reliability and performance that Service Broker provides to SQL Server applications, the fact that Service Broker is built into SQL Server means that it works only for SQL Server applications.

Service Broker also supports only transactional messaging. Transactional messaging is the only way to ensure that messages are processed exactly once and in order. Because it is part of the database, Service Broker can do transactional messaging significantly better than messaging systems that aren't built into the database. If the application doesn't require transactional reliability, however, this is unnecessary overhead.

Service Broker and MSMQ

Because it is built into SQL Server, Service Broker messaging has some significant advantages over MSMQ transactional messaging:

- Service Broker can commit updates to the message queue, database data, and application state in a simple database transaction. MSMQ requires a two-phase commit to do the same thing.

- Service Broker messages can be processed by any application that can establish a database connection to the SQL Server database. Applications that process MSMQ transactional messages must run on the same physical machine as the queue.

- MSMQ message ordering is assured within a single transaction. Service Broker message ordering in a dialog is assured across transactions, sending applications, and receiving applications.

- The maximum MSMQ message size is 4 MB. The maximum Service Broker message size is 2 GB.

- Service Broker activates another queue reader process only when the current processes aren't keeping up with the load, whereas MSMQ triggers fire for every message that arrives.

On the other hand, MSMQ has some significant features that Service Broker doesn't have:

- MSMQ offers express, reliable, and transactional message styles, whereas Service Broker is transactional only.

- MSMQ can communicate between virtually any pair of Windows applications. Service Broker can communicate only between applications connected to SQL Server.

- MSMQ offers both a TCP/IP binary protocol and an HTTP SOAP protocol for communications. Service Broker is binary TCP/IP only in SQL Server 2008.

Service Broker and BizTalk

Service Broker and BizTalk don't have a lot in common other than reliable message delivery and database queues. Service Broker can reliably deliver a message to another SQL Server instance with exactly-once-in-order assurances. BizTalk does this also, but in addition it can manipulate the contents of messages, map message formats, manage message processing, manage workflows, manage state, send messages over multiple different transports, and so on. If your application doesn't use any of these features and just requires reliable delivery of XML documents from one SQL Server instance to another, Service Broker is probably a better alternative. However, if your application requires the more advanced BizTalk features, you will need to use BizTalk or write the logic yourself.

Service Broker and Windows Communication Foundation

Service Broker supports reliable, transactional messaging over TCP/IP using a proprietary protocol between SQL Server instances. Windows Communication Foundation (WCF) supports many messaging styles over a variety of standards-based protocols between Windows and any operating system that implements the standard protocols that WCF supports. Although WCF can't match Service Broker when it comes to connecting SQL Server applications together reliably, its total feature set and connectivity options go far beyond what Service Broker offers. You can combine the Service Broker asynchronous, reliable database platform capabilities with WCF's interoperability to build reliable, heterogeneous applications.

Conclusion

Service Broker brings the advantages of asynchronous execution and reliable messaging to SQL Server applications. Service Broker's message ordering, correlation, and activation features are unequaled by any messaging system. When combined with CLR integration, database mirroring, and the new XML features, Service Broker makes SQL Server 2008 a viable platform for building database applications and services that offer unprecedented levels of reliability and fault tolerance.

Appendix A
Companion to CLR Routines

This book has common language runtime (CLR) code scattered in multiple chapters. CLR routine code for functions, stored procedures, and triggers appears in four chapters (2, 3, 4, and 8). For your convenience and for reference purposes, I centralized all routine code from the four chapters in this appendix.

CLR user-defined types (UDTs) are covered in Chapter 11. The CLR code coverage there is already centralized and independent, so I didn't see any value in providing it in this appendix as well. Note that CLR user-defined aggregates (UDAs) are discussed in the prequel to this book, *T-SQL Querying*.

You will also be provided with step-by-step instructions on how to develop and deploy the solutions in both C# and Microsoft Visual Basic. You will be instructed to implement some of the steps in Microsoft Visual Studio 2008, and some in Microsoft SQL Server 2008.

In general, you develop .NET routines by following these steps:

- Create a test database (SQL Server).
- Develop .NET code (Visual Studio):
  - ❏ Create a project.
  - ❏ Develop code.
- Deploy and test the solution (Visual Studio and SQL Server):
  - ❏ Build and deploy the solution.
  - ❏ Test the solution.

In this appendix, I'll follow these steps in detail for the CLR routines from this book.

For your reference, the step-by-step instructions are followed by listings that contain the complete CLR and T-SQL code that appears in the four chapters.

For a better learning experience, you might find it convenient to first follow the steps described in this appendix to create all routines that are included in the book. Then, as you read a chapter, you won't have to follow the same steps repeatedly to add each routine. Instead, you can focus on the code snippets provided inline in the chapter.

Create the CLRUtilities Database: SQL Server

All CLR routines covered in the book are created in the CLRUtilities database, which you create by running the code in Listing A-1. The code also creates the table T1, which will be used for the CLR trigger example.

Development: Visual Studio

Following are step-by-step instructions you should follow to develop the solution. All development is done in Visual Studio 2008. Follow the relevant instructions based on your language of preference (C# or Visual Basic). Note that in some editions of Visual Studio, like Professional, you can work with the SQL Server Project template, which allows you to deploy the assembly and the routines in SQL Server automatically. In any edition of Visual Studio you can use the Class Library project template. This template allows you to develop and build the assembly in Visual Studio, in which case you will have to follow with a manual process of deployment in SQL Server using T-SQL code. Both options are covered in the step-by-step instructions.

If this is the first time you're developing .NET code for SQL Server, I'd recommend experimenting with both template options (assuming both are available to you).

Create a Project

1. Create a new project using your preferred language (C# or Visual Basic):

   (File | New | Project | Visual C# or Visual Basic)

2. Choose a project template based on the Visual Studio edition.

   For the Professional or higher edition:

   Use either the Database SQL Server template (Database | SQL Server Project) or the Class Library template (Windows | Class Library).

   For the Standard edition:

   Use the Class Library template (Windows | Class Library).

3. Specify the following details in the New Project dialog box:

   ❑   Name   CLRUtilities

   ❑   Location   C:\ (or your folder of preference)

   ❑   Solution Name   CLRUtilities

   And then click OK.

4. Create a database reference in the Add Database Reference dialog box (relevant only if you chose the SQL Server Project template).

Create a new database reference to the CLRUtilities database, or choose an existing reference if you created one already.

Do not confirm SQL/CLR debugging on this connection.

Develop Code

1. Add or rename the class.

   SQL Server Project template:

   (Project | Add Class | Class | Name: CLRUtilities.cs or CLRUtilities.vb | Add)

   Class Library template:

   (Rename Class1.cs to CLRUtilities.cs or Class1.vb to CLRUtilities.vb in Solution Explorer)

2. Replace the code in the class with the code from Listing A-2 (C#) or Listing A-3 (Visual Basic).

Deployment and Testing: Visual Studio and SQL Server

When you're done with the code development, you need to deploy the assembly and the routines into a SQL Server database:

1. Build the project into an assembly—a .DLL file on disk with the Intermediate Language (IL) code.

2. Deploy the assembly into a SQL Server database. The IL code is loaded from the .DLL file into the database, and after the load, you no longer need the external file.

3. Create routines (functions, stored procedures, and triggers) in the SQL Server database. This process essentially registers routines from the assembly, which already resides in the database.

All these steps can be achieved from Visual Studio with an automated process if you're working with the SQL Server Project template. If you're working with the Class Library template, from Visual Studio, you can only build the assembly. The deployment will be a manual process in SQL Server using T-SQL CREATE ASSEMBLY and CREATE FUNCTION | PROCEDURE | TRIGGER commands.

The following sections describe the step-by-step instructions for both templates.

Build and Deploy the Solution

- SQL Server Project template: (Build | Deploy)

  Done

- Class Library template: (Build | Build)

   In SQL Server, run the CREATE ASSEMBLY | FUNCTION | PROCEDURE | TRIGGER code in Listing A-4 (C#), A-5 (Visual Basic) (relevant only for the Class Library template).

When you're done with deployment, you can test and use your new routines.

Test the Solution

Run the test code in Listing A-4 (C#), A-5 (Visual Basic) without the CREATE statements.

LISTING A-1 T-SQL code to enable CLR and create CLRUtilities database and T1 table

```
SET NOCOUNT ON;
USE master;
EXEC sp_configure 'clr enabled', 1;
RECONFIGURE;
GO
IF DB_ID('CLRUtilities') IS NOT NULL
  DROP DATABASE CLRUtilities;
GO
CREATE DATABASE CLRUtilities;
GO
USE CLRUtilities;
GO

-- Create T1 table
IF OBJECT_ID('dbo.T1', 'U') IS NOT NULL DROP TABLE dbo.T1;

CREATE TABLE dbo.T1
(
  keycol  INT        NOT NULL PRIMARY KEY,
  datacol VARCHAR(10) NOT NULL
);
```

LISTING A-2 C# code for CLRUtilities class

```
using System;
using System.Data;
using System.Data.SqlClient;
using System.Data.SqlTypes;
using Microsoft.SqlServer.Server;
using System.Text;
using System.Text.RegularExpressions;
using System.Collections;
using System.Collections.Generic;
using System.Diagnostics;
using System.Reflection;
```

```csharp
public partial class CLRUtilities
{
  // RegexIsMatch function
  // Validates input string against regular expression
  [SqlFunction(IsDeterministic = true, DataAccess = DataAccessKind.None)]
  public static SqlBoolean RegexIsMatch(SqlString input,
    SqlString pattern)
  {
      if (input.IsNull || pattern.IsNull)
         return SqlBoolean.Null;
      else
         return (SqlBoolean)Regex.IsMatch(input.Value, pattern.Value,
            RegexOptions.CultureInvariant);
  }


  // RegexReplace function
  // String replacement based on regular expression
  [SqlFunction(IsDeterministic = true, DataAccess = DataAccessKind.None)]
  public static SqlString RegexReplace(
      SqlString input, SqlString pattern, SqlString replacement)
  {
    if (input.IsNull || pattern.IsNull || replacement.IsNull)
       return SqlString.Null;
    else
      return (SqlString)Regex.Replace(
        input.Value, pattern.Value, replacement.Value);
  }


  // FormatDatetime function
  // Formats a DATETIME value based on a format string
  [Microsoft.SqlServer.Server.SqlFunction]
  public static SqlString FormatDatetime(SqlDateTime dt, SqlString formatstring)
  {
    if (dt.IsNull || formatstring.IsNull)
      return SqlString.Null;
    else
      return (SqlString)dt.Value.ToString(formatstring.Value);
  }


  // Compare implicit vs. explicit casting
  [SqlFunction(IsDeterministic = true, DataAccess = DataAccessKind.None)]
  public static string ImpCast(string inpStr)
  {
    return inpStr.Substring(2, 3);
  }


  [SqlFunction(IsDeterministic = true, DataAccess = DataAccessKind.None)]
  public static SqlString ExpCast(SqlString inpStr)
  {
    return (SqlString)inpStr.ToString().Substring(2, 3);
  }
```

```csharp
// SQLSigCLR Funcion
// Produces SQL Signature from an input query string
[SqlFunction(IsDeterministic = true, DataAccess = DataAccessKind.None)]
public static SqlString SQLSigCLR(SqlString inpRawString,
  SqlInt32 inpParseLength)
{
  if (inpRawString.IsNull)
    return SqlString.Null;
  int pos = 0;
  string mode = "command";
  string RawString = inpRawString.Value;
  int maxlength = RawString.Length;
  StringBuilder p2 = new StringBuilder();
  char currchar = ' ';
  char nextchar = ' ';
  int ParseLength = RawString.Length;
  if (!inpParseLength.IsNull)
    ParseLength = inpParseLength.Value;
  if (RawString.Length > ParseLength)
  {
    maxlength = ParseLength;
  }
  while (pos < maxlength)
  {
    currchar = RawString[pos];
    if (pos < maxlength - 1)
    {
      nextchar = RawString[pos + 1];
    }
    else
    {
      nextchar = RawString[pos];
    }
    if (mode == "command")
    {
      p2.Append(currchar);
      if ((",( =<>!".IndexOf(currchar) >= 0)
          &&
          (nextchar >= '0' && nextchar <= '9'))
      {
        mode = "number";
        p2.Append('#');
      }
      if (currchar == '\'')
      {
        mode = "literal";
        p2.Append("#'");
      }
    }
    else if ((mode == "number")
             &&
             (",( =<>!".IndexOf(nextchar) >= 0))
    {
      mode = "command";
    }
```

```csharp
      else if ((mode == "literal") && (currchar == '\''))
      {
        mode = "command";
      }
      pos++;
  }
  return p2.ToString();
}


// Struct used in SplitCLR function
struct row_item
{
  public string item;
  public int pos;
}


// SplitCLR Function
// Splits separated list of values and returns a table
// FillRowMethodName = "ArrSplitFillRow"
[SqlFunction(FillRowMethodName = "ArrSplitFillRow",
 DataAccess = DataAccessKind.None,
 TableDefinition = "pos INT, element NVARCHAR(4000) ")]
public static IEnumerable SplitCLR(SqlString inpStr,
    SqlString charSeparator)
{
  string locStr;
  string[] splitStr;
  char[] locSeparator = new char[1];
  locSeparator[0] = (char)charSeparator.Value[0];
  if (inpStr.IsNull)
    locStr = "";
  else
    locStr = inpStr.Value;
  splitStr = locStr.Split(locSeparator,
      StringSplitOptions.RemoveEmptyEntries);
  //locStr.Split(charSeparator.ToString()[0]);
  List<row_item> SplitString = new List<row_item>();
  int i = 1;
  foreach (string s in splitStr)
  {
    row_item r = new row_item();
    r.item = s;
    r.pos = i;
    SplitString.Add(r);
    ++i;
  }
  return SplitString;
}


public static void ArrSplitFillRow(
  Object obj, out int pos, out string item)
{
  pos = ((row_item)obj).pos;
  item = ((row_item)obj).item;
}
```

```
// GetEnvInfo Procedure
// Returns environment info in tabular format
[SqlProcedure]
public static void GetEnvInfo()
{
  // Create a record - object representation of a row
  // Include the metadata for the SQL table
  SqlDataRecord record = new SqlDataRecord(
      new SqlMetaData("EnvProperty", SqlDbType.NVarChar, 20),
      new SqlMetaData("Value", SqlDbType.NVarChar, 256));
  // Marks the beginning of the result set to be sent back to the client
  // The record parameter is used to construct the metadata
  // for the result set
  SqlContext.Pipe.SendResultsStart(record);
  // Populate some records and send them through the pipe
  record.SetSqlString(0, @"Machine Name");
  record.SetSqlString(1, Environment.MachineName);
  SqlContext.Pipe.SendResultsRow(record);
  record.SetSqlString(0, @"Processors");
  record.SetSqlString(1, Environment.ProcessorCount.ToString());
  SqlContext.Pipe.SendResultsRow(record);
  record.SetSqlString(0, @"OS Version");
  record.SetSqlString(1, Environment.OSVersion.ToString());
  SqlContext.Pipe.SendResultsRow(record);
  record.SetSqlString(0, @"CLR Version");
  record.SetSqlString(1, Environment.Version.ToString());
  SqlContext.Pipe.SendResultsRow(record);
  // End of result set
  SqlContext.Pipe.SendResultsEnd();
}


// GetAssemblyInfo Procedure
// Returns assembly info, uses Reflection
[SqlProcedure]
public static void GetAssemblyInfo(SqlString asmName)
{
  // Retrieve the clr name of the assembly
  String clrName = null;
  // Get the context
  using (SqlConnection connection =
          new SqlConnection("Context connection = true"))
  {
    connection.Open();
    using (SqlCommand command = new SqlCommand())
    {
      // Get the assembly and load it
      command.Connection = connection;
      command.CommandText =
        "SELECT clr_name FROM sys.assemblies WHERE name = @asmName";
      command.Parameters.Add("@asmName", SqlDbType.NVarChar);
      command.Parameters[0].Value = asmName;
      clrName = (String)command.ExecuteScalar();
      if (clrName == null)
      {
        throw new ArgumentException("Invalid assembly name!");
      }
```

```
        Assembly myAsm = Assembly.Load(clrName);
        // Create a record - object representation of a row
        // Include the metadata for the SQL table
        SqlDataRecord record = new SqlDataRecord(
            new SqlMetaData("Type", SqlDbType.NVarChar, 50),
            new SqlMetaData("Name", SqlDbType.NVarChar, 256));
        // Marks the beginning of the result set to be sent back
        // to the client
        // The record parameter is used to construct the metadata
        // for the result set
        SqlContext.Pipe.SendResultsStart(record);
        // Get all types in the assembly
        Type[] typesArr = myAsm.GetTypes();
        foreach (Type t in typesArr)
        {
          // The type should be Class or Structure
          if (t.IsClass == true)
          {
            record.SetSqlString(0, @"Class");
          }
          else
          {
            record.SetSqlString(0, @"Structure");
          }
          record.SetSqlString(1, t.FullName);
          SqlContext.Pipe.SendResultsRow(record);
          // Find all public static methods
          MethodInfo[] miArr = t.GetMethods();
          foreach (MethodInfo mi in miArr)
          {
            if (mi.IsPublic && mi.IsStatic)
            {
              record.SetSqlString(0, @"  Method");
              record.SetSqlString(1, mi.Name);
              SqlContext.Pipe.SendResultsRow(record);
            }
          }
        }
        // End of result set
        SqlContext.Pipe.SendResultsEnd();
    }
  }
}


// trg_GenericDMLAudit Trigger
// Generic trigger for auditing DML statements
// trigger will write first 200 characters from all columns
// in an XML format to App Event Log
[SqlTrigger(Name = @"trg_GenericDMLAudit", Target = "T1",
   Event = "FOR INSERT, UPDATE, DELETE")]
public static void trg_GenericDMLAudit()
{
  // Get the trigger context to get info about the action type
  SqlTriggerContext triggContext = SqlContext.TriggerContext;
```

```
// Prepare the command and pipe objects
SqlCommand command;
SqlPipe pipe = SqlContext.Pipe;

// Check type of action
switch (triggContext.TriggerAction)
{
  case TriggerAction.Insert:
    // Retrieve the connection that the trigger is using
    using (SqlConnection connection
      = new SqlConnection(@"context connection=true"))
    {
      connection.Open();
      // Collect all columns into an XML type, cast it
      // to nvarchar and select only a substring from it
      // Info from Inserted
      command = new SqlCommand(
        @"SELECT 'New data: '
            + REPLACE(
                SUBSTRING(CAST(a.InsertedContents AS NVARCHAR(MAX))
                  ,1,200),
                CHAR(39), CHAR(39)+CHAR(39)) AS InsertedContents200
          FROM (SELECT * FROM Inserted FOR XML AUTO, TYPE)
            AS a(InsertedContents);",
          connection);
      // Store info collected to a string variable
      string msg;
      msg = (string)command.ExecuteScalar();
      // Write the audit info to the event log
      EventLogEntryType entry = new EventLogEntryType();
      entry = EventLogEntryType.SuccessAudit;
      // Note: if the following line would use
      // Environment.MachineName instead of "." to refer to
      // the local machine event log, the assembly would need
      // the UNSAFE permission set
      EventLog ev = new EventLog(@"Application",
        ".", @"GenericDMLAudit Trigger");
      ev.WriteEntry(msg, entry);
      // send the audit info to the user
      pipe.Send(msg);
    }
    break;
  case TriggerAction.Update:
    // Retrieve the connection that the trigger is using
    using (SqlConnection connection
      = new SqlConnection(@"context connection=true"))
    {
      connection.Open();
      // Collect all columns into an XML type,
      // cast it to nvarchar and select only a substring from it
      // Info from Deleted
      command = new SqlCommand(
        @"SELECT 'Old data: '
            + REPLACE(
```

```
                  SUBSTRING(CAST(a.DeletedContents AS NVARCHAR(MAX))
                   ,1,200),
                  CHAR(39), CHAR(39)+CHAR(39)) AS DeletedContents200
          FROM (SELECT * FROM Deleted FOR XML AUTO, TYPE)
            AS a(DeletedContents);",
        connection);
      // Store info collected to a string variable
      string msg;
      msg = (string)command.ExecuteScalar();
      // Info from Inserted
      command.CommandText =
        @"SELECT ' // New data: '
            + REPLACE(
                SUBSTRING(CAST(a.InsertedContents AS NVARCHAR(MAX))
                 ,1,200),
                CHAR(39), CHAR(39)+CHAR(39)) AS InsertedContents200
          FROM (SELECT * FROM Inserted FOR XML AUTO, TYPE)
            AS a(InsertedContents);";
      msg = msg + (string)command.ExecuteScalar();
      // Write the audit info to the event log
      EventLogEntryType entry = new EventLogEntryType();
      entry = EventLogEntryType.SuccessAudit;
      EventLog ev = new EventLog(@"Application",
        ".", @"GenericDMLAudit Trigger");
      ev.WriteEntry(msg, entry);
      // send the audit info to the user
      pipe.Send(msg);
    }
    break;
case TriggerAction.Delete:
  // Retrieve the connection that the trigger is using
  using (SqlConnection connection
    = new SqlConnection(@"context connection=true"))
  {
    connection.Open();
    // Collect all columns into an XML type,
    // cast it to nvarchar and select only a substring from it
    // Info from Deleted
    command = new SqlCommand(
      @"SELECT 'Old data: '
          + REPLACE(
              SUBSTRING(CAST(a. DeletedContents AS NVARCHAR(MAX))
               ,1,200),
              CHAR(39), CHAR(39)+CHAR(39)) AS DeletedContents200
        FROM (SELECT * FROM Deleted FOR XML AUTO, TYPE)
            AS a(DeletedContents);",
        connection);
    // Store info collected to a string variable
    string msg;
    msg = (string)command.ExecuteScalar();
    // Write the audit info to the event log
    EventLogEntryType entry = new EventLogEntryType();
    entry = EventLogEntryType.SuccessAudit;
    EventLog ev = new EventLog(@"Application",
      ".", @"GenericDMLAudit Trigger");
```

```
        ev.WriteEntry(msg, entry);
        // send the audit info to the user
        pipe.Send(msg);
      }
      break;
    default:
      // Just to be sure - this part should never fire
      pipe.Send(@"Nothing happened");
      break;
  }
}

// SalesRunningSum Procedure
// Queries dbo.Sales, returns running sum of qty for each empid, dt
[Microsoft.SqlServer.Server.SqlProcedure]
public static void SalesRunningSum()
{
  using (SqlConnection conn = new SqlConnection("context connection=true;"))
  {
    SqlCommand comm = new SqlCommand();
    comm.Connection = conn;
    comm.CommandText = "" +
        "SELECT empid, dt, qty " +
        "FROM dbo.Sales " +
        "ORDER BY empid, dt;";

    SqlMetaData[] columns = new SqlMetaData[4];
    columns[0] = new SqlMetaData("empid", SqlDbType.Int);
    columns[1] = new SqlMetaData("dt", SqlDbType.DateTime);
    columns[2] = new SqlMetaData("qty", SqlDbType.Int);
    columns[3] = new SqlMetaData("sumqty", SqlDbType.BigInt);

    SqlDataRecord record = new SqlDataRecord(columns);

    SqlContext.Pipe.SendResultsStart(record);

    conn.Open();

    SqlDataReader reader = comm.ExecuteReader();

    SqlInt32 prvempid = 0;
    SqlInt64 sumqty = 0;

    while (reader.Read())
    {
      SqlInt32 empid = reader.GetSqlInt32(0);
      SqlInt32 qty = reader.GetSqlInt32(2);

      if (empid == prvempid)
      {
        sumqty += qty;
      }
      else
      {
        sumqty = qty;
      }
```

```
        prvempid = empid;

      record.SetSqlInt32(0, reader.GetSqlInt32(0));
      record.SetSqlDateTime(1, reader.GetSqlDateTime(1));
      record.SetSqlInt32(2, qty);
      record.SetSqlInt64(3, sumqty);

      SqlContext.Pipe.SendResultsRow(record);
    }

    SqlContext.Pipe.SendResultsEnd();
  }
 }
};
```

LISTING A-3 Visual Basic code for CLRUtilities class

```
Imports System
Imports System.Data
Imports System.Data.SqlClient
Imports System.Data.SqlTypes
Imports Microsoft.SqlServer.Server
Imports System.Text
Imports System.Text.RegularExpressions
Imports System.Collections
Imports System.Collections.Generic
Imports System.Diagnostics
Imports System.Reflection
Imports System.Runtime.InteropServices

Partial Public Class CLRUtilities

  ' RegexIsMatch function
  ' Validates input string against regular expression
  <SqlFunction(IsDeterministic:=True, DataAccess:=DataAccessKind.None)> _
  Public Shared Function RegexIsMatch(ByVal input As SqlString, _
    ByVal pattern As SqlString) As SqlBoolean
      If (input.IsNull Or pattern.IsNull) Then
          Return SqlBoolean.Null
      Else
          Return CType(Regex.IsMatch(input.Value, pattern.Value, _
            RegexOptions.CultureInvariant), SqlBoolean)
      End If
  End Function

  ' RegexReplace function
  ' String replacement based on regular expression
  <SqlFunction(IsDeterministic:=True, DataAccess:=DataAccessKind.None)> _
  Public Shared Function RegexReplace( _
    ByVal input As SqlString, ByVal pattern As SqlString, _
    ByVal replacement As SqlString) As SqlString

    If (input.IsNull Or pattern.IsNull Or replacement.IsNull) Then
      Return SqlString.Null
```

```vb
    Else
      Return CType(Regex.Replace( _
        input.Value, pattern.Value, replacement.Value), SqlString)
    End If
End Function


' FormatDatetime function
' Formats a DATETIME value based on a format string
<SqlFunction(IsDeterministic:=True, DataAccess:=DataAccessKind.None)> _
Public Shared Function FormatDatetime( _
  ByVal dt As SqlDateTime, ByVal formatstring As SqlString) As SqlString

  If (dt.IsNull Or formatstring.IsNull) Then
    Return SqlString.Null
  Else
    Return CType(dt.Value.ToString(formatstring.Value), SqlString)
  End If
End Function


' Compare implicit vs. explicit casting
<SqlFunction(IsDeterministic:=True, DataAccess:=DataAccessKind.None)> _
Public Shared Function ImpCast(ByVal inpStr As String) As String
  Return inpStr.Substring(2, 3)
End Function


<SqlFunction(IsDeterministic:=True, DataAccess:=DataAccessKind.None)> _
Public Shared Function ExpCast(ByVal inpStr As SqlString) As SqlString
  Return CType(inpStr.ToString().Substring(2, 3), SqlString)
End Function

' SQLSigCLR Funcion
' Produces SQL Signature from an input query string
<SqlFunction(IsDeterministic:=True, DataAccess:=DataAccessKind.None)> _
Public Shared Function SQLSigCLR(ByVal inpRawString As SqlString, _
  ByVal inpParseLength As SqlInt32) As SqlString
  If inpRawString.IsNull Then
    Return SqlString.Null
  End If
  Dim pos As Integer = 0
  Dim mode As String = "command"
  Dim RawString As String = inpRawString.Value
  Dim maxlength As Integer = RawString.Length
  Dim p2 As StringBuilder = New StringBuilder()
  Dim currchar As Char = " "c
  Dim nextchar As Char = " "c
  Dim ParseLength As Integer = RawString.Length
  If (Not inpParseLength.IsNull) Then
    ParseLength = inpParseLength.Value
  End If
  If (RawString.Length > ParseLength) Then
    maxlength = ParseLength
  End If
  While (pos < maxlength)
    currchar = RawString(pos)
```

```
      If (pos < maxlength - 1) Then
        nextchar = RawString(pos + 1)
      Else
        nextchar = RawString(pos)
      End If
      If (mode = "command") Then
        p2.Append(currchar)
        If ((",( =<>!".IndexOf(currchar) >= 0) _
            And _
            (nextchar >= "0"c And nextchar <= "9"c)) Then
          mode = "number"
          p2.Append("#")
        End If
        If (currchar = "'"c) Then
          mode = "literal"
          p2.Append("#")
        End If
      ElseIf ((mode = "number") And _
              (",( =<>!".IndexOf(nextchar) >= 0)) Then
        mode = "command"
      ElseIf ((mode = "literal") And _
              (currchar = "'"c)) Then
        mode = "command"
      End If
      pos = pos + 1
    End While
    Return p2.ToString
  End Function


  'Struct used in SplitCLR function
  Structure row_item
    Dim item As String
    Dim pos As Integer
  End Structure


  ' SplitCLR Function
  ' Splits separated list of values and returns a table
  ' FillRowMethodName = "ArrSplitFillRow"
  <SqlFunction(FillRowMethodName:="ArrSplitFillRow", _
    DataAccess:=DataAccessKind.None, _
    TableDefinition:="pos INT, element NVARCHAR(4000) ")> _
  Public Shared Function SplitCLR(ByVal inpStr As SqlString, _
    ByVal charSeparator As SqlString) As IEnumerable
    Dim locStr As String
    Dim splitStr() As String
    Dim locSeparator(0) As Char
    locSeparator(0) = CChar(charSeparator.Value(0))
    If (inpStr.IsNull) Then
      locStr = ""
    Else
      locStr = inpStr.Value
    End If
    splitStr = locStr.Split(locSeparator, _
      StringSplitOptions.RemoveEmptyEntries)
```

```vb
  Dim SplitString As New List(Of row_item)
  Dim i As Integer = 1
  For Each s As String In splitStr
    Dim r As New row_item
    r.item = s
    r.pos = i
    SplitString.Add(r)
    i = i + 1
  Next
  Return SplitString
End Function

Public Shared Sub ArrSplitFillRow( _
ByVal obj As Object, <Out()> ByRef pos As Integer, _
  <Out()> ByRef item As String)
  pos = CType(obj, row_item).pos
  item = CType(obj, row_item).item
End Sub

' GetEnvInfo Procedure
' Returns environment info in tabular format
<SqlProcedure()> _
Public Shared Sub GetEnvInfo()
  ' Create a record - object representation of a row
  ' Include the metadata for the SQL table
  Dim record As New SqlDataRecord( _
      New SqlMetaData("EnvProperty", SqlDbType.NVarChar, 20), _
      New SqlMetaData("Value", SqlDbType.NVarChar, 256))
  ' Marks the beginning of the result set to be sent back to the client
  ' The record parameter is used to construct the metadata for
  ' the result set
  SqlContext.Pipe.SendResultsStart(record)
  '' Populate some records and send them through the pipe
  record.SetSqlString(0, "Machine Name")
  record.SetSqlString(1, Environment.MachineName)
  SqlContext.Pipe.SendResultsRow(record)
  record.SetSqlString(0, "Processors")
  record.SetSqlString(1, Environment.ProcessorCount.ToString())
  SqlContext.Pipe.SendResultsRow(record)
  record.SetSqlString(0, "OS Version")
  record.SetSqlString(1, Environment.OSVersion.ToString())
  SqlContext.Pipe.SendResultsRow(record)
  record.SetSqlString(0, "CLR Version")
  record.SetSqlString(1, Environment.Version.ToString())
  SqlContext.Pipe.SendResultsRow(record)
  ' End of result set
  SqlContext.Pipe.SendResultsEnd()
End Sub

' GetAssemblyInfo Procedure
' Returns assembly info, uses Reflection
<SqlProcedure()> _
Public Shared Sub GetAssemblyInfo(ByVal asmName As SqlString)
  ' Retrieve the clr name of the assembly
```

```vb
   Dim clrName As String = Nothing
   ' Get the context
   Using connection As New SqlConnection("Context connection = true")
     connection.Open()
     Using command As New SqlCommand
       ' Get the assembly and load it
       command.Connection = connection
       command.CommandText = _
         "SELECT clr_name FROM sys.assemblies WHERE name = @asmName"
       command.Parameters.Add("@asmName", SqlDbType.NVarChar)
       command.Parameters(0).Value = asmName
       clrName = CStr(command.ExecuteScalar())
       If (clrName = Nothing) Then
         Throw New ArgumentException("Invalid assembly name!")
       End If
       Dim myAsm As Assembly = Assembly.Load(clrName)
       ' Create a record - object representation of a row
       ' Include the metadata for the SQL table
       Dim record As New SqlDataRecord( _
           New SqlMetaData("Type", SqlDbType.NVarChar, 50), _
           New SqlMetaData("Name", SqlDbType.NVarChar, 256))
       ' Marks the beginning of the result set to be sent back
       ' to the client
       ' The record parameter is used to construct the metadata
       ' for the result set
       SqlContext.Pipe.SendResultsStart(record)
       ' Get all types in the assembly
       Dim typesArr() As Type = myAsm.GetTypes()
       For Each t As Type In typesArr
         ' The type should be Class or Structure
         If (t.IsClass = True) Then
           record.SetSqlString(0, "Class")
         Else
           record.SetSqlString(0, "Structure")
         End If
         record.SetSqlString(1, t.FullName)
         SqlContext.Pipe.SendResultsRow(record)
         ' Find all public static methods
         Dim miArr() As MethodInfo = t.GetMethods
         For Each mi As MethodInfo In miArr
           If (mi.IsPublic And mi.IsStatic) Then
             record.SetSqlString(0, "  Method")
             record.SetSqlString(1, mi.Name)
             SqlContext.Pipe.SendResultsRow(record)
           End If
         Next
       Next
       ' End of result set
       SqlContext.Pipe.SendResultsEnd()
     End Using
   End Using
End Sub

' trg_GenericDMLAudit Trigger
' Generic trigger for auditing DML statements
```

```vb
' trigger will write first 200 characters from all columns
' in an XML format to App Event Log
<SqlTrigger(Name:="trg_GenericDMLAudit", Target:="T1", _
  Event:="FOR INSERT, UPDATE, DELETE")> _
Public Shared Sub trg_GenericDMLAudit()
  ' Get the trigger context to get info about the action type
  Dim triggContext As SqlTriggerContext = SqlContext.TriggerContext
  ' Prepare the command and pipe objects
  Dim command As SqlCommand
  Dim pipe As SqlPipe = SqlContext.Pipe

  ' Check type of action
  Select Case triggContext.TriggerAction
    Case TriggerAction.Insert
      ' Retrieve the connection that the trigger is using
      Using connection _
        As New SqlConnection("Context connection = true")
        connection.Open()
        ' Collect all columns into an XML type,
        ' cast it to nvarchar and select only a substring from it
        ' Info from Inserted
        command = New SqlCommand( _
          "SELECT 'New data: ' + REPLACE(" & _
          "SUBSTRING(CAST(a.InsertedContents AS NVARCHAR(MAX)" & _
          "),1,200), CHAR(39), CHAR(39)+CHAR(39)) AS InsertedContents200 " & _
          "FROM (SELECT * FROM Inserted FOR XML AUTO, TYPE) " & _
          "AS a(InsertedContents);", _
           connection)
        ' Store info collected to a string variable
        Dim msg As String
        msg = CStr(command.ExecuteScalar())
        ' Write the audit info to the event log
        Dim entry As EventLogEntryType
        entry = EventLogEntryType.SuccessAudit
        ' Note: if the following line would use
        ' Environment.MachineName instead of "." to refer to
        ' the local machine event log, the assembly would need
        ' the UNSAFE permission set
        Dim ev As New EventLog("Application", _
          ".", "GenericDMLAudit Trigger")
        ev.WriteEntry(msg, entry)
        ' send the audit info to the user
        pipe.Send(msg)
      End Using
    Case TriggerAction.Update
      ' Retrieve the connection that the trigger is using
      Using connection _
        As New SqlConnection("Context connection = true")
        connection.Open()
        ' Collect all columns into an XML type,
        ' cast it to nvarchar and select only a substring from it
        ' Info from Deleted
        command = New SqlCommand( _
          "SELECT 'Old data: ' + REPLACE(" & _
          "SUBSTRING(CAST(a.DeletedContents AS NVARCHAR(MAX)" & _
          "),1,200), CHAR(39), CHAR(39)+CHAR(39)) AS DeletedContents200 " & _
```

```vb
          "FROM (SELECT * FROM Deleted FOR XML AUTO, TYPE) " & _
          "AS a(DeletedContents);", _
           connection)
        ' Store info collected to a string variable
        Dim msg As String
        msg = CStr(command.ExecuteScalar())
        ' Info from Inserted
        command.CommandText = _
          "SELECT ' // New data: ' + REPLACE(" & _
          "SUBSTRING(CAST(a.InsertedContents AS NVARCHAR(MAX)" & _
          "),1,200), CHAR(39), CHAR(39)+CHAR(39)) AS InsertedContents200 " & _
          "FROM (SELECT * FROM Inserted FOR XML AUTO, TYPE) " & _
          "AS a(InsertedContents);"
        msg = msg + CStr(command.ExecuteScalar())
        ' Write the audit info to the event log
        Dim entry As EventLogEntryType
        entry = EventLogEntryType.SuccessAudit
        Dim ev As New EventLog("Application", _
          ".", "GenericDMLAudit Trigger")
        ev.WriteEntry(msg, entry)
        ' send the audit info to the user
        pipe.Send(msg)
      End Using
    Case TriggerAction.Delete
      ' Retrieve the connection that the trigger is using
      Using connection _
        As New SqlConnection("Context connection = true")
        connection.Open()
        ' Collect all columns into an XML type,
        ' cast it to nvarchar and select only a substring from it
        ' Info from Deleted
        command = New SqlCommand( _
          "SELECT 'Old data: ' + REPLACE(" & _
          "SUBSTRING(CAST(a.DeletedContents AS NVARCHAR(MAX)" & _
          "),1,200), CHAR(39), CHAR(39)+CHAR(39)) AS DeletedContents200 " & _
          "FROM (SELECT * FROM Deleted FOR XML AUTO, TYPE) " & _
          "AS a(DeletedContents);", _
           connection)
        ' Store info collected to a string variable
        Dim msg As String
        msg = CStr(command.ExecuteScalar())
        ' Write the audit info to the event log
        Dim entry As EventLogEntryType
        entry = EventLogEntryType.SuccessAudit
        Dim ev As New EventLog("Application", _
          ".", "GenericDMLAudit Trigger")
        ev.WriteEntry(msg, entry)
        ' send the audit info to the user
        pipe.Send(msg)
      End Using
    Case Else
      ' Just to be sure - this part should never fire
      pipe.Send("Nothing happened")
  End Select
End Sub
```

```vb
' SalesRunningSum Procedure
' Queries dbo.Sales, returns running sum of qty for each empid, dt
<Microsoft.SqlServer.Server.SqlProcedure()> _
Public Shared Sub SalesRunningSum()

    Using conn As New SqlConnection("context connection=true")
        Dim comm As New SqlCommand
        comm.Connection = conn
        comm.CommandText = "" & _
            "SELECT empid, dt, qty " & _
            "FROM dbo.Sales " & _
            "ORDER BY empid, dt;"

        Dim columns() As SqlMetaData = New SqlMetaData(3) {}
        columns(0) = New SqlMetaData("empid", SqlDbType.Int)
        columns(1) = New SqlMetaData("dt", SqlDbType.DateTime)
        columns(2) = New SqlMetaData("qty", SqlDbType.Int)
        columns(3) = New SqlMetaData("sumqty", SqlDbType.BigInt)

        Dim record As New SqlDataRecord(columns)

        SqlContext.Pipe.SendResultsStart(record)

        conn.Open()

        Dim reader As SqlDataReader = comm.ExecuteReader

        Dim prvempid As SqlInt32 = 0
        Dim sumqty As SqlInt64 = 0

        While (reader.Read())
            Dim empid As SqlInt32 = reader.GetSqlInt32(0)
            Dim qty As SqlInt32 = reader.GetSqlInt32(2)

            If (empid = prvempid) Then
                sumqty = sumqty + qty
            Else
                sumqty = qty
            End If

            prvempid = empid

            record.SetSqlInt32(0, reader.GetSqlInt32(0))
            record.SetSqlDateTime(1, reader.GetSqlDateTime(1))
            record.SetSqlInt32(2, qty)
            record.SetSqlInt64(3, sumqty)

            SqlContext.Pipe.SendResultsRow(record)
        End While

        SqlContext.Pipe.SendResultsEnd()
    End Using

End Sub
End Class
```

LISTING A-4 C# code to deploy and test CLR routines

```
USE CLRUtilities;
GO


-- Create assembly
CREATE ASSEMBLY CLRUtilities
FROM 'C:\CLRUtilities\CLRUtilities\bin\Debug\CLRUtilities.dll'
WITH PERMISSION_SET = SAFE;
-- If no Debug folder, use instead:
-- FROM 'C:\CLRUtilities\CLRUtilities\bin\CLRUtilities.dll'
GO


----------------------------------------------------------------------
-- Scalar Function: RegexIsMatch
----------------------------------------------------------------------


-- Create RegexIsMatch function
CREATE FUNCTION dbo.RegexIsMatch
  (@inpstr AS NVARCHAR(MAX), @regexstr AS NVARCHAR(MAX))
RETURNS BIT
WITH RETURNS NULL ON NULL INPUT
EXTERNAL NAME CLRUtilities.CLRUtilities.RegexIsMatch;
GO

-- Note: By default, automatic deployment with VS will create functions
-- with the option CALLED ON NULL INPUT
-- and not with RETURNS NULL ON NULL INPUT

-- Test RegexIsMatch function
SELECT dbo.RegexIsMatch(
  N'dejan@solidq.com',
  N'^([\w-]+\.)*?[\w-]+@[\w-]+\.([\w-]+\.)*?[\w]+$');
GO


----------------------------------------------------------------------
-- Scalar Function: RegexReplace
----------------------------------------------------------------------


-- Create RegexReplace function
CREATE FUNCTION dbo.RegexReplace(
  @input       AS NVARCHAR(MAX),
  @pattern     AS NVARCHAR(MAX),
  @replacement AS NVARCHAR(MAX))
RETURNS NVARCHAR(MAX)
WITH RETURNS NULL ON NULL INPUT
EXTERNAL NAME CLRUtilities.CLRUtilities.RegexReplace;
GO

-- Test RegexReplace function
SELECT dbo.RegexReplace('(123)-456-789', '[^0-9]', '');
GO


----------------------------------------------------------------------
-- Scalar Function: FormatDatetime
----------------------------------------------------------------------
```

```
-- Create FormatDatetime function
CREATE FUNCTION dbo.FormatDatetime
  (@dt AS DATETIME, @formatstring AS NVARCHAR(500))
RETURNS NVARCHAR(500)
WITH RETURNS NULL ON NULL INPUT
EXTERNAL NAME CLRUtilities.CLRUtilities.FormatDatetime;
GO

-- Test FormatDatetime function
SELECT dbo.FormatDatetime(GETDATE(), 'MM/dd/yyyy');
GO


---------------------------------------------------------------------
-- Scalar Functions: ImpCast, ExpCast
---------------------------------------------------------------------


-- Create ImpCast function
CREATE FUNCTION dbo.ImpCast(@inpstr AS NVARCHAR(4000))
RETURNS NVARCHAR(4000)
EXTERNAL NAME CLRUtilities.CLRUtilities.ImpCast;
GO
-- Create ExpCast function
CREATE FUNCTION dbo.ExpCast(@inpstr AS NVARCHAR(4000))
RETURNS NVARCHAR(4000)
EXTERNAL NAME CLRUtilities.CLRUtilities.ExpCast;
GO

-- Test ImpCast and ExpCast functions
SELECT dbo.ImpCast(N'123456'), dbo.ExpCast(N'123456');
GO


---------------------------------------------------------------------
-- Scalar Function: SQLSigCLR
---------------------------------------------------------------------


-- Create SQLSigCLR function
CREATE FUNCTION dbo.SQLSigCLR
  (@rawstring AS NVARCHAR(MAX), @parselength AS INT)
RETURNS NVARCHAR(MAX)
EXTERNAL NAME CLRUtilities.CLRUtilities.SQLSigCLR;
GO

-- Test SQLSigCLR function
SELECT dbo.SQLSigCLR
  (N'SELECT * FROM dbo.T1 WHERE col1 = 3 AND col2 > 78', 4000);
GO


---------------------------------------------------------------------
-- Table Function: SplitCLR
---------------------------------------------------------------------


-- Create SplitCLR function
CREATE FUNCTION dbo.SplitCLR
  (@string AS NVARCHAR(4000), @separator AS NCHAR(1))
```

```
RETURNS TABLE(pos INT, element NVARCHAR(4000))
EXTERNAL NAME CLRUtilities.CLRUtilities.SplitCLR;
GO


-- Test SplitCLR function
SELECT pos, element FROM dbo.SplitCLR(N'a,b,c', N',');
GO


-- Create SplitCLR_OrderByPos function
CREATE FUNCTION dbo.SplitCLR_OrderByPos
  (@string AS NVARCHAR(4000), @separator AS NCHAR(1))
RETURNS TABLE(pos INT, element NVARCHAR(4000))
ORDER(pos) -- new in SQL Server 2008
EXTERNAL NAME CLRUtilities.CLRUtilities.SplitCLR;
GO


-- Test SplitCLR_OrderByPos function
SELECT *
FROM dbo.SplitCLR_OrderByPos(N'a,b,c,d,e,f,g,h,i,j,k,l,m,n,o,p,q,r,s,t,u,v,
w,x,y,z', N',')
ORDER BY pos;
GO


---------------------------------------------------------------------
-- Stored Procedure: GetEnvInfo
---------------------------------------------------------------------


-- Database option TRUSTWORTHY needs to be ON for EXTERNAL_ACCESS
ALTER DATABASE CLRUtilities SET TRUSTWORTHY ON;
GO
-- Alter assembly with PERMISSION_SET = EXTERNAL_ACCESS
ALTER ASSEMBLY CLRUtilities
WITH PERMISSION_SET = EXTERNAL_ACCESS;
GO


/*
-- Safer alternative:

-- Create an asymmetric key from the signed assembly
-- Note: you have to sign the assembly using a strong name key file
USE master;
GO
CREATE ASYMMETRIC KEY CLRUtilitiesKey
  FROM EXECUTABLE FILE =
    'C:\CLRUtilities\CLRUtilities\bin\Debug\CLRUtilities.dll';
-- Create login and grant it with external access permission level
CREATE LOGIN CLRUtilitiesLogin FROM ASYMMETRIC KEY CLRUtilitiesKey;
GRANT EXTERNAL ACCESS ASSEMBLY TO CLRUtilitiesLogin;
GO
*/


-- Create GetEnvInfo stored procedure
CREATE PROCEDURE dbo.GetEnvInfo
AS EXTERNAL NAME CLRUtilities.CLRUtilities.GetEnvInfo;
GO
```

```
-- Test GetEnvInfo stored procedure
EXEC dbo.GetEnvInfo;
GO


---------------------------------------------------------------------
-- Stored Procedure: GetAssemblyInfo
---------------------------------------------------------------------

-- Create GetAssemblyInfo stored procedure
CREATE PROCEDURE GetAssemblyInfo
  @asmName AS sysname
AS EXTERNAL NAME CLRUtilities.CLRUtilities.GetAssemblyInfo;
GO

-- Test GetAssemblyInfo stored procedure
EXEC GetAssemblyInfo N'CLRUtilities';
GO


---------------------------------------------------------------------
-- Trigger: trg_GenericDMLAudit
---------------------------------------------------------------------

IF OBJECT_ID('dbo.T1', 'U') IS NOT NULL DROP TABLE dbo.T1;

CREATE TABLE dbo.T1
(
  keycol  INT         NOT NULL PRIMARY KEY,
  datacol VARCHAR(10) NOT NULL
);
GO

-- Database option TRUSTWORTHY needs to be ON for EXTERNAL_ACCESS
ALTER DATABASE CLRUtilities SET TRUSTWORTHY ON;
GO
-- Alter assembly with PERMISSION_SET = EXTERNAL_ACCESS
ALTER ASSEMBLY CLRUtilities
WITH PERMISSION_SET = EXTERNAL_ACCESS;
GO

/*
-- Safer alternative:

-- Create an asymmetric key from the signed assembly
-- Note: you have to sign the assembly using a strong name key file
USE master;
GO
CREATE ASYMMETRIC KEY CLRUtilitiesKey
  FROM EXECUTABLE FILE =
    'C:\CLRUtilities\CLRUtilities\bin\Debug\CLRUtilities.dll';
-- Create login and grant it with external access permission level
CREATE LOGIN CLRUtilitiesLogin FROM ASYMMETRIC KEY CLRUtilitiesKey;
GRANT EXTERNAL ACCESS ASSEMBLY TO CLRUtilitiesLogin;
GO
*/
```

```
-- Create trg_T1_iud_GenericDMLAudit trigger
USE CLRUtilities;
GO

CREATE TRIGGER trg_T1_iud_GenericDMLAudit
 ON dbo.T1 FOR INSERT, UPDATE, DELETE
AS
EXTERNAL NAME CLRUtilities.CLRUtilities.trg_GenericDMLAudit;
GO

-- Test trg_GenericDMLAudit trigger
INSERT INTO dbo.T1(keycol, datacol) VALUES(1, N'A');
UPDATE dbo.T1 SET datacol = N'B' WHERE keycol = 1;
DELETE FROM dbo.T1 WHERE keycol = 1;
-- Examine Windows Application Log
GO


---------------------------------------------------------------------
-- Stored Procedure: SalesRunningSum
---------------------------------------------------------------------

-- Create and populate Sales table
IF OBJECT_ID('dbo.Sales', 'U') IS NOT NULL DROP TABLE dbo.Sales;

CREATE TABLE dbo.Sales
(
  empid INT     NOT NULL,               -- partitioning column
  dt    DATETIME NOT NULL,              -- ordering column
  qty   INT     NOT NULL DEFAULT (1),   -- measure 1
  val   MONEY   NOT NULL DEFAULT (1.00), -- measure 2
  CONSTRAINT PK_Sales PRIMARY KEY(empid, dt)
);
GO

INSERT INTO dbo.Sales(empid, dt, qty, val) VALUES
  (1, '20100212', 10, 100.00),
  (1, '20100213', 30, 330.00),
  (1, '20100214', 20, 200.00),
  (2, '20100212', 40, 450.00),
  (2, '20100213', 10, 100.00),
  (2, '20100214', 50, 560.00);
GO

-- Create SalesRunningSum procedure
CREATE PROCEDURE dbo.SalesRunningSum
AS EXTERNAL NAME CLRUtilities.CLRUtilities.SalesRunningSum;
GO

-- Test SalesRunningSum procedure
EXEC dbo.SalesRunningSum;
GO
```

LISTING A-5 Visual Basic code to deploy and test CLR routines

```
USE CLRutilities;
GO


-- Create assembly
CREATE ASSEMBLY CLRUtilities
FROM 'C:\CLRUtilities\CLRUtilities\bin\Debug\CLRUtilities.dll'
WITH PERMISSION_SET = SAFE;
-- If no Debug folder, use instead:
-- FROM 'C:\CLRUtilities\CLRUtilities\bin\CLRUtilities.dll'
GO


-------------------------------------------------------------------
-- Scalar Function: RegexIsMatch
-------------------------------------------------------------------


-- Create RegexIsMatch function
CREATE FUNCTION dbo.RegexIsMatch
  (@inpstr AS NVARCHAR(MAX), @regexstr AS NVARCHAR(MAX))
RETURNS BIT
WITH RETURNS NULL ON NULL INPUT
EXTERNAL NAME CLRUtilities.[CLRUtilities.CLRUtilities].RegexIsMatch;
GO


-- Note: By default, automatic deployment with VS will create functions
-- with the option CALLED ON NULL INPUT
-- and not with RETURNS NULL ON NULL INPUT


-- Test RegexIsMatch function
SELECT dbo.RegexIsMatch(
  N'dejan@solidq.com',
  N'^([\w-]+\.)*?[\w-]+@[\w-]+\.([\w-]+\.)*?[\w]+$');
GO


-------------------------------------------------------------------
-- Scalar Function: RegexReplace
-------------------------------------------------------------------


-- Create RegexReplace function
CREATE FUNCTION dbo.RegexReplace(
  @input       AS NVARCHAR(MAX),
  @pattern     AS NVARCHAR(MAX),
  @replacement AS NVARCHAR(MAX))
RETURNS NVARCHAR(MAX)
WITH RETURNS NULL ON NULL INPUT
EXTERNAL NAME CLRUtilities.[CLRUtilities.CLRUtilities].RegexReplace;
GO


-- Test RegexReplace function
SELECT dbo.RegexReplace('(123)-456-789', '[^0-9]', '');
GO


-------------------------------------------------------------------
-- Scalar Function: FormatDatetime
-------------------------------------------------------------------
```

```
-- Create FormatDatetime function
CREATE FUNCTION dbo.FormatDatetime
  (@dt AS DATETIME, @formatstring AS NVARCHAR(500))
RETURNS NVARCHAR(500)
WITH RETURNS NULL ON NULL INPUT
EXTERNAL NAME CLRUtilities.[CLRUtilities.CLRUtilities].FormatDatetime;
GO

-- Test FormatDatetime function
SELECT dbo.FormatDatetime(GETDATE(), 'MM/dd/yyyy');
GO


------------------------------------------------------------------------
-- Scalar Functions: ImpCast, ExpCast
------------------------------------------------------------------------


-- Create ImpCast function
CREATE FUNCTION dbo.ImpCast(@inpstr AS NVARCHAR(4000))
RETURNS NVARCHAR(4000)
EXTERNAL NAME CLRUtilities.[CLRUtilities.CLRUtilities].ImpCast;
GO
-- Create ExpCast function
CREATE FUNCTION dbo.ExpCast(@inpstr AS NVARCHAR(4000))
RETURNS NVARCHAR(4000)
EXTERNAL NAME CLRUtilities.[CLRUtilities.CLRUtilities].ExpCast;
GO

-- Test ImpCast and ExpCast functions
SELECT dbo.ImpCast(N'123456'), dbo.ExpCast(N'123456');
GO


------------------------------------------------------------------------
-- Scalar Function: SQLSigCLR
------------------------------------------------------------------------


-- Create SQLSigCLR function
CREATE FUNCTION dbo.SQLSigCLR
  (@rawstring AS NVARCHAR(MAX), @parselength AS INT)
RETURNS NVARCHAR(MAX)
EXTERNAL NAME CLRUtilities.[CLRUtilities.CLRUtilities].SQLSigCLR;
GO

-- Test SQLSigCLR function
SELECT dbo.SQLSigCLR
  (N'SELECT * FROM dbo.T1 WHERE col1 = 3 AND col2 > 78', 4000);
GO


------------------------------------------------------------------------
-- Table Function: SplitCLR
------------------------------------------------------------------------


-- Create SplitCLR function
CREATE FUNCTION dbo.SplitCLR
  (@string AS NVARCHAR(4000), @separator AS NCHAR(1))
```

```
RETURNS TABLE(pos INT, element NVARCHAR(4000))
EXTERNAL NAME CLRUtilities.[CLRUtilities.CLRUtilities].SplitCLR;
GO


-- Test SplitCLR function
SELECT pos, element FROM dbo.SplitCLR(N'a,b,c', N',');
GO


-- Create SplitCLR_OrderByPos function
CREATE FUNCTION dbo.SplitCLR_OrderByPos
  (@string AS NVARCHAR(4000), @separator AS NCHAR(1))
RETURNS TABLE(pos INT, element NVARCHAR(4000))
ORDER(pos)
EXTERNAL NAME CLRUtilities.[CLRUtilities.CLRUtilities].SplitCLR;
GO


-- Test SplitCLR_OrderByPos function
SELECT *
FROM dbo.SplitCLR_OrderByPos(N'a,b,c,d,e,f,g,h,i,j,k,l,m,n,o,p,q,r,s,t,u,
v,w,x,y,z', N',')
ORDER BY pos;
GO


---------------------------------------------------------------------
-- Stored Procedure: GetEnvInfo
---------------------------------------------------------------------


-- Database option TRUSTWORTHY needs to be ON for EXTERNAL_ACCESS
ALTER DATABASE CLRUtilities SET TRUSTWORTHY ON;
GO
-- Alter assembly with PERMISSION_SET = EXTERNAL_ACCESS
ALTER ASSEMBLY CLRUtilities
WITH PERMISSION_SET = EXTERNAL_ACCESS;
GO


/*
-- Safer alternative:

-- Create an asymmetric key from the signed assembly
-- Note: you have to sign the assembly using a strong name key file
USE master;
GO
CREATE ASYMMETRIC KEY CLRUtilitiesKey
  FROM EXECUTABLE FILE =
    'C:\CLRUtilities\CLRUtilities\bin\Debug\CLRUtilities.dll';
-- Create login and grant it with external access permission level
CREATE LOGIN CLRUtilitiesLogin FROM ASYMMETRIC KEY CLRUtilitiesKey;
GRANT EXTERNAL ACCESS ASSEMBLY TO CLRUtilitiesLogin;
GO
*/


-- Create GetEnvInfo stored procedure
CREATE PROCEDURE dbo.GetEnvInfo
AS EXTERNAL NAME
  CLRUtilities.[CLRUtilities.CLRUtilities].GetEnvInfo;
GO
```

```
-- Test GetEnvInfo stored procedure
EXEC dbo.GetEnvInfo;
GO


-------------------------------------------------------------------
-- Stored Procedure: GetAssemblyInfo
-------------------------------------------------------------------


-- Create GetAssemblyInfo stored procedure
CREATE PROCEDURE GetAssemblyInfo
  @asmName AS sysname
AS EXTERNAL NAME
  CLRUtilities.[CLRUtilities.CLRUtilities].GetAssemblyInfo;
GO

-- Test GetAssemblyInfo stored procedure
EXEC GetAssemblyInfo N'CLRUtilities';
GO


-------------------------------------------------------------------
-- Trigger: trg_GenericDMLAudit
-------------------------------------------------------------------


-- Create T1 table
IF OBJECT_ID('dbo.T1', 'U') IS NOT NULL DROP TABLE dbo.T1;

CREATE TABLE dbo.T1
(
  keycol  INT         NOT NULL PRIMARY KEY,
  datacol VARCHAR(10) NOT NULL
);
GO

-- Database option TRUSTWORTHY needs to be ON for EXTERNAL_ACCESS
ALTER DATABASE CLRUtilities SET TRUSTWORTHY ON;
GO
-- Alter assembly with PERMISSION_SET = EXTERNAL_ACCESS
ALTER ASSEMBLY CLRUtilities
WITH PERMISSION_SET = EXTERNAL_ACCESS;
GO


/*
-- Safer alternative:

-- Create an asymmetric key from the signed assembly
-- Note: you have to sign the assembly using a strong name key file
USE master;
GO
CREATE ASYMMETRIC KEY CLRUtilitiesKey
  FROM EXECUTABLE FILE =
    'C:\CLRUtilities\CLRUtilities\bin\Debug\CLRUtilities.dll';
-- Create login and grant it with external access permission level
CREATE LOGIN CLRUtilitiesLogin FROM ASYMMETRIC KEY CLRUtilitiesKey;
GRANT EXTERNAL ACCESS ASSEMBLY TO CLRUtilitiesLogin;
GO
*/
```

```
-- Create trg_T1_iud_GenericDMLAudit trigger
USE CLRUtilities;
GO

CREATE TRIGGER trg_T1_iud_GenericDMLAudit
  ON dbo.T1 FOR INSERT, UPDATE, DELETE
AS
EXTERNAL NAME
  CLRUtilities.[CLRUtilities.CLRUtilities].trg_GenericDMLAudit;
GO

-- Test trg_GenericDMLAudit trigger
INSERT INTO dbo.T1(keycol, datacol) VALUES(1, N'A');
UPDATE dbo.T1 SET datacol = N'B' WHERE keycol = 1;
DELETE FROM dbo.T1 WHERE keycol = 1;
-- Examine Windows Application Log
GO


---------------------------------------------------------------------
-- Stored Procedure: SalesRunningSum
---------------------------------------------------------------------

-- Create and populate Sales table
IF OBJECT_ID('dbo.Sales', 'U') IS NOT NULL DROP TABLE dbo.Sales;

CREATE TABLE dbo.Sales
(
  empid INT      NOT NULL,              -- partitioning column
  dt    DATETIME NOT NULL,              -- ordering column
  qty   INT      NOT NULL DEFAULT (1),    -- measure 1
  val   MONEY    NOT NULL DEFAULT (1.00), -- measure 2
  CONSTRAINT PK_Sales PRIMARY KEY(empid, dt)
);
GO

INSERT INTO dbo.Sales(empid, dt, qty, val) VALUES
  (1, '20100212', 10, 100.00),
  (1, '20100213', 30, 330.00),
  (1, '20100214', 20, 200.00),
  (2, '20100212', 40, 450.00),
  (2, '20100213', 10, 100.00),
  (2, '20100214', 50, 560.00);
GO

-- Create SalesRunningSum procedure
CREATE PROCEDURE dbo.SalesRunningSum
AS EXTERNAL NAME CLRUtilities.[CLRUtilities.CLRUtilities].SalesRunningSum;
GO

-- Test SalesRunningSum procedure
EXEC dbo.SalesRunningSum;
GO
```

Index

Symbols and Numbers

[ ] (square brackets), 512
- (minus) operator, 378
(single number) symbol, 89, 247
(double number) symbol, 89, 257
#endregion, 424
#region, 424
$ (dollar sign), 517
& (ampersand), 492
( ) (parentheses), 512
* (asterisk), 3, 511
   in SCHEMABINDING option, 20–21
   in SELECT statements, 6
   in strings, 40
.dbf file, 551, 593
.NET language, 61
   .NET SqlTypes, 419
   Common Language Runtime triggers in, 181–90
   for creating user-defined types, 416
   native types, 54–55
   string replacement, 51
   T-SQL language compared to, 44
.NET SQL types, 54–55
.prj file, 551
.shp file, 551, 593
.shx file, 551, 593
/ (slash character), 500, 510
/i1all/i0 functions, in change data capture, 670
/i1net/i0 functions, in change data capture, 670
/i1package0/i0 packages, 629
/i1SecAudit /i0packages, 629
/i1to /i0attribute, 446–48
/i1to/i0 attribute, 441
; semicolon, 84, 492, 507
– (question mark), 492
@ character, 500, 511
@@ERROR function, 225–26
@@rowcount function, 150, 226
@dialog, 688, 696
@mode variable, 58
@module, 122
@p1 parameter, 58
@params, 122–24, 326
@parselength, 58
@separator, 66
@stmt, 326
@string, 66
__$update_mask columns, 669
+ (plus) operator, 378
< (less than), 492
> (greater than), 492
6NF (sixth normal form), 479, 487–88

A

ABP (adjacent broker protocol), 731–32, 734–37
abstraction mechanism, use of views as an, 1
access
   indirect, 650–51
   parameterized, 651
   tracking, 625
accessor methods, 417, 557
Accumulate method, 615
ACID (Atomicity, Consistency, Isolation,
     and Durability), 191
ACS (Audit Collection Service), 651
actions, 631–33, 646
activation, 698–706
   external, 702–06
   internal, 699–702
   sample dialog, 714–16
ACTIVATION parameter, 699, 701
AddLine, 618
AddOne function, 36–38
ADDRESS, 738
addresses, Server Broker, 739
adjacency list model, 411, 523
adjacent broker protocol (ABP), 731–32, 734–37
ADO.NET Sync Services, 627, 662–65
AES (advanced encryption standard) algorithm, 733
AFTER triggers, 145–46, 172
age, calculating, 395–98
aggregate concatenation technique, 33
aggregate functions, 509, 611–13
aggregations
   custom, 291–92
   running, 292–300
algorithms
   /i1greedy/i0 matching, 312–14
   encryption, 733
aliases, in XML, 493, 500
allocation order scan, 203–05
ALTER ANY DATABASE AUDIT permission, 646
ALTER ANY SERVER AUDIT permission, 643, 645
ALTER ASSEMBLY command, 430
ALTER DATABASE statement, 654
ALTER ENDPOINT statement, 732–33
ALTER EVENT SESSION, 635
ALTER permissions, 118
ALTER QUEUE statement, 685, 699
ALTER statement, 23
ALTER TABLE DISABLE TRIGGER command, 152
ALTER TABLE SWITCH statement, 660
ampersand (&), 492
analysis, inconsistent, 201
angular measures, 546

About the Authors

Itzik Ben-Gan is a mentor and cofounder of Solid Quality Mentors. A SQL Server Microsoft MVP (Most Valuable Professional) since 1999, Itzik has delivered numerous training events around the world focused on T-SQL querying, query tuning, and programming. Itzik is the author of several books about T-SQL. He has written many articles for *SQL Server Magazine* as well as articles and white papers for MSDN. Itzik's speaking engagements include Tech Ed, DevWeek, PASS, SQL Server Magazine Connections, various user groups around the world, and Solid Quality Mentors events.

Dejan Sarka focuses on development of database and business intelligence applications. Besides projects, he spends about half of the time on training and mentoring. He is a frequent speaker on some of the most important international conferences such as PASS, TechEd, and SqlDevCon. He is also indispensable on regional MS events, for example on the NT Conference, the biggest MS conference in Central and Eastern Europe. He is the founder of the Slovenian SQL Server and .NET Users Group. Dejan Sarka is the main author, coauthor, or guest author of seven books about databases and SQL Server. Dejan Sarka also developed two courses for Solid Quality Learning—Data Modeling Essentials and Data Mining with SQL Server 2008.

Roger Wolter is an architect on the Microsoft IT MDM project team. He has 30 years of experience in various aspects of the computer industry including jobs at Unisys, Infospan, Fourth Shift, and the last 10 years as a Program Manager at Microsoft. His projects at Microsoft include SQLXML, the Soap Toolkit, the SQL Server Service Broker, SQL Server Express, and Master Data Services. He is currently working on a project to master all of Microsoft's customer and partner data.

Greg Low is a consultant and trainer, best known for his SQL Down Under podcast *(www.sqldownunder.com)* and for his work as the director of global chapter operations for PASS. Greg is the country lead for Solid Quality Mentors in Australia *(www.solidq.com.au)*, a SQL Server MVP, and a Microsoft Regional Director. He holds a PhD in computer science from QUT and has written a number of books on SQL Server and on building technical communities. For Microsoft, he has written SQL Server white papers and training materials and is one of a handful of trainers chosen to deliver the Microsoft Certified Masters program for SQL Server 2008.

Ed Katibah is a program manager on the Microsoft SQL Server Strategy, Infrastructure and Architecture team. Ed began his professional career over 34 years ago while working in a University of California, Berkeley, research group at the Space Sciences Laboratory. Ed has extensive experience in the spatial industry with jobs ranging from research, software development, consulting, application programming, and large-scale spatial database production systems. Since 1996, Ed has worked exclusively on spatially enabled database systems for Informix, IBM, and now Microsoft.

Isaac Kunen is a program manager on the SQL Server engine programmability team. Since joining Microsoft in 2005, he has worked on the type system, SQL CLR integration, and database extensibility. His most prominent project to date is the spatial data support in SQL Server 2008. Isaac is currently focusing on reducing the complexity of database application development, deployment, and management.

Resources for SQL Server 2008

Microsoft® SQL Server® 2008 Administrator's Pocket Consultant
William R. Stanek
ISBN 9780735625891

Programming Microsoft SQL Server 2008
Leonard Lobel, Andrew J. Brust, Stephen Forte
ISBN 9780735625990

Microsoft SQL Server 2008 Step by Step
Mike Hotek
ISBN 9780735626041

Microsoft SQL Server 2008 T-SQL Fundamentals
Itzik Ben-Gan
ISBN 9780735626010

MCTS Self-Paced Training Kit (Exam 70-432) Microsoft SQL Server 2008 Implementation and Maintenance
Mike Hotek
ISBN 9780735626058

Smart Business Intelligence Solutions with Microsoft SQL Server 2008
Lynn Langit, Kevin S. Goff, Davide Mauri, Sahil Malik
ISBN 9780735625808

ALSO SEE

Microsoft SQL Server 2008 Internals
Kalen Delaney et al.
ISBN 9780735626249

Inside Microsoft SQL Server 2008: T-SQL Querying
Itzik Ben-Gan, Lubor Kollar, Dejan Sarka, Steve Kass
ISBN 9780735626034

Inside Microsoft SQL Server 2008: T-SQL Programming
Itzik Ben-Gan, Dejan Sarka, Roger Wolter, Greg Low, Ed Katibah, Isaac Kunen
ISBN 9780735626027

Microsoft SQL Server 2008 MDX Step by Step
Bryan C. Smith, C. Ryan Clay, Hitachi Consulting
ISBN 9780735626188

Microsoft SQL Server 2008 Reporting Services Step by Step
Stacia Misner
ISBN 9780735626478

Microsoft SQL Server 2008 Analysis Services Step by Step
Scott Cameron, Hitachi Consulting
ISBN 9780735626201

microsoft.com/mspress

Collaborative Technologies— Resources for Developers

Inside Microsoft® Windows® SharePoint® Services 3.0

Ted Pattison, Daniel Larson

ISBN 9780735623200

Get the in-depth architectural insights, task-oriented guidance, and extensive code samples you need to build robust, enterprise content-management solutions.

Inside Microsoft Office SharePoint Server 2007

Patrick Tisseghem

ISBN 9780735623682

Led by an expert in collaboration technologies, you'll plumb the internals of SharePoint Server 2007—and master the intricacies of developing intranets, extranets, and Web-based applications.

Inside the Index and Search Engines: Microsoft Office SharePoint Server 2007

Patrick Tisseghem, Lars Fastrup

ISBN 9780735625358

Customize and extend the enterprise search capabilities in SharePoint Server 2007—and optimize the user experience—with guidance from two recognized SharePoint experts.

Working with Microsoft Dynamics® CRM 4.0, Second Edition

Mike Snyder, Jim Steger

ISBN 9780735623781

Whether you're an IT professional, a developer, or a power user, get real-world guidance on how to make Microsoft Dynamics CRM work the way you do—with or without programming.

Programming Microsoft Dynamics CRM 4.0

Jim Steger *et al.*

ISBN 9780735625945

Apply the design and coding practices that leading CRM consultants use to customize, integrate, and extend Microsoft Dynamics CRM 4.0 for specific business needs.

ALSO SEE

Inside Microsoft Dynamics AX 2009
ISBN 9780735626454

6 Microsoft Office Business Applications for Office SharePoint Server 2007
ISBN 9780735622760

Programming Microsoft Office Business Applications
ISBN 9780735625365

Inside Microsoft Exchange Server 2007 Web Services
ISBN 9780735623927

microsoft.com/mspress

What do you think of this book?

We want to hear from you!

To participate in a brief online survey, please visit:

microsoft.com/learning/booksurvey

Tell us how well this book meets your needs—what works effectively, and what we can do better. Your feedback will help us continually improve our books and learning resources for you.

Thank you in advance for your input!

Stay in touch!

To subscribe to the *Microsoft Press® Book Connection Newsletter*—for news on upcoming books, events, and special offers—please visit:

microsoft.com/learning/books/newsletter